Lecture Notes in Computer Scien

Commenced Publication in 1973
Founding and Former Series Editors:
Gerhard Goos, Juris Hartmanis, and Jan van Leeuwen

Maura Cerioli (Ed.)

Fundamental Approaches to Software Engineering

8th International Conference, FASE 2005
Held as Part of the Joint European Conferences
on Theory and Practice of Software, ETAPS 2005
Edinburgh, UK, April 4-8, 2005
Proceedings

 Springer

Volume Editor

Maura Cerioli
Università di Genova, DISI
Via Dodecaneso 35, 16146 Genova, Italy
E-mail: cerioli@disi.unige.it

Library of Congress Control Number: 2005922879

CR Subject Classification (1998): D.2, F.3, D.3

ISSN   0302-9743
ISBN-10   3-540-25420-X Springer Berlin Heidelberg New York
ISBN-13   978-3-540-25420-1 Springer Berlin Heidelberg New York

Springer is a part of Springer Science+Business Media

springeronline.com

© Springer-Verlag Berlin Heidelberg 2005
Printed in Germany

Typesetting: Camera-ready by author, data conversion by Scientific Publishing Services, Chennai, India
Printed on acid-free paper   SPIN: 11405955   06/3142   5 4 3 2 1 0

Foreword

ETAPS 2005 was the eighth instance of the European Joint Conferences on Theory and Practice of Software. ETAPS is an annual federated conference that was established in 1998 by combining a number of existing and new conferences. This year it comprised five conferences (CC, ESOP, FASE, FOSSACS, TACAS), 17 satellite workshops (AVIS, BYTECODE, CEES, CLASE, CMSB, COCV, FAC, FESCA, FINCO, GCW-DSE, GLPL, LDTA, QAPL, SC, SLAP, TGC, UITP), seven invited lectures (not including those that were specific to the satellite events), and several tutorials. We received over 550 submissions to the five conferences this year, giving acceptance rates below 30% for each one. Congratulations to all the authors who made it to the final program! I hope that most of the other authors still found a way of participating in this exciting event and I hope you will continue submitting.

The events that comprise ETAPS address various aspects of the system development process, including specification, design, implementation, analysis and improvement. The languages, methodologies and tools which support these activities are all well within its scope. Different blends of theory and practice are represented, with an inclination towards theory with a practical motivation on the one hand and soundly based practice on the other. Many of the issues involved in software design apply to systems in general, including hardware systems, and the emphasis on software is not intended to be exclusive.

ETAPS is a loose confederation in which each event retains its own identity, with a separate program committee and proceedings. Its format is open-ended, allowing it to grow and evolve as time goes by. Contributed talks and system demonstrations are in synchronized parallel sessions, with invited lectures in plenary sessions. Two of the invited lectures are reserved for "unifying" talks on topics of interest to the whole range of ETAPS attendees. The aim of cramming all this activity into a single one-week meeting is to create a strong magnet for academic and industrial researchers working on topics within its scope, giving them the opportunity to learn about research in related areas, and thereby to foster new and existing links between work in areas that were formerly addressed in separate meetings.

ETAPS 2005 was organized by the School of Informatics of the University of Edinburgh, in cooperation with

- European Association for Theoretical Computer Science (EATCS);
- European Association for Programming Languages and Systems (EAPLS);
- European Association of Software Science and Technology (EASST).

The organizing team comprised:

- Chair: Don Sannella
- Publicity: David Aspinall
- Satellite Events: Massimo Felici

- Secretariat: Dyane Goodchild
- Local Arrangements: Monika-Jeannette Lekuse
- Tutorials: Alberto Momigliano
- Finances: Ian Stark
- Website: Jennifer Tenzer, Daniel Winterstein
- Fundraising: Phil Wadler

ETAPS 2005 received support from the University of Edinburgh.

Overall planning for ETAPS conferences is the responsibility of its Steering Committee, whose current membership is:

Perdita Stevens (Edinburgh, Chair), Luca Aceto (Aalborg and Reykjavík), Rastislav Bodik (Berkeley), Maura Cerioli (Genoa), Evelyn Duesterwald (IBM, USA), Hartmut Ehrig (Berlin), José Fiadeiro (Leicester), Marie-Claude Gaudel (Paris), Roberto Gorrieri (Bologna), Reiko Heckel (Paderborn), Holger Hermanns (Saarbrücken), Joost-Pieter Katoen (Aachen), Paul Klint (Amsterdam), Jens Knoop (Vienna), Kim Larsen (Aalborg), Tiziana Margaria (Dortmund), Ugo Montanari (Pisa), Hanne Riis Nielson (Copenhagen), Fernando Orejas (Barcelona), Mooly Sagiv (Tel Aviv), Don Sannella (Edinburgh), Vladimiro Sassone (Sussex), Peter Sestoft (Copenhagen), Michel Wermelinger (Lisbon), Igor Walukiewicz (Bordeaux), Andreas Zeller (Saarbrücken), Lenore Zuck (Chicago).

I would like to express my sincere gratitude to all of these people and organizations, the program committee chairs and PC members of the ETAPS conferences, the organizers of the satellite events, the speakers themselves, the many reviewers, and Springer for agreeing to publish the ETAPS proceedings. Finally, I would like to thank the organizer of ETAPS 2005, Don Sannella. He has been instrumental in the development of ETAPS since its beginning; it is quite beyond the limits of what might be expected that, in addition to all the work he has done as the original ETAPS Steering Committee Chairman and current ETAPS Treasurer, he has been prepared to take on the task of organizing this instance of ETAPS. It gives me particular pleasure to thank him for organizing ETAPS in this wonderful city of Edinburgh in this my first year as ETAPS Steering Committee Chair.

Edinburgh, January 2005   Perdita Stevens
                                            ETAPS Steering Committee Chair

Preface

The conference on Fundamental Approaches to Software Engineering (FASE) is one of the European Joint Conferences on Theory and Practice of Software (ETAPS). As such, it provides a common forum for practitioners and researchers to discuss theories for supporting and improving software engineering practices and their practical application in real contexts.

Contributions were sought targeting both pragmatic concepts and their formal foundations which could lead to new engineering practices and a higher level of reliability, robustness, and evolvability of heterogeneous software federations.

The record submission of 99 research papers and 6 tool demos was the response of the scientific community, with contributions ranging from theoretical aspects, such as graph grammars, graph transformation, agent theory and algebraic specification languages, to applications to industrially used languages, methods, technologies, and tools, including UML, Web services, product lines, component-based development, Java, and Java cards.

The scientific program was complemented by the invited lectures of Gérard Berry on *Esterel v7: from Verified Formal Specification to Efficient Industrial Designs* and of Thomas A. Henzinger on *Checking Memory Safety with Blast*.

The authors of the submissions were from 29 countries, both within Europe (Belgium, Denmark, Finland, France, Germany, Hungary, Ireland, Italy, Luxembourg, Macedonia, Portugal, Spain, Sweden, Switzerland, The Netherlands, United Kingdom) and outside (Australia, Brazil, Canada, China, India, Japan, Korea, Pakistan, Russia, Thailand, Tunisia, Turkey, USA). It is a pleasure to note the increasing number of submissions from eastern Europe and from outside Europe altogether, showing that FASE is gaining importance as a world-wide conference.

The help of the Program Committee was invaluable in selecting just 25 papers (3 of them tool demos) from the large number of high-quality submissions, and I take the opportunity to thank warmly all its members and the other referees for supporting the selection process with their precious time.

FASE 2005 was held in Edinburgh, hosted and organized by the School of Informatics of the University of Edinburgh. Next year FASE will take place in Vienna (Austria).

Being part of ETAPS, FASE shares the sponsoring and support described by the ETAPS Chair in the Foreword. Heartfelt thanks are also due to José Fiadeiro and Perdita Stevens for their great efforts in the global ETAPS organization and to Don Sannella and his staff for the wonderful job as local organizers.

Finally, a special thanks to the contributors to and participants of FASE, who in the end are the people making the conference worthwhile.

Genoa, January 2005   Maura Cerioli

Organization

Program Committee

Silvia Teresita Acuña (Universidad Autónoma de Madrid, Spain)
Leonor Barroca (Open University, UK)
Yolande Berbers (Katholieke Universiteit Leuven, Belgium)
Jean Bézivin (University of Nantes, France)
Jean-Michel Bruel (University of Pau, France)
Maura Cerioli (Università di Genova, Italy)
Marsha Chechik (University of Toronto, Canada)
Gianpaolo Cugola (Politecnico di Milano, Italy)
Colin Fidge (University of Queensland, Australia)
Anthony Finkelstein (University College London, UK)
Chris George (UNU/IIST, Macao 1, China)
Martin Große-Rhode (Fraunhofer-Institut für Software und
    Systemtechnik, Germany)
Tomasz Janowski (University of Gdańsk, Poland)
Mehdi Jazayeri (Technical University of Vienna, Austria)
Cliff Jones (University of Newcastle upon Tyne, UK)
Antónia Lopes (University of Lisbon, Portugal)
Tiziana Margaria (University of Dortmund, Germany)
Stephan Merz (INRIA Lorraine, LORIA, France)
Carlo Montangero (Università di Pisa, Italy)
Doron Peled (University of Warwick, UK)
Ernesto Pimentel (Universidad de Málaga, Spain)
Michel Wermelinger (Universidade Nova de Lisboa, Portugal)
Roel Wieringa (University of Twente, The Netherlands)
Alexander Wolf (University of Colorado at Boulder, USA)

Reviewers

Vincenzo Ambriola
Jonathan Amir
Giovanni Cignoni
Joey Coleman
Maya Daneva
Valeria de Castro
Juan de Lara
Benet Devereux
Manuel Díaz

Oscar Dieste
Francisco Durán
Rik Eshuis
Pascal Fenkam
Fabio Gadducci
Vincenzo Gervasi
Mihaela Gheorghiu
Vittoria Gianuzzi
Arie Gurfinkel

Markus Hardt
David N. Jansen
Ioannis Kassios
Engin Kirda
Giovanni Lagorio
Albert Lai
José A. Macías Iglesias
Paola Magillo
Antonio Maña

Table of Contents

Product Lines

Theory

Code Understanding and Validation

The UML

Automatic Proofs and Provers

Esterel v7: From Verified Formal Specification to Efficient Industrial Designs

Gérard Berry

Chief Scientist, Esterel Technologies Member, Academie des Sciences

Synchronous languages were developed in the mid-80's specifically to deal with embedded systems. They are based on mathematical semantics and support formal compilation to classical software or hardware languages as well as formal verification. Esterel v7 is a major industrial evolution of the original Esterel synchronous language, mostly directed to complex hardware applications. The language is supported by the Esterel Studio integrated development environment, which provides a smooth path from verifiable executable specification to efficient circuit synthesis. The graphical Safe States Machines derived from Esterel are also used in the SCADE tool which is widely used for safety-critical software applications in avionics.

Through the examples of Esterel v7 and SCADE, we discuss the impact and evolution of formal methods for actual industrial design. In particular, we discuss some issues that are central for actual applications but are usually either not considered as such or viewed as too difficult to handle in research or R&D projects. We demonstrate that the difference between industrial success and failure often lies in precisely these aspects.

M. Cerioli (Ed.): FASE 2005, LNCS 3442, p. 1, 2005.

Checking Memory Safety with Blast[*]

Dirk Beyer[1], Thomas A. Henzinger[1,2], Ranjit Jhala[3],
and Rupak Majumdar[4]

[1] EPFL, Switzerland
[2] University of California, Berkeley
[3] University of California, San Diego
[4] University of California, Los Angeles

Abstract. BLAST is an automatic verification tool for checking temporal safety properties of C programs. Given a C program and a temporal
safety property, BLAST statically proves that either the program satisfies the safety property or the program has an execution trace that
exhibits a violation of the property. BLAST constructs, explores, and refines abstractions of the program state space based on lazy predicate
abstraction and interpolation-based predicate discovery. We show how
BLAST can be used to statically prove memory safety for C programs.
We take a two-step approach. First, we use CCURED, a type-based memory safety analyzer, to annotate with run-time checks all program points
that cannot be proved memory safe by the type system. Second, we use
BLAST to remove as many of the run-time checks as possible (by proving
that these checks never fail), and to generate for the remaining run-time
checks execution traces that witness them fail. Our experience shows
that BLAST can remove many of the run-time checks added by CCURED
and provide useful information to the programmer about many of the
remaining checks.

1 Introduction

Invalid memory access is a major source of program failures. If a program statement dereferences a pointer that points to an invalid memory cell, the program
is either aborted by the operating system or, often worse, the program continues to run with an undefined behavior. To avoid the latter, one can perform
checks before every memory access at run time. For some programming languages
(e.g., Java) this is done automatically by the compiler/run-time environment.
For the language C, neither the compiler nor the run-time environment enforces
memory-safety policies. CCURED [7, 24] is a program-transformation tool for C
which transforms any given C program to a memory-safe version. CCURED uses
a type-based program analysis to prove as many memory accesses as possible

---

[*] This research was supported in part by the NSF grants CCR-0234690, CCR-0225610,
and ITR-0326577.

M. Cerioli (Ed.): FASE 2005, LNCS 3442, pp. 2–18, 2005.

memory safe, and it inserts run-time checks before the remaining memory accesses. The resulting, "cured" C program is memory safe in the sense that it alarms the user if the program was about to execute an unsafe operation. Despite the manyfold advantages of this approach, it has two drawbacks: first, the run-time checks consume additional processor time, and second, the checks give late feedback, just before the program aborts.

We address these two points by combining CCURED with a more powerful, path-sensitive program analysis. The additional analysis is performed by the model checker BLAST [19]. For each memory access that the type-based analysis of CCURED fails to prove safe, we invoke the more precise, more expensive analysis of BLAST. There are three possible outcomes. First, BLAST may be able to prove that the memory access is safe (even though CCURED was not able to prove this). In this case, no run-time check needs to be inserted, thus reducing the overhead in the cured program. Second, BLAST may be able to generate an execution trace to an invalid pointer dereference at the considered control location, i.e., an execution trace along which the run-time check inserted by CCURED would fail. This may expose a program bug, which can, based on the error trace provided by BLAST, then be fixed by the programmer. Third, BLAST may time-out attempting to check whether or not a given memory access is always safe. In this case, the run-time check inserted by CCURED remains in the cured program. It is important to note that BLAST, even though often more powerful than CCURED, is not invoked by itself, but only after a type-based pointer analysis fails. This is because where successful, the CCURED analysis is more efficient, and it may also succeed in cases that overwhelm the model checker. However, the combination of CCURED and BLAST guarantees memory-safe programs with less run-time overhead than the use of CCURED alone, and it provides useful compile-time feedback about memory-safety violations to the programmer.

BLAST performs an abstract reachability analysis to check if a given error location of a C program can be visited during program execution. All paths of the program are checked symbolically and abstractly, by tracking only some relevant facts (called *predicates*) about program variables, instead of the full program state. If a path to the error location is found, the path may be due to the imprecision in the abstraction (a so-called *spurious* counterexample) or it may correspond to a feasible program path (a *genuine* counterexample). In the former case, additional relevant predicates are discovered automatically to remove the spurious error trace. The process is repeated, by tracking an increasing number of predicates, until either a genuine error trace (program bug) is found, or the abstraction is precise enough to prove the absence of error traces. This scheme of counterexample-guided predicate abstraction refinement was first implemented for verifying software by the SLAM project [3]. BLAST improves on the general scheme in two main ways. First, relevant predicates are discovered locally and independently at each program location as interpolants between the past and the future fragments of a spurious error trace [15]. Second, the discovered new predicates are added and tracked locally only in those parts of an abstract reachability tree where the spurious error trace occurred (*lazy abstraction*) [18]. This emphasis on parsimonious, nonuniform abstractions renders the analysis scalable beyond 100,000 lines of code [15].

Much recent interest has focused on the addition of run-time checks to improve the memory safety and security of C programs [2, 12, 21], often coupled with a static analysis to reduce the run-time overhead by eliminating dynamic checks [4, 7, 14, 23, 26]. However, to our knowledge, model checking has not been used previously in the elimination of these run-time checks, even though the model checking of software has been a very active area of research in recent years [1, 3, 6, 8, 11, 13, 20, 22] (for more related work on software model checking, see [17]).

2   The Software Model Checker BLAST

We illustrate how BLAST combines lazy abstraction and interpolation-based, localized predicate discovery on the example shown in Figure 1.

Example Program. The program consists of three functions. Function altInit has three formal parameters: size, pval1, and pval2. It allocates and initializes a global array a. The size of the allocated array is given by size. The array is initialized with an alternating sequence of two values, pointed to by the pointers pval1 and pval2. After the initialization is completed, the last value of the sequence is the value returned to the caller. Function main is a test driver for function altInit. It reads in an integer number from standard input and ensures that it gets a value greater than zero. Then it calls function altInit with the read value as parameter for the size as well as for the two initial values. Finally, the stub function myscanf models the behavior of the C library function scanf, which reads input values. The stub myscanf models arbitrary user input by returning a random integer value.

Control-Flow Automata. Internally, this program is represented by control-flow automata (CFA), one for each function of the program. A CFA is a directed graph, with locations corresponding to control points of the program (program-counter values), and edges corresponding to program operations. An edge between two locations is labeled by the instruction that executes when control moves from the source to the destination; an instruction is either a *basic block* of assignments, an *assume predicate* corresponding to the condition that must hold for control to go across the edge, a *function call* with call-by-value parameters (BLAST also handles call-by-reference, but this is omitted from this exposition for simplicity), or a *return* instruction. Figures 2 and 3 show the control-flow automata for the functions main and altInit, respectively.

Memory Safety. We wish to prove that our program is memory safe, in particular, that there is no null-pointer dereference. In our example, we focus on one particular pointer dereference in the program: the dereference of the pointer ptr at the end of the function altInit (on line 19). We wish to prove that along all executions of the program, this pointer dereference is valid, that is, the value of ptr is not null. Notice that this property holds for our program: along every

```
#include <stdio.h>
#include <stdlib.h>
int *a;

void myscanf(const char* format, int* arg) {
  *arg = rand();
}

int altInit(int size, int *pval1, int *pval2){
 1:   int i, *ptr;
 2:   a = (int *) malloc(sizeof(int) * size);
 3:   if (a == 0) {
 4:     printf("Memory exhausted.");
 5:     exit(1);
 6:   }
 7:   i = 0;
 8:   while(i < size) {
 9:     i = i + 1;
10:     if (i % 2 == 0) {
11:        ptr = pval1;
12:     } else {
13:        ptr = pval2;
14:     }
15:     a[i] = *ptr;
16:     printf("%d. iteration", i);
17:   }
18:   if (ptr == 0) ERR: ;
19:   return *ptr;
}

int main(int argc, char *argv []){
20:   int *pval = (int *) malloc(sizeof(int));
21:   if (pval == 0) {
22:     printf("Memory exhausted.");
23:     exit(1);
24:   }
25:   *pval = 0;
26:   while(*pval <= 0) {
27:     printf("Give a number greater zero: ");
28:     myscanf("%d", pval);
29:   }
30:   return altInit(*pval, pval, pval);
}
```

Fig. 1. The example C program

execution path to line 19, the pointer `ptr` equals either `pval1` or `pval2`. Moreover, when `altInit` is called from `main`, the actual arguments passed to `pval1` and `pval2` are both `pval` (line 30). We have allocated space for `pval` in `main` (line 20), and we have already checked that the allocation succeeded (the test on line 21 and the code on lines 22–23 ensures that the program exits if `pval` is null). While the actual reason for correctness is simple, the example shows that the analysis to prove safety must be interprocedural and path-sensitive.

We have instrumented the program to check for this property (line 18), by checking whether the pointer `ptr` is null immediately before the dereference. In the next section, we will describe how such instrumentations are inserted automatically by a memory-safety analysis. With the instrumentation, the label ERR on line 18 is reached if and only if the pointer `ptr` is null and about to be dereferenced at line 19. In Figure 3 the error location with label 1#22 is depicted by a filled ellipse. We now describe how BLAST checks that the label ERR (or

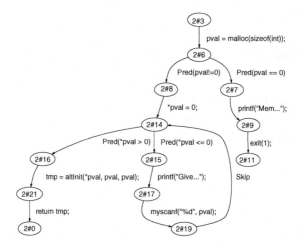

Fig. 2. Control-flow automaton for function `main`

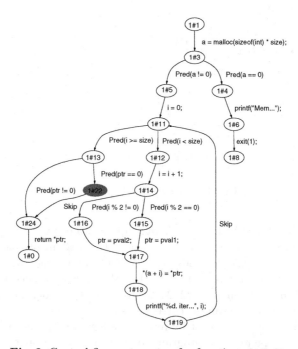

Fig. 3. Control-flow automaton for function `altInit`

equivalently, the location 1#22 of the CFA) is not reached along any execution of the program, and thus proves that the dereference on line 19 never fails.

Abstract Reachability Trees. In order to prove that the label ERR is never reached, BLAST constructs an abstract reachability tree (ART). An ART is a labeled tree that represents a portion of the reachable state space of the program. Each node of the ART is labeled with a location of a CFA, the current call stack (a sequence of CFA nodes representing return addresses), and a boolean formula (called the *reachable region*) representing a set of data states. We denote a labeled tree node as $\mathbf{n} : (q, s, \varphi)$, where $\mathbf{n}$ is the tree node, q is the CFA node, s is the call stack, and φ is the reachable region. Each edge of the tree is marked with a basic block, an assume predicate, a function call, or a return. A path in the reachability tree corresponds to a program execution. The reachable region of a node describes an overapproximation of the reachable states of the program assuming execution follows the sequence of operations labeling the path from the root of the tree to the node.

Given a region (set of data states) φ and program operation (basic block or assume predicate) op, let $post(\varphi, \mathsf{op})$ be the set of states reachable from φ by executing the operation op. For a function call op, let $post(\varphi, \mathsf{op})$ be the set of states reachable from φ by assigning the actual parameters to the formal parameters of the called function. For a return instruction op and variable x, let $post(\varphi, \mathsf{op}, \mathsf{x})$ be the set of states reachable from φ by assigning the return value to x. An ART is *complete* if (1) the root is labeled with the initial states of the program; (2) the tree is closed under postconditions, that is, for every internal node $\mathbf{n} : (q, s, \varphi)$ of the tree with $\varphi \neq \emptyset$,

(2a) if $q \xrightarrow{\mathsf{op}} q'$ is an edge in the CFA of q and op is a basic block or assume predicate, then there is a successor node $\mathbf{n}' : (q', s, \varphi')$ of $\mathbf{n}$ in the tree such that the edge $(\mathbf{n}, \mathbf{n}')$ is marked with op and $post(\varphi, \mathsf{op}) \subseteq \varphi'$,

(2b) if $q \xrightarrow{\mathsf{op}} q'$ is a CFA edge and op is a function call, then there is an op-successor $\mathbf{n}' : (q'', s', \varphi')$ in the tree such that q'' is the initial location of the called function, the call stack s' results from pushing the return location q' together with the left-hand-side variable of the function call onto s, and $post(\varphi, \mathsf{op}) \subseteq \varphi'$,

(2c) if $q \xrightarrow{\mathsf{op}} q'$ is a CFA edge and op is a return instruction, then there is an op-successor $\mathbf{n}' : (q'', s', \varphi')$ in the tree such that (q'', x) is the top of the call stack s, the new call stack s' results from popping the top of s, and $post(\varphi, \mathsf{op}, \mathsf{x}) \subseteq \varphi'$;

and (3) for every leaf node $\mathbf{n} : (q, s, \varphi)$ of the tree, either q has no outgoing edge in its CFA, or $\varphi = \emptyset$, or there exists an internal tree node $\mathbf{n}' : (q, s, \varphi')$ such that $\varphi \subseteq \varphi'$. In the last case, we say that $\mathbf{n}$ is *covered* by $\mathbf{n}'$, as every program execution from $\mathbf{n}$ is also possible from $\mathbf{n}'$. A complete ART overapproximates the set of reachable states of a program. A complete ART is *safe* with respect to a CFA location q (the *error* location) if for every node $\mathbf{n} : (q, \cdot, \varphi)$ in the tree, we have $\varphi = \emptyset$. A complete ART that is safe for q serves as a certificate (proof) that q cannot be reached by any execution of the program [16].

Figure 4 shows a complete ART for our example program. We omit the call stack for clarity. Each node of the tree is labeled with a CFA node, and the

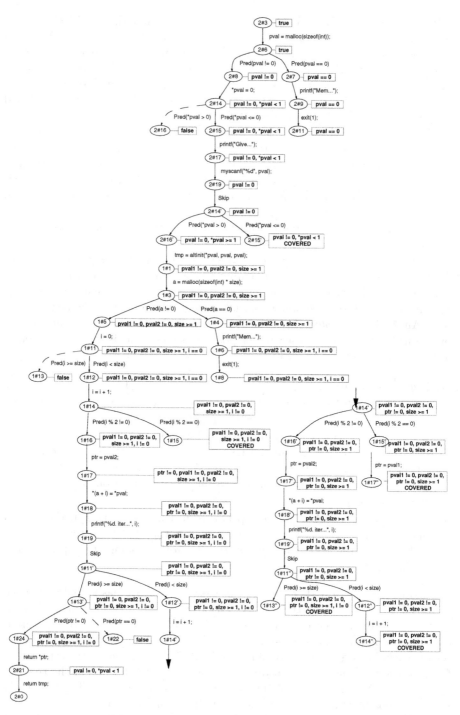

Fig. 4. Complete abstract reachability tree

reachable region is depicted in the associated rectangular box. The reachable region is the conjunction of the list of predicates in each box. Notice that some leaf nodes in the tree are marked "COVERED". Since this ART is safe for the error location 1#22, this proves that ERR cannot be reached in the program. Notice that the reachable region at a node is an overapproximation of the concretely reachable states in terms of some suitably chosen set of predicates. For example, consider the edge 1#16 $\xrightarrow{\texttt{ptr=pval2}}$ 1#17 in the CFA. Starting from the region

$$\texttt{pval1} \neq 0 \wedge \texttt{pval2} \neq 0 \wedge \texttt{size} \geq 1 \wedge \texttt{i} \neq 0,$$

the set of states that can be reached by the assignment ptr=pval2 is

$$\texttt{pval1} \neq 0 \wedge \texttt{pval2} \neq 0 \wedge \texttt{size} \geq 1 \wedge \texttt{i} \neq 0 \wedge \texttt{ptr} = \texttt{pval2}.$$

However, the tree maintains an overapproximation of this set of states, namely,

$$\texttt{pval1} \neq 0 \wedge \texttt{pval2} \neq 0 \wedge \texttt{size} \geq 1 \wedge \texttt{i} \neq 0 \wedge \texttt{ptr} \neq 0,$$

which loses the fact that ptr now contains the same address as pval2. This overapproximation is precise enough to show that the ART is safe for the location 1#22. Overapproximating is crucial in making the analysis scale, as the cost of the analysis grows rapidly with increased precision. Thus, the safety-verification algorithm must (1) find an abstraction (a mapping of control locations to predicates) which is precise enough to prove the property of interest, yet coarse enough to allow the model checker to succeed, and (2) efficiently explore (i.e., model check) the abstract state space of the program.

Counterexample-Guided Abstraction Refinement. BLAST solves these problems in the following way. It starts with a coarse abstraction of the state space and attempts to construct a complete ART with the coarse abstraction. If this complete ART is safe for the error location, then the program is safe. However, the imprecision of the abstraction may result in the analysis finding paths in the ART leading to the error location which are infeasible during the execution of the program. We call such paths spurious counterexamples. In this case, BLAST refines the current abstraction by running a counterexample-analysis algorithm that determines whether the path to the error location is genuine (that is, there is a bug) or spurious. The counterexample-analysis algorithm uses an interpolation-based predicate-discovery algorithm which adds predicates locally to rule out spurious counterexamples [15]. For a given abstraction (mapping of control locations to predicates), BLAST constructs the ART on-the-fly, stopping and running the counterexample analysis whenever a path to the error location is found in the ART. The refinement procedure refines the abstraction locally, and the search is resumed on the nodes of the ART where the abstraction has been refined. The parts of the ART that have not been affected by the refinement are left intact. This algorithm is called *lazy abstraction* [18]; we now describe how it works on our example.

Constructing the ART. Initially, BLAST starts with no predicates, and attempts to construct an ART. The ART construction proceeds by unrolling the

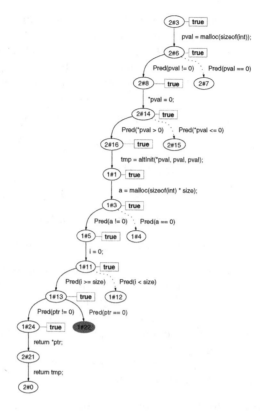

Fig. 5. Abstract reachability tree when the first spurious error path is found

CFAs and keeping track of the reachable region at each CFA node. We start with the initial location of `main`, with the reachable region *true* (which represents an arbitrary initial data state). For a tree node $n : (q, s, \varphi)$, we construct successor nodes of n in the tree for all edges $q \xrightarrow{\text{op}} q'$ in the CFA of q. The successor nodes are labeled with overapproximations of the set of states reachable from (q, s, φ) when the corresponding operations `op` are performed. To handle function calls and returns, BLAST implements a context-free reachability algorithm [25]. For our first iteration, since we do not track any facts (predicates) about variable values, all reachable regions are overapproximated by *true* (that is, the abstraction assumes that every data state is possible). With this abstraction, BLAST finds that the error location may be reachable. Figure 5 shows the ART when BLAST finds the first path to the error location. This ART is not complete, because some nodes have not been processed yet. In the figure, all nodes with incoming dotted edges (e.g., the node 2#7) have not been processed. However, the incomplete ART already contains an error path from node 2#3 to 1#22 (the error node is depicted as a filled ellipse).

$$\left.\begin{array}{l} \langle \mathtt{pval}, 1 \rangle = \mathtt{malloc}_0 \wedge \langle \mathtt{pval}, 1 \rangle \neq 0 \wedge \\ \langle *(\langle \mathtt{pval}, 1 \rangle), 1 \rangle = 0 \wedge \langle *(\langle \mathtt{pval}, 1 \rangle), 1 \rangle > 0 \wedge \end{array}\right\} \text{ function } \mathtt{main}$$

$$\left.\begin{array}{l} \langle \mathtt{size}, 1 \rangle = \langle *(\langle \mathtt{pval}, 1 \rangle), 1 \rangle \wedge \\ \langle \mathtt{pval1}, 1 \rangle = \langle \mathtt{pval}, 1 \rangle \wedge \\ \langle \mathtt{pval2}, 1 \rangle = \langle \mathtt{pval}, 1 \rangle \wedge \end{array}\right\} \text{ formals assigned actuals}$$

$$\left.\begin{array}{l} \langle \mathtt{a}, 1 \rangle = \mathtt{malloc}_1 \wedge \langle \mathtt{a}, 1 \rangle \neq 0 \wedge \\ \langle \mathtt{i}, 1 \rangle = 0 \wedge \langle \mathtt{i}, 1 \rangle \geq \langle \mathtt{size}, 1 \rangle \wedge \\ \langle \mathtt{ptr}, 1 \rangle = 0 \end{array}\right\} \text{ function } \mathtt{altInit}$$

Fig. 6. Trace formula for the error path of Figure 5

Counterexample Analysis. At this point, BLAST invokes the counterexample-analysis algorithm which checks if the error path is feasible in the concrete program (i.e., the program has a bug), or whether it arises because the current abstraction is too coarse. To analyze the error path, BLAST creates a set of constraints (called the *trace formula*) which is satisfiable if and only if the path is feasible in the concrete program. The trace formula is built by transforming the error path to single-assignment form [10] (every variable is assigned a value at most once, which is achieved by introducing new variables) and then generating constraints for each operation along the path. For the error path of the example, the trace formula is given in Figure 6. Note that in this example, each program variable occurs only once at the left-hand-side of an assignment; if, for instance, the program variable pval were assigned a value twice along the path, then the result of the first assignment would be denoted by the new variable $\langle \mathtt{pval}, 1 \rangle$ and the result of the second assignment would be denoted by the new variable $\langle \mathtt{pval}, 2 \rangle$. The trace formula is unsatisfiable, and hence the error path is not feasible. There are several reasons why this path is not feasible. First, we set *pval to 0 in main, and then take the branch where *pval > 0. Further, we check in main that *pval > 0, and pass *pval as the argument size to altInit. Hence, size > 0. Now, we set i to 0, and then check that i ≥ size. This check cannot succeed, because i is zero, while size is greater than 0. Thus, the path cannot be executed and represents a spurious counterexample.

Predicate Discovery. The predicate-discovery algorithm takes the trace formula and finds new predicates that must be added to the abstraction in order to rule out the spurious counterexample. New predicates are obtained at each location along the spurious error path using an interpolation procedure. For a pair of formulas φ^- and φ^+ such that $\varphi^- \wedge \varphi^+$ is unsatisfiable, a *Craig interpolant* ψ is a formula such that (1) the implication $\varphi^- \Rightarrow \psi$ is valid, (2) the conjunction $\psi \wedge \varphi^+$ is unsatisfiable, and (3) ψ only contains symbols that are common to both φ^- and φ^+. Given an appropriate logical theory, such interpolants always exist [9]. BLAST cuts the infeasible path at every location. At each cut point, the part of the trace formula corresponding to the path fragment up to the cut point is φ^-, and the part of the formula corresponding to the path fragment after the cut point is φ^+. Then, the interpolant at the cut point represents a formula over the live program variables that contains the reachable region after the path up to the cut point is executed (by property (1)), and is sufficient to show that the rest of the path is unfeasible (by property (2)). The live program variables are represented by those new variables which occur both up to and after the cut point (by property (3)).

For example, consider the cut at location 2#16. For this cut, φ^- is

$$\langle \mathtt{pval}, 1 \rangle = \mathtt{malloc}_0 \wedge \langle \mathtt{pval}, 1 \rangle \neq 0 \wedge \langle *(\langle \mathtt{pval}, 1 \rangle), 1 \rangle = 0 \wedge \langle *(\langle \mathtt{pval}, 1 \rangle), 1 \rangle > 0,$$

and φ^+ is

$$\langle \mathtt{size}, 1 \rangle = \langle *(\langle \mathtt{pval}, 1 \rangle), 1 \rangle \wedge \langle \mathtt{pval1}, 1 \rangle = \langle \mathtt{pval}, 1 \rangle \wedge \langle \mathtt{pval2}, 1 \rangle = \langle \mathtt{pval}, 1 \rangle \wedge$$
$$\langle \mathtt{a}, 1 \rangle = \mathtt{malloc}_1 \wedge \langle \mathtt{a}, 1 \rangle \neq 0 \wedge \langle \mathtt{i}, 1 \rangle = 0 \wedge \langle \mathtt{i}, 1 \rangle \geq \langle \mathtt{size}, 1 \rangle \wedge \langle \mathtt{ptr}, 1 \rangle = 0.$$

The only common symbol across the cut is $\langle *(\langle \mathtt{pval}, 1 \rangle), 1 \rangle$, and the interpolant is $\langle *(\mathtt{pval}, 1), 1 \rangle \geq 1$. Relating the new variable $\langle *(\mathtt{pval}, 1), 1 \rangle$ back to the program variable *pval, this suggests that the fact *pval ≥ 1 suffices to prove the error path infeasible. This predicate is henceforth tracked at location 2#16. Similarly, at nodes 1#1, 1#3, and 1#5, BLAST discovers that the predicate size ≥ 1 is useful, and at location 1#11, the predicates size ≥ 1 and i $= 0$ are found. After adding these predicates, BLAST refines the ART, now tracking the truth or falsehood of the newly found predicates at the locations where they are useful.

Refining the ART. When BLAST refines the ART with the new abstraction, it only reconstructs subtrees that are rooted at nodes where new predicates have been added. In the example, a second error path is found; Figure 7 shows the ART when this happens. Notice that this time, the reachable regions are not all *true*; instead they are overapproximations, at each node of the ART, of the reachable data states in terms of the predicates that are tracked at the node. For example, the reachable region at the first occurrence of location 2#14 in the ART is *pval < 1 (the negation of the tracked predicate *pval ≥ 1), because *pval is set to 0 when going from 2#8 to 2#14, and *pval < 1 is the abstraction of *pval $= 0$ in terms of the tracked predicates. This more precise reachable region disallows certain CFA paths from being explored. For example, again at the first occurrence of location 2#14, the ART has no left successor with location 2#16, because no data state in the reachable region *pval < 1 can take the program branch with the condition *pval > 0 (recall that *pval is an integer).

On the second error path, the counterexample analysis discovers the new predicates pval $= 0$, pval2 $= 0$, and ptr $= 0$. In the next iteration, BLAST finds a third error path, shown in Figure 8, for which it finds the predicate pval1 $= 0$.

With these predicates, BLAST constructs the complete ART shown in Figure 4. Since this tree is safe for the error location 1#22, this proves that ERR can never be reached by executing the program. Note that some leaf nodes in the tree are covered: as no new states can be reached by exploring states from covered nodes, BLAST stops the ART construction at such nodes, and the whole process terminates.

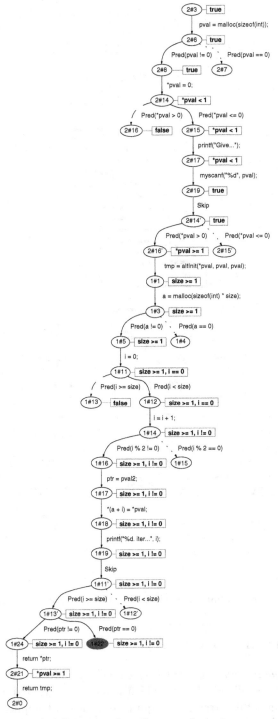

Fig. 7. Abstract reachability tree when the second spurious error path is found

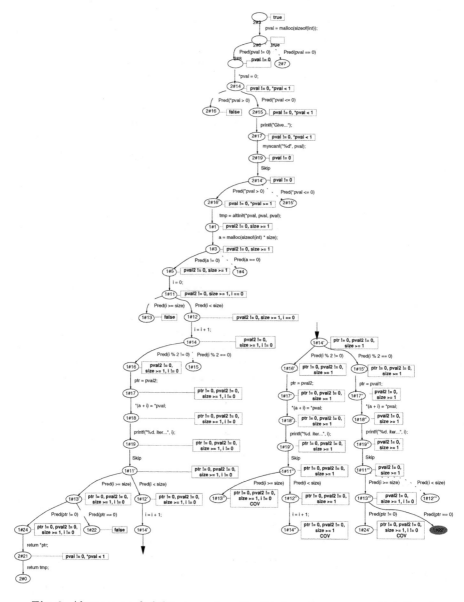

Fig. 8. Abstract reachability tree when the third spurious error path is found

3   Checking Memory Safety

A program is *memory safe* if it only accesses memory addresses within the bounds
of the objects it has allocated or to which it has been granted access. Memory
safety is a fundamental correctness requirement for most applications. We consider one particular aspect of memory safety: null-pointer dereferencing. Pointers

in C programs can be null (i.e., not pointing to a valid address), or point to an allocated object. Dereferencing a null pointer can cause an arbitrary value to be read, or the program to crash with a segmentation fault.

The absence of null-pointer dereferences is a safety property. In principle, we can annotate every dereference operation in the program with a check that the dereferenced pointer is not null, and run BLAST on the annotated program to verify that no such check fails. However, this strategy does not scale well. First, many accesses can be proved memory safe using an inexpensive type-based approach, and using an expensive analysis like BLAST is overkill. Second, each annotation should be checked independently, so that the abstractions required to prove each annotation do not interfere and result in a large state space. Therefore, we use CCURED [7, 24], a type-based memory-safety analysis, to classify the pointers according to usage and annotate the program with run-time checks. CCURED analyzes C programs with respect to a sound type system which ensures that well-typed programs are memory safe. When the type system cannot prove that a pointer variable is always used safely, CCURED inserts run-time checks in the program which monitor correct pointer usage at execution time. In particular, each dereference of a potentially unsafe (i.e., not proved safe by the type system) pointer is annotated with a check that the pointer is non-null. The run-time checks abort the program safely, instead of running into undefined configurations. However, each run-time check constitutes overhead at execution time, and CCURED implements many optimizations that remove redundant run-time checks based on simple data-flow analyses. Typically, the CCURED optimizations remove over 50% of the run-time checks inserted by the type system, and the optimized programs run within a factor of two of their original execution time. We wish to check how many of the remaining run-time checks can be removed by the more sophisticated analysis implemented in BLAST.

Specifically, for each potentially unsafe pointer dereference *p in the program, CCURED introduces a call __CHECK_NULL(p) which checks that the pointer p is non-null. The function __CHECK_NULL terminates the program if its argument is null, and simply returns if the argument is non-null. Thus, if the actual argument p at a call site is non-null along all execution paths, then this function call can be removed without affecting the behavior of the program. To check if a call to __CHECK_NULL can be removed from the program, BLAST does the following. First, it replaces the call to __CHECK_NULL with a call to __BLAST__CHECK_NULL with the same argument, where __BLAST__CHECK_NULL is the following function:

```
void __BLAST__CHECK_NULL(void *p) {
   if (!p) { __BLAST_ERROR: ; }
}
```

Second, BLAST checks if the location labeled with __BLAST_ERROR is reachable. Both steps are performed independently for each call to __CHECK_NULL in the program body. Each call of BLAST has three possible outcomes.

The first outcome is that BLAST reports that the label __BLAST_ERROR is not reachable. In this case, the function call can be removed, since the corresponding check will not fail at run time.

The second possible outcome is that BLAST produces an error trace that gives a program execution in which __BLAST__CHECK_NULL is called with a null argument, which indicates a situation where the run-time check fails. In this case, the check must remain in the program to terminate the program safely should the check fail. This may also indicate a program error, in which case the feedback provided by BLAST (the error trace) provides useful information for fixing the bug. We often encountered error traces of the form that the programmer forgot to check the return value of `malloc`: if the memory allocation fails, then the next dereference of the pointer is unsafe. BLAST assumes that `malloc` may return a null pointer and discovers the problem. However, not every error trace found by BLAST necessarily indicates a program error, because BLAST makes conservative assumptions about library functions.

There is a third possible outcome, namely, that BLAST fails to declare whether the considered run-time check is superfluous or necessary, due to time or space limitations. In this case, we say that BLAST *fails*, and we will provide the failure rate for the experiments below. If BLAST fails on a run-time check, then the check must of course remain in the program. Notice that by changing each call to __CHECK_NULL separately, BLAST checks if a run-time check is necessary independently from all other checks. These checks can be run in parallel and often lead to different program abstractions.

We ran our method on several examples. The first seven programs are from the Olden v1.0 benchmark suite [5]. We included the programs for the Bitonic Sort algorithm (bisort), the Electromagnetic Problem in Three Dimensions (em3d), the Power Pricing problem (power), the Tree Add example (treeadd), the Traveling Salesman problem (tsp), the Perimeters algorithm (perimeter), and the Minimum Spanning Tree problem (mst). Finally, we processed the scheduler for Unix systems fcron, version 2.9.5, and the Lisp interpreter (li) from the Spec95 benchmark suite. We ran BLAST on each run-time check inserted by CCURED separately, and fixed a time-out of 200 s for each check; that is, a run of the model checker is stopped after 200 s with *failure*, and the studied run-time check is conservatively declared necessary.

Table 1 presents the results of our experiments. The first column lists the program name, the second and third columns give the number of lines of the original program ("LOC orig.") and of the instrumented program after preprocessing and CCURED instrumentation ("LOC cured"). The three columns of "run-time checks" lists the number of run-time checks inserted by the CCURED type system (column "inserted"), the number of remaining checks after the CCURED optimizer removes redundant checks (column "optim."), and finally the number of remaining checks after BLAST is used to remove run-time checks (column "BLAST"). The column "proved safe by BLAST" is the difference between the "optim." and "BLAST" columns: it shows the number of checks remaining after the CCURED optimizer which BLAST proves will never fail.

Table 1. Verification of run-time checks

Program	LOC		run-time checks			proved safe	potential
	orig.	cured	inserted	optim.	BLAST	by BLAST	errors found
bisort	684	2,510	51	21	6	15	6
em3d	561	2,831	33	20	9	11	9
power	763	2,891	149	24	24	0	24
power-fixed	763	2,901	149	24	24	12	12
treeadd	370	2,246	11	7	6	1	6
tsp	565	2,560	93	59	44	15	4
perimeter	395	2,292	49	18	8	10	5
mst	582	2,932	54	34	19	15	18
fcron 2.9.5	11,994	38,080	877	455	222	233	74
li	6,343	39,289	1,715	915	361	554	11

The remaining checks, which cannot be removed by BLAST, fall into two categories. First, the column "potential errors found" lists the number of checks for which BLAST found an error trace leading to a violation of the run-time check; those are potential bugs and the error traces give useful information to the programmer. For example, we took the program with the most potential errors found, namely power, and analyzed its error traces. In many of them, a call to `malloc` occurs without a check whether there is enough memory available. So we inserted after each call to `malloc` a null-pointer check to ensure that the program execution does not proceed in such a case. Analyzing the fixed program (with null-pointer checks inserted after each `malloc`), we can remove 12 more run-time checks. To give an example of the performance of BLAST, in the case of power-fixed, the cured program was checked in 15.6 s of processor time on a 3 GHz Linux machine.

Second, the difference between the columns "BLAST" and "potential errors found" gives the number of run-time checks on which the model checker fails (times out) without an answer. The number of these failures is not shown explicitly in the table; it is zero for the first five programs. Since BLAST gives no information about these checks, they must remain in the program.

Acknowledgments. We thank George Necula and Matt Harren for help with CCURED.

References

1. T. Andrews, S. Qadeer, S.K. Rajamani, J. Rehof, and Y. Xie. ZING: A model checker for concurrent software. In *Proc. CAV*, LNCS 3114, pages 484–487. Springer, 2004.
2. T.M. Austin, S.E. Breach, and G.S. Sohi. Efficient detection of all pointer and array access errors. In *Proc. PLDI*, pages 290–301. ACM, 1994.
3. T. Ball and S.K. Rajamani. The SLAM project: Debugging system software via static analysis. In *Proc. POPL*, pages 1–3. ACM, 2002.

4. R. Bodik, R. Gupta, and V. Sarkar. ABCD: Eliminating array bounds checks on demand. In *Proc. PLDI*, pages 321–333. ACM, 2000.
5. M.C. Carlisle. *Olden: Parallelizing Programs with Dynamic Data Structures on Distributed Memory Machines*. PhD thesis, Princeton University, 1996.
6. S. Chaki, E.M. Clarke, A. Groce, S. Jha, and H. Veith. Modular verification of software components in C. *IEEE Trans. Software Engineering*, 30:388–402, 2004.
7. J. Condit, M. Harren, S. McPeak, G.C. Necula, and W. Weimer. CCURED in the real world. In *Proc. PLDI*, pages 232–244. ACM, 2003.
8. J.C. Corbett, M.B. Dwyer, J. Hatcliff, C. Pasareanu, Robby, S. Laubach, and H. Zheng. BANDERA: Extracting finite-state models from Java source code. In *Proc. ICSE*, pages 439–448. ACM, 2000.
9. W. Craig. Linear reasoning. *J. Symbolic Logic*, 22:250–268, 1957.
10. R. Cytron, J. Ferrante, B.K. Rosen, M.N. Wegman, and F.K. Zadek. Efficiently computing static single-assignment form and the program dependence graph. *ACM Trans. Programming Languages and Systems*, 13:451–490, 1991.
11. P. Godefroid. Model checking for programming languages using VERISOFT. In *Proc. POPL*, pages 174–186. ACM, 1997.
12. R. Hastings and B. Joyce. Purify: Fast detection of memory leaks and access errors. In *Proc. USENIX*, pages 125–136, 1992.
13. K. Havelund and T. Pressburger. Model checking Java programs using Java PATHFINDER. *Software Tools for Technology Transfer*, 2:72–84, 2000.
14. F. Henglein. Global tagging optimization by type inference. In *Proc. LISP and Functional Programming*, pages 205–215. ACM, 1992.
15. T.A. Henzinger, R. Jhala, R. Majumdar, and K.L. McMillan. Abstractions from proofs. In *Proc. POPL*, pages 232–244. ACM, 2004.
16. T.A. Henzinger, R. Jhala, R. Majumdar, G.C. Necula, G. Sutre, and W. Weimer. Temporal-safety proofs for systems code. In *Proc. CAV*, LNCS 2404, pages 526–538. Springer, 2002.
17. T.A. Henzinger, R. Jhala, R. Majumdar, and M.A.A. Sanvido. Extreme model checking. In *International Symposium on Verification: Theory and Practice*, LNCS 2772, pages 332–358. Springer, 2003.
18. T.A. Henzinger, R. Jhala, R. Majumdar, and G. Sutre. Lazy abstraction. In *Proc. POPL*, pages 58–70. ACM, 2002.
19. T.A. Henzinger, R. Jhala, R. Majumdar, and G. Sutre. Software verification with BLAST. In *Proc. SPIN*, LNCS 2648, pages 235–239. Springer, 2003.
20. G.J. Holzmann. *The SPIN Model Checker: Primer and Reference Manual*. Addison-Wesley, 2003.
21. S. Kaufer, R. Lopez, and S. Pratap. SABER-C: An interpreter-based programming environment for the C language. In *Proc. USENIX*, pages 161–171, 1988.
22. M. Musuvathi, D.Y.W. Park, A. Chou, D.R. Engler, and D.L. Dill. CMC: A pragmatic approach to model checking real code. In *Proc. OSDI*. USENIX, 2002.
23. G.C. Necula and P. Lee. Efficient representation and validation of proofs. In *Proc. LICS*, pages 93–104. IEEE, 1998.
24. G.C. Necula, S. McPeak, and W. Weimer. CCURED: Type-safe retrofitting of legacy code. In *Proc. POPL*, pages 128–139. ACM, 2002.
25. T. Reps, S. Horwitz, and M. Sagiv. Precise interprocedural dataflow analysis via graph reachability. In *Proc. POPL*, pages 49–61. ACM, 1995.
26. N. Suzuki and K. Ishihata. Implementation of an array bound checker. In *Proc. POPL*, pages 132–143. ACM, 1977.

Analyzing Web Service Based Business Processes

Axel Martens

Humboldt-Universität zu Berlin,
Department of Computer Sciece, Berlin (Adlershof), Germany
IBM T. J. Watson Research Center,
Component Systems Group, Hawthorne (NY), USA
martens@informatik.hu-berlin.de *amarten@us.ibm.com*

Abstract. This paper is concerned with the application of Web services
to distributed, cross-organizational business processes. In this scenario,
it is crucial to answer the following questions: Do two Web services fit
together in a way such that the composed system is deadlock-free? –
the question of *compatibility*. Can one Web service be replaced by another while the remaining components stay untouched? – the question of
equivalence. Can we reason about the soundness of one given Web service
without considering the actual environment it will by used in?
This paper defines the notion of *usability* – an intuitive and locally provable soundness criterion for a given Web services. Based on this notion,
this paper demonstrates how the other questions could be answered.
The presented method is based on Petri nets, because this formalism is
widely used for modeling and analyzing business processes. Due to the
existing Petri net semantics for BPEL4WS – a language that is in the
very act of becoming the industrial standard for Web service based business processes – the results are directly applicable to real world examples.

Keywords: Business Process Modeling, Web Service, BPEL4WS, Tool
based Verification, Petri nets.

1   Introduction

Over the past years, the Internet has evolved from just a communication media
into a platform for B2B integration. Emerging technologies and industrial standards in the field of *Web services* enable a much faster and easier cooperation
of distributed partners. This paper is concerned with the application of Web
services to distributed, cross-organizational business processes.

The Scenario. A *Web service* [1] is a self-describing, self-contained modular
application that can be published, located, and invoked over a network, e. g. the
Internet. A Web service performs an encapsulated function and can be accessed
via a standardized interface. In this paper, each local sub-process of each participating company is realized through one Web service. The composition of all
Web services of all participating companies realizes the global business process.

M. Cerioli (Ed.): FASE 2005, LNCS 3442, pp. 19–33, 2005.

Instead of *one* new specific technology, the Web service approach provides a stack of closely related technologies [4] to cover heterogeneity and distribution underneath a homogenous concept of components and composition. Among other things, the language BPEL4WS [2] belongs to this stack. Due to this layered architecture, the presented analysis method can be focussed on the Web service's BPEL process model without losing generality or practical relevance.

The Goal. The Web service technologies define a technical framework to implement distributed business processes while a minimum of *syntactic* consistency is guaranteed. But as this paper will show, there is a need for more advanced analysis, and there exist effective methods that are able to support the development of Web services and Web service based business processes according to the *Service oriented architecture* (SOA [9]).

The service oriented architecture describes three roles: The *service provider* implements the Web service and publishes its description (the Web service model) to one or more repositories for potential users to locate. For him, it is crucial to determine errors and weaknesses of his service prior to publication. Hence, this paper presents the notion *usability* – a locally provable soundness criterion for a given Web service – that prevents publication of erroneous services.

The *service requestor* is searching for a Web service that he could bind to his own components. For him, it is crucial to determine whether or not a given Web service does interact properly with his components. Hence, this paper defines the criterion of *semantic compatibility* and provides its verification.

Finally, the *service broker* manages a repository and allows the service requestor to find an adequate service. According to the *query-by-example* approach, he compares the actual Web service model (published by provider) with an abstract Web service model submitted by the requestor. Beside other use cases, the presented *equivalence* criterion provides a basis for the necessary *matchmaking*.

The Method. Many of the Web services technologies are still in the standardization process, and therefore some specifications will likely be changed several times until a consistent status is reached. Hence, the presented method refrains from the actual syntax of any proposed Web service modeling languages. Instead, it applies a generic formalism of *Petri nets* [16] to addresses the core problems of distributed business processes. This formal method is widely used for modeling and analyzing business processes and Web services [21, 5, 6]. Applying the rich theory of distributed systems, the presented method is able to define and verify *usability*, *compatibility* and *equivalence* of Web services. Moreover, the presented results can easily be adopted to almost any concrete modeling language (e. g. WS-CDL [7], OWL-S [25] or YAWL [23]). In particular, there exists already a Petri net semantics for BPEL4WS [18] – a language that is in the very act of becoming the industrial standard for modeling Web service based business processes. Hence, the method is directly applicable to real world examples.

The remaining paper is structured as follows: Section 2 gives a short introduction to Petri nets and describes the structure and composition of *workflow modules* – the formal model of a Web Sevice. Section 3, discusses and defines the notion of *usability* by help of examples, and derives the properties of *compatibility* and *equivalence*. Section 4 establishes the core section of this paper: Applied to an example, the verification algorithm is presented. Finally, Section 5 summarizes the results and discusses their correlation to other published approaches.

2   Modeling

The *Business Process Execution Language for Web Services* BPEL4WS [2] provides a syntax to describe Web service process models. But, its semantics so far is defined only by English prose or encoded into middleware components, more ore less accurately. To verify properties like properties compatibility or equivalence of two models a formal semantics of all its concepts is needed. The presented method is based on a Petri net semantics [18]. Petri nets are a well established method for modeling and analyzing (cross-organizational) business processes [20, 21, 8]. They possess an intuitive graphical representation as well as an algebraic foundation, and therefore Petri nets allow an effective analysis. Other recent research projects apply Petri nets to Web Services [6, 15], too.

In contrast to the mentioned Petri net semantics, the current approach abstracts from data aspects. This is an usual procedure in the field of computer aided verification. On the one hand, a model without data has the disadvantage of less precision (i. e. a more general behavior), but on the other hand, this enables analysis methods yielding important results that are not applicable to models with full expressive power of arbitrary data objects. The mapping of a BPEL process model into an analyzable Petri net is explained in [13].

2.1   Modeling with Petri Nets

Figure 1 shows Petri net models of three Web service: A route planning service, a services that acts as mediator and a customer's service. These examples will be used to demonstrate the modeling method, and to visualize composition and compatibility of Web services. But first, some basic Petri net notions have to be introduced:

Petri Nets. A *Petri net* $N = (P, T, F)$ consists of a set of *transitions* T (boxes), a set of *places* P (ellipses), and a *flow relation* F (arcs) [16]. A transition represents a dynamic element, i. e. an activity of a business process (e. g. Get Itinerary). A place represents a static element, i. e. the causality between activities or a message channel (e. g. Itinerary). The *marking* (i. e. state) of a Petri net is represented by black *tokens* distributed over the places (see places p0, q0 and s0). A transition t is enabled if on each place $p, (p, t) \in F$ there is at least one token. If an enabled transition t fires, t removes one token from each place $p_1, (p_1, t) \in F$ and produces one token on each place $p_2, (t, p_2) \in F$. Based on this *firing rule*, it is possible to reason about the behavior of a Petri net in term of *firing sequences*, *reachable states* and/or *concurrent runs* (cf. [17]).

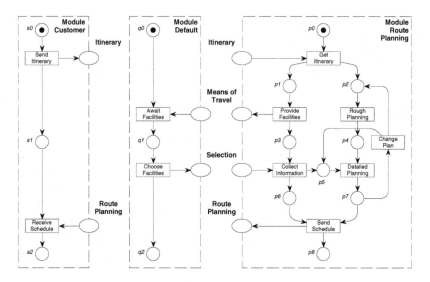

Fig. 1. Modeling with Petri nets

Workflow Modules. A stateful Web service defines an internal process (i.e. activities building its internal structure), and an interface to communicate with other Web services. Hence, the Petri net model of such a Web service consists of a *workflow net* – a special Petri net that has two distinguished places $(\alpha, \omega \in P)$ to denote the begin and the end of a process [21] – supplemented by a set of interface places – each of them representing one directed message channel. Such a model is called *workflow module*.

Definition 1 (Module). *A finite Petri net $M = (P, T, F)$ is called* workflow module *(or just* module*) if the following conditions hold:*

(i) The set of places is divided into three disjoint sets: internal places P^N, input places P^I *and* output places P^O.
(ii) The flow relation is divided into internal flow $F^N \subseteq (P^N \times T) \cup (T \times P^N)$ *and* communication flow $F^C \subseteq (P^I \times T) \cup (T \times P^O)$.
(iii) The net $PM = (P^N, T, F^N)$ is a workflow net.
(iv) No transitions is connected both to an input place and an output place.

Within a workflow module M, the workflow net PM is called the *internal process* of M and the tuple $\mathcal{I}(M) = (P^I, P^O)$ is called its *interface*. Lets have a closer look on the module Route Planning shown in Figure 1. The internal process is triggered by an incoming Itinerary. Then the control flow splits into two concurrent threads. On the left side, an available Means of travel are offered to the customer and the service awaits his Selection. Meanwhile, on the right side, a Rough Planning may happen. The Detailed Planning requires information from the customer. Finally, the service sends a Route Planning to the customer.

2.2   Composing Workflow Modules

A distributed business process is realized by the composition of a set of Web services. The following section defines the pairwise composition of workflow modules. Because this yields another workflow module, composition of more than two modules is realized by recurrent application of pairwise composition.

Compatibility. Figure 1 shows the module Default in the middle. The purpose of this service is to unburden the customer from making a selection: The module consumes the message on available Means of travel and returns a default Selection. Intuitively, it looks like the modules Default and Route Planning could be composed. Formally, we will define the property of *syntactic compatibility* as a precondition for composition of two modules.

Definition 2 (Syntactic compatibility). *Two workflow modules are called* syntactically compatible *if both internal processes are disjoint, and each common place is an output place of one module and an input place of the other.*

Referring to previous definition, the modules Default and Route Planning are syntactically compatible. Nevertheless, this is not a sufficient criterion for proper interaction between two partners. Lets consider a workflow module of an online shop and a workflow module of a customer: The customer sends the payment after he has received the ordered product, whereas the online shop waits for payment before sending the product. Both modules have a syntactically compatible interface, but the resulting distributed process leads to a deadlock. To avoid such errors, Section 3.2 will define the property of *semantic compatibility*.

Composition. As the example has shown, two syntactically compatible modules do not need to have a completely matching interface. They might even have a completely disjoint interface. When two modules are composed, the common places are merged and the dangling input and output places become the new interface. To achieve a syntactically correct workflow module, it is necessary to add new components for initialization and termination.

Definition 3 (Composed system). *Let $A = (P_a, T_a, F_a)$ and $B = (P_b, T_b, F_b)$ be two syntactically compatible modules. Let $\alpha_s, \omega_s \notin (P_a \cup P_b)$ two new places and $t_\alpha, t_\omega \notin (T_a \cup T_b)$ two new transitions. The composed system $\Pi = A \oplus B$ is given by (P_s, T_s, F_s), such that: $P_s = P_a \cup P_b \cup \{\alpha_s, \omega_s\}$, $T_s = T_a \cup T_b \cup \{t_\alpha, t_\omega\}$ and $F_s = F_a \cup F_b \cup \{(\alpha_s, t_\alpha), (t_\alpha, \alpha_a), (t_\alpha, \alpha_b), (\omega_a, t_\omega), (\omega_b, t_\omega), (t_\omega, \omega_s)\}$.*

If the composed system contains more than one components for initialization and termination, the corresponding elements are merged.

It can be easily proven that the composition of two syntactically compatible workflow modules always yield a workflow module, too. This is because of the additional components for initialization and termination. If more than two modules are composed, it is important to guarantee *associativity* of pairwise composition (i. e. $(A \oplus B) \oplus C = A \oplus (B \oplus C)$). Hence, if there are already such syntactic components, they are merged while composition (cf. Figure 2(b)). In

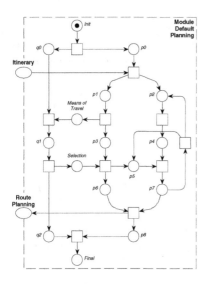

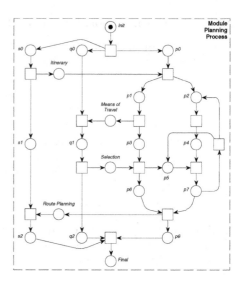

(a) A composed Web service model   (b) A composed business process model

Fig. 2. Composition of workflow modules

Figure 2(a), the workflow module Default Planning is shown – the model of the composed Web service Route Planning ⊕ Default. This service offers a simpler interface to the customer: He only has to submit the Itinerary to obtain the Route Planning information. To use this service, it is not relevant for a customer wether or not the actual service was deployed at once or was formed by composition.

Environment. The composition of two workflow modules A and B yields a model of a distributed business process, if both sets of interface places completely match, i.e. the composed system $\Pi = A \oplus B$ has an empty interface. With other words, Π is also a workflow net. In that case, module A is called an *environment* of module B – obviously, this notion is symmetric.

The module Customer shown in Figure 1 is an environment of the (composed) module Default Planning and vice versa. Figure 2(b) shows the resulting workflow net. While composing both modules, the existing and the new added components for initialization and termination are merged, as already mentioned.

Given a workflow module and its environment, it is possible to reason about the *soundness* of the composed process model. This notion is an established quality criterion for workflow nets [21]. Basically, it requires each initiated process to reach eventually a proper final state. Additionally, each transition should be relevant, i.e. there should be at least one firing sequence of the process in which this transition participates. Although the second requirement was reasonable if a business process was modeled from scratch, in the Web service approach, a process arises from composition of several predefined components. Due to this, a workflow net is acceptable even if not all functionality of each specific component is used in that system. Hence, a slightly alleviated criterion is used in this paper.

Definition 4 (Weak soundness). *A workflow net* (P, T, F) *with the final place* $\omega \in P$ *is called* weak sound *if the following conditions hold:*

(i) For each reachable marking m holds: the final marking $[\omega]$ is reachable.
(ii) For each reachable marking m with $m \geq [\omega]$ holds: $m = [\omega]$.

The weak soundness of the module Planning Process shown in Figure 2(b) can be easily proven. Because of that, intuitively, the modules Default Planning and Customer seem to be *semantically compatible*. In Section 3.1, the core notion of *usability* will be discuss and precisely defined. Based on this notion, definition of *semantic compatibility* can be derived that meets this intuition.

3   Properties

This section discusses the property of *usability* – the proposed soundness criterion for workflow modules – and derives the definitions of *compatibility* and *equivalence*. Obviously, the purpose of a Web service is to be bound to other components such that a proper realization of a distributed business process arises. Hence, the purpose of a workflow module is to be composed with an environment such that the resulting workflow net is at least weak sound. But, for a given module there might exist infinitely many possible environments. The question is: How many of these environments have to match to call the given module *usable*?

3.1   Usability

An example of a ticket service and a customer is used to address the question above. Figure 3(a) shows a workflow module C1 representing the customer and a module T1, which models the ticket service. The ticket service initiates the communication by sending a Ticket and waits for payment (either VISA or eCash). By receiving the Ticket, the customer solves an internal conflict and determines the kind of payment. The composed system C1 ⊕ T1 is weak sound, and therefore it seems reasonable to call these two modules *semantically compatible*. Is this enough to call both modules *usable*, as well?

Figure 3(b) shows two slightly modified workflow modules C2 and T2. The ticket service solves an internal conflict and sends the Ticket. Thereafter, module T2 is either in state p1 waiting for eCash only, or in state p2 waiting for VISA only. The customer receives the Ticket and has the choice between the two kinds of payment. But, he does not know the internal state of the ticket service module. Hence, he might choose the "wrong" payment, and the composed system C2 ⊕ T2 ends up in a deadlock, i. e. it is not weak sound.

Obviously, these two modules are *not* semantically compatible. To locate the modeling error, lets consider the other two possible combinations: The system C2 ⊕ T1 is also weak sound, whereas the system C1 ⊕ T2 may reach a deadlock,

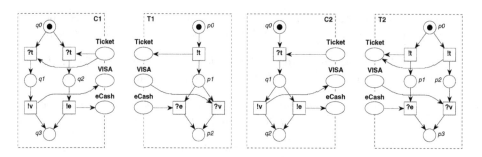

(a) An usable ticket service   (b) A non usable ticket service

Fig. 3. Usability of workflow modules

too. Hence, there are two compatible environments for module T1 and no compatible environment for module T2. By help of the developed analysis method (cf. Section 4), it can be proven that there can't be any environment that forms a weak sound composed system together with module T2. This is because of a severe error in module T2: An internal decision is made and not communicated properly to the environment. This type of errors is known in the literature as the *non local choice problem* [3]. Consequently, the module T2 is *not usable*.

For both modules C1 and C2, there is one compatible environment (T1) and one incompatible environment (T2). One might think of calling a module *usable* if *all* possible environments form a weak sound composed system together with that module. In that case, both modules C1 and C2 would be *not* usable – because of the environment T2. However, this definition is unfair: the error within the module T2 should not determine the quality of module C1. Moreover, for each given module it is possible to construct a *malicious environment* (cf. [12]). Hence, this paper proposes a more appropriate definition of usability:

Definition 5 (Usability). *Let M be a workflow module. An environment U utilizes module M if the composed system $\Pi = M \oplus U$ is weak sound. Module M is called* usable *if there exists at least one environment U that utilizes M.*

Thus, the modules C1, C2 and T1 are called usable. Section 4 presents the algorithm to decide usability of a workflow module by creating an utilizing environment (if possible). A further discussion on usability can be found in [11].

3.2   Compatibility

In the previous section, the notion of *semantic compatibility* has already be mentioned. Now, a definition of this notion shall be derived. There are two cases: If a workflow module and its environment are given, obviously, they are semantically compatible if the composed system is weak sound. But, if there are two arbitrary modules (e.g. modules Default and Route Planning shown in Figure 1), a different definition is required. Obviously, two modules are *not* compatible in case the composed system has an error, i.e. the resulting module is *not* usable. Hence, this paper proposes the following definition.

Definition 6 (Semantic compatibility). *Two syntactically compatible workflow modules A and B are called* semantically compatible *if the composed system $A \oplus B$ is usable.*

Thus, the modules Default and Route Planning are semantically compatible. Moreover, this definition also cover the composition of a module and its environment: Because the composition of those two modules yields workflow module with an empty interface (cf. Figure 2(b)), it is easy to find an utilizing environment – with an empty interface, too. Consequently, each weak sound composed system is usable. Hence, the modules Default Planning and Customer are semantically compatible. More details on compatibility can be found in [10].

3.3   Equivalence

There are many use cases, where it is crucial to decide whether two Web services behave similar, i.e. their models are *equivalent*. Beside the already mentioned problem of discovery (cf. Section 1), the problem arises if a Web service – being already part of a global business process – needs to be replaced, e.g. because of efficiency. Of course, all other participating components should stay untouched.

Intuitively, two Web services are equivalent if in a *comparable situation* one Web service *behaves like* the other and vice versa. Concerned with various formal methods, there are countless approaches published dealing with the comparison of behavior in terms of simulation or equivalence. This variety results from different interpretations of the terms "comparable situation" and "behave like" ([24] gives a substantial overview on equivalence notions). But, none of them seems to fit exactly to this field of application: The purpose of a Web service is to be used by an environment. Hence, an adequate notion of simulation or equivalence, first of all, should be derived semantically from the field of application.

Definition 7 (Simulation/Equivalence). *A workflow module A* simulates *a workflow module B if each utilizing environment of module B is an utilizing environment of module A, too. Two workflow modules A and and B are called* equivalent, *if module A simulates module B and module B simulates module A.*

This definition exactly meets the requirement of the cross-organizational business process scenario: Lets consider a workflow module M and an utilizing environment E. For each module M' simulating M and for each module E' simulating E holds: E' is an utilizing environment of M' and vice versa. This property follows directly from Definition 7.

In this approach, the verification of equivalence is based on a formal simulation relation between the *communication graphs* of both workflow modules – the explicit representation of the module's externally visible behavior, explain in the following section. Because of limited space a detailed discussion is omitted here, but some results are presented: The workflow modules C1 and C2 (shown in Figure 3) can be proven equivalent, whereas e.g. classical *bisimulation* does not yield this result. In contrast, the workflow modules T1 and T2 are proven to be not equivalent, whereas referred to *trace equivalence* those modules can't be distinguished. These examples, the comparison of selected notions of equivalence and the precise definition of the verification algorithm can be found in [13].

4   Analysis

The usability of a workflow module is defined through the existence of an utilizing environment. Hence, the definition does not describe how to disprove the usability of a given Web service. This section provides a different approach: First, an adequate representation of the Web service's external behavior is derived – called the *communication graph*. Second, the usable behavior of the Web service is determined – called the *u-graph*. Finally, the usability of a given workflow module and the algorithmic constructing its usability graph are related within the core theorem, such that usability can be decided effectively.

4.1   Reflecting the Behavior

A workflow module is a reactive system, it consumes messages from the environment and produces answers depending on its internal state. Problems may arise because an environment has no *explicit* information on the internal state of the module. But each environment can derive some information by considering the communication towards the module. Hence, an environment has some *implicit* information. We reflect exactly that kind of information within a data structure – called the *communication graph* (abbr. *c-graph*).

Definition 8 (Communication graph/c-graph). *A communication graph* $((V, H, E), m)$ *is a directed, strongly connected, labeled, bipartite graph such that:*

- *The graph has two kinds of nodes:* visible *nodes* V *and* hidden *nodes* H.
- *Each edge* $e \in E$ *connects two nodes of different kinds.*
- *The graph has a definite root node* $v_0 \in V$, *each leaf is a visible node, too.*
- *The labeling* m *maps each visible node to a set of states of the corresponding Petri net, and each edge to a bag of messages.*

Figure 4 presents the c-graphs of those workflow modules shown in Figure 3; Section 4.2 will explain why one graph is drawn with dashed lines. Lets have a closer look on the graph C(C1). The root node v0 is labeled with the initial state of the module $[q0]$[1].

Each edge, starting at a visible node, is labeled with a bag of messages sent by the environment – called *input*. In the initial state, the module C1 is able to consume only the message Ticket. Each edge, starting at a hidden node, is labeled

---

[1] The actual labeling of the node $v0$ is $\{ [q0] \}$ – the singleton containing the state $[q0]$. For reasons of simplicity, we omit these extra braces as well as the brackets around the bags of messages.

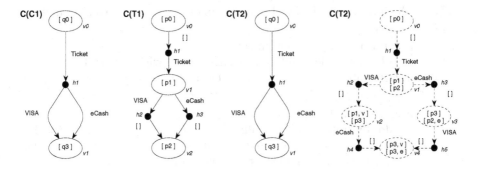

Fig. 4. Communication and usability graphs

with a bag of messages sent by the module – called *output*. In the example, the customer replies to the Ticket by paying either with VISA or with eCash. An edge may be labeled with an empty bag as well, denoted by [ ]. Each path from the root to a leaf represents a complete communication sequence between the module an an environment. In general, a visible node may be labeled with more than one state (e. g. v1 in C(T2)), and an edge may be labeled with more than on message (not present in the chosen examples). The c-graph of a given workflow module is well defined, and it can be calculated based on the following notions:

Activated input: Referring to a given state, an activated input is a bag of input messages that are consumed by the module along a firing sequence, whereas no output message was produced and the firing sequence ends either in the module's final state or in a state that enables a transition that can produce an output message. The function INP yields the set of activated inputs.

Successor state: Referring to a given state, a successor state is a maximal reachable state w. r. t. one possible behavior (i. e. one *concurred run* [17]) of the module. The function NXT yields the set of successor states.

Possible output: Referring to a given state, a possible output is the bag of output message that was produced while reaching one successor state. The function OUT yields the set of possible outputs.

Communication step: A four-tuple (z, i, o, z') is called communication step if z, z' are states of a module, i is an input and o is an output, and $(z' + o)$ is a successor state of $(z + i)$. $\mathcal{S}(M)$ denotes the set of all communication steps.

The c-graph of a workflow module may contain cycles. That doesn't affect the presented analysis method as long as the graph is finite. But, workflow modules with an infinite c-graph always contain an severe modeling error. The precise, mathematical definition of all notions mentioned above, a discussion on the complexity of the algorithm and possible optimizations, and the problem of infinite graphs is discussed in [12]. Applying these notions, we are now able to present the construction of the c-graph. The algorithm starts with the root node v_0 labeled with the initial state:

1. For each state within the label of v_k calculate the set of activated inputs: $\bigcup_{z \in m(v_k)} \text{INP}(z)$.
2. For each activated input i within this set:
   (a) Add a hidden node h, add a new edge (v_k, h) with the label i.
   (b) For each state within the label of v_k calculate the set of possible outputs: $\bigcup_{z \in m(v_k)} \text{OUT}(z + i)$.
   (c) For each possible output o within this set:
      i. Add a visible node v_{k+1}, add a new edge (h, v_{k+1}) with the label o.
      ii. For each state $z \in m(v_k)$ and for each communication step $(z, i, o, z') \in \mathcal{S}(M)$ add z' to the label of v_{k+1}.
      iii. If there exists a visible node v such that $m(v_{k+1}) = m(v)$ then merge v and v_{k+1}. Otherwise, goto step 1 with node v_{k+1}.

The c-graph of a workflow module contains the maximal information an environment can derive. The environment always sends only those messages the module is able to consume (in at least one of the possible reached states), but enough to achieve an answer or to terminate the process in a proper state. By considering all reachable successor states (and all possible outputs), the choices within the module are not restricted.

4.2   Analyzing the Behavior

In general, the c-graph may have several leaf nodes. But in each c-graph, there is at most one leaf node that is labeled with the defined final state of the workflow module. All other leaf nodes contain at least one state, where there are messages left or which is a deadlock state of the module (e.g. v4 in C(T2)). Consequently, if an environment was communicating with the module according to the labels along the path towards such a leaf node, this environment would not be an utilizing environment. The elimination of all such erroneous sequences yields a (possibly empty) subgraph that can be regarded as directions for using the module – called the *usability graph* (abbr. *u-graph*). of that module.

Definition 9 (Usability graph/u-graph). *A finite, non-empty subgraph U of the c-graph C is called* usability graph *if the following conditions hold:*

- *U contains the root node of C and only that leaf node of C, which is labeled with the defined final state of the workflow module.*
- *For each hidden node of C that is in U, all outgoing edges are in U, as well.*
- *Each node within U lies on a path between the root and the defined leaf node.*

An u-graph arises by removing only those edges (and succeeding nodes) that start at a visible node. Hence, it restricts the behavior of an utilizing environment (some *inputs* are removed), but it does not restrict the behavior of the module (all *output* are still available). In that sense, an u-graph of a workflow module describes a *instruction manual* for a possible environment.

In Figure 4, those parts of the c-graphs that does not belong to any u-graph are drawn with dashed lines. The graph C(T2) does not contain any u-graphs.

Hence, this module is not usable. Referring to modules C1 and C2, the whole c-graph is their only u-graph. But in general, a c-graph may contain several u-graphs. The whole graph C(T1) is an u-graph, and removing the hidden node h2 (or h3, resp.) yields another u-graph, i. e. this ticket module can be used as well by a customer who exclusively pays with eCash (or VISA, resp.). To find the maximal u-graph, the algorithm walks backwards through the c-graph, and removes nodes according to Definition 9.

4.3   Theorem of usability

An u-graph U of a module M can easily be transformed into an environment of the M: Each node of the graph becomes a place, each edge starting at a visible node becomes a sending transition, and each remaining edge becomes a receiving transition of the environment. The resulting module is called the *constructed environment*, denoted by $\Gamma(U)$. Based on the restrictions of U, it is easy to prove that the composed workflow module $M \oplus \Gamma(U)$ does not contain any deadlock. If $M \oplus \Gamma(U)$ also does not contain any livelock (i. e. the composed module always can terminate), the constructed environment $\Gamma(U)$ is an utilizing environment of M. The following theorem formulates the correlation between the usability of a workflow module and the existence of an u-graph:

Theorem 1 (Usability). *Let M be a workflow module and let C be the c-graph of M. The module M is usable, if and only if C contains at least one u-graph U and the composed system $M \oplus \Gamma(U)$ always can terminate.*

The entire proof can be found in [12]. The following paragraph sketches its idea. *Implication*: As already mentioned, it can be proven easily that $M \oplus \Gamma(U)$ does not contain any deadlock. Hence, if the composed system terminates, it must have reached the desired final state, otherwise it would have reached a deadlock. Thus, $\Gamma(U)$ is an utilizing environment of M. In case M is an acyclic module, termination is granted, and the theorem only requires the existence of an u-graph. *Revers implication*: If the module M is usable, there is at least one utilizing environment E. Based on this property it is possible to project the all reachable states of the composed system $M \oplus E$ to the c-graph of M (without sticking to one specific environment). This yields a subgraph $C' \subseteq C$, which can be proven to meet the requirements of Definition 9. Hence, $\Gamma(C')$ is an utilizing environment of M.

The theorem on usability makes it possible to decide usability in many cases: An acyclic workflow module has a finite c-graph. Thus, we can search for an u-graph and decide usability. The most cyclic modules have a finite c-graph, too. Even if an usable cyclic module has an infinite c-graph, there exists a finite u-graph. Applying breadth-first-search, this graph will be found after finite time.

5   Summary

In this paper, a framework for modeling and analyzing Web service based business processes by help of Petri nets was presented [12]. Each Web service has an interface and an internal process structure. Hence, a Web service is modeled in terms of a *workflow module* – a workflow net with a set of interface places. Based on this formalism, the notion of *usability* was defined – an intuitive and locally provable soundness criterion for workflow modules. On top of usability, the questions *compatibility* and *equivalence* could be precisely addressed, and there are effective algorithms to verify all these properties. Due to the available Petri net semantic of BPEL4WS [18], the method is directly applicable to real world examples.

Of course, the current work was inspired by many other approaches, dealing with the problems of cross-organizational workflow and Web services. Some approaches also use Petri nets [20, 6] and/or specify the global interaction by help of *Message Sequence Charts* (MSC) [22, 8]. But, none of them presents such a focussed view on a components externally visible behavior as the *communication graph* does. Due to this representation, the comparison of behavior is more adequate w. r. t. the field of application than traces [24] or automaton [26].

All presented algorithms are implemented within the prototype WOMBAT4WS [27]. Currently, the work is focussed on improving the algorithms' efficiency by the application of *partial order reduction* techniques [19]. Moreover, up to a certain degree the integration of data aspects into the formalism is planned. Especially the dependencies between the content of incoming message and internal decisions made by the process are the focussed target. Applying technologies of static program analysis (e. g. *slicing* [14]), it seems possible, to achieve a higher level of precision in mapping a given process model into a Petri net, without loosing the possibility of efficient analysis.

References

1. Gustavo Alonso, Fabio Casati, Harumi Kuno, and Vijay Machiraju. *Web Services.* Springer-Verlag, December 2002.
2. Andrews, Curbera, Dholakia, Goland, Klein, Leymann, Liu, Roller, Smith, Thatte, Trickovic, and Weerawarana. *BPEL4WS – Business Process Execution Language for Web Services.* OASIS, Standard proposal, Version 1.1, July 2002.
3. H. Ben-Abdallah and S. Leue. Syntactic detection of process divergence and non-local choice in message sequence charts. LNCS 1217. Springer Verlag, 1997.
4. Karl Gottschalk. *Web Services architecture overview.* IBM developerWorks, Whitepaper, September 2000. http://ibm.com/developerWorks.
5. Paul W.P.J. Grefen and Samuil Angelov. *Three-Level Process Specification for Dynamic Service Outsourcing.* LNCS 2472. Springer-Verlag, 2003.
6. Rachid Hamadi and Boualem Benatallah. *A Petri Net based Model for Web Service Composition.* In *Proc. of ADC 2003.* Australian Computer Society, Inc., 2003.
7. Kavantzas, Burdett, Ritzinger, and Lafon. *Web Services Choreography Description Language.* W3C Working Draft, Version 1.0, October 2004.
8. E. Kindler, A. Martens, and W. Reisig. *Inter-operability of Workshop Applications – Local Criteria for Global Soundness.* LNCS 1806. Springer-Verlag, 2000.
9. Heather Kreger. *WSCA – Web Services Conceptual Architecture.* IBM Software Group, Whitepaper, 2001. http://ibm.com/webservices/pdf/WSCA.pdf.

10. Axel Martens. On compatibility of web services. *Petri Net Newsletter*, 65:12–20, October 2003.

11. Axel Martens. *On Usability of Web Services*. In Calero, Diaz, and Piattini, editors, *Proc. of Intl. Conference Workshop WQW 2003*, Rome, Italy, December 2003.

12. Axel Martens. *Verteilte Geschäftsprozesse – Modellierung und Verifikation mit Hilfe von Web Services*. PhD thesis, WiKu-Verlag Stuttgart, 2004.

13. Axel Martens. Simulation and equivalence between bpel process models. In *Proc. of Intl. Conference DASD'05*, San Diego, California, April 2005.

14. Flemming Nielson, Hanne R. Nielson, and Chris Hankin. *Principles of Program Analysis*. Springer-Verlag, 1999.

15. Alexander Norta. *Web Supported Enactment of Petri-Net Based Workflows with XRL/flower*. LNCS 3099. Springer-Verlag, June 2004.

16. W. Reisig. *Petri Nets*. Springer-Verlag, 1985.

17. W. Reisig. *Elements of Distributed Algorithms – Modeling and Analysis with Petri Nets*. Springer-Verlag, 1998.

18. K. Schmidt and Ch. Stahl. A Petri net semantic for BPEL. In Ekkart Kindler, editor, *Proc. of 11th Workshop AWPN*. Paderborn University, October 2004.

19. Karsten Schmidt. *Explicit State Space Verification*. Postdoctoral thesis, Humboldt-Universität zu Berlin, 2002.

20. W. M. P. van der Aalst. *Modeling and Analyzing Interorganizational Workflows*. In *Proc. of CSD'98*. IEEE Computer Society Press, 1998.

21. W. M. P. van der Aalst. The Application of Petri Nets to Workflow Management. *Journal of Circuits, Systems and Computers*, 8(1):21–66, 1998.

22. W. M. P. van der Aalst. Interorganizational Workflows – An Approach based on MSC and Petri Nets. *Systems Analysis - Modelling - Simulation*, 34(3), 1999.

23. W.M.P. van der Aalst and A.H.M. ter Hofstede. Yawl: Yet another workflow language. Qut technical report, fit-tr-2003-04, Queensland University of Technology, Brisbane, Australia, 2003.

24. Rob J. van Glabbeek. *The Linear Time - Branching Time Spectrum*. In Baeten and Klop, editors, *Proceedings CONCUR 90*, LNCS 458. Springer-Verlag, 1990.

25. Web-Ontology Working Group. *Ontology Web Language for Web Services*. OWL-S 1.1, November 2004.

26. A. Wombacher, P. Fankhauser, B. Mahleko, and E. Neuhold. *Matchmaking for Business Processes*. In *Proc. of EEE-04*. IEEE Computer Society, 2004.

27. WOMBAT4WS. *Workflow Modeling and Business Analysis Toolkit for Web Services*. hompage, http://www.informatik.hu-berlin.de/top/wombat/.

Automatic Conformance Testing of Web Services

Reiko Heckel and Leonardo Mariani

Department of Mathematics and Computer Science,
University of Paderborn,
33095 Paderborn, Germany
{heckel, mariani}@upb.de

Abstract. Web Services are the basic building blocks of next generation Internet applications, based on dynamic service discovery and composition. Dedicated *discovery services* will store both syntactic and behavioral descriptions of available services and guarantee their compatibility with the requirements expressed by clients. In practice, however, interactions may still fail because the Web Service's implementation may be faulty. In fact, the client has no guarantee on the *quality* of the implementation associated to any service description.

In this paper, we propose the idea of *high-quality service discovery* incorporating *automatic testing* for validating Web Services before allowing their registration. First, the discovery service automatically generates conformance test cases from the provided service description, then runs the test cases on the target Web Service, and only if the test is successfully passed, the service is registered.

In this way, clients bind with Web Services providing a compatible signature, a suitable behavior, and a high-quality implementation.

1 Introduction

Internet and the WWW provide a huge amount of services accessible from every connected machine. Most of these services are designed for human users, and only a strict subset can be easily discovered by search engines. This scenario is in contradiction to that of a machine-readable Web that exploits dynamic and automatic composition of services [1].

Web Services and the Service Oriented Architecture (SOA) represent a step toward the Internet as computational infrastructure [2, 3]. Web Services are software applications identified by URIs, whose interfaces and bindings are defined and discovered through XML documents. A Web Service supports direct interactions with other software agents using XML-based messages exchanged via Internet-based protocols [2]. The SOA provides the basic infrastructure for the discovery and dynamic binding of Web Services by defining the roles of *provider*, *requestor* and *discovery service*. A provider offering a service publishes its description at the discovery service. The requestor queries the discovery service in order to find a suitable service it can interact with to perform a certain task. The discovery service provides functions for storing, classifying, and browsing registered services [3].

M. Cerioli (Ed.): FASE 2005, LNCS 3442, pp. 34–48, 2005.

With this basic scenario, several problems remain open. First of all, service description and discovery is largely syntactic, reduced to the signatures of operations and simple classifications. Thus, there is no guarantee that the returned service operates in the way expected by the client. This problem can be overcome by augmenting the syntactic description by a behavioral specification of the service. Rather than logic or algebraic techniques we prefer graph transformation rules for this purpose because they blend well with UML, the standard software modeling language, thus keeping the additional effort manageable [5].

Graph transformation rules have been proposed for modeling both the behavior of the provided service and the client's requirements [4]. The provider uploads (an XML representation of) these models together with the syntactic service description, while the requestor uses a requirements model to specify its query. Then, service discovery includes the matching of these models at the discovery service: If the provided model satisfies the requirements, binding is allowed; otherwise another Web Service must be selected.

This new scenario increases the reliability of the binding between the requestor and the provider. However, another problem still exists. Can the client trust the implementation of the service description? The provider may register a suitable model, but provide a faulty implementation; for instance because of insufficient testing. Moreover, service providers could maliciously provide "models better than services". Since a faulty interaction can affect a distributed computation, clients dynamically binding to faulty Web Services can encounter serious problems, e.g., a complex business transaction may lead to expensive recovery procedures. Therefore, requestors exploiting dynamic and automatic discovery and binding require high-quality Web Services. To reach this goal we foresee the introduction of *High-Quality Service Discovery* agencies, i.e., discovery services with added functionality for behavioral matching and *automatic testing*.

High-quality service discovery automatically tests a Web Service with respect to a provided model consisting of GT rules that specify the individual operations of the service. The registration of services is allowed only if testing is passed, otherwise a report is generated and sent to the service provider. The developer of the Web Service can use the report to refine either the rules of the models or the implementation, depending on the origin of the problem.

Clients that use a high-quality service discovery agency have the guarantee that any discovered Web Service has passed the testing phase, therefore it can rely on both the interface compatibility and the implementation of the service.

2   Registration Scenario

We focus on the scenario taking place during the registration of a new service. The discovery and binding phases have been discussed in [4].

Let us assume the existence of a provider P and a discovery service U. P provides a Web Service ws that is described by means of both a syntactic interface description (e.g., a WSDL descriptor) and GT rules specifying the offered behavior. The registration phase includes the following steps (see Figure 1):

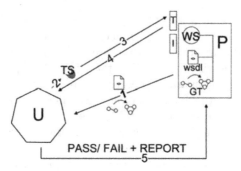

Fig. 1. The registration process for a new Web Service

1. The provider P uploads both the WSDL document and the GT rules to the discovery service U. See Section 3 for details on the specification of Web Services by GT rules.
2. The discovery service U automatically generates a set of test specifications from the GT rules. Tests cover validation of both single operations and sequences. See Section 4 for details.
3. Concrete test cases are generated and remotely executed using a *testing interface* T provided by the Web Service ws. This resembles the normal interface, but includes additional functions facilitating the execution of the test cases. See Section 5 for details.
4. Results of test cases are judged based on the returned results and the conceptual state of the service after completing the operation. The latter is read through the testing interface which provides access to an abstraction of the internal data state. See Section 5 for details.
5. If all test cases have been passed, the discovery service U registers the new Web Service with both the WSDL document and the GT rules for matching against the requirements of requestors. Finally, the service provider replaces the testing interface by the ordinary one. If test cases have failed, the discovery service U generates a report that is sent to the provider P.

3   Specification of Web Services by GT Rules

A Web Service provides a coherent set of operations based on a common data model, i.e., an XML schema. Together with the operation's signatures this makes up the WSDL description of the service. Extending this syntactic description, the behavioral specification of operations by means of GT rules is based on the data model of the service interface as well as a conceptual model of the internal state of the service. At the model level, the state is represented by an attributed graph, visualized as an UML object diagram [6].

A GT rule refines the signature of the service, specifying how parameters and internal data are used and modified. Each service is associated to a set of production rules representing the different computations that can take place

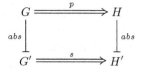

Fig. 2. Relation between conceptual and implementation state transformation

when the service is executed with different input values at different states. A production rule has a precondition and an effect. If the precondition is satisfied, the rule can be applied. The effect consists of objects and links that are deleted and added, and attribute values that are modified. A graph can satisfy the preconditions of multiple rules, in such case the choice is non-deterministic.

In this paper, we visualize graph transformations by the notation proposed in [7], see Figure 3 for an example. The semantics of the adopted graphical notation is the following one: nodes and edges fully contained inside the triangle are part of the pre-condition: they must be present and are not deleted by the application; edges and nodes partially or fully present at the left-hand side of the triangle are part of the pre-condition, too, but they are deleted when the rule is applied; nodes and edges partially or fully present on the right-hand side of the triangle are created by the rule; and finally, edges and nodes partially or fully present below the triangle form a negative application condition: they must not be present in the given graph. Parameters are distinguished from objects in the state of the server by a gray background. Finally, at the bottom of the graphical notation, guard conditions and assignment are provided. The guard is a Boolean expression over attributes: a production rule can take place only if the guard is evaluated to **true**. The assignment is responsible for updating values of attributes.

Graph transformations specify the behavior of a Web Service at the conceptual level. Therefore, the state of the service whose evolution is described does not coincide with the concrete data state, whose representation may involve Java objects and attributes or database tables, depending on the used implementation technology. Testing is performed on the *implementation* of the Web Service, hence it refers to the concrete data state. However, test cases are generated from the *specification*, thus they refer to the conceptual state. Figure 2 captures this situation where G' is the concrete state of the service, and G represents the abstract state that corresponds to G' [8]. G can be obtained from G' by an abstraction function abs that extracts a high-level representation of the actual state. A production rule p can be applied to the abstract state to obtain a new abstract state H. In the same way, the corresponding service s can be executed on the concrete state G' to obtain a new concrete state H'.

Testing is used to demonstrate the *conformance* of the specification with the implementation. We define conformance in terms of the following conditions.

Completeness: For each concrete state G' of service s, if $abs(G') = G$ satisfies the precondition of an associated rule p, then there exists a transformation $G' \stackrel{s}{\Longrightarrow} H'$ on the concrete state such that $G \stackrel{p}{\Longrightarrow} H = abs(H')$.

Soundness: A service s does not perform unspecified operations, with the exception of errors leaving the state unchanged, i.e., $G' \overset{s}{\Longrightarrow} H'$ implies $G' = H'$ or there exists an associated rule p with $abs(G') = G \overset{p}{\Longrightarrow} H = abs(H')$.

We initially validate completeness and soundness by deriving test cases for single rules. Completeness is validated by generating test cases inside the input domain of the rules, while soundness is checked through test cases outside the rules' domain.

Unfortunately, testing single rules is not enough to ascertain the conformance of the specification with the implementation. The execution of sequences of operations can reveal additional implementation faults related to details that are not present in the conceptual state. We account for such cases by defining different types of dependencies among rules and deriving test cases where these dependencies are exercised.

Throughout the paper we consider the example of a Web Service providing simplified banking functions. Figure 3 shows production rules corresponding to the creation of a new account, the withdrawal of money, the charging of an account with a set of payments, the deposit of money, and the closing of the account.

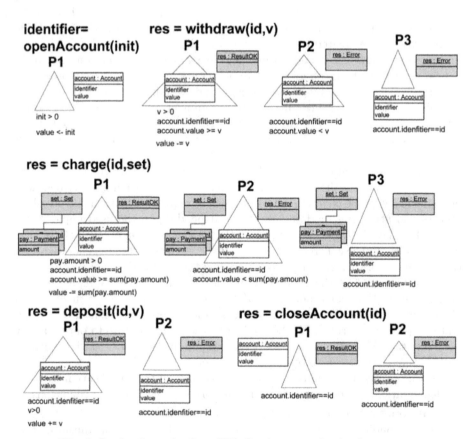

Fig. 3. Production rules for a Web Service managing bank accounts

4   Test Case Generation

We generate test cases for testing conformance of the implementation with individual rules by selecting "promising" inputs. Moreover, we generate test sequences stressing the interaction among rules.

Generation of Test Cases for Single Services. A WSDL description defines the input parameters and domains for the operations of a service. Possible inputs are further constrained by the preconditions of the GT rules. This suggests the derivation of test cases using a domain-based strategy, known as partition testing [9], which is an established technique successfully used in several contexts [10, 11]. The idea is to select test cases by dividing the *input domain* into (possibly overlapping) subsets and choosing one or more elements from each *domain* [10].

Partition testing has been used neither in the context of Web Services nor with respect to GT rules. Hence, our approach reuses standard ideas of testing in a new context. This requires a notion of input domain which combines the concrete input parameters of operations with the conceptual state of the Web Service before it is applied.

Formally, the *input domain* of a service s is the set of all parameter-state pairs $ID(s) = \{\langle par, st \rangle \mid par$ satisfies the WSDL description$\}$. The presence of both input and state in the domain is required because services are triggered by a combination of the two. Samples from $ID(s)$ can thus invoke all possible behaviors.

We identified the following fault-based guidelines [10] as strategy for designing the domains from each of which at least one test case should be chosen. The idea is that "small" partitions where several insidious faults can be present, and "larger" partitions where no assumptions about specific implementation threats can be performed are identified. Inside a partition all inputs have the same bias to be faulty. The discovery service administrator can exactly set the number of test cases that are sampled for each domain in a way to find the right balance between coverage and time consumed on testing. Experimental work aiming at finding the best number of test cases that should be selected from each domain is part of future work.

- The input domain of a rule p, given by the set of all parameter-state pairs $\langle par, st \rangle$ satisfying the pre-condition of the rule, defines a domain $D(p)$.
- Parameter-state pairs $\langle par, st \rangle$ simultaneously enabling two different rules p_1, p_2 form an input domain $D(p_1, p_2) = D(p_1) \cap D(p_2)$ because they require an internal decision (possibly non-deterministic) to decide which behavior must take place. This decision may be complex and its implementation incorrect.
- Input parameters and objects in the conceptual states carry attributes that are constrained by types and attribute conditions. Faults are likely when dealing with values at the boundary of their domains [9]. Thus, we define separate domains for inputs where at least one attribute has a boundary value. Note that the same attribute can have multiple boundary values.

- A production rule can also contain multi-objects which, upon application, are expanded to a set of objects whose cardinality depends on the current input. In order to validate this mechanism, we consider the inputs leading to expansions with zero, one, and multiple elements.
- Inputs outside the specification should create a response to notifies the client, but without modifying the state of the server. Failures to check for incorrect inputs can lead to follow-up faults which are very difficult to detect. We therefore consider a domain for values that do not belong to the input of any rule, but are correctly typed with regard to the WSDL description of s, i.e., $ID(s) \setminus \bigcup_{p_i \in s} D(p_i)$.

Note that these domains are not disjoint, but can overlap. It happens because different problems with different probabilities to be faulty can apply to the same concrete input elements.

A test case specification is composed of three parts: the *precondition*, the *test sequence*, and the *expected result*. The *precondition* specifies constraints that are expected to hold for the state of the server when the test case is executed. It is derived from the left-hand sides of the rules that must be tested. Conditions on parameters are not considered as part of the precondition, but contained in the *test sequence* which specifies conditions on input parameters together with the order of service invocations. Conditions on parameters are extracted from the left-hand sides of rules, too. The *expected result* is obtained by executing the rule for the generated input values. Note that a parameter-state pair can trigger multiple rules associated to the same service. In this case, we accept as correct any result produced by any of the applicable rules.

If we apply the defined criteria to the service `charge` in Figure 3, we obtain the following domains.

- The service is specified by three production rules; hence we have domains $D(p_1), D(p_2), D(p_3)$ generated from their left-hand sides.
- There is no non-determinism, i.e., the three domains are pair wise disjoint.
- Considering rule p_1, there are three attributes that can be defined: `payment`, `sum(pay.amount)`[1] and `account.value`. Test cases are generated by fixing a boundary value for at least one of them and randomly generating the other two values. The same applies to rules p_2 and p_3.
- Each multi-object produces domains for zero, one, and many instances. Thus, three test cases are generated for each rule: one with an empty set of payments, one with a set containing one payment, and one with a set containing n payments.
- Incorrect inputs are generated for each rule by choosing attribute values that violate the guard conditions. For instance, p_1 generates a test case with negative payments.

---

[1] values obtained by the application of common mathematical functions on multi-objects are handled as attributes, thus avoiding the use of problem solvers even for simple cases.

Currently we limit the generation of random values to linear constraints. Extensions to non-linear constraints have already been proposed in [11].

Generation of Tests for Sequences of Operations. The execution of an operation can alter parts of the service's state that are used by other operations. GT rules specify state modifications at a conceptual level. By analyzing these rules we can thus understand dependencies and conflicts between operations without looking into their actual implementation.

Data flow analysis is frequently used to generate test cases. The idea is to exercise paths in the code that include combinations of variable *definition* and *uses* [12]. This problem has been extensively investigated and several coverage criteria have been defined [13]. In particular, a widely used coverage criterion is "all def-use pairs" [14], which requires a test suite that executes all possible pairs of definition and uses for variables in the program under test.

Conceptually, each operation (rule) can add or remove nodes and edges to or from the conceptual state, and can change the values of attributes. The principles of data-flow testing can be reused to test the interaction among production rules if creation of nodes and edges is interpreted as "definition" and deletion as "use". We expect that sequences of operations that include the creation of a (conceptual) entity and its subsequent use are likely to expose (state-based) faults. The formalization of this intuition is given by the relations of conflicts and casual dependencies between rules.

Given two transformations $G \xrightarrow{p_1} H_1$ and $G \xrightarrow{p_2} H_2$ like in Figure 4, they are *parallel independent* if the application of one does not disable the other. That means, one transformation does not delete anything necessary for the application of the other, does not add anything forbidden by the negative application condition of the other, and does not modify attribute values used in the guard condition of the other rule.

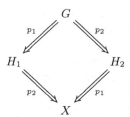

Fig. 4. Independence of transformation steps

Given a sequence of two transformations $G \xrightarrow{p_1} H_1 \xrightarrow{p_2} X$ like in Figure 4, they are *sequentially independent* if they can be exchanged. This means, as in the parallel case, that their occurrences do only overlap in such elements that are preserved by both transformations, and that application and guard conditions are not affected.

Thus, parallel and sequential independence are defined with respect to given graphs and occurrences, that is, using run-time concepts. To derive test cases from specifications, however, a static definition of *potential* conflicts and dependencies is required. Therefore, the above notions have to be lifted to the level of rules. For two rules $p_1 : L_1 \to R_1$ and $p_2 : L_2 \to R_2$ we say that

- p_2 *may disable* p_1 if there exist transformation steps $G \overset{p_1}{\Longrightarrow} H_1$ and $G \overset{p_2}{\Longrightarrow} H_2$ like in Figure 4, such that $G \overset{p_1}{\Longrightarrow} H_1$ is *not* independent of $G \overset{p_2}{\Longrightarrow} H_2$,
- p_1 *may cause* p_2 if there exist transformation steps $G \overset{p_1}{\Longrightarrow} H_1 \overset{p_2}{\Longrightarrow} X$ like in Figure 4, such that $H_1 \overset{p_2}{\Longrightarrow} X$ is *not* independent of $G \overset{p_1}{\Longrightarrow} H_1$.

The *may-disable* relation captures possible conflicts among rules and is used to test sequences of actions that should lead to an error when the last request is issued, but that can erroneously produce some side effects on the actual state. The *may-cause* relation captures possible structural and attribute dependencies among rules. The may-disable relation is used to test completeness of rules, while the may-cause relation is used to test the consistency of rules. Formal definitions for dependencies among rules can be found in [15].

The criterion for generating test cases consists of covering the execution of all pairs of rules (p_s, p_t), where p_s *may disable/cause* p_t. However, it may be impossible to immediately execute p_t after p_s. Therefore, a sequence $p_s, p_1, \ldots p_n, p_t$ must be generated, where p_s *may disable/cause* p_t and the overall effect of the sequence $p_1, \ldots, p_n$ does not entirely "invalidates" the *may disable/cause* relation.

The relation between two rules is based on a set of nodes that have been deleted or added, or on a set of attributes that have been modified: the *entities of the relation*. If further rules are executed between the execution of the two related rules (p_s, p_t), the effect of the intermediate rules can overwrite the part of the state where p_s and p_t interact, i.e., the entities of the relation can be modified. In our case, if the effect of $p_1, \ldots, p_n$ modifies all entities of the relation, $p_1, \ldots, p_n$ entirely invalidates the relation. For the purpose of test case generation, it makes sense to cover the execution of only those pairs that effectively interact, i.e., the dependencies have not been overwritten and the conflicts have not been removed by other rules.

Also in this case, a test case specification is composed of three parts: the *precondition*, the *test sequence*, and the *expected result*. The *precondition* for a particular invocation sequence is obtained by anticipating the preconditions of all rules in the sequence [16]. The *test sequence* is given by the sequence of operations that must be executed and the conditions over the parameters that must be used for their invocation. Finally, the *expected result* is obtained by executing the rules over the concrete values. The concrete test cases are obtained by randomly generating concrete values that satisfy the constraints.

Potential conflicts and dependencies between rules are automatically computed by the AGG tool [17]. The additional relations deriving from attribute values can be obtained by simple data-flow analysis over constraints and assignments. If we apply this criterion to the running example and focus on rule p_1 of the service **withdraw**, we derive that the target service is dependent on rule p_1 of **openAccount**, on rule p_1 of **charge**, on rule p_1 of **deposit**, and on rule p_1 of service **withdraw**. Therefore, test cases for opening the account and withdrawing money, charging payments and withdrawing money, depositing and withdrawing money, and withdrawing money twice are generated. Moreover, rule p_1 of the **withdrawing** service is in conflict with itself and with rule p_1 of the **closeAccount** service. Thus, a test case that closes the account before withdrawing money and a test case that withdraws money twice leading the current deposit to a negative value are generated for testing soundness (attributes and parameters for the latter test case are obtained by randomly generating values that satisfy all rule constraints and the negation of the condition **account.value**$\geq$v in p_1). In a similar way, we proceed for the other rules.

The Certified Level of Quality. Once a Web Service has passed the pre-registration testing phase, the client can rely on a high-quality implementation of the discovered services. In particular, the test cases generated for single services validate that all specified scenarios are implemented and that the implementation behaves according to the specification, at least for some inputs. Moreover, test cases validate that any internal decision taken by the Web Service satisfies the specification. Test cases for boundary values and multi-objects also certify that a range of values representing the normal operation of the service is defined and that collections are correctly managed in the cases of 0, 1 and multiple elements. Finally, test cases that violate guard conditions certify that guard conditions are implemented according to the specification and that a proper reaction mechanism is provided for incorrect inputs.

Test cases for sequences of operations validate that the state of the component evolves according to the specification at least for pairs of service invocation. Moreover, test cases check that the Web Service prevents reaching unsound states by multiple invocation of services.

Some interferences among operations, e.g., the definitions and uses of some state variables that cannot be deduced from the specification, cannot be automatically tested. However, clients of high-quality Web Services can rely on both the implementation of all specified behaviors and the existence of guard mechanisms for identifying incorrect inputs and effects.

5   Generation of Invocation Sequences

A test case has a precondition that consists of a set of constraints that must be satisfied by the actual state. Thus, the Web Service must be set to a state that satisfies the precondition of the test case. We assume that a Web Service facilitates this goal by providing a testing interface with three basic additional features:

- the possibility to setting the initial state of the service, possibly choosing from a set of alternatives representing different situations,
- a set of creator/destructor operations that enable the modification of the state of the server (if necessary),
- an implementation of the abstraction function.

A state that enables the execution of a given test case is reached by choosing an initial state from the set of states provided by the Web Service, and searching for a suitable sequence of requests that turns the chosen state into one satisfying the precondition of the test case. Dedicated creator/destructor operations are not required if the "normal" service interface already enables sufficiently free creation and deletion of objects on the server.

A similar problem arises in testing sequences of operations, where a transformation sequence must be generated enabling the execution of pairs of related rules. Both search problems are solved by building a search tree rooted at the selected initial state(s) and then incrementally considering the different rules. Each node is labeled with a path condition, i.e., the constraints that must be satisfied by the state variables to enable the sequence starting from the root and ending with the considered node. The path condition is derived by merging and simplifying both the guards and the assignments of single rules. When a state that satisfies the given properties is identified, the search stops, and the corresponding sequence is used in the test case. This is essentially the strategy employed by [18], the first work on model-based testing with GT rules we are aware of. In that paper, the search tree is in fact the concurrent unfolding of a grammar.

The search problem is realistic because not all rules can be applied at all steps and the overall number of rules is generally small for Web Services. For instance, a meaningful subset of the Amazon Web Service has been specified with 11 GT rules (see Section 6). Moreover, the service provider can further restrict the search space by uploading a specification of the Web Service interaction protocol [19]. Goal directed search strategies can heavily increase performance of the search by considering the structure of the current state, the modifications performed by the GT rules, and the structure of the final state in the search. However, a discussion over effective search strategies is out of the scope of this paper.

Tool support for execution, depth-first search, and bounded state space construction for GT rules is already in place. In particular, PROGRESS allows specifications based on rules with attributes and various application conditions and implements search by means of backtracking [20]. GROOVE [21] can generate bounded fragments of the transition system described by a set of rules in which paths to states with particular properties can be detected. Since the tool does not support attributed graphs, it would have to be complemented with a theorem prover to collect and combine the guard conditions and assignments for the identified sequence.

Concrete test cases are obtained by randomly generating attribute values that satisfy the path condition of the test sequence. Once concrete values have been generated, the expected result can be obtained by executing the rules over the concrete values. When a test case is executed, the final state of the Web Service is retrieved using the abstraction function of the testing interface. If the retrieved final state corresponds to the final state generated by the rules, the test case has been passed. The conformance relation (see Section 3) requires that the result obtained by applying the rule on the conceptual state coincides with that obtained by the abstraction function on the concrete state reached after the execution of the test case.

The implementation of this function can be simplified by developing the system behind the Web Service with the Model-View-Controller (MVC) design pattern [22]. The design pattern isolates the state of the application (model) from the rest of the system, i.e., the control logic and the presentation layer. This strategy simplifies the access to the actual state and reduces the effort required to the developer for implementing the abstraction function.

Both the specification and the implementation of a service are furnished by the service provider who can, in principle, "cheat" by providing specifications and implementations that do not correspond with the final service, but that can easily pass the testing phase. However, specifications are used by clients for dynamically discovering services. Therefore, if the specification differs from the concrete service, the service cannot be successfully used by clients. In the same way, if the implementation is modified without repeating the testing phase, the registered specification will not match the provided service and interactions with clients will not be possible. Thus, the running version of the service, its specification and the tested implementation must be kept synchronized by the service provider.

6   Early Experience

We performed a number of small experiments in test case generation for real Web Services, initially considering two simple Web Services, the *Weather - Temperature* Web Service available at www.xmethods.com and the *Kayak Paddle Guide* available at `www.terawave.ca/webservices/paddle.html`. The former provides the current temperature in a given U.S. region. The latter computes the recommended length of a paddle, given the height of the person who will use it. Both Web Services provide one single simple operation. We derived the GT specification from the informal description available on Web. Then we generated test cases for single operations by sampling two values from each domain. The *Weather - Temperature* Web Service has been covered with 4 test cases and passed the test. The *Kayak Paddle Guide* has been covered with 6 test cases and failed the test. The technique discovered a fault for values that are expected to represent incorrect heights for a person, e.g., 600cm. In this case, the Web Service returns the longest paddle instead of signaling the incorrect input.

The two Web Services are very simple examples, but their complexity is representative for a large set of Web Services currently available on the Web. However, we decided to move to an example closer to the current state of the art for the Web Service technology. Thus, we considered the Amazon Web Service at `www.amazon.com/gp/aws/landing.html`, which provides a full set of functionalities for browsing and purchasing all items available in the Amazon Web Shop. In our experiment, we considered a comprehensive subset of the provided operations and we derived the GT specification from the online documentation provided by Amazon. In case of failing test cases, we inspected the fault to understand whether the cause is either a fault or an error in the inferred specification. The operations selected for testing have included the search for DVDs based on the director's name and usual operations for cart management, i.e., item addition, item modification, item deletion, and clearing of the cart. We overcame the necessity of constructor methods for creating DVDs in the catalog by taking advantage of the knowledge of the content of the catalog. In a real scenario, the Web Service should have offered constructor methods for the creation of DVDs that could be then purchased.

The definition of the rules was straightforward, the five operations were specified by 11 GT rules. For testing of single rules, we sampled 2 values for each domain and we obtained 65 test cases. For testing of sequences, 14 dependent pairs and 3 conflicting pairs were identified. All pairs can be directly executed without requiring the generation of an intermediate sequence of operations. For test cases of both single rules and pairs, the initial sequence enabling the execution of the test case was always generated by the initial addition of a proper set of items in the cart. In a real scenario, the sequence would include also the invocation of constructor methods for the creation of DVDs.

Test case execution - which has been performed with a Java client - revealed an incompatibility between the rules and the Web Service. The incompatibility arose from a fault in the specification. In fact, in contrast with our rules, the operation for adding an item did not increase the quantity of items that were already in the cart, but overwrote the quantity instead, e.g., adding a DVD in the cart twice results on a single DVD in the cart. Thus, we modified the rule and generated the test cases again. This time the Web Service passed the test.

Our early experience with the testing of Web Services provided important insights: The technique is useful with respect to the complexity of current Web Services; the inspected Web Services do not require the generation of long initialization sequences, thus the search space that must be inspected is very limited; the number of generated test cases is suitable for a discovery service that automatically performs testing; both test cases for consistency, such as the repeated addition of items in the cart for the Amazon Web Service, and completeness, such as the incorrect input height for the Kayak Web Service, revealed to be useful.

7   Related Work and Conclusions

To our knowledge, there is only one approach to test case generation based on GT rules [18]. We advance research in this area by proposing two novel ideas: (1) the application of existing domain-based testing techniques to the case of graph transformations and (2) the execution of *automatic testing* for validating Web Services. The application of domain-based testing requires the management of the server state as part of the domain, when adapted to graph transformations. Moreover, data-flow testing needs to be reinterpreted in terms of dependencies and conflicts among rules. Finally, the idea of using agencies which automatically test Web Services before registering them is new.

In contrast with graph-based testing, behavioral descriptions based on UML sequence diagrams and state charts can be used to generate test cases [23, 24]. However, the generated test cases fail to capture the concrete complexity of the exchanged parameters that often are restricted to few simple types, see for instance [24]. Moreover, due to the lack of precise semantics, UML diagrams cannot precisely describe the evolution of the state of the service. Graph transformations instead are suitable to unambiguously correlate the concrete states of the objects involved in an interaction with the behavior of a service. This kind of description enables the automatic generation of test cases that cover complex parameter passing and behaviors that are activated only for given internal states.

The design of GT rules has been demonstrated to be convenient when combined with a development methodology based on UML [5]. Therefore, the additional effort on behalf of the service developer for providing high-quality services is limited to the implementation of the abstraction function and to the eventual definition of additional constructor methods. The result is the publication of the Web Service in discovery services that aim at the dynamic composition of high-quality systems.

References

1. Berners-Lee, T., Hendler, J., Lassila, O.: The Semantic Web. Scientific American **284** (2001) 34–43
2. W3C Web Services Architecture Working Group: Web Services architecture requirements. W3C working draft, World Wide Web Consortium (2002)
3. Booth, D., Haas, H., McCabe, F., Newcomer, E., Champion, M., Ferris, C., Orchard, D.: Web Services architecture. W3C working group note, W3C (2004)
4. Hausmann, J.H., Heckel, R., Lohmann, M.: Model-based discovery of Web Services. In: Intl. Conference on Web Services. (2004)
5. Baresi, L., Heckel, R.: Tutorial introduction to graph transformation: a software engineering perspective. In: Intl. Conference on Graph Transformation. Volume 1 of LNCS., Springer (2002)
6. Jacobson, I., Booch, G., Rumbaugh, J.: The Unified Software Development Process. Addison-Wesley (1999)
7. Kaplan, S., Loyall, J., Goering, S.: Specifying concurrent languages and systems with δ-grammars. In Ehrig, H., Kreowski, H.J., Rozenberg, G., eds.: Proc. 4th Intl. Workshop on Graph Grammars and Their Application to Computer Science. Volume 532 of LNCS., Springer (1991) 475–489
8. de Roever, W.P., Engelhardt, K.: Data Refinement: Model-Oriented Proof Methods and Their Comparison. Volume 47 of Cambridge Tracts in Theoretical Computer Science. Cambridge University Press (1998)
9. White, L., Cohen, E.J.: A domain strategy for computer program testing. IEEE Transactions on Software Engineering **6** (1980) 247–257
10. Weyuker, E., Jeng, B.: Analyzing partition testing strategies. IEEE Transactions on Software Engineering **17** (1991) 703–711
11. Jeng, B., Weyuker, E.J.: A simplified domain-testing strategy. ACM Transactions on Software Engineering Methodology **3** (1994) 254–270

12. Rapps, S., Wejuker, E.: Data flow analysis techniques for program test data selection. In: 6th Intl. Conference on Software Engineering. (1982) 272–278
13. Frankl, P.G., Weyuker, E.J.: An applicable family of data flow testing criteria. IEEE Transactions on Software Engineering **14** (1988) 1483–1498
14. Pande, H.D., Landi, W.A., Ryder, B.G.: Interprocedural def-use associations for C systems with single level pointers. IEEE Transactions on Software Engineering **20** (1994) 385–403
15. Hausmann, J., Heckel, R., Taentzer, G.: Detecting conflicting functional requirements in a use case driven approach: a static analysis technique based on graph transformation. In: Intl. Conference on Software Engineering. (2002) 105–155
16. Rozenberg, G., ed.: Handbook of Graph Grammars and Computing by Graph Transformation. Volume Volume 1 - Foundations. World Scientific (1997)
17. Technical University Berlin: The attributed graph grammar system (AGG). http://tfs.cs.tu-berlin.de/agg/ (Visited in 2004)
18. Baldan, P., König, B., Stürmer, I.: Generating test cases for code generators by unfolding graph transformation systems. In: Proc. 2nd Intl. Conference on Graph Transformation, Rome, Italy (2004)
19. Bochmann, G.V., Petrenko, A.: Protocol testing: review of methods and relevance for software testing. In: Proceedings of the 1994 ACM SIGSOFT Intl. Symposium on Software Testing and Analysis, ACM Press (1994) 109–124
20. Schürr, A., Winter, A.J., Zündorf, A.: The PROGRES approach: language and environment. In: Handbook of graph grammars and computing by graph transformation: vol.2: applications, languages, and tools, World Scientific (1999) 487–550
21. Rensink, A.: The GROOVE simulator: A tool for state space generation. In: 2nd Intl. Workshop on Applications of Graph Transformations with Industrial Relevance. Volume 3062 of LNCS., Springer (2004) 479–485
22. Singh, I., Stearns, B., Johnson, M., Enterprise Team: Designing Enterprise Applications with the J2EE Platform. 2nd edn. Addison-Wesley (2002)
23. Fraikin, F., Leonhardt, T.: SeDiTeC - testing based on sequence diagram. In: IEEE Intl. Conference on Automated Software Engineering. (2002)
24. Hartmann, J., Imoberdorf, C., Meisinger, M.: Uml-based integration testing. In: Intl. Symposium on Software Testing and Analysis, ACM Press (2000) 60–70

Termination Criteria for Model Transformation*

Hartmut Ehrig[1], Karsten Ehrig[1], Juan de Lara[2], Gabriele Taentzer[1],
Dániel Varró[3], and Szilvia Varró-Gyapay[3]

[1] Technische Universität Berlin, Germany
{ehrig, karstene, gabi}@cs.tu-berlin.de
[2] Universidad Autonoma of Madrid, Spain
Juan.Lara@ii.uam.es
[3] Budapest University of Technology and Economics, Hungary
{varro, gyapay}@mit.bme.hu

Abstract. *Model Transformation* has become central to most software
engineering activities. It refers to the process of modifying a (usually
graphical) model for the purpose of analysis (by its transformation to
some other domain), optimization, evolution, migration or even code
generation. In this work, we show *termination criteria* for model transformation based on *graph transformation*. This framework offers visual
and formal techniques based on rules, in such a way that model transformations can be subject to analysis. Previous results on graph transformation are extended by proving the termination of a transformation
if the rules applied meet certain criteria. We show the suitability of the
approach by an example in which we translate a simplified version of
Statecharts into Petri nets for functional correctness analysis.

1 Introduction

Diagrams are ever more frequently used in our everyday work as a means for
problem solving, specification and comprehension. Their use is pervasive in areas
such as computer science, with the increasing tool support and popularity of
notations (such as UML), and model-based development processes (such as the
one proposed by the MDA [23]). In this area, we are witnessing a paradigm shift,
where models are no longer mere (passive) documentation, but are used for code
generation, analysis and simulation as well.

Whereas the syntax of most notations is usually well-defined (sometimes by
means of a meta-model), semantics are often specified in a semi-formal way,
which prevents the use of analysis methods. Moreover, sometimes modelling is
easier using a certain notation, but the formalism lacks certain analysis techniques to solve some of the user problems. One way to solve these difficulties
is by specifying transformations from the initial source formalism into a target

---

* Juan de Lara, Dániel Varró and Szilvia Varró-Gyapay were partially supported by
the Segravis Research Training Network.

M. Cerioli (Ed.): FASE 2005, LNCS 3442, pp. 49–63, 2005.

notation [9]. Once the model is translated, we can use the target notation analysis techniques to solve the initial problem. There are many other scenarios in which model transformations are present, such as model evolution, migration (for example between different database schemata or between different versions of the UML meta-model) or model optimization. Even code generation can be seen as a transformation into the abstract syntax of the target textual language.

Problem Statement. An important question is *how to specify such model transformations*. A recent initiative of the Object Management Group aims at developing a standard for describing Queries, Views and Transformations (QVT) [19] for UML (in fact, any MOF-based) models. Although the submitted approaches vary a lot (e.g. in providing textual [26] vs. graphical specifications [22] for transformations), high-level, graph-based and declarative specifications are proposed in many of the submissions.

The correctness of model transformations, namely, to *guarantee that certain semantic properties hold for a transformation*, is also a crucial aspect of transformation engineering. For instance, when transforming UML models into mathematical domains, the results of a formal analysis can be invalidated by erroneous model transformations as the systems engineers cannot distinguish whether an error is in the design or in the transformation. Most typical correctness properties of a model transformation are termination, uniqueness (confluence) and behaviour preservation.

Objectives. In the paper, we propose the use of graph transformation [24] over typed and attributed graphs that provides rule and pattern-based manipulation of graph models generalizing Chomsky grammars from strings to graphs. The algebraic approach to graph transformation is based on concepts of *category theory* (see [11]), and has a rich body of theoretical results that have been developed in the last 30 years (see [24]). In this way, transformations expressed as graph grammars become not only graphical and intuitive but also formal, declarative and high-level models, subject themselves to analysis.

While the use of graph transformation for specifying model transformations has been under intensive research, the main result of the paper is concerned with the *termination of model transformations*. Although termination is undecidable for graph grammars in general [21], in this paper we show that if graph grammars with negative application conditions (see [14]) meet suitable termination criteria, we can conclude that they are terminating. The criteria we propose are based on assigning a *layer* to each rule, node and edge label (type).

Structure of the Paper. The rest of the paper is organized as follows: Sec. 2 presents a running example, in which we specify (with graph grammar rules) a transformation from a restricted version of Statecharts into Petri nets, with the aim of subsequent analysis. Sec. 3 details the critera for termination of layered graph grammars. Sec. 4 discusses the application of the criteria to the running example, and sketches how the criteria can easily be applied to other interesting model transformation examples. Sec. 5 discusses related work and finally Sec. 6 presents our conclusions and proposals for future work.

2   Motivating Example: From Statecharts to Petri Nets

In order to illustrate the idea of the proposed criteria for termination of model transformation we introduce a model transformation from UML statecharts into Petri nets. The running example is a simplified version of the original transformation that was designed and implemented in the VIATRA system [29] as part of a Hungarian research project (IKTA 065/2000 – A framework for the modelling and analysis of dependable and safety critical systems) and discussed in more details in [28]. The transformation aims at formal verification of safety critical applications designed by UML statecharts using semi-decision analysis methods of Petri nets [20] and it was applied on various UML models provided by the industrial partners of the project. Similar transformations into various classes of Petri nets carry out dependability and performance analysis for the system model in early stages of design and their termination could be validated by the proposed techniques.

2.1   Source Modelling Language: UML statecharts

UML statecharts are an object-oriented variant of classical Harel statecharts [15] that describe behavioural aspects of (any instance of) a class in the system under design. In fact, the statechart formalism itself is an extension of finite state machines to allow a decomposition of states into a state hierarchy with parallel regions that greatly enhance the readability and scalability of state models.

An extract of the metamodel of UML statecharts is depicted in the upper left part of Fig. 1 (abbreviated as SC). In fact, this metamodel is a proper extension of the standard UML metamodel (for which we assume the reader's familiarity) that explicitly introduces several notions of statecharts that are only implicitly present in the standard (such as state configurations, queues, etc.). The necessity and the guideline of these extensions to obtain a formal operational semantics of statecharts is discussed in [28, 27].

In the paper, we consider a network of statemachines SM, each of which having an associated event queue. A single statemachine captures the behaviour of any object of a specific class by flattening the state hierarchy into *state configurations* and grouping parallel transitions into *steps*. [1]

A Configuration is composed of a set of States that can be active at a time. The activeness of a state is indicated by the isAct edge, while the initial configuration is identified by the initConf association.

A Step is composed of non-conflicting Transitions (which are, in turn, binary relations between states) that can be fired in parallel. A step is leading from a configuration fromConf to a configuration toConf, and it is triggered by a common Event for all its transitions. The effect of a step is a sequence of Actions. For the paper, we only consider *send actions* which send a message to a target (receiver) queue in the form of a corresponding event.

---

[1] Note that configurations and steps can be collected at compile time, i.e. prior to the statecharts to Petri nets model transformation (see [28] for further details).

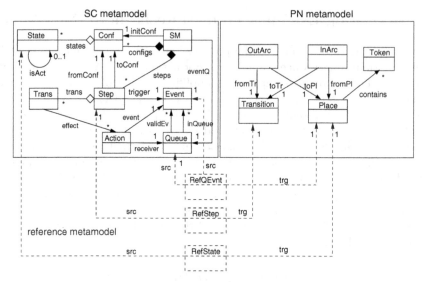

Fig. 1. The combined metamodel of statecharts and Petri nets

Each statemachine has exactly one associated event Queue (handled as sets and not FIFOs for presentation purposes) that store Events. The inQueue association denotes if a certain event is present in the corresponding event queue. The set of acceptable events in a certain queue is denoted by the association validEv.

2.2 Target Modelling Language: Petri Nets

Petri nets (abbreviated as PN) are widely used to formally capture the dynamic semantics of concurrent systems due to their easy-to-understand visual notation and the wide range of available analysis tools. From a system modelling point of view, transforming UML models to Petri nets may provide correctness, dependability and performance analysis for the system model in early stages of design.

Petri nets are bipartite graphs, with two disjoint sets of nodes: Places and Transitions. Places may contain an arbitrary number of Tokens. A token distribution defines the state of the modelled system. The state of the net can be changed by firing enabled transitions. A transition is *enabled* if each of its input places contains at least one token (if no arc weights are considered). When firing a transition, we remove a token from all input places (connected to the transition by InArcs) and add a token to all output places (as defined by OutArcs). A Petri net metamodel is shown in the upper right corner of Fig. 1.

Reference Metamodel. In order to interrelate the source and target modelling languages, we use reference metamodels [29]. For instance, a reference node of type RefState (in Fig. 1) relates a source State to a target Place.

2.3   Transforming State Machines into Petri Nets

An Informal Overview of Graph Transformation. The model transformation from state machines into Petri nets is specified by graph transformation rules.

Graph transformation [24] (for the formal treatment see Sec. 3) provides a rule-based manipulation of graph models. A *graph transformation rule* consists of a left-hand side (LHS) graph L, right-hand side (RHS) graph R, and (an optional) negative application condition N. Informally, L and N of a rule define the *precondition* while R defines the *postcondition*.

The *application* of a rule to a *host model graph* G (e.g., a UML model built by the user) alters the model graph by replacing the pattern defined by L with the pattern of the R. This is performed by (i) *finding a match* of the L pattern in model G; (ii) *checking the negative application conditions* N which prohibits the presence of certain model elements; (iii) *removing* a part of the model M that can be mapped to the L pattern but not the R pattern yielding an intermediate graph D; (iv) *adding* new elements to the intermediate graph D which exist in the R but not in L yielding the derived graph H. In our example we follow the *Double Pushout Approach* [7, 13]. Technical details are given as far as necessary in Sec. 3.

For a more compact presentation of the rules, we abbreviate the L, N and R graphs of a rule into one, and we only mark which (the images of) graph elements need to be removed (del), or created (new). Due to the special structure imposed by nondeleting rules (to be discussed in Sec. 3), all elements in the negative application condition N should also be present in R. Therefore, we assume for the current model transformation that R and N are isomorphic, and we simply omit the neg tags for the sake of clarity. The graph transformation rule generating a PN transition for a SC step is depicted in both the mathematical and the abbreviated notation in the upper-most part of Fig. 2.

The UML Statechart to Petri Net Transformation. Transforming our flattened UML statechart representation (with configurations and steps) into Petri nets is relatively simple (see the transformation rules and an example in Fig. 2).

- Each SC state is modeled with a respective place in the target PN model where a token in such a place denotes that the corresponding state is active initially (rules ActState2TokenR, State2PlaceR). In addition, places are generated to model messages stored in event queues of a state machine. A separate place is generated for each valid event accepted by a certain queue, and initialized according to the presence of corresponding events (QueueEvent2PlaceR: the general case; InQueueEvent2TokenR: a special case).
- Each SC step is projected into a PN transition (Step2TransR). Naturally, the Petri net should simulate how to exit and enter the corresponding states in the statechart, therefore input and output arcs of the transition should be generated accordingly (see StepFrom2InArcR and StepTo2OutArcR). Furthermore, firing a transition should consume the token of the trigger event (Trigger2InArcR), and should generate tokens to (the places related to) the target (receiver) event queues according to the actions (Action2OutArc).

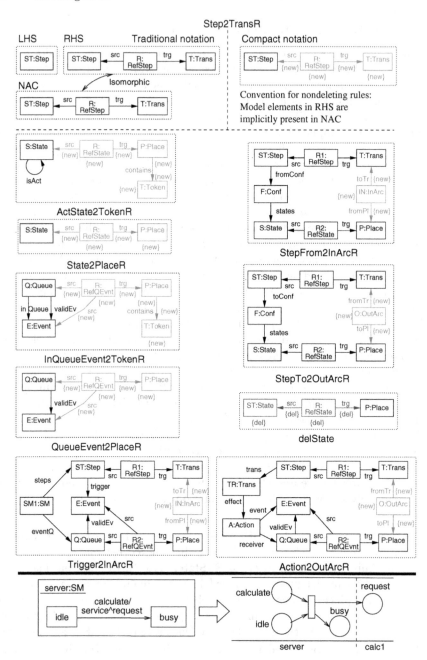

Fig. 2. From state machines to Petri nets

– Finally, we clear up the joint model by removing all model elements from
the source and the reference metamodel by another set of graph transformation rules. For instance, rule delState deletes a State with a corresponding

RefState, if the state is not active. All the other deleting rules of similar kind (including those removing reference nodes and edges) are omitted for space considerations.

3 Termination Criteria for Layered Graph Transformation Systems

In this section we present and prove termination criteria for layered graph transformation systems, which will be used in the next section to show termination of our running example. In fact, our termination criteria are valid for a broad class of graph transformation systems. The criteria for nondeleting rules are based on the single – or double pushout approach (see [7]). For the applications in Sec. 2 and 4 we use in this paper typed attributed graph transformation (see [16, 12]) with injective rule morphisms $l : K \to L, r : K \to R$ and injective matches $m : L \to G$. Moreover we use negative application conditions (NACs) given by an injective morphism $n : L \to N$. The match $m : L \to G$ satisfies the NAC if there is no injective morphism $q : N \to G$ with $m = q \circ n$. Rule morphisms are depicted (in Fig. 2) by using the same node identifiers in LHS, NAC and RHS. Labels LAB can be defined in the traditional way by label sets or in correspondence with the metamodel.

Now we define layered graph grammars with deletion and nondeletion layers. Informally, the deletion layer conditions express that the last creation of a node with a certain label should precede the first deletion of a node with the same label. On the other hand, nondeletion layer conditions ensure that if an element of label l occurs in the LHS of a rule then all elements of the same label were already created in previous layers.

Definition 1 (Layered Graph Grammar). *A graph grammar with rules RUL and labels LAB is called* layered graph grammar *if for each rule $r \in RUL$ we have a rule layer $rl(r) = k$ with $0 \le k \le k_0$ ($k, k_0 \in \mathbb{N}$) where k_0 is the number of layers. Moreover for each label $l \in LAB$ we have a creation and a deletion layer $cl(l), dl(l) \in \mathbb{N}$ and each layer k is either a deletion layer or a nondeletion layer satisfying the following conditions for all $r \in RUL$ with $rl(r) = k$:*

If k is a deletion layer Deletion Layer Conditions	If k is a nondeletion layer Nondeletion Layer Conditions
1. r is deleting at least one item	1. r is nondeleting, i.e. $K = L$ s.t. $r : L \to R$
2. $0 \le cl(l) \le dl(l) \le k_0$ for all $l \in LAB$	2. r has NAC $n : L \to N$ and there is an injective $n' : N \to R$ with $n' \circ n = r$
3. r deletes $l \Rightarrow dl(l) \le rl(r)$	3. $x \in L \Rightarrow cl(label(x)) \le rl(r)$
4. r creates $l \Rightarrow cl(l) > rl(r)$	4. r creates $l \Rightarrow cl(l) > rl(r)$

For the SC2PN transformation the layer conditions mean, for instance, that rules creating Place nodes cannot be in the same layer with rule StepFrom2InArcR: since Place nodes can be used as a pre-condition by a rule (StepFrom2InArcR) only if its creation has finished, i.e. there are no more rules creating Place nodes in the same layer or above. Thus rules ActState2TokenR, State2PlaceR, InQueueEvent2TokenR, and QueueEvent2PlaceR has to precede rule StepFrom2InArcR.

The termination of layered graph grammars expresses that no infinite derivation sequences exist starting from an initial graph if rules are applied within layers as long as possible.

Definition 2 (Termination of Layered Graph Grammars). *A layered graph grammar with finite start graph G_0 and rules RUL terminates, if there is no infinite derivation sequence from G_0 via $RUL = [RUL_k = \{r \in RUL \mid rl(r) = k\}]_{k=0..k_0}$, where starting with layer $k = 0$ rules $r \in RUL_k$ are applied as long as possible before going over to layer $k + 1 \leq k_0$.*

The termination of layered graph grammars are proved separately for the deletion and the nondeletion layers.

Lemma 1 (Termination of Layered Graph Grammars with Deletion). *Each layered graph grammar with deletion terminates.*

Proof (Lemma 1).
Step 0: Let $c_0 = card\{x \in G_0 | dl(label(x)) = 0\}$.
By deletion layer conditions 1,3 the application of a rule r to G_0 with $rl(r) = 0$ deletes at least one item $x \in G_0$ with label $l = label(x)$ and $dl(l) = 0$.
Moreover by deletion layer condition 4 each of the rules r can only create items x with $label(x) = l$, where $cl(l) > 0$. This means by using deletion layer condition 2 that only items x with $label(x) = l$ and $dl(l) \geq cl(l) > 0$ can be created. Hence at most c_0 applications of rules $r \in RUL_0$ are possible in layer 0 leading to $G_0 \Rightarrow^* G_1$ via RUL_0.
Step k: Given graph G_k as result of step $(k - 1)$ for $1 \leq k \leq k_0$ then define $c_k = card\{x \in G_k \mid dl(label(x)) \leq k\}$. Using now rules r with $rl(r) = k$ each $r \in RUL_k$ deletes at least one item $x \in G_k$ with $dl(label(x)) \leq k$ by deletion layer conditions 1 and 3 and creates at most items x with $cl(label(x)) > k$ by deletion layer condition 4 which implies $dl(label(x)) \geq cl(label(x)) > k$ by deletion layer condition 2. Hence at most c_k applications of rules $r \in RUL_k$ are possible in layer k leading to $G_k \Rightarrow^* G_{k+1}$ via RUL_k.
After step n we have at most $c = \Sigma_{k=0}^{k_0} c_k$ applications of rules $r \in R$ leading to $G_0 \Rightarrow^* G_{k_0+1}$, which implies termination.   □

Before proving termination for nondeletion layers, we need to define the notion of essential matches. Informally, an essential match m_0 of a match m_1 : $L \to H_1$ for a transformation $G_0 \Rightarrow^* H_1$ with $G_0 \subseteq H_1$ means that m_1 can be restricted to $m_0 : L \to G_0$.

Definition 3 (Transformation and Essential Match). *Given a nondeleting graph grammar with injective matches a nondeleting rule r is given by an* *injective morphism $r : L \to R$, and a match $m : L \to G$ is an injective morphism leading to a transformation step $G \Rightarrow H$ via (r, m) defined by the pushout (1) of r and m, where $d : G \to H$ is called <u>tracking morphism</u> of $G \Rightarrow H$ via (r, m).*

$$
\begin{array}{ccc}
L & \xrightarrow{\ r\ } & R \\
m \downarrow & (1) & \downarrow m^* \\
G & \xrightarrow[\ d\ ]{} & H
\end{array}
$$

Since r and m are injective morphisms, pushout properties (1) imply that also d and m^* are injective. Given a transformation $G_0 \Rightarrow^* H_1$ i.e. a sequence of transformation steps with induced injective tracking morphism $d_1 : G_0 \to H_1$ a match $m_1 : L \to H_1$ of L in H_1 has an <u>essential match</u> $m_0 : L \to G_0$ of L in G_0 if we have $d_1 \circ m_0 = m_1$. Note, that there is at most one essential match m_0 for m_1, because d_1 is injective.

The following lemma (which is proved in Appendix A) states that rules can be applied at most once with the same essential match.

Lemma 2. *In each derivation sequence starting from G_0 of a nondeleting layered graph grammar with injective matches, each rule $r : L \to R$ with $r \in RUL_0$ can be applied at most once with the same essential match $m_0 : L \to G_0$ and $m_0 \models NAC$.*

Lemma 3 (Termination of Nondeleting Layered Graph Grammars).
Each nondeleting layered graph grammar with injective matches terminates.

Proof (Lemma 3).
Step 0 Given the start Graph G_0 we count for each $r \in RUL_0$ with $r : L \to R$ and NAC the number of possible matches $m : L \to G_0$ with $m \models NAC$

$$
c_r^0 = card\{m_0 | m_0 : L \to G_0 \text{ match with } m_0 \models NAC\}
$$

We will show the following:

The application of rules $r \in RUL_0$ creates by nondeletion layer condition 4 only new items x with $cl(label(x)) > rl(r) = 0$, while each item $x \in L$ for any rule $r \in RUL_0$ has $cl(label(x)) \leq rl(r) = 0$ by nondeleting layer condition 3. This means that for each derivation sequence $G_0 \Rightarrow^* H_1$ via RUL_0 with injective matches and injective morphism $d_1 : G_0 \to H_1$ (induced from $G_0 \Rightarrow^* H_1$ by nondeleting layer condition 1) each match $m_1 : L \to H_1$ of some $r \in RUL_0$ must have an 'essential match' $m_0 : L \to G_0$ with $d_1 \circ m_0 = m_1$.

From Lemma 2 we conclude that in step 0 we have at most

$$
c_0 = \sum_{r \in RUL_0} c_r^0
$$

application of rules $r \in RUL_0$ leading to $G_0 \Rightarrow^* G_1$ via RUL_0.
Step k Given graph G_k as result of step $(k - 1)$ for $1 \leq k \leq k_0$ then define for each $r \in RUL_k$ with $r : L \to R$ and NAC

$$c_r^k = card\{m_k \mid m_k : L \to G_k \text{ match with } m \models NAC\}.$$

Similar to step 0 each $r \in RUL_k$ creates only new items x with $cl(label(x)) > rl(r) = k$, while each item $x \in L$ has $cl(label(x)) \le rl(r) = k$. Now we can apply Lemma 2 for G_k, RUL_k, and m_k instead of G_0, RUL_0, and m_0 and can conclude to have at most $c_k = \sum_{r \in RUL_k} c_r^k$ application of rules leading to $G_k \Rightarrow^* G_{k+1}$, via RUL_k.

After step n we have at most $c = \sum_{k=0}^{k_0} c_k$ applications of rules $r \in RUL$ leading to $G_0 \Rightarrow^* G_{k_0+1}$, which implies termination.

This completes the proof of Lemma 3. □

Theorem 1 (Termination of Layered Graph Grammars). *Each layered graph grammar with injective matches terminates.*

Proof (Theorem 1). Starting with $k = 0$ we can apply for each deletion layer the deletion layer conditions (see Lemma 1) and for each nondeletion layer the nondeletion layer conditions (see Lemma 3). □

4   Termination Analysis

4.1   Termination Analysis of the Running Example

Now we apply the results (of Sec. 3) to prove the termination of the model transformation of Sec. 2 from UML statecharts to Petri nets. Therefore, we first assign the rules of Fig. 2 to four layers (three nondeletion and one deletion layer). Then the creation and deletion layers of labels (types) in the metamodel of Fig. 1 are set to respect Def. 1. Finally, the check of the conditions in Def. 1 yields the termination of the transformation according to Theorem 1.

Assigning Rule Layers. Let us define four layers for the model transformation rules of Fig. 2 as follows:

Layer 0	Layer 1	Layer 2	Layer 3
nondeletion	nondeletion	nondeletion	deletion
$rl(r) = 0$	$rl(r) = 1$	$rl(r) = 2$	$rl(r) = 3$
Step2TransR	State2PlaceR	StepFrom2InArcR	delState
ActState2TokenR	QueueEvent2PlaceR	StepTo2OutArcR	
	InQueueEvent2TokenR	Trigger2InArcR	
		Action2OutArcR	

Assigning Layers to Labels (Types). We define a possible way to automatically assign creation and deletion layers to each label (type) in the metamodel based upon the previous layer definitions for rules.

Definition 4 (Layer assignments). *If we have a start graph G_0 with start labels $T_0 \subseteq LAB$ and then we can define for each $l \in LAB$ the creation and deletion layers as follows*

$$cl(l) = \textit{if } l \in T_0 \textit{ then } 0 \textit{ else } max\{rl(r)|r \textit{ creates } l\} + 1$$
$$dl(l) = \textit{if } l \textit{ is deleted by some } r \textit{ then } min\{rl(r)|r \textit{ deletes } l\} \textit{ else } k_0$$

As only the elements in the source language are present initially in a model transformations, exactly those labels are included in the start labels T_0. Now the creation and deletion layer of labels are assigned as follows (only a subset of labels are considered due to space limitations).

Src label l_s	$cl(l)$	$dl(l)$	Ref label l_r	$cl(l)$	$dl(l)$	Trg label l_t	$cl(l)$	$dl(l)$
State	0	3	RefState	2	3	Place	2	4
Step	0	3	RefStep	1	3	Trans	1	4
Queue	0	3	RefQEvnt	2	3	Token	2	4
Event	0	3				InArc	3	4
Conf	0	3				OutArc	3	4

Checking Conditions of Termination. Finally we show how the sufficient conditions of deletion and nondeletion layers in Def. 1 are fulfilled by the previous layer assignments.

- *Nondeletion Layer Conditions.* First, we notice that Conditions 1 and 2 are straightforwardly guaranteed by the construction (as NAC is isomorphic/identical with RHS). Now we only show the validity of Condition 3 and 4 for a single rule, namely, $r = $ StepFrom2InArcR (while the rest of the rules can be checked similarly). In Condition 3, for each graph element x in the LHS, we need to check $cl(label(x)) \leq rl(r)$, which holds according to the layer assignments above (as $max_{x \in L}\{cl(label(x))\} = 2$ and $rl(r) = 2$). Condition 4 states that $cl(l) > rl(r)$ for all l created by r which is justified by $cl(\mathsf{InArc}) = 3$ and $rl(r) = 2$ (and similar reasoning on edges).
- *Deletion Layer Conditions.* As a first observation, Condition 1 trivially holds for the deletion rules of Layer 3. Condition 2 can be verified according to the table above. Since all deletion rules in Fig. 2 are included in the last layer, Condition 3 holds directly. Finally, the fact that these deletion rules do not create new elements implies Condition 4.

Furthermore, we carried out critical pair analysis using the AGG system [1], which builds upon the confluence results of [13]. As the graph transformation rules within a single layer are free of critical pairs (potential conflicts), we can conclude that our model transformation is a well-defined function from the class of statecharts to that of Petri nets (i.e. it yields a unique result).

4.2 Further Case Studies

From the General Resource Model (GRM) to Petri Nets. In order to provide Petri net-based simultaneous optimization and verification of resource allocation problems, in [8] we aim at generating the application specific Petri net model from a variant of the *General Resource Modeling framework (GRM)* [18] using attributed graph transformation. The graph transformation system (implemented in AGG [1]) consists of five rule layers as follows (where layers 0 and 2 are nondeletion layers while the others are deletion layers):

1. Target model elements are derived from core GRM elements like resource types, activities, and control flow elements;
2. Petri net transitions and arcs are created between the already transformed Petri net items according to the control flow in the source model;
3. The start and the end points of the process are marked by auxiliary edges;
4. The quantitative attributes of the Petri net elements are set;
5. All the auxiliary edges and the source model elements are deleted.

Since the rules are applied to the host graph using injective matches only, and the GTS with a valid source model satisfies the Layered Graph Grammar Definition (Def. 1), the graph grammar fulfills the termination criteria of Theorem 1 hence the graph grammar terminates.

From Process Interaction Diagrams to Timed Petri Nets. In [9], a model transformation from a Process Interaction notation to Timed Transition Petri nets is specified using graph transformation. The source language is customized towards the area of manufacturing and allows building and simulating networks of machines and queues through which pieces can flow. For the mapping, timed transitions depict service times of machines, places are used to model queues and machine states, and finally pieces are mapped to tokens. The transformation was divided in four layers, the first one being nondeleting, while the rest are deleting. The first layer creates Petri net elements connected to the source elements. Rules in the second layer delete the pieces in the model, creating tokens in the appropriate places. In the third layer, we connect the Petri net elements following the connectivity of the source language elements. In addition, the connectivity of the Process Interaction elements is deleted. Finally, the last layer deletes the Process Interaction elements. The languages and the transformation were defined with the AToM^3 tool [10], and then analyzed using AGG.

5   Related Work

Termination of graph transformation systems is undecidable in general [21], but several approaches have been considered to restrict a graph transformation system such that termination can be shown. The classical approach of proving termination is to construct a monotone function that measures graph properties, and to show that the value of such a function decreases with every rule application. Concrete criteria such as the number of nodes and edges of certain types have already been considered by Aßman in [2]. However, he sticks to these concrete criteria, while Bottoni et.al. [5] developed a general approach to termination based on measurement functions.

With respect to termination for graph transformation systems, the current work generalizes and formalizes the work begun at [9]. This, in fact, is an extension of the layering conditions for deleting grammars proposed in [6], which were used for parsing.

With respect to the transformation from Statecharts into Petri nets, in [10] graph grammars were also used to describe the translation. In that approach, Statecharts were restricted to be flat (no hierarchy), termination was not proven and intermediate elements for linking source and target language elements were not formally defined.

6   Conclusion

In this paper, we have presented termination criteria for model transformation expressed as graph transformation. The criteria are based on dividing the grammar in (deleting or nondeleting) layers. A running example, showing a transformation from Statecharts into Petri nets was verified to be terminating. The applicability of the criteria to other examples was also discussed. The proposed termination checks are available in AGG Version 1.2.4 [1].

We believe that our results can also be useful for proving the correctness of QVT-based model transformations. For instance, triple graph grammars (TGG) [25] provide a declarative means to specify model transformations, and show a strong conceptual correspondence with bidirectional QVT mappings. Moreover, a pair of traditional (operational) graph transformations can be easily derived for each TGG rule, and then our termination criteria become directly applicable.

In the future, it will be interesting to extend the termination criteria to graph grammars with *abstract rules* [3]. These rules may contain nodes whose typing is abstract, and are equivalent to all the rules resulting from the substitution of the abstract nodes by nodes in its inheritance tree. This extension would allow to use type graphs with inheritance for the definition of the source and target languages in a model transformation.

References

1. AGG Homepage, http://tfs.cs.tu-berlin.de/agg.
2. Aßmann, U. 2000. *Graph Rewrite Systems for Program Optimization.* ACM TOPLAS, vol. 22(4), pp. 583–637, ACM Press, New York.
3. Bardohl, R., Ehrig, H., de Lara J., and Taentzer, G. 2004. *Integrating Meta Modelling with Graph Transformation for Efficient Visual Language Definition and Model Manipulation.* In *Proc. FASE'04*, LNCS 2984, pp. 214–228. Springer.
4. Baresi, L., Pezzé, M. 2001. *Improving UML with Petri-Nets.* ENTCS 44 (4).
5. Bottoni, P., Koch, M., Parisi-Presicce, F., Taentzer, G. 2004. *Termination of High-Level Replacement Units with Application to Model Transformation.* In proceedings of VLFM'04, ENTCS.
6. Bottoni, P., Taentzer, G., Schürr, A. 2000. *Efficient Parsing of Visual Languages based on Critical Pair Analysis and Contextual Layered Graph Transformation.* In Proc. Visual Languages 2000 IEEE Computer Society. pp.: 59-60.

7. A. Corradini, U. Montanari, F. Rossi, H. Ehrig, R. Heckel, and M. Löwe. *In [24]*, chap. Algebraic Approaches to Graph Transformation — Part I: Basic Concepts and Double Pushout Approach, pp. 163–245. World Scientific, 1997.

8. S. Gyapay. Model transformation from General Resource Models to Petri nets using graph transformation. Tech. rep., Technical University of Berlin, Dept. of Computer Science, July, 2004.

9. de Lara, J., Taentzer, G. 2004. *Automated Model Transformation and its Validation with AToM³ and AGG.* In DIAGRAMS'2004 (Cambridge, UK). Lecture Notes in Artificial Intelligence 2980, pp.: 182–198. Springer.

10. de Lara, J., Vangheluwe, H. 2002 *Computer Aided Multi-Paradigm Modelling to process Petri-Nets and Statecharts.* In ICGT'2002. LNCS 2505. pp.: 239–253. Springer.

11. Ehrig, H. 1979. *Introduction to the Algebraic Theory of Graph Grammars.* In V. Claus, H. Ehrig, and G. Rozenberg (eds.), 1st Graph Grammar Workshop, pages 1-69. Springer LNCS 73, 1979.

12. Ehrig, H., Habel, A., Padberg, J., Prange, U. 2004. *Adhesive High-Level Replacement Categories and Systems.* In Proc. 2nd Int. Conference on Graph Transformation (ICGT'04). Springer LNCS 3256, pp. 144–160.

13. Ehrig, H., Prange, U., Taentzer, G. 2004. *Fundamental Theory for Typed Attributed Graph Transformation.* In Proc. 2nd Int. Conference on Graph Transformation (ICGT'04). Springer LNCS 3256, pp. 161–177.

14. Habel, A., Heckel, R., Taentzer, G. 1996. *Graph Grammars with Negative Application Conditions*, Special issue of Fundamenta Informaticae 26(3-4): 287-313.

15. Harel, D. Statecharts: A visual formalism for complex systems. *Science of Computer Programming*, vol. 8(3):pp. 231–274, 1987.

16. Heckel, R., Küster, J., Taentzer, G. 2002. *Towards Automatic Translation of UML Models into Semantic Domains*. In Proc. of APPLIGRAPH Workshop on Applied Graph Transformation (AGT 2002).

17. Heckel, R., Küster, J. M., Taentzer, G. Confluence of typed attributed graph transformation systems. In *Proc. ICGT 2002: First Int. Conference on Graph Transformation*, vol. 2505 of *LNCS*, pp. 161–176. Springer, Barcelona, Spain, 2002.

18. Object Management Group. *UML Profile for Schedulability, Performance and Time.* http://www.omg.org.

19. Object Management Group. *QVT: Request for Proposal for Queries, Views and Transformations.* http://www.omg.org.

20. Pataricza, A. Semi-decisions in the validation of dependable systems. In *Suppl. Proc. DSN 2001: The International IEEE Conference on Dependable Systems and Networks*, pp. 114–115. Göteborg, Sweden, 2001.

21. Plump, D. 1998. *Termination of Graph Rewriting is Undecidable.* Fundamenta Informaticae 33(2):201-209.

22. QVT-Partners. *Revised submission for MOF 2.0 Query / Views / Transformations RFP.* http://qvtp.org.

23. Raistrick, C., Francis, P., Wright, J., Carter, C., Wilkie, I. 2004. *Model Driven Architecture with Executable UML.* Cambridge University Press. Cambridge, UK. See also the MDA home page at OMG web site: http://www.omg.org/mda/.

24. Rozenberg, G. (ed) 1997. *Handbook of Graph Grammars and Computing by Graph Transformation.* World Scientific. Volume 1.

25. Schürr, A. Specification of Graph Translators with Triple Graph Grammars. In *Proc. WG94: Int. Workshop on Graph-Theoretic Concepts in Computer Science*, vol. 903 of *LNCS*, pp. 151–163. Springer-Verlag, 1994.

26. Süß, J.G., Leicher, A., Busse, S. 2003. *OCLPrime – Environment and Language for Model Query, Views and Transformations.* In OCL Workshop at UML'2003. San Francisco.
27. Varró, D. A formal semantics of UML Statecharts by model transition systems. In *Proc. ICGT 2002: First Int. Conference on Graph Transformation,* vol. 2505 of *LNCS,* pp. 378–392. Springer-Verlag, Barcelona, Spain, 2002.
28. Varró, D. *Automated Model Transformations for the Analysis of IT Systems.* Ph.D. thesis, Budapest Univ. of Technology and Economics, Dept. of Measurement and Information Systems, 2004.
29. Varró, D., Varró, G., Pataricza, A. Designing the automatic transformation of visual languages. *Science of Computer Programming,* vol. 44(2):pp. 205–227, 2002.

A   Proofs

Lemma 2. *In each derivation sequence starting from G_0 each rule $r : L \to R$ with $r \in RUL_0$ can be applied at most once with the same 'essential match' $m_0 : L \to G_0$ and $m_0 \models NAC$.*

Proof (Lemma 2). Assume that in $G_0 \Rightarrow^* H_1$ rule r has been applied with the same 'essential match' m_0 already. This means we can decompose $G_0 \Rightarrow^* H_1$ into $G_0 \Rightarrow^* G \Rightarrow H \Rightarrow^* H_1$ with pushout(1) and injective morphisms $G_0 \xrightarrow{g} G \xrightarrow{d} H \xrightarrow{h_1} H_1$ satisfying $d_1 = h_1 \circ d \circ g$ and $d_1 \circ m_0 = m_1$ in Figure 3.

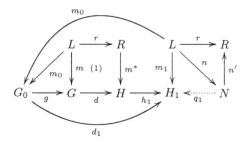

Fig. 3. Second Application of Rule r with same essential match m_0

In order to prove the lemma now it is sufficient to show that $m_1 : L \to H_1$ does not satisfy the NAC of r, i.e. $m_1 \not\models NAC$, where the NAC is given by an injective morphism $n : L \to N$ with $n' : N \to R$ injective satisfying $n' \circ n = r$ by condition 2. In fact we are able to construct an injective $q_1 : N \to H_1$ with $q_1 \circ n = m_1$.

Let $q_1 = h_1 \circ m^* \circ n'$, then q_1 is injective because n', m^* and h_1 are injective and injectivity of m^* follows from injectivity of match m. Moreover we have:

$$q_1 \circ n = h_1 \circ m^* \circ n' \circ n = h_1 \circ m^* \circ r = h_1 \circ d \circ m = h_1 \circ d \circ g \circ m_0 = d_1 \circ m_0 = m_1$$

This completes the proof of lemma 2.   □

Ensuring Structural Constraints in Graph-Based Models with Type Inheritance

Gabriele Taentzer[1] and Arend Rensink[2]

[1] Computer Science Department, Technical University of Berlin,
Franklinstr. 28/29, 10587 Berlin, Germany
[2] Computer Science Department, University of Twente,
P.O. Box 217, 7500 AE Enschede, The Netherlands

Abstract. Graphs are a common means to represent structures in models and meta-models of software systems. In this context, the description of model domains by classifying the domain entities and their relations using *class diagrams* or *type graphs* has emerged as a very valuable principle. The constraints that can be imposed by pure typing are, however, relatively weak; it is therefore common practice to enrich type information with *structural properties* (such as local invariants or multiplicity conditions) or *inheritance*.

In this paper, we show how to formulate structural properties using *graph constraints* in type graphs with inheritance, and we show how to translate constrained type graphs with inheritance to equivalent constrained simple type graphs. From existing theory it then follows that graph constraints can be translated into pre-conditions for productions of a typed graph transformation system which ensures those graph constraints. This result can be regarded as a further important step of integrating graph transformation with object-orientation concepts.

1 Introduction

Graphs and graphical representations play a central role in modeling and meta-modeling of software systems. Graphs are used to describe essential structures of entities and their relations. Their representation ranges from simply formatted, graph-like notations such as class diagrams, Petri nets, automata, etc. to more elaborated diagram kinds such as message sequence charts and to more application-specific notations for modeling, e.g., for industrial production processes.

In graph-based modeling and meta-modeling, graphs are used to define the static structure, such as class and object structures, data base schemes, as well as visual symbols and interrelations, i.e., visual alphabets and sentences. Graph manipulations describe the dynamic changes of these structures. Classifying the possible entities and interrelations in static system structures or visual language constructs isas a valuable principle for the description of model domains. In the object-oriented approach, *class diagrams* are the basic means to specify classification structures; e.g., in UML (Unified Modeling Language) [11] for software systems and MOF (Meta Object Facility) [11] for visual language specification. When applying graph transformation for modeling or meta-modeling, *type graphs* are used to classify graph nodes and edges.

M. Cerioli (Ed.): FASE 2005, LNCS 3442, pp. 64–79, 2005.

One of the main principles to handle complex classification structures comes from the object-orientation paradigm: class inheritance enhances the typing principle by adding more abstract types on top of the ones concretely used in the (meta)models. Inheritance allows much more compact representations by reducing redundancy. The principle of inheritance has been carried over and formalized for graph transformation in [2]; there we have shown that node inheritance in typed graph transformation leads to a denser form of a graph transformation system, by a simular reduction of redundancy.

The power of pure typing to describe and constrain the static structure is, however, relatively weak (and is not enhanced by inheritance). It is therefore common practice to enrich type information with *structural properties* which further constrain the correct instances. A typical class of such structural properties are *multiplicity conditions*, which restrict correctly typed structures to those where the numbers of entities and interrelations are within given ranges. Further constraints can be *local invariants* which require, e.g., the existence or non-existence of certain substructures. In class diagrams, some of these constraint kinds are built-in, like multiplicities, while others have to be stated by separate constraints using, e.g., OCL [11]. On the other hand, typed graphs can be equipped with *graph constraints*, as proposed first in [9], which can be used to describe a variety of local invariants. Note, however, that graph constraints have so far been studied for *flat* graphs only (i.e., without node type inheritance).

The object-oriented and graph transformation approaches can be integrated by identifying classes with node types, and associations with edge types. In this way, class inheritance naturally corresponds to node type inheritance. In this paper we show how to express multiplicities and *edge inheritance* by graph constraints over type graphs with inheritance. Furthermore, we give a translation of constrained type graphs with inheritance to constrained flat type graphs. From existing theory [6] it then follows that graph constraints can be translated into (necessary and sufficient) pre-conditions for typed graph transformation rules. Our result can be regarded as a necessary further step of integrating graph transformation with object-orientation concepts. Application areas for the resulting theory are for instance: *operational semantics* for object-oriented systems as in [4] (leading to a theory of behavioral verification) and *refactoring* as in [10] (leading to a formal underpinning). We use a running example from the former area.

The paper is organized as follows: In the next section, we recall type graphs with node type inheritance as introduced in [2]; this will be the basis for further development. In Section 3 defined graph constraints over type graphs with inheritance and presents a translation to constraints over simple type graphs. Then Section 4 shows that multiplicities and edge inheritance are expressible by graph constraints. Section 5 describes how graph constraints can be ensured by typed graph transformation systems, reusing and extending the results in [6]. All proofs are omitted due to lack of space.

2   Type Graphs with Node Type Inheritance

The basic idea for specifying node type hierarchies is to introduce a special kind of (directed) edges, called *inheritance edges*, into type graphs. The source node of an inheritance edge is said to be a sub-type of the target node, which is called the former one's super-type. Moreover, nodes are marked either as *concrete* or *abstract*; we will

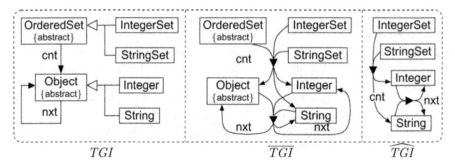

Fig. 1. A sample type graph with node type inheritance, and its abstract and concrete closure

see that only concrete type nodes can have direct instances. In host graphs only nodes of concrete types shall occur, while graphs in rules may contain nodes of both types.

Definition 1 (type graph with inheritance). *A type graph with inheritance is a triple* $TGI = (TG, I, A)$ *consisting of a type graph* $TG = (N, E, s, t)$ *(with a set N of nodes, a set E of edges, source and target functions $s, t : E \rightarrow N$), an acyclic inheritance relation $I \subseteq N \times N$, and a set $A \subseteq N$, called abstract nodes. For each $x \in N$, the inheritance clan is defined by $clan_I(x) = \{y \in N \mid (y, x) \in I^*\}$, where I^* is the reflexive-transitive closure of I.*

Example 1. As sample type graph we use TGI in Fig. 1. This describes a special kind of sets, namely ordered sets, which contain a number of objecs (indicated by cnt-edges from OrderedSet-nodes to Object-nodes) which can be put into some order (indicated by nxt-edges among the object). We consider two possible specializations of ordered sets, namely StringSet and IntegerSet, which are intended to contain Strings and Integers, respectively. Note that the type graph by itself does not yet enforce this constraint: that is, it does not rule out that StringSets contain also Integers, and vice versa.

To benefit from the existing theory of graph transformation [5], which does not recognize the notion of inheritance, we define the *flattening* or *closure* of type graphs with inheritance to ordinary ones.

Definition 2 (Closure of type graph with inheritance). *Let* $TGI = (TG, I, A)$ *be a type graph with inheritance, and let* $TG = (N, E, src, tar)$. *The abstract closure of* TGI *is the graph* $\overline{TGI} = (N, \overline{E}, \overline{src}, \overline{tar})$ *with*

- $\overline{E} = \{(n_1, e, n_2) \mid e \in E, n_1 \in clan_I(src(e)), n_2 \in clan_I(tar(e))\}$;
- $\overline{src}((n_1, e, n_2)) = n_1$;
- $\overline{tar}((n_1, e, n_2)) = n_2$.

The concrete closure of TGI *is the graph* $\widehat{TGI} = \overline{TGI}|_{N-A}$.[3]

---

[3] Given a graph $G = (N, E, s, t)$ and a set $X \subseteq N$, we denote by $G|_X$ the sub-graph $(X, E_X = \{e \in E \mid s(e), t(e) \in X\}, s|_{E_X}, t|_{E_X})$.

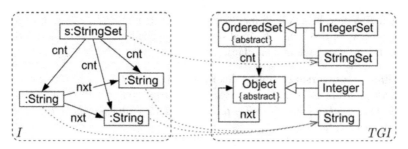

Fig. 2. Sample clan-typed graph

Example 2. Fig. 1 also shows the abstract and concrete closure of the type graph with inheritance TGI. Please note that for better readability of the closures, the edge types are bundled using auxiliary nodes. Note that the inheritance edges are no longer present in the closure, and the abstract node types and adjacent edge types are absent from the concrete closure. Instead, for all combinations of corresponding sub-types a new edge type is inserted — including those which do not follow our intuition, like edge type nxt between String and Integer. We will use structural graph properties in addition to rule out those unwanted structures.

The distinction between the abstract and the concrete closure of a type graph is necessary, since they give rise to different instances. We will define abstract graph transformation rules of which the left hand and right hand sides are typed over the abstract closure (see Sect. 5), whereas ordinary host graphs and concrete rules are typed over the concrete closure.

Definition 3 (instance graph). *An abstract instance graph* (G, tp_A) *of a type graph with inheritance TGI is an instance graph of $\overline{TGI}$; i.e., $tp_A\colon G \to \overline{TGI}$. Analogously, a concrete instance graph* (G, tp_C) *of TGI is a graph typed over $\widehat{TGI}$.*

Note that, due to the canonical inclusion $inc_{TG}\colon \widehat{TGI} \hookrightarrow \overline{TGI}$, all concrete instance graphs are abstract instance graphs. The construction of the closure in Def. 2 gives rise to a characterization of instance graphs directly on type graphs with inheritance. Namely, instance graphs can be typed over the type graph with inheritance by a pair of functions, from nodes to node types and from edges to edge types, respectively. This pair of functions does not constitute a graph morphism, but will be called *clan morphism*; it uniquely characterizes the type morphism into the flattened type graph.

Definition 4 (clan morphism). *Let $TGI = (TG, I, A)$ be a type graph with inheritance. A* clan-morphism *from G to TGI is a pair ctp $= (ctp_N\colon N_G \to N_{TG}, ctp_E\colon E_G \to E_{TG})$ such that for all $e \in E_G$ the following holds:*

- *$ctp_N \circ s_G(e) \in clan_I(s_{TG} \circ ctp_E(e))$ and*
- *$ctp_N \circ t_G(e) \in clan_I(t_{TG} \circ ctp_E(e))$.*

(G, ctp) is called a clan-typed graph. *ctp is called* concrete *if $ctp_N^{-1}(A) = \emptyset$.*

Example 3. Fig. 2 shows a sample instance graph typed over TGI of Fig. 1. The edge typing is not shown explicitly, but follows uniquely from the node typing. The typing is done by a clan morphism which maps each node to its node type and each edge to an edge type between potentially more abstract node types holding the source and target types of the instance edge in their clans.

Proposition 1 (universal clan morphism, see [1]). *Let $TGI = (TG, I, A)$ be a type graph with inheritance. There is a universal clan morphism $u_{TG} \colon \overline{TGI} \to TG$ such that for each clan morphism $ctp \colon G \to TG$ there is a unique graph morphism $tp \colon G \to \overline{TGI}$ with $u_{TG} \circ tp = ctp$.*

We often write G for the clan-typed graph (G, ctp_G). To formalize the relationship between abstract and concrete rules (see Sect. 5), we introduce the notion of *type refinement*. This imposes an order over the set of clan morphisms of a given instance graph: one clan morphism is said to be *finer* than another if it assigns more concrete node types to the instance graph nodes.

Definition 5 (type refinement and typed graph morphism). *Let $TGI = (TG, I, A)$ be a type graph with inheritance, and let $ctp, ctp' \colon G \to TG$ be clan typings. ctp is a refinement of ctp', denoted $ctp \leq ctp'$, if*

- $ctp_N(n) \in clan_I(ctp'_N(n))$ *for all $n \in N_G$, and*
- $ctp_E = ctp'_E$.

Given clan-typed graphs (G, ctp_G) and (H, ctp_H) over TGI, a morphism $g \colon G \to H$ is called type-refining *if $g \circ ctp_H \leq ctp_G$, and* type-preserving *if $g \circ ctp_H = ctp_G$.*

We write $(G, ctp_G) \leq (H, ctp_H)$ if $G = H$ and $ctp_G \leq ctp_H$. We write $g \colon G \to_c H$ to denote that G and H are both concrete and g is an injective type-preserving morphism, and $g \colon G \to_a H$ to denote that g is an injective type-refining morphism. The following proposition states some facts regarding type-refining and type-preserving morphisms.

Proposition 2. *Let G, H be clan-typed graphs, and let $g \colon G \to H$ be type refining.*

1. *There is a unique clan-typed graph $K \leq G$ such that $g \colon K \to H$ is type-preserving;*
2. *For any clan-typed graph $K \geq G$, $g \colon K \to H$ is type-refining.*
3. *For any clan-typed graph $K \leq H$, $g \colon G \to K$ is type-refining.*

3   Structural Properties over Type Graphs with Inheritance

The following definition extends the concept of graph constraints, originally introduced in [9] (where they are called consistency constraints). There are two points of change:

- We define constraints over concrete clan-typed graphs rather than ordinary typed graphs. However, this is not a real extension since (due to Prop. 1), there is a one-to-one correspondence between concrete clan morphisms and type morphisms to the concrete closure of the type graph.
- We allow constraints with multiple, disjunctively interpreted conclusions, rather than a single conclusion, as in [9, 6]. This is a real extension, as it properly enlarges the set of properties expressible through graph constraints.

Whenever we mention "clan-typed graphs" in the following, we mean graphs with a clan morphism to some implicit, globally given type graph with inheritance TGI.

Definition 6 (graph atoms and formulae). *Let* L, G *be clan-typed graphs, such that* G *is concrete.*

- *A concrete [abstract] graph atom* A *over* L *is a tuple* $(n: L \rightarrow_c P, Con)$ $[(n: L \rightarrow_a P, Con)]$*, where* n *is an injective type-preserving [type-refining] morphism, and* Con *is a set of injective type-preserving [type-refining] morphisms starting in* P*. If* $L = \emptyset$ *we also write* (P, Con) *for* A*.*
- A *is said to be satisfied by an injective type-preserving [type-refining] morphism* $m: L \rightarrow_c G$ $[m: L \rightarrow_a G]$*, denoted* $m \models^c A$ $[m \models^a A]$*, if for all injective type-preserving [type-refining] morphisms* $p: P \rightarrow_c G$ $[p: P \rightarrow_a G]$ *such that* $m = p \circ n$*, there is a* $(q: P \rightarrow C) \in Con$ *and an injective type-preserving [type-refining] morphism* $c: C \rightarrow_c G$ $[c: C \rightarrow_a G]$ *such that* $p = c \circ q$*. If* $L = \emptyset$ *(i.e., the empty graph) then we also write* $G \models^c A$ $[G \models^a A]$*.*
- *A concrete [abstract] graph formula* F *over* L *is a boolean formula over concrete [abstract] graph atoms over* L*. The satisfaction relation* $\models^c$ $[\models^a]$ *is extended to graph formulae by defining the semantics of the boolean operators in the usual way. We call* F *a* constraint *if* $L = \emptyset$*, and an* application condition *otherwise.*

Example 4. Fig. 3 shows three atoms over the type graph with inheritance TGI in Fig. 1. In this and later pictures we depict graph atoms $(L \rightarrow P, \{P \rightarrow C_i\}_i)$ more compactly as $L \rightarrow P \rightarrow \{C_i\}_i$.

- A_1 is satisfied by a morphism that selects an element without an outgoing nxt-edge;
- A_2 is satisfied by a graph if every OrderedSet is empty, i.e., contains no elements;
- A_3 is satisfied by a graph if for every OrderedSet and every pair of distinct elements contained in it, (at least) one element as an outgoing nxt-edge. Note that the graphs in the set on the right hand side are to be interpreted disjunctively.

A_2 and A_3 range over the same graph L, viz. the empty graph: in fact, they are *constraints* and can be combined into the formula $A_2 \wedge A_3$. A_1, on the other hand, cannot be combined with A_2 or A_3 into one formula, since they are atoms over different graphs.

We can now define the flattening of an abstract atom and an abstract formula.

Definition 7 (flattening). *Let* K, L *be clan-typed graphs such that* $K \leq L$ *and* K *is concrete.*

- *For any abstract graph atom* $A = \langle n: L \rightarrow_a Q, Con \rangle$*, the* K*-flattening of* A *is defined by:*

$$flat_K(A) = \bigwedge \{(n: K \rightarrow_c P, flat_P(Con)) \mid P \leq Q\}$$
$$flat_P(Con) = \{q: P \rightarrow_c C \mid (q: Q \rightarrow_a D) \in Con, C \leq D\} \ .$$

- *For any abstract graph formula* F *over* L*, the* K*-flattening* $flat_K(F)$ *is defined by replacing each abstract graph atom* A *occurring in* F *by the corresponding* K*-flattening* $flat_K(A)$*.*

In the next secion we give some examples of flattening. The following theorem is the main contribution of this paper. It states that satisfaction of an abstract atom or formula over an abstract clan-typed graph L by a type-refining morphism $m: L \rightarrow_a G$ is equivalent to satisfaction of the flattening of that atom or formula with respect to the concrete clan-typed graph $K \leq L$ for which $m: K \rightarrow_c G$ is type-preserving (which uniquely exists due to Prop. 2.1). This allows us to re-use existing theory on concrete graph formulae.

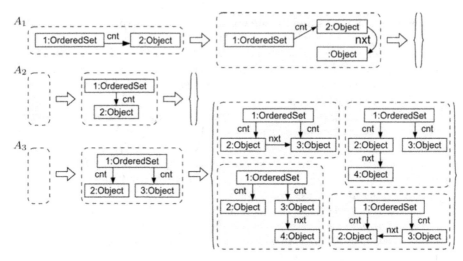

Fig. 3. Three example graph atoms

Theorem 1 (flattening of abstract graph formulae). *Let K, L, G be clan-typed graphs such that $K \leq L$, and let $m\colon K \to_c G$. For any abstract graph atom A and graph formula F over L the following holds:*

$$(m\colon L \to_a G) \models^a A \text{ iff } (m\colon K \to_c G) \models^c flat_K(A)$$
$$(m\colon L \to_a G) \models^a F \text{ iff } (m\colon K \to_c G) \models^c flat_K(F) \ .$$

The proof relies on the fact that the flattening defined in Def. 7 "predicts" all concrete ways in which the abstract atom and formula could be satisfied, by taking conjunctions resp. disjunction over all concrete instance graphs that are $\leq$-predecessors of the abstract premises and conclusions.

4   Multiplicities and Edge Inheritance as Graph Formulae

In this section we show that two existing classes of constraints on type graphs with inheritance can be translated to abstract graph formulae. This serves to give some intuition about graph formulae, and to demonstrate that they are expressive enough to cover practically useful examples. (It should be noted, however, that there are many graph constraints that do not fall into either of these classes: for instance, A_3 in Fig. 3 cannot be expressed through multiplicities or edge inheritance.)

Multiplicities. By enriching a type graph with multiplicities we can restrict the class of instance graphs to those which are not only correctly typed but also satisfy additional constraints concerning the number of nodes and edges for each type. These constraints are expressed using so-called *multiplicities*.

Definition 8 (multiplicities). *A multiplicity is a pair $[i, j] \in \mathcal{N} \times (\mathcal{N} \cup \{*\})$ with $i \leq j$ or $j = *$. The set of multiplicities is denoted Mult. The special value $*$ indicates that* *the maximum number of nodes or edges is not constrained. For an arbitrary finite set X and $[i, j] \in Mult$, we write $|X| \in [i, j]$ if $i \leq |X|$ and either $j = *$ or $|X| \leq j$.*

As usual, we use multiplicities to decorate the nodes and edges of type graphs. For the nodes, the multiplicity indicates the total number of instances; for the edges, we use multiplicities expressing the number of incoming, respectively outgoing edges *for each target, respectively source instance.*

Definition 9 (Type graph with multiplicities). *A type graph with multiplicities is a tuple $TGM = (TGI, m_N, m_{src}, m_{tar})$ consisting of a type graph with inheritance TGI and additional functions $m_N : N_{TGI} \rightarrow Mult$, called* node multiplicity function, *and $m_{src}, m_{tar} : E_{TGI} \rightarrow Mult$, called* edge multiplicity functions.

The satisfaction of multiplicity constraints is expressed by counting inverse images with respect to the clan typing.

Definition 10 (Semantics of type graphs with multiplicities). *A clan-typed graph G over $TGI = (TG, I, A)$ is said to* satisfy *a type graph with multiplicities $(TGI, m_N, m_{src}, m_{tar})$ if the following conditions hold:*

- *for all $n \in N_{TG}$, $|ctp_G^{-1}(clan_I(n))| \in m_N(n)$;*
- *for all $e \in E_{TG}$ and $p \in ctp_G^{-1}(clan_I(src(e)))$, $|ctp_G^{-1}(e) \cap src_G^{-1}(p)| \in m_{tar}(e)$;*
- *for all $e \in E_{TG}$ and $p \in ctp_G^{-1}(clan_I(tar(e)))$, $|ctp_G^{-1}(e) \cap tar_G^{-1}(p)| \in m_{src}(e)$.*

We now show how a type graph with multiplicities TGM can be translated to an abstract graph formula that is satisfied by precisely those clan-typed graphs that also satisfy TGM. In order to do that, we introduce two special types of graphs: for all $i \in \mathcal{N}$,

- For all $n \in N$, G_i^n is the graph consisting of i distinct n-typed nodes.
- For all $e \in E$, $\mathcal{G}_i^{e, src}$ is the *set* of graphs with i distinct e-typed edges and all source nodes glued together; dually, $\mathcal{G}_i^{e, tar}$ is the set of graphs with i distinct e-typed edges and all target nodes glued together.

Definition 11 (Multiplicities as abstract graph formulae). *Given a type graph with multiplicities $TGM = (TGI, m_N, m_{src}, m_{tar})$, we define*

$$F_{TGM} = \bigwedge\nolimits_{n \in N_{TGI}} F_n \wedge \bigwedge\nolimits_{e \in E_{TGI}} (F_e^{src} \wedge F_e^{tar})$$

where F_n, F_e^{src} and F_e^{tar} are abstract graph formulae defined as follows:

- *F_n regulates the node multiplicity of n. Let $m_N(n) = [i, j]$; then $F_n = A_{n \geq i} \wedge A_{n \leq j}$ if $j \neq *$ and $F_n = A_{n \geq i}$ otherwise, where*

$$A_{n \geq i} = (\emptyset, \{\emptyset \rightarrow G_i^n\})$$
$$A_{n \leq j} = (G_{j+1}^n, \emptyset) \ .$$

- *F_e^{src} regulates the edge source multiplicity of e. Let $m_{src}(e) = [i, j]$; then $F_e^{src} = A_{e \geq i}^{src} \wedge F_{e \leq j}^{src}$ if $j \neq *$ and $F_e^{src} = A_{e \geq i}^{src}$ otherwise, where*

$$A_{e \geq i}^{src} = (G_1^{tar(e)}, \{q^{tar} : G_1^{tar(e)} \rightarrow H \mid H \in \mathcal{G}_i^{e, tar}\})$$
$$F_{e \leq j}^{src} = \bigwedge \{(H, \emptyset) \mid H \in \mathcal{G}_{j+1}^{e, tar}\}$$

with q^{tar} mapping the sole node of $G_1^{tar(e)}$ to the unique target node of H.

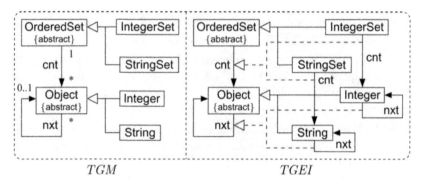

$$TGM \qquad\qquad\qquad\qquad TGEI$$

Fig. 4. Type graph with multiplicities, respectively edge inheritance

- F_e^{tar} regulates the edge target multiplicity of e, and is the exact dual of F_e^{src} (obtained by switching src and tar everywhere in the above definition).

The following theorem states that this formula indeed expresses the multiplicity semantics according to Def. 10. The proof is omitted here.

Theorem 2 (semantics of multiplicities). *For all type graphs with multiplicity TGM and all graphs G clan-typed over TGI, G satisfies TGM (in the sense of Def. 10) if and only if* $G \models^a F_{TGM}$.

Example 5 (multiplicity constraints). In Figure 4 (left hand side), the type graph *TGI* of Fig. 1 has been extended with multiplicities at edge types. For the notation of multiplicities we follow UML. Each object has always to belong to precisely one ordered set. This statement contains two constraints: a lower and an upper bound, which in this case are both equal to 1. Vice versa, ordered sets are allowed to contain arbitrarily many objects, which is indicated by an asterisk. The nxt relation on objects is constrained to a partial order where at most one object is nxt, but each object may have arbitrarily many predecessors. This results in the five graph constraints depicted in Figure 5. (Note that we have omitted the empty initial graph.) The first constraint states that every object is contained in a set (which is a *positive* constraint), the next two that an object is not allowed to have two outgoing containment edges, neither to different nor to the same OrderedSet node (which are *negative* constraints), and the last two constraints (also negative) express that an object does not have two successor objects.

The next step is to flatten these graph constraints; i.e., we formulate graph constraints w.r.t. the concrete closure $\widehat{TGI}$ also given in Fig. 1. Some representatives of the flattened constraints are shown in Fig. 6. The first of these is the complete flattening of the first constraint in Fig. 5; the second and third show two of the four atomic constraints that constitute the flattening of the second constraint in Fig. 5.

Edge Inheritance. As we have seen, node inheritance is used to formulate a compact type graph in the sense that edge types between super types stand for all combinations of edge types between their sub-types (including themselves). This might lead to a type graph with too loose type information concerning edges. In the following, we introduce *edge type inheritance*, which aims at restricting the combinations of sub-types allowed.

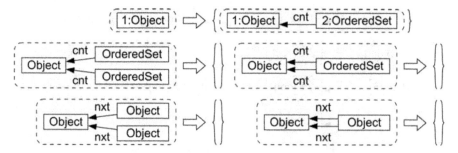

Fig. 5. Multiplicity constraints as abstract graph atoms

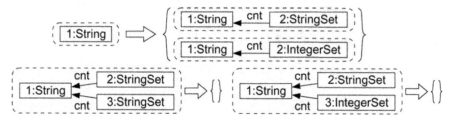

Fig. 6. Flattened multiplicity constraints

Definition 12 (type graph with edge inheritance). *A type graph with edge inheritance is a tuple* (TG, I, A) *where* $I \subseteq (N \times N) \cup (E \times E)$ *is an acyclic relation such that* $TGI = (TG, I|_N, A)$ *is a type graph with (node) inheritance, and moreover,* $(e, f) \in I \cap (E \times E)$ *implies* $src(e) \in clan_I(src(f))$ *and* $tar(e) \in clan_I(tar(f))$.

The idea is that if a type edge e inherits from another type edge f, then f can occur as an edge type only for concrete graph edges whose source and target node types are not in the clan of the source type, resp. target of e. The semantics of edge inheritance can either be expressed by redefining the closure, or directly as a constraint on the clan morphism. In other words, if the source or target node of an edge would allow e as an edge type, then no proper super-type of e may be used.

Definition 13 (semantics of type graphs with edge inheritance). *A clan-typed graph* G *over* TGI *is said to* satisfy *a type graph with edge inheritance* (TG, I, A) *for which* $TGI = (TG, I|_N, A)$ *if for all* $x \in E_G$ *and* $(e, ctp_G(x)) \in I$, $ctp_G(src_G(x)) \notin clan_I(src_{TG}(e))$ *and* $ctp_G(tar_G(x)) \notin clan_I(tar_{TG}(e))$.

We now construct an abstract graph formula which expresses the same constraint.

Definition 14 (edge inheritance as an abstract formula). *Given a type graph with edge inheritance* $TGEI = (TG, I, A)$, *define* $F_{TGEI} = \bigwedge_{(e,f) \in I_E} A_{e,f}^{src} \wedge A_{e,f}^{tar}$ *where*

$$A_{e,f}^{src} = (G^{src(e),f,tar(f)}, \{q_{e,f} : G^{src(e),f,tar(f)} \rightarrow G^{src(e),e,tar(e)}\})$$
$$A_{e,f}^{tar} = (G^{src(f),f,tar(e)}, \{q_{e,f} : G^{src(f),f,tar(e)} \rightarrow G^{src(e),e,tar(e)}\}) \; .$$

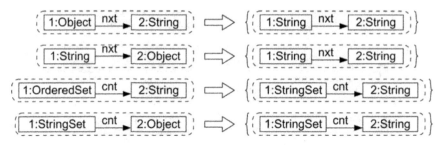

Fig. 7. Edge inheritance as graph constraints

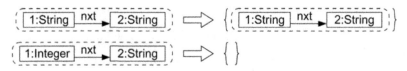

Fig. 8. Flattened edge inheritance constraints

with G^{n_1,e,n_2} for $n_1 \in clan_I(src(e))$ and $n_2 \in clan_I(tar(e))$ being the graph consisting of two nodes typed over n_1 and n_2, and one edge typed over e. $q_{e,f}$ is the unique type-refining morphism between the source and target graph.

The following theorem states that this formula indeed expresses the satisfaction of the edge inheritance relation, according to Def. 13. The proof is omitted here.

Theorem 3 (semantics of edge inheritance). *For all type graphs with edge inheritance* $TGEI = (TG, I, A)$ *and all graphs* G *clan-typed over* $(TG, I|_N, A)$, G *satisfies* $TGEI$ *(in the sense of Def. 13) if and only if* $G \models^a F_{TGEI}$.

Example 6 (edge inheritance constraints). In Figure 4 (right hand side) we extended the type graph of Fig. 1 with edge type inheritance, depicted by (dashed) inheritance arrows between edges. Hence this type graph expresses (among other things) that an instance may not contain a nxt-edge from a String-typed node to anything but another String-typed node — in particular not to an Integer-typed node — or to a node typed by a subtype of String(of which there are none in this example).

Similarly to the example above, we flatten these graph constraints, i.e., we formulate graph constraints w.r.t. the concrete closure $\widehat{TGI}$ given in Fig. 1. The constraints shown in Fig. 8 are the complete flattening of the first constraint in Fig. 7. Note that the first flattened constraint is always true, and the second describes a handle not allowed by the edge inheritances.

5   Ensuring Abstract Graph Formulae

Having defined the concept of abstract graph formulae and shown their utility in formalizing node multiplicities and edge inheritance, we now turn to the issue of *ensuring* graph constraints (not arbitrary formulae) in a given graph transformation system. A graph transformation system is said to ensure a graph constraint if all the graphs that can be derived satisfy the constraint; in other words, if the constraint is an invariant on the derivable graphs. The method for enforcing a constraint is by including appropriate *preconditions* (which are themselves graph formulae) in the rules, using a technique worked out recently for sub-classes of concrete constraints in [6].

We first define abstract and concrete rules with application conditions, and their matching. The following definition extends that in [2].

Definition 15 (abstract and concrete rules). *An* abstract *rule typed over a type graph* $TGI = (TG, I, A)$ *with inheritance is given by* $p = (L \xleftarrow{l} K \xrightarrow{r} R, F_L, F_R)$, *where* L, K, R *are abstract clan-typed graphs,* l *and* r *are type-preserving graph morphisms,* F_L *and* F_R *are abstract graph formulae, and* $ctp_R^{-1}(A) \subseteq r(N_K)$.

p is called concrete *if* L, K, R *are concrete clan-typed graphs and* F_L, F_R *are concrete graph formulae.*

Concrete rule p' *refines abstract rule* p, *if* $L' \leq L, K' \leq K, R' \leq R$ *and* $ctp'_R|_{N'_R} = ctp_R|_{N'_R}$, *and moreover,* $F'_L = flat_{L'}(F_L)$ *and* $F'_R = flat_{R'}(F_R)$. *The set of all concrete refinements of an abstract rule* p *is denoted by* $\widehat{p}$.

Example 7 (abstract rules). Fig. 9 shows two abstract rules, modelling the insertion of a new string into an ordered set. InsertFirstString inserts a string into an empty set (the emptyness is ensured by the application condition), whereas InsertNextString handles the case of a non-empty set: an existing object will become the predecessor of the newly inserted String. Note that, if this existing object already has a successor, application of the rule will violate the multiplicity constraint in Fig. 5. We will show below (Ex. 8) that this condition is obtained automatically by translation from the multiplicity constraints. (Note that Fig. 9 only shows the left and right hand sides; the interface graph can be deduced from the node identities.)

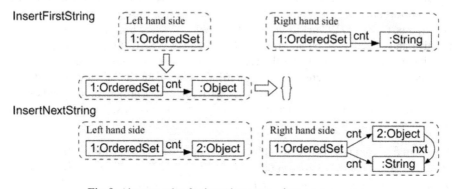

Fig. 9. Abstract rules for inserting a String into an OrderedSet

Definition 16 (rule matching and application). *Let* $p = (L \xleftarrow{l} K \xrightarrow{r} R, F_L, F_R)$ *be a derivation rule,* G *and* H *concrete clan-typed graphs, and* $m: L \to G$ *a type-preserving graph morphism.*

– *If* p *is a concrete rule, then* m *is a* match *of* p *in* G *if*

- m is a match of the untyped rule $\langle L \xleftarrow{l} K \xrightarrow{r} R \rangle$ in the untyped graph G,
- $m \models^c F_L$.

Given a match m, a concrete direct derivation $G \overset{p,m}{\Longrightarrow} H$ exists if there is a span of type-preserving morphisms $G \leftarrow D \rightarrow H$ and a co-match $m^* : R \rightarrow H$ of p in H that give rise to a derivation in the classical theory of (untyped) graph transformations [5]. The derivation is valid if $m^* \models^c F_R$.

- If p is an abstract rule, then m is a match of p in G if
  - m is a match of the untyped rule $\langle L \xleftarrow{l} K \xrightarrow{r} R \rangle$ in the untyped graph G;
  - $t_K(x_1) = t_K(x_2)$ for $t_K = ctp_G \circ m \circ l$ and $x_1, x_2 \in N_K$ with $r(x_1) = r(x_2)$;
  - $m \models^a F_L$.

Given a match m, an abstract direct derivation $G \overset{p,m}{\Longrightarrow} H$ exists if there is a span of type-preserving morphisms $G \leftarrow D \rightarrow H$ and a co-match $m^* : R \rightarrow H$ of p in H that give rise to a derivation in the sense of [2]. The derivation is valid if $m^* \models^a F_R$.

The following is the main theorem of [1], extended to the more general application conditions used in the paper. It can be proved using Theorem 1.

Theorem 4 (equivalence of abstract and concrete derivations). *Given an abstract rule* $p_a = (L \leftarrow K \rightarrow R, F_L, F_R)$, *concrete clan-typed graph* G, H *and a structural match morphism* $m : L \rightarrow G$ *(i.e. a match with respect to the untyped rule* $\langle L \leftarrow K \rightarrow R \rangle$), *the following statements are equivalent:*

1. *m is a match of p_a in G, yielding a valid abstract direct derivation:* $G \overset{p_a,m}{\Longrightarrow} H$.
2. *m is a match of the concrete rule* $p_c = (L_c \leftarrow K_c \rightarrow R_c, F_L^c, F_R^c)$ *in G with* $p_c \in \hat{p}_a$ *and* $m : L_c \rightarrow_c G$ *type-preserving, yielding a valid concrete direct derivation:* $G \overset{p_c,m}{\Longrightarrow} H$.

In the following, we want to use the translation of graph constraints to application conditions of graph rules as described in [6]. Therefore, we have to restrict the class of graph formulae we use to the ones defined in [6]. If we restrict our concrete graph constraints $GC = (P, Con)$ to those with $|Con| \leq 1$, they become equivalent to the positive and negative graph constraints of [6]: the case of $|Con| = 1$ corresponds to positive graph constraints, while the case of $|Con| = 0$ correspond to negative graph constraints.[4] Another difference is that, in [6], the morphisms in Con are allowed to be arbitrary, but that does not add expressiveness (although it does add compactness) to those we have defined here, which have injective morphisms only. The following is the relevant result from [6].

Theorem 5 (from concrete constraints to left application conditions). *Given a concrete constraint GC and a concrete rule* $p = \langle L \leftarrow K \rightarrow R \rangle$, *there is a left application condition* acc_L *such that for all direct derivations* $G \overset{p,m}{\Longrightarrow} H$ *we have:* $m \models^c acc_L \Leftrightarrow H \models^c GC$.

By combining this with Theorems 1 and 4, we can prove the following.

---

[4] The result of [6] has since been extended in [8] to and beyond our graph formulae, namely to arbitrarily nested formulae as in [13], which means that the results below also hold for arbitrary formulae.

Concrete application conditions for InsertFirstString

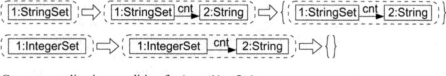

Concrete application condition for InsertNextString

Fig. 10. Derived application conditions

Theorem 6 (from abstract constraints to left application conditions). *Given an abstract constraint GC_a and an abstract rule p_a with left hand side L_a, there is a set S of concrete application conditions such that for all direct derivations $G \overset{p_a,m}{\Longrightarrow} H$ we have: $(\exists F \in S : m \models^c F) \Leftrightarrow H \models^a GC_a$.*

Thus, given some abstract graph constraint formula F_a typed over type graph TGI with inheritance, we can flatten it to a concrete graph formula F_c as described in Section 3. F_c can be considered as simply typed over concrete closure $\widehat{TGI}$ and translated to a concrete left application condition acc_L that guarantees F_a. Note that acc_L is also typed over $\widehat{TGI}$. Unfortunately, there is no straightforward way to translate acc_L to an abstract application condition.

Example 8 (additional application constraints for abstract rules). Consider the constraints in Figs. 5 and 7, respectively and the abstract rules in Fig. 9. Fig. 10 shows some of the elements of S derived for this case according to Th. 6.

For rule InsertFirstString, the multiplicity constraints (Fig. 5) do not lead to interesting application conditions, since the left-hand side does not contain an Object; but the edge inheritance constraints (Fig. 7) induce the two application conditions shown in the figure. These essentially express that the OrderedSet involved has to be a StringSet. For rule InsertNextString, the multiplicity constraint on nxt-edges leads to the third application condition of Fig. 10 (among others). This expresses that the node with identity 2 in the left hand side of the rule (which has the abstract type Object in the rule but concrete type String in the condition) may not have an outgoing nxt-edge; see also Fig. 3.

6   Conclusions

In the literature, a variety of formal integrations of object-orientation and formal specification techniques exist. They are considered in the context of precise semantics for UML as well as for precise meta-modeling. It is the declared aim of the precise UML group [12] to come up with a precise standard semantics of the whole language UML, and then to use it for verification purposes. There are various approaches being developed, each formalizing certain aspects of UML with the intention of using the resulting precision for formal reasoning. In [3], the authors are especially concerned with the formalization of classes and their relations, inheritance and constraints on the basis of *description logics*. This work is dedicated entirely to the static part and does not regard the dynamic behavior of objects. Precise meta-modeling is considered in [14], where MOF and graph transformation concepts are integrated. While the aim and the basic ideas are similar to ours, the formalization chosen in [14] is different and not as comprehensive; in particular, it does not deal with constraints.

In addition to *formulating* a precise semantics, one has also to consider the process by which constraints are *enforced*. In this paper we have shown one way in which this can be done (by translation to application conditions). We are not aware of other approaches in the literature.

Summarizing, in this paper we have obtained a further, important step of integrating graph transformation with object-orientation concepts: now, type inheritance, constraints, and graph transformation concepts are integrated in one comprehensive formal framework. This offers the possibility to check properties for object-oriented software models. On the meta-model level, the results in our paper can be used to check constraints for model transformation. Further work is needed to carry over other analysis techniques to typed graph transformation with inheritance, to come up with a comprehensive visual and precise framework for object-oriented modeling and meta-modeling.

References

1. R. Bardohl, H. Ehrig, J. de Lara, O. Runge, G. Taentzer, and I. Weinhold. Node Type Inheritance Concepts for Typed Graph Transformation. Technical Report 2003–19, Technical University Berlin, Dept. of Computer Science, November 2003.
2. R. Bardohl, H. Ehrig, J. de Lara, and G. Taentzer. Integrating Meta Modelling with Graph Transformation for Efficient Visual Language Definition and Model Manipulation. In M. Wermelinger and T. Margaria-Steffens, editors, *Fundamental Aspects of Software Engineering (FASE)*, volume 2984 of *LNCS*. Springer, 2004.
3. A. Calœ, D. Calvanese, G. De Giacomo, and M. Lenzerini. A formal framework for reasoning on UML class diagrams. In *Int. Symp. on Methodologies for Intelligent Systems (ISMIS 2002)*, volume 2366 of *LNCS*, pages 503–513. Springer, 2002.
4. A. Corradini, F. L. Dotti, L. Foss, and L. Ribeiro. Translating Java into graph transformation systems. In Ehrig et al. [7], pages 383–389.
5. A. Corradini, U. Montanari, and F. Rossi. Graph Processes. *Special Issue of Fundamenta Informaticae*, 26(3,4):241–266, 1996.
6. H. Ehrig, K. Ehrig, A. Habel, and K.-H. Pennemann. Constraints and application conditions: From graphs to high-level structures. In Ehrig et al. [7].
7. H. Ehrig, G. Engels, F. Parisi-Presicce, and G. Rozenberg, editors. *Second International Conference on Graph Transformation (ICGT)*, volume 3256 of *LNCS*. Springer, 2004.
8. A. Habel. Private communication, 2004.
9. R. Heckel and A. Wagner. Ensuring Consistency of Conditional Graph Grammars – A constructive Approach. *Proc. of SEGRAGRA'95 "Graph Rewriting and Computation", Electronic Notes of TCS*, 2, 1995. http://www.elsevier.nl/locate/entcs/volume2.html.

10. T. Mens, S. Demeyer, and D. Janssens. Formalising behaviour preserving program trans-
    formations. In A. Corradini, H. Ehrig, H.-J. Kreowski, and G. Rozenberg, editors, *First
    International Conference on Graph Transformation (ICGT)*, volume 2505 of *LNCS*, pages
    286–301. Springer, 2002.
11. OMG. *MDA, MOF, UML and OCL specifications*. OMG, 2004. at the OMG web page:
    http://www.omg.org/.
12. pUML. *The precise UML group http://www.puml.org/*, 2004.
13. A. Rensink. Representing first-order logic using graphs. In Ehrig et al. [7], pages 319–335.
14. D. Varró and A. Pataricza. VPM: A visual, precise and multilevel metamodeling framework
    for describing mathematical domains and UML. *Journal of Software and Systems Modelling*,
    1:1–24, 2003.

Modelling Parametric Contracts
and the State Space of Composite Components
by Graph Grammars

Ralf H. Reussner[1], Jens Happe[1], and Annegret Habel[2]

[1] Software Engineering Group (Fax ++49 441 9722 502)
[2] Formal Languages Group (Fax ++ 49 441 798 2965)
University of Oldenburg, Germany
{ralf.reussner, jens.happe,
annegret.habel}@informatik.uni-oldenburg.de

Abstract. Modeling the dependencies between provided and required services within a software component is necessary for several reasons, such as automated component adaptation and architectural dependency analysis. Parametric contracts for software components specify such dependencies and were successfully used for automated protocol adaptation and quality of service prediction. In this paper, a novel model for parametric contracts based on graph grammars is presented and a first definition of the compositionality of parametric contracts is given. Compared to the previously used finite state machine based formalism, the graph grammar formalism allows a more elegant formulation of parametric contract applications and considerably simpler implementations.

1   Introduction

Specifications should not be a means by themselves, but should have beneficial applications (besides of being a specification of something). Applications of software component specifications and software architecture specifications include automated test case generation, architectural dependency analysis [18] and component adaptation [14]. In any of these applications, additional information on a component (besides their interfaces) is beneficial which, on a first glance, seems to contradict the black-box use of components. However, the conflict between the need of additional information and black-box component (re-)use does not exist, as long as two conditions are fulfilled: Information on the component (beyond the interfaces) does not (a) have to be understood by human users, and (b) expose the intellectual property of the component creator. In addition, it is beneficial, if information on the component can be easily specified or even generated out of the component's code.

Parametric contracts [14, 15] support automated component protocol adaptation, quality of service prediction [16] and architectural dependency analysis by giving additional information on the inner structure of the component. In more detail, parametric contracts request so-called *service effect specifications* for specifying inner-component dependencies between provided and required services. These dependencies are simple to model as lists in case of signature-list interfaces (which required services are needed

M. Cerioli (Ed.): FASE 2005, LNCS 3442, pp. 80–95, 2005.

by a provided service). In case of protocol modelling interfaces things are more complicated, as one needs to specify sets of call sequences (which call sequences are needed
to provide a service). As service effect specifications are an abstraction of a component's implementation's control-flow graph, it can automatically be extracted out of a
component's code by control-flow analysis [10].

To make a component model compositional, all properties attached to a component
should be present for a composite component as well (i.e., there is not difference between
a basic and a composite component when neglecting the inner structure) and, in addition,
the properties of a composite component should be derivable from the properties of the
inner component plus the composition structure.

In this paper we discuss the compositionality of parametric contracts, in particular
of parametric contracts used for protocol modeling interfaces. We use graph grammars
to rewrite the graphical representation of a transition function of a finite state machine
(FSM) modelling such sets of call sequences.

The contribution of this paper is twofold: Firstly, we show in detail how parametric
contracts are modelled by a graph grammar. This is a novel contribution, as until now
parametric contracts were described by a state machines and predicates. This directly
leads to using graph grammars to component protocol adaptation. In particular, the graph
grammar model leads to simpler implementations for the practically relevant adaptation
of provides interfaces. Secondly, we show how service effect specifications of parametric
contracts are composed by using graph grammars. This is the most important contribution
with respect to applications, as until now, there was no compositional component model
for components using parametric contracts. It should be emphasised that the contribution
lies in the fruitful application of existing graph grammar formalisms to component based
software engineering, not in the extension of the formalisms themselves.

This paper is organised as follows. In section 2 we review parametric contracts, their
state machine models and give a brief introduction of the graph grammar notion used in
this paper. In section 3 we show in general how graph grammars can be used to rewrite
FSMs by interpreting their transition function as a graph. In section 4 we apply this
idea to the main topic of this paper, namely protocol adaptation by parametric contracts
and component state space composition. In section 5 we conclude by summarising the
achievements of the paper, showing the limitations of our approach and discussing future
work on open questions. Related work is discussed throughout the whole paper where
appropriate.

2   Fundamentals

2.1   The Contractual Use of Components

The essence of design-by-contract[11] can be summarised as: If the client fulfils the
precondition of the supplier, the supplier will fulfil its postcondition.

Much of the confusion about the term "contractual use" of a component comes from
the double meaning of the term "use" of a component. The "use" of a component can
mean either:

The usage of a component during run-time. This is, calling a service of a component.
Therefore it should be evident that this type of contractual component use is nothing

different as using a method contractually. Thus this case should be called the use of a *component service* instead of the use of a *component*. As the contractual use of methods is well elaborated in literature [11], we do not consider this case here.

The usage of a component during composition time. This is, placing a component in a new reuse-context, like it happens when architecting systems, or reconfiguring existing systems (e.g., updating the component).

Depending on the above case, contracts play different roles. The usage of components at composition time is the actual important case when discussing the contractual use of components. Consider a component C acting as supplier, and the environment acting as client. The component offers services to the environment (i.e., the components connected to C's provides interface(s)). According to the above discussion of contracts, these offered services are the postcondition of the component, because this is, what the client can expect from a working component. According to Meyer's above description of contracts, the precondition specifies what the component expects from its environment to be provided in order to enable C to offer its services (as stated in its postcondition). Hence, the precondition of a component is stated in its requires interfaces.

Analogous to the above single sentence formulation of a contract, we can state:

> If the user of a component fulfils the components' requires interface (offers the right environment) the component will offer its services as described in the provides interface.

Checking the satisfaction of a requires interface includes checking for each required service whether its service contract is a a sub-contract of the service contracts of the corresponding provided service. Subcontracts are elobaroated in [12–p. 573].

2.2   Parametric Contracts

For a component developer it is hard to foresee all possible reuse contexts of a component in advance (i.e., during design-time). One of the severe consequences for component oriented programming is that one cannot provide the component with all the config-uration possibilities which will be required for making the component fit into future reuse contexts. Coming back to our discussion about component contracts, this means, that in practice one single pre- and postcondition of a component will not be sufficient. Consider the following two scenarios:

1. the precondition of a component is not satisfied by a specific environment while the component itself would be able to provide a meaningful subset of its functionality.
2. a weaker postcondition of a component is sufficient in a specific reuse context (i.e., not the full functionality of a component will be used). Due to that, the component will itself require less functionality at its requires interface(s), i.e., will be satisfied by a weaker precondition.

As a consequence, we do not need statically fixed pre- and postconditions, but *parametric contracts* to be evaluated during deployment-time. In the first case a parametric contract computes the postcondition which is computed in dependency of the strongest precondition guaranteed by a specific reuse context (hence the postcondition is param-eterised by the precondition). In the second case the parametric contract computes the precondition in dependency of the post-condition (which acts as a parameter of the pre-condition). Due to this parametric mutual dependencies between the pre-condiction and the post-condition these contracts are called "parametric" contracts. For components a parametric contracts means, that provides- and requires-interfaces are not fixed. A provides interface is computed in dependency of the actual functionality a component receives at its requires interface, and a requires interface is computed in dependency of the functionality actually requested from a component in a specific reuse context. Hence, opposed to classical contracts, one can say:

> Parametric contracts link the provides- and requires-interface(s) of the same component. They have a range of possible results (i.e., new interfaces).

Interoperability is a special case now: if a component is interoperable with its environment, its provides interface will not change. If the interoperability check fails, a new provides interface will be computed.

Mathematically, parametric contracts are modelled by a function p mapping a provides interface P to the minimal requires interface $R = p(P) = R_C$ specifying the needs of P. Hence p is a function of the set Prov_C of all possible provides interfaces of C to the set Req_C of all possible requires interfaces of C. A possible provides interface is any interface offering a subset of the functionality implemented in C, the set of all possible requires interfaces is the image of Prov_C under p. Note that p not necessarily is an injective function: several different provides interfaces may be mapped to the same requires interface. Consequently, the inverse mapping, associates to each requires interface of $R \in \text{Req}_C$ a *set* of supported provides interfaces. To yield a single provides interface, we use the "maximum" element of this set. Formally, this element is the smallest upper bound of the set $p^{-1}(R)$. This smallest upper bound is the join of the elements of $p^{-1}(R)$ which exists because if provides interfaces P_1 and P_2 are elements of $p^{-1}(R)$ each of their elements (i.e., services, service call sequences, services with QoS annotations) is supported, consequently, the interface describing the set of all these elements is also itself element of $p^{-1}(R)$ ($P_1, P_2 \in p^{-1}(R) \Rightarrow P_1 \cup P_2 \in p^{-1}(R)$). For later use, we define the shorthand inv-$p : \text{Req}_C \to \text{Prov}_C$ as inv-$p(R) := \bigcup_{E \in p^{-1}(R)} E$. (Note that we use the more intuitive set-oriented notion of $\cup$ for the join-operator which is commonly referred to as $\sqcap$ in literature on lattices, etc.)

Like for a classical contracts, the actual parametric contract specification depends on the actual interface model[19] and should be statically computable. In any case, there's no need for the software developer to foresee possible reuse contexts. Only the specification of a bidirectional mapping between provides- and requires-interfaces is necessary.

2.3   Finite State Machines and Component Protocols

The protocol of the services offered by a component is defined as (a subset of) the set of valid call sequences. A *valid* call sequence is a call sequence which is actually supported by the component. For example for a file `open-read-close` is a valid call sequence, while `read-open` is not. The specified set of valid call sequences is called the provides-protocol.

Analogously, the protocol of the services required by a component is a set of call sequences by which the component calls external methods. This set of sequences of calls to external component services is called the requires-protocol.

The provides- and the requires-protocols are considered as sets of sequences. State machines are well-known notations for protocol specification [2, 9, 13, 20]. The benefits of a state machine specification of protocols are the representation of protocols in a compact and precise manner and the possibility of an efficient automatic formal analysis of protocols.

Definition 1 (Finite State Machine). *A finite state machine (FSM) is a system $A = (I, Z, F, z_0, \delta)$ where I is an input alphabet, Z is a finite set of states, $F \subseteq Z$ is a set of final states, $z_0 \in Z$ is a start state, and $\delta : Z \times I \to Z$ is a total transition function.*

Not that every partial transition function can be extended to a total one by adding a state $\perp$ and assigning $\perp$ whenever the partial function yields undefied or the state in consideration is $\perp$.

By P-FSM we denote the FSM specifying the provides protocol of a component, while the *component-requires-FSM* (CR-FSM) gives the requires protocol. The P-FSMs input alphabet is the set of methods provides by the component. In the reverse, the input alphabet of the the CR-FSM is the set of (external) methods required by the component. Since our implementation utilises a state-machine based approach we identify state-machines and protocols.

When modelling call sequences, we model for each state which methods are callable in this state. In many cases, a method call changes the state of the state machine, i.e., some other methods are callable after the call, while others, callable in the old state, are not callable in the new state. An example of the P-FSM of an exemplary video-stream component is shown in figure 1(a). The protocol described by this FSM represents the maximum functionality which can be offered by the video-stream. Note that the video-stream offers to manipulate the sound and the picture while playing and while pausing the video.

2.4   Graph Grammars

Graph transformation systems and graph grammars generalize string rewriting systems and Chomsky grammars, respectively: The objects are graphs, the rules are graph replacement rules, and the application of a rule to a graph yields a graph. Graph transformation systems and graph grammars are well-studied and applied to several areas of computer science (see, e.g. [17, 4, 5]). In the following, we provide the basic notions on graphs and graph grammars needed in the paper. Details and pointers to the literature can be found e.g. in [6, 8].

We consider directed, edge-labelled graphs with a finite set of nodes and edges. Source and target nodes of an edge are given by the source and target functions; the labelling of an edge is given by the labelling function.

Definition 2 (Graph). *A graph over an alphabet C is a system $G = (V, E, s, t, l)$ consisting of two finite sets V and E of nodes (or vertices) and edges, two source and target functions $s, t : E \to V$, and a labelling function $l : E \to C$. The components of*

G are denoted by V_G, E_G, s_G, t_G, and l_G, respectively. The set of all graphs is over C is denoted by $\mathcal{G}_C$.

A graph morphism relates graphs. A graph morphism $g: G \to H$ between graphs G and H consists of two functions $g_V: V_G \to V_H$ and $g_E: E_G \to E_H$ that preserve sources, targets and labels, that is, $s_H \circ g_E = g_V \circ s_G$, $t_H \circ g_E = g_V \circ t_G$, and $l_H \circ g = l_G$. A morphism g is an inclusion if g_V and g_E are inclusions and an isomorphism if g_V and g_E are injective and surjective. In the latter case, G and H are isomorphic denoted by $G \cong H$. A graph replacement rule consists of two graphs, the left-hand side and right-hand side of the rule. The left- and right-hand side are related by two inclusions from a common graph into the left- and the right-hand side.

Definition 3 (Rule). *A rule* $r = \langle L \leftarrow K \to R \rangle$ *consists of two graphs L and R, the left-hand side and the right-hand side of r, and two inclusions $K \to L$ and $K \to R$ from a common graph K. A rule r is an edge replacement rule if L is a graph with two nodes and a connecting edge and K is obtained from L by removing the connecting edge. The application of a rule r to a graph G amounts to the following steps:*

(1) Find a graph morphism $g: L \to G$ and check the following two conditions.
   Dangling condition: No edge in $G - g(L)$ is incident to a node in $g(L - K)$.
   Identification condition: For all distinct items $x, y \in L$, $g(x) = g(y)$ only if $x, y \in K$. (This condition is understood to hold separately for nodes and edges.)
(2) Remove $g(L - K)$ from G, yielding a graph $D = G - g(L - K)$.
(3) Add $R - K$ to tD, yielding a graph $H = D + (R - K)$.

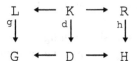

An example of the application of a rule to a graph is given in figure 2.

The graph G directly derives H via r and g, denoted by $G \Rightarrow_{r,g} H$ or $G \Rightarrow H$. A sequence of direct derivations $G = G_0 \Rightarrow_{r_1,g_1} \cdots \Rightarrow_{r_n,g_n} G_n \cong H$ via $r_1, \ldots r_n \in \mathcal{R}$ is a derivation from G to H (of length n), denoted by $G \Rightarrow_{\mathcal{R}}^* H$. If the derivation is of length at least one, we also write $G \Rightarrow_{\mathcal{R}}^+ H$.

A graph grammar consists of an alphabet, a nonterminal alphabet, a set of rules, and a start graph. The generated language consists of all graphs without nonterminal labels derivable from the start graph via the rules of the grammar.

Definition 4 (Graph Grammar). *A graph grammar is a system $\mathcal{G} = \langle C, N, \mathcal{R}, S \rangle$, where C and $N \subseteq C$ are alphabets, $\mathcal{R}$ is a finite set of rules, and S is a start graph. If $\mathcal{R}$ is a set of edge replacement rules, $\mathcal{G}$ is an edge replacement graph grammar. The graph language $L(\mathcal{G})$ generated by $\mathcal{G}$ consists of all graphs without nonterminal labels which can be derived from S by applying the rules of $\mathcal{R}$: $L(\mathcal{G}) = \{ G \in \mathcal{G}_{C-N} \mid S \Rightarrow_{\mathcal{R}}^* G \}$.*

3   Refining Finite State Machines by Graph Grammars

3.1   Finite State Machines as Graphs

Usually, a finite state machine is drawn as a graph with additional information concerning the start and the final states. It can be represented as a graph by adding two nodes begin and end and edges with label Start and Final, respectively, from begin to the start state and the final states to end.

Let $A = (I, Z, F, z_0, \delta)$ be a finite state machine. Then $G(A) = (V, E, s, t, l)$ denotes the graph over the alphabet $C = I \cup \{\text{Start}, \text{Final}\}$ with node set $V = Z \cup \{\text{begin}, \text{end}\}$, edge set $E = Z \times I \cup \{e_{z_0}\} \cup \{e_f \mid f \in F\}$, and source, target, and labelling functions s, t, and l with

(1) $s(z, i) = z$, $t(z, i) = \delta(z, i)$, and $l(z, i) = i$ for all $z \in Z$ and $i \in I$,
(2) $l(e_{z_0}) = \text{Start}$, $\text{begin} = s(e_{z_0})$, and $t(e_{z_0}) = z_0$,
(3) $l(e_f) = \text{Final}$, $f = s(e_f)$, and $t(e_f) = \text{end}$ for all $f \in F$.

For convenience, start and final states are depicted in the classical way, that is, by an arrow pointing to the start state and a black dot inside each final state. The nodes begin and end are not drawn. An example of the representation of a FSM as a graph using the drawing conventions is given in figure 1(a).

3.2   Substuitution of Transitions in Finite State Machines

Substitutions of transitions in a finite state machine by finite state machines will be implemented by edge replacement graph grammars.

Example 1 (Substitution of Transitions by FSMs). Consider the FSM in figure 1(a). The transition b from the start state to the final state shall be replaced by the FSM given in figure 1(b).

The result of the substitution is shown in figure 1(c). The ε-transitions are needed to maintain the structure of the original finite state machine. Without these ε-transitions

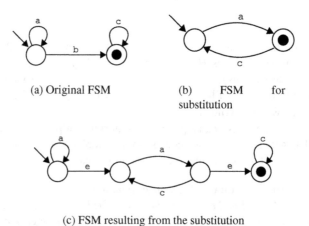

(a) Original FSM   (b)   FSM   for
                          substitution

(c) FSM resulting from the substitution

Fig. 1. Substitution of transitions by FSMs

(by just linking the transitions connected to the start state with the source of transition b and the ones connected to the final state with the destination of transition b) it would be possible to go from the final state back to the start state. This contradicts the structure of the original FSM.

The implementation of the substitution of transitions by FSMs by an edge replacement graph grammar is done as follows: The FSMs are transformed into graphs and a set of substituting rules is defined.

Let A be a FSM, $I' \subseteq I$ a subset of input symbols selected for substitution, and sub: $I' \to \mathcal{A}$ a mapping assigning a FSM of the set of FSMs $\mathcal{A}$ to each selected input symbol. For $i \in I'$, let $A_i = \mathrm{sub}(i)$ denote the FSM associated with the input symbol i. Then the edge replacement graph grammar $\mathcal{G} = \langle C, N, \mathcal{R}, S \rangle$ associated with A and sub is as follows: $S = G(A)$ is the start graph, $N = I'$ is the set of input symbols selected for substitution, and $\mathcal{R} = \{r_i \mid i \in I'\}$ is a set of rules where, for $i \in I'$, $r_i = \langle L_i \leftarrow K_i \to R_i \rangle$ is constructed as follows. L_i is the handle induced by i, that is the graph $(\{v_1, v_2\}, \{e\}, s, t, l)$ with $s(e) = v_1, t(e) = v_2$, and $l(e) = i$, K_i is obtained from L_i by removing the edge e, and R_i is the graph $G_\varepsilon(A_i)$ obtained form $G(A_i)$ by replacing the symbols Start and Final by the symbol ε. The label alphabet C consists of all symbols occurring in the start graph or some rules.

Example 2 (Application of Rules). The rule for the substitution in example in figure 1(b) is shown at the top of figure 2. The application of the rule to the graph of the FSM in figure 1(a) results in the direct derivation $G \Rightarrow H$ shown in figure 2.

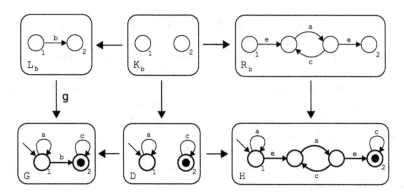

Fig. 2. Application of a rule

There is a close relationship between the iterated application of a substitution and the application of rules induced by the substitution [6]. We use the relationship for defining the iterated application of a substitution of transitions by FSMs.

Definition 5 (Substitution of Transitions by FSMs). *Let A be a FSM, sub a substitution, and $\mathcal{G} = \langle C, N, \mathcal{R}, G(A) \rangle$ the associated edge replacement graph grammar. Then the iterated application of sub to A is the graph language $L(\mathcal{G}) = \{H \in \mathcal{G}_{C-N} \mid G(A) \Rightarrow_\mathcal{R}^* H\}$.*

The edge replacement graph grammar starts in the graph of the FSM and replaces nonterminal labeled edges as long as possible. If the edge replacement graph grammar is non-recursive[3], then there are no infinite derivations from the start graph. Moreover, the rewrite relation $\Rightarrow_\mathcal{R}$ satisfies the diamond property, that is for every pair of direct derivation $G \Rightarrow_\mathcal{R} H_1$ and $G \Rightarrow_\mathcal{R} H_2$ with $H_1 \not\cong H_2$ for some M there are direct derivations $H_1 \Rightarrow_\mathcal{R} M$ and $H_2 \Rightarrow_\mathcal{R} M$.

Fact 1. Let $\mathcal{G}$ be a non-recursive edge replacement graph grammar associated with a FSM and a substitution. Then $L(\mathcal{G})$ has exactly one element.

If the edge replacement graph grammar is recursive, then there is a symbol i with derivation $G \Rightarrow^+ H$ from the handle of i to a graph containing the symbol i. Since every symbol, in particular i, occurs in the start graph, there is an infinite derivation beginning with the start graph. Since there is exactly one rule for each nonterminal symbol, there is no chance to derive a terminal graph.

Fact 2. Let $\mathcal{G}$ be a recursive edge replacement graph grammar associated with a FSM and a substitution. Then $L(\mathcal{G})$ is empty.

For every non-recursive edge replacement graph grammar $\mathcal{G}$, we can find a linear ordering on the nonterminals such that every rule is strictly order-preserving, that is the symbol on the left-hand side is less that the nonterminal symbols on the right-hand side. Vice versa, if we can find such an ordering, then the grammar is non-recursive. Thus, we obtain the following.

Lemma 1. *It is decidable whether an edge replacement graph grammar is recursive.*

Proof. Similar to the proof for left-recursive context-free string grammars in [1]. If the edge replacement grammar is a non-recursive, then there is a linear order $<$ on the nonterminal symbols such that for every rule, the nonterminal symbol on the left-hand side is less than all nonterminal symbols on the right-hand side: Let $\lhd$ be the relation $A \lhd B$ if and only if $G \Rightarrow^* H$ where G is a handle with label A and H is a graph containing the label B. By definition of recursion, $\lhd$ is a partial order. (Transitivity is easy to show.) $\lhd$ can be extended to a linear order $<$ with the desired property. If $<$ is a linear order on the nonterminal symbols such that for every rule, the nonterminal symbol in the left-hand side is greater than all nonterminal symbols in the right-hand side, then there does not exist a nonterminal symbol A with derivation $G \Rightarrow^+ H$ from a handle G with label A to a graph H containing the nonterminal symbol A, i.e. the grammar is non-recursive.

If one considers a transition as function call, this problem can be seen as recursion of a function. In the context of function calls and parametric contracts it has been solved in [14].

---

[3] A symbol i in an edge replacement graph grammar is recursive if there exists a derivation $G \Rightarrow_\mathcal{R}^+ H$ from the handle of i to a graph containing the symbol i. An edge replacement edge replacement graph grammar with at least one recursive symbol is recursive.

4   Applications to Protocol Adaptation with Parametric Contracts and Component Composition

Parametric contracts enable the deployer of a software component to determine the services a software component can provide in its current environment. Therefore, the requires interface is computed out of the components provides interfaces and service-effect-specifications. The result is intersected with the interfaces provided by the component's environment yielding an interface that contains only the services (of the component's requires interface) the environment can offer. This reduced requires interface is transformed into a reduced provides interface that includes only the services the component can provide in the current context.

It is also possible to compute the requirements of a component depending on the services needed by its environment. Therefore, the provides interfaces of a component are intersected with the (joined) interfaces required by its environment yielding a reduced provides interface that contains only the services that are needed by the environment. The result and the service-effect-specifications of the component are used to determine a reduced requires interface that asks only the services from the environment that are currently needed.

4.1   Computation of Requires Interfaces

The CR-FSM of a component can be derived from its P-FSM and its service-effect-specifications. Therefore, each transition in the P-FSM representing a service call is substituted by the associated service-effect-specification. This results in a new protocol consisting of the external services used by the component.

More formally speaking we have a P-FSM A_P and a set of service-effect-specifications $\mathcal{A}$, all given as finite state machines. Additionally, the function $v : I_P \rightarrow \mathcal{A}$ associates every input symbol of A_P with a service-effect-specification in $\mathcal{A}$.

Informally, we proceed as follows. Firstly, a graph grammar $\mathcal{G}$ is defined substituting each transition with the associated service-effect-specification. (The substitution without graph grammars is described in [14, 15].) The definition of $\mathcal{G}$ is similar to the one given in section 3 except that no ϵ-transitions are used for integrating the FSM into its new context, but special calling and return transitions. The requires protocol is a projection of this protocol where the calling and return transitions will be replaced by ϵ-symbols. But for the moment, they are needed for the construction of the adapted provides interface as described in section 4.2. Secondly, we apply this graph-grammar $\mathcal{G}$ to the provides protocol. The result of this application forms the requires protocol. Hence, the "algorithm" of computing the requires protocol is simply the application of $\mathcal{G}$ to the provides protocol. This is the minimal requires interface, as no substitution performed by $\mathcal{G}$ is superfluous. The time-complexity of this approach is bounded by the number of transitions of the P-FSM.

More formally, let $\mathcal{G}$ be a graph grammar according to section 3 with the original FSM A_p, the FSM set for substitution $\mathcal{A}$, and the mapping function v. Instead of defining E_s and E_f for the right-hand side of rule r_i (the rule associated with input symbol i in I_P) as above, set $E_s = \{e | s(e) = n_1, l_V'(t(e)) = Start, l_E(e) = i'\}$ and $E_f = \{e | l_V'(s_{R_i}(e)) = Final, t(e) = n_2, l_E(e) = return\}$, where $i', return \notin$

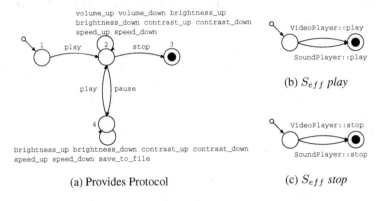

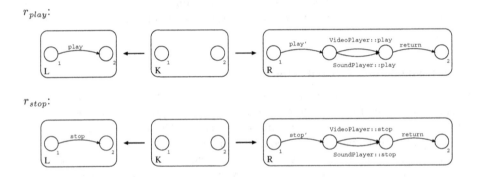

(a) Provides Protocol

(b) S_{eff} play

(c) S_{eff} stop

Fig. 3. Substitution of transitions by FSMs

Fig. 4. Rules for substitution

$I_P \bigcup_{A_i \in \mathcal{A}_i} I_i$ are new edge labels and l_V' is the node label function of G_{A_i}. E_s contains exactly one edge from the source of the substituted edge i to the node associated with the start state of A_i. Instead of labelling it with ϵ as above, a new edge label i' is defined marking the transition as a service call. E_f consist of edges from all nodes corresponding to the final states of A_i to the destination the substituted edge. The ϵ label used in section 3 is replaced by a general $return$ label tagging the edge as a return-transition from a called service.

As an example of the approach described above, consider the provides automaton of a video-stream component shown in figure 3(a). The video-stream component maps its provided services on a video-player and sound-player component. The service-effect-specifications for play and stop are given in figures 3(b) and 3(c).

Now, we create a graph grammar $\mathcal{G}$ that substitutes the transitions of the P-FSM as described above. Therefore, the start graph S of $\mathcal{G}$ is set to the graph representation of the provides automaton A_P shown in figure 3(a) and the non terminal alphabet N_E is set to the input alphabet $I_P = \{play, \ stop, \ \dots\}$ of A_P. The total label alphabet contains I_P, the input symbols of the service-effect-specifications, and a set of new

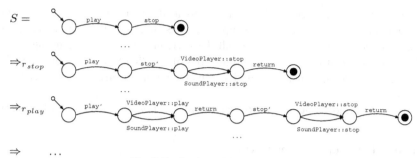

Fig. 5. Derivation of the CR-FSM

input symbols $I'_P = \{\texttt{return, play'}, \ \texttt{stop'} \ \dots\}$. Last but not least, the rules are created as shown in figure 4. For rule r_{play} the play-transition is replaced by the service-effect-specification of play. The transition play' on the right-hand side of the rule indicates that the service called play is executed. After this transition follows the start-state of the service-effect-specification of play, the calls to the video player and sound player components and the final-state which is connected to the target of the play-transition with a return-transition. The structure of r_{stop} and all other rules is analogous.

The computation of the requires protocol from the start-graph of $\mathcal{G}$ amounts in the derivation shown in figure 5. First, rule r_{stop} is applied on start-graph S, the graph representation of the provides automaton (it is only partially depicted) and the transition stop is substituted by the corresponding service-effect-specification. Next, rule r_{play} is applied. This process is continued until all provided services are replaced by its service-effect-specifications.

The result of the application of $\mathcal{G}$ on S is a FSM that can be easily transformed to the requires protocol of the video stream component. Therefore, the symbols introduced above ($I'_P = \{\texttt{return, play'}, \ \texttt{stop'} \ \dots\}$) are substituted by ϵ. The resulting FSM describes the service calls made by the component to its environment. Transforming this ϵ-FSM into a deterministic FSM and minimising the result leads to a good representation of the call sequences used by the component. For parametric contracts, the next step is to intersect the result with the P-FSMs of the component's environment as described in the beginning of this section.

4.2   Computation of Provides Interfaces

We are not only interested in the services required by a component depending on its environment, but also in the services that can be provided in the current environment. Therefore, we need to determine the P-FSM of the component depending on the protocols and services offered by its environment. This is done by intersecting the CR-FSM of the component with P-FSMs of its environment. The result is a CR-FSM containing only those services that are required by the component **and** can be provided by its environment. This reduced CR-FSM is used to determine a reduced P-FSM containing only those call sequences that can by provided by the component in the current context.

Therefore, we need to reconstruct a graph that has a structure similar to the result of our graph grammar $\mathcal{G}$ given in section 4.1. We can use this graph to apply the inverse rules of $\mathcal{G}$ and derive the reduced P-FSM of the component. Finally, we need to intersect the result with the original P-FSM to clean up all service-effect-specifications that could not be transformed back to a single service call. This is required since during the intersection with the environment some states and transitions of the CR-FSM are removed and thus, some service-effect-specifications are incomplete and the inverse rules of $\mathcal{G}$ cannot be applied.

For the first step we define an *asymmetric intersection* between two finite state machines:

Definition 1 (Asymmetric Intersection)
Let $A = (I_A, Z_A, F_A, z_{0\,A}, \delta_A)$ and $B = (I_B, Z_B, F_B, z_{0\,B}, \delta_B)$ be two finite state machines with $I_A \subseteq I_B$, and $I'_B \subseteq I_B - I_A$. The asymmetric intersection of A and B is given by $A \times B = (I_B, Z_A \times Z_B, F, (z_{0\,A}, z_{0\,B}), \delta_{A\times B})$. Where $(z_1, z_2) \in F$, if $z_1 \in F_A$ and $z_2 \in F_B$. The state transition function $\delta_{A\times B}$ is given by

$$\delta_{A\times B}((z_1, z_2), i) = \begin{cases} (\delta_A(z_1, i), \delta_B(z_2, i)), & if\, i \in I_A \\ (z_1, \delta_B(z_2, i)), & if\, i \in I'_B \\ undefined, & otherwise \end{cases}$$

The asymmetric intersection creates a new FSM whose accepted language $L(A \times B)$ is a subset of $L(B)$ but (usually) not of $L(A)$. One can consider it as a finite state machine accepting the common language of A and B while ignoring all input symbols in I'_B for automaton A. Note, if I'_B is the empty set, the asymmetric intersection matches the regular FSM intersection.

Let G_{Req} be the result of the application of $\mathcal{G}$, G'_{Req} the result of the intersection, and A_{Req} and A'_{Req} the corresponding FSMs. Then, set $A = A'_{Req}$, $B = A_{Req}$ and I'_B to the symbols newly introduced by the construction of $\mathcal{G}$ (for example return, play' and stop' for the video-stream component). Then the result of the asymmetric intersection is structural similar to the result of the application of $\mathcal{G}$, but does contain only the service calls that are supported by the environment. So, we can use the inverse graph grammar $\mathcal{G}^{-1}$ of $\mathcal{G}$ for the construction of the reduced P-FSM.

The inverse graph grammar $\mathcal{G}^{-1}$ of $\mathcal{G}$ is constructed by inverting all rules of $\mathcal{G}$. The inverse rule r^{-1} of r is given by $L^{-1} = R$, $K^{-1} = K$, and $R^{-1} = L$. So, only the left-hand and right-hand side of the rules are exchanged.

The application of $\mathcal{G}^{-1}$ on the result of the asymmetric intersection is a graph whose complete service-effect-specifications have been substituted by the corresponding service calls and whose incomplete ones still exist. Hence, the final step is to clean up the result by intersecting it with the original P-FSM. This yields a reduced P-FSM containing only the call sequences that can be provided by the component in its current context.

The resulting P-FSM is maximal, as all provided service sequences are included. This is because all possible substitutions are performed by $\mathcal{G}^{-1}$ which means that an implemented services is available in all states where its requires call sequences (i.e., the left-hand side of the rule in $\mathcal{G}^{-1}$ corresponding to the service) are present in the CR-FSM.

The time-complexity is bounded by the number of substitutions to be performed which is approximately the number of transitions of the CR-FSM divided the average number of edges ("transitions") of the left-hand sides of the rules of $\mathcal{G}^{-1}$. (This is in principle the same time-complexity as the computation of the requires-protocol, however, in the latter case the number of edges in the left-hand sides of the rules in $\mathcal{G}$ is is one, while the number of edges in the left-hand sides of the rules in $\mathcal{G}^{-1}$ is higher than one, as the left-hand sides in $\mathcal{G}^{-1}$ are service effect automata.

4.3   Compositional State Spaces

As mentioned, service effect automata are an abstraction of a component's internal state space. As transitions model calls to external services, all internal computations in-between two calls of an external service, are modelled by a single state of the service effect automaton. As service effect automata are part of our component model and component models should be compositional, in the following we will apply the above described mechanism of substituting a transition of a FSM by another FSM to the compositionality of components with service effect automata. Compositionality relates to a composition operator $\mathcal{O}$ taking two or more components and compsiting it to a new (composed) component. We consider as composition operator the use-relationship. We denote a component using others as C_1 and set set of components $C_2 \ldots C_n$ *directly* connected to its requires interface(s) as $\mathcal{C}$. Hence, $\mathcal{O}(C_1, \mathcal{C}) =: C_c$ denotes the composition of $C_1 \ldots C_n$. As this composition is again a component, it can be itself a parameter to the composition operator which if one wishes to include components indirectly used by C_1 in the composition. As C_c offers the same services as C_1 does, we are now interested in the service effect automata of C_c for these services. Formally speaking we have a service effect automaton A_P of a service s of component C_1 and a set of service-effect-specifications $\mathcal{A}$, all describing the bahaviour of services implemented by components $\mathcal{C}$. We are now interested in the service effect automaton of service s of the composed component C_c. Like in the other applications of edge substitution, the function $v : I_P \rightarrow \mathcal{A}$ associates every input symbol of A_P with a service-effect-specification in $\mathcal{A}$. Now we proceed like on the above construction of requires interfaces (section 4.1) with the only difference that A_P denotes a service effect automaton (and not a provides protocol) and the result of the substitution is the service effect automaton of service s of component C_c. For computing the requires protocol of component C_c, we use the provides protocol of C_c (which is per definition identical to the provides protocol of C_1) and all service effect automata of C_c (constructed as described above) and proceed as shown in section 4.1.

Note that the here presented approach to compositionality is not restricted to service effect automata. Muchmore, any state model with a partial function from transitions to a set of state models to be substituted can be composed by the approach described.

5   Conclusion and Future Work

We presented three applications of a graph grammar approach to finite state machine rewriting, namely (a) computation of requires protocols in dependency of provides protocols given invariant service effect automata, (b) the inverse: computation of provides protocols in dependency of requires protocols given invariant service effect automata and (c) the composition of service effect automata of components connected by a direct use-relationship. These computations form the base for various applications in component based software engineering, such as automated component adaptation [14] and analyses of component based architectures [18]. The main benefits of using edge replacent graph grammars are (a) a unified formal base of the above computations, (b) an important theory comparable with the theory on context-free string grammars [6], and (c) its simplicity (compared to the existing state machine based approach [14, 15]). In the future, we plan to explore the application of using hierarchical graph transformation [3] to model recursively inserted service effect automata.

References

1. Alfred V. Aho and Jeffrey D. Ullman. *The Theory of Parsing, Translation, and Compiling, Vol. I: Parsing*. Prentice-Hall, Englewood-Cliffs, New Jersey, 1972.
2. Luca de Alfaro and Thomas A. Henzinger. Interface automata. In Volker Gruhn, editor, *Proceedings of the Joint 8th European Software Engeneering Conference and 9th ACM SIG-SOFT Symposium on the Foundation of Software Engeneering (ESEC/FSE-01)*, volume 26, 5 of *SOFTWARE ENGINEERING NOTES*, pages 109–120, New York, September 10–14 2001. ACM Press.
3. Frank Drewes, Berthold Hoffmann, and Detlef Plump. Hierarchical graph transformation. *Journal of Computer and System Sciences*, 64:249–283, 2002.
4. Hartmut Ehrig, Gregor Engels, Hans-Jörg Kreowski, and Grzegorz Rozenberg, editors. *Handbook of Graph Grammars and Computing by Graph Transformation*, volume 2: Applications, Languages and Tools. World Scientific, 1999.
5. Hartmut Ehrig, Hans-Jörg Kreowski, Ugo Montanari, and Grzegorz Rozenberg, editors. *Handbook of Graph Grammars and Computing by Graph Transformation*, volume 3: Concurrency, Parallelism, and Distribution. World Scientific, 1999.
6. Annegret Habel. *Hyperedge Replacement: Grammars and Languages*, volume 643 of *Lecture Notes in Computer Science*. Springer-Verlag, Berlin, 1992.
7. Annegret Habel. Hypergraph grammars: Transformational and algorithmic aspects. *Journal of Information Processing and Cybernetics EIK*, 28:241–277, 1992.
8. Annegret Habel, Jürgen Müller, and Detlef Plump. Double-pushout graph transformation revisited. *Mathematical Structures in Computer Science*, 11(5):637–688, 2001.
9. Gerald J. Holzmann. *Design and Validation of Computer Protocols*. Prentice Hall, Englewood Cliffs, NJ, USA, 1991.
10. Gunnar Hunzelmann. Generierung von Protokollinformation für Softwarekomponenten-schnittstellen aus annotiertem Java-Code. Diplomarbeit, Fakultät für Informatik, Universität Karlsruhe (TH), Germany, April 2001.
11. Bertrand Meyer. Applying "Design by Contract". *IEEE Computer*, 25(10):40–51, October 1992.
12. Bertrand Meyer. *Object-Oriented Software Construction*. Prentice Hall, Englewood Cliffs, NJ, USA, 2 edition, 1997.
13. Oscar Nierstrasz. Regular types for active objects. In *Proceedings of the 8th ACM Conference on Object-Oriented Programming Systems, Languages and Applications (OOPSLA-93)*, volume 28, 10 of *ACM SIGPLAN Notices*, pages 1–15, October 1993.
14. Ralf H. Reussner. *Parametrisierte Verträge zur Protokolladaption bei Software-Komponenten*. Logos Verlag, Berlin, 2001.
15. Ralf H. Reussner. Automatic Component Protocol Adaptation with the CoCoNut Tool Suite. *Future Generation Computer Systems*, 19:627–639, July 2003.

16. Ralf H. Reussner, Iman H. Poernomo, and Heinz W. Schmidt. Reasoning on software architectures with contractually specified components. In A. Cechich, M. Piattini, and A. Vallecillo, editors, *Component-Based Software Quality: Methods and Techniques*, number 2693 in LNCS, pages 287–325. Springer-Verlag, Berlin, Germany, 2003.
17. Grzegorz Rozenberg, editor. *Handbook of Graph Grammars and Computing by Graph Transformation*, volume 1: Foundations. World Scientific, 1997.
18. Judith A. Stafford, Alexander L. Wolf, and Mauro Capuroscio. The application of dependence analysis to software architecture descriptions. In M. Bernardo and P. Inverardi, editors, *Formal Methods to Software Architects*, volume 2804 of *Lecture Notes in Computer Science*, pages 52–62. Springer-Verlag, Berlin, Germany, 2003.
19. A. Vallecillo, J. Hernández, and J.M. Troya. Object interoperability. In A. Moreira and S. Demeyer, editors, *Object Oriented Technology – ECOOP '99 Workshop Reader*, number 1743 in LNCS, pages 1–21. Springer-Verlag, Berlin, Germany, 1999.
20. D. Yellin and R. Strom. Protocol Specifications and Component Adaptors. *ACM Transactions on Programming Languages and Systems*, 19(2):292–333, 1997.

Improving the Build Architecture of Legacy C/C++ Software Systems

Homayoun Dayani-Fard[1], Yijun Yu[2], John Mylopoulos[2],
and Periklis Andritsos[2]

[1] IBM Canada
[2] University of Toronto

Abstract. The build architecture of legacy C/C++ software systems, groups program files in directories to represent logical components. The interfaces of these components are loosely defined by a set of header files that are typically grouped in one common include directory. As legacy systems evolve, these interfaces decay, which contribute to an increase in the build time and the number of conflict in parallel developments. This paper presents an empirical study of the build architecture of large commercial software systems, introduces a restructuring approach, based on Reflexion models and automatic clustering, and reports on a case study using VIM open source editor.

1   Introduction

In large software development, it is a common practice to organize programs into components (or sub-systems), which group a number of related files. Components can be identified by a simple naming convention, a directory, or using configuration items in more sophisticated configuration management tools. Each component exposes its interface to other components through a number of header files. This grouping of files and components, and their logical and syntactic inter-dependencies, constitute the build architecture of a system. The build architecture provides division of responsibility and ownership among teams as it facilitates the development of new features [1].

To ensure the stability of the software [2], as program files are changed, these and other files dependent on them need to be recompiled to create a new version of the software. As software systems evolve, the number of files, the number of components, and the dependencies among them grow. The result is a decaying build architecture, where the original objectives may no longer be valid, interfaces lose their integrity, and compilation times increase rapidly.

The solution, can broadly be stated as a (semi-)automatic approach to improving the build architecture of C/C++ software systems. More succinctly, a solution that partitions a software system into components with the following goals.

1. Components must have clean interfaces, where changes to one component do not require unnecessary recompilations of other components. This contributes to faster build as well as easier migration to parallel code management environment such as Rational ClearCase.

M. Cerioli (Ed.): FASE 2005, LNCS 3442, pp. 96–110, 2005.

2. Components must follow a reference architectural pattern reflecting an architecture discovered from the code [3]. This can contribute to a controlled evolution of the architecture in light of future growth.

To achieve the first goal, we remove redundancies (i.e., program entities or units that are declared but not used in the preprocessed files) and false dependencies (i.e., unnecessary program entities included from header files) [4]. As for the second goal, we combine the architectural repair [5] and the reflexion model [6].

To ease the discussion, we use VIM, an open source editor as our case study. First, VIM is representative of small to average size components in commercial software systems that we have studied. Second, VIM is continually evolving and growing (e.g., +5% from version 6.1 to 6.2 [7]). Third, availability of existing studies on the repair of VIM architecture enables us to compare our approach to others. Though VIM is written in C, our approach can be applied to C++ programs. Elsewhere [8], we reported the application of our tool on a large C++ component of a commercial software product, which is the basis of the motivation in Section 2.

The rest of the paper is structured as follows. Section 2 presents motivations behind the stated problems by reporting on our study of the growth of commercial software systems. Section 3 outlines our approach. Section 4 reports on the results of a case study (e.g., VIM) and its experimental results. Section 5 evaluates the componentization process and the case study. Section 6 summarizes related work in architectural discovery and repair as well as some VIM case studies. Section 7 concludes the findings.

2   Motivation

The curiosity arises from a study of a number of commercial software systems and their build architecture. These systems are implemented using C/C++. The number of program source files vary from several hundred to several thousands, which are organized into components. On average each component has 30 to 50 files and is owned by a development manager. The development model resembles synch and stabilize [2], where the programs are compiled and linked on a daily basis.

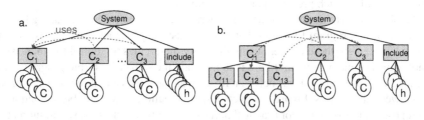

Fig. 1. The build architectures of a software before (a) and after (b) the componentization

Program files are organized in directories, each of which represent a component. All header files are placed in a separate include directory (Figure 1a). Initially, such a layout with proper protocols could sustain changes due to the addition of new features or the repairs of existing defects. However, as the software evolved, the interdependencies increased, which made manual protocols ineffective. Modern languages, such as Java, provide other mechanisms (e.g., packages) to organize files and components, as well as controlling access among components. However, such mechanisms are absent in legacy C/C++ software systems and must be created manually.

While control is a prime reason for repairing the architecture of legacy software, the compilation time is also pressing. In particular, our study revealed that on average between 80 to 90% of extra program entities (i.e. units such as, function, data, and type declarations) are included through unused header files. On average, each file included 60% of all header files multiple times. In an average size component, 172KLOC or 2.8% of entire programs, the average number of header files included by program files was 543 (directly and through transitive inclusion). The average size of program files was 37KB, whereas the average size of preprocessed file was 1.96 MB. While the compiler will discard unused entities, the preprocessor and the parser are penalized for opening, reading through , and closing the files. Even in case of conditional compilation, while the entire file is discarded, all lines must be read to determine the end of conditional guard. Such rate of dependency can significantly slow the compilation process in a software with thousands of program files.

Another reason for the repair reflects the changing needs of the development team. In our example, the number of files in the system has been growing steadily for the past four years, with jumps near major new releases. Similarly, the number of actual dependencies have grown as well as the average number of header files included by program files. Figure 2 shows the growth of the number of program entities (broken down into functions, variables and types), source files, included header files, and component dependencies for several major releases of the software.

To improve productivity, teams need to work in parallel. This can be accomplished if components are smaller and their interfaces minimized. Each component needs to know only the interface of the components that it uses and parallel development can proceed. When the interface of a component changes, all other components that use it must update their definitions. In our example, any time the interface of a component changes, the components that use it must synchronize (recompile, re-test). As components become larger and their interfaces degrade, the number of synchronizations increases rapidly, which prevents parallel development.

Our objective is to generate component hierarchies (Figure 1b) by leveraging hidden structures in the program files. In other words, clustering files according to some criteria and implement these clusters using directory hierarchies to control the increasing complexity. The main constraint here is to maintain the semantics of the programs: we can only move program entities between files, create new files and directories, or move files between directories. Figure 1 depicts a sample build architecture before and after the proposed improvement. For practical purposes, the process must be semi-automatic: it accepts as input a hypothesis about the layout of components and connectors (i.e., a reference architecture) and leverages automatic clustering to satisfy it.

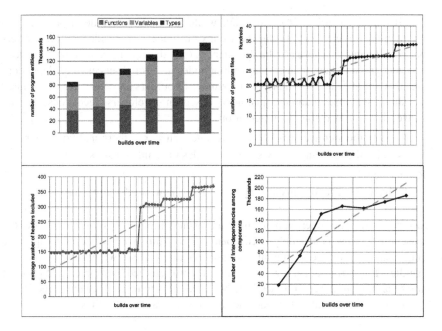

Fig. 2. The growth of an industrial software

3   Componentization Process

The componentization process described in this section relies on data extracted from the programs and an initial architectural pattern. The former is automatically generated, while the latter is the input from the developers providing a high level build architecture. If there is no overall build architecture, we can use automatic clustering to propose possible build architectures. The componentization process involves three steps, where at each step mechanisms are provided for manual intervention.

1. Form an initial hypothesis: $H = < D, A, M >$ where
   - D is the program dependency graph, which captures the dependencies among program units, e.g. functions, variables, and types. This graph is automatically constructed from the program source [4]. It contains all possible dependencies among program units and provides an invariant logical view of the program that must not change by restructuring.
   - A is a high-level architecture, which captures the structure of the program. This is a graph where nodes are high-level clusters (or components) and the edges are inter-dependencies among them. If there are no high-level architectures, we use the *information loss minimizing clustering* algorithm [3] on the program dependency graph D to create an initial architecture.
   - M is a one-to-many mapping, which maps nodes of D to a node in A. This mapping can be provided by the developers or an initial mapping can be obtained from the clustering algorithm (as specified in the creation of A above). M may not cover all nodes in D.

2. The dependency graph D is invariant, while the architecture description A and its mapping M can vary. Using the Reflexion model [6] we identify the outliers between D and A. These are the divergences (e.g. dependencies that exist between nodes in graph D but not in corresponding nodes in A) or absences (e.g., dependencies that are in D but not in A). If the number of outliers exceeds a pre-determined threshold, we make manual adjustments based on developers' feedbacks, naming conventions, or available documentation.

    – Modify the architecture A by adding a new cluster or merging two clusters.

    – Modify the mapping M by grouping nodes in D into clusters in A.

    Repeat step 2.

3. Each cluster in A represents a component in our new build architecture.

To demonstrate the operation of the componentization process, we use VIM 6.2 as a case study. VIM is a widely used open source editor whose size is comparable to components of average or medium size in commercial software systems that we have studies. Furthermore, earlier version of VIM was studied by Tran et al [5] for the purpose of architectural repair. Elsewhere, we used VIM to investigate the reduction of build time by removing false dependencies among program header files [8].

Constructing program dependency graphs. The program dependency graph was obtained as a by-product of our header restructuring algorithm [4]. There are two types of dependency graphs. A file-level dependency graph (FDG) $G = < V, E >$ is a graph where its vertices V represent files (program files or header files) and its edges represent inclusion directions between files (i.e., #include directives). A snippet of this graph for VIM 6.2 is shown below.

```
buffer.c <- vim.h
vim.h <- globals.h
...
```

A program unit dependency graph (PUDG) $G = < V, E >$ contains more detailed information about the program. Its vertices are program units (e.g. entities with one definition and multiple declarations) and its edges are syntax dependencies among the program units. A snippet of the PUDG for VIM 6.2 is shown below.

```
func:AppendCharToRedobuff <- func:add_char_buff
func:AppendCharToRedobuff <- var:block_redo
...
```

After restructuring VIM 6.2 header files, 956 header files (numbered by a natural number) were generated, which were included by 46 compilation units. This results in an updated FDG with 1002 nodes and 5546 vertexes. The respective PUDG has 26389 nodes and 72056 edges. The PUDG captures all low-level call graph, use-def relations, type dependencies, etc. in one graph. Both FDG and PUDG can be constructed using a C/C++ parser. They can be clustered into components to improve cohesion and reduce coupling among the resulting components.

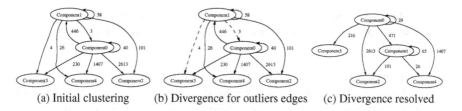

(a) Initial clustering   (b) Divergence for outliers edges   (c) Divergence resolved

Fig. 3. The reflexion models as a result of LIMBO clustering on the restructured header file dependency graph. An edge label is the number of inclusions between two clusters. The final model can be seen as MVC model after merging "c0" and "c3" as "Controller", merging "c1" and "c4" as "View" and regarding "c2" as "Model"

Clustering dependency graphs. The reference architecture explored by Tran et al. [5] was not based on the VIM documentation. Furthermore, VIM has evolved through several major revisions from 5.7 to 6.2 and it is not clear whether the reference architecture proposed by Tran et al. still fits the code. Therefore, we tried two different paths to see if we can converge on the same architecture: (1) use FDG to reveal an initial architecture based on information loss minimizing clustering; (2) use PUDG to reveal the architecture through repairing a reference architecture.

We performed an initial clustering of the updated FDG of the restructured program using the LIMBO algorithm [3]. Chosen $N = 5$ as the desired number of clusters, the output of the algorithm gave a partition of the involved files as follows:

```
c0={*.c except for buffer.c (41 files) 151.h 152.h ...(24 files)}
c1={buffer.c 1.h 156.h ... (143 files) }
c2={10.h 103.h ... (365 files) }
c3={110.h 150.h ... (96 files) }
c4={0.h 101.h ... (298 files)}
```

To apply jRMTool (the reflexion model tool) [6], we prepared a mapping with the following format:

```
[ file=<fileName> mapTo=<componentName> ]
```

where fileName can be given as a regular expression to match multiple files using the patterns from naming conventions. After feeding the rules found by the clustering mapping into jRMTool, a reflexion model is created as shown in figure 3a.

The divergences and absences are indications that either the high level model does not present a good fit or the mapping is not correct. Adjusting the high level model requires better understanding of the architecture.

Although there is no divergence in the above model, two edges in the high-level model, namely c1→ c0 and c1 → c3, have only very few instances in the source model. We consider them as outliers. After removing them in the high-level model, we have two divergences as shown in figure 3b. These divergences arise from two sets of misclassified headers, we reclassified them into the more appropriate cluster:

```
c0 -> c1: {153.h 159.h 43.h}
c3 -> c1: {110.h 116.h 200.h 210.h}
```

Applying the above adjustments on the reflexion mappings, we obtain a new high-level model as shown in figure 3c. It is worth noting that the clustering leads to an architecture that is similar to the model-view-controller (MVC) pattern.

Selecting a reference architecture. We begin by using the architecture from Tran et al for VIM 5.7 [5] as a reference architecture and compare the results of the reflexion model with the PUDG for VIM 6.2. We convert the "contain.rsf" used in Tran's result into an initial high-level model A with the initial mapping M. Here, we only use the call-graph, a subgraph of the PUDG where the edges are function calls, in order to compare VIM 6.2 with results reported for VIM 5.7 [5]. Figure 4a shows the result of this comparison. As this reflexion model shows, there are many divergences and absences. These are due to the changes made to the programs between the two releases. Adding the new functions to the original mapping and merging the sub-components "CHAR" and "MISC" with their parent components "Terminal" and "Utility" respectively, we obtain a new reference architecture, as shown in Figure 4b. Furthermore, we merge "Lang_Interface" into "Terminal" and "Utility" into "FILE", and adjusted some clusterings by changing the mappings. The repaired architecture is shown in Figure 5b, where three divergences are fully repaired by merging "Terminal" and "GUI" into "View", part of "FILE" and "OS_Interface" into "Model" and "Command" and rest of "FILE" into "Controller".

Componentization of VIM. Both automated clustering and manual creation of a reference architecture suggest an MVC architectural style for VIM 6.2. We partition the program files into three components, each of which is implemented as a directory. As for PUDG for VIM 6.2, we use the results of earlier header restructuring [4]. To fit the MVC architecture on VIM 6.2, we leverage the Reflexion Model [6]. We gave the reference architecture as a high-level model and the converted dependency graph as the source-level model. In addition, we gave the mapping from the compilation units to the clusters.

According to the reflexion mappings, the 46 compilation units are mapped into 3 directories: 4 in Model, 24 in View and 18 in Controller. Then, we copy the 956 generated headers into these directories that are directly or indirectly included by the implement files: 126 headers in Model, 868 in View and 862 in Controller. There are duplicated headers among them, namely 109 headers are common to all the three directories, for the remaining 759 headers in View and 753 headers in Controller, there are 665 in common. We create two additional directories for common headers. Next, we put these headers into an interface for the components to obtain just 5 headers, the file inclusion dependencies for the directory restructured VIM becomes:

```
common.h -> model.h -> 4 .c files
         -> common_vc.h -> view.h       -> 24 .c
                        -> controller.h-> 18 .c
```

4   Experimental Results

We adapted the GCC 3.4.0 compiler (1) to remove redundancies through a *precompilation* option: -dump-program-units; (2) to remove false dependencies through a

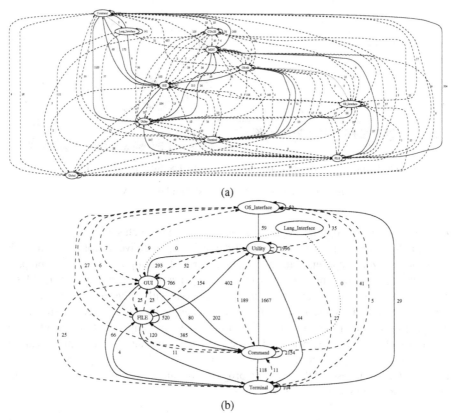

Fig. 4. The initial reflexion model is based on Tran's architecture of VIM 5.7. Figure 4a shows the initial model without considering new functions in VIM 6.2, and figure 4b shows the model with the new functions. Here an edge label shows the number of function calls among two clusters

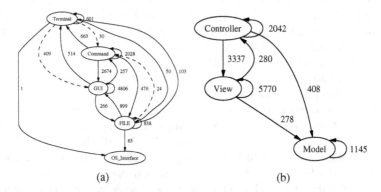

Fig. 5. The reflexion model after architecture repairing, where three divergences are inevitable while the clusters were fixed. If we merge "Terminal" and "GUI" as "View", merge part of "FILE" with "OS_Interface" as "Model" and "Command" and part of "FILE" as "Controller", a MVC model can be obtained which resolves all the divergences/absences

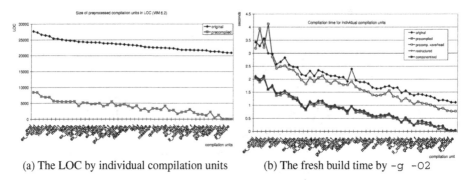

(a) The LOC by individual compilation units   (b) The fresh build time by -g -O2

Fig. 6. Break down LOC and fresh build time of VIM

header restructuring option: -dump-headers; (3) and to cluster generated headers into smaller number of headers and adjust the inclusion directives accordingly through a *componentization* option: -dump-components. These options serve as a preparing step before a real compilation. As a result, the generated compilation units (.c files), header units (.h files) and component units (directories with a clustered header file) are saved into temporary files. These temporary files can be used by the second run of the compiler to speedup its compilation. The build process is completely transparent to the developers. It is not necessary to modify the Makefile because the new options can be given to make through an argument, e.g., CC = "gcc -dump-program-units". For VIM 6.2, we measured the resulting programs by our pre-compilation, restructuring and componentization respectively.

Measuring fresh builds. The experiments were carried out on a number of networked Linux workstations. The host machine for the compilations is a 2.20 GHz Intel Pentium 4 workstation, with 512 KB cache. We also used the servers available in the local area network of our campus lab. The compilation farm can use up to 8 processors: 2 x 2.8GHz, 4 x 2.4GHz, 1 x 2.2GHz (the local workstation) and 1 x 1.6GHz. All machines use the same operating system. The times are measured as the average of 10 separate runs of the same settings. The default compilation takes around 70 seconds, whereas the build time with all the tuning options turned on reduces drastically to around 2 seconds (39.5x speedup). Our techniques are also shown to be orthogonal to other tuning techniques such as parallel build and compilation cache [8].

To make a fair comparison of the code bases, we preprocessed the original code base using the -E -P options so that no preprocessing time is compared. The average size of preprocessed files was reduced from 708.9 KB to 104.71 KB. The overall build size is reduced from 33.9 MB to 5.01 MB. The saving comparisons of individual compilation units are shown in Figure 6a. The data items are horizontally sorted by the original preprocessed file size. The similar shapes of the two curves indicate that the reduction is almost uniform to every compilation unit. The time savings and their comparisons are shown in Figure 6b. Here, the data items are still sorted by the descending order of the original preprocessed file size. In this manner, we can not only see the correlation between the curves in this chart, but also the correlation between the preprocessed file size and the compilation time. The compilation time is almost uniformly reduced for each unit, since almost every compilation unit in VIM includes the `vim.h`. The net speedup by precompilation is 2.51. The precompilation overhead is needed for the first fresh build. Even taking it into account, the precompilation plus a fresh build is still 12.6% faster than the original fresh build. If the precompiled code is compiled N times, then the overhead can be divided by N. The restructured and componentized code has a little less time reduction in fresh build, as shown in Figure 6b.

Measuring incremental builds. When a line of code is changed, all files dependent on it must recompile. Since pre-compilation generates preprocessed files, one must rely on the original file inclusion dependency to judge whether a compilation unit needs to be recompiled. On the other hand, the header restructuring generates new header inclusions that have no false dependencies, the number of recompilations is reduced to the minimum. However, the larger number of headers generated by the restructuring hampers the fresh build execution time because of increased file open/close operations, thus the componentization can be employed to reduce the number of headers. The cost of doing so is the increasing number of recompilations. To verify the above rationale, we performed a simulation based on concrete numbers gathered from the time spent on individual compilation units under various options, and also based on the FDG implied by the generated inclusion relationships.

Since the change data of VIM at each incremental build is not available[3], a probability analysis is used by assuming that a program per incremental build changes ΔL lines of code and the probability of change for each line is uniform: $\Delta L/L$ where L is the total lines of code (LOC).

Consider a file dependency graph (FDG), and measure the line of code for each file as L_{H_i} for headers H_i or L_{C_i} for compilation units C_i. The probability of changing a header H_i or a compilation unit C_i is $L_{H_i}\Delta L/L$ or $L_{C_i}\Delta L/L$ respectively. For every change in a header file H_i, all the dependent compilation units $\mathcal{D}(i)$ require re-compilation, whereas for each changed compilation unit, only itself must be recompiled. In the original code base, a compilation unit C_i needs a re-compilation if either its implementation is changed, or any of its dependent headers is changed. If we measure the time for its re-compilation as t_i, then the overall incremental build time is

$$\Delta t = \sum_i p_i t_i \text{ where } p_i = [L(C_i) + \sum_{j|i\in\mathcal{D}(H_j)} L(H_j)]\Delta L/L \qquad (1)$$

Equation (1) is used with a different parameter L and a different FDG for restructured and componentized code bases, since the restructuring and clustering needs to be done only once during the incremental build.

The precompiled programs use the same FDG as original, but Equation (1) is adjusted as Equation (2) since the directly changed compilation unit needs an overhead of t_i' to redo the pre-compilation, while indirectly changed compilation unit can quickly recompile with the precompiled code.

---

[3] The publicly committed CVS log does not match the real development changes since not all changes were committed to the repository.

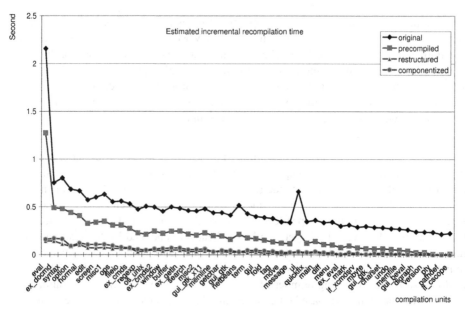

Fig. 7. Break down the required recompilation time as a line is changed per incremental build

$$\Delta t = \sum_i [p_i^c(t_i + t_i') + (1 - p_i^c)p_i^h t_i] \, , p_i^c = L(C_i)\Delta L/L \, ,$$
$$p_i^h = \sum_{j|i \in \mathcal{D}(H_j)} L(H_j)\Delta L/L \tag{2}$$

Having the LOC of source files (Figure 6a) and the timing of the compilation units (Figure 6b), the incremental build time analysis of the *original, precompiled, restructured* and *componentized* code bases is shown in Figure 7. In total, for the *original, precompiled, restructured* and *componentized* code base, an incremental build when changing one line of code takes respectively 22.73, 10.06, 1.76 and 2.46 seconds of recompilation (see Figure 7), whereas the fresh build takes 97.89, 39.04, 41.1 and 40.91 seconds respectively (see Figure 6b).

Finally, we verified both the header restructured and componentized VIM programs by executing all 51 test cases and comparing the results with that of original VIM. 49 test cases ran cleanly and produced identical results, while 2 test cases failed due to dependencies on Win32 platform. The original VIM also failed these two test cases in our environment.

5   Discussion

The goals of improving a build architecture are many-fold and some are conflicting. In particular, the improvement of build time through reduction of redundancies and the number of header files that conflict with one another. Other goals contribute to our overall objectives to varying degrees. Figure 8 depicts various objectives, issues, concerns and operations as a soft-goal interdependency graph [9]. In this graph, the cloud nodes are high-level soft-goals, those not directly affecting the correct functionality of the system. At the root level we have the goal of improving build architecture. The

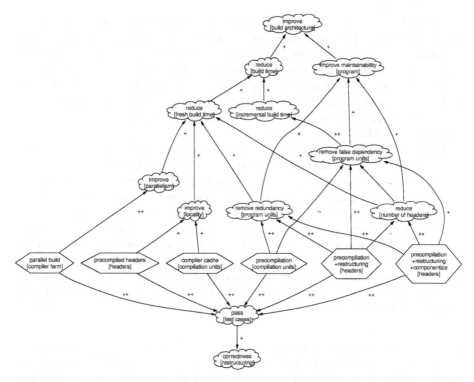

Fig. 8. Rationale of improving the architecture for the build process

intermediate goals represent issues and concerns that contribute to our root goal, e.g., reducing the build time. Similarly, the lower level goals contribute to their respective parents. The hexagon nodes are the operationalization of higher-level goals: the actions or tasks that assist in achieving goals.

Precompilation and header restructuring are both fully automated with little overhead. Other steps of our componentization process provide facilities for manual input. This combination facilitates an exploratory approach to improving the build architecture, where the developers have complete control through creation of a reference architecture and appropriate mappings. Using similar goal models, developers can balance the trade offs in the architectural repair process.

6   Related Work

Architecture views and the MVC pattern.   Different views of software architecture support different tasks in software development. Typical examples of views include the "4+1" view [10], Siemens Four view [11] , and Business Component Factory [12]. In a recent book, Clements et al [1] provide a treatment of various views, their definitions, and their audience in a software development project. Furthermore, the authors describe conditions under which various views may be merged together. This paper focuses on two such views: module view and allocation view. Module views focus on physical program units, e.g. functions, classes, or a group thereof, and their relationships. The allocation view (more specifically the implementation styles) focus on how a module is allocated to the code management system. In its simplest form, this can be a directory, or in more elaborate configuration management, a configuration item. While the module view is necessary for understanding the static properties of the software system, the allocation view enables project managers to assign work responsibilities or divide the resources for build and testing activities.

Various architectural patterns have been documented (e.g. Clements et al [1]). Such patterns provide clues to developers' intentions and help speed up the communication among the team. The patterns are loosely defined. In this paper, we used the idea of patterns as a reference architecture that was the input to our componentization process. In our case study of VIM, we used the Model-View-Controller (MVC) pattern, which was proposed by the Smalltalk community as a reference architecture for graphical editors [13]. In this pattern, the Model keeps the data structures of the documents being edited, the View shows the model to the user, and updates the view whenever there is a change in the model, the Controller calls appropriate actions based on the user's command. Thus, both View and Controller need to interact with the Model and each other. Such patterns can be loosely defined and modified by reflecting different views.

Reflexion Model and architectural repair. There are many reverse engineering tools to compare an architecture against the low-level code artifacts [6, 14, 15, 5]. Among them, we choose Murphy et al's reflexion model [6] and Tran's architecture repair [5] for the reverse engineering. The reason for the choice is not only to recover the architecture, but also allows for maintaining it through monitoring and repairing.

This paper uses the reflexion model to verify the mappings or clusterings after the architecture discovery and during the architecture repair. Unlike other work that uses call-graphs as the source model, we compute the program dependency graphs as the source model to reduce the build time through removal of false dependencies.

Tran et al [5] proposed a way of repairing an architecture through manual clustering. The idea is similar to the reflexion model [6], which also requires a mapping between a high level model (e.g., architecture) and a low level source model (e.g., call graphs). The architecture repair aims at adjusting the high-level models as well as low-level source models so that the number of divergences is kept small. Tran et al studies VIM 5.7 as one of their case studies. In this paper, we investigated whether the same architecture is still followed by VIM 6.2, and moreover, how much repair is needed to remove divergences.

Architecture discovery through clustering. There are several approaches in literature [3, 16,17,18] to cluster software artifacts into architectures. Among them, we chose LIMBO, a scalable algorithm developed by Andritsos et al [3] that discovers clusters from code facts automatically. The algorithm computes the information content of the data at hand and its objective is to minimize the loss of information as code artifacts are placed into clusters. Intuitively, when a code artifact is given, LIMBO tries to minimize the uncertainty of identifying the cluster to which this artifact belongs. The reason for choosing LIMBO, is that our artifacts collected from header restructuring are dependency graphs that can be expressed into input for the algorithm, and the algorithm allows for an unbiased clustering with a single parameter N: the number of desired clusters.

In a program fact graph with nodes and links, each node is annotated by a set of neighboring nodes through its links to them, *i.e.*, each node becomes a vector over the nodes with which it is connected. Then, the distance between two particular nodes is defined as the loss of information we would incur if their vectors were merged into a single vector, representative of the two. Therefore, during the first steps of the algorithm, vectors with no information loss are merged. These are the vectors that contain identical sets of code facts. Given a threshold for the information that can be lost, the algorithm proceeds with more vector merges and stops when a desired number of clusters is reached. In this paper, LIMBO was used as an initial step to discover an architecture based on program dependency graph rather than a call-graph. Some further repair is needed to remove divergences from automatically generated clusters.

Build speedup through header restructuring. Large legacy C/C++ software systems typically consist of header files (.h files) and compilation units (.c files). Ideally an compilation unit includes only the declarations that it uses. However, a header file can be included by multiple files and as such may contain declarations and definitions that are not used by all compilation units that include it [19]. In such cases, false dependencies are created. Another problem is that symbols may be declared in more than one places. As systems evolve, such redundant declarations tend to become common.

Redundancies and false dependencies do not affect the functionality of a system, but they do affect the efficiency of the development process. The longer the build process takes, the longer developers have to wait to integrate their changes. Large software systems that contain millions of lines of code may take several hours to build. Redundancies increase the size of the code and may cause inconsistencies. A false dependency between a compilation unit and its header exacerbates the problem by causing unnecessary compilation of the unit when an independent part of the header file has changed. This problem is particularly important in light of the popularity of the sync-and-stabilize development paradigm [20], where software systems undergo frequent, often daily, builds. Earlier [4], we reported an algorithm to remove false code dependences and redundancies through header restructuring.

7   Conclusion

As legacy software systems evolve, their build architectures decay, which result in inefficiencies that can hamper the development process. However, repairing the build architecture requires balancing a number of objectives. This paper presented a study of commercial software systems evolution and the impact on their build architecture. Furthermore, it outlined the key requirements for repairing the architecture of a large system. In particular, the approach facilitates exploration, where the developers provide some input and the process automatically carries out the restructuring. The componentization process was carried out on a case study, VIM 6.2, whose build architecture closely follows small to medium size components of legacy software systems that we studied. After improving the build architecture, we found that technically, such a componentization can reduce the incremental build time more than 10x while reducing its fresh build time more than 2x, and perhaps more importantly, the restructured VIM follows the MVC pattern facilitating better understanding of the program and its maintenance.

References

1. Clements, P., Bachmann, F., Bass, L., Garlan, D., Ivers, J., Little, R., Nord, R., Stafford, J.: Documenting Software Architectures: Views and Beyond. Addison Wesley (2002)
2. Selby, R.W., Cusumano, M.A.: Microsoft secrets. Simon and Schuster (1998)
3. Andritsos, P., Tzerpos, V.: Software clustering based on information loss minimization. In: 10th Working Conference on Reverse Engineering. (2003) 334–344
4. Yu, Y., Dayani-Fard, H., Mylopoulos, J.: Removing false code dependencies to speedup software development processes. In: Proceedings of CASCON. (2003) 288–297
5. Tran, J., Godfrey, M., Lee, E., Holt, R.: Architectural repair of open source software. In: IWPC 2000. (2000)
6. Murphy, G.C., Notkin, D., Sullivan, K.J.: Software reflexion models: Bridging the gap between design and implementation. IEEE Trans. Software Eng **27** (2001) 364–380
7. Moolenaar, B.: Vim 6.2, http://www.vim.org (2003)
8. Yu, Y., Dayani-Fard, H., Mylopoulos, J., Andritsos, P.: Reducing build time through precompilations for large-scale software. Technical Report CSRG-504, Department of Computer Science, University of Toronto (2004)
9. Mylopoulos, J., Chung, L., Nixon, B.: Representing and using nonfunctional requirements: A process-oriented approach. IEEE Trans. on Softw. Eng. **18** (1992) 483–497
10. Kruchten, P.: Architectural blueprints – the "4+1" view model of software architecture. IEEE Software **12** (1995) 42 – 50
11. Hofmeister, C., Nord, R., Soni, D.: Applied software architecture. Addison-Wesley (2000)
12. Herzum, P., Sims, O.: Business Component Factory: A Comprehensive Overview of Component-Based Development for the Enterprise. John Wiley and Sons (1999)
13. Krasner, G.E., S.T.Pope: A cookbook for using the model-view-controller user interface paradigm in smalltalk-80. Journal of Object-Oriented Programming **1** (1988) 26–49
14. Eixelsberger, W., Ogris, M., Gall, H., Bellay, B.: Software architecture recovery of a program family. In: Proceedings of the 20th ICSE, IEEE Computer Society (1998) 508–511
15. Bellay, B., Gall, H.: An evaluation of reverse engineering tool capabilities. Journal of Software Maintenance: Research and Practice **10** (1998) 305–32
16. Maletic, J., Valluri, N.: Automatic software clustering via latent semantic analysis. In: Proceeding of ASE'99. (1999) 251–254
17. Mitchell, B.S., Mancoridis, S.: Modeling the search landscape of metaheuristic software clustering algorithms. In: GECCO-03, LNCS 2724, Chicago (2003) 2499–2510
18. Mitchell, B.S., Gansner, E.R., Mancoridis, S., Chen, Y.: Bunch: A clustering tool for the recovery and maintenance of software system structures. In: ICSM'99. (1999)
19. Borison, E.A.: Program Changes and the Cost of Selective Recompilation. PhD thesis, Carnegie Mellon University (1989)
20. Cusumano, M.A., Selby, R.W.: How Microsoft builds software. CACM **40** (1997)

Using Scenarios to Predict the Reliability of Concurrent Component-Based Software Systems

Genaína Rodrigues[1], David Rosenblum[1], and Sebastian Uchitel[2]

[1] Department of Computer Science,
London Software Systems,
University College London,
Gower Street, WC1E 6BT, UK
[2] Department of Computing,
London Software Systems,
Imperial College London,
180 Queen's Gate, SW7 2RH, U.K

Abstract. Scenarios are a popular means for capturing behavioural requirements of software systems early in the lifecycle. Scenarios show how components interact to provide system level functionality. If component reliability information is available, scenarios can be used to perform early system reliability assessment. In this paper we present a novel automated approach for predicting software system reliability. The approach involves extending a scenario specification to model (1) the probability of component *failure*, and (2) *scenario transition probabilities* derived from an operational profile of the system. From the extended scenario specification, probabilistic behaviour models are synthesized for each component and are then composed in parallel into a model for the system. Finally, a user-oriented reliability model described by Cheung is used to compute a reliability prediction from the system behaviour model. The contribution of this paper is a reliability prediction technique that takes into account the component structure exhibited in the scenarios and the concurrent nature of component-based systems. We also show how implied scenarios induced by the component structure and system behaviour described in the scenarios can be used to evolve the reliability prediction.

1   Introduction

Software reliability engineering is an important aspect of many system development efforts, and consequently there has been a great deal of research in this area [15, 10]. One important activity included in software reliability engineering is *reliability prediction* [11]. There has been much recent work in reliability engineering that has addressed reliability modeling and prediction of architecture- and component-based software [8, 19]. Components both simplify and complicate reliability prediction. They simplify because accurate component reliability estimates may be available to aid reliability prediction early in the development lifecycle. They complicate due to the need for a sound compositional approach

M. Cerioli (Ed.): FASE 2005, LNCS 3442, pp. 111–126, 2005.

to reliability prediction. A promising compositional approach to predicting reliability of component-based systems early in the lifecycle is to base the prediction on scenarios of system usage.

Scenarios have been widely adopted as a way to capture system behavioral requirements. *Message Sequence Charts* (MSCs) [9] and their UML counterpart, Sequence Diagrams (SDs) [16] are widely accepted notations for scenario-based specification.

There has been some previous work on using scenarios to predict the reliability of component-based software [4, 27], but they use imprecise, coarse-grained, sequential models of system architecture as the basis for prediction. In this paper, we present a novel scenario-based approach to reliability prediction in which a more precise, fine-grained, concurrent system architecture model is synthesised for computing a reliability prediction. The approach starts with a set of scenarios and a high-level message sequence chart (HMSC). The HMSC is annotated with *scenario transition probabilities* derived from an operational profile of the system [14], which accounts for the relative frequency with which system usage results in a transition from one scenario to another. We synthesise from the scenarios a deterministic probabilititistic behaviour model for each system component. Each component model is then extended to model the probability of component *failure*. The resulting probabilistic models are composed in parallel and used to predict the reliability of the component-based system according to Cheung's user-oriented reliability model [3].

The contribution of this paper is a reliability prediction technique that takes into account the component structure exhibited in the scenarios and the concurrent nature of component-based systems. We also show how as a result of this implied scenarios can impact the result of reliability analysis.

The paper is structured as follows: In Section 2, we briefly present some background information about the different elements of our approach. In Section 3 we describe in detail our scenario-based method for predicting software system reliability and an extensive illustration of our approach. In Section 4 we show how implied scenarios detection can be used to improve reliability prediction for concurrent software systems. In Section 5 we compare our approach to other efforts for analysing reliability of component-based software and discuss the main differences between our approach and other scenario-based reliability analysis models. Finally, in Section 6 we present our conclusions and discuss several future directions for our work.

2   Background

In this section we briefly review the two main concepts on which we base our method for predicting the reliability of component-based software: scenario specifications, and Cheung's user-oriented software reliability model. Note that we adopt Szyperski's definition of component as a unit of independent development and deployment. We further view components as being large-grained system entities (as opposed to small-scale components such as GUI widgets) for which one may reasonably expect to have reliability data, which in turn can be established through reliability testing [6].

2.1   Scenarios

Scenario notations such as Message Sequence Charts [9] are used at early stages of development to document, elicit and describe system behaviour. Scenarios are partial descriptions of how components interact to provide system level functionality. A *scenario specification* is formed by composing multiple scenarios possibly from different stakeholders.

The underlying notion of scenario composition is that simple scenarios can be used as building blocks to describe new, more complex, scenarios. Simple sequences of behavior are described using *Basic Message Sequence Charts* (BMSCs). A BMSC is formed by vertical lines representing component time lines and horizontal arrows representing interactions between components. In this paper, we interpret each interaction as a synchronous communication between components. Because a BMSC can represent concurrent activity among the components it portrays, it denotes a partial ordering of activities, which in turn under an interleaving semantics determines a corresponding set of finite sequences of interactions.

Three fundamental constructs for combining BMSCs are *vertical composition* (where two BMSCs can be combined sequentially), *alternative composition* (defining that the system could alternatively choose one of the BMSCs to follow) and *iterative composition* (which composes a BMSC sequentially with itself). The *high-level MSC* (HMSC) is a widely adopted syntactic construct for describing scenario composition. An HMSC is a directed graph, whose nodes refer to BMSCs and whose edges indicate the acceptable ordering of the BMSCs. HMSCs allow stakeholders to reuse scenarios within a specification and to introduce sequences, loops and alternatives of BMSCs. The semantics of an HMSC is the set of sequences of interactions that follow some maximal path through the HMSC.

Throughout this paper we use a variant of the Boiler Control system example presented by Uchitel et al. [25]. As shown in Figure 1, the Boiler Control system consists of four components: *Sensor, Control, Database* and *Actuator*. In the top portion of the figure, we depict the HMSC specification of the Boiler, which composes five BMSCs: *Initialise, Register, Analyse, Terminate* and *End*, which are depicted in Figure 1, excluding the upper-left corner where the HMSC is. Note that the variables appearing in curly brackets in the figure are an extension to MSCs that we explain in Section 3.

2.2   The Cheung User-Oriented Reliability Model

In order to predict software system reliability, we need a reliability model that expresses system reliability as a function of the reliability of the components and the frequency of utilization of those components. Using Cheung's approach [3], the reliability of the system can be computed as a function of both the deterministic properties of the structure of the program and the stochastic properties of the utilisation and failure of its components.

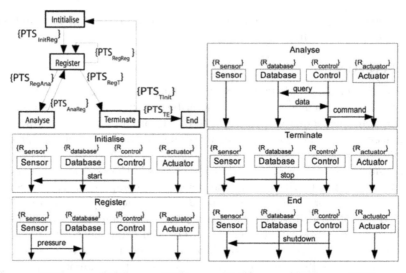

Fig. 1. The Message Sequence Chart Specification for the Boiler Control System, with Example Probability Values

Essentially, the Cheung model is a Markov reliability model that uses a program flow graph to represent the structure of the system. Every node N_i in the flow graph of the Cheung model represents a program module and a direct branch (N_i, N_j) represents a possible transfer of control from N_i to N_j. A probability P_{ij} that transition (N_i, N_j) will happen is attached to every directed branch. R_i is the reliability of node N_i. The original transition (N_i, N_j) in the flow graph is then modified into $R_i P_{ij}$, which represents the probability that the execution of module N_i produces the correct result and control is transferred to module N_j. The reliability of the program is, therefore, the probability of reaching the correct termination of the program flow graph from its initial state in the following way: Let $N = \{C, F, N_1, N_2, ..., N_n\}$ be the states of the model, where N_1 is the start state of the program control flow graph, the N_i are intermediate states, N_n is the last (non-absorbing) state reached in any successful execution of the system, and C and F are absorbing states representing the terminal states Correct (to which there is a transition from N_n) and Fault. Let the transition matrix be M' where M'_{ij} represents the probability of transition from state i to state j:

$$
M' =
\begin{array}{c}
\\ C \\ F \\ N_1 \\ N_2 \\ \vdots \\ N_n
\end{array}
\begin{array}{cccccc}
C & F & N_1 & N_2 & \dots & N_n \\
\left(\begin{array}{cccccc}
1 & 0 & 0 & 0 & \dots & 0 \\
0 & 1 & 0 & 0 & \dots & 0 \\
0 & 1-R_1 & 0 & R_1 P_{12} & \dots & R_1 P_{1n} \\
0 & 1-R_2 & 0 & R_2 P_{22} & \dots & R_2 P_{2n} \\
\vdots & \vdots & \vdots & \vdots & \vdots & \vdots \\
R_n & 1-R_n & 0 & 0 & \dots & 0
\end{array} \right)
\end{array}
$$

Let M be the matrix obtained from M' by deleting the rows and columns corresponding to the absorbing states C and F. Let S be a matrix such that:

$$S = I + M + M^2 + M^3 + \ldots\ldots = \sum_{k=0}^{\infty} M^k = (I - M)^{-1}$$

where I is the identity matrix with same dimension of M. Cheung shows that the system reliability is $Rel = S(1,n) \times R_n$, which is the probability of successfully transitioning from N_1 to N_n in any execution times the probability of successfully reaching C from N_n. Equivalently, Cheung shows that $S(1,n)$ can be computed as

$$S(1,n) = (-1)^{n+1} \frac{|M|}{|I - M|} \tag{1}$$

where $|M|$ and $|I - M|$ represent the determinant of M and $I - M$, respectively. We refer the reader to Cheung [3] for further details on the description and derivation of these formulae.

In the next section, we show how we weave the concepts presented in this section into a method for predicting the reliability of component-based software.

3   Reliability Analysis Using Scenarios

In this section we describe a method to predict software system reliability as a function of component reliability estimates. We annotate a scenario specification with probabilistic properties and use a probabilistic labelled transition system (LTS) synthesised from the scenario specification for the software reliability prediction. The method is depicted in Figure 2 as five major steps: (1) annotation of the scenarios, (2) synthesis of the probabilistic LTS, (3) construction of the stochastic matrix, (4) system reliability prediction, and (5) implied scenario detection.

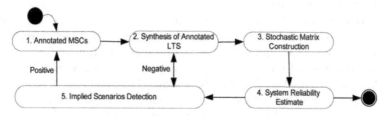

Fig. 2. The Reliability Prediction Method

Four key assumptions underlie our method:

1. The transfer of control between components has the Markov property, meaning that the transition from one execution state to another is dependent only on the source state and its available transitions and not on the past history

of state transitions. This is a traditional assumption that simplifies in work on reliability analysis and it greatly simplifies the computation of reliability estimates.

2. Failures are independent across transitions. Again, this assumption simplifies the computation of reliability estimates.

3. A message from component C to component C' represents an invocation by C of a service offered by C'. The reliability with which this service is performed is thus the reliability of C', $R_{C'}$. Additionally, the execution time of the invocation is assumed to be so short as not to be a factor in the component's reliability. In other words, $R_{C'}$ is the probability of successful completion of an invocation of any service offered by C', irrespective of the execution time of the service. This assumption is simply a modeling choice that is made without loss of generality. For instance, we could just as easily accommodate method-level reliabilities, and/or communication reliabilities (as is done, for instance, in Yacoub et.al [27])

4. There is only one initial and one final scenario for the system in the HMSC. Multiple initial and final scenarios can be combined by introducing a *super-initial* and a *super-final* scenario, analogously to the *super-initial state* and *super-final state* proposed by Wang et al. [26].

3.1   The Annotated Scenarios

In the first step, we annotate the scenarios (i.e., the HMSC and BMSCs) with two kinds of probabilities, *the probability of transitions between scenarios PTS_{ij}* and *the reliability of the components R_C*.

The transition probability PTS_{ij} is the probability that execution control transfers directly from scenario S_i to scenario S_j. This information would be normally derived from an operational profile for the system [14]. Thus, from scenario S_i, the sum of the probabilities PTS_{ij} for all successor scenarios S_j is equal to one. As the PTS_{ij} relates to the transition between scenarios, these probabilities are annotated on the corresponding edges of the HMSC, as shown on the HMSC of Figure 1.

The component reliabilities R_C are annotated on the BMSCs, as also shown in Figure 1. Without loss of generality, this paper uses coarse-grained, single values for the overall component reliabilities; in general, we could associate reliabilities with individual messages and/or segments of component timelines.

For the purposes of illustrating our method on the Boiler example, we use the values depicted in Figure 1 for the PTS_{ij}. The values for the PTS_{ij} are based on the assumption that the system executes the scenario *Register* (which causes sensor readings to be entered into the database) far more frequently than the scenarios *Analyse* and *Terminate*, and that when it does execute *Terminate* there is an equal probability of reinitialising and shutting down.

The values on Figure 1 for the reliability of the components reflect the assumption that the *Database* is a highly reliable commercial software product, that the *Sensor* and *Actuator* are components whose hardware interface to the sensed/actuated phenomena will eventually fail, and that *Control* is a complex software subsystem that still contains latent faults.

3.2   Synthesis of the Probabilistic LTS

The second step of our method is to synthesise a probabilistic LTS from the annotated scenario specification. This step is an extension of the synthesis approach of Uchitel et al. [24], which consists of the following steps:

1. For each component C_i and each BMSC S_j, a *labelled transition system* (LTS) $C_i\_S_j$ is constructed by projecting the local behaviour of C_i within S_j. In particular, each message with an action a that C_i sends or receives in S_j is synthesised as a transition with action a in $C_i\_S_j$, and the sequence of transitions in $C_i\_S_j$ corresponds with the sequence of messages sent or received by C_i in S_j.
2. For each component C_i, the set of LTSs constructed for C_i in step 1 are composed into a *component LTS* for C_i according to the structure of the HMSC, with hidden transitions (τ actions) linking the final state of $C_i\_S_j$ to the start state of $C_i\_S_{j'}$ whenever there is a transition from S_j to $S_{j'}$ in the HMSC. The resulting LTS includes a new start state corresponding to the start state of the HMSC.
3. Each component LTS constructed in step 2 is reduced to a trace-equivalent deterministic, minimal LTS. This is consistent with the delayed choice semantics of the ITU MSC standard [9].
4. The architecture model for the system is taken as the parallel composition of the minimised component LTSs constructed in step 3.

Our extension of this approach exploits recent probabilistic extensions to the LTS formalism [2] and involves enhancements to each step listed above. The enhancements have the effect of mapping the probability annotations of the scenario specification into probability weights for transitions in the synthesised architecture model. In step 1, for each transition in a $C_i\_S_j$ representing the invocation of a service offered by C_i, an additional transition from the same source state is added with the target state being the global ERROR state. The resulting pair of transitions forms a probabilistic choice, with the former transition having probability R_{C_i} and the latter transition having probability $1 - R_{C_i}$.

In step 2, the scenario transition probabilities PTS_{ij} are mapped to probability weights on the hidden transitions linking the $C_i\_S_j$. Figure 3 illustrates the LTS of component *Control* that would be synthesised as a result of applying steps 1 and 2 of our synthesis method. Each shaded area contains an LTS synthesised in step 1 from a BMSC of Figure 1 and thus models the behaviour of *Control* within that BMSC. The transitions linking these different LTS are synthesised in step 2 and correspond to the transitions between BMSCs defined in the HMSC of Figure 1. Note that the probability weights on the τ transitions are the same as the corresponding transitions in the HMSC of Figure 1. Note also that because *data* is a message received by *Control* in scenario *Analyse*, it is synthesised as two transitions, the "successful" transition being weighted with probability R_{ctrl} and the transition to the ERROR state (labelled -1 in the figure) being weighted with probability $1 - R_{ctrl}$. This action only applies to transitions labelled with *data* as it is an application of assumption three we

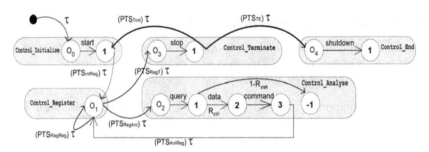

Fig. 3. Probabilistic LTS Synthesised for Component *Control*

explained earlier in this section. Note that the final state of the model is state 1 in the top right part of the figure.

Continuing with our extensions, in step 3, the probability weights must be handled correctly in the process of reducing each component LTS to its deterministic, minimal form. Intuitively, the elimination of a τ transition results in the merging of the transition's target state with its source state, with the outgoing transitions of the target state becoming outgoing transitions of the source state. Since there may be multiple τ transitions from the original source state (each with probability weight less than one), the probability weight of an eliminated τ transition must be "pushed" to the newly accumulated outgoing transitions, with the new weight on each such outgoing transition equal to its old weight times the weight on the eliminated τ transition. In the presence of τ self-loops (such as the τ self-loop on state 0 of *Control_Register* in Figure 4), it can be shown that such transitions can be eliminated entirely without any of the above merging or pushing of its weight. At the end of the elimination of outgoing τ transitions from a state, the weights on the outgoing transitions of the resulting state may not sum to one, in which case the weights must be normalised so that they do sum to one.

Using the example parameters presented previously in Figure 1, the resulting minimised LTS for component *Control* is depicted in Figure 4.

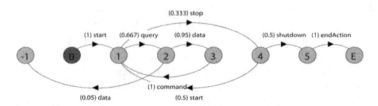

Fig. 4. Minimised Component LTS for Component *Control*

Finally, in step 4, the system architecture model is constructed as the parallel composition of the LTSs synthesized for each component. The probability weights of the composed LTS are computed according to the notion of *generative*

```
ArchitectureModel = Q0,
Q0    = ( (0.01) control.sensor.start -> ERROR
      | (0.99) control.sensor.start -> Q1),
Q1    = ( (0.001) sensor.database.pressure -> ERROR
      | (0.999) sensor.database.pressure -> Q2),
Q2    = ( (0.001) sensor.database.pressure -> ERROR
      | (0.809) sensor.database.pressure -> Q2
      | (0.152) control.database.query -> Q3
      | (0.038) control.sensor.stop -> Q10),
Q3    = ( (0.05) database.control.data -> ERROR
      | (0.95) database.control.data -> Q4),
Q4    = ( (0.005) control.actuator.command -> ERROR
      | (0.521) control.actuator.command -> Q5
      | (0.474) sensor.database.pressure -> Q9),
Q5    = ( (0.964) sensor.database.pressure -> Q2
      | (0.036) control.sensor.stop -> Q6),
Q6    = ( (0.005) control.sensor.start -> ERROR
      | (0.005) control.sensor.shutdown -> ERROR
      | (0.495) control.sensor.start -> Q1
      | (0.495) control.sensor.shutdown -> Q7),
Q7    = ( (1.0) endAction -> Q8),
Q8    = STOP,
Q9    = ( (0.006) control.actuator.command -> ERROR
      | (0.616) control.actuator.command -> Q2
      | (0.378) sensor.database.pressure -> Q9),
Q10   = ( (0.005) control.sensor.start -> ERROR
      | (0.005) control.sensor.shutdown -> ERROR
      | (0.495) control.sensor.shutdown -> Q7
      | (0.495) control.sensor.start -> Q11),
Q11   = ( (0.855) sensor.database.pressure -> Q2
      | (0.145) control.database.query -> Q12),
Q12   = ( (0.05) database.control.data -> ERROR
      | (0.95) database.control.data -> Q13),
Q13   = ( (0.005) control.actuator.command -> ERROR
      | (0.471) control.actuator.command -> Q1
      | (0.524) sensor.database.pressure -> Q9).
```

Fig. 5. The FSP of the Architecture Model

parallel composition defined by D'Argenio et al. [5]. At the end of this step, it follows that for each node of the synthesized architecture model, $\sum_{j=1}^{n} PA_{ij} = 1$, where n is the number of states in the LTS architecture model and PA_{ij} is the probability of transition between state S_i and S_j of the composed LTS. Otherwise, $PA_{ij} = 0$ if the transition (S_i, S_j) does not exist.

The architecture model for the Boiler Control system resulting from the application of all four steps of our extended synthesis method is depicted in Figure 5. For the sake of readability, we present the model in textual form as a specification expressed in FSP (Finite State Processes), the modelling notation of the LTSA tool (Labelled Transition System Analyser) [23]. FSP serves both as a modelling notation for end users, and as an intermediate form used in the automated synthesis of LTS models. As shown in the figure, a side-effect of the synthesis is the use of the auxiliary action *endAction* as the final action in a terminating path through the LTS.

3.3   Computing the Reliability Prediction

In this final step of our prediction method, the architecture model synthesised in the previous step is interpreted as a Markov model, and we apply the method of Cheung to compute the reliability prediction. In particular, the transition

$$\begin{pmatrix}
0 & 0.99 & 0 & 0 & 0 & 0 & 0 & 0 & 0 & 0 & 0 & 0 & 0 & 0 \\
0 & 0 & 0.999 & 0 & 0 & 0 & 0 & 0 & 0 & 0 & 0 & 0 & 0 & 0 \\
0 & 0 & 0.809 & 0.152 & 0 & 0 & 0 & 0 & 0 & 0 & 0.038 & 0 & 0 & 0 \\
0 & 0 & 0 & 0 & 0.95 & 0 & 0 & 0 & 0 & 0 & 0 & 0 & 0 & 0 \\
0 & 0 & 0 & 0 & 0 & 0.521 & 0 & 0 & 0 & 0.474 & 0 & 0 & 0 & 0 \\
0 & 0 & 0.964 & 0 & 0 & 0 & 0.036 & 0 & 0 & 0 & 0 & 0 & 0 & 0 \\
0 & 0.495 & 0 & 0 & 0 & 0 & 0 & 0 & 0 & 0 & 0 & 0 & 0.495 & 0 \\
0 & 0 & 0 & 0 & 0 & 0 & 0 & 0 & 0.95 & 0 & 0 & 0 & 0 & 0 \\
0 & 0.471 & 0 & 0 & 0 & 0 & 0 & 0 & 0.524 & 0 & 0 & 0 & 0 & 0 \\
0 & 0 & 0.616 & 0 & 0 & 0 & 0 & 0 & 0.378 & 0 & 0 & 0 & 0 & 0 \\
0 & 0 & 0 & 0 & 0 & 0 & 0 & 0 & 0 & 0 & 0.495 & 0.495 & 0 & 0 \\
0 & 0 & 0.855 & 0 & 0 & 0 & 0 & 0.145 & 0 & 0 & 0 & 0 & 0 & 0 \\
0 & 0 & 0 & 0 & 0 & 0 & 0 & 0 & 0 & 0 & 0 & 0 & 0 & 1 \\
0 & 0 & 0 & 0 & 0 & 0 & 0 & 0 & 0 & 0 & 0 & 0 & 0 & 0
\end{pmatrix}$$

Fig. 6. The Matrix Derived from the Synthesized Boiler LTS

probability weights of the architecture model are mapped into a square transition matrix M' whose row entries sum to one. This is used as the matrix M' described in Section 2.2, with $N = \{E, -1, 0, 1, ..., n - 1\}$ the set of states in the synthesised LTS, E the terminal state of correct execution (corresponding to state C described in Section 2.2), -1 the terminal fault state (state F of Section 2.2), and $n - 1$ the state from which a transition to state E is made upon action *endAction* (state N_n of Section 2.2). Note that the numeric state labels produced by LTSA may need to be renumbered so that the state leading to state E is the highest numbered state, as required by Cheung's model.

In Figure 6 we depict the transition matrix derived from the synthesised architecture model presented in Figure 5; note that this is actually the reduced matrix M, with the rows and columns for states E and -1 eliminated as in Section 2.2. Additionally, we point out for the fact that the rows in the sparse matrix in Figure 6 will sum to one if we add the transitions to the *ERROR* state. Applying the Cheung model to that matrix, we compute the reliability prediction for the Boiler Control system as $Rel= 0.649 = 64.9\%$.

4   Implied Scenarios

Scenarios describe two aspects of a system. On the one hand, they describe a set of system traces the system is intended to exhibit. On the other, it describes the components that will provide system level functionality and their interfaces (the messages these components can use to interact between each other to provide system level functionality). In the example in Figure 1, we see that the Boiler Control System is expected to exhibit a trace "*start, pressure, query, data, command ...*" and that component Control interacts with *Database* only through messages *query* and *data*.

It has been shown [1, 25] that given a scenario specification, it may be impossible to build a set of components that communicate exclusively through the interfaces described and that exhibit only the specified traces when running in parallel. The additional unspecified traces that are exhibited by the composed system are all called implied scenarios and are the result of specifying the be-

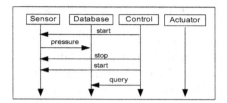

Fig. 7. Implied Scenario Detected

havior of a system from a global perspective yet expecting it to be provided by independent entities with a local system view. If the interaction mechanisms do not provide components with a rich enough local view of what is happening at a system level, they may not be able to enforce the intended system behavior. Effectively, what may occur is that each component may, from its local perspective, believe that it is behaving correctly, yet from a system perspective the behavior may not be what is intended.

The Boiler Control System of Figure 1 has implied scenarios, Figure 7 shows one of them. From the specification it is simple to see that after initialising *Sensor* there must be some pressure data registered into the *Database* before any queries can be done. However, in the implied scenario of Figure 7 a query is being performed immediately after start.

Why is this occurring? The cause is an inadequate architecture for the traces specified in the MSC specification. The *Control* component cannot observe when the Sensor has registered data in the *Database*, thus if it is to query the *Database* after data has been registered at least once, it must rely on the Database to enable and disable queries when appropriate. However, as the *Database* cannot tell when the *Sensor* has been turned on or off, it cannot distinguish a first registration of data from others. Thus, it cannot enable and disable queries appropriately. Succinctly, components do not have enough local information to prevent the system execution shown in Figure 7. Note that each component is behaving correctly from its local point of view, i.e. it is behaving according to some valid sequence of BMSCs. The problem is that each component is following a different sequence of BMSCs! The *Sensor, Control* and *Actuator* are going through scenarios *Initialise, Register, Terminate, Initialise, Analysis, Register*. However, the *Database* is performing *Initialise, Register, Analysis, Register*.

Implied scenarios indicate gaps in a scenario-based specification. They can represent intended system behaviour that was missing from the inherently partial scenario specification or undesired behaviour that should be avoided by changing the architecture of the system. Hence, implied scenarios need to be validated (identifying them as positive or negative system behaviour) and the scenario specification elaborated accordingly.

The existence of an implied scenario means that the reliability prediction for the Boiler Control System described above has been applied on a scenario specification that has a mismatch between behaviour and architecture. The behaviour model constructed in the previous section to predict reliability can exhibit behaviour (an implied scenairo) that has not yet been validated and that, acording to whether it described intended or unintended system behaviour, can impact system reliability.

As an example, suppose that the rate at which the sensor checks pressure information and saves it in the database is high enough that the probability of occurence of the trace in Figure 7 is negligible. Then reliability should be predicted on the behaviour model of Figure 5 constrained in such a way that the implied scenario cannot occur. We can use the approach described in [25] to build such a constraint.

If we calculate the reliability of the resulting constrained model in the same way as described in Section 3 then we obtain 86.2%.

On the other hand, the implied scenario may be undesired behaviour that needs to be avoided through a change in the architecture of the system. In this case, different or additional components will be needed, and the reliability performance will have to be recalculated from scratch.

Either way shows that implied scenarios can impact the reliability prediction significantly and that they should be validated before reliability is calculated.

More generally, the existence of implied scenarios as a result of the close relation that exists between behaviour and architecture in scenario-based specifications supports our claim that taking into account behaviour and architecture when performing reliability prediction is important.

5   Discussion and Related Work

Several previous architecture-based approaches to reliability engineering of component-based systems have been reported. They can be divided into two main categories, *state-based* approaches and *path-based* approaches. Goševa-Popstojanova and Trivedi provide a comprehensive survey of the various approaches [8]. For the sake of brevity, we provide here a brief view of the approaches of greatest interest to the scope of this work.

State-based models [3, 7] use a control flow graph to represent the system architecture. In such models it is assumed that the transfer of control among the components can be modelled as a Markov chain, with future behaviour of the system dependent only on the current state and not on past behaviour. Gokhale et al. use a regression test suite to experimentally determine the architecture of the software and the reliabilities of its components. As described in Section 2, Cheung's model takes into account the reliability of each component and the operational profile. In general, relying the analysis of the software reliability on provided state-machines may not be accurate. In our model, the system states are generated by the LTSA based on the precision of a model checker. Although scenarios are provided as a basis for the analysis, we explore the expressiveness of the given scenarios by checking if the existence of implied scenarios that could impact negatively during the system execution.

Path-based models [20, 27] compute the reliability of the system by enumerating possible execution paths of the program. The scenario-based method of Yacoub et al. [27] is perhaps closest in spirit to our own approach. In many ways their method is a hybrid approach in which a state-based model of the system is constructed from a scenario specification (a set of basic scenarios plus a graph representing the composition of basic scenarios), and then paths through the model are enumerated until a threshold execution time is reached along each path. Their approach reveals the pitfalls of using imprecise, coarse-grained behaviour models of system architecture. The model used in their approach is the *component dependence graph* (CDG), a state-machine model in which the states represent execution inside a particular component (with one state per component), and the transitions represent the transfer of control from one component to another (with a transition from one component to another representing a merge of all messages sent by the former to the latter in the scenarios). Because the representation of component behaviour in the CDG is at the level of whole components, it is an inherently sequential model of system behavior in which one component executes at a time, meaning that any concurrency inherent in the scenario specification is lost. Furthermore, a CDG can exhibit sequences of component transitions not found in the scenarios from which it is derived. In a sense such sequences are implied scenarios, but they arise not as an artefact of components having limited local knowledge of global behaviour. Instead, they are merely a consequence of modelling the system architecture imprecisely at the granularity of whole components rather than at the granularity of the component interactions specified in the scenarios. Finally, it can happen that a component in a CDG is represented by an absorbing state, even though the scenario specification itself is able to progress beyond any interactions with the "absorbing" component. Indeed, we attempted to model the Boiler Control system using the approach of Yacoub et al., with the result that the *Actuator* was an absorbing component from which we had to add transitions artificially to other components in order to construct a model that was able to progress to the final state.

In previous work we show how reliability engineering of component-based software systems can be carried out following a model-driven approach [17, 18]. It would be fair to say that the Unified Modeling Language (UML) has had a considerable influence to make viable model driven analysis approach such as [22], where design and analysis of software architecture can be specified, visualized, constructed and documented using one common notation. Since its first version, UML has been enriched in order to become more precise syntactically and semantically. The ultimate goal is to support automated or semi-automated transformation of design models to code, raising the level of abstraction at which automated code generation is applied. A major challenge for model-driven development will be finding ways of enforcing or preserving properties established early in development, particularly non-functional properties such as reliability predictions.

Other work can be situated in the area of a model-driven analysis technique: [12, 13, 4]. These approaches also propose a framework for automatic generation of reliability models from software specifications, bringing reliability analysis to early stages of the software lifecycle. István et al. [12, 13] shed some light on ways to fully automate dependability analysis, applied to the Fault-Tolerant

CORBA, using graph transformations into their VIATRA framework. The work from Singh et al. [21] provides a prediction algorithm to analyse the reliability of the system prior to its construction. Their approach requires the user to provide global behavior scenarios other than the local behavior of the components interactions. However, this feature may turn out to be unsuitable for the system modularity and therefore hindering systems maintainability.

6   Conclusion and Future Work

In this paper, we have presented a framework to quantitatively assess software reliability using scenario specifications, thus applicable to early phases of the software life cycle. Our major contribution lies on a reliability prediction technique that takes into account the component structure exhibited in the scenarios and the concurrent nature of component-based systems.

In the approach we present, we have extended scenario specification to model the probability of component *failure*, and *scenario transition probabilities* derived from an operational profile of the system. From the extended scenario specification, probabilisitic behaviour models were synthesised for each componenet and then composed in parallel into a model for the system. The Cheung model for software reliability was then used to compute a reliability prediction from the system behaviour model. The importance of implied scenarios detection in the software reliability analysis was then addressed so that the intended system behaviour could be enforced despite the local view of the components. We numerically showed how the detection of implied scenarios can improve the reliability assurance of the software system.

For future work, we will use our framework to enhance software system reliability using software architecture models. In doing this, we can use our framework for the purpose of model driven development to construct deployment profiles and generate implementation code configured to the desired reliability assurance for software systems. Another promising direction includes the use of the synthesized component LTS to predict component reliability. This may be useful when there are uncertainties associated with a component s operational profile coming out from lack of implementation artifacts. In Section 4 we presented initial evidence of how important is to consider implied scenarios when assessing provided scenario specifications for reliability. However, additional work is needed to explore methods and techniques that can fully reveal the effect of implied scenarios on system reliability. Finally, we plan to apply our approach on case studies of larger, more realistic systems in order to evaluate its scalability and the accuracy of the predictions it produces.

Acknowledgment

David Rosenblum holds a Wolfson Research Merit Award from the Royal Society. Sebastian Uchitel was partially funded by EPSRC grant READS GR/S03270/01 and Genaína Rodrigues was funded by CAPES, under grant number 108201-9.

We would like to thank Rami Bahsoon, Philip Cook and the anonymous referees for their helpful suggestions on improving the manuscript.

References

1. R. Alur, K. Etessami, and M. Yannakakis. Inference of message sequence charts. In *Proc. of the* 22nd *ICSE*, pages 304–313. ACM Press, 2000.
2. T. Ayles, A. Field, J. Magee, and A. Bennett. Adding performance evaluation to the LTSA tool (tool demonstration). In *Proc. 13th Performance Tools*, September 2003.
3. R. C. Cheung. A User-Oriented Software Reliability Model. In *IEEE Transactions on Software Engineering*, volume 6(2), pages 118–125. IEEE, Mar. 1980.
4. V. Cortellessa, H. Singh, and B. Cukic. Early reliability assessment of uml based software models. In *Proceedings of the* 3rd *WOSP*, pages 302–309. ACM Press, 2002.
5. P. R. D'Argenio, H. Hermanns, and J.-P. Katoen. On generative parallel composition. In C. Baier, M. Huth, M. Kwiatkowska, and M. Ryan, editors, *Electronic Notes in Theoretical Computer Science*, volume 22. Elsevier, 2000.
6. P. Frankl, R. Hamlet, B. Littlewood, and L. Strigini. Evaluating testing methods by delivered reliability. *IEEE Transactions on Software Engineering*, 24(8):586–601, 1998.
7. S. Gokhale, M. Lyu, and K. Trivedi. Reliability Simulation of Component Based Software Systems. In *Reliability Simulation of Component Based Sofware Systems*, pages 192–201. Proc. of the 9th ISSRE, 1998.
8. K. Goševa-Popstojanova and K. S. Trivedi. Architecture-Based Approach to Reliability Assessment of Software Systems. In *Performance Evaluation Journal*. Elsevier Science, 2001.
9. ITU. ITU-T Recommendation Z.120 Message Sequence Charts (MSC'99). Technical report, ITU Telecommunication Standardization Sector, Geneva, 1996.
10. M. R. Lyu. *Software Reliability Modeling*. World Scientific Publishing Company, 1991.
11. M. R. Lyu. *Handbook of Software Reliability Engineering*. IEEE Computer Society Press and McGraw-Hill, 1996.
12. I. Majzik and G. Huszerl. Towards dependability modeling of FT-CORBA architectures. In *Proc. 4th EDCC, Toulouse)*, pages 121–139. Springer–Verlag, 2002.
13. I. Majzik, A. Pataricza, and A. Bondavalli. Stochastic Dependability Analysis of System Architecture Based on UML Models. In R. de Lemos, C. Gacek, and A. Romanovsky, editors, *Architecting Dependable Systems, LNCS-2667*, pages 219–244. Springer Verlag, 2003.
14. J. D. Musa. Operational profiles in software-reliability engineering. *IEEE Softw.*, 10(2):14–32, 1993.
15. J. D. Musa, A. Iannino, and K. Okumoto. *Software reliability: measurement, prediction, application*. McGraw-Hill, Inc., 1987.
16. Object Management Group. Unified Modeling Language Specification version 2.0:Superstructure. Technical report, http://www.omg.org/docs/ptc/03-08-02.pdf, 2003.
17. G. Rodrigues. A Model Driven Approach for Software Systems Reliability. In *Proc. of the Doctoral Symposium of the* 26th *ICSE, May 2004 - Edinburgh, Scotland*. IEEE Computer Society, May 2004.

18. G. Rodrigues, G. Roberts, and W. Emmerich. Reliability Support for the Model Driven Architecture. In R. de Lemos, C. Gacek, and A. Romanovsky, editors, *To Appear in: Architecting Dependable Systems II –LNCS*. Springer Verlag, 2004.
19. R. Roshandel and N. Medvidovic. Toward Archtitecture-Based Reliability Estimation. In *ICSE/WADS 2004, Edinburgh, UK.*, pages 2–6. IEEE Computer Society, May 2003.
20. M. Shooman. Structural Models for Software Reliability Prediction. In *Proc. of the 2nd ICSE*, pages 268–280, 1976.
21. H. Singh, V. Cortellessa, B. Cukic, E. Gunel, and V. Bharadwaj. A bayesian approach to reliability prediction and assessment of component based systems. In *Proc. of the 12th IEEE ISSRE*, pages 12–21. IEEE, 2001.
22. J. Skene and W. Emmerich. A Model Driven Architecture Approach to Analysis of Non-Functional Properties of Software Architecture. In *Proc. of the 18th ASE. Toronto, CA*. IEEE Computer Society, Oct. 2001.
23. S. Uchitel, R. Chatley, J. Kramer, and J.Magee. LTSA-MSC: Tool Support for Behaviour Model Elaboration Using Implied Scenarios. In *Proc. of 9th TACAS, Warsaw*, Apr. 2003.
24. S. Uchitel, J. Kramer, and J.Magee. Synthesis on Behavioral Models from Scenarios. In *IEEE Transactions on Software Engineering*, volume 29(2), pages 99–115. IEEE, Feb. 2003.
25. S. Uchitel, J. Kramer, and J.Magee. Incremental Elaboration of Scenarios-Based Specifications and Behavior Models Using Implied Scenarios. In *ACM Transactions on Software Engineering and Methodologies*, volume 13(1), pages 37–85. ACM Press, Jan. 2004.
26. W. L. Wang, Y. Wu, and M. H. Chen. An Architecture-Based Software Reliability Model. In *Proc. Pacific Rim International Symposium on Dependable Computing. Washington, DC , USA*, pages 143–150. IEEE Computer Society, 1999.
27. S. M. Yacoub, B. Cukic, and H. H. Ammar. Scenario-Based Reliability Analysis of Component-Based Software. In *Proc. of the 10th ISSRE, Boca Raton, FL, USA*. IEEE, Nov. 1999.

Augmenting UML Models for Composition Conflict Analysis

Andreas Leicher and Jörn Guy Süß

Technische Universität Berlin, Germany,
Computergestützte InformationsSysteme (CIS)
{aleicher, jgsuess}@cs.tu-berlin.de

Abstract. Component reuse is inhibited by two factors: Lack of an adequate modeling representation of components and lack of a method to predict properties of a composition of application components. In this paper, we propose a framework for conflict identification. The framework is primarily based on a taxonomy describing communication and technology related properties. Conflict identification is based on inference rules. Furthermore, we aim to integrate conflict reasoning in the software development process. We will show that the Unified Modeling Language and the Resource Description Framework can be combined to provide a solution to the representation problems, without resorting to extension mechanisms, and without limiting to a specific component platform. As a real life example, we model the connection of an .Net Serviced Component to an Enterprise Java Bean as part of a mortgage bank's enterprise architecture and prove its viability.

1 Introduction

The advantages of buying a fitting component to provide a part of a solution over custom construction are long established [7]. The number of components we can consider to build a solution depends on the size of the market [14] from which we can buy the solution. Unfortunately, platform boundaries subdivide this market, because we can not evaluate if components of different technologies are compatible or not.

Each technology can be described by properties relevant for communication. We aim to support conflict analysis for middleware components based on such properties. We reuse an adapted version of the connector taxonomy proposed by Medvidovic/Mehta as this taxonomy provides more fine grained properties compared to other approaches. As this taxonomy is designed platform independently, we customized the taxonomy for particular middleware technologies. Based on this taxonomy, developers can estimate on the fly, how complicated a particular composition will be.

Furthermore, we aim to support component analysis in the context of the software design process. Design is often based on abstract models, that are represented by diagrams in a graphical notation like that of the UML. We perceive a method to quickly estimate component compatibility in the context of these tools valuable, because

M. Cerioli (Ed.): FASE 2005, LNCS 3442, pp. 127–140, 2005.

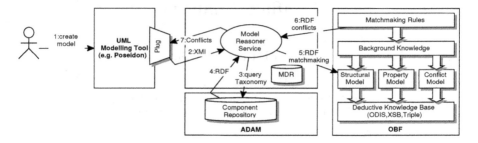

Fig. 1. Architecture of the Ontology-Based Framework

- developers can decide on the fly how complex a composition is.
- analysis can be carried out in the normal development process, without the need to transfer data into a specialized analysis tool.

While the metamodel of the UML is designed to accommodate object-oriented languages, it does not offer straightforward support for deductive logic, which we would need to draw conclusions about the compatibility of components.

We propose to attach only the necessary information about components to elements in a model, and then reason about this information externally against our domain-specific background knowledge. Our approach provides the ability to check that this additional meta-information fulfills structural constraints like type specifications, and thus guarantees the validity of input to services based on such information.

Figure 1 shows an overview of the overall process. Execution proceeds as follows: Within a UML tool - in this case Poseidon UML - we create a component model[1]. Components are annotated with the property information available. This includes properties describing the technologies as well as other properties that are known to the developer (see figure 2 for an example). We connect the components with an association and attach a comment which indicates to the service that this association is to be processed (1). Then we submit the model to the Model Reasoner Service embedded in EVE[2] [22] (2). The service extracts the annotations in the model and attaches itself to a repository designed to hold Analytical Data on Architectures and Models (ADAM). The service extracts the addressed part of the knowledge base (3/4) and passes it to the reasoner, combined with the information extracted from the model(5). The reasoner calculates the match and returns its characteristics to the service(6). The service embeds the resulting information in the model, attached to the association (7). If the result is a conflict, a conflict description is generated. If the result is a match, the service can fill in implied property information for each component, if desired by the user.

---

[1] In principle, this can be done either with UML 1.x or 2.0. However, most existing tools support only UML 1.x so that we use a profile to describe components.

[2] EVE is a framework to support tool independent manipulation of UML models.

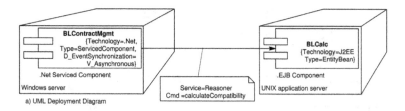

Fig. 2. Integrating two heterogeneous components, initial step

Example component annotations can be found in figure 2. Both components are part of a customer information system of a large European mortgage bank: the simulation of financial development for different forms of mortgage contracts, predicting expected savings for combinations of financial products. The system consists of two components, a management component which acts as a customer facade and a set of worker components, which provide the calculation. The calculation functionality ('BLCalc') is implemented in a piece of Java code originally developed for a standalone application. To share the functionality the code was encapsulated as an EntityBean component and deployed on a UNIX application server. The 'BLContractMgmt' Component was implemented as a .Net Serviced Component on a windows server.

The rest of the paper is structured as follows: In section 2 we discuss our platform independent framework for reasoning about component matches and its schema. Section 3 discusses the state of the art regarding background knowledge in UML diagrams and introduces our RDF-based solution. Section 4 summarizes the approach and widens the discussion to include other fields of application.

2   Conflict Identification for Component Composition

In this section, we first provide an overview of existing approaches to classify component-based systems as well as of approaches to identify conflicts. We then introduce our framework for conflict identification, explain the compatibility relationship used to identify conflicts and discuss some results obtained by analyzing our running example.

2.1   Existing Approaches

Architectural Styles were one of the early approaches in software architecture to classify systems. A style specifies the parts of a system as well as properties that need to be satisfied in a system configuration. Bass et. al. [2] define an architectural style as follows:

> By a particular style we mean a set of design rules that identify the kinds of components and connectors that may be used to compose a system or subsystem, together with local or global constraints on the way composition is done.

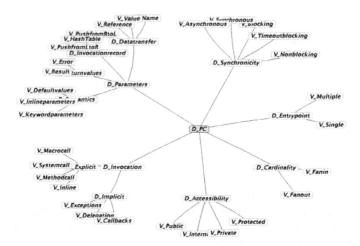

Fig. 3. Procedure Call: Starting from the Connector Type Procedure Call, including Dimensions and Values as defined by Mehta

One possible application area of styles is the classification of systems regarding the composition of their constituting parts. Shaw [19, 20] provides such a classification. A style is represented by a set of values that describe the kinds of components and connectors, the control and data flow as well as their interactions in a system. Another application area infers resulting properties of a particular style. A style, for example, is indicative of such aspects as system reconfiguration, component exchange, and component adaptation.

In general, an architectural style takes a kind of 'macro' view of a system. It describes 'coarse grained' properties that must hold for a whole system. These are helpful, if we investigate the system as a whole. However, only a few of these properties are relevant for deciding compatibility of single components. Unfortunately, the classification provided by Architectural Styles is not useful for analyzing middleware technologies such as CORBA, J2EE etc. These systems show almost no differences in the classification. Middleware systems aim for similar goals and are designed with similar architecture in mind.

Medvidovic/Mehta [15, 17, 16] propose a sophisticated taxonomy to describe communication properties of connectors. Part of this taxonomy, rendered by our ODIS tool [5] is shown in figure 3. It describes relevant properties for a procedure call. This taxonomy consists of eight connector types, each of which is described by several dimensions (complex properties) that consist of subdimensions and values. Each connector can provide four kinds of services: communication, coordination, conversion, and facilitation. Connectors in programming languages and middleware technologies can be described by deriving and extending the taxonomy.

The analysis of middleware technologies in the context of Mehta's connector taxonomy also reveals several problems: The terms used in the taxonomy are not explicitly defined. For a number of terms, a lot of different definitions are available. Some terms are ambiguous as different interpretations in the taxonomy can be chosen. For example Exceptions can refer to a method that throws

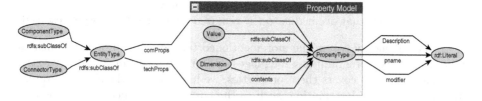

Fig. 4. The Property Model of the Framework

an exception or one that is activated because of an exception. The taxonomy describes connector types as part of the taxonomy. We feel that these types should not be included in the taxonomy, because connector types are the entities that are described by properties, but they themselves are not properties.

Other approaches aim to automatically discover mismatches based on conflicting characteristics [10, 9, 1, 12, 24, 16]. Most of these approaches concentrate on architectural mismatches. They do not handle technologies directly as well as structural and behavioral specifications. They can be classified in approaches using only a structure such as a table to describe properties [1, 16] and in approaches which additionally provide reasoning support [10, 9, 12]. Approaches providing reasoning support often only support a subset of properties available in the former category.

2.2   Property Model

To analyse the relationships of communication and technology related properties, we need to define a means of notation. Our property model shown in figure 4 defines a structure to create hierarchically connected properties. Each property is described as a feature that can either be optional or mandatory. A feature can contain several sub-features. Sub-features can be grouped by two operators 'xor' and 'or' to describe possible feature combinations. Furthermore, each feature can be associated with attributes (FeatureAttributes) to state additional requirements. 'EntityTypes' can be associated with 'Features' by two relationships: one to describe communication properties (comProps) and one to state technology related properties (techProps).

To organize the space of component properties, we decided to reuse the existing taxonomy by Medvidovic/Mehta, as it provides the most fine grained properties. Unfortunately, this taxonomy is designed on a platform independent level. Therefore, we needed to analyse platform specific connectors for middleware systems of interest. We modified the original taxonomy in the following way:

- Platform specific properties that describe communication in Java, Jini, J2EE and .Net were added.
- A modifier for conflict analysis was introduced. It describes whether a property is 'mandatory' or 'optional' in a given context.
- The meaning of properties was exactly defined: A definition is associated with every property.

- Connector types were removed from the taxonomy.
- Name clashes that occur due to the removed connector types were resolved.

A second taxonomy covers the aforementioned technological properties such as platforms (OSs), programming languages, etc. As we have not found any existing taxonomy that covers these properties, we have defined them from scratch. Technology-related information, such as the language, in which a component is written, platform availability or resulting cost provide additional information regarding the complexity of a connector. For example, it may describe if a composition of two components requires a distributed connector, or if they can be composed by a local connector. We do not detail this taxonomy in this paper, as it does not relevantly contribute to the topic at hand.

2.3   The Role of Communication Properties Regarding Composition

The communication taxonomy describes properties in the context of connector types. However, for our example, we also need to interpret communication properties in the context of component types.

If we represent each technology (EJB, ServicedComponents) by a middleware component, i.e. a binary artifact, each application component (BLCalc, BLContractMgmt) is bound via a precisely defined mechanism to that middleware and cannot be used independently. Figure 5 shows a typical mechanism that uses stub and skeleton objects to integrate components with respect to a particular middleware. Here, middleware plays a dual role: It is at the same time a connector that facilitates the communication and a component that can be physically deployed in an appropriate location.

Consequently, application components (BLCalc, BLContractMgmt) are restricted by the properties offered by their technologies. As we have described communication properties of EntityBeans and ServicedComponents [11], we are able to annotate application components (BLCalc, BLContractMgmt).

Regarding a composition, components are either the initiators of a communication or the receiver. Conflict identification needs to only consider the relevant properties for such a constellation. For example, an EntityBean is annotated with properties concerning data access to a underlying database. In a communication where the EntityBean is called by a client, however, these properties need not to be considered, because the client is not concerned with database issues.

Figure 6 shows the example components annotated with communication properties relevant for communication initiated by the 'BLContractMgmt' component.

2.4   Conflict Identification

We assume that the connector taxonomy as well as the taxonomy for technology related properties contain all relevant properties for communication. Component comparison is based on the comparison of annotated properties based on their type (either optional or mandatory). Two entities are compatible, if for all vertices they either require a property or do not support it. For example, two

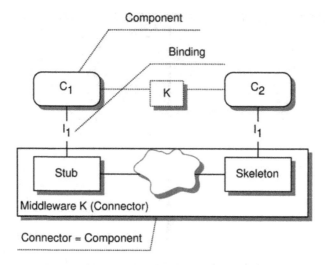

Fig. 5. Component Binding in Subject to the Underlying Middleware

components C_1 and C_2 are compatible, if the predicate $comp(C_1, C_2)$ evaluates to true:

$$\forall n \in \{C_1.r.comProps \cup C_1.r.techProps\}$$
$$isMandatoryFeature(n) \rightarrow$$
$$\exists m \in \{C_2.q.comProps \cup C_2.q.techProps\}. \tag{1}$$
$$n.fname = m.fname \wedge$$
$$isMandatoryFeature(m)$$

Unfortunately, this approach suffers several problems:

1. Often, it is difficult to decide if a property is required in a particular technology or not. Middleware specifications describe communication protocols coarse grained only. Lower level properties are often not or only partially described. Consequently, we need to deal with unknown properties.
2. Technologies support several communication mechanisms that may be used by application components, but are not compulsory. Consequently, we must distinguish between a property that is supported as an option or that is required (mandatory).

In response to these problems each feature can be described by one the following states:

Optional: The property can be supported by the component.
Unsupported: The component does not support this property.
Mandatory: The component requires this property for communication.

As a result, we get a compatibility matrix (shown in table 1) describing valid and invalid property combinations between the two components to be composed. We

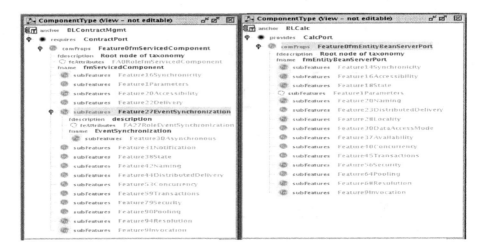

Fig. 6. View of the Communication Properties of the Example Components in Their Middleware Context

Table 1. Compatibility Matrix between two Components

Component vs. Component	mandatory	optional	unsupported
mandatory	√	w	f
optional	w	w	w
unsupported	f	w	√
w = warning			
f = failure			

distinguish conflicts of two categories: Failures are generated if properties definitely do not match, e.g. 'unsupported' vs. 'mandatory'. Warnings are generated due to 'optional' properties. For example, if 'BLCalc' is annotated with an 'optional' property it is unclear if it actually supports the property or not. Consequently, a warning needs to be generated. Optional properties are often annotated to connector types and middleware components such as the EntityBean component type. They describe the communication mechanism provided by a technology. These mechanisms may be used by application components but are not required.

To express conflict rules we require a logical formalism. As the component descriptions can be viewed as instances of a more general component schema, a formalism like F-Logic [13], which distinguishes between instance data and schema information (types/classes) would be advantageous.

Triple [21] satisfies these conditions. It is a language designed for reasoning in the semantic web. Triple states facts as quadruples (S,P,O,C): S for subject, the entity to be described. P is a predicate that states the relation of interest, O stands for an Object, which is either a Literal or another quadruple. C describes the context within which the tuple is valid. Thus, Triple facts are RDF statements extended by the 'context', which allows specifying views of an object in different contexts. This feature is extremely helpful, because it divides up fact bases into chunks that can be used as separate units.

In addition Triple provides two further advantages: It allows universal identification of resources through introduction of URIs. Section 3 shows how this can be applied. Also Triple allows the creation of new contexts on the fly by definition of mapping rules. We have applied this to transform a UML model containing platform independent components into different EJB component realizations. The concrete transformation is implicitly selected by requirements stated as parameters to the transformation rule[6].

Conflicts are generated by 'Triple' rules of the following kind:

```
forall ?c,?s,?f,?n,?pc,?ps unsupportedMandatoryFeatures(?c,?pc,?s,?ps,?f)<-
    getComFeatures(?c,?pc,?f) and
    hasOnlyMandatoryParentFeatures(?f) and
    getFeatureName(?f,?n) and
    isFeatureNotBound(?s,?ps,?n).

forall C,S,PC,PS @failure(C,S,PC,PS) {
    forall ?x, ?f, ?ns
        ?ns:?x[sys:directType->core:FeatureConflict;
            core:concerns->C;
            core:relates->S;
            core:concernsFeature->?ns:?f;
            core:cause->'Mandatory feature of client unsupported by server.']
    <-
        unsupportedMandatoryFeatures(C,PC,S,PS,?ns:?f)@core and
        concatConflict(?x,?f,'Failure').
}
```

The first rule identifies mismatched properties. The second rule (a mapping) generates conflict statements. These statements can be directly converted to plain RDF and handed back to the modeling tool.

2.5   Conflicts in the Example

Analysis of the example components yields several conflicts, part of them shown in figure 7. For example, a failure concerns Event support (Feature30Asynchronous). An EntityBean cannot handle events. These are covered by MessageBeans in J2EE. Furthermore, naming schemes (Feature21Structurebased, Feature22Hierarchical) are handled differently in both technologies: J2EE uses a structure based naming mechanism, .Net an attribute based scheme. Furthermore, a lot of warnings (not shown) are generated, because most property values are imported directly from the underlying component types (EntityBean and ServicedComponent). As discussed above these components are often 'optional'. So, it cannot be inferred that they actually match.

As shown in figure 1 conflicts are handed back to the EVE Service (6). The results are attached to the association (7) and presented to the developer. Conflicts

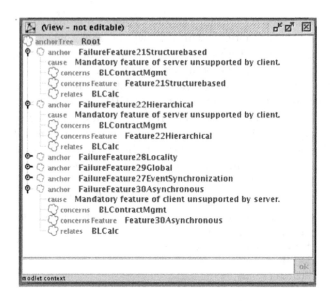

Fig. 7. Conflicts Generated by Comparing Both Components

need to be interpreted by a developer. She needs to select important properties and prune superfluous properties. In any case, it should be possible for a developer to infer, what is actually needed for composition and how this impacts on cost and resources.

3   Augmenting the UML with an Overlaid RDF Structure

In UML 1.x, external resources like files can only be represented as components and artifacts, which can only be used in component and deployment diagrams.To make statements about such external resources, an association is drawn from the element which is assigned the property to the artifact which represents the associated resource. These associations rarely appear in diagrams, because they cut across diagram types, making their practical application difficult. In addition, the choice of component types available is limited and the extension of that type space involves the creation of UML profiles. If only one profile is allowed under the version of UML in use, the modeler has to choose to either apply the profile she uses for her primary problem domain and drop detailed modeling of the types of background resources, or model the background resources in detail and drop the profile for the domain, or manually create a unified profile, which may lead to clashes between stereotype constraints. In any case, all the information which one merely wanted to attach has to be included in the model in a tedious way, because it involves substantial indirection: Information about the external resource is linked to a Model Element that is created solely to act as a placeholder for that type of metadata.

Even in today's UML 2.0, there is no simple mechanism to attach background knowledge to the model. Some case tools like Rational Rose work around this limitation by introducing links to other resources as a new type of Model Element residing in Packages next to other Model Elements. These link-based extensions, apart from being proprietary to the tool, have several disadvantages:

- The meaning of the resource that the link points to is only weakly defined. For example, if a link, which points to an HTML page about a Java library, resides in package "x", implications are unclear. It could mean that the library realizes package "x" or that the model relies on package "x" or that the author of this model used patterns described on the page to create the contents of that package.
- Links are also limited because they can only be directly attached to Packages and no other Model Elements. For example, to state that a Class acted in the role of a ConcreteCommand in the Command Pattern, one would need to create a link in the Package and additionally describe the relationship to that link on a Comment attached to the Class. Furthermore, such a Comment may be ignored when interpreting the model elsewhere, since a Comment "has no semantic force but may contain information useful to the modeler." [18–pp.2-28]

While the previously described extensions of plain UML are either tedious and problematic, like the creation of profiles for resource description, or unprecise like the use of unqualified package links, the extension mechanism offers the Tagged Value - a useful yet simple feature[18–pp. 2-68]: "An arbitrary property attached to the Model Element. The tag is the name of the property and the value is an arbitrary value. The interpretation of the Tagged Value is outside the scope of the UML metamodel." However, Tagged Values do not have any descriptive power with regards to outside resources. But this can be introduced by defining a convention describing how to link and type such resources. In fact, the definition of Tagged Values can be interpreted similarly to the representation of knowledge about resources in the Resource Description Framework (RDF) [23–3.11]: "The underlying structure of any expression in RDF is a collection of triples, each consisting of a subject, a predicate and an object. A set of such triples is called an RDF graph ... Each triple represents a statement of a relationship between the things denoted by the nodes that it links." So to join Tagged Values and RDF we only need a bijective function, which maps Tagged Values to RDF statements and vice versa.

In a nutshell, our approach involves the following steps: Assign a Tagged Value to each Model Element to be annotated. Choose its Name to be the Uniform Resource Identifier (URI)[3] of the properties' definition and the Value to be the URL of the resource. Extract the RDF. Query or reason in logic.

3.1   RDF Statements

The example in listing 1.1 shows how the .Net Calculation component is described as supporting asynchronous communication by linking it with an external resource via a semantically well-defined relationship. This relationship is expressed by an RDF triple which describes a Tagged Value. The parts of the triple are the equivalent of a sentence with subject, predicate and object. The grammatical elements are:

Subject. There is a Component named "BLContractMgmt" which resides in the UML model in a Package named "Business Apps".

Predicate. It can be described in terms of event synchronization support, as defined in the core of the .Net Serviced Component Taxonomy of the CIS group.

Object. From the different choices on event synchronization, it does only support asynchronous message transfer.

Listing 1.1. An RDF description of a component's transaction capability

```
1 (S)  <.#Business%20Apps::BLContractMgmt>
2 (P)  <http://cis.cs.tu-berlin.de/picm/core/
        ServicedComponent#EventSynchronization>
3 (O)  <http://cis.cs.tu-berlin.de/picm/core/
        ServicedComponent#Asynchronous> .
```

Listing 1.1 might require some explanation: The statement is written in a simple RDF-equivalent notation called N3 [4]. Each element is a URI. Primarily these serve to identify resources for the purpose of retrieval. In that role they function as a Uniform Resource Locator (URL) as can be seen in line one: The subject of the description, which is the "BLContractMgmt" component, can be accessed by navigating into the Namespace element called "Business Apps" to the Model Element called "BLContractMgmt" within the current document.

Thus, to use this approach to describe an organization's own concepts it has to decide on the types of properties it would like to apply to its models. Then URIs, keyed off of the organizations Internet domain name, can be assigned to represent the desired properties[3].

3.2   Extraction of RDF Statements from Tagged Values

The extraction service follows this algorithm: Extract each model element, and see if any Tagged Values exist. If so, convert its name into a URI as follows: Take as root the relative or absolute URL, describing the location of the model file. Append as path the model-internal path based on the Namespace of the Model Element. Append the name of the Model Element. This results in unique URIs because of the scoping of Model Elements within Namespaces[18–pp. 2-38]: "The pathname of Namespace or ModelElement names starting from the root package provides a unique designation for every ModelElement." The model element forms the subject of the RDF statement. The predicate is the name of the associated tagged value. The object is the value of the tagged value. As a result, RDF statements as defined in section 3.1 are created.

---

[3] Please note that a URI must not link to a web representation. It is a concept used to uniquely identify resources.

Our implementation of extraction is a JMI-based service which uses the Jena[8] framework. We call that service 'Fringe' because it extracts information pointing from the fringes of the UML model to external resources, rather than at structures within the model.

4 Conclusion

This paper has discussed a framework based on a connector taxonomy to enable an adequate modeling representation of components and provide a method to discover conflicts in compositions of those components. The framework is based on a taxonomy by Mehta. It describes communication and technology related properties and provides conflict identification based on inference rules. We have discussed how to integrate such conflict reasoning into the software development process. To this end, we have shown how the Unified Modeling Language and the Resource Description Framework can be combined via Tagged Values to provide a solution to representation problems, without resorting to extension mechanisms, and without limiting to a specific component platform. As a real life example, we have modeled the connection of a .Net Serviced Component to an Enterprise Java Bean in UML and identified inherent conflicts using the Triple-based framework.

We plan to augment the conflict reasoning framework to suggest solutions to conflicts based on existing connectors that are registered in our knowledge base. Furthermore, type checks and behavior checks are to be integrated with the matchmaking process.

References

1. Robert Allen and David Garlan. A formal basis for architectural connection. *ACM Transactions on Software Engineering and Methodology (TOSEM)*, 6(3):213–249, 1997.
2. Len Bass, Paul Clements, and Rick Kazman. *Software Architecture in Practice*. Software Engineering Institute. Addison-Wesley, 1998. ISBN 0-201-19930-0.
3. T. Berners-Lee, R. Fielding, and L. Masinter. RFC 2396: Uniform Resource Identifiers (URI): Generic syntax, 1998. Status: DRAFT STANDARD.
4. Tim Berners-Lee. Notation 3 - ideas about web architecture, 2001. `http://www.w3.org/DesignIssues/Notation3.html`.
5. Andreas Billig. ODIS - Ein Domänenrepository auf der Basis von Semantic Web Technologien. In *Tagungsband der Berliner XML Tage*. XML-Clearinghouse, 2003. english version: http://www.isst.fhg.de/~abillig/Odis/xsw2003.
6. Andreas Billig, Susanne Busse, Andreas Leicher, and Jrn Guy S. Platform independent model transformation based on triple. Middleware 2004, October 2004.
7. Jr. Frederic P. Brooks. *The Mythical Man Month*. ISBN: 0-201-83595-9, anniversary edition, 1995.
8. Jeremy J. Carroll, Ian Dickinson, Chris Dollin, Dave Reynolds, Andy Seaborne, and Kevin Wilkinson. Jena: Implementing the semantic web recommendations. Technical Report HPL-2003-146, Hewlett Packard Laboratories, 24 2003.

9. L. Davis, D. Flagg, R. Gamble, and C. Karatas. Classifying interoperability conflicts. In T. Weng H. Erdogmus, editor, *COTS-Based Software Systems: Second International Conference, ICCBSS 2003 Ottawa, Canada*, number 2580 in LNCS, pages 62–71. SPRINGER, 2003.

10. L. Davis, R. Gamble, and J. Payton. The impact of component architectures on interoperability. *Journal of Systems and Software*, 61(1):31–45, 2002. based on the Technical Report UTULSA-MCS-99-30.

11. Jan Gädicke. Metadatengestützte analyse der kommunikationsfähigkeit von enterprise java beans und .net. Master's thesis, TU Berlin, 2004. german.

12. A. Kelkar and R.F. Gamble. Understanding the architectural characteristics behind middleware choices. In *1st International Conference in Information Reuse and Integration, 1999.*, 1999.

13. M. Kifer, G. Lausen, and J. Wu. Logical foundations of object-oriented and frame-based languages. *Journal of the ACM*, 42:741–843, Juli 1995.

14. M.D. McIlroy. Mass produced software components. In P.Naur and B. Randel, editors, *NATO Conference on Software Engineering*. NATO Science Commitee, Oktober 1968.

15. Nikunj R. Mehta. Software connectors: A taxonomy approach. In *Workshop on Evaluating Software Architectural Solutions 2000*. Institute for Software Research University of California, Irvine, 2000.

16. Nikunj R. Mehta and Nenad Medvidovic. Understanding software connector compatibilites using a connector taxonomy. In *In Proceedings of First Workshop on Software Design and Architecture (SoDA02), Bangalore, India*, December 2002.

17. Nikunj R. Mehta, Nenad Medvidovic, and Sandeep Phadke. Towards a taxonomy of software connectors. In *Proceedings of the 22nd international conference on Software engineering*, pages 178–187, 2000.

18. Object Management Group (OMG). *Unified Modeling Language Specification, Version 1.3*, March 2000. http://cgi.omg.org/docs/formal/00-03-01.pdf.

19. Mary Shaw and Paul C. Clements. A field guide to boxology: Preliminary classification of architectural styles for software systems. In *Proceedings of the 21st International Computer Software and Applications Conference*, pages 6–13. IEEE Computer Society, 1997.

20. Mary Shaw and David Garlan. *Software Architecture: Perspectives on an Emerging Discipline*. PH, April 1996. ISBN 0131829572.

21. Michael Sintek and Stefan Decker. TRIPLE - A Query, Inference, and Transformation Language for the Semantic Web. In *Proceedings of International Semantic Web Conference ISWC 2002*. Lecture Notes in Computer Science, Bd. 2342, Springer, 2002.

22. Jörn Guy Süß, Andreas Leicher, Herbert Weber, and Ralf-D. Kutsche. Model-centric engineering with the evolution and validation environment. In Perdita Stevens, Jon Whittle, and Grady Booch, editors, *UML 2003 - The Unified Modeling Language: Modeling Languages and Applications, 6th International Conference, San Francisco, CA, USA*, volume 2863 of *LNCS*, pages 31 – 43. Springer, 2003.

23. World Wide Web Consortium. *Resource Description Framework (RDF) Model and Syntax Specification*, 1999. statut : W3C Recommandation, errata REC-rdf-syntax-19990222 , http://www.w3.org/TR/REC-rdf-syntax/.

24. Daniil Yakimovich, James M. Bieman, and Victor R. Basili. Software architecture classification for estimating the cost of cots integration. In *Proceedings of the 21st international conference on Software engineering*, pages 296–302. IEEE Computer Society Press, 1999.

A Tool to Automate Component Clustering and Identification[1]

Soo Ho Chang, Man Jib Han, and Soo Dong Kim

Department of Computer Science,
Soongsil University,
1-1 Sangdo-Dong, Dongjak-Ku, Seoul, Korea 156-743
{shchang, mjhan}@otlab.ssu.ac.kr
sdkim@comp.ssu.ac.kr

Abstract. It is a key activity in CBD to identify high-quality components which have high cohesion and low coupling. However, component clustering is carried out in manual fashion by developers, resulting excessive time consumption and generating errors. In this article, we present an implementation of a tool which automates a component clustering and identification method. We show how we realize a clustering method as a tool and explain techniques applied in the implementation. Using the tool, component identification can be automated, and one can generate and navigate multiple configurations to find the most appropriate one for the project effortlessly.

1 Introduction

Component-based development (CBD) has been widely accepted as one of the representative reuse development paradigm. A component is a basic unit for reuse and provides a relatively coarse-grained functionality. A component typically consists of several related objects which collaborate to carry out system operations. Hence it is a key activity in CBD to identify high-quality components which have high cohesion and low coupling[1][2].

Several methods for identifying components have been proposed, but the manual application of the methods by developers is time-consuming and prone to generate errors. Hence, it is desirable to have tools to automate the process of the methods.

In this article, we present an implementation of a tool which automates a component clustering and identification method. We show how we modified the method for the purpose of realizing in a tool and key techniques applied in the implementation.

2 A Method for Clustering Component

The method that we chose for our implementation is known as one of the systematic methods with guidelines [3], and it consists of four steps as in figure 1. This method

[1] This work was supported by Korea Research Foundation Grant. (KRF-2004-005-D00172)

M. Cerioli (Ed.): FASE 2005, LNCS 3442, pp. 141–144, 2005.

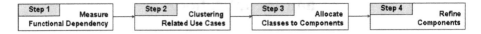

Fig. 1. The Overall Process

assumes that the fundamental artifacts of object-oriented modeling such as use case model, object model and dynamic model are available.

In this method, three types of relationships are considered for identifying components. In steps 1 and 2, functional dependency between use cases is used as the fundamental means to cluster related functions. The dependencies are measured with four criteria in step1 and related use cases are clustered in step 2. In step 3, functionality-to-data relationships expressed in a dynamic model such as sequence diagram are taken to assign related classes to candidate components. In step 4, dependency or coupling between classes is used to verify and refine the identified components. If there are two closely related classes which are separated into two components, it is identified and refined in this step

3   Implementation of the Tool

We develop the tool on Visual Studio .NET framework using C# language and MS Office Access. Hence, the tool runs on .NET framework with Office Access database installed. We applied a simplified version of object-oriented method. The tool has four modules, shown with «subsystem» stereotype in Figure 2; *Initializer*, *Configurator*, *Custerer*, and *Navigator*.

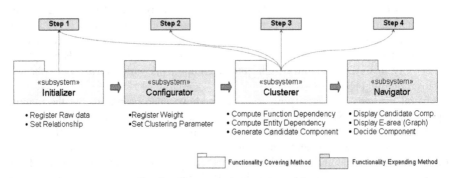

Fig. 2. Method and Subsystems of Tool

Initializer and *Clusterer* directly cover steps of the method, and *Configurator* and *Navigator* support additional functionalities for clustering in various conditions.

The *Initializer* module implements the step 1 of the method. It is to gather raw data needed for clustering; actors, use cases, classes, and to set the relationships among them. The *Configurator* module extends the step 1 with a functionality to register weight values for the metrics computing functional dependency (FD) and entity dependency (ED) and to set various parameters for resolving clustering conflicts.

The *Clusterer* module is to compute FD and ED, to cluster use cases into candidate components, and to assign classes into the components. Conflict occurrence during automatic clustering is a common problem, and we use the following algorithm to resolve the conflicts mechanically.

...
// Classify conflict use case and duplicated use cases
For all use cases UC_i
    Search conflict components for a use case.
        If the number of conflict components >=
                            numOfConf then
        conflictUC.usecaseList = UC_j
        conflictUC.conflictComponentsList =
                        conflict components.
 	
        add conflictUCList(conflictUC)
    Else if the number of conflict components
                                > 1 then
        duplicatedUC.usecase = UC_j
        duplicatedUC.conflictComponentsList
                        = conflict components.
	add duplicatedUCList(duplicatedUC).
	        End if
	Loop
	// Discard subset of conflict component list.
	..
	// Make new component from conflict component list
	.
	..
	// Assign duplicated use case
	For i = 1 to duplicatedUCList.cnt
	    // Form resolving use case conflict
	    // for In-house Component
	    AssignConflictUsecase(duplicateUCList[i].usecase,
	                    duplicateUCList[i].candiateComponentList)
	    Loop

The *Navigator* module is to display multiple configurations of component set, and to let the user browse them and select the most appropriate configuration. The module computes and displays various measures about multiple component sets, so that users can made more logical decisions based on these measures.

4   Case Study with Rental Management

The rental management system is for managing rental operations in various rental-related businesses such as library, movie rental, and car rental. There is a good degree of commonality among these applications, and we were able to identify several components for this commonality.Our object-oriented analysis model only for entity layer includes 33 use cases and 6 entity classes. Figure 3 is a snapshot of *Initializer* showing the raw data of these use cases and classes entered.

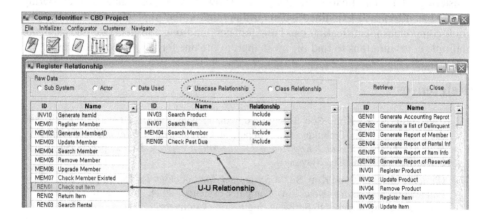

Fig. 3. Initialization

After *Configurator* gets parameters for resolving conflicts, *Cluster* computes automatically FD and ED and derives candidate components, as shown on the left-hand side of figure 4. The tool generates multiple configurations of component sets. Finally, the Navigator plots *economic area graph*s as shown in figure 4. It shows two relationships; one between the number of components and the value of 't' threshold, and the other between the granularity of components and the value of 't'. Using this information, user chooses a component set that best satisfies the requirement.

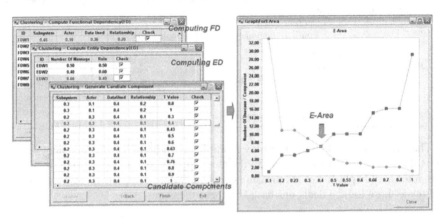

Fig. 4. Computation by *Clusterer* and Analysis by *Navigator*

5 Concluding Remarks

It is an essential activity in CBD to identify high-quality components which have high cohesion and low coupling. However, component clustering is carried out in manual fashion by developers, resulting excessive time consumption and generating errors. In this article, we presented an implementation of a tool which automates a component clustering and identification method. We showed how we realized a clustering method as a tool and explained techniques applied in the implementation. Using the tool, component identification can be automated, and one can generate and navigate multiple configurations to find the most appropriate one for the project effortlessly.

References

[1] Cho, Eun Sook, Kim, Soo Dong, and, Rhew, Sung Yul, "Domain Analysis and Preliminary Design Technique for Component Development", *International Journal of Software Engineering and Knowledge Engineering*, Vol. 14, No. 2, p.221-254, World Scientific Publishing Co., May 2004

[2] Choi, S., Chang, S., and Kim, S., "A Systematic Methodology for Developing Component Frameworks," Lecture Notes in Computer Science 2984, Proceedings of the 7th Fundamental Approaches to Software Engineering Conference, 2004

[3] Kim, S., Chang, S., "A Systematic Method to Identify Software Components," Proceedings of APSEC 2004, Nov. 2004.

Managing Variability Using Heterogeneous Feature Variation Patterns

Imed Hammouda, Juha Hautamäki, Mika Pussinen,
and Kai Koskimies

Institute of Software Systems, Tampere University of Technology,
P.O.BOX 553, FIN-33101 Tampere, Finland
{firstname.lastname, juha.o.hautamaki}@tut.fi

Abstract. Feature-driven variability is viewed as an instance of multi-dimensional separation of concerns. We argue that feature variation concerns can be presented as pattern-like entities - called feature variation patterns - cross-cutting heterogeneous artifacts. We show that a feature variation pattern, covering a wide range of artifact types from a feature model to implementation, can be used to manage feature-driven variability in a software development process. A prototype tool environment has been developed to demonstrate the idea, supporting the specification and use of heterogeneous feature variation patterns. We illustrate the idea with a small example taken from J2EE, and further study the practical applicability of the approach in an industrial product-line.

1   Introduction

The software engineering community is becoming increasingly aware of the nature of software systems as multi-dimensionally structured collections of artifacts: no single structuring principle can cover all the possible concerns of the stakeholders of a software system. This observation has far-reaching implications on how we construct, understand and manage software systems. Multi-dimensional approaches to software engineering have been the target of active research for a long time [1, 2, 3].

In the context of software product-lines [4, 5], one of the central concerns is variability management. The aim of variability management is to change, customize or configure a software system for use in a particular context [6]. In feature-driven variability management, variations of software products are expressed in terms of feature models (e.g. [7]). Selections of certain variants in a feature model are reflected in the design and implementation of the resulting product. Thus, a feature and its variation points constitute a slice of the entire system, cross-cutting various system artifacts ranging from feature models to implementation. Although variability management has been recognized as one of the key issues of software product-lines, its tool support lacks systematic approaches: most tools used in the industry are specific to a particular domain or product-line platform. Typically, automated support for variability management

M. Cerioli (Ed.): FASE 2005, LNCS 3442, pp. 145–159, 2005.

is based on product specifications given in, say, XML, used to generate the actual product by a proprietary tool.

A particular challenge for more systematic tool support for variability management is the fact that variability concerns span different kinds of artifacts and different phases of the development process. Even if we forget informal documents, the artifacts involved in variability concerns may include formal requirement specifications, design models, Java source files, XML files, scripts, make files, etc. The languages these artifacts are expressed in vary from graphical notations like UML [8] to various textual languages. Within UML, so-called profiles can be further used to create specialized modeling languages as extensions of UML for various purposes. Thus, we need a tool concept for variability concerns which is easily adapted to any reasonable artifact format.

In our previous work [9, 10, 11, 12] we have studied how a generic pattern concept can be used as a basis of tool support for various cross-cutting concerns like framework's specialization interfaces, maintenance concerns, and comprehension concerns within artifacts of a particular kind (e.g. UML design models or Java source code files). Here the term pattern [1] refers to a specification of a collection of related software entities capturing a concern in a software system; a pattern consists of roles which are bound to the concrete entities.

In this paper we generalize the pattern concept to allow multiple artifact types within the same pattern, thus satisfying the needs of feature variation patterns. We argue that the pattern concept is particularly amenable to present such heterogeneous patterns, since the basic pattern mechanisms are independent of the representation format of the artifacts, as long as there is a way to bind certain elements appearing in the artifacts to the roles of the pattern. This is in contrast to traditional aspects [13] which are presented using language-dependent mechanisms. The main contributions of this paper are the following:

- An approach to provide tool support for representing concerns within heterogeneous artifact types covering different phases of the development process
- The concept of a feature variation pattern as a model for tool-supported feature-driven variability management
- A prototype tool environment allowing the specification and use of feature variation patterns, together with early experiments

We proceed as follows. In the next section we briefly sketch the main idea. In Section 3, we explain the basic structuring device our approach is based on, the pattern concept. In Section 4, we give an overview of our current prototype environment supporting heterogeneous patterns. In Section 5, we illustrate our approach with an example concerning feature variation management in the J2EE environment. In Section 6, we present a small case study where we have applied the idea of feature variation patterns to a product-line provided by our industrial partner. Related areas in software engineering are discussed in Section 7. Finally, we summarize our work in Section 8.

---

[1] Our pattern concept has little to do with, say, design patterns: a pattern is a low-level mechanism that can be used to represent a design pattern or some other concern.

2   Basic Idea

We propose that feature variability can be managed using an artifact-neutral structuring device, a feature variation pattern. We will explain the pattern concept in more detail in the next section. Basically, a pattern consists of roles which are bound to actual system elements located in various artifacts; the pattern defines the required relationships between the elements bound to its roles. A feature variation pattern collects together elements relevant for realizing the anticipated variability of a feature across multiple artifacts. Ranging from requirements descriptions to actual implementation, these artifacts may be created in different phases of the software development process, and manipulated by different tools.

A single tool is used to manage the patterns, communicating with artifact-specific tools through their APIs. The existence of a feature variation pattern makes it possible for the tool to guide the product developer in exploiting the variability provided by a product-line platform, to assist in the generation of product-specific parts of the system, to make sure that the product has been developed according to the assumptions of the platform, to trace design-level variability support back to requirements, and to extract a system slice representing a single feature variation concern. This paper focuses on the two first issues. The general idea of the tool concept is illustrated in Figure 1.

Our approach is conservative in the sense that we do not make assumptions about languages or design methods: the only thing we assume is that the tools used to process the relevant system artifacts offer an API which allows the pattern tool to access the elements of those artifacts and to catch certain events (e.g. when an artifact has been modified). This assumption holds for many modern tools; in this work we have used Rational Rose for UML models and Eclipse for Java and XML. The artifacts can be freely edited through their dedicated tools: if an artifact is modified, the worst that can happen is that some bindings in an existing pattern become invalid or certain constraints defined by the pattern are violated. In this case, the pattern tool warns the developer about the inconsistencies and proposes corrective actions. It is then up to the developer to either correct the situation or ignore the warning. A prototype tool environment is presented in more detail in Section 4.

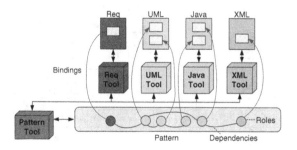

Fig. 1. The pattern-based approach to managing feature variability

3   Patterns

We view a feature variation pattern as an organized collection of software elements capturing any concern in a software system related to the variation of a particular feature. The target system could be a software product-line, or a single product with anticipated needs for feature variation.

Figure 2 depicts a conceptual model in UML for (feature variation) patterns. A pattern is a collection of hierarchically organized *roles*. A pattern is instantiated in a particular context by binding the roles to certain elements of concrete artifacts. Each role can be associated with a set of *constraints* expressing conditions that must be satisfied by the element bound to a role.

Artifacts contain models which can be expressed in different notations following well-defined metamodels. Here we regard any formal presentation describing some system properties as a model, including, say, UML models and source code. A metamodel is assumed to define a containment relationship between the model elements. In any binding, the containment relationships of the bound elements must respect the hierarchy of the roles.

The metamodels of the notations used in a model define properties for the model elements that can be checked by constraints. Constraints may refer to the elements bound to other roles, implying *dependencies* between the roles. For example, in a pattern which covers UML models, a constraint of an association role may require that the association bound to this role must appear between the classes bound to certain class roles, thus implying a dependency from the association role to the two class roles.

A role is associated with a *type*, which determines the kind of model elements that can be bound to the role. A role type typically corresponds to a metaclass in the metamodel of a given notation. As indicated in the lower part of Figure 2, a pattern can be associated with multiple sets of role types (for example UML, Java, etc). Each set groups together related role types. For example, there is a set

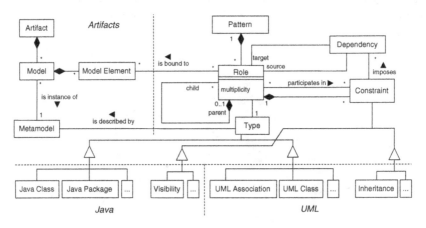

Fig. 2. Conceptual model for feature variation patterns

of role types for representing UML model elements. In this paper, we use patterns with role types covering a subset of UML (for representing feature models and design models), Java (for representing the actual implementation), and general text (for representing deployment descriptors). Each set of role types can be associated with specialized constraints applicable only for the roles in that set. For example, a Visibility constraint checks the visibility option of classes and their members in Java.

A *multiplicity* is defined for each role. The multiplicity of a role gives the lower and upper limits for the number of elements playing the role in an instantiation of the pattern. For example, if a class role has multiplicity [0..1], the class is optional in the pattern, because the lower limit is 0.

4   A Prototype Environment - MADE

Our experimental environment supporting feature variability management is the result of the integration of several existing tools. Eclipse [14] is used as a platform for JavaFrames [9] that implements the previously described generic pattern concept for Java role types. Eclipse acts also as a Java IDE in our work. The pattern engine of JavaFrames has been lately exploited in the MADE tool for creating a pattern-driven UML modeling environment [12]. This has been done by adding UML specific role types and integrating the resulting UML pattern tool with Rational Rose [15]. We have further extended the pattern tool with simple text file role types, allowing text files or their tagged elements to be bound to the roles as well. Thus, we can bind the roles to, say, XML files or items.

The MADE tool transforms a partially bound pattern into a task list. This is done by generating a task for each unbound role that can be bound in the current situation, taking into account the dependencies and multiplicities of roles. By performing a task, the designer effectively binds a role to an element. In order to use patterns as a generative mechanism (as in this paper), a *default element* can be defined for every role. If a role with a default element specification is to be bound during the pattern instantiation process, the binding can be carried out by first generating the default element according to the specification, and then binding the role to this element. The pattern engine updates the task list after a task has been performed, usually creating new tasks. When updating the task list, the pattern engine also checks that the constraints of the roles are satisfied, and generates corrective tasks if this is not the case.

A main principle in the design of our environment has been avoiding any kind of compulsive working mode of the designer. The existence of patterns does not prevent normal editing of, say, UML models or Java code; the purpose of the patterns is to offer additional support rather than a strait-jacket. If some constraint of a pattern bound to an element (or the binding itself) is broken as a result of an editing action, the tool generates immediately a new task to repair the broken constraint or rebind the role. In many cases the tool can even offer an automated repairing option.

5   Illustrative Example: Managing Persistence in J2EE

We illustrate the idea of feature variation patterns with a simple J2EE application. A typical J2EE application makes use of a persistent data storage which can be realized by different database products. We assume that the developers of the application want to make it easy to select the most suitable database solution for different customers. Thus, the possible variations of the database solution are specified in the feature model, and the design is given in such a way that all the desired variations can be easily achieved.

Assuming bean-managed persistence, the bean should be able to decide for optimization reasons which data source implementation to use. After the right implementation has been established, the bean can rely on a standard interface (DAO, Data Access Object) implemented by all the different data sources. There are two common solutions to select a data source implementation. The first is to hardcode the name of the implementation class in a specific method in the bean. When the data source changes, the implementation of that method should be changed so that it would return the proper implementation class. Another solution is to store the name of the implementation class in the deployment descriptor of the bean, as an environment variable. The bean decides at run-time which data source to use by looking up the value of this environment variable.

In both techniques, either the Java code or the deployment descriptor should change according to the data source selected. However, even if the developer decides to hardcode the implementation class in the bean code, storing the information of the used data source in the deployment descriptor might serve other purposes such as application documentation. In addition, the design model of the application should change in the sense that a class corresponding to the selected data source is added to the model filling the variation point.

5.1   Representing Database Selection as a Feature Variation Pattern

The above situation can be described using a feature variation pattern. The pattern has roles representing concrete elements at four abstraction levels: feature model, design model, Java source code, and deployment descriptor (XML). The pattern is given using a dedicated editor in MADE; however, we illustrate the pattern in Figure 3 with a dependency graph. The four different artifact types are represented by circular shapes. Roles are denoted by rounded rectangles, with role type marks (<<role type>>). Prebound roles are shaded. Role dependencies are drawn as broken arrows, while containment relationships are presented with diamond edges.

In the feature model part, there is a role named 'ConcreteDatasource'. This role represents the data source variant to be used. In the design model part, the UML class role named 'BeanDAOImplementation' stands for the model element indicating the proper DAO implementation. This role should be bound to a UML class in the application design model. Role 'Implementation' is used to reflect the data source decision at the code level. This role should be bound to a Java

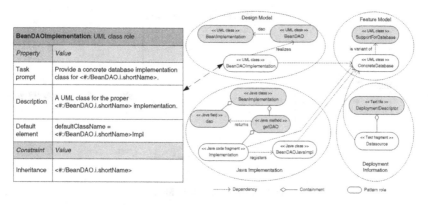

Fig. 3. Pattern role diagram

code fragment that specifies the proper DAO Java implementation. Furthermore, there is a role for storing the data source decision in the deployment descriptor of the bean. This role is named 'Datasource' and should be bound to a text fragment providing the right descriptor XML tags. All these roles depend on the database variant and are bound during the specialization process.

In addition to these roles, the pattern defines prebound roles specifying the context of the above roles. The 'DeploymentDescriptor' role, for instance, is bound to the deployment descriptor file where the generated XML text fragment should be inserted. Similarly, the Java class role 'BeanImplementation' represents the bean implementation class where the concrete DAO implementation should be registered.

There is a dependency from the four roles 'Datasource', 'Implementation', 'BeanDAOJavaImpl', and 'BeanDAOImplementation' to 'ConcreteDatasource' since the concrete elements bound to these four roles depend on the chosen data source implementation. The pattern tool generates the tasks following the partial order defined by the dependency relationships of the roles.

The actual pattern specification defines a set of tool-related properties for each role such as the task prompt, an informal description of the task (shown to the user together with the task prompt), and the possible default element generated prior to binding. The table in Figure 3 illustrates how these properties of the roles are specified in MADE. The table presents the properties of role 'BeanDAOImplementation'. Note that the specifications refer to the names of the elements bound to other roles using the $< \# : ... >$ notation, an expression of a simple scripting language used in our tool.

Due to such references, the values of these textual properties of the role are adapted to the current binding situation; for example, the task prompt and task description always use the application-specific names. In this case the default element is a template for the UML class of the proper DAO implementation. The template gives the name of the DAO implementation class and refers to the concrete name of the DAO class. In addition to role properties, the table in Figure 3 includes an example inheritance constraint which is used to check the

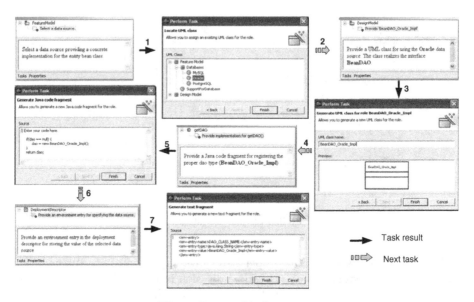

Fig. 4. Pattern binding steps

generalization/specialization relationship between the UML class bound to role 'BeanDAOImplementation' and the UML class bound to role 'BeanDAO'.

5.2   Using the Pattern

Figure 4 shows a scenario for applying the pattern. The MADE tool transforms an unbound role into a task, shown as a textual prompt. The execution of the task results in binding the role. The figure includes four tasks and their outcome.

The scenario starts from the left upper corner. First, a task prompt asks the user to select the data source to be used. The user is shown the list of available data sources: MySQL, Oracle, and PostgreSQL (1). The user decides to use the Oracle database. Next, a new task for providing a UML class named 'Bean-DAO_Oracle_Impl' is shown (2). The UML class stands for the implementation class of the DAO interface. Note that the environment adapts the task description to the context of the user: the selected database name 'Oracle' is used in the default name of the UML class (3). The next task is to register the DAO Java implementation class to be used by the bean (4). A Java code fragment is then generated (5). The code creates a new instance of class 'BeanDAO_Oracle_Impl' and assigns it to the bean field holding the DAO object. Finally, the last task is to store the name of the DAO implementation class in the deployment descriptor of the bean (6). For this purpose, a new environment entry 'DAO_CLASS_NAME' is generated. The value of the entry is 'BeanDAO_Oracle_Impl' (7).

Figure 5 shows an overall view of our environment after the tasks described above have been carried out. In the upper half of the screen, Rose displays the feature model (on the left) and the design model (on the right) as UML class diagrams. In the lower half of the screen, the Eclipse Java environment displays

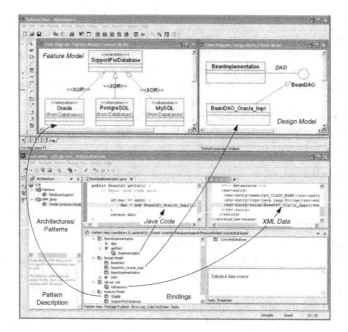

Fig. 5. A prototype environment

two textual editors (above) and the integrated pattern tool (below). The latter is further divided into three panes: the pattern view showing the roles in a containment tree (left), the task view (upper) and the instruction view (lower). The textual editors are for Java code and for XML.

When a pattern is selected in the pattern view, the task view displays the tasks generated by that pattern. In Figure 5, however, no doable tasks are shown since the pattern is fully bound. Instead, the view reveals a description of a task (data source selection) that has already been carried out. The outcome of every performed task can be retrieved in this way at any time. The bindings, visualized with the arrows in Figure 5, show how a pattern acts as a connecting artifact between different model levels.

6   Case Study - Nokia GUI Platform

6.1   Target System

Nokia produces a family of NMS (Network Management System) and EM (Element Manager) applications, which are software systems used to manage networks and network elements. For this purpose, the company has developed a Java GUI (Graphical User Interface) platform to support the implementation of the GUI parts for the variants of this product family. The platform is used as an object-oriented Java framework, in which the application is created by deriving new subclasses and by using the components and services of the framework.

The platform provides a number of services useful for GUI applications. There are services for system logging, online help, user authentication, product internationalization, clipboard usage, CORBA-based communication, and licensing. Depending on the environment used, each service may have different implementations. Applications, built on top of the GUI platform, get a reference to the proper service implementation from a registry file. It is essential that product developers register the right service implementation. Due to the confidential nature of the platform, detailed descriptions about its architecture are omitted.

6.2   Experiment

The goal of the case study was threefold: identifying variability in the GUI platform, expressing the identified variation points in terms of feature models, and using our pattern concept and prototype tool to achieve an environment where variability is managed across multiple artifacts.

Our first step was to analyze the platform documentation and interview several of the platform users. As a result, we have identified a number of variability issues regarding how platform services are being used. The next step was to construct feature models realizing the variability issues we have identified. Figure 6 depicts, in lighter color, a feature model representing the main services provided by the GUI platform. All services are optional. It is up to the product developer to decide which services to use. The 'I18n' service stands for the internationalization service.

As a third step, we have developed a system of feature variation patterns for expressing which platform services are used and which service implementations are considered. Because a service is regarded as a separate concern in the platform, a pattern (or a set of related patterns) is used to represent that service. The patterns cover four abstraction levels: the feature model representing the services, the design model of the product, the Java implementation of the application, and the product service registry files.

When instantiating the patterns, developers decide which services the application should incorporate and which service implementation to use. If a service is selected, MADE uses the corresponding pattern to generate tasks for registering the service in the application service registry. Furthermore, the pattern ensures that the right service implementation is added to the design model of the application, that the Java implementation exists, and that the right (and only one per service) service implementation is registered to the property files.

Each of the services shown in Figure 6 in lighter color can be further represented by its own feature models. The figure, for example, depicts, in darker color, a feature model specifying how application GUI components can use the on-line help service. First, the variant 'User_Event' indicates that the call resulted from a user request whereas 'System_Event' indicates that the call originated from the application. GUI components can support either event types but not both at the same time. Second, developers must specify what type of help service is requested. There are five variants for such service type. 'Contents', for example indicates that the target of the request is a table of contents whereas 'Search'

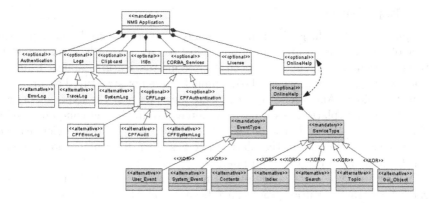

Fig. 6. Feature models for platform services and online help service

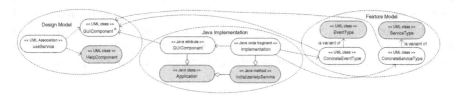

Fig. 7. Role diagram for the OnlineHelp pattern

indicates that the target of the request is a search page. Similarly, the choice of the service type is exclusive.

A feature variation pattern is used for representing the feature model for online help. The pattern is used to generate tasks for selecting the GUI components which incorporate a help service and the help event and service types associated with those components. In addition, it ensures that only one variant is selected and that it is correctly represented in the Java implementation. Furthermore, the pattern is used to associate, in the design model, the help service with the selected GUI components.

The role structure of the pattern is shown in Figure 7. The two roles named 'ConcreteEventType' and 'ConcreteServiceType' represent the event and service type variants to be used. In the design model, role 'GUIComponent' should be bound to a UML class representing the GUI components associated with the help service. The '+' symbol in front of the role name stands for the multiplicity value meaning, in this case, that there can be any number of GUI components (UML classes) bound to the role. At the implementation level, the pattern uses the variants in the feature model to generate a Java code fragment for registering the proper help service to the selected GUI components. This is illustrated by role 'Implementation'. The code fragment is inserted in an initialization method of the application.

6.3   Experiences

As explained earlier the goals of the case study have been to study the expressive power of our formalism and the applicability of our approach in an industrial setting. Our first challenge has been to dig up the feature models from the platform documentation, where the documents were not structured according to our methodology. Another problem, during this phase of the experiment, was the fact that the platform is used by different groups in the company having different interests towards the product line. Thus, we had to interview each of these parties. Furthermore, the platform comes with different versions making it harder to identify the variation points.

The variability aspects of the platform were mostly specified in Word documents. An attractive option would have been to link the relevant parts of these documents to the feature variation patterns, rather than (or in addition to) feature models. However, this would require different structuring of the Word documents and new role types covering elements in these documents. In the case study, we have specified all platform services as optional features, even though services such as internationalization or online help are in practice required. At this stage, we could conveniently present a number of variation points in the platform with a set of heterogeneous patterns. However, we still need to construct more patterns in order to cover variability in other platform components.

7   Related Approaches

Feature Variability Management
One of the key issues in software product lines is variability management. A product line architecture makes it easier to manage the product family as it promotes the variation between different products, i.e., the use of variants and variation points [16]. The software community has taken different approaches to variability management. Our methodology is based on feature models [7]. Other methodologies include architecture description languages (ADLs) [17] and different XML-based program specification [18].

Framed aspects [19] are another approach for representing features in software product lines. The purpose of the method is to support evolution in product lines rather than the development of products. First, aspects are used to encapsulate tangled features. Then, frames are used to provide parameterization and reconfiguration support for the features. Compared to our approach, framed aspects are applied at the implementation level only.

Model-Driven Engineering
MDD (Model-Driven Development) [20] promotes an approach where models of the same system are usually derived from each other leading to better alignment between the models. MDA (Model-Driven Architecture) [21] is a recent initiative by OMG for supporting MDD principles. MDA defines three views of a system: a Computation Independent Model (CIM), which is a representation of a system from a business viewpoint, a Platform Independent Model (PIM), which is a rep-

resentation of a system ignoring platform specific details, and Platform Specific Model (PSM), which is a model of a system that covers both platform independent information and details about a specific platform. Compared to MDA, our feature models correspond to CIM whereas other model kinds can be viewed as PSM. In this paper we do not discuss support for PIM. An MDA-oriented approach, using our pattern concept, is presented in [22].

Batory et al. take an approach to feature oriented programming where models are treated as a series of layered refinements [23]. Features are composed together in a step-wise refinement fashion to form complex models. Models can be programs or other non-code representations. To support their concepts, the authors have developed a number of tools for feature composition, called AHEAD toolset. The toolset provides similar functions to those of MADE. MADE environment solves two problems not otherwise addressed in [23]: tracing features across different artifacts and checking the validity of models.

Separation of Concerns Across Artifacts

The idea of representing concerns within and across different artifacts has been addressed in the work on multi-dimensional separation of concerns [2]. The authors present a model for encapsulating concerns using so-called hyperslices. These are entities independent of any artifact formalism. Our heterogeneous pattern concept can be considered as a concrete realization of the hyperslice concept. Other concepts such as subjects [24], aspects [1], and viewpoints [25] also resemble our patterns. Subjects are class hierarchies representing a particular view point of a domain model. Thus subjects deal only with object-oriented artifacts. Aspects, on the other hand, have been mostly used to represent concerns at the programming level. Viewpoints, in turn, are used to represent developers' views at the requirements level. Different viewpoints can be described using different notations. Compared to these concepts, our pattern approach is not bound to a specific artifact type but can be used to capture concerns cross-cutting different phases of the development process.

Tool Support for Traceability

The ability to track relationships between artifacts has been a central aim in requirements engineering [26]. Rational RequisitePro [27] is a market-leading requirement management tool. In RequisitePro, use cases are written as Word documents which are stored into a relational database. Use case diagrams can be associated with use case documents; sequence diagrams implementing the use cases can be linked to the use case diagrams, and class diagrams can be linked to the sequence diagrams. A related approach has been proposed to achieve traceability in software product families [28], linking requirements, architecture, components, and source code. In both works, traceability is based mainly on explicitly created links. In our approach there are no explicit links between the artifacts themselves, but instead we specify a particular concern as a pattern and bind the roles of the pattern to certain elements of the artifacts.

8   Concluding Remarks

We have developed a prototype environment supporting the representation of concerns cross-cutting not only components but also various artifacts produced in different phases of a software development process. Our first experiences with the environment are encouraging: we could conveniently present variation points in a product-line with a heterogeneous pattern covering multiple artifact types. Using existing tool technology for pattern-driven software development, we could achieve an environment where the pattern guides variation management from feature model to actual implementation.

However, feature variation management is just one example of the potential benefits of our environment. The main point is that the pattern stores the information of the existence of a concern among the artifacts. This information can be exploited in many ways. For example, it is often useful simply to generate a single view where all the fragments related to a particular concern can be browsed, a kind of concern visualizer. This kind of support is readily available in our tool. Heterogeneous patterns can be used for tracing as well: the designer can follow the dependencies between the roles of a pattern and find out why, for example, a particular class has been introduced in the design model.

In order to support new representation formats of artifacts, we are working at transforming the tool into a framework for constructing new role types. Other future directions include enhancing the alignment and traceability between the various artifact types, and proceeding with the case studies provided by our industrial partners.

Acknowledgments

This work is supported financially by the Academy of Finland (project 51528) and by the National Technology Agency of Finland (projects 40183/03 and 40226/04), and is partly (first author) funded by Nokia Foundation.

References

1. Elrad, T., Filman, R.E., Bader, A., Editors: Communications of the ACM. Special issue on Aspect-Oriented Programming, 44:10 (2001)
2. Tarr, P., Ossher, H., Harrison, W., and Sutton, Jr., S. M: N degrees of separation: Multi-dimensional separation of concerns. In: Proc. ICSE 1999, Los Angeles, CA, USA, ACM Press (1999) 107–119
3. Parnas, D.L.: On the criteria to be used in decomposing systems into modules. Communications of the ACM **15** (1972) 1053–1058
4. Bosch, J.: Design and Use of Software Architectures: Adopting and Evolving a Product-line Approach. Addison.Wesley (2000)
5. Clements, P., Northrop, L.: Software Product Lines: Practices and Patterns. Addison-Wesley (2002)
6. Van Gurp, J., Bosch, J., Svahnberg, M.: On the notion of variability in software product lines. In: Proc. WICSA 2001, Amsterdam, The Netherlands (2001) 45–55

7. Czarnecki, K., Eisenecker, U.: Generative Programming, Methods, Tools and Applications. Addison Wesley (2000)
8. OMG: UML WWW site. At URL http://www.uml.org/ (2005)
9. Hakala M., Hautamäki J., Koskimies K., Paakki J., Viljamaa A., and Viljamaa J: Generating application development environments for Java frameworks. In: Proc. GCSE 2001, Erfurt, Germany, Springer, LNCS 2186 (2001) 163–176
10. Hammouda, I., Harsu, M.: Documenting maintenance tasks using maintenance patterns. In: Proc. CSMR 2004. (2004) 37–47
11. Hammouda, I., Guldogan, O., Koskimies, K., Systä, T.: Tool-supported customization of uml class diagrams for learning complex system models. In: Proc. IWPC 2004, Bari, Italy (2004) 24–33
12. Hammouda, I., Koskinen, J., Pussinen, M., Katara, M., Mikkonen, T.: Adaptable concern-based framework specialization in UML. In: Proc. ASE 2004, Linz, Austria (2004) 78–87
13. Eclipse: AspectJ WWW site. At URL http://eclipse.org/aspectj/ (2005)
14. Eclipse: Eclipse WWW site. At URL http://www.eclipse.org (2005)
15. IBM Rational: Rational software. At URL http://www-306.ibm.com/software/rational/ (2005)
16. Jacobson, I., Griss, M., Jonsson, P.: Software Reuse - Architecture, Process and Organization for Business Success. Addison-Wesley (1997)
17. Van der Hoek, A.: Capturing product line architectures. In: Proc. ISAW-4, Limerick, Ireland (2000) 95–99
18. Cleaveland, J.: Program Generators with XML and Java. Prentice-Hall (2001)
19. Loughran, N., Rashid, A., Zhang, W., Jarzabek, S.: Supporting product line evolution with framed aspects. ACP4IS Workshop AOSD 04 (2004)
20. Mellor, S., Clark, A., Futagami, T.: Model-driven development. IEEE Software 20 (2003) 14–18
21. OMG: MDA guide version 1.0.1. At URL http://www.omg.org/docs/omg/03-06-01.pdf (2003)
22. Siikarla, M., Koskimies, K., Systä, T.: Open MDA using transformational patterns. In: Proc. MDAFA 2004, Linköping, Sweden (2004) 92–106
23. Batory, D., Sarvela, J.N., Rauschmayer, A.: Scaling stepwise refinement. In: Proc. ICSE 2003, Portland, USA (2003) 187–197
24. Clarke, S., Harrison, W., Ossher, H., and Tarr, P: Subject-oriented design: towards improved alignment of requirements, design, and code. ACM SIGPLAN Notices 34 (1999) 325–339
25. Nuseibeh, B., Kramer, J., Finkelstein, A.: A framework for expressing the relationships between multiple views in requirements specifications. Transactions on Software Engineering 20 (1994) 760–773
26. Leffingwell, D., Widrig, D.: Managing Software Requirements. Addison.Wesley (2000)
27. IBM Rational: Rational RequisitePro. At URL http://www3.software.ibm.com/ibmdl/pub/software/rational/web/datasheets/version6/reqpro.pdf (2005)
28. Lago, P., Niemel, E., Van Vliet, H.: Tool support for traceable product evolution. In: Proc. CSMR 2004, Tampere, Finland (2004) 261–269

Color-Blind Specifications for Transformations of Reactive Synchronous Programs

Kim G. Larsen[1], Ulrik Larsen[1], and Andrzej Wąsowski[2]

[1] CISS, Aalborg University, Denmark
{kgl,ulrikl}@cs.aau.dk
[2] IT University of Copenhagen, Denmark
wasowski@itu.dk

Abstract. Execution environments are used as specifications for specialization of input-output programs in the derivation of product lines. These environments, formalized as color-blind I/O-alternating transition systems, are tolerant to mutations in a given program's outputs. Execution environments enable new compiler optimizations, vastly exceeding usual reductions. We propose a notion of context-dependent refinement for I/O-alternating transition systems, which supports composition and hierarchical reuse. The framework is demonstrated by discussing adaptations to realistic design languages and by presenting an example of a product line.

1 Introduction

Modern software becomes increasingly customizable. This especially affects embedded software, since embedded devices are typically produced in multiple variants. Our long-term goal is to provide a theoretical foundation, tools, and methodology for maintaining a family of software for reactive synchronous systems. In the present work we focus on the theoretical basis for specifying correctness of transformations used in automatic derivation of family members.

A single general model is used as a description of all available functionality. Hierarchically organized specifications of environments define the family members by restricting input and output abilities of the general model. I/O alternating transition systems are used to model the semantics of both environments and the general model. Our environments are novel in that they not only restrict possible input traces, but also exhibit inabilities in distinguishing output traces. Some outputs are indistinguishable for a given environment in the same way as a color-blind person cannot distinguish some colors. Color-blindness can be used to model surprisingly many aspects of realistic environments (for example causality between the firing and timing-out of a stop-watch, boolean memory flags, or the use of a single actuator in place of two). The general model can be transformed according to the behavior of a specific environment, and individually optimized for that particular environment and purpose.

Section 2 motivates our work using a popular reactive language. I/O alternating transition systems are introduced in section 3, color-blindness in section 4, and composition operators in section 5. Remaining sections focus on practical

M. Cerioli (Ed.): FASE 2005, LNCS 3442, pp. 160–174, 2005.

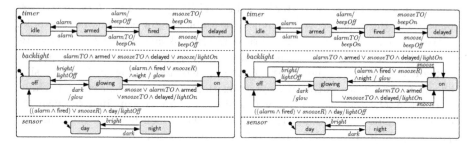

Fig. 1. Initial state/event model C_0 **Fig. 2.** The specialized model C_1

applications: adaptation to realistic design languages (section 6) and an example of a product line (section 7). Sections 8-9 refer the related work and conclude.

2   State/Event Systems

Let *Event* and *Action* be finite sets of environment stimuli and system outputs respectively. A *state/event machine* $M_i = (S_i, s_i^0, T_i)$ is a triple comprising a set of local states S_i, the initial state $s_i^0 \in S_i$ and a set of syntactic transitions T_i. A *state/event system* consists of n machines $\mathcal{M} = \{M_1, \ldots, M_n\}$ with mutually disjoint sets of states. A global state of the system is a tuple of local states: $State = S_1 \times S_2 \times \cdots \times S_n$. Transitions in $T_i \subseteq S_i \times Event \times Guard \times Action \times S_i$ describe reactions undertaken by M_i in reply to a given event, in a given local and global state. Global states are described by transition guards: simple Boolean expressions over activity of states, which can be evaluated in any given global state, giving rise to a natural satisfaction relation $\vDash \subseteq State \times Guard$.

State/event systems are *input-enabled*: the local transition relation includes not only the syntactical transitions but also self loops for all configurations for which reactions are not specified. We write $s \xrightarrow{e \quad o}_i s_i'$, meaning that the reaction of machine M_i to arrival of event e in global state s is, to change the local state to s_i' and generate the set of actions o:

$$s \xrightarrow{e \quad \{a\}}_i s' \qquad \text{iff } \exists g.\ (\pi_i(s), e, g, a, s_i') \in T_i \wedge s \vDash g$$

$$s \xrightarrow{e \quad \emptyset}_i \pi_i(s) \qquad \text{otherwise (where } \pi_i(s) \text{ denotes the } i\text{'th projection of } s)$$

The global transition relation $T \subseteq State \times Event \times \mathcal{P}(Action) \times State$ subsumes all local reactions: $s \xrightarrow{e \quad o} s' \Leftrightarrow_{def} \forall i.s \xrightarrow{e \quad o_i}_i \pi_i(s')$ where $o = o_1 \cup \ldots \cup o_n$.

Fig. 1 depicts a state/event model C_0 of an alarm clock. The essentials of the alarm clock are handled by the *timer* machine. If the *timer* is in the armed state and the hardware sends an alarm time-out event (*alarmTO*) then the beeper is turned on. The user can postpone the alarm by pressing the snooze button (event *snooze*), which allows him to continue sleeping until the snooze timer times out (*snoozeTO*). Releasing the button sends a *snoozeR* event to the model. The *backlight* machine controls the built-in lamps. Only a faint light is displayed in the glowing state, such that the display can be read in the dark. The full light is on while the alarm is beeping or the snooze button is being pressed. The *sensor* machine models the current external light level. Proper events (*dark, bright*) are generated by the sensor driver whenever the ambient light passes some threshold.

We would like to support automatic derivation of variants for discrete control systems like the alarm clock. One such variant $\mathcal{C}_1$, which does not activate the backlight in reaction to the *snooze* button, is depicted on Fig. 2. Note the simplification of guards and the two new transitions in the *backlight* state machine. What is the relation between the two models? Both models are indistinguishable for some execution environment, namely the one, which becomes blind for the *lightOn* action immediately after producing the *snooze* event.

3   I/O Alternating Transition Systems

The reactive synchronous paradigm seems to be predominant in development of embedded software. The state/event systems of the previous section [17, 11] are just an example chosen from a multitude of available formalisms, like Esterel [2], statecharts [7], or Java Card [24]. A common assumption about these systems is that they react to any input event at any time. Each reaction occurs infinitely fast, so that the system is always able to observe the arrival of the next event. Such semantics is conveniently captured by *I/O-alternating transition systems*:

Definition 1. *An I/O-alternating transition system, or IOATS, is a tuple* $(In,$ $Out, Gen, Obs, \xrightarrow{!}, \xrightarrow{?}, s^0)$*, where In and Out are sets of inputs and outputs, Gen and Obs are finite sets of generators and observers,* $\xrightarrow{!} \subseteq Gen \times Out \times Obs$ *is a generation relation,* $\xrightarrow{?} \subseteq Obs \times In \times Gen$ *is an observation relation, and* $s^0 \in Gen \cup Obs$ *is the initial state.*

We have distinguished two transition relations: $\xrightarrow{!}$ is a generation relation advancing from a generator to an observer, while $\xrightarrow{?}$ is an observation relation advancing from an observer to a generator. This alternation is inherent to the way synchronous systems operate. We write $S \xrightarrow{o!} s$, instead of $(S, o, s) \in \xrightarrow{!}$ and $s \xrightarrow{i?} S$ instead of $(s, i, S) \in \xrightarrow{?}$. Small letters are used for observers and capital letters for generators. In addition observers are required to be input-enabled:

$$\forall s \in Obs. \ \forall i \in In. \ \exists S, o, s'. \ s \xrightarrow{i?} S \wedge S \xrightarrow{o!} s' \tag{1}$$

With these assumptions we can propose a simulation based refinement relation:

Definition 2. *Let* $\mathcal{S}_1 = (In, Out, Gen_1, Obs_1, \xrightarrow{!}_1, \xrightarrow{?}_1, s_1^0)$ *and* $\mathcal{S}_2 = (In, Out,$ $Gen_2, Obs_2, \xrightarrow{!}_2, \xrightarrow{?}_2, s_2^0)$ *be IOATSs. A binary relation* $R \in Obs_1 \times Obs_2$ *constitutes a simulation on observers of* $\mathcal{S}_1$ *and* $\mathcal{S}_2$ *iff* $(s_1, s_2) \in R$ *implies that:*

whenever $s_1 \xrightarrow{i?} S_1 \wedge S_1 \xrightarrow{o!} s_1'$ *then also* $s_2 \xrightarrow{i?} S_2 \wedge S_2 \xrightarrow{o!} s_2'$ *and* $(s_1', s_2') \in R$.

Let R be the largest of such relations ordered by inclusion. An observer s_2 *simulates an observer* s_1*, written* $s_1 \leqslant s_2$*, iff* $(s_1, s_2) \in R$*. Finally* $\mathcal{S}_2$ *simulates* $\mathcal{S}_1$*, written* $\mathcal{S}_1 \leqslant \mathcal{S}_2$*, iff* $s_1^0 \leqslant s_2^0$*.*

We distinguish the actual systems from the environments, in which they operate. Environments are free in choice of inputs, while systems independently determine the outputs. A system $\mathcal{S} = (In_{\mathcal{S}}, Out_{\mathcal{S}}, Gen_{\mathcal{S}}, Obs_{\mathcal{S}}, \xrightarrow{!}_{\mathcal{S}}, \xrightarrow{?}_{\mathcal{S}}, s_{\mathcal{S}})$ operates embedded in some environment $\mathcal{E} = (In_\mathcal{E}, Out_\mathcal{E}, Gen_\mathcal{E}, Obs_\mathcal{E}, \overset{!}{\longrightarrow}_\mathcal{E}, \overset{?}{\longrightarrow}_\mathcal{E}, s_\mathcal{E})$. Systems always begin execution in an observer state, so $s_S \in Obs_S$. Environments always begin execution in a generator state, so $s_\mathcal{E} \in Gen_\mathcal{E}$. System $\mathcal{S}$ is *compatible* with the environment $\mathcal{E}$ if $In_S = Out_\mathcal{E}$ and $Out_S = In_\mathcal{E}$. Composition of a system $\mathcal{S}$ with a compatible environment $\mathcal{E}$ is defined in the usual way, by synchronization on identical labels (and complimentary transition types). The initial observer of the system is composed with the initial generator of the environment. Due to the compatibility requirement and input-enabledness of observers, the closed system is able to advance for any input that can be generated by the environment. For a closed system it is known, which of its states cannot be exercised by the environment. A given environment may not be able to distinguish two systems from each other, even though they are not identical. We capture this with a notion of *relativized simulation*:

Definition 3. *Consider three IOATSs: an environment* $\mathcal{E} = (Out, In, Gen, Obs, \overset{!}{\longrightarrow}, \overset{?}{\longrightarrow}, E^0)$ *and two systems:* $\mathcal{S}_1 = (In, Out, Gen_1, Obs_1, \overset{!}{\longrightarrow}_1, \overset{?}{\longrightarrow}_1, s_1^0)$ *and* $\mathcal{S}_2 = (In, Out, Gen_2, Obs_2, \overset{!}{\longrightarrow}_2, \overset{?}{\longrightarrow}_2, s_2^0)$. *A Gen-indexed family of binary relations* $R\colon Gen \to \mathcal{P}(Obs_1 \times Obs_2)$ *is a relativized simulation iff* $(s_1, s_2) \in R_E$ *implies that:*

$$whenever\ E \overset{i!}{\longrightarrow} e \wedge e \overset{o?}{\longrightarrow} E'$$
$$then\ whenever\ s_1 \overset{i?}{\longrightarrow} S_1 \wedge S_1 \overset{o!}{\longrightarrow} s_1'$$
$$then\ also\ s_2 \overset{i?}{\longrightarrow} S_2 \wedge S_2 \overset{o!}{\longrightarrow} s_2'\ and\ (s_1', s_2') \in R_{E'}.$$

Let R be the largest of such families ordered by component-wise inclusion. We say that an observer s_2 *simulates an observer* s_1 *in the generator E, written* $s_1 \leqslant_E s_2$, *iff* $(s_1, s_2) \in R_E$. *The system* $\mathcal{S}_2$ *simulates* $\mathcal{S}_1$ *in the context of* $\mathcal{E}$, *written* $\mathcal{S}_1 \leqslant_\mathcal{E} \mathcal{S}_2$, *iff* $s_1^0 \leqslant_{E^0} s_2^0$.

The choice of simulation as the preorder underlying our methodology is somewhat arbitrary. Most other behavioral preorders of the linear-time/branching-time hierarchy of van Glabbeek [6] would be adequate, such as testing preorder, $^2/_3$ bisimulation (ready simulation) and bisimulation. What is important is that the particular preorder preserves properties of interest and that the preorder may be relativized with respect to environmental restrictions.

4   Color-Blind I/O-Alternating Transition Systems

In the previous section we were able to state that two systems are in a refinement relation with respect to a certain context if this context cannot activate their incompatible parts. However, in industrial development, it often happens that the environment cannot distinguish two systems, not because it makes incompatible parts unreachable, but because its ability to distinguish the *different outputs* it observes might be limited depending on its actual state. A variant of the alarm clock may have only one physical lamp installed, which should be lit whenever the backlight is on or glowing. The environment, being a model of the hardware in this case, will treat the two outputs *glow* and *lightOn* as being identical, allowing for powerful optimizations when generating code for this specific type of hardware. For this particular example, the distinguishing capability of the environment is clearly static and hence the specification of code optimization is realizable using simple process algebraic operations such as relabelling and hiding. However, environmental restrictions can be dynamically changing as was the case for the environment leading to the specialized model C_1 (Fig. 2). Here the environment only becomes blind for the *lightOn* action after the production of the *snooze* event. To give a proper treatment of such situations we relax the equivalence of labels in relativized simulation and label observation transitions of environments with sets of inputs called *observation classes*. Such transitions can be taken in the presence of any of the inputs in their observation class.

Definition 4. *A color-blind IOATS is a tuple* $\mathcal{E} = (In, Out, Gen, Obs, \xrightarrow{!}, \xrightarrow{?}, E^0)$, *where In and Out are sets of inputs and outputs, Gen and Obs are finite sets of generators and color-blind observers,* $\xrightarrow{!} \subseteq Gen \times Out \times Obs$ *is a generation relation,* $\xrightarrow{?} \subseteq Obs \times \mathcal{P}(In) \times Gen$ *is a color-blind observation relation, and* $E^0 \in Gen$ *is the initial state.*

A color-blind environment $\mathcal{E} = (In_{\mathcal{E}}, Out_{\mathcal{E}}, Gen_{\mathcal{E}}, Obs_{\mathcal{E}}, \xrightarrow{!}_{\mathcal{E}}, \xrightarrow{?}_{\mathcal{E}}, E)$ and a usual IOATS $\mathcal{S} = (In_{\mathcal{S}}, Out_{\mathcal{S}}, Gen_{\mathcal{S}}, Obs_{\mathcal{S}}, \xrightarrow{!}_{\mathcal{S}}, \xrightarrow{?}_{\mathcal{S}}, s)$ are compatible if their signatures match: $In_{\mathcal{E}} = Out_{\mathcal{S}} \wedge Out_{\mathcal{E}} = In_{\mathcal{S}}$. Since we only consider compatible systems and environments, we fix the meaning of the input and output, choosing the system's perspective. We denote the set of inputs of the system by In (which is also the set of outputs of the environment). Similarly Out is the set of outputs of the system (but the set of inputs for the environment). A single input will be denoted by i, single output by o, and classes of outputs by capital O. We still write $E \xrightarrow{i!} e$ instead of $(E, i, e) \in \xrightarrow{!}$ and $e \xrightarrow{O?} E$ instead of $(e, O, E) \in \xrightarrow{?}$.

We require that the observers in color-blind IOATS are deterministic and input enabled, so that the observation classes on the transitions outgoing from a single state form a partitioning of the inputs into equivalence classes. Formally:

$$\forall e \in Obs_{\mathcal{E}}.\forall O_1, O_2 \subseteq Out.\forall E_1, E_2 \in Gen_{\mathcal{E}}.\ e \xrightarrow{O_1?} E_1 \wedge e \xrightarrow{O_2?} E_2$$
$$\Rightarrow O_1 \cap O_2 = \emptyset \vee (O_1 = O_2 \wedge E_1 = E_2)$$
$$\forall e \in Obs_{\mathcal{E}}.\forall o \in Out.\exists O \subseteq Out.\exists E \in Gen_{\mathcal{E}}.e \xrightarrow{O?} E \wedge o \in O. \tag{2}$$

The generation relation should also be deterministic: $\forall E \in Gen_{\mathcal{E}}.\ \forall i \in In.$ $\forall e_1, e_2 \in Obs_{\mathcal{E}}.E \xrightarrow{i!} e_1 \wedge E \xrightarrow{i!} e_2 \Rightarrow e_1 = e_2$. Note that determinism in this sense does not limit the freedom of the environment in choosing inputs, but means that each input choice uniquely determines the target state.

Consider a blind environment $\mathcal{B}$ with two states, a generator **B** and an observer **b**. Intuitively $\mathcal{B}$ can execute all parts of the system, but does not care about the responses it gets: $\forall i \in In.$ **B** $\xrightarrow{i!}$ **b** and **b** $\xrightarrow{Out?}$ **B**. Dually, a perfect vision environment $\mathcal{V}$ observes all the outputs: $\forall i \in In.$**V** $\xrightarrow{i!}$ **v** and $\forall o \in Out.$**v** $\xrightarrow{\{o\}?}$ **V**.

A compatible environment–system pair forms a closed system, advancing in lock-steps. However, now the generation transition of the system, synchronizes with the observation transition of the environment, whenever the output produced falls into the right observation class. We enrich our previous definition of relativized simulation to accommodate this new synchronization principle:

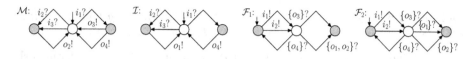

Fig. 3. Systems $\mathcal{M}$ and $\mathcal{I}$ and compatible environments $\mathcal{F}_1$, $\mathcal{F}_2$

Definition 5. *Let $\mathcal{E}=(Out, In, Gen, Obs, \xrightarrow{!}, \xrightarrow{?}, E^0)$ be a color-blind environment IOATS and $\mathcal{S}_1=(In, Out, Gen_1, Obs_1, \xrightarrow{!}_1, \xrightarrow{?}_1, s_1^0)$, $\mathcal{S}_2=(In, Out, Gen_2, Obs_2, \xrightarrow{!}_2, \xrightarrow{?}_2, s_2^0)$ be two system IOATSs. A Gen-indexed family of relations $R: Gen \to \mathcal{P}(Obs_1 \times Obs_2)$ is a relativized simulation iff $(s_1, s_2) \in R_E$ implies that:*

whenever $E \xrightarrow{i!} e \wedge e \xrightarrow{O?} E'$

then whenever $s_1 \xrightarrow{i?} S_1 \wedge S_1 \xrightarrow{o_1!} s_1' \wedge o_1 \in O$

then also $s_2 \xrightarrow{i?} S_2 \wedge S_2 \xrightarrow{o_2!} s_2' \wedge o_2 \in O$ and $(s_1', s_2') \in R_{E'}$.

Let R be the largest of such families ordered by component-wise inclusion. An observer s_2 simulates an observer s_1 in the context of generator E, written $s_1 \leqslant_E s_2$, iff $(s_1, s_2) \in R_E$. An IOATS $\mathcal{S}_2$ simulates another IOATS $\mathcal{S}_1$ in the context of a compatible color-blind IOATS $\mathcal{E}$, written $\mathcal{S}_1 \leqslant_{\mathcal{E}} \mathcal{S}_2$, iff $s_1^0 \leqslant_{E^0} s_2^0$. Finally $\mathcal{S}_1$ is equivalent to $\mathcal{S}_2$ in the context of $\mathcal{E}$, written $\mathcal{S}_1 \lesssim_{\mathcal{E}} \mathcal{S}_2$, iff $\mathcal{S}_1 \leqslant_{\mathcal{E}} \mathcal{S}_2$ and $\mathcal{S}_2 \leqslant_{\mathcal{E}} \mathcal{S}_1$.

Even though we have initially postulated that most of the execution contexts do not exercise all possible traces of the system, we shall now require that environments can always produce any of the inputs in *In*. This requirement surprisingly does not defeat our initial goal. We can direct all transitions producing impossible inputs to the observer **b** and embed the blind environment $\mathcal{B}$ in every environment. Instead of specifying that the environment cannot produce i, we state that i can be produced, but the subsequent system behavior is irrelevant. Proposition 1 states this formally:

Proposition 1. *For any two observers S_1, S_2 of the same IOATS $S_1 \leqslant_\mathbf{B} S_2$.*

Fig. 3 presents two systems and two compatible color-blind environments. Environment transitions from generators to the blind observer **b** have been omitted. There is one such transition for each input–generator pair, for which the transition is not drawn. Observe that the system $\mathcal{M}$ simulates $\mathcal{I}$ in the environment $\mathcal{F}_1$ ($\mathcal{I} \leqslant_{\mathcal{F}_1} \mathcal{M}$) not due to the fact that $\mathcal{F}_1$ is not able to exercise the differing parts of the two systems, but because $\mathcal{F}_1$ cannot distinguish between the outputs (o_1, o_2) produced by $\mathcal{I}$ and $\mathcal{M}$. The $\mathcal{F}_2$ environment distinguishes $\mathcal{I}$ and $\mathcal{M}$, by observing the outputs o_1 and o_2 with two separate transitions.

Relativized simulation is a weaker notion than usual simulation and the perfect vision environment $\mathcal{V}$ is the most discriminating environment:

Proposition 2. *For any two systems $\mathcal{S}_1$, $\mathcal{S}_2$ and for any compatible color-blind environment $\mathcal{E}$ it holds that $\mathcal{S}_1 \leqslant \mathcal{S}_2 \Rightarrow \mathcal{S}_1 \leqslant_{\mathcal{E}} \mathcal{S}_2$ and $\mathcal{S}_1 \leqslant \mathcal{S}_2 \iff \mathcal{S}_1 \leqslant_{\mathcal{V}} \mathcal{S}_2$.*

With the above propositions we have hinted at the notion of *discrimination*— the ability of environment to distinguish systems from each other:

Definition 6. *A color-blind IOATS $\mathcal{F}$ is more discriminating than $\mathcal{E}$, written $\mathcal{E} \sqsubseteq \mathcal{F}$, iff $\mathcal{F}$ distinguishes more processes: $\mathcal{E} \sqsubseteq \mathcal{F}$ iff $\forall S_1, S_2. S_1 \leqslant_{\mathcal{F}} S_2 \Rightarrow S_1 \leqslant_{\mathcal{E}} S_2$.*

The blind environment $\mathcal{B}$ is the least discriminating—it cannot distinguish any two systems from each other (proposition 1). By proposition 2 the perfect vision environment $\mathcal{V}$ is the most discriminating one.

The notion of discrimination will soon prove fundamental for our developments. We shall use it to design composition operators for behavioral properties, facilitating hierarchical modeling of product lines. Unfortunately the definition of the discrimination is rather abstract. The quantification over all systems, makes it infeasible for mechanical treatment. To remedy this obstacle we introduce a new preorder on environments: a simulation for color-blind IOATSs.

Definition 7. *Let $\mathcal{E} = (Out, In, Gen_{\mathcal{E}}, Obs_{\mathcal{E}}, \overset{!}{\longrightarrow}_{\mathcal{E}}, \overset{?}{\longrightarrow}_{\mathcal{E}}, E^0)$ and $\mathcal{F} = (Out, In, Gen_{\mathcal{F}}, Obs_{\mathcal{F}}, \overset{!}{\longrightarrow}_{\mathcal{F}}, \overset{?}{\longrightarrow}_{\mathcal{F}}, F^0)$ be color-blind environments. A pair of binary relations, $R_1 \subseteq Gen_{\mathcal{E}} \times Gen_{\mathcal{F}}$ and $R_2 \subseteq Obs_{\mathcal{F}} \times Obs_{\mathcal{E}}$, constitutes a simulation between states of color-blind IOATSs iff $(E, F) \in R_1$ implies that*

$$\text{whenever } E \overset{i!}{\longrightarrow} e \text{ then also } F \overset{i!}{\longrightarrow} f \text{ and } (f, e) \in R_2 \ ,$$

and $(f, e) \in R_2$ implies that whenever $f \overset{O_f?}{\longrightarrow} F$

$$\text{then also } e \overset{O_e?}{\longrightarrow} E \text{ and } O_f \subseteq O_e \text{ and } (E, F) \in R_1 \ .$$

Let (R_1, R_2) be the largest such pair of relations (ordered by point-wise inclusion). A generator F simulates a generator E, written $E \leqslant F$, iff $(E, F) \in R_1$. An observer e simulates an observer f, written $f \leqslant e$, iff $(f, e) \in R_2$. An environment $\mathcal{F}$ simulates $\mathcal{E}$, written $\mathcal{E} \leqslant \mathcal{F}$, iff $E^0 \leqslant F^0$.

The simulation preorder can be established mechanically for finite state systems using state exploration techniques [3]. Thanks to the following central result, these techniques can also be used to verify discrimination properties:

Theorem 1. *For any two color-blind environments $\mathcal{E}$ and $\mathcal{F}$: $\mathcal{E} \sqsubseteq \mathcal{F}$ iff $\mathcal{E} \leqslant \mathcal{F}$.*

5   Composition of Behavioral Properties

Typical code generators do not use any context information, assuming that the model is combined with the perfect vision environment $\mathcal{V}$. Another extreme would be a program synthesis tool requiring a precise environment model, imposing a significant burden on engineers. We propose light-weight, composable, partial specifications of environments in the form of behavioral properties like: that certain events always come interleaved (e.g. on/off switch), or that there is causality between an input and an output (e.g. a timer only timeouts after it has been started). Each property can be expressed as a simple color-blind IOATS. In this section we consider ways of composing such properties.

As said before, every observer e of a color-blind IOATS induces a partitioning of Out into observation classes. Let us denote this partitioning by P_e. The set of all equivalence relations (and hence the set of all partitionings) over Out, ordered by inclusion, forms a complete lattice. Consequently for any set of partitionings $\{P_k\}_{k\in L}$ there exist the greatest lower bound $\bigcap_{k\in L} P_k$, which is the coarsest partitioning finer than any of P_k and the least upper bound $\bigsqcup_{k\in L} P_k$, which is the finest partitioning coarser than all P_k.

The composition is defined for environments with the same I/O signatures. We consider two kinds of composition: a sum and a product. Sums intuitively correspond to disjunction of properties (or sums in CCS [19]). Products correspond to conjunctions (or synchronous composition in CSP [9]).

$$\frac{E_1\overset{i!}{\longrightarrow}e_1 \ldots E_n\overset{i!}{\longrightarrow}e_n}{\sum_{k=1}^{n} E_k\overset{i!}{\longrightarrow}\prod_{k=1}^{n} e_k}\ (\mathrm{SG}) \qquad \frac{O\in\bigsqcup_{k=1}^{n}P_{e_k} \quad \mathbb{E} = \{E|\exists 1\leq k\leq n.\exists O' \subseteq O.e_k\overset{O'?}{\longrightarrow}E\}}{\sum_{k=1}^{n} e_k\overset{O?}{\longrightarrow}\prod\mathbb{E}}\ (\mathrm{SO})$$

$$\frac{E_1\overset{i!}{\longrightarrow}e_1 \ldots E_n\overset{i!}{\longrightarrow}e_n}{\prod_{k=1}^{n} E_k\overset{i!}{\longrightarrow}\sum_{k=1}^{n} e_k}\ (\mathrm{PG}) \qquad \frac{O\in\bigcap_{k=1}^{n}P_{e_k} \quad \mathbb{E}=\{E|\exists 1\leq k\leq n.\exists O'\subseteq Out.e_k\overset{O'?}{\longrightarrow}E\wedge O\subseteq O'\}}{\prod_{k=1}^{n} e_k\overset{O?}{\longrightarrow}\sum\mathbb{E}}\ (\mathrm{PO})$$

The result of a composition is a well-formed color-blind IOATS. The rules for the sum of generators (SG) and for the product of generators (PG) are very simple, due to the determinism and input-enabledness of our generators. The composition is synchronous: all composed generators take identical steps simultaneously. From the system's perspective a single input is generated. The observer rules are more complex, due to the embedding of determinisation. Consider the product of observers (PO) first. The observation classes O of the composed environment will be finer than observation classes of any of the composed processes. Whenever any o is observed by the result of the composition we advance to the state $\mathbb{E}$ composed of states reachable by o from all e_k's. Since O is finer than some class in any of these observers there is always exactly n such reachable generators. Dually in the sum (SO) observational classes are coarser than classes of any of the composed observers. The transition relation follows to those generators that can be reached by any output belonging to such an extended class. The size of $\mathbb{E}$ can exceed the number of original observers n.

Our compositions enjoy the following essential property:

Theorem 2. $\sum_{k=1}^{n}\{\mathcal{E}_k\}$ *is the least environment, which simulates all summands, while* $\prod_{k=1}^{n}\{\mathcal{E}_k\}$ *is the greatest environment, which is simulated by all the factors.*

Since discrimination and simulation coincide (Thm. 1) $\sqsubseteq$ can replace $\leqslant$ in the above theorem: *The sum of environments is the least discriminating environment, more discriminating than each of the summands. The product is the most discriminating environment, less discriminating than each of the factors.* These in turn are standard expectations about conjunction and disjunction. A conjunction (product) of two properties expressing inability to observe two behaviors, will result in a property expressing inability to observe either. Disjunction (sum) of two properties expressing ability to observe something, results in a property expressing the ability to observe both. See example on Fig. 4.

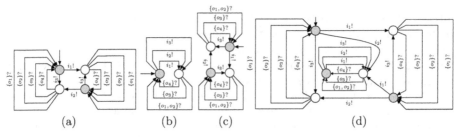

Fig. 4. Environments *Interleave* i_1 i_2 (a) and *Equiv* o_1 o_2 (b), their product (c) and sum (d) ($In = \{i_1, i_2, i_3\}$, $Out = \{o_1, \ldots, o_4\}$). Transitions to the **b** observer are suppressed. The product only generates what both of the factors could generate. It can distinguish only what both of them could. The sum can generate what any of the summands could observe, and it observers what any of them could. In particular o_1 and o_2 are distinguished in the traces for which the *Interleave* property is preserved and not otherwise

6   Toward Realistic Design Languages

Until now we have assumed that outputs of systems are atomic. This assumption however often does not hold for realistic languages, which typically support structured output: sets, multisets, sequences or even sequences of sets of atomic actions produced in a single step. We have successfully applied our framework to the semantics of languages producing sets (state/event systems of section 2, Harel's statecharts [7], synchronous languages [2]) and sequences (Java Card [24], UML state diagrams [21]). We describe some intricacies of the latter here, while simpler set-based environments are demonstrated by example in section 7.

Let *Event* and *Action* be finite sets of atomic events and actions respectively. Each observation transition of the system awaits a single input from *Event*, while each generation transition produces an output which is a finite sequence of actions from *Action*: $In = Event$ and $Out = Action^*$. The first step in adapting the theory is linking the concrete states of models (for example state configurations in statecharts, or variable store in Java Card) to abstract states of the IOATS. This can normally be done in a direct way (at least for finite state models). Subsequently the observation and generation relations must be extracted from the semantics of the language in question. Observation classes on the environment side (color-blind) become sets of sequences of actions. Partitioning of $Action^*$ into classes that are regular languages can be described by a finite automaton.

Definition 8. *A classifier DFA over alphabet A is a quadruple $c = (S, A, s, \rightarrow)$, where S is a finite set of states, A is a finite set of symbols, $s \in S$ is an initial state and $\rightarrow \in S \rightarrow A \rightarrow S$ is an input-enabled transition function, meaning that for every $s \in S$ function $\rightarrow(s)$ is defined for each element of its domain A. We usually write $s \xrightarrow{a} s'$ instead of $\rightarrow(s)(a) = s'$.*

A classifier DFA consecutively applies $\longrightarrow$ to a state and the head of the input sequence obtaining a new state and input sequence. An execution over a list of symbols $s \xrightarrow{a_1} s_1 \xrightarrow{a_2} \ldots \xrightarrow{a_n} s_n$ is abbreviated with $s \xrightarrow{a_1 \ldots a_n} {}^* s_n$.

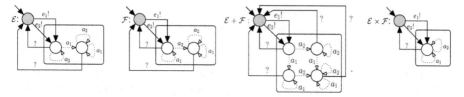

Fig. 5. Environments $\mathcal{E}$ and $\mathcal{F}$ observing sequences, their sum and product

Definition 9. *Let $c = (S, A, s, \rightarrow)$ be a classifier. Sequences $\sigma_1, \sigma_2 \in A^*$ are equivalent with respect to c if both advance c to the same state: $\exists s'. s \xrightarrow{\sigma_1}{}^* s' \wedge s \xrightarrow{\sigma_2}{}^* s'$.*

The equivalence with respect to a classifier is an equivalence relation and partitions A^* into a finite set of classes, isomorphic with the reachable states.

For a classifier $e = (S_e, Action, s_e, \rightarrow_e)$ consider a mapping of its states to generators $\gamma_e : S_e \rightarrow Gen$. Each observer of the environment comprises a classifier and a generator mapping. Environments advance from an observer (e, γ_e) to a generator $\gamma_e(s)$ if it observes a sequence σ advancing the classifier to a state s:

$$(e, \gamma_e) \xrightarrow{\{\sigma \mid s_e \xrightarrow{\sigma}{}^* s\}\ ?} \gamma_e(s) \ .$$

Fig. 5 shows two color-blind IOATSs $\mathcal{E}$ and $\mathcal{F}$ of signature: $Event = \{e_1, e_2\}$ and $Action = \{a_1, a_2\}$. $\mathcal{E}$ distinguishes reactions containing at least one occurrence of a_1 from those not containing a_1 at all. Similarly $\mathcal{F}$ distinguishes between sequences containing at least one a_2 from those not containing a_2 at all. Observers are drawn as boxes containing classifier DFAs. Classifier transitions are represented as dotted arrows to distinguish them from IOATS transitions.

The product of classifiers is a central construction in computing products of observers, supporting composition of environments:

Definition 10. *Let $e = (S_e, A, s_e, \rightarrow_e)$ and $f = (S_f, A, s_f, \rightarrow_f)$ be classifiers. A product of e and f is a classifier $e \otimes f = (S_e \times S_f, A, (s_e, s_f), \rightarrow)$, where $(s_e, s_f) \xrightarrow{a} (s'_e, s'_f)$ if $s_e \xrightarrow{a} s'_e$ and $s_f \xrightarrow{a} s'_f$.*

Proposition 3. *Let $\sim_e$ and $\sim_f$ be two equivalences on $Action^*$ induced by classifiers e and f. Their greatest lower bound $\sim_e \sqcap \sim_f$ exists and is induced by $e \otimes f$.*

Figure 5 presents the sum $\mathcal{E} + \mathcal{F}$ obtained by application of operational rules of section 5 (SG,PO) and the above proposition. $\mathcal{E} + \mathcal{F}$ distinguishes four classes of outputs: an empty sequence, sequences consisting of occurrences of a_1, consisting of occurrences of a_2, and containing occurrences of both a_1 and a_2.

The least upper bound of two partitionings $\sim_e \sqcup \sim_f$ is usually computed using a Union-Find algorithm, which unifies any two overlapping classes, until all classes are disjoint. In our case classes are represented by states in the classifiers e and f. We need to apply the algorithm to states of e and f, ultimately producing a classifier, whose states are sets of states of f and e. The two classes s_1 and s_2 overlap, whenever there is an output sequence, that can advance one classifier to a state in s_1, and the other classifier to a state in s_2. The initial set of classes is given by reachable states of the product classifier $e \otimes f$:

i. $S := \{\{e_i, f_j\} \mid (e_i, f_j) \text{ is reachable in } e \otimes f\}$.
ii. If there exist $s_1, s_2 \in S$ such that $s_1 \cap s_2 \neq \emptyset$ then $S := S \setminus \{s_1, s_2\} \cup \{s_1 \cup s_2\}$.
iii. Repeat (ii) until no more classes can be unified.

The final value of S is the set of states of the new classifier DFA. The initial state is the class that contains initial states of e and f (note that both of them will be in the same class). The transition function $\rightarrow$ is a sum of transition functions $\rightarrow_e$ and $\rightarrow_f$ lifted to sets of states. For $s_1, s_2 \in S$: $s_1 \xrightarrow{a} s_2$ if $\exists.p_1 \in S_1.\exists p_2 \in S_2.p_1 \xrightarrow{a}_e p_2 \vee p_1 \xrightarrow{a}_f p_2$. The following proposition claims that this function is well-defined, deterministic and input-enabled:

Proposition 4. *Let $s_1, s_2 \in S$ be any two of the sets of states (not necessarily distinct) constructed with the above algorithm. Then for any states $p_1, p_2 \in s_1$, $p'_1, p'_2 \in s_2$ of the original classifiers and any symbol a: $p_1 \xrightarrow{a}_1 p'_1$ and $p'_1 \in s_2$ iff $p_2 \xrightarrow{a}_2 p'_2$ and $s'_2 \in s_2$, where $\rightarrow_i$ denotes $\rightarrow_e$ if $s_i \in S_e$ or $\rightarrow_f$ if $s_i \in S_f$.*

It follows that the classifier $g = (S, A, s, \rightarrow)$ constructed above is a well defined classifier DFA. Moreover, the observation classes that it induces are coarser than any class of $\sim_e$ and $\sim_f$. Due to the properties of the union-find algorithm, $\sim_g$ is actually the least equivalence encompassing both $\sim_e$ and $\sim_f$:

Proposition 5. *Let $\sim_e$ and $\sim_f$ be equivalences over $Action^*$, induced by classifiers $e = (S_e, Action, s_e, \rightarrow_e)$ and $f = (S_f, Action, s_f, \rightarrow_f)$. The equivalence $\sim_e \sqcup \sim_f$ is induced by a classifier g such that its states are computed applying the UNION-FIND algorithm to the set $\{ \{e_i, f_j\} \mid (e_i, f_j) \text{ reachable in } e \otimes f \}$, where two sets s_1, s_2 are unifiable if $s_1 \cap s_2$ is not empty. The union operation is a set union, the initial state is the set containing initial states of e and f, and the transition function is a sum of transition functions lifted to sets of states.*

The rightmost IOATS on Fig. 5 is a product of $\mathcal{E}$ and $\mathcal{F}$ obtained by application of the composition rules from section 5 (PG,SO) and the above algorithm. This product gives rise to the observer which does not distinguish any sequences.

7 Environment Driven Specialization

We shall now broaden the meaning of a model of a system to encompass a family of systems, and let it represent functionality, which in its entire richness may not be present in any of the actual members being produced. Particular family members will be specified using models of environments, and derived by transformations preserving relativized equivalence in a given color-blind environment. We shall informally demonstrate a product line derivation scenario, hinting at what techniques could be used to make such automatic derivation viable.

Our family will consist of several state/event systems. The transition relation of state/event systems (see section 2) produces sets of actions during a single reaction step. In such a setting the observational classes of environments become sets of sets (powersets) of actions.

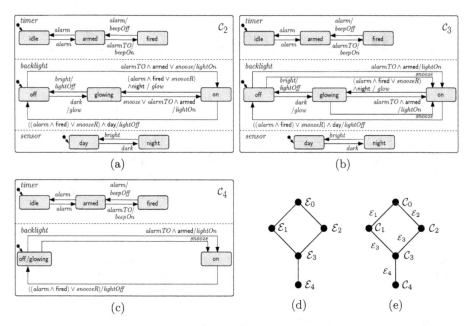

Fig. 6. Specialized models $\mathcal{C}_2$ (a), $\mathcal{C}_3$ (b) and $\mathcal{C}_4$ (c). Overview of the relationship between the environments (d) and the specialized models (e)

For a set $A \subseteq Action$ let *ignore A* denote observation classes, which ignore elements of A, but distinguish all the other actions:

$$ignore\ A = \big\{ \{o \cup o' | o' \in \mathcal{P}(A)\} \mid o \in \mathcal{P}(Action \setminus A)\big\}$$

Note that ignoring the empty set, *ignore $\emptyset$*, means observing all differences in outputs. Another abbreviation *equiv A* denotes observation classes, which are unable to distinguish between any actions in A:

$$equiv\ A = \big\{ \{o \cup o' | o' \in \mathcal{P}(A) \setminus \emptyset\} \mid o \in \mathcal{P}(Action \setminus A)\big\} \cup \{o \mid o \in \mathcal{P}(Action \setminus A)\}$$

We shall begin with stating general requirements, which hold for all the environments used to execute the alarm clock. These general requirements usually reflect the physical nature of actuators and sensors. In the case of our alarm clock events *dark/bright* and *snooze/snoozeR* are always generated in an alternating fashion: $\mathcal{E}_0 = Interleave\ snooze\ snoozeR\ \wedge\ Interleave\ dark\ bright$. Figure 7a demonstrates how *Interleave* could be defined using a set-based semantics.

The first member of the family $\mathcal{C}_1$ was introduced in section 2 (Fig. 2). This model operates in an environment, which becomes blind for the *lightOn* action right after generating the *snooze* event. Formally $\mathcal{E}_1 = \mathcal{E}_0 \wedge \mathcal{E}'$, where $\mathcal{E}'$ is defined on Fig. 7b. Figure 6a presents a new clock $\mathcal{C}_2$, which is devoid of the actual snooze function. The user of this clock can still press the snooze button, but the only effect it has is turning the backlight on for a short while. This

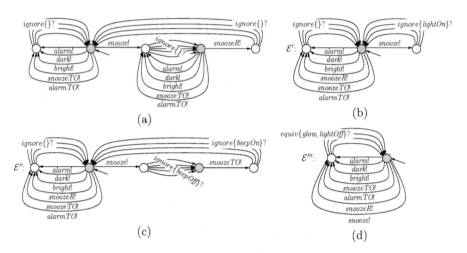

Fig. 7. (a) *Interleave snooze snoozeR*. (b) Environment $\mathcal{E}'$ ignoring the *lightOn* output produced in reaction to the *snooze* button. (c) Environment $\mathcal{E}''$ ignoring the snooze function of the clock. (d) Environment $\mathcal{E}'''$ *Equiv glow lightOff*

user becomes blind to *beepOn* and *beepOff* actions initiated by the *snooze* and *snoozeTO* events. Formally $\mathcal{E}_2 = \mathcal{E}_0 \wedge \mathcal{E}''$, where $\mathcal{E}''$ is defined on Fig. 7c.

The third clock variant $\mathcal{C}_3$ is a combination of $\mathcal{C}_1$ and $\mathcal{C}_2$. It has neither the snooze function nor the snooze activated backlight function. We obtain it by specialization against the $\mathcal{E}_3$ environment, where $\mathcal{E}_3 = \mathcal{E}_1 \wedge \mathcal{E}_2$. The model is presented on Fig. 6b. Note that this clock still needs a snooze button, which exhibits a slight anomaly in turning on the glow mode, namely that the glow mode will not be activated, while this button is pressed. This is a perfectly correct reminiscence of our original model, which could be easily remedied by adding another constraint to the environment, that event *snooze* never occurs.

We would like to consider yet another restriction of the clock behavior. The clock denoted $\mathcal{C}_4$, shall be deprived of the glowing mode (Fig. 6c). The glow-mode lamp is not installed and the *glow* action is reimplemented to turn off the main lamp instead. A corresponding environment $\mathcal{E}'''$ is defined on Fig. 7d. This environment is itself interesting as it specifies a less shiny alarm clock, which may find its happy customers. Nevertheless, we decided to combine its characteristics with the restrictions of $\mathcal{E}_3$, giving rise to an even more simple alarm clock with neither the snooze related functions nor the glow mode: $\mathcal{E}_4 = \mathcal{E}_3 \wedge \mathcal{E}'''$.

One can describe surprisingly many more reasonable variants even for such a simple system as our alarm clock. Figures 6d-6e present an overview of environments and systems in our product line. Edges represent simulation and relativized simulation. Proposition 6 explains how to interpret transitivity in the hierarchy of systems (Fig. 6e).

Proposition 6. *For any systems $\mathcal{S}_1$, $\mathcal{S}_2$ and $\mathcal{S}_3$ and any two compatible color-blind environments $\mathcal{E}$ and $\mathcal{F}$ it holds that: $\mathcal{S}_1 \leqslant_{\mathcal{E}} \mathcal{S}_2 \wedge \mathcal{S}_2 \leqslant_{\mathcal{F}} \mathcal{S}_3 \wedge \mathcal{E} \leqslant \mathcal{F} \Rightarrow \mathcal{S}_1 \leqslant_{\mathcal{E}} \mathcal{S}_3$.*

8   Related Work

Derivation of product lines is conventionally associated with partial evaluation [13, 4, 8]. There have been limited approaches to enable partial evaluation based on execution traces instead of fixed input values [10, 20, 5], nevertheless they were never implemented for realistic languages. We fear that these transformations, designed for abstract process calculi, can be barely applied in such contexts. This is why we intend to define transformations on the language level, and only prove correctness on the abstract level. Our framework allows more transformations than known before due to the color-blindness, which allows some non-reductive mutations in the program.

Previously Wąsowski [25] presented a static framework for specifying environments for reactive models, which relies solely on state independent properties. The present paper provides a theoretical foundation for a product line management setup similar to Wasowski's [25], but based on behavioral properties.

Relativized simulation has been originally introduced by Larsen [16, 15, 14]. Our framework is modeled after this work, rephrased in the setting of I/O alternating transition systems and extended with the notion of color-blindness. In Larsen's formulation, based on simple labeled transition systems [19], it was impossible to express an environment's inability to distinguish outputs.

The study of behaviors of systems embedded into execution contexts is relatively mature [15, 1, 18, 22, 12]. Our work stems out from this series, by its extended support for observability specifications via color-blindness. This support is needed, if the tools based on this framework, are to be useful for development of product lines of embedded systems.

9   Conclusion and Future Work

We have presented the semantics of a specification language for environments of reactive synchronous systems, together with a notion of context-dependent refinement based on color-blindness. This refinement relation is more liberal than usual in allowing some mutations to program outputs, instead of bare reductions. We have explained and demonstrated how partial specifications of behaviors can be composed and used to define families of products. The framework was designed as a core of an upcoming tool for compact code generation and product line derivation for discrete control embedded systems. Our specifications shall be used as preconditions for advanced model optimizers/specializers. We have thoroughly discussed issues, which arise in the implementation of the theory for realistic languages, especially focusing on languages with sequences as outputs.

An implementation [23] of a powerful context-aware optimizer for models based on model-checking and program analysis is currently underway. This prototype tool is supposed to be compatible with an industrial development environment for embedded systems [11], which will allow for realistic case studies.

We would like to attempt a formulation of a corresponding theory for distributed asynchronous systems. We hope that a similarly appealing construction can be proposed for such systems. The main difficulty appears to be a notion of simulation between nondeterministic color-blind environments. The simulation of definition 7 is too weak to imply theorem 1 in a nondeterministic setting.

References

1. L. de Alfaro and T. A. Henzinger. Interface automata. In *Foundations of Software Engineering (FSE)*, pp. 109–120, Vienna, September 2001. ACM Press.
2. G. Berry. The foundations of Esterel. In G. Plotkin, etal. eds., *Proof, Language and Interaction. Essays in Honour of Robin Milner*, pp. 425–454. MIT Press, 2000.
3. E. M. Clarke. *Model Checking*. The MIT Press, 1999.
4. O. Danvy et al. eds., *Partial Evaluation, LNCS* 1110, Feb. 1996. Springer-Verlag.
5. S. Etalle and M. Gabbrieli. Partial evaluation of concurrent constraint languages. *ACM Computing Surveys*, 30(3es), September 1998.
6. Rob van Glabbeek. The linear time–branching time spectrum In J.C.M Beaten and J.W. Klop eds., *CONCUR'90, LNCS* 458, Springer–Verlag
7. D. Harel. Statecharts: A visual formalism for complex systems. *Science of Computer Programming*, 8:231–274, 1987.
8. J. Hatcliff, T. Æ. Mogensen, and P. Thiemann, editors. *Partial Evaluation: Practice and Theory, LNCS 1706*. Springer-Verlag, Copenhagen, Denmark, 1999.
9. C.A.R. Hoare. *Communicating Sequential Processes*. Prentice Hall, 1985.
10. H. Hosoya, N. Kobayashi, A. Yonezawa. Partial evaluation scheme for concurrent languages and its correctness. In L. Bougé et al eds., *Euro-Par'96, LNCS* 1123.
11. IAR Inc. IAR visualSTATE®. http://www.iar.com/Products/VS/.
12. A. Igarashi and N. Kobayashi. A generic type system for the pi-calculus. In *POPL 2001*. ACM Press.
13. Neil D. Jones, Carsten K. Gomard, and Peter Sestoft. *Partial Evaluation and Automatic Program Generation*. Prentice Hall, 1993.
14. K.G. Larsen and R. Milner. A compositional protocol verification using relativized bisimulation. *Information and Computation*, 99(1):80–108, 1992.
15. K. Larsen. *Context Dependent Bisimulation Between Processes*. PhD thesis, Edinburgh University, 1986.
16. K. Larsen. A context dependent equivalence between processes. *Theoretical Computer Science*, 49:184–215, 1987.
17. J. Lind-Nielsen, H. R. Andersen, H. Hulgaard, G. Behrmann, K. Kristoffersen, and K. G. Larsen. Verification of large state/event systems using compositionality and dependency analysis. *Formal Methods in System Design*, 18(1):5–23, 2001.
18. N. Lynch. I/O automata: A model for discrete event systems. In *Annual Conference on Information Sciences and Systems*, pp. 29–38, Princeton, N.J., 1988.
19. R. Milner. *Communication and Concurrency*. Prentice Hall, 1989.
20. M. Murakami. Partial evaluation of reactive communciating processes using temporal logic formulas. In *Algebraic and Object-Oriented Approaches to Software Science*, 1995.
21. Object Management Group. OMG Unified Modelling Language specification, 1999.
22. S. K. Rajamani, J. Rehof. Conformance checking for models of asynchronous message passing software. In *CAV'02*, LNCS 2404, Springer-Verlag.
23. Scope: a statechart compiler. http://www.mini.pw.edu.pl/~wasowski/scope.
24. Sun Microsystems, Inc. Java Card(TM) specification. http://java.sun.com/.
25. A. Wąsowski. Automatic generation of program families by model restrictions. In *SPLC 2004*, LNCS 3154, Boston, USA, September 2004. Springer-Verlag.

On the Correspondence Between Conformance Testing and Regular Inference

Therese Berg[1], Olga Grinchtein[1], Bengt Jonsson[1],
Martin Leucker[2], Harald Raffelt[3], and Bernhard Steffen[3]

[1] Department of Computer Systems, Uppsala University, Sweden
{thereseb, olgag, bengt}@it.uu.se
[2] Institute of Informatics, TU Munich, Germany
leucker@in.tum.de
[3] LS V, Universität Dortmund, Germany
{raffelt, steffen}@cs.uni-dortmund.de

Abstract. Conformance testing for finite state machines and regular inference both aim at identifying the model structure underlying a *black box system* on the basis of a limited set of observations. Whereas the former technique *checks* for equivalence with a *given* conjecture model, the latter techniques addresses the corresponding *synthesis* problem by means of techniques adopted from automata learning. In this paper we establish a common framework to investigate the similarities of these techniques by showing how results in one area can be transferred to results in the other and to explain the reasons for their differences.

1 Introduction

The two areas of conformance testing for finite state machines and regular inference both share the same problem of deducing an unknown finite state machine from a limited set of observations. Whereas the former technique justifies a given conjecture, the latter techniques aims at constructing conjectures by observation. In this paper we establish a common framework to investigate the similarities of these techniques by showing how results in one area can be transferred to results in the other and to explain the reasons for their differences.

The area of testing reactive systems has witnessed significant advances in the last decades. A model problem in this area is that of black-box protocol testing, where one assumes given a finite-state machine specification of the intended behavior of a protocol, and would like to derive a test suite which checks that an implementation conforms to such a specification. There are several techniques for generating test suites that guarantee that an implementation under test (IUT) conforms to a specification, under certain hypotheses [Cho78, FvBK+91, SD88, VCI90].

A more recent line of development concerns checking whether an IUT satisfies certain correctness properties, in the absence of a model or specification. Recent work has employed techniques of automata learning, or regular inference [GPY02, HHNS02, HNS03, PVY99].

M. Cerioli (Ed.): FASE 2005, LNCS 3442, pp. 175–189, 2005.

Both of the above approaches solve the problem of inferring a finite state machine from observations of its behavior, with different modalities. In conformance testing, the purpose is to check that it is equivalent to a given finite state specification. In automata learning, the purpose is to infer an unknown finite state machine. Both approaches must solve the problem of how to infer a finite state machine from a limited set of observations. Thus, techniques for conformance testing and automata learning must decide what is "enough information" to deduce that an IUT is equivalent to a certain finite state machine. In conformance testing, one goal is to minimize the cost (e.g., the number of observations or their total length) of the observations that are needed to infer that the IUT is equivalent to a specification. In automata learning, one goal has been to understand when "enough information" is obtained to make a conjecture about the structure of an IUT.

Let us make the preceding discussion a little more elaborate. In conformance testing we are given an FSM $\mathcal{M}$, playing the role of a specification, and we want to verify that the IUT is equivalent to $\mathcal{M}$. We construct a test suite with the property that any FSM $\mathcal{A}$ which passes the test suite is equivalent to $\mathcal{M}$. Of course, this can not be achieved unless some additional assumptions about $\mathcal{A}$ are introduced. A common such assumption is that $\mathcal{A}$ has at most as many states as $\mathcal{M}$. We will then say that the test suite is a conformance test suite for $\mathcal{M}$ under these assumptions.

In Automata Learning, we are given a set of observations generated by a test suite or a set of queries, and want to construct an FSM which is an "as good as possible explanation" of the observations, hopefully being close to the structure of the actual IUT. Since there are an infinite number of such FSMs, we should also here add assumptions. Typical assumptions are of the form to give an upper bound the number of states, or to ask for an automaton with a minimum number of states; note that there may be several such automata.

The problem of constructing conformant finite automata was studied by many people [Ang81, Ang87, BDG97, Gol67, Gol78, OG92] and others. Several of these works present conditions on observations that allow a unique minimum automaton to be constructed with modest effort (e.g., in polynomial time).

From the above discussion, it follows that in principle, we can relate conformance testing and automata learning in the following way:

- If the observations form a conformance test suite for an FSM $\mathcal{M}$, given some assumptions, then under the same assumptions we can infer the FSM $\mathcal{M}$ from these observations using automata learning techniques.
- If the FSM $\mathcal{A}$ is inferred from the observations under some assumptions, and furthermore $\mathcal{A}$ is the only such automaton, then under the same assumptions the observations form a conformance test suite for $\mathcal{A}$.

The above statements are rather general, and "kind of obvious". In this paper, we shall compare results in these two areas, and make the link between these two areas explicit. One goal is to relate existing techniques for conformance testing and automata learning by showing that they use very similar concepts of "enough information" in order to infer the structure of an IUT. We will also make a comparison of the difference in complexity between the two approaches in different settings.

From a different point of view, one can understand our contribution as clarifying the following question: What is the core information of an automaton in terms of observations/traces needed to identify it uniquely? We do this in the framework of conformance testing as well as in the framework of learning and show that both domains (nearly) identify the same type of information.

For our comparison, we must bridge several differences in the models typically used. In conformance testing, the most common model is the Mealy machine, which generates output on each transition. In automata learning, the most common model is deterministic finite automata (DFA), which merely accept or reject a given input string. We therefore define a unifying notion of finite state machine which has an abstract notion of "output" in response to a received sequence of input symbols. This notion can be instantiated to Mealy machines by letting the output be the sequence of symbols generated in response to the input, to DFAs outputting a verdict "accepted" or "not accepted".

An important vehicle in the comparison is a general theorem, which shows that under certain conditions on a set of observations, a small finite state machine that satisfies these observations must have a certain structure.

Related Work. The relationship between machine learning and conformance testing was observed by Lee and Yannakakis [LY96–p. 1118], who stated that Angluin's algorithm can be used for fault detection. Note that [LY96] employ learning techniques for conformance testing while we study their similarities. [LY96] also suggested as an interesting subject of study the relationship between conformance testing without reset (surveyed in [LY96]), and corresponding work on machine learning by Rivest and Schapire [RS93].

Organization of this Paper. In the next section, we define our model of Finite State Machines, aiming to unify Mealy machines, DFAs, and some other models. In Section 3, we state a general theorem which shows how a set of observations limits the set of machines that may be inferred from it. Section 4 describes some existing techniques for deriving conformance test suites, and Section 5 describes some existing techniques for learning automata from observations. Results for these methods are shown to follow from the general theorem in Section 3. The techniques of these two sections are thereafter related in Section 6.

2   Preliminaries

We will first define two variants of finite state machines: Mealy machines, commonly used in the conformance testing literature, and finite automata, commonly used in automata learning literature. They differ in how they respond to input sequences: Mealy machines produce an output symbol in response to each received input symbol, whereas finite automata merely accept or reject a given input string. We will define a unifying more general model of finite state machines, that produce a more abstractly defined form of output, which can be specialized to both Mealy machines and finite automata.

We assume a finite set Σ of *input symbols*, usually denoted by $a, b, a_1, a_2, \ldots$. Elements of Σ^* are (input) *strings* or *words*. Given $u, v \in \Sigma^*$, u is said to be a *prefix* of v if $v = uw$ for some $w \in \Sigma^*$.

Mealy Machines. A *Mealy machine* over Σ is a tuple $M = \langle O, Q, q_0, \delta, \lambda \rangle$ where O is a finite nonempty set of *output symbols*, Q is a finite nonempty set of *states*, $q_0 \in Q$ is the *initial state*, $\delta : Q \times \Sigma \to Q$ is the *state transition function*, and $\lambda : Q \times \Sigma \to O$ is the *output function*.

An intuitive interpretation of a Mealy machine is as follows. At any point in time, the machine is in one state $q \in Q$. It is possible to give inputs to the machine, by applying an input symbol a. The machine responds by producing an output symbol $\lambda(q, a)$ and transforming itself to the new state $\delta(q, a)$. We can depict Mealy machines as directed labeled graphs, where Q is the set of vertices. For each state $q \in Q$ and input symbol $a \in \Sigma$, there is an edge from q to $\delta(q, a)$ labeled by "a/b", where b is the output symbol $\lambda(q, a)$. See Figure 1 for an example of a Mealy machine. Note that the letters a and b are used in two ways. In the text they are metasymbols denoting arbitrary input and output symbols, whereas in examples they denote specific input or output symbols.

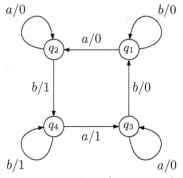

Fig. 1. A Mealy machine with states $Q = \{q_1, q_2, q_3, q_4\}$, input symbols $I = \Sigma = \{a, b\}$, and output symbols $O = \{0, 1\}$

Applying an input sequence $u = a_1 a_2 \cdots a_k \in \Sigma^*$ starting in a state q_1 takes the machine successively to a sequence of states $q_2, q_3, \ldots, q_{k+1}$, denoted $\delta(q_i, u)$, where $q_{i+1} = \delta(q_i, a_i)$ for $i = 1, \cdots, k$, and produces a sequence of output symbols $b_1 b_2 \cdots b_k \in O^*$, where $b_i = \lambda(q_i, a_i)$ for $i = 1, \cdots, k$. We extend the transition and output functions from input symbols to sequences of input symbols, by defining $\delta(q_1, u) = q_{k+1}$ and $\lambda(q_1, u) = b_1 b_2 \cdots b_k$. A more precise recursive definition is as follows:

$$\delta(q, \varepsilon) = q \qquad\qquad \lambda(q, \varepsilon) = \varepsilon$$
$$\delta(q, ua) = \delta(\delta(q, u), a) \qquad\qquad \lambda(q, ua) = \lambda(q, u)\lambda(\delta(q, u), a)$$

Finite Automata. A *deterministic finite automaton* (*DFA*) over Σ is a structure $\mathcal{A} = (Q, \delta, q_0, F)$ where Q is a non-empty finite set of *states*, $q_0 \in Q$ is the *initial state*, $\delta : Q \times \Sigma \to Q$ is the *transition function*, and $F \subseteq Q$ is the set of *accepting states*.

Just as for Mealy machines, we extend the transition function from input symbols to sequences of input symbols, by defining

$$\delta(q, \varepsilon) = q$$
$$\delta(q, ua) = \delta(\delta(q, u), a)$$

An input string u is *accepted* iff $\delta(q_0, u) \in F$. The *language* accepted by $\mathcal{A}$, denoted by $\mathcal{L}(\mathcal{A})$, is the set of accepted input strings.

Unifying Formalism. In order to unify the two above types of state machines, we define a more abstract notion of output produced by a finite state machine. Let an *output domain* be a semi-group $\mathcal{D}$ equipped with an associative binary operation, which we denote by juxtaposition. The intended intuition is that an FSM when inputing a sequence of inputs u outputs an element in $\mathcal{D}$. If the FSM outputs x after inputing u and thereafter outputs y in response to v, then the entire output in response to uv is the element xy.

Definition 1. *A finite state machine (FSM) over Σ is a structure $(\mathcal{D}, Q, \delta, q_0, \lambda)$ where $\mathcal{D}$ is an output domain, Q is a non-empty finite set of* states, $q_0 \in Q$ is *the* initial state, $\delta : Q \times \Sigma \to Q$ is the *transition function, and* $\lambda : Q \times \Sigma^* \to \mathcal{D}$ *is an* output function, *which satisfies the following* homomorphism *property:*

- $\lambda(q, uv) = \lambda(q, u)\lambda(\delta(q, u), v)$ *for any $q \in Q$ and $u, v \in \Sigma^*$.*   □

By the homomorphism property, it is enough to define the output function for input sequences of length 0 and 1, i.e., to define $\lambda(q, \varepsilon)$ and $\lambda(q, a)$ for $a \in \Sigma$.

In this paper, we will consider only FSMs which are *suffix-observable*, meaning that from only the output $\lambda(q_0, uv)$ produced by applying the input sequence uv, we can uniquely extract the output generated by the suffix v, which we denote by $\lambda(q_0, uv)|_v$, so that $\lambda(q_0, uv)|_v = \lambda(\delta(q_0, u), v)$. For the Mealy machine and DFA models, this assumption trivially holds.

To see how our definition of finite state machines generalizes Mealy machines and finite automata, let us specialize it first to Mealy machines. Here, the output domain is the set O^* with the binary string concatenation operation. The output function is the same as that defined for Mealy machines, lifted to strings.

To specialize to finite automata, let $\mathcal{D}$ be the set $\{+, -\}$, where intuitively $+$ denotes "accept" and $-$ denotes "not accept". The semi-group operation maps a pair of arguments onto the second one, i.e., it can be defined by the following table.

$$+\, + \; = \; + \qquad\qquad +\, - \; = \; -$$
$$-\, + \; = \; + \qquad\qquad -\, - \; = \; -$$

The output function of a DFA is defined by

$$\lambda(q, \varepsilon) = \begin{cases} + & \text{if} \quad q \in F \\ - & \text{if} \quad q \notin F \end{cases}$$
$$\lambda(q, u) = \lambda(\delta(q, u), \varepsilon)$$

where the last equality follows from the particular definition of the semi-group operation, which makes the left argument irrelevant.

Looking at the examples of Mealy machines and finite automata, we can identify two special subclasses of FSM, characterized by the forms of their output functions:

- FSMs that generate output only at transitions, where $\lambda(q, \varepsilon)$ is a unit element of $\mathcal{D}$ for any state q. Mealy machines are an example with ε as unit element.
- FSMs that generate output only at the last state, i.e., $\lambda(q, u) = \lambda(\delta(q, u), \varepsilon)$, implying that we only need to specify $\lambda(q, \varepsilon)$ for any state q. An example is DFAs.

3   Characterizing FSMs by Observations

In this section, we provide general definitions and results concerning how FSMs can be uniquely inferred from or characterized by observations or tests. Let $\mathcal{D}$ from now on be a fixed particular output domain.

Let us consider the process of observing or testing a black-box IUT, whose behavior can be represented as an FSM. This consists in applying a set of input sequences to the IUT, whereby the corresponding outputs are observed and recorded. The recorded observations can be represented as a partial *observation function* $\mathcal{O}$ from Σ^* to $\mathcal{D}$, whose domain $Dom(\mathcal{O})$ is the set of input sequences that have been applied to the IUT.

In conformance testing, the observation function should represent a test suite which is obtained from an FSM $\mathcal{M} = (\mathcal{D}, Q, \delta, q_0, \lambda)$ which plays the role of a specification, and a set $\mathcal{I} \subseteq \Sigma^*$ of input sequences. Define $\mathcal{M}|_{\mathcal{I}}$ as the observation function $\mathcal{O}$ with $Dom(\mathcal{O}) = \mathcal{I}$, such that $\mathcal{O}(u)$ is defined and equal to $\lambda(q_0, u)$ whenever $u \in \mathcal{I}$. We say that an FSM $\mathcal{A} = (\mathcal{D}, Q, \delta, q_0, \lambda)$ is *conformant* with an observation function $\mathcal{O}$, denoted $\mathcal{A} \models \mathcal{O}$, if $\mathcal{O}(u) = \lambda(q_0, u)$ whenever $u \in Dom(\mathcal{O})$. We trivially have $\mathcal{M} \models \mathcal{M}|_{\mathcal{I}}$ for any $\mathcal{M}$ and $\mathcal{I}$.

Definition 2. *$\mathcal{O}$ is a conformance test suite for $\mathcal{M}$ if any FSM $\mathcal{A}$ with at most as many states as $\mathcal{M}$, such that $\mathcal{A} \models \mathcal{O}$, is isomorphic to $\mathcal{M}$.*

In automata learning, we are given an observation function $\mathcal{O}$, and want to construct an FSM which is an "as good as possible explanation" of the observations, hopefully being close to the actual IUT. An obvious criterion is that the FSM should be conformant with $\mathcal{O}$.[1] Since there are an infinite number of such FSMs,

---

[1] However, not all works on automata learning guarantee to generate conformant FSMs.

we should also here add assumptions. A natural choice is to ask for an automaton with a minimum number of states. Note that there may be several such automata.

Definition 3. *Let $\mathcal{O}$ be an observation function. We say that the FSM $\mathcal{A}$ is inferred from $\mathcal{O}$ if $\mathcal{A} \models \mathcal{O}$ and any other $\mathcal{A}'$ with $\mathcal{A}' \models \mathcal{O}$ has at least as many states as $\mathcal{A}$. We say that $\mathcal{A}$ is* uniquely inferred *from $\mathcal{O}$ if $\mathcal{A}$ is the only such FSM.*

We observe the following propositions,

- if $\mathcal{O}$ is a conformance test suite for $\mathcal{M}$ then $\mathcal{M}$ is uniquely inferred from $\mathcal{O}$, and
- if $\mathcal{A}$ is uniquely inferred from $\mathcal{O}$ then $\mathcal{O}$ is a conformance test suite for $\mathcal{A}$.

By these propositions, both conformance testing and automata learning must in some sense prescribe how to transform an observation function $\mathcal{O}$ into an automaton which is conformant with $\mathcal{O}$. A natural approach is to define an equivalence relation on the prefixes of $Dom(\mathcal{O})$, and let each equivalence class be a state of an automaton. If the equivalence is properly constructed, the transition and output functions can be obtained from $\mathcal{O}$. In general, however, the number of possible equivalences is too large for this to be an efficient procedure. The problem of finding the minimal FSM (i.e., with the smallest number of states) which is conformant with a given observation function is NP-complete [Gol78]. But several works [Gol67, Gol78, Ang81, Ang87, OG92, BDG97] overcome this obstacle by presenting conditions on the observations that allow a unique minimum automaton to be constructed. The conditions exploit the property of suffix-observability, by regarding each input sequence as the concatenation of a prefix and a suffix (possibly in several ways).

So, let the set of observations be given by an *observation structure*, which is a partial function $\mathcal{T}$ from a set $Dom(\mathcal{T}) \subseteq \Sigma^*$ of prefixes, which must include ε. For each $u \in Dom(\mathcal{T})$, $\mathcal{T}(u)$ is a partial function from a set $Dom(\mathcal{T}(u)) \subseteq \Sigma^*$ of suffixes, which must include ε, to $\mathcal{D}$. Intuitively, $\mathcal{T}(u)(v)$, for $v \neq \varepsilon$, is the output produced in response to the suffix v in a situation where the input sequence uv is applied to the IUT. Note that this output can be uniquely extracted by the assumption of suffix-observability. In contrast, we let $\mathcal{T}(u)(\varepsilon)$ be the entire output produced by the IUT in response to the input sequence u. Note that $\mathcal{T}(u)(\varepsilon)$ has a meaning which differs from that of $\mathcal{T}(u)(v)$ for $v \neq \varepsilon$.

An observation structure $\mathcal{T}$ represents the observation function $\mathcal{O}_\mathcal{T}$ with

- $Dom(\mathcal{O}_\mathcal{T}) = \{uv \ : \ u \in Dom(\mathcal{T}) \text{ and } v \in Dom(\mathcal{T}(u))\}$, and
- $\mathcal{O}_\mathcal{T}(uv) = \mathcal{T}(u)(\varepsilon) \, \mathcal{T}(u)(v)$.

Conversely, an observation function $\mathcal{O}$ can, given a set $U \subseteq Dom(\mathcal{O})$, be represented by the observation structure $\mathcal{T}_{\mathcal{O},U}$ with

- $Dom(\mathcal{T}_{\mathcal{O},U}) = U$ and $Dom(\mathcal{T}_{\mathcal{O},U}(u)) = \{v \ : \ uv \in Dom(\mathcal{O})\}$,
- $\mathcal{T}_{\mathcal{O},U}(u)(\varepsilon) = \mathcal{O}(u)$ for $u \in U$, and
- $\mathcal{T}_{\mathcal{O},U}(u)(v) = \mathcal{O}(uv)|_v$ for $v \neq \varepsilon$, $u \in U$, and $v \in Dom(\mathcal{T}_{\mathcal{O},U}(u))$,

where $\mathcal{O}(uv)|_v$ is the output produced in response to the suffix v, obtained from the result $\mathcal{O}(uv)$ of applying uv to the IUT.

When constructing an automaton from observations, the prefixes in $Dom(T)$ are candidates for representing states of the automaton, whereas the suffixes in the sets $Dom(T(u))$ are used to determine which prefixes should represent the same state.

Let $T(u) \approx T(u')$ denote that for any $v \in (Dom(T(u)) \cap Dom(T(u')))$ we have $T(u)(v) = T(u')(v)$. Let $T(u) \subseteq T(u')$ denote that $Dom(T(u)) \subseteq Dom(T(u'))$ and $T(u) \approx T(u')$. Let $T(u) = T(u')$ denote that $T(u) \subseteq T(u')$ and $T(u') \subseteq T(u)$.

Define an *access string* of T, to be an input sequence $u \in Dom(T)$ such that $ua \in Dom(T)$ for each $a \in \Sigma$. We say that an equivalence $\equiv$ on $Dom(T)$ is *U-closed* if each equivalence class contains a string in U. We say that an equivalence $\equiv$ on $Dom(T)$ is *U-consistent* if whenever $u \equiv u'$ for $u, u' \in U$ and $ua, u'a \in Dom(T)$ for any $a \in \Sigma$, then $ua \equiv u'a$ and $T(ua)(\varepsilon)|_a = T(u'a)(\varepsilon)|_a$.

Definition 4. *Let T be an observation structure, let U be a set of access strings of T containing ε. If $\equiv$ is a U-closed and U-consistent equivalence relation on $Dom(T)$, define the automaton $\langle T, U \rangle / \equiv$ as $(\mathcal{D}, Q, \delta, q_0, \lambda)$, where*

- $Q = Dom(T)/ \equiv$,
- $\delta([u], a) = [ua]$ *for* $u \in U$,
- $q_0 = [\varepsilon]$,
- $\lambda([u], a) = \mathcal{O}_T(u, a)|_a$ *for* $u \in U$.   □

We are now ready to state a general theorem that gives constraints on any FSM that is conformant with an observation function.

Theorem 1 (Characterization Theorem). *Let T be an observation structure, and let U be a set of access strings of T. If the relation $\approx$ on $Dom(T)$ contains a unique maximal equivalence relation $\equiv$, which is U-closed, then (letting n be the number of equivalence classes of $\equiv$)*

1. *any FSM which is conformant with $\mathcal{O}_T$ has at least n states,*
2. *if $\mathcal{A} \models \mathcal{O}_T$ and $\mathcal{A}$ has at most n states, then $\equiv$ is U-consistent, and*
   (a) *$\mathcal{A}$ is isomorphic to $\langle T, U \rangle / \equiv$,*
   (b) *T is a conformance test for $\mathcal{A}$*
   (c) *$\mathcal{A}$ is uniquely inferred from T.*

Proof. If $\mathcal{A} = (\mathcal{D}, Q', \delta', q_0', \lambda') \models \mathcal{O}_T$, then each of its states can correspond to at most one equivalence class of $\equiv$, i.e., $u \equiv u'$ if $\delta'(q_0', u) = \delta'(q_0', u')$ for $u, u' \in Dom(T)$. If $\mathcal{A}$ has n states, this correspondence must be exact, and the theorem follows.   □

Intuitively, Theorem 1 gives necessary constraints on an FSM that is conformant with the observations represented by an observation structure T. If there is a unique maximal equivalence with n classes, then any conformant automaton has at least n states. In general, there is no guarantee that a conformant FSM with n states actually exists, but if it does, Theorem 1 states that it must be isomorphic to $\langle T, U \rangle / \equiv$. Later, in Theorem 4 we shall give extra conditions on T which guarantee the existence of a conformant n-state automaton.

The condition "contains a unique maximal equivalence relation" in Theorem 1 is not so constructive. More concrete sufficient conditions on T are given by the following proposition.

Proposition 1. *Let T be an observation structure, and let U be a set of access strings of T. If*

- *$T(u) \not\approx T(u')$ for $u, u' \in U$ with $u \neq u'$, and*
- *for each $u \in Dom(T)$ there is a $u' \in U$ with $T(u) \subseteq T(u')$,*

then $\approx$ is a unique maximal equivalence on $Dom(T)$, and is closed. □

4 Conformance Testing

In this section, we consider some standard techniques for constructing conformance test suites: the W-method by Vasilevski [Vas73] and Chow [Cho78], an optimization by Fujiwara et al. [FvBK+91] called the partial W-method (or Wp-method), and another optimization described by Lee and Yannakakis [LY96].

Definition 5. *Let $\mathcal{M} = (\mathcal{D}, Q, \delta, q_0, \lambda)$ be an FSM. A set U of input sequences containing ε is called*

- *a state cover set if for each state $q \in Q$ there is an input sequence $u \in U$ with $\delta(q_0, u) = q$, i.e., for each state of $\mathcal{M}$, some sequence in U leads to it*
- *a transition cover set if whenever $\delta(q, a) = q'$ for some $q, q' \in Q$ and $a \in \Sigma$, there is an input sequence u with $\delta(q_0, u) = q$ such that both $u \in U$ and $ua \in U$.* □

The literature has slight differences in how such sequences can be chosen. For instance, Lee and Yannakakis [LY96] consider state and transition cover sets that are generated by a spanning tree for $\mathcal{M}$.

Say that a sequence $w \in \Sigma^*$ separates the states q and q' if $\lambda(q, w) \neq \lambda(q, w')$.

Definition 6. *Let $\mathcal{M} = (\mathcal{D}, Q, \delta, q_0, \lambda)$ be an FSM.*

- *A set W of sequences is a characterizing set for $\mathcal{M}$ (or separating set) if for each pair $q, q' \in Q$ of states it contains a sequence $w \in W$ which separates q and q'.*
- *A collection $\{W_q\}_{q \in Q}$ of sets of sequences W_q, one for each $q \in Q$, is called*
  - *a separating family [LY96] for $\mathcal{M}$ if for each pair $q, q' \in Q$ of states there is a sequence $w \in W_q \cap W_{q'}$ which separates q and q',*
  - *a family of identification sets for $\mathcal{M}$ if for each pair $q, q' \in Q$ of states, the set W_q contains a sequence $w \in W_q$ that separates q from q',* □

A separating family is also a family of identification sets, but not vice versa. A family of identification sets can be transformed into a separating family by adding the necessary sequences to the sets. A characterizing set can be thought of as a separating family, where all sets are identical. A characterizing set (and hence also a separating family) exists for every machine that is minimized.

In the following, fix an FSM $\mathcal{M} = (\mathcal{D}, Q, \delta, q_0, \lambda)$. Let

- V be a transition cover set; we denote by $v_{q,a}$ the sequence leading to q such that both $v_{q,a} \in V$ and $v_{q,a}a \in V$,
- U be a state cover set included in V; we denote by u_q the sequence leading to q (i.e., $u_q = v_{q,a}$ for some a),
- W be a characterizing set,
- $\{Z_q\}_{q \in Q}$ be a separating family,
- $\{W_q\}_{q \in Q}$ be a family of identification sets.

Definition 7. *A set $\mathcal{I} \subseteq \Sigma^*$ is called*

- *A W-set if it is of form* VW,
- *A Wp-set if it is of form*

$$U \left(\bigcup_{q \in Q} W_q \right) \cup \bigcup_{q \in Q, a \in \Sigma} v_{q,a} a W_{\delta(q,a)}$$

- *A Z-set if it is of form*

$$\bigcup_{q \in Q} v_{q,a} Z_q \cup \bigcup_{q \in Q, a \in \Sigma} v_{q,a} a Z_{\delta(q,a)}$$

□

Theorem 2 (Conformance Test Suites). *Let $\mathcal{M} = \langle Q, \delta, q_0, \lambda \rangle$ be an FSM and let $\mathcal{I} \subseteq \Sigma^*$ be a W-set, a Wp-set, or a Z-set. Then the observation function $\mathcal{M}|_{\mathcal{I}}$ is a conformance test suite for $\mathcal{M}$.*

Proof. We consider the case of Wp-set; the other cases are analogous. Let $\mathcal{T}$ be the observation structure defined by $Dom(\mathcal{T}) = U \cup \{v_{q,a}a : q \in Q, a \in \Sigma\}$, where $Dom(\mathcal{T}(u_q)) = \bigcup_{q \in Q} W_q$ for $u_q \in U$ and $Dom(\mathcal{T}(v_{q,a}a)) = W_{\delta(q,a)}$ for $v_{q,a} \in \{v_{q,a} : q \in Q, a \in \Sigma\} \setminus U$, such that $\mathcal{O}_{\mathcal{T}} = \mathcal{M}|_{\mathcal{I}}$. Since the observation structure is derived from $\mathcal{M}$, and by the properties of identification sets, it follows that U is a set of access strings such that the conditions in Proposition 1 are satisfied. Hence the conclusions of Theorem 1 hold, from which the result follows.   □

The W-method by Vasilevski [Vas73] and Chow [Cho78] uses W-sets. The Wp-method by Fujiwara et al. [FvBK+91] optimizes by using (hopefully smaller) identifications sets to reduce the size of the test suite; another optimization, using separating families (here defined using what we call Z-sets) is described by Lee and Yannakakis [LY96]. Since in the worst case, each identification set W_q has the same cardinality as the characterizing set W, upper bounds on sizes of the test suite generated by the three methods are the same: $O(n^2 |\Sigma|)$.

5   Automata Learning

We here briefly review some techniques of Automata Learning. The techniques reviewed here work by making queries about the output of an IUT in response to a set of input sequences, and recording the results in what can be represented as an observation structure T. When T has been developed so that it satisfies certain properties, then an automaton is conjectured from T. This conjecture is then compared by other means (idealized by a so-called "equivalence query") with the IUT. If the conjecture is equivalent to the IUT, the learning process stops, otherwise the equivalence query returns an input sequence on which the conjecture and the IUT disagree, and the learning process continues. It is desirable that each hypothesis has strictly more states than the previous one, in order that the process monotonically converges to a correct conjecture in reasonable time. This can be ensured if the properties required for making a hypothesis ensure that only one automaton can be inferred from T.

In this section, we present conditions on T that are defined by the L^* algorithm of Angluin [Ang87] using *observation tables*, and the *observation packs* defined by Balcázar et al. [BDG97].

Let T be an observation structure. Two situations are particularly interesting and separately well-studied in the literature

Definition 8. *Let T be an observation structure, where $Dom(T) = U \cup U\Sigma$ for a set U of access strings. T is an*

- **observation table** *if $Dom(T)$ is prefix-closed, and all $Dom(T(u))$ for $u \in Dom(T)$ are equal and suffix-closed.*
- **observation pack** *if $\varepsilon \in U$, and*
  - *$T(u) \not\approx T(u')$ for $u, u' \in U$ with $u \neq u'$, and*
  - *for each $u \in Dom(T)$ there is a $u' \in U$ with $T(u) = T(u')$.*   □

Based on these definitions, we obtain:

Theorem 3 (Uniqueness Theorem). *Let T be an observation structure with U as in Definition 8. If T is either*

- *an observation table, where $\approx$ is U-closed and U-consistent, or*
- *an observation pack, where $\approx$ is U-closed,*

then the relation $\approx$ on $Dom(T)$ is an equivalence relation. Let n be the number of equivalence classes of $\equiv$. Then any automaton A with at most n states, which is conformant with $\mathcal{O}_T$, is isomorphic to $\langle T, U \rangle / \equiv$.

Proof. It follows from Definition 8 that $\approx$ is an equivalence relation. The rest follows immediately from the Characterization Theorem 1   □

Please note that the Uniqueness Theorem does not guarantee the existence of a conformant automaton with n states. However, for observation tables we can give such a guarantee.

Theorem 4 (Existence Theorem). *Let T be an observation table with U as in Definition 8, where $\approx$ is U-closed and U-consistent. Then $\langle T, U \rangle / \approx \models \mathcal{O}_T$.*

This theorem is proved in [Gol78, Ang87]. Our Existence Theorem is a straightforward generalization.

6 Relating Testing and Learning Techniques

Conformance testing and learning are both concerned with establishing a relationship between a formal model and a black box system. Both techniques work by constructing a particular set of tests serving for the observation of the black box system. These conceptual similarities should be clear from the previous sections.

In fact, this similarity even reaches down to the level of technical detail of observation structures:

From Automata Learning to Conformance Testing

- Let T be an observation table with U as in Definition 8, such that $\approx$ is U-closed and U-consistent. Let W denote $Dom(T(u))$ for some $u \in U$ (the choice of u is irrelevant by Definition 8). If $\mathcal{M}$ is isomorphic to $\langle T, U \rangle / \approx$, then the set $(U \cup U\Sigma)W$ is a W-set for $\mathcal{M}$.
- Let T be an observation pack with U as in Definition 8, such that $\approx$ is U-closed. If $\mathcal{M} = \langle T, U \rangle / \approx$ is conformant with $\mathcal{O}_T$, then the set

$$\bigcup_{u \in U} u\, Dom(T(u)) \quad \cup \quad \bigcup_{u \in U, a \in \Sigma} ua\, Dom(T(ua))$$

is a Z-set for $\mathcal{M}$.

From Conformance Testing to Automata Learning Let $\mathcal{M} = \langle Q, \delta, q_0, \lambda \rangle$ be an FSM and let U be a state cover set of $\mathcal{M}$, and $U\Sigma$ the corresponding transition cover set.

- If U is prefix-closed, and W is a suffix-closed characterizing set, then the observation structure T defined by $Dom(T) = U \cup U\Sigma$ and $Dom(T(u)) = W$ for any $u \in U$, with $\mathcal{O}_T = \mathcal{M}|_{(U \cup U\Sigma)W}$, is an observation table where $\approx$ is U-closed and U-consistent, such that $\mathcal{M}$ is isomorphic to $\langle T, U \rangle / \approx$ and $\mathcal{M} \models \mathcal{O}_T$.
- If $\{Z_q\}_{q \in Q}$ is a separating family and

$$\mathcal{I} = \bigcup_{q \in Q} u_q Z_q \quad \cup \quad \bigcup_{q \in Q, a \in \Sigma} u_q a Z_{\delta(q,a)}$$

is a corresponding Z-set, then the observation structure T defined by $Dom(T) = U \cup U\Sigma$ and $Dom(T(u)) = Z_{\delta(q_0, u)}$ for $u \in U \cup U\Sigma$, with $\mathcal{O}_T = \mathcal{M}|_{\mathcal{I}}$, is an observation pack where $\approx$ is U-closed, such that $\mathcal{M}$ is isomorphic to $\langle T, U \rangle / \approx$ and $\mathcal{M} \models \mathcal{O}_T$.

Thus the observation table technique is strongly related to the W-method and the observation pack technique to the conformance testing technique described in [LY96].

However, there is also an intrinsic conceptual difference:

- conformance testing solves a *checking* problem: given a model and a black box system, it checks for conformance of the two. This allows us to systematically construct the tests from the given model, and
- learning solves a *synthesis* problem: given a black box, it synthesizes a model on the basis of a systematic experimentation process. The tests used here must be generated online in parallel with the model synthesis.

This conceptual difference becomes particularly clear under the often used assumption that the number of states of the black box system is known to be at most the number of states of the model n. In this case, we have:

The construction of a conformance test suite is a systematic and rather efficient process ($O\left(n^2 |\Sigma|\right)$) that extracts sufficiently many tests from the model to characterize the model up to isomorphism.

The process of generating tests during the learning process is much more involved, as there is no model for orientation. Thus we are essentially left with a systematic search problem. Angluins assumption of an equivalence oracle, which provides a (minimal) counter example in case of failure, draws a nice dividing line between the efficient and expensive part:

- *Complexity relative to the equivalence oracle:* Angluins observation table only grows polynomially in the size of the resulting model. The original proof for $O\left(n^3 |\Sigma|\right)$ can straightforwardly be extended to FSMs. Thus there is only an additional factor n in comparison to the conformance test suite generation. This factor is due to the fact that one must maintain many strings as potential state representatives as their redundancy can only be decided after the learning process has terminated.
- *Complexity for realizing/approximating the equivalence oracle:* In general it is impossible to implement an equivalence oracle, and even if the size of the black box system is known the problem is exponential in this size. Thus the equivalence oracle is the true bottleneck of automata learning. However, also here are similarities to conformance testing: a conformance test suite capturing IUTs which may have k states more than the model also grows exponentially in k. In fact, one could consider conformance testing of this more general kind as a good approximation of the equivalence oracle.[2]

7   Discussion

In this paper, we have established a common framework for investigating the similarities of conformance testing and automata learning by showing how re-

---

[2] Note, this is usually the line where the interplay of learning and conformance testing is mentioned.

sults in one area can be transferred to results in the other and to explain the reasons for their differences. Both techniques aim at identifying the model structure underlying a *black box system* on the basis of a limited set of observations. Whereas the former technique aims at *checking* for equivalence with a *given* conjecture model, the latter techniques addresses the corresponding *synthesis* problem: given a system, it aims at inferring a corresponding model. Our unified framework makes it possible to directly transfer results between these two communities or, more concretely, to build tools that easily specialize to tools for conformance testing or automata learning, respectively.

Beyond this rather technical match, our contribution also directly addresses the following question: What is the essential information about an automaton in terms of observations/traces? The similarity of the corresponding characterizations in the two domains mark them as a 'natural' choice. And, in fact, the state of the art here does not seem to leave much room for further optimizations, at least for the general setting. In particular when considering automata learning this means that major performance gains, a necessary precondition for a significant practical impact of this technology, are only possible for restricted scenarios. In other words, learning will only scale to practically relevant system scenarios, if its is possible to steer the learning process on the basis of complementary knowledge, e.g. about the structure of the black box systems, its intended behavior or certain other behavioral characteristics like input enabledness or output determinism. Our first experiments [HNS03, SH03] indicate the power of exploiting such knowledge, which does not only reduce the learning effort, but also the size of the model representation. We are currently investigating, how similar considerations may also be used to minimize conformance test suites.

References

[Ang81]   Dana Angluin. A note on the number of queries needed to identify regular languages. *Information and Control*, 51(1):76–87, 1981.

[Ang87]   Dana Angluin. Learning regular sets from queries and counterexamples. *Information and Computation*, 75(2):87–106, 1987.

[BDG97]   José L. Balcázar, Josep Díaz, and Ricard Gavaldá. Algorithms for learning finite automata from queries: A unified view. In *Advances in Algorithms, Languages, and Complexity*, pages 53–72. Kluwer, 1997.

[Cho78]   Tsun S. Chow. Testing software design modeled by finite-state machines. *IEEE Trans. on Software Engineering*, 4(3):178–187, May 1978. Special collection based on COMPSAC.

[FvBK+91] S. Fujiwara, G. v. Bochmann, F. Khendek, M. Amalou, and A. Ghedamsi. Test selection based on finite state models. *IEEE Trans. on Software Engineering*, 17(6):591–603, June 1991.

[Gol67]   E. M. Gold. Language identification in the limit. *Information and Control*, 10(5):447–474, 1967.

[Gol78]   E. M. Gold. Complexity of automaton identification from given data. *Information and Control*, 37(3):302–320, 1978.

[GPY02]   A. Groce, D. Peled, and M. Yannakakis. Adaptive model checking. In J.-P. Katoen and P. Stevens, editors, *Proc. TACAS '02, 8th Int. Conf. on Tools and Algorithms for the Construction and Analysis of Systems*, volume 2280 of *Lecture Notes in Computer Science*, pages 357–370. Springer Verlag, 2002.

[HHNS02]   A. Hagerer, H. Hungar, O. Niese, and B. Steffen. Model generation by moderated regular extrapolation. In R.-D. Kutsche and H. Weber, editors, *Proc. FASE '02, 5th Int. Conf. on Fundamental Approaches to Software Engineering*, volume 2306 of *Lecture Notes in Computer Science*, pages 80–95. Springer Verlag, 2002.

[HNS03]   Hardi Hungar, Oliver Niese, and Bernhard Steffen. Domain-specific optimization in automata learning. In *Proc. 15th Int. Conf. on Computer Aided Verification*, volume 2725 of *Lecture Notes in Computer Science*, pages 315–327, 2003.

[LY96]   D. Lee and M. Yannakakis. Principles and methods of testing finite state machines – a survey. *Proc. IEEE*, 84(8):1090–1126, 1996.

[OG92]   J. Oncina and P. García. Inferring regular languages in polynomial update time. In *Pattern Recognition and Image Analysis*, volume 1 of *Series in Machine Perception and Artificial Intelligence*, pages 49–61. World Scientific, 1992.

[PVY99]   Doron Peled, Moshe Y. Vardi, and Mihalis Yannakakis. Black box checking. In Jianping Wu, Samuel T. Chanson, and Qiang Gao, editors, *Formal Methods for Protocol Engineering and Distributed Systems, FORTE/PSTV*, pages 225–240, Beijing, China, 1999. Kluwer.

[RS93]   R.L. Rivest and R.E. Schapire. Inference of finite automata using homing sequences. *Information and Computation*, 103:299–347, 1993.

[SD88]   Krishan Sabnani and Anton Dahbura. A protocol test generation procedure. *Computer Networks and ISDN Systems*, 15(4):285–297, September 1988.

[SH03]   Bernhard Steffen and Hardi Hungar. Behavior-based model construction. In *VMCAI 2003: Proceedings of the 4th International Conference on Verification, Model Checking, and Abstract Interpretation*, volume 2575 of *Lecture Notes in Computer Science*, pages 5–19. Springer-Verlag, 2003.

[Vas73]   M. P. Vasilevski. Failure diagnosis of automata. *Cybernetic*, 9(4):653–665, 1973.

[VCI90]   S.T. Vuong, W.Y.L. Chan, and M.R. Ito. The UIOv-method for protocol test sequence generation. In *Proc. 2nd Int. Workshop on Protocol Test Systems*, pages 161–176. North-Holland, 1990.

Observational Purity and Encapsulation

David A. Naumann[*]

Department of Computer Science, Stevens Institute of Technology
naumann@cs.stevens.edu

Abstract. Practical specification languages for imperative and object-oriented programs, such as JML, Eiffel, and Spec#, allow the use of program expressions including method calls in specification formulas. For coherent semantics of specifications, and to avoid anomalies with runtime assertion checking, expressions in specifications and assertions are typically required to be strongly pure in the sense that their evaluation has no effect on the state of preexisting objects. For specification of large systems using standard libraries this restriction is impractical: it disallows many standard methods that mutate state for purposes such as caching or lazy initialization. Calls of such methods can sensibly be used for specifications and annotations in contexts where their effects cannot be observed. This paper formalizes and extends a recently proposed notion of observational purity, reducing the proof obligation to a familiar one for equivalence of two class implementations.

1 Introduction

There are a number of uses for identifying pure expressions, i.e., those without side effects. For example, they admit transformations such as re-ordering and they may be used without difficulty in program specifications. For verification of programs in object oriented languages such as Java, it is important to allow annotations (including specifications and intermediate assertions) to invoke methods whose calls are pure in a more liberal sense: allowing construction of fresh objects. For example, to return a pair of values, a pair objects may be created. This notion of purity is used in the JML behavioral interface specification language [12].

Many software libraries include methods that one would expect to be pure, such as `String.equals` in Java, but which in fact mutate preexisting objects for purposes such as memoization, caching, or lazy initialization. The solution adopted in JML is to duplicate such library methods with pure ones to be used in specifications, but this is awkward at best. It has recently been proposed to liberalize the notion further, to allow methods that have "benign" side effects, i.e., mutation of preexisting objects so long as these effects are not visible in the context where the method is treated as pure.

Allowing benign side effects is important for specification and program transformation to scale up to large systems, but it poses challenges: How do such effects interact

---

[*] Partially supported by the National Science Foundation under grants CCR-0208984 and CCF-0429894 and by Microsoft Research.

M. Cerioli (Ed.): FASE 2005, LNCS 3442, pp. 190–204, 2005.

```
class Cell {
    public val : int;
    proc pos(c : Cell) : bool { return c.val > 0; }    }
class D {
    private f, arg, farg : int;
    proc pureProd(s : D, n : int) : Cell {
        x : Cell := new Cell; x.val := s.f * n;  return x; }
    proc memoProd(s : D, n : int) : Cell {
        x : Cell := new Cell;
        if n = 0 then x.val := 0; return x;
        elseif s.arg ≠ n then s.arg := n; s.farg := s.f * n;  end;
        x.val := s.farg;  return x; }
    proc get(s : D) : int { return s.f }
    proc set(s : D, v : int) {s.f := v; s.arg := 0; }    }
```

Fig. 1. Example program in simple language with class-bound procedures. It maintains an invariant: $o.arg \neq 0$ implies $o.farg = o.f * o.arg$ for all D-objects o

with "modifies" specifications? What is the meaning of an effectful predicate in a precondition? How do effects interact with runtime assertion checking?

A definition of observational purity is proposed by Barnett et al. [6] along with a static analysis based on secure information flow [18] combined with verified program assertions. But the definition has been criticized as ad hoc and obscure and the checking technique seems rather specialized. In this paper we disentangle and extend the ideas, showing how observational purity can be formulated in terms of established notions of abstraction and encapsulation. This opens the way to using existing methods to verify observational purity. Moreover, we obtain a sound and general theory without the need to prove the hardest of the results from scratch.

The key idea is that an observationally pure method is equivalent to one that is strongly pure in the sense of allowing allocation of new objects but no mutation of preexisting ones. This requires an account of strong purity, which we have not seen in the literature. Our account is set in the context of partial correctness; in the conclusion we describe how the approach can be adapted to total correctness using refinement. The core difficulties and ideas are already present in the partial correctness setting.

As a simple and general way to justify the use of pure method calls in specifications and annotations we seek conditions under which "**assert** Q" is equivalent to "**skip**", where Q is a boolean expression that may include method invocations as well as specification constructs such as quantifiers. The notion of equivalence must be compositional, i.e., a congruence, and correctness-preserving. We base our theory on simulation, the standard technique for proving equivalence of implementations that differ in their data representation.

In the sequel a simple but representative example is used; see Figure 1. This program memoizes a product $f * arg$ in a field $farg$. In the context of some class B with access to $d : D$ and $i : int$ one might find expression $pos(pureProd(d, i))$ in a specification. The argument for allowing this is that, although it has an effect on the heap, it changes no preexisting objects and thus cannot interfere with the meaning of other terms of the asserted formula. Another argument for allowing it is that one could turn runtime assertion checking on or off without affecting the outcome from the program: the fresh object returned by *pureProd* is examined in evaluating the asserted formula but then discarded. This could have an effect, e.g., via out-of-memory condition; or via pointer arithmetic because it affects where the next allocation takes place. But for many purposes none of these sorts of observation are of interest. It is under such idealization that our results are of interest.

Strong purity is a property of a procedure in isolation. Observational purity is a property of a class (or module) in which the effects of the observationally pure procedure are encapsulated. Procedure *memoProd* in Figure 1 is observationally pure, but this depends on cooperation by the other procedures, which neither interfere with the cache nor expose it. Moveover, *memoProd* is observationally pure *outside* its declaring class D, meaning that if it occurs in Q then **assert** Q is equivalent to **skip** only in the context of a class other than D.

Outline. Section 2 formalizes a simple language sufficient to illustrate the ideas. Section 3 defines strong purity which admits *pureProd* in Figure 1. A notion of equivalence is defined and justified, such that **assert** Q is equivalent to **skip** for strongly pure Q. Section 4 adds visibility to the language in order to formalize a notion of observational purity. It is shown that **assert** Q is equivalent to **skip** for observationally pure Q, but for a notion of visible equivalence that is not a congruence. Section 5 generalizes equivalence to simulations, which are congruences. Section 6 concludes. Most proofs are omitted for lack of space.

Notation. We write $f\ v$ for application of function f to v. Application associates to the left and binds more tightly than other binary operators. For subset X of the domain of f, we write $X \triangleleft f$ for the restriction of f to X. And $v \triangleleft\!\!\!- f$ denotes f with v removed from its domain. We write $[f \mid v \mapsto u]$ for overriding or extending f to map v to u. Relational operators like $\sim$ bind less tightly than others such as $\triangleleft$, e.g., $\operatorname{dom} h \triangleleft k \sim h$ is parsed as $((\operatorname{dom} h) \triangleleft k) \sim h$. The product of relations α, β is written $\alpha \cdot \beta$.

2   Illustrative Language

We consider a procedural language with dynamically allocated mutable objects, as this suffices to expose the main ideas. The syntax is given in Table 1. A program consists of a collection of class and procedure declarations The declaration of a class named C gives its fields. A distinguished field, type, gives the class name of an object; it is not allowed to be the target of assignment. Because we do not consider subclassing, we need not distinguish a "self" parameter for special treatment. In fact for simplicity in the formalism we consider only procedures that return a value and have exactly one parameter (passed by value). For each procedure p a term, body p, should be given. In Section 4 we add visibility control for fields and thus associate procedures with classes as in Figure 1. Non-local variables and static fields are omitted. In order to avoid unilluminating complications in the proofs, we assume there are no recursive procedures. It should be straightforward to extend the results to these and other program constructs

Table 1. Grammar of effectful terms

$C, D \in \mathit{ClassName}$ $p \in \mathit{ProcedureName}$ $x, y \in \mathit{VarName}$ $f \in \mathit{FieldName}$

$M, N, Q ::= \mathbf{assert}\ M$

	$M = M$	equality test, for values
	x	read local variable
	$x := M$	write local variable
	$M.f$	read field of heap object
	$x.f := M$	write field of heap object
	$\mathbf{new}\ C$	reference to freshly allocated object of class C
	$p(M)$	invoke procedure p on argument M
	$\mathbf{null} \mid \mathbf{skip} \mid M; M \mid \mathbf{if}\ M\ \mathbf{then}\ M\ \mathbf{else}\ M \mid \mathbf{while}\ M\ \mathbf{do}\ M \mid \mathbf{var}\ x\ \mathbf{in}\ M$	

as well as specification constructs such as quantifiers and regular path expressions. What we need is that the language satisfies Propositions 1 and 20 in the sequel.

The details of typing, although important to preclude pointer arithmetic, are ignored in the formalism due to space limitation.

Because we focus on side effects of expressions, we refrain from distinguishing between expressions and commands; the short word *term* is used for both.

Semantics. The language is deterministic; in particular an arbitrary but deterministic memory allocator is used. Purity, which is about effects, does not depend on determinacy. Of course determinacy for assertions is important to facilitate reasoning.

A *store* is a finite mapping from identifiers to primitive values (booleans, integers, locations). An *object state* is just a store; the domain is the object's field names including the distinguished name, type, that records the class of the object. A *heap* is a finite mapping from locations to object states. A *state* is a pair (h, s) where h is a heap and s is a store. The idea is that the domain of s has local variables and parameters for a particular procedure.

A special variable, res, is present in the store part of every state, but is not allowed to occur in the program text. It is used in the semantics like a temporary register, to record the value of a term. This formalization helps streamline subsequent definitions, e.g., a single definition for equivalence of stores serves for both the value and effect of a term.

For partial correctness it suffices to use a relational (evaluation) semantics; Table 2 gives representative cases. For term M, the relation $M, \cdot \to \cdot$ on states is written $M, h, s \to k, t$ and interpreted to mean that in initial state (h, s) execution of M can yield outcome (k, t). To model that M diverges from (h, s), there is no (k, t) such that $M, h, s \to k, t$.

For invocation of a procedure named p, execution of the body of p affects the variables in scope for the body, namely res and the parameter, but only the value of res is needed for semantics of the invocation. The auxiliary relation $-\!|p|\!\to$ is defined by

$$h, s -\!|p|\!\to k, v \iff M, h, s \to k, t \text{ and } v = t(\text{res}) \text{ for some } t, \text{ where } M = \text{body } p.$$

This gives the meaning of a procedure in terms of its local state.

The semantics makes $\mathbf{assert}\ M$ yield a final state only if M yields a final state (k, u) in which $u(\text{res})$ is true. The final state of the $\mathbf{assert}$ retains the effect of M on

Table 2. Semantics for selected terms. We assume that *fresh* is a total function from heaps to locations such that *fresh* $h \notin$ dom h. We abbreviate a nested update to field f by $[h \mid o.f \mapsto v]$

If M is ...	then $M, h, s \to k, t$ iff ...
null	$k = h$ and $t = [s \mid \text{res} \mapsto \textbf{null}]$
skip	$k = h$ and $t = s$
x	$k = h$ and $t = [s \mid \text{res} \mapsto s\,x]$
$x := N$	$N, h, s \to k, u$ and $t = [u \mid x \mapsto u(\text{res}), \text{res} \mapsto s(\text{res})]$ for some u
$N.f$	$N, h, s \to k, u$ and $u(\text{res}) \neq \textbf{null}$ and $t = [u \mid \text{res} \mapsto k(u(\text{res})).f]$ for some u
$x.f := N$	$s\,x \neq \textbf{null}$ and $N, h, s \to g, u$ and $t = [u \mid \text{res} \mapsto s(\text{res})]$
	and $k = [g \mid s\,x.f \mapsto u(\text{res})]$ for some g, u
assert N	$N, h, s \to k, u$ for some u with $u(\text{res}) = true$, and $t = [u \mid \text{res} \mapsto s(\text{res})]$
new C	$k = [h \mid o \mapsto default\_C\_state]$ and $t = [s \mid \text{res} \mapsto o]$ where $o = fresh\ h$
$p(N)$	$N, h, s \to g, r$ and $g, \arg(r(\text{res})) -\!\|p\|\!\mapsto k, v$ and $t = [r \mid \text{res} \mapsto v]$
	for some g, r, v, where $\arg(y) \hat{=} [x \mapsto y, \text{res} \mapsto default]$ and x is the parameter of p

the heap and on the store, except that res has its initial value —otherwise an **assert** could never be equivalent to **skip**.

As an illustrative but otherwise useless example, consider execution of the term "$x.f$; **assert** $((y := 1) = 2)$" from initial state (h, s). Evaluation of $x.f$ changes the store to $[s \mid \text{res} \mapsto v]$ where v is the value of field f of object $s\,x$ (i.e., $v = h(s\,x).f$) and there is no outcome if $s\,x$ is null. Next, $y := 1$ is executed, updating y but restoring res to v. Then the equality is evaluated, comparing v with 2. If they are equal, the final store is $[s \mid \text{res}, y \mapsto v, 1]$ because the semantics of **assert**, like $:=$, discards the intermediate res values. If $v \neq 2$ there is no outcome.

The semantic definitions do not explicitly impose the obvious condition that terms are evaluated in the context of a suitable initial store (that includes all free variables of the term) or that the final store has the same domain. Like typing, the precise conditions can easily be provided by the interested reader. To prove the results in the sequel, it is important to confine attention to *closed states* (h, s), i.e., those such that every location that occurs in s or in an object field in h is in dom h. (More precisely, if o is in rng s or in rng r for some object state r in rng h then o is in dom h.) The following is easily proved for the language in Table 1.

Proposition 1. If $M, h, s \to k, t$ and (h, s) is closed then (k, t) is closed, dom $s =$ dom t, and dom $h \subseteq$ dom k.

3   Strong Purity

A strongly pure term is one that does not write fields of any initially existing objects. Nor does it write any local variables except possibly res.

Definition 2. Term M is *strongly pure* iff $M, h, s \to k, t$ implies dom $h \triangleleft k = h$ and res$\triangleleft t =$ res$\triangleleft s$. Procedure p is *strongly pure* iff $h, s -\!|p|\!\mapsto k, v$ implies dom $h \triangleleft k = h$.

In this and subsequent definitions we abuse notation for brevity, omitting universal quantifiers (e.g., for h, s, k, t after the first "iff").

As an example, *pureProd* from Figure 1 is strongly pure, but *memoProd* is not. In general, strong purity allows that in the final store res may point to a new object from which other new objects are reachable, and these may point to preexisting objects —but preexisting objects are not mutated and in particular do not point to the new ones. The update $x.f := y$ is not strongly pure but $\{\mathbf{var}\ x\ \mathbf{in}\ x := \mathbf{new}\ C;\ x.f := y\}$ is. A conservative static analysis for strong purity is easy: check for complete absence of assignments and field updates (except initializers). To admit cases in which new objects are repeatedly updated, pointer analysis can be used [19].

For a procedure p, a sufficient condition for p to be strongly pure is that body p is a strongly pure term. This is not necessary because body p could assign to the parameters but only the final value of res is used. The important fact is that if p and M are strongly pure then so is the invocation $p(M)$.

Equivalence Modulo Renaming. Our objective is to justify invocations of pure methods in assertions by showing that such an assertion is the same as **skip**. For this purpose we need a suitable notion of equivalence. For example, **assert** $pos(pureProd(a, i))$ is not semantically equal to **skip**, because it allocates a new *Cell* object. This object is only used in evaluation of the asserted formula; afterward it is unreachable, but nonetheless the final state is not identical to the final state after **skip**.

To formalize a suitable notion of equivalence we adopt a standard technique: state (h, s) is equivalent to (h', s') if there is a bijective renaming from dom h to dom h' by which s, s' correspond and so do all object states. We use the term *location bijection* for a partial bijective relation on locations.

Definition 3. $(\sim_\beta)$ Let β be a location bijection. Define relation $\sim_\beta$ on values by $v \sim_\beta v'$ iff either v, v' have primitive type and $v = v'$, or $v = \mathbf{null} = v'$, or $(v, v') \in \beta$. For stores with the same domain, define $s \sim_\beta s'$ iff $s\,x \sim_\beta s'\,x$ for all $x \in$ dom s. For heaps, $h \sim_\beta h'$ iff dom $\beta \subseteq$ dom h, rng $\beta \subseteq$ dom h', and $h\,o \sim_\beta h'\,o'$ for all $(o, o') \in \beta$. For states, $(h, s) \sim_\beta (h', s')$ iff $h \sim_\beta h'$ and $s \sim_\beta s'$.

Note that every variable in a store must be related. Hence if a pair of locations o, o' are related by β then locations in all fields of $h\,o$ and $h'\,o'$ must be related. In particular, $h\,o$ type $= h'\,o'$ type, as we treat the classname-valued field type like a primitive type. But there may be locations in dom h and in object fields in h that are not in the domain of β (and in dom h' but outside the range of β).

These relations are easily shown to be symmetric and we use this without remark in the sequel. A kind of transitivity holds, via composing bijections; what we need is in Lemma 12 in the sequel. A kind of reflexivity holds: $(h, s) \sim_{\delta h} (h, s)$ where $\delta\,h$ denotes the identity relation on dom h. The notation $\delta\,h$ is used extensively in the sequel. For example, it lets us reformulate strong purity as follows.

Lemma 4. M is strongly pure iff $M, h, s \to k, t$ implies $k \sim_{\delta h} h$ and res $\triangleleft t \sim_{\delta h}$ res $\triangleleft s$.

Equivalence for states is lifted to terms in a straightforward way, suited to partial correctness and dynamic allocation.

Definition 5. $(\approx)$ For terms M, M' to be equivalent, written $M \approx M'$, means that if $(h, s) \sim_\beta (h', s')$, $M, h, s \to k, t$, and $M', h', s' \to k', t'$ then there is $\gamma \supseteq \beta$ such that $(k, t) \sim_\gamma (k', t')$.

Here the implicitly universally quantified β, γ range over location bijections, so γ is the same as β for preexisting locations.

As an example, **new** C is not equivalent to **skip** because **new** updates res. On the other hand, **skip** is equivalent to the block $\{\textbf{var } x \textbf{ in } x := \textbf{new } C; \}$ which allocates an object that is unreachable in the final state. From initial bijection β the witnessing γ is also β, which does not have the fresh object in its domain. As another example, $x := \textbf{new } C; x1 := \textbf{new } D \approx x1 := \textbf{new } D; x := \textbf{new } C$. This can be shown by taking $\gamma = \beta \cup \{(a, d), (b, c)\}$ if the left side allocates objects a, b and the right allocates c, d (in that order). Note that $\{\textbf{var } x \textbf{ in } x := \textbf{new } C\}$ would not be equivalent to **skip** if we used a semantics for assignment that had an effect on res.

Theorem 6. If Q is strongly pure then **assert** $Q \approx \textbf{skip}$.

Proof. Suppose $(h, s) \sim_\beta (h', s')$, $(\textbf{assert } Q), h, s \to k, t$, and $\textbf{skip}, h', s' \to k', t'$. We must choose $\gamma \supseteq \beta$ and show $(k, t) \sim_\gamma (k', t')$; we choose $\gamma = \beta$. By semantics of **assert** we have $Q, h, s \to k, u$ for some u. By strong purity of Q we have $dom\, h \triangleleft k = h$. By Definition 3 we have $dom\, \beta \subseteq dom\, h$, whence, using $dom\, h \triangleleft k = h$ and $h \sim_\beta h'$, we obtain $k \sim_\beta h'$. Hence $(k, s) \sim_\beta (h', s')$. By strong purity of Q we have res $\triangleleft u = $ res $\triangleleft s$ and by semantics of **assert** we have $t = [u \mid \text{res} \mapsto s(\text{res})]$, hence $t = s$. By semantics of **skip** we have $(h', s') = (k', t')$, so we conclude that $(k, t) \sim_\beta (k', t')$. $\qquad\square$

What remains is to justify that this equivalence is respected by any context and to justify that the equivalence relation is not too coarse. Regarding contexts, we have the following which is straightforward to prove for the language in Table 1. (It is instructive to prove the case for $p(M)$ because it fails for the relation $\approx^C$ in the sequel.)

Proposition 7. *(congruence)* If $M \approx N$ then $C[M] \approx C[N]$ for all contexts $C[-]$.

Observation and Specification. Unreachable objects cannot be detected by ordinary source program constructs, but what about the predicate $(\exists o \bullet o.\text{type} = C)$? Two implementations that are related by $\approx$ might be distinguished by a specification with postcondition $(\exists o \bullet o.\text{type} = C)$. The could also be distinguished by a postcondition involving address arithmetic. (Congruence would also be broken.)

The decision in languages like JML to allow strongly pure method calls in specifications is only sound if predicates are restricted so they cannot make undesired distinctions. We aim for results that are generally applicable so we aim for minimal semantic conditions rather than considering syntax for formulas. This is important because verification systems often use a shallow embedding of formulas in the language of a theorem prover. One condition is that predicates should not depend on particular locations, i.e., they should respect bijective renaming. Another condition is garbage-insensitivity, which would disallow the example above.

Let $reach(h, s)$ be the set of locations reached transitively from s. We define $gc(h, s) = (reach(h, s) \triangleleft h, s)$. For set ψ of states, we say that ψ is *healthy* iff $(h, s) \in \psi$ implies $(k, t) \in \psi$ whenever $gc(h, s) \sim_\beta gc(k, t)$.

Lemma 8. (a) If $(h, s) \sim_\beta (h', s')$ then $gc(h, s) \sim_\gamma gc(h', s')$ where γ is obtained by restricting β, to wit $\gamma = \beta \cap (reach(h, s) \times reach(h', s'))$.
(b) Suppose $M \approx N$, $M, h, s \rightarrow k, t$, and $N, h, s \rightarrow k', t'$. If ψ is healthy then $(k, t) \in \psi$ iff $(k', t') \in \psi$.

A straightforward consequence of Lemma 8(b) is the following. We refrain from spelling out the straightforward notion of satisfaction for partial correctness.

Corollary 9. Suppose $M \approx N$. Then for any $pre, post$ specification where $post$ is healthy, M satisfies the specification iff N does.

Strongly Pure Terms in Context. A direct consequence of Proposition 7 and Theorem 6 is the following.

Corollary 10. If Q is strongly pure then $C[\textbf{assert } Q] \approx C[\textbf{skip}]$ for all $C[-]$.

With this we have justified the use of calls to strongly pure procedures in assertions. If method calls in Q are strongly pure then Q is so; and then by Corollary 10 the **assert** can be replaced by **skip**. This replacement is correctness-preserving, by Corollary 9.

4   Observational Purity

Our objective is to find a notion of purity that validates a result like Corollary 10 but allows updates of preexisting fields. Clearly not all updates can be allowed. For example, suppose Q is an invocation $p(x)$ where boolean-valued p checks whether $x.f$ is positive but also sets $x.f$ to 0. For the context $-; y := x.f$ we then have **assert** $Q; y := x.f \not\approx$ **skip**; $y := x.f$ Sensible updates are to encapsulated state as in Figure 1.

Visibility. A familiar notion of encapsulation suffices for our purposes. A field f of class C may or may not be visible in methods of class D. Two heaps are equivalent, as viewed in code of class C, if corresponding objects have corresponding values for all visible fields. It is well known that field access is inadequate to achieve encapsulation; additional restrictions on heap sharing are needed to prevent interference with *objects* that are intended to be private. For our purposes we need not formalize a discipline such as ownership types [9, 1] to control aliasing. The requisite assumptions can be expressed using the location bijection; a location not visible in a particular context is not in the bijection.

To impose visibility restrictions, we assume that each procedure p is declared in some class, denoted class p. Furthermore, for each class C there is a set vis C of fields visible in C. (We assume that distinct classes have disjoint field names and we are not modelling subclasses or inheritance). This encoding can represent private, global, and module-scoped visibility. For an object $o \in$ dom h, vis $C \lhd h\, o$ is the part of the object state $h\, o$ that is visible in code of class C. If class $p = C$ then the only fields that may be read or written in body p are those in vis C. The semantics is revised in a straightforward way, writing $C, M, h, s \rightarrow k, t$ to make explicit that M is executed as a constituent of a procedure of class C.

Definition 11. $(\sim_{\beta}^{C}, \approx^{C})$ For heaps, define $h \sim_{\beta}^{C} h'$ iff $\mathrm{dom}\,\beta \subseteq \mathrm{dom}\,h$, $\mathrm{rng}\,\beta \subseteq \mathrm{dom}\,h'$, and $\mathrm{vis}\,C \triangleleft h\,o \sim_{\beta} \mathrm{vis}\,C \triangleleft h'\,o'$ for all $(o, o') \in \beta$. For states, define $(h, s) \sim_{\beta}^{C} (h', s')$ iff $s \sim_{\beta} s'$ and $h \sim_{\beta}^{C} h'$. For terms, $M \approx^{C} M'$ iff $(h, s) \sim_{\beta}^{C} (h', s')$, $C, M, h, s \rightarrow k, t$, and $C, M', h', s' \rightarrow k', t'$ implies there is $\gamma \supseteq \beta$ such that $(k, t) \sim_{\gamma}^{C} (k', t')$.

Note that $\sim_{\beta} \subseteq \sim_{\beta}^{C}$, because $\sim_{\beta}^{C}$ is $\sim_{\beta}$ with no fields hidden. Note also that for the store component of a state it suffices to use relation $s \sim_{\beta} s'$ because the store models local variables and parameters. (We omit global variables and static fields.) The following technical results are needed for later proofs.

Lemma 12. If $h \sim_{\alpha} g$ and $g \sim_{\beta}^{C} k$ then $h \sim_{\alpha \cdot \beta}^{C} k$. If $\delta h \subseteq \beta$, $h \sim_{\delta h} g$, and $g \sim_{\beta}^{C} k$ then $h \sim_{\delta h}^{C} k$. If $h \sim_{\beta}^{C} k$ and $\gamma \supseteq \beta$ then $h \sim_{\gamma}^{C} k$ provided that $\mathrm{dom}\,\gamma \subseteq \mathrm{dom}\,h$ and $\mathrm{rng}\,\gamma \subseteq \mathrm{dom}\,k$. Similarly for stores.

Observational Purity. Our goal is for **assert** $Q \approx^{C}$ **skip** to hold provided that Q has no effect observable in class C —e.g., Q is a call $p(x)$ that changes fields of x but only fields private to D with $D \neq C$. Following the pattern of Lemma 4 we adapt the definition of strong purity to one using the visible relations.

Definition 13. Term M is *observationally pure outside* D provided that the following holds for all $C \neq D$. If $C, M, h, s \rightarrow k, t$ then $k \sim_{\delta h}^{C} h$ and $\mathrm{res} \triangleleft t \sim_{\delta h} \mathrm{res} \triangleleft s$.

Procedure p is *observationally pure outside* D iff $h, s \dashv p \mapsto k, v$ implies $k \sim_{\delta h}^{C} h$ for all $C \neq D$.

Procedure *memoProd* of class D in Figure 1 is observationally pure outside D. It updates fields of preexisting objects but those fields are not visible outside D and the updates do not make it possible to reach the newly allocated object (return value). For initial heap h, the new object is not in the range of δh.

As in the case of strong purity, a sufficient but not necessary condition for a procedure to be observationally pure is that its body is. Moreover, if p and M are observationally pure outside D then so is $p(M)$.

Fact 14. If Q is observationally pure outside D then **assert** $Q \approx^{C}$ **skip** for all $C \neq D$.

This result is not yet satisfactory, however, because unlike the case of strong purity we do not get congruence in general. That is, $M \approx^{C} M'$ does not imply $\mathcal{C}[M] \approx^{C} \mathcal{C}[M']$ (compare Proposition 7).

Example 15. Consider the term $pos(memoProd(y, i))$, evaluation of which may well update $y.arg$ and $y.farg$. By Fact 14, **assert** $pos(memoProd(y, i)) \approx^{C}$ **skip** Moreover the procedures of D do not leak information about fields updated by *memoProd*, so for example we have (**assert** $pos(memoProd(y, i))$); $get(y) \approx^{C}$ **skip**; $get(y)$. But suppose D declared procedure $leak(self : D) : \mathbf{int}\{\,\mathbf{return}\,self.arg\}$. Then

$$\mathbf{assert}\ pos(memoProd(y, i)); leak(y) \not\approx^{C} \mathbf{skip}; leak(y)$$

because the result of $leak(y)$ after $memoProd(y, i)$ is i whereas after **skip** it is the initial value of $y.arg$. The problem is that $leak$ violates encapsulation and makes the cache indirectly visible.   □

A related problem is that even if $h \sim^C_\beta h'$ for all $C \neq D$, it is possible for there to be $(o, o') \in \beta$ with $h\ o$ type $= D$ and moreover $h\ o\ arg = h'\ o'\ arg$ but $h\ o\ farg \neq h'\ o'\ farg$ because these fields are not visible outside D. From such a pair of states, the corresponding pair of results from $memoProd$ are $Cell$-objects with different val field; thus $\not\sim^C$ for the final state. Thus $memoProd \not\approx^C memoProd$.

In general the problem with congruence is that if $p \not\approx^C p$ then $M \approx^C N$ does not imply $p(M) \approx^C p(N)$. The problem is solved in section 5.

A shortcoming of Definition 13 is that checking it appears to be a nontrivial and nonstandard problem. In fact, the check can be reduced to equivalence.

Theorem 16. Suppose $M \approx^C N$ for all $C \neq D$, and suppose N is strongly pure. If N terminates when M does[1] then M is observationally pure outside D.

As an example, procedure $memoProd$ is equivalent to $pureProd$ which is strongly pure and terminates when $memoProd$ does. The termination antecedent is necessary. As an extreme case, if N never terminates then it is strongly pure and $M \approx^D N$ for any M whatsoever.

A standard technique for proving program equivalence in the presence of encapsulated state is to use simulation relations —unlike mere visible equivalence, a simulation can track correspondence of internals and impose invariants [14, 10]. Using a simulation to establish the antecedent of Theorem 16 has the added benefit of congruence.

5   Observational Purity via Simulation

This section gives the main result, equivalence of $C[\textbf{assert}\ Q]$ and $C[\textbf{skip}]$ for observationally pure Q. To this end, we generalize from specific equivalences on states to an arbitrary relation subject to some conditions. As before, the relation involves renaming of locations. So what we consider is a ternary relation, written $\asymp$ and read "couples", on two heaps and a bijection —or what amounts to the same, a family, indexed by bijections, of binary relations $\asymp_\beta$ on heaps.

Example 17. In the context of Figure 1, define $\asymp$ by $h \asymp_\beta h'$ iff (a) $h \sim^C_\beta h'$ for any $C \neq D$, and (b) for all $(o, o') \in \beta$, if $h\ o$ type $= D$ then $h\ o.f = h'\ o'.f$ and both $h\ o$ and $h'\ o'$ satisfy the invariant mentioned in the caption of Figure 1. From two states related by $\asymp_\beta$, $memoProd$ gives the same results, indeed that is true for all the procedures of D.   □

If the cache involved other objects, an encapsulation condition would be imposed on them as well, e.g., via ownership [9, 5]. In our formulation, encapsulation at the level of classes is sufficient; it need not be instance-based.

To express healthiness conditions on $\asymp$ we use the following routine extensions.

---

[1] $M, h, s \Downarrow$ implies $N, h, s \Downarrow$, where $M, h, s \Downarrow$ means there exists k, t with $M, h, s \rightarrow k, t$.

Definition 18. Gived a bijection-indexed family of relations $\asymp_\beta$ on heaps, define $\asymp_\beta$ on states by $(h, s) \asymp_\beta (h', s')$ iff $h \asymp_\beta h'$ and $s \sim_\beta s'$. For terms, $M \asymp M'$ iff $(h, s) \asymp_\beta (h', s')$, $C, M, h, s \to k, t$, and $C, M', h', s' \to k', t'$ implies there is $\gamma \supseteq \beta$ such that $(k, t) \asymp_\gamma (k', t')$. Finally, $p \asymp p'$ iff $(h, s) \asymp_\beta (h', s')$, $h, s \dashv p \vdash k, v$, and $h', s' \dashv p' \vdash k', v'$ implies there is $\gamma \supseteq \beta$ such that $k \asymp_\gamma k'$ and $v \sim_\gamma v'$.

Definition 19 (coupling, simulation). A D-*coupling* is $\asymp$ such that

(a) if $h \asymp_\beta k$ then $\mathrm{dom}\,\beta \subseteq \mathrm{dom}\,h$ and $\mathrm{rng}\,\beta \subseteq \mathrm{dom}\,k$
(b) $h \asymp_\alpha g$ and $g \sim_\beta k$ implies $h \asymp_{\alpha \cdot \beta} k$
(c) $h \asymp_\beta k$ implies $h \sim_\beta^C k$ for all $C \neq D$

A D-*simulation* is a D-coupling such that

(d) there is a term *Init* such that for any C, β, h, s, h', s', if $(h, s) \sim_\beta^C (h', s')$ then there is some k, t, k', t', γ with $C, Init, h, s \to k, s$ and $C, Init, h', s' \to k', s'$ and $\gamma \supseteq \beta$ and $(k, s) \asymp_\gamma (k', s')$.
(e) $p \asymp p$ for every procedure p (in every class)

Items (a) and (b) are simple healthiness conditions (compare Definition 3 and healthy predicates in Section 3). Item (c) says that the relation reduces to equality modulo renaming, for classes other than D. A consequence is that $(h, s) \asymp_\beta (h', s')$ implies $(h, s) \sim_\beta^C (h', s')$ for all $C \neq D$.

As usual, the role of initialization is to establish a relation which does not simply follow from $(h, s) \sim_\beta^C (h', s')$ because $\sim_\beta^C$ allows arbitrary difference in non-visible fields. Item (d) is a simple formalization of initialization that follows the pattern used in the literature for single-instance modules [10]. For dynamic allocation, it is the object constructor (or default values) that established the relation [2, 8]. To cater for this in our simple setup, one can take *Init* to be an assertion of a predicate like "all existing D-objects have $arg = 0 = f$", or even "no D-objects exist".[2]

Item (e) requires all procedures to preserve $\asymp$. It precludes *leak* in Example 15. All procedures in Figure 1 preserve the relation in Example 17. Item (e) appears alarmingly strong. But for programs using suitable encapsulation, $p \asymp p$ holds for all p provided that it holds for all p of class D. This is the core of the theory of representation independence which has been well studied; see Section 6. The preservation result in such a theory yields the following.

Proposition 20. Suppose $\asymp$ is a D-simulation. If $M \asymp N$ then $C[M] \asymp C[N]$.

We shall take this as an assumption. Such a result depends on several things: conditions on the relation; conformance of the program with rules to ensure encapsulation (e.g., absence of pointer arithmetic, alias confinement); and preservation by the methods of D, which have privileged access to encapsulated state.

---

[2] This is not a healthy predicate as defined in Section 3, but there is no problem because the healthiness condition is not needed for preconditions.

5.1   Using D-Simulations for Purity

Definition 21. Let $\asymp$ be a D-coupling. Then M is *observationally pure for* $\asymp$ iff for all $C \neq D$, if $C, M, h, s \rightarrow k, t$ then $k \asymp_{\delta h} h$ and $\text{res} \triangleleft t \sim_{\delta h} \text{res} \triangleleft s$.

p is *observationally pure for* $\asymp$ if $h, s \dashv |p| \mapsto k, v$ implies that $h \asymp_{\delta h} k$.

Fact 22. Suppose M is observationally pure for some D-coupling $\asymp$. Then it is observationally pure outside D.

This Fact, together with Fact 14, implies **assert** $M \approx^C$ **skip** for $C \neq D$. But Theorem 16 suggests that for interchangeability of an **assert** with **skip**, it is enough to formulate observational purity as in Definition 13. The role of a coupling is then to prove the antecedent equivalence of the Theorem and in addition to enjoy a congruence property. This is worked out in our main result to follow.

Analogous to Theorem 16, one might expect the following: If $M \asymp N$ for N is strongly pure, and N terminates when M does, then M is observationally pure outside D. But the property $M \asymp N$ is only applicable to a pair of initially related states and the relation need not be reflexive, so the proof of Theorem 16 does not directly generalize. However, we can prove the following Fact. It uses the termination condition that would be imposed everywhere for simulations in a total-correctness setting.

Definition 23. N *terminates when* M *does, modulo* $\asymp$, iff $(h, s) \asymp_\beta (h', s')$ and $C, M, h, s \Downarrow$ implies $C, N, h', s' \Downarrow$.

Fact 24. If $M \asymp N$ and N is strongly pure then **assert** $M \asymp$ **skip** provided that $\asymp$ is a D-coupling and N terminates when M does, modulo $\asymp$.

5.2   Main Result

Two more ingredients are needed. The first is equivalence for properly initialized programs. The step from simulation to program equivalence requires that the programs proved equivalent are properly initialized, so that from equivalence of initial states one gets the coupled states needed to exploit the simulation. In the setting of our formalization, the following is suitable. It can be justified by an analysis of specifications as in Section 3 but taking into account visibility restrictions on specifications. For lack of space we omit the details of the justification.

Definition 25 ($\dot{\approx}^C$). Suppose *Init* is given as in Definition 19. Define $M \dot{\approx}^C M'$ iff *Init*; $M \approx^C$ *Init*; M'.

The point of using simulations is to get both congruence and the following which expresses how simulation implies equivalence.

Theorem 26. If $M \asymp N$ and $\asymp$ is a D-simulation then $M \dot{\approx}^C N$ for any $C \neq D$.

The last ingredient needed for the main result is a way to compose the main relations. We have defined several relations on terms and they enjoy various composition properties, most of which turn out not to help. What we need is the following.

Lemma 27. Suppose $\asymp$ is a D-simulation and N terminates when M does, modulo $\asymp$. If $M \stackrel{\cdot}{\approx}^{C} N$ and $N \approx Q$ then $M \stackrel{\cdot}{\approx}^{C} Q$.

Theorem 28. Suppose $\asymp$ is a D-simulation and N terminates when Q does, modulo $\asymp$. If $Q \asymp N$ and N is strongly pure then $C[\text{assert } Q] \stackrel{\cdot}{\approx}^{C} C[\text{skip}]$ for all contexts C and classes $C \neq D$.

Proof. From $Q \asymp N$ we get $C[\text{assert } Q] \asymp C[\text{assert } N]$ by congruence Proposition 20. Thus $C[\text{assert } Q] \stackrel{\cdot}{\approx}^{C} C[\text{assert } N]$ by Theorem 26. By strong purity of N and Corollary 10 we have $C[\text{assert } N] \approx C[\text{skip}]$. Because all constructs of the language are monotonic with respect to termination, we have that $C[\text{assert } N]$ terminates when $C[\text{assert } Q]$ does, modulo $\asymp$. Thus Lemma 27 applies to yield the result. □

Our main Theorem 28 avoids the need to use the notions of observational purity or observational purity for $\asymp$ but it comes at the cost of proving simulation with a strongly pure term. The alternative is to use observational purity following the pattern of Corollary 10. This depends on a transitivity condition on simulations that is satisfied in all the observational purity examples we have considered. It is not included in Definition 19 because no other results depend on it. Transitivity does not make sense for simulations used for changes of data representation, where the source and target of the relation are different state spaces.

Theorem 29. Suppose $\asymp$ is a D-simulation such that $\asymp_\alpha \cdot \asymp_\beta = \asymp_{\alpha \cdot \beta}$ for all α, β. If Q is observationally pure for $\asymp$ then $\text{assert } Q \asymp \text{skip}$.

Corollary 30. *Suppose $\asymp$ is a D-simulation such that $\asymp_\alpha \cdot \asymp_\beta = \asymp_{\alpha \cdot \beta}$. If Q is observationally pure for $\asymp$ then for any context $C[-]$ and any class $C \neq D$ we have $C[\text{assert } Q] \stackrel{\cdot}{\approx}^{C} C[\text{skip}]$.*

Proof. By Theorem 29, Proposition 20, and Theorem 26. □

6   Conclusion

To avoid logical anomalies and misleading results from runtime assertion checking, practical verification systems impose various purity requirements for specifications and annotations: no invocations allowed (ESC/Java [11]), strong purity checking (JML [12]), or unchecked advice to programmers (Eiffel [13]). But for verification to scale to large systems it is important to consider as pure even procedures which, for reasons such as caching, update preexisting objects, provided that the updates are unobservable. Absence of anomalies for formula Q can be made precise by equating **assert** Q with **skip** — the presence of Q has no effect on the properties of following code— using a notion of equivalence that is a congruence and correctness-preserving.

Our main result shows that Q satisfies the equivalence, in the context of some class C, provided that it simulates, in the context of a different class D, a strongly pure term. The main application is where Q invokes procedures of D and is used to reason about procedures of C. The result reduces admissibility of Q to a proof obligation (simulation) together with static analysis for strong purity rather than a more specialized analysis. To apply our results one needs a method for defining D-simulations. In particular, it is essential that condition (e) in Definition 19 need only be checked for procedures of D; for procedures of $C \neq D$ it should follow by a preservation/congruence theorem. Such theories (analogs of our Proposition 20 and Theorem 26) have been developed for many sorts of languages [14, 10]). For Java-like languages, Banerjee and Naumann [2] give such a theory under the assumption of suitable alias control which can be achieved using static analysis [2, 15, 9]; a similar result has recently been given [4] using state-based enforcement of encapsulation [5, 16]. Such results are difficult to prove for complex languages so it is fortunate that we could treat observational purity in terms of existing formulations.

In justifying the choice of program equivalence we have uncovered an issue for strong purity. If, in postconditions, it is allowed to use quantification over all allocated objects, even unreachable ones, then pre/post specifications can "observe" allocation and even strong purity is not sound. Quantifications over all allocated objects have been used in some settings, e.g., the program invariants of the Boogie discipline [5, 16], but in that context programmer-defined predicates are in fact restricted to reachability in terms of auxiliary fields. Pierik et al. [17] advocate global invariants such as "there is at most one C-object" which are apparently incompatible with strong purity.

The most closely related work is that of Barnett et al. [6], where a seemingly ad hoc condition combining Definitions 13 and 21 is proposed. Rather than drawing on the general theory of encapsulation and simulation, the work uses the noninterference property from information security. There may be some advantage to that approach in avoiding the full generality of simulation theory. It is being explored as part of the Spec#/Boogie project [5]. The full version of [6] will include examples of observationally pure procedurs from the .NET libraries. Leavens et al. [12] discuss the rationale and static analysis for strong purity in JML. Sălcianu and Rinard [19] give a more precise static analysis for the strong purity condition. Program equivalence modulo garbage collection has been studied by Calcagno et al. [7] and others [2].

To extend observational purity to total correctness, equivalence is replaced by refinement of **assert** Q by **skip**. Suitable simulation theory for a Java-like languages can be adapted from existing work [8, 2, 4]. We conjecture that the extension to concurrency is also straightforward. Procedures called in assertions need to be deterministic in order to apply logical reasoning, but our theory depends in no way on determinacy.

We leave open the question of completeness: if M is observationally pure outside D then is it simulated by some stongly pure N? Given such M, it is straightforward to define a relation R such that R is strongly pure (semantically) and suitably coupled with M. But the coupling needs to be a simulation for all procedures of D and R needs to be denoted by a term in the language.

References

1. J. Aldrich and C. Chambers. Ownership domains: Separating aliasing policy from mechanism. In *European Conference on Object-Oriented Programming*, pages 1–25, 2004.

2. A. Banerjee and D. A. Naumann. Ownership confinement ensures representation independence for object-oriented programs. *Journal of the ACM*, 2002. Accepted, revision pending. Extended version of [3].

3. A. Banerjee and D. A. Naumann. Representation independence, confinement and access control. In *ACM Symp. on Princ. of Program. Lang. (POPL)*, pages 166–177, 2002.

4. A. Banerjee and D. A. Naumann. State based ownership, reentrance, and encapsulation. Submitted, Dec. 2004.

5. M. Barnett, R. DeLine, M. Fähndrich, K. R. M. Leino, and W. Schulte. Verification of object-oriented programs with invariants. *Journal of Object Technology*, 3(6):27–56, 2004.

6. M. Barnett, D. A. Naumann, W. Schulte, and Q. Sun. 99.44% pure: Useful abstractions in specifications. In *ECOOP workshop on Formal Techniques for Java-like Programs (FTfJP)*, 2004. Technical Report NIII-R0426, University of Nijmegen.

7. C. Calcagno, P. O'Hearn, and R. Bornat. Program logic and equivalence in the presence of garbage collection. *Theoretical Comput. Sci.*, 298(3):557–581, 2003.

8. A. L. C. Cavalcanti and D. A. Naumann. Forward simulation for data refinement of classes. In *Formal Methods Europe*, volume 2391 of *LNCS*, pages 471–490, 2002.

9. D. Clarke and S. Drossopoulou. Ownership, encapsulation and the disjointness of type and effect. In *OOPSLA*, pages 292–310, Nov. 2002.

10. W.-P. de Roever and K. Engelhardt. *Data Refinement: Model-Oriented Proof Methods and their Comparison*. Cambridge University Press, 1998.

11. C. Flanagan, K. R. M. Leino, M. Lillibridge, G. Nelson, J. B. Saxe, and R. Stata. Extended static checking for Java. In *ACM Conf. on Program. Lang. Design and Implementation (PLDI)*, pages 234–245, 2002.

12. G. T. Leavens, Y. Cheon, C. Clifton, C. Ruby, and D. R. Cok. How the design of JML accommodates both runtime assertion checking and formal verification. In *Formal Methods for Components and Objects (FMCO 2002)*, volume 2852 of *LNCS*, pages 262–284, 2003.

13. B. Meyer. *Object-oriented Software Construction*. Prentice Hall, New York, second edition, 1997.

14. J. C. Mitchell. *Foundations for Programming Languages*. MIT Press, 1996.

15. P. Müller. *Modular Specification and Verification of Object-Oriented Programs*. Number 2262 in *LNCS*. Springer, 2002.

16. D. A. Naumann and M. Barnett. Towards imperative modules: Reasoning about invariants and sharing of mutable state (extended abstract). In *IEEE Symp. on Logic in Computer Science (LICS)*, pages 313–323, 2004.

17. C. Pierik, D. Clarke, and F. S. de Boer. Creational invariants. In *Proceedings of ECOOP workshop on Formal Techniques for Java-like Programs (FTfJP)*, 2004. Technical Report NIII-R0426, University of Nijmegen.

18. A. Sabelfeld and A. C. Myers. Language-based information-flow security. *IEEE J. Selected Areas in Communications*, 21(1):5–19, Jan. 2003.

19. A. Sălcianu and M. Rinard. A combined pointer and purity analysis for Java programs. Technical Report MIT-CSAIL-TR-949, Department of Computer Science, Massachusetts Institute of Technology, May 2004.

Towards a Theory on the Role of Ontologies in Software Engineering Problem Solving

Conclusions from a Theoretical Model of Methodological Works

José M. Cañete* and Francisco J. Galán

Faculty of Computer Science,
University of Sevilla (Spain).

Abstract. We present and validate a theoretical model of methodological works in Software Engineering that, without claiming for completeness, allows us to investigate the role of ontologies in the problem solving process related with the development of software. Our main conclusion is the potential of ontologies as resources for an individual to *think* during problem solving. We argument that suitable ontologies can support solving strategies as well as motivate their invention. We also conclude the importance of accompany an ontology with knowledge that guides the engineer in reasoning with its concepts.

The model regards a methodological work as an heterogeneous theory about a class of problems and about a number of conceptual elements. Some of the elements are ontologies, which play the role of identifying and relating aspects of the knowledge about the class of problems, making up novel perspectives on the problems that may promote solving strategies.

For illustration purposes, we take Jackson's "Problem Frames" as a case study. We analyse this work through the former model, identifying the ontologies, guides, and promoted strategies. Then we propose an alternative ontology, based on that used in the KAOS approach; we reformulate some parts of Jackson's work through this ontology and propose a strategy as well as some guides.

Keywords: Ontologies, Methodologies, Modelling, Problem Solving, Cognitive Science.

1   Introduction

Modelling languages have been used for years in Software Engineering, and they are currently broadly extended. Textbooks and papers are plenty of modelling-

* Corresponding author. Contact at jmcv@us.es or at José Miguel Cañete Valdeón, ETS de Ingeniería Informática, Avda Reina Mercedes, S/N, 41012, Sevilla, Spain.
This work has been partially funded by the research project TIC 2003-02737-C02-01.

M. Cerioli (Ed.): FASE 2005, LNCS 3442, pp. 205–219, 2005.

related concepts as "model-driven engineering", "Model-Driven Architecture", and "Unified Modeling Language". In a previous paper we investigated the uses of these languages in the context of several software development methodologies, finding that the most popular use is that of *description* (Cañete et al., [1]). Frequently described subjects are the system-to-be and its environment. However, we also discovered that the models created with some languages are used for *reasoning* about some aspect of the development *problem*, allowing to obtain useful conclusions that, in some cases, could even motivate some design decision[1]. This fact leads to an interesting question: *what is the relation between modelling languages and human reasoning during problem solving?* This paper aims to contribute to answer this question. The followed approach is the study of ontologies in methodological works. We base this decision on three arguments.

First, the semantic conceptualization that is the basis of any modelling language can be regarded an ontology. Second, ontologies allow to acquire, organize, represent, and deal with *knowledge*. These activities are important for anybody that is solving a problem. Besides, in the case of solving a software development problem, it is necessary to have general knowledge about aspects of the class which the problem belongs to. And it is also useful to have some general knowledge about heuristics and other kinds of well-founded guides that suggest how to address the problems in the class. In conclusion, knowledge is important in problem solving, and ontologies are good instruments for managing knowledge. Therefore, a software engineer is likely to use several kinds of ontologies while she reasons in the resolution of a problem. The third argument to base our approach is that methodological works can be regarded as sources for the previously cited general knowledge (we will prove this later in this paper). In conclusion: ontologies and methodological knowledge are software engineer's tools in reasoning during problem solving. Their study seems a promising starting point for answering the question that we have formulated at the beginning of this section.

To this aim, we propose and validate a theoretical model of methodological works and we use it as an instrument for investigation. We obtain a number of predictions from the theoretical model, including the claim that ontologies may promote reasoning strategies for problem solving. The methodological work "Problem Frames" (Jackson, [11]) is used throughout this paper for illustration purposes.

The rest of the paper is organized as follows. Section 2 contains some background terms from Philosophy of Science that are necessary for the remaining parts. Section 3 describes and validates the theoretical model. In Section 4 we reason with the model and obtain a number of predictions. Section 5 summarizes the conclusions and exposes our current works. We close in Appendix A with an example of reasoning with ontologies.

---

[1] Note that we are not referring to languages intended to *describe* the reasoning process; this aspect constitutes an interesting research area in which important contributions have been made, particularly those by Potts and Bruns ([17]), and by Ramesh and Dhar ([18]).

2 Scientific Theories, Models, Hypotheses, and Ontologies

In this section we review some terms that we use in the rest of this paper, from the perspective of Philosophy of Science. The central concept is that of *"scientific theory"*. There are several philosophical approaches to what a theory is. A broadly accepted approach is the so-called "semantic view". It considers that a theory can be defined by a class of structures that provide an interpretation for it (a *semantics*); these structures are called *theoretical models* or, simply, *models*. Models can be defined in a variety of languages, none of which is the basic or unique expression of the theory. Some contributions to the semantic view are those by Suppes ([21, 22]), Suppe ([20]), van Fraasen ([7]), and Giere ([8]).

In particular, Giere's approach ([8]) understands a theory as comprising two elements: (1) a family of interrelated *theoretical models*, and (2) various *theoretical hypotheses* that claim the *similarity* among models in the family and parts of the real world, in indicated respects and to some specified degrees of accuracy. Giere's theoretical models are conceptual, idealised systems (e.g. those discussed in mechanics texts) that jointly provide the semantics of a theory. Hypotheses are true if the models do fit the world in the indicated respects and degrees, and they are false otherwise. Theoretical models of the same family are related between them by similarity relations ("resemblance" –Giere, [8], p. 86); in some cases, they may constitute different approximations to a real world situation.

Morgan and Morrison ([14]) argue that scientific models are instruments for investigation, and they point out several functions of models as instruments. One of these functions is to aid in theory construction. The theoretical model that we have proposed (Section 3) is intended to investigate the relationship between ontologies and reasoning during the resolution of problems; therefore, the model contributes to the development of a theory about such relationship.

Giere ([9]) argues that theoretical models can be used for making *predictions* about the reality that they represent. If the model is proven to fit the world in certain respects and to some specified degrees of accuracy, then the predictions made from the model are also true in the world. Predictions, in turn, allow to *learn* with the model, another of the characteristics pointed out by Morgan and Morrison ([14]). Section 4 describes some predictions obtained from our proposed model of methodological works.

Ontology is a branch of Philosophy concerned with the study of what exists. In Computer Science, ontologies are of great interest for knowledge acquisition and representation, and recently also for Semantic Web. A popular ontology definition is that by Gruber ([10]): an ontology provides *"an explicit specification of a conceptualization"*. Mylopoulos ([15]) emphasizes the role of ontologies in acquiring the right concepts to model a world for which one would like to do computations or knowledge management operations. Jurisica, Mylopoulos, and Yu ([12]) classify ontologies for knowledge representation into four broad categories: static, dynamic, intentional, and social.

3   A Theoretical Model of Methodological Works

In this section we present and validate a theoretical model that fits a class of methodological works. In spite of its simplicity, the model has been an adequate instrument for investigation of the role of ontologies in problem solving, allowing us to obtain a number of conclusions in the form of predictions, which are exposed in the next section. The reality to be modelled is constituted by the methodological works in Software Engineering. A methodological work is that aimed to be applied by a practising engineer to any problem in a class, with the hope of contributing to its resolution. They form a conceptual reality, and we can find descriptions of them in research papers and textbooks.

3.1   Description of the Model

The first component of our model is a study of the class of problems that are intended to be solved. The analysis covers different aspects of the problems, which probably constitute novel approaches to the study of the class. Several concepts are defined, and the study of some of the identified aspects is presented through these concepts. Sets of interrelated concepts are grouped in ontologies.

The model also incorporates a number of guides, which are suggestions for the practising engineer of activities to do. Some of these guides are specific for several of the former ontologies, suggesting how to use them to achieve some purpose which, in turn, contributes to the resolution of the problems in the class. A special type of guides is constituted by logical schemes that, when they are instantiated by the practising engineer on a concrete problem, result in conclusions that contribute to the problem resolution (e.g. to conclude to make some design decision). The ontologies with guides may have a textual or graphical syntax associated to their concepts, although it is not strictly necessary.

The concepts introduced to study the class of problems can have properties on their own, from an abstract point of view. A last component of the model is constituted by these properties, together with the properties derivable from the former guides.

The above components are related by a constraint: the concepts and guides must actually contribute to the resolution of the class of problems. If this constrains holds and the former studies are correct, the methodological work is considered to be valid.

3.2   Validation of the Theoretical Model

Giere ([9]) proposes a program to validate theoretical hypotheses, and, hence, theoretical models. The program is based on making predictions from the theoretical model. If such predictions do not agree with experimental data, then the model does not fit the world and the hypothesis is false. Otherwise, the hypothesis is considered to be true if there are no alternative models that explain the same predictions.

Seven predictions from our model are presented in the next section where we also reason the soundness of each one, thus contributing to the validation of the

Table 1. Some of the problem aspects studied in "Problem Frames"

Aspect	Description
A_1	There exist classes of typical software problems. Some of these classes have typical decompositions in terms of others.
A_2	The physical, spatial extension of software problems.
A_3	The extension of software problems from the viewpoint of the customer's needs.
A_4	The different roles played by the physical elements of a software problem.
A_5	The variability in each class of softw. problems from a physical perspective.
A_6	The diversity in the domain nature and its impact in each class of software problems.
A_7	The logical correction of each class of software problems.
A_8	The impact of the failure of a reliable domain in a software problem.

Table 2. Some of the concepts defined in "Problem Frames" for studying each problem aspect. We have put together each group of related concepts in an ontology

Aspect	Concepts	Ontology
A_1	Problem Frame, Information Display Frame, ...	O_1
A_2	Domain, Interface, Phenomenon, Description, ...	O_2
A_3	Requirement, Customer's Authority, Customer's Responsibility	O_3
A_4	Operator, Machine, Display, Real World, Workpieces, ...	O_4
A_5	Variant, Description Variant, Operator Variant, ...	O_5
A_6	Flavour, Static Flavour, Dynamic Flavour, ...	O_6
$A_7, A_8, ...$	Concern, Frame Concern (A_7), Reliability Concern (A_8), ...	O_7

whole model. We have not found an alternative theoretical model that explains all the predictions.

Besides, our model agrees with Wieringa's account on design-related research (Wieringa, [26]). He reasons that, during any design process, both the problem properties and the solution properties must be studied. According to the author, this is also applicable to the design of methods.

3.3   Example: Modelling the "Problem Frames" Methodological Work

The preface of "Problem Frames" (Jackson, [11]) states on page xii: "*The central idea of this book is to use problem frames in problem analysis and structure*". A "software problem" is a general and incomplete specification of the responsibilities of a software system in the context of a composite system[2] in which it is immersed. Analysis is the problem of identifying the concerns and difficulties of a software problem. Structure is the problem of designing a correct decomposition of a software problem into subproblems, which ideally contributes to an easier

---

[2] A composite system includes people, hardware, software, and lexical entities.

Table 3. The fist column indicates some guides included in "Problem Frames". The second column specifies the ontologies that are directly involved in each guide. The page and chapter references are relative to (Jackson, [11])

Guides	Ontologies
$\mathcal{G}_1$ (*heuristic*): identify ancillary problems. This guide is based on the knowledge that in most software problems there are ancillary subproblems surrounding the core (p. 293).	$\mathcal{O}_1$
$\mathcal{G}_2$ (*heuristic*): identify and address the concerns of the frames that have already been identified for a problem. This guide is based on the knowledge that each problem frame has a number of typical concerns (chapter 9).	$\mathcal{O}_1 + \mathcal{O}_7$
$\mathcal{G}_3$ (*heuristic*): study the software problem beyond the software system interface. This guide is based on the knowledge that the software problem is immersed in and interacts with a composite system (pp. 7–10).	$\mathcal{O}_2$
$\mathcal{G}_4$ (*heuristic*): expand your study of the composite system to the extent that the customer's responsibilities are covered, without trespassing the customer's authority. This guide is based on the knowledge that the software problem requirements must not be too small in relation to the customer's responsibilities, and that the customer's authority limits the scope of what the software system may legitimately be designed to do (pp. 29–33).	$\mathcal{O}_2 + \mathcal{O}_3$
$\mathcal{G}_5$ (*heuristic*): a valid way to address the failure detection in the reliability concern of a problem is to insert an information subproblem to audit failures. This guide is based on knowledge about the reliability concern (pp. 248–257).	$\mathcal{O}_1$ + Reliability Concern ($\mathcal{O}_7$)

development of the software. Therefore, we can summarize the class of problems which the methodological work is intended for as: "*how to analyse and structure software problems?*".

The approach includes a vast study of numerous aspects of the cited class of problems. Table 1 shows a possible relation of some of these aspects; other classifications can also be valid. Several concepts defined in the method for the study of each aspect have been collected in Table 2, where we have also proposed a possible grouping of the concepts in different ontologies. The main concept is "Problem Frame", which is a synonym for a known class of software problems. The only concepts in Table 2 that have an associated syntax are those of ontology $\mathcal{O}_2$ together with the concept "Requirement" (in $\mathcal{O}_3$).

As we will prove in Section 4.1, some ontological concepts, in addition to be useful for the study of the class of problems, are also intended to contribute to the engineer's reasoning in solving any particular problem of the class. Such ontologies are associated with guides. In "Problem Frames" we can find guides to be used with several ontologies, including $\mathcal{O}_1$, $\mathcal{O}_2$, $\mathcal{O}_3$, $\mathcal{O}_4$, and $\mathcal{O}_7$; Table 3 shows some of them. Some guides as $\mathcal{G}_2$ require concepts from several ontologies.

Note that the ontologies without an associated syntax may also have associated guides (e.g. $\mathcal{O}_1$).

One of the guides intended to help in locating and bounding software problems is related with the customer's authority and responsibility (pp. 31–33). We have identified it as $\mathcal{G}_4$ in Table 3. The "customer" is a notional person representing all the people who are entitled to contribute to the requirement in a software problem (Jackson, [11], p. 363). The guide is intended to be used with the so-called "context diagrams", which are elaborated from the concepts of ontology $\mathcal{O}_2$. It suggests that the domains that must be considered in analysing a software problem must be limited by the customer's authority, while covering the customer's responsibility. But the ontology $\mathcal{O}_2$ does not make explicit the concept of "Domain Responsibility", so we find that, in practice, the guide is difficult to be used with $\mathcal{O}_2$. We will return to this topic in Section 4.5.

"Problem Frames" includes some properties of the ontological concepts from an abstract point of view (third component of the model). For example, those concepts with an associated syntax (e.g. those in $\mathcal{O}_2$) have a set of abstract properties that allow to combine instances of them, forming different graphical models (diagrams). A sample property is that two instances of "Domain" cannot be directly associated but they need an instance of "Interface".

4   Predictions from the Theoretical Model

In this section we present seven predictions inferred from the theoretical model previously introduced. We argument the validity of each obtained prediction, thus contributing to the validation of the whole theoretical model (Section 3.2).

4.1   Ontologies may Promote Strategies

Research from Cognitive Psychology shows that individuals develop and use *strategies* to solve problems, not necessarily in a conscious manner (Schaeken et al., [19]; Van der Henst et al., [23]). We propose the following working definition: a strategy is a particular reasoning approach towards the resolution of a problem in a certain class of related problems. We are interested in those strategies that can be applied not only to a particular problem instance in the class, but to all of them or, at least, to a number of them.

In his famous problem-solving method from 1945, George Polya emphasizes the importance of considering different aspects of the problem and combining them to form novel perspectives, which may lead to a solution strategy: *"Consider your problem from various sides. Emphasize different parts, examine different details, examine the same details repeatedly but in different ways, combine the details differently, approach them from different sides. Try to see some new meaning in each detail, some new interpretation of the whole.[...]"* (Polya, [16], p. 34). Our theoretical model of methodological works agrees with this principle: the concepts in the ontologies consider different aspects of the problems and they allow to study these aspects together. Therefore, ontologies that capture aspects

Table 4. The two main strategies in "Problem Frames". Note that S_2 is a sub-strategy for realizing S_1. Page numbers refer to (Jackson, [11])

Ontology	Strategy
O_1	S_1: Analyse a software problem by reducing it to a combination of known class of problems. Design a structure for a software problem by composing known classes of problems (pp. 59–61).
O_2	S_2: Ground the analysis and structure of software problems in observable, physical phenomena: this will help to check whether we are really satisfying the requirements or not (pp. 22–23).

of the problem may inspire the emerging of new strategies to address the problem. The hypothesis that considering novel aspects and combining them can lead to new ideas is consistent with the creativity theory by the psychologist Boden ([2, 3]), who defends the association of concepts as a valid process of emerging of new ideas. Ward et al. ([24]) refer to this process as "conceptual combination".

According to our initial definition, a strategy may contribute only to some respect of the overall resolution of the problem. Therefore, a number of strategies may be necessary to constitute a complete method for a class of problems; this is one of the reasons why the theoretical model allows several ontologies (another reason will be explained in Section 4.5). For example, sometimes a strategy is needed to carry out a higher-level strategy. This happens in Jackson's Problem Frames (see the example below).

From the preceding discussion we can conclude that it is possible to design ontologies that motivate the invention of strategies that contribute to the resolution of some problem. At the moment we do not have a theory that fully characterizes the class of ontologies that promote strategies. However, in this section we have proven that ontologies that explore different perspectives of problems are good candidates for promoting useful strategies.

Example: Strategies in "Problem Frames". Table 4 show the two main strategies proposed by the "Problem Frames" approach. The observation that there exist classes of typical software problems (aspect A_1 in Table 1) has motivated strategy S_1. This strategy is quite general, and it needs at least another one to be realized; S_2 proposes a possible way of achieving S_1. It has been motivated by the observation that each class of software problems has a defined spatial structure (aspect A_2).

4.2   Guides Suggest How to Carry Out Strategies Promoted by Ontologies

The former prediction has proven that ontologies included in the theoretical model of Section 3.1 may inspire strategies. The theoretical model also includes guides related to the use of the ontologies. In this section we will prove that these guides are the methodologist's suggestions for carrying out the corresponding strategies promoted by the ontologies.

Consider an ontology without associated guides. According to the problem-solving approach and creativity theory exposed in the previous section, the practising engineer could still invent her own strategy while experimenting with an ontology on a concrete problem, even in the absence of guides. However, in the general case, it is not possible to prove the contribution of such an ontology to the resolution of the class of problems, implying that the methodological work could not be validated. As validation of the method is one requirement of our model, the role of ontologies without guides is restricted to the study of some aspect of the class of problems.

4.3   Ontologies in Methods are Reasoning Instruments

Ontologies are intended to be used by the practising engineer, together with guides that help her to carry out the related strategies. To applying an strategy means that the practising engineer must *reason* with the concepts in the corresponding ontology. Guides help her in this reasoning to a certain extent, specially those that we have called "logical schemes" in Section 3.1.

4.4   Strategies Promoted by Ontologies Apply Knowledge to the Resolution of Problems

The ontologies of the theoretical model have two kinds of associated knowledge. On the one hand, a portion of the study on the class of problems: the one related to the problem aspects that the ontological concepts represent. On the other hand, the abstract properties of the concepts. Therefore, any strategy promoted by some ontology is based on and applies the knowledge associated to its ontology.

4.5   A Method may Have Alternative Strategies

We have reasoned in Section 4.1 that our model allows that several strategies coexist, each one contributing to solve some respect of the whole problem. However, the model does not impede that two strategies contribute to the resolution of the *same* respect. Each one could apply a different portion of the method knowledge, and each one could be driven by different sets of guides. If, in dealing with a concrete problem, strategy A has failed in solving a subproblem or it is not applicable to the concrete case, the practising engineer could try strategy B for solving the same subproblem. Below we present an example of an alternative strategy to S_2.

Example: Introduction of A New Strategy in "Problem Frames". The different roles introduced by Jackson (aspect A_4, ontology O_4) denote different *responsibilities* of the domains with respect to the composite system. The fulfillment of the responsibilities causes the appearance of an *emergent behavior* (Wieringa, [25]), which may or may not be what the customer expects. The study of responsibilities in composite systems has a long tradition in Software Engineering (Feather, [5]). A related concept is that of *Goal*, which has been proven to be a useful resource for this kind of analysis, particularly in the KAOS

Agent an active system component (or "processor") which may have choice of behaviour to ensure the goals it is assigned to (Feather, [5]).

And/Or Goal Reduction a mechanism for goal refinement: g is a reduction of G iff achieving goal g possibly with other subgoals is among the alternative ways of achieving goal G (Dardenne et al, [4]).

Goal an objective to be achieved by the system under consideration (Letier and van Lamsweerde, [13]). "System" refers to the composite system consisting of the software-to-be together with its environment (Fickas and Helm, [6]).

Goal Pattern classification based on the temporal behaviour required by the goal. It can be *achieve, cease, maintain,* and *avoid* (Dardenne et al, [4]).

Responsibility Assignment assigning responsibility to an agent means that this agent must restrict its behaviour so as to ensure the goal (Dardenne et al, [4]).

Fig. 1. Some concepts of the KAOS ontology ($\mathcal{O}_G$)

approach (Dardenne, Fickas, and Lamsweerde, [4]). This has encouraged us to borrow the KAOS ontology from (Letier and Lamsweerde, [13]), and to use it to study the class of problems addressed in (Jackson, [11]). Figure 1 defines some of the concepts in the cited ontology, which we will denote as $\mathcal{O}_G$.

This study revealed that each problem frame has a defined structure in terms of goals. For example, Figure 2 shows the goal structure of the "Information Display Frame". The figure describes two alternative ways of achieving the goal Maintain[ReportingWorldInformation], which is the higher-level goal of the frame. The left goal tree requires the collaboration of three agents: Machine, Real world, and Display. The right goal tree does not require the Display, because the data about the real world are represented as pure information (in a lexical domain).

The fact that each problem frame has a corresponding goal structure, motivated us for defining the following strategy, which contributes to achieve the general strategy $\mathcal{S}_1$:

> $\mathcal{S}_G$: in problem analysis, identify problem frames by looking for the goals and responsibilities in the problem; in problem structure, design subproblems by thinking about goals that must be satisfied by lower-level goals, which will be ultimately realized by agents. For both purposes, use the knowledge of the goal structure of problem frames.

In order to realize this strategy, we have proposed a number of guides related with $\mathcal{O}_1$ and $\mathcal{O}_G$. Table 5 shows some of these guides. Figure 3 in Appendix A shows an example of reasoning with $\mathcal{O}_G$ in analysing and structuring the "package router control problem" (p. 270 of Jackson, [11]). Note also that $\mathcal{O}_G$ allows a more easy application of guide $\mathcal{G}_4$ (Section 3.3.), as it makes explicit the responsibilities assigned to each Domain (Agent).

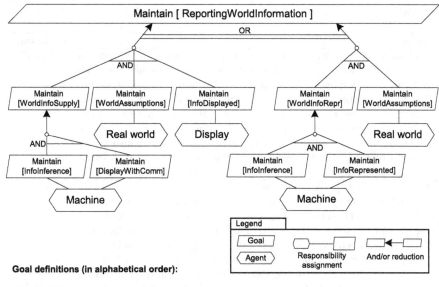

Goal definitions (in alphabetical order):

Maintain[DisplayWithComm] = Inferred information is translated to display commands.
Maintain[InfoDisplayed] = Display what is indicated through commands.
Maintain[InfoInference] = Information of interest about the world is inferred from observed data.
Maintain[InfoRepresented] = Inferred information is represented in a lexical domain.
Maintain[ReportingWorldInformation] = Certain information of interest about the world is continually needed at the required place in the required form.
Maintain[WorldAssumptions] = Assumptions about the world used on inference are never violated.
Maintain[WorldInfoRepr] = Information of interest about the world in represented in a lexical domain.
Maintain[WorldInfoSuppy] = Information of interest about the world is supplied to Display in the form of displaying commands.

Fig. 2. Goal structure for the "Information Display Frame". The figure includes the legend for the some concepts in $\mathcal{O}_G$

4.6   Methods Can be Regarded as Scientific Theories

If we recall the description of the theoretical model (Section 3.1), it contains a study of the problems in a class. Such class is a reality, so the study can be considered as a theory that claims that the obtained results fit such reality.

Other elements in the model are ontologies and guides. They may exist previously in another context, or they may be invented by the methodologist when she developed the method. In any case, they constitute conceptual realities. The model contains a study of the properties of these elements; as before, this study can be regarded as a theory about a reality. It is necessary for proving the correctness of the methodological work (Section 3.1).

In conclusion, the model can be interpreted as consisting of two theories: one referred to the class of problems, and the other one referred to conceptual elements (ontologies and guides).

Table 5. Some proposed guides for reasoning with $O_1 + O_G$ to realize $\mathcal{S}_G$

Guides	Ontologies
$\mathcal{G}_6$ (*logical scheme*): we have realized that some goal g, which appears as assigned to the software system in the initial statement of some problem p, corresponds to the higher-level goal in the goal structure of a certain problem frame F. Therefore, it is unlikely that the software system alone could operationalise g on its own. Therefore, let us assume that our problem p fits frame F. Applying the goal structure of F to p, we discover the remaining agents and their responsibilities in terms of sub-goals. We verify our initial assumption by checking that the assigned goals make sense in the context of p.	$\mathcal{O}_1 + \mathcal{O}_G$
$\mathcal{G}_7$ (*logical scheme*): We are in doubt about if a certain problem frame F fits our problem p. Let us assume it fits. Applying the goal structure of F, we obtain the relation of agents that should participate and their responsibilities in terms of operationalisation of goals. *If* we find that (1) either some goal demands more than its agent in p is able to do, or (2) several goals demand too little from their associated agents in p, wasting their capabilities, *then* we can conclude that the initial assumption is probably false.	$\mathcal{O}_1 + \mathcal{O}_G$

4.7   The Study of Problems is Central to the Design of a Method

According to the model prediction of Section 4.1, the study of the class of problems under different concepts may motivate the invention of resolution strategies, and therefore it is central to the design of methods. The study is also necessary to prove that the methodological work is valid; this is described in the constraint stated in the theoretical model (Section 3.1). This reason has been also pointed out by Wieringa ([26]).

5   Conclusions and Current Work

This paper has presented a contribution to the relation between ontologies that constitute modelling languages and an individual's reasoning process during problem solving in Software Engineering. Our research method has been to make predictions from a theoretical model of methodological works. This approach has led to a number of interesting conclusions (Section 4), including the property that ontologies may inspire solving strategies, and hence they are essential instruments for reasoning during problem solving. In particular, this property establishes that it is possible to design modelling languages that help the engineer to reason in the problem solving process of software development. However, we do not have a complete theory that characterizes the whole class of ontologies that motivate reasoning strategies. Our current work is to advance in this research area.

Acknowledgments. We want to thank the anonymous reviewers for their work in reading the first version of this paper and for their useful comments. We also want to thank María del Carmen Serrano Jiménez for the English grammatical revision of this work.

References

[1] Cañete, J.M., Galán, F.J., Toro, M. (2004). Some Problems of Current Modelling Languages that Obstruct to Obtain Models as Instruments. *Proceedings of the IX Spanish Conference on Software Engineering and Databases (JISBD'2004).*

[2] Boden, M. (1990) *The Creative Mind: Myths & Mechanisms.* Basic Books.

[3] Boden, M. (1994). What is creativity? In M. A. Boden (Ed.), *Dimensions of creativity* (pp. 75-117). The MIT Press.

[4] Dardenne, A., van Lamsweerde, A., Fickas, S. (1993). Goal-Directed Requirements Acquisition. *Science of Computer Programming*, 20, 3–50.

[5] Feather, M. (1987). Language Support for the Specification and Development of Composite Systems. *ACM Transactions on Programming Languages and Systems*, 9:2, 198–234.

[6] Fickas, S., Helm, R. (1992). Knowledge Representation and Reasoning in the Design of Composite Systems. *IEEE Transactions on Software Engineering*, 18:6, 470–482.

[7] Fraasen, B. van (1980). *The Scientific Image.* Clarendon Press.

[8] Giere, R. (1988). *Explaining Science.A Cognitive Approach.*University of Chicago Press.

[9] Giere, R. (1997). *Understanding Scientific Reasoning.* Fourth Edition. Harcourt Brace College Publishers.

[10] Gruber, T.R. (1993). A translation approach to portable ontology specifications. *Knowledge Acquisition*, 5, 199–220.

[11] Jackson, M. (2001). *Problem Frames. Analyzing and structuring software development problems.* Addison-Wesley.

[12] Jurisica, I., Mylopoulos, J. Yu, E. (2004). Ontologies for Knowledge Management: An Information Systems Perspective. *Knowledge and Information Systems*, 6, 380–401.

[13] Letier, E., van Lamsweerde, A. (2002). Agent-Based Tactics for Goal-Oriented Requirements Elaboration. *Proceedings of the 24th International Conference on Software Engineering* (ICSE'2002). ACM Press.

[14] Morgan, M. and Morrison, M. (1999). Models as mediating instruments. *Models as Mediators. Perspectives on Natural and Social Science*, pp. 10–37. Cambridge University Press.

[15] Mylopoulos, J. (1998) Information Modeling in the Time of the Revolution. *Information Systems 23 (3-4), 127-155.*

[16] Polya, G. (1945) *How to Solve It. A New Aspect of Mathematical Method.* Princeton University Press.

[17] Potts, C. and Bruns, G. (1988). Recording the Reasons for Design Decisions. *Proceedings of the 10th International Conference on Software Engineering*, pp. 418–427.

[18] Ramesh, B. and Dhar, V. (1992) Supporting Systems Development by Capturing Deliberations During Requirements Engineering. *IEEE Transactions on Software Engineering*, 18(6), 498–510.

[19] Schaeken, W., De Vooght, G., Vandierendonck, A., d'Ydewalle, G. (2000). *Deductive reasoning and strategies*. Lawrence Erlbaum Associates.

[20] Suppe, F. (1977). *The Structure of Scientific Theories*. University of Illinois Press.

[21] Suppes, P. (1961). A Comparison of the Meanaing and Use of Models in the Mathematical and Empirical Sciences. *The Concept and Role of the Model in Mathematics and Natural and Social Sciences*, pp. 163–167. Reidel.

[22] Suppes, P. (1967). What is a Scientific Theory? *Philosophy of Science Today*, pp. 55–67. Basic Books.

[23] Van der Henst, J.B., Yang, Y., Johnson-Laird, P.N. (2002). Strategies in sentential reasoning. *Cognitive Science*, 26, 425–468.

[24] Ward, T. B., Finke, R. A., Smith, S. M. (1995). *Creativity and the mind: Discovering the genius within*. Plenum Press.

[25] Wieringa, R. (2003). *Design Methods for Reactive Systems: Yourdon, Statemate and the UML*. Morgan Kaufmann.

[26] Wieringa, R. (2004). Requirements engineering research is the study of design. Internal report. Department of Computer Science, University of Twente, the Netherlands.

A   An Example of Reasoning with Ontologies

We show a simple example of reasoning with ontologies $\mathcal{O}_1$ and $\mathcal{O}_G$. The aim is to analyse and structure the "package router control problem", which also solved in pp. 270–291 of (Jackson, [11]) with strategies $\mathcal{S}_1$ and $\mathcal{S}_2$. The following problem statement has been extracted from page 270 of the same reference:

A package router is a large mechanical device used by postal and delivery organisations to sort packages into bins according to their destinations. The packages carry bar-coded labels. They move along a conveyor to a reading station where their package-ids and destinations are read. They then slide by gravity down pipes fitted with sensors at top and bottom. The pipes are connected by two-position switches that the computer can flip (where no package is present between the incoming and outgoing pipes). At the leaves of the tree of pipes are destination bins, corresponding to the bar-coded destinations. A package cannot overtake another either in a pipe or a switch. Also, the pipes are bent near the sensors so that the sensors are guaranteed to detect each package separately. However, packages slide at unpredictable speeds, and may get too close together to allow a switch to be set correctly. A misrouted package may be routed to any bin, an appropriate message being displayed. There are control buttons by which an operator can command the controlling computer to stop and start the conveyor.

The problem is to build the controlling computer to obey the operator's commands, to route packages to their destination bins by setting the switches appropriately, and to report misrouted packages.

Thinking in terms of $\mathcal{O}_G$, we can identify three goals from the problem statement, which appear as assigned to the software system (box 1 in Figure 3). Reasoning with the knowledge from guide $\mathcal{G}_6$, we conclude that the goal Report misrouted packages may be the high-level goal of an Information Display Frame. Hence, it is unlikely that the Machine could operationalise this goal only by itself. Box 2 in Figure 3 shows the identified frame, which is an instance of the Information Display Frame concept in $\mathcal{O}_1$. Next, according to the suggestion of

$\mathcal{G}_2$, we realize that the Reliability Concern is important for this problem: the assumptions about the packages may likely fail, and this would bring undesirable consequences for the composite system (we cannot trust in agent Router & packages to satisfy its goal). Following guide $\mathcal{G}_5$, we introduce a new Information Display frame that audits these possible failures (box 3 in Figure 3).

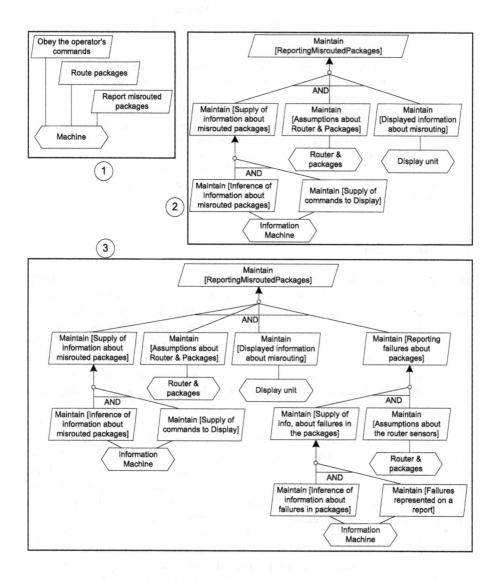

Fig. 3. A simple example of reasoning with $\mathcal{O}_1$ and $\mathcal{O}_G$

A Framework for Counterexample Generation and Exploration

Marsha Chechik and Arie Gurfinkel

Department of Computer Science, University of Toronto,
Toronto, ON M5S 3G4, Canada
{chechik, arie}@cs.toronto.edu

Abstract. Model-checking is becoming an accepted technique for debugging hardware and software systems. Debugging is based on the "Check / Analyze / Fix" loop: check the system against a desired property, producing a counterexample when the property fails to hold; analyze the generated counterexample to locate the source of the error; fix the flawed artifact – the property or the model. The success of model-checking non-trivial systems critically depends on making this Check / Analyze / Fix loop as tight as possible. In this paper, we concentrate on the Analyze part of the debugging loop. To this end, we present a framework for generating, structuring and exploring counterexamples either interactively or with the help of user-specified strategies.

1   Introduction

Model-checking is an automated verification technique that receives a finite-state description of a system and a temporal logic property and decides whether the property holds in the system. Model-checking is rapidly becoming an accepted technique for analyzing software and hardware system. In addition to telling the user whether the desired temporal property holds, it can also generate a counterexample, explaining the *reason why* this property failed. Typically, counterexamples are given in terms of states and transitions of the model and can be effectively used for debugging. The counterexample generation ability has been one of the major advantages of model-checking when compared to other verification methods.

During debugging, a model-checker is used as a part of the Check / Analyze / Fix loop: check the model, analyze the produced counterexample, fix the model or the property. Copty et al. [7] describe several stages of debugging: (1) the specification debugging stage, during which we fix the properties to make them trustworthy; (2) the model debugging stage, during which the actual bugs in the model are being found; and (3) the quality assurance stage which addresses the problem of "regression verification" – making sure that fixing one error does not introduce new ones.

Counterexamples can also be used for *design exploration* [2]. A model-checker enables the user to specify scenarios of interest without specifying the exact input sequences leading to them, and can also reason about multiple executions of the system in parallel. Thus, the user can provide a set of constraints in the form of a temporal logic property that an "interesting" trace through the system should satisfy, and the model-checker computes such traces while checking the property.

M. Cerioli (Ed.): FASE 2005, LNCS 3442, pp. 220–236, 2005.

Explaining why a property p fails to hold (a *counterexample*) is the same as explaining why a property $\neg p$ holds (a *witness*). In this paper, we often use witnesses and counterexamples interchangeably, referring to them collectively as *evidence*.

Some version of the Check/Analyze/Fix loop frequently applies, and the goal of this work is to make this loop tighter. The Check phase involves running a model-checker, which is an exponential algorithm that often takes hours to run even for moderately-sized models [7]. So, it is desirable to minimize the number of model-checking runs while maximizing the information obtained from each run.

The Analyze phase is measured in terms of the time that an engineer spends exploring the generated evidence, and thus is costly as well. It is possible for model-checkers to generate too much evidence [9], flooding the user with information, and making it hard to build a mental picture of what is going on. In this case, the user may spend too much time and energy trying to reach the portion of interest or get confused about the purpose of a given sub-trace in the overall explanation. Also, since the size of the property under analysis is typically much smaller than the size of the system, formula-specific patterns often repeat themselves throughout the evidence [9], and users fail to notice them. It is therefore desirable to have control over just how much evidence is generated by the model-checker. This can be accomplished via *interactive explanations* – evidence generation based on user preferences. Interactive explanations can allow users to put a bound on the time that the model-checker spends computing the evidence, and continue exploring it manually; control which option is used to facilitate the generation of "interesting" evidence; and control the amount of information that is generated and presented by restricting the scope of exploration according to some criterion of interest. Clearly, interactive explanations makes the problem of generating and understanding evidence tractable:

- The amount of evidence generated is based on what the user is willing to understand. This helps scalability of our approach to large models.
- The amount of evidence displayed makes it easier to identify "interesting" cases and helps with debugging.

Since model-checking runs are expensive, it is desirable to enable users to fix as many errors as possible before repeating the verification, rather than eliminating one counterexample at a time. For example, we would like to know that $f \wedge g$ fails to hold because *both* f and g are false. To this end, providing the user with all disjoint counterexamples to a given property can significantly shorten the debugging time.

Contributions of this Paper. In this paper, we propose a framework for structuring and interactively exploring evidence. The framework is based on the idea that the most general type of evidence to why a property holds or fails to hold is a *proof*. Such proofs can be presented to the user in the form of proof-like counterexamples [12] without sacrificing any of the intuitiveness and close relation to the model that users have learned to expect from model-checkers. Basing the evidence on proofs allows us to unify a number of existing ad-hoc approaches to exploring counterexamples. In particular, notions of forward and backward exploration as well as starting and stopping conditions are natural in the proof setting. Proofs can also be used to control what kind of evidence is being generated. The primary sources of such choices are:

1. determining which part of the property to explain (e.g., if the property is $p \lor q$, should the presented evidence be for p or for q?) and
2. determining which part of the model to use for the explanation (e.g., if the property is "there exists a next state where p holds" and the model has several such states, which should be presented?).

The above choices can be made by the user interactively or automated in the form of *strategies* (e.g., if faced with a choice of states for the explanation, always choose the one where some predicate x holds). The application of strategies is implemented in our framework by changing the proof rules used to generate evidence. The modification of proof rules can be *permanent* for the duration of the entire run of the model-checker, and thus can be facilitated by *history-free strategies*. Alternatively, the application of strategies can depend on the previously-observed behaviour of the system. For example, to see the infinite alternation between x and y, we may want to specify a strategy that oscillates between preferring a state where x holds and a state where y holds.

Finally, from the software engineering point of view, our framework provides a simple, unified way to interact with the counterexample generator. The interaction is based on defining strategies that combine property-based and model-based choices. For example, we can specify a strategy that prefers the part of the model that the user has explored previously, while attempting to satisfy a part of the property for which the witness is the shortest.

Clearly, most users cannot understand large proofs. In our framework, proofs are used in the back-end. They help generate and navigate through the evidence, without the need to be presented to the user. Instead, users see witnesses and counterexamples. Furthermore, large proofs are never computed in our approach since proof fragments are generated from the model-checking runs as part of interactive explorations to facilitate user-understanding. Application of strategies for dynamic proof generation is the major technical contribution of this paper, when compared to our previous work reported in [12].

In this paper, we *illustrate* the framework using a simple example rather than *validating* its effectiveness via a sizable case study. Here, we draw on industrial experience [7] that being able to limit the amount of evidence shown and generating several counterexamples at once is extremely effective in reducing the effort that engineers spend looking for a real cause of an error. Our framework unifies a number of existing approaches and allows users to create additional strategies that may further improve the debugging process. Thus, it can be used for explaining the reason why the property failed or succeeded, determining whether the property was correct ("specification debugging"), and for general model exploration.

Related Work. The problem of generating and analyzing counterexamples for model-checking can be divided into three categories: generating the counterexample efficiently, obtaining a visual presentation suitable for interactive exploration, and automatically analyzing the counterexample to extract the exact source of the error.

The original counterexample generation algorithm, implemented in most symbolic model-checkers, was proposed by Clarke et al. [5], and was later extended to handle arbitrary universal properties [6, 12], i.e., properties that quantify over all paths of the model. An alternative approach was independently suggested by Namjoshi [13] and Tan and Cleaveland [16] with the goal to extend the counterexample generation technique to all (as opposed to just universal) branching temporal properties. The proposed methods identify what information must be stored from the intermediate run of the model-checker to reconstruct the proof of correctness of the result. A similar technique for linear properties was explored by Peled et al. [14].

The problem of the visual *presentation* of generated counterexamples was addressed by Dong et al. [9, 8]. The authors developed a tool that simplifies the counterexample exploration by presenting evidence through various graphical views. In particular, they found that one of the most important parts of the visualization process is highlighting the correspondence between the analyzed property and the generated counterexample.

The problem of the automatic analysis of counterexamples was addressed by many researchers but space limitations do not allow us to survey them here. Many of these techniques (e.g. [11, 1]) are based on comparing all counterexamples to a safety property (i.e., a temporal property where a counterexample has a finite number of steps) to identify the common cause of the error.

The goal of our work is to develop a unifying framework for combining various visualization and analysis techniques. In that, the work of Copty et al. [7] is the closest to ours. The authors report on a "counterexample wizard" – a tool for counterexample exploration for safety properties. The key idea of the approach is to compute and compactly store all counterexamples to a given property. Users can then visualize the result in various ways, replay several counterexamples in parallel, and apply different automatic analysis techniques.

Organization. The rest of this paper is organized as follows: We discuss CTL model-checking in Section 2 and the framework from the user perspective in Section 3. In Section 4, we discuss the internals of the framework. In Section 5, we enrich the framework with additional proof strategies that allow the user to control which counterexample gets generated. In Section 6, we discuss how to use our framework to generate several counterexamples at once. We conclude in Section 7 with the summary of the paper and discussion of future research directions.

2   CTL Model-Checking

Model-checking is an automated verification technique that receives a system K and a temporal logic property φ and decides whether φ holds in K. In this paper, we assume that K is a Kripke structure consisting of a finite set of states S, a designated initial state s_0, a set of atomic propositions A, a total transition relation $R \subseteq S \times S$, and a labeling function $I : S \rightarrow 2^A$ that assigns a truth value to each atomic proposition in each state. An example Kripke structure is shown in Figure 1(a).

We specify properties in *Computation Tree Logic* (CTL) [4], defined below:

$$\varphi = a \mid \varphi \vee \varphi \mid \varphi \wedge \varphi \mid \neg\varphi \mid EX\varphi \mid AX\varphi \mid EF\varphi \mid AF\varphi \mid EG\varphi \mid AG\varphi \mid E[\varphi \ U \ \varphi] \mid A[\varphi \ U \ \varphi]$$

where a is an atomic proposition. The meaning of the temporal operators is: given a state and paths emanating from it, φ holds in one (EX) or all (AX) next states; φ holds in some future state along one (EF) or all (AF) paths, φ holds globally along one (EG) or

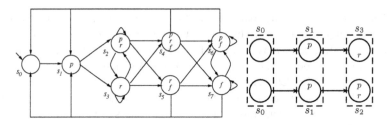

Fig. 1. (a) State machine for the module Button; (b) Two witnesses of length 3 for $[\![EFr]\!](s_0)$ for this statemachine

$$AX\varphi \triangleq \neg EX\neg\varphi \qquad AF\varphi \triangleq A[\text{true } U \ \varphi] \quad E[\varphi U_0\psi] \triangleq \psi$$
$$EF\varphi \triangleq E[\text{true } U \ \varphi] \quad AG\varphi \triangleq \neg EF\neg\varphi \qquad E[\varphi U_i\psi] \triangleq \psi \vee (\varphi \wedge EXE[\varphi U_{i-1} \ \psi])$$
$$A[\varphi \ U \ \psi] \triangleq \neg E[\neg\psi \ U \ \neg\varphi \wedge \neg\psi] \wedge \neg EG\neg\psi$$

Fig. 2. Definitions of CTL operators

all (AG) paths, and φ holds until a point where ψ holds along one (EU) or all (AU) paths. Some properties of the model in Figure 1(a) are: "it is possible to generate a request" (EFr) and "once a button is pressed, a request will be generated" ($AG(p \Rightarrow AFr)$).

We write $[\![\varphi]\!]^K(s)$ to indicate the value of φ in the state s of K, and $[\![\varphi]\!](s)$ when K is clear from the context. A formula φ is satisfied in a Kripke structure K if and only if it is satisfied in its initial state. The operators EX, EG, and EU form an adequate set, i.e. all other operators can be defined from them, as shown in Figure 2. Semantics EX, EG and EU is formally in defined as follows:

$[\![EX\varphi]\!](s)$ **iff** $\exists t \in S \cdot R(s,t) \wedge [\![\varphi]\!](t)$
$[\![E[\varphi U\psi]]\!](s)$ **iff** there exists a path $s_0, \ldots, s_n$ such that $s = s_0$ and $[\![\psi]\!](s_n)$ and $\forall i < n \cdot [\![\varphi]\!](s_i)$
$[\![EG\varphi]\!](s)$ **iff** there exists an infinite path $s_0, s_1, \ldots$ such that $s_0 = s$ and $\forall i \in nat \cdot [\![\varphi]\!](s_i)$

We also introduce a bounded version of the EU operator, that restricts path quantification to paths of bounded length, as shown in Figure 2.

3   User View of The Framework

In this section, we illustrate the framework from the user perspective on a familiar example of an elevator controller system.

3.1   Elevator Controller System

An elevator controller system consists of a single elevator which accepts requests made by users pressing buttons at the floor landings or inside the elevator. The elevator moves up and down between floors and opens and closes its doors in response to these requests.

We use the model specified in SMV by Plath & Ryan [15]. We do not present the state-machine model here because the purpose of our use of counterexamples is model

(a)   (b)   (c)

Fig. 3. Possible witnesses for EGp in state s: (a) a looping witness, (b) a path followed by a loop, and (c) two witnesses combining cases (a) and (b)

debugging and model understanding. However, to illustrate a few concepts, we do provide a state machine for a module Button, shown in Figure 1(a). One instance of the Button module is produced for each button inside the elevator and on floor landings.

Variable f determines when the request has been fulfilled and the button can be reset. We model the latching explicitly: variable p determines the state of the button (pressed or released), whereas r determines whether the request to move to the desired floor has been generated. We further assume that a request cannot be fulfilled before it has been generated, i.e., f cannot become true if r is false. In Figure 1(a), we only show true variables; thus, in state s_0, p, r, and f are false.

3.2   Witnesses and Counterexamples

Suppose we are interested in checking the following property of the Button module: "it is never the case that a request can be fulfilled", expressed in CTL as $AG\neg f$. The counterexample to this property is a finite path that starts in the initial state (s_0) and arrives at the state where f is true, e.g., s_0, s_1, s_2, s_5. Note that this path is also a witness to the negation of the above property: EFf, i.e., "it is possible to fulfill a request".

Consider another property: "whenever a request is generated, it will eventually be fulfilled", formalized in CTL as $AG(r \Rightarrow AFf)$. The counterexample to this property, or a witness to the equivalent property $EF(r \wedge EG\neg f)$, is an infinite behavior that describes (1) how the system can reach a state where r holds and from then on (2) how it can avoid entering a state in which f holds. One such path is s_0, s_1, s_2 (reaching r), followed by a loop at s_2 (so f is always false).

Unlike traditional model checkers, our framework does not automatically generate a single counterexample. Instead, it automates the process of dynamically constructing one, or several, starting from the initial state. Further, it gives two separate views of the counterexample: the low-level view, which describes each state explicitly, naming its variables, and a high-level view that shows the complete trace and annotates each state with additional information, which we refer to as *summaries*, describing the significance of the state with respect to the overall property, and summarizing the rest of the trace.

3.3   Exploring the Elevator Controller Model

We now describe user interactions with the framework while debugging and exploring the Elevator model.

Generating Several Counterexamples at Once. When we start verifying the system using the model-checker, it is usually the case that the property we are trying to check is wrong. Consider the property: "from any state, all paths go through a state where the elevator is on the third floor and doors are open" ($AGAF(\text{floor} = 3 \wedge \text{doors} = \text{open})$). The first counterexample tells us that it is possible to start on the first floor and stay there forever. We may conclude that the first floor is "special", and instead check that our desired configuration is reachable from any floor except the first one: $AG(\text{floor} \neq 1 \Rightarrow AF(\text{floor} = 3 \wedge \text{doors} = \text{open}))$. The counterexample we get in this case would lead us to the second floor and remain there forever, or possibly oscillate between the first and the second floor, without ever reaching the third. Seeing all three counterexamples at once would have helped us determine that the elevator never gets to the third floor unless a request for this floor has been made, and the property should have been updated to $AG(\text{btn3}.r \Rightarrow AF(\text{floor} = 3 \wedge \text{door} = \text{open}))$.

Excluding a Known Counterexample via Strategies. Consider the above example. Instead of modifying the property to exclude our first counterexample, which is often difficult for engineers, we specify a strategy that attempts to avoid the state where floor = 1, if possible. A success of this strategy allows us to discover further counterexamples without modifying the property.

Preferring/Avoiding the Explored Part of the Model. Our model of the elevator controller comes with a number of desired properties, e.g., "the elevator never moves with its doors open", "every request for the elevator is eventually fulfilled", etc. When analyzing a few of these, we quickly get familiar with part of the model, e.g., we discover that the elevator can stay in a state where floor=1, doors are closed, the state of the controller is notMoving, and the direction of the elevator is up. We call this state Idle.

Strategies allow engineers to use their knowledge of "designated" states, such as Idle, to guide the counterexample generator towards them in the case where an AF property is false. In particular, using the information about the state of the doors, the direction of the movement, and the state of the controller, we define a *distance* function between the Idle state and the current state of the model and specify a strategy that picks a state where this distance is minimized.

Note that an additional benefit of using this strategy during debugging is that we can stay within a better-understood part of the model. On the other hand, if the goal of model-checking is model exploration [2], we may instead choose to avoid the known behavior by maximizing the distance between the next state in the proof and Idle.

Choosing the "Best" Loop Using Summaries. Generating the shortest counterexample for an arbitrary temporal property is NP-hard [5], and thus conventional model-checkers apply a greedy strategy by computing the shortest counterexample to each subformula. In the case of counterexamples to AFp (or witnesses to $EG\neg p$), even this strategy is hard to implement. Instead, model-checkers consider a state s to satisfy EGp if either there is a path on which p holds in each state that loops around s (see Figure 3(a)) or there is a successor of s in which p holds and there is a looping path of p-states around it (see Figure 3(b)). Thus, the algorithm to compute a witness to EGp in state s checks whether there is a path that leads back to s and on which p holds in each state, terminates if such a path is found, and otherwise picks a successor of s where EGp holds as the new state and continues. Such an algorithm picks the *first* loop on a path, even if it is long and hard to explore. We illustrate this scenario in Figure 3(c): the dashed loop around s' may be short and simple, whereas conventional model-checkers always return the solid loop around s, if one exists, as the witness to EGp.

Our framework allows the user to define strategies to loop around a familiar state (e.g., Idle) or use state summaries to choose the most interesting loop. Consider the witness to a property EGp in the state s_1 of the model in Figure 1(a). Clearly, there are several paths that satisfy it: s_1, followed by a loop around s_2; a loop s_1, s_2, s_4, s_1; a loop s_1, s_2, s_4, s_6, s_1, etc. The framework displays the state s_1 and indicates that EGp holds in it; this is the current "explanation" of the state s_1. Clicking on EGp produces further explanations of why EGp holds in s_1: (1) s_1 is part of a three-state loop and p holds in each state of the loop; (2) there is a successor state of s_1 from which we can explain EGp. Clicking on the second explanation tells us that the successor state of interest is s_2, and EGp holds in it. Clicking on this EGp tells us the reason: (2a): there is a self-loop (a loop of length 0) around s_2 and p holds in s_2; (2b): there is a successor state of s_2 in which EGp holds. At this point, we can either go back to the first explanation and in a few clicks reveal the three states of the loop, or decide that the self-loop around s_2 provides the better explanation. Of course, we can continue looking for other explanations until all possible p-loops have been discovered.

Alternatively, after the first explanation that tells us that s_1 is part of a three-state loop, we may choose to define a strategy that examines the model from state s_1 up to depth three to see whether there are other witnesses to EGp and how long the corresponding loops are, and then chooses the shortest such loop to explore.

4   Framework

The framework for generating and visualizing counterexamples is shown in Figure 4. Dashed lines indicate optional inputs. The user interaction with the framework starts by providing a proof keeper with a model K and a property φ. The proof keeper is the central part of the framework, responsible for generating (a fragment of) the proof and presenting it to the user. First, it calls a model-checker to find out whether φ is satisfied or violated by the model. It then uses the database of proof rules, according to a user-specified proof strategy, to prove that fact. In this step, it uses the model-checker to decide which proof rules are applicable and to ensure the soundness of the proof. (Additional runs of the model-checker can be avoided by efficiently computing and storing evidence, as discussed in [16, 13, 12].) The current proof fragment produced by the proof keeper is shown to the user via a visualization engine. The interaction of the user with this part of the framework is captured by user-supplied visualization strategies. In the rest of this section we discuss the framework in more detail. The framework augmented with additional proof strategies is described in Section 5.

4.1   Proof Rules

Several proof rules from the CTL proof system are given in Figure 5. These include all proof rules of the propositional logic that deal with disjunction and conjunction, such as the $\land$-, $\lor$-rules, i.e., to prove $a \land b$, we need to prove a and b separately, and to prove $a \lor b$, we need to prove either a or b. Additionally, our proof system uses the axiomatization of the given Kripke structure K, describing its transition relation R and values of each atomic proposition in each state. For example, some of the axioms of the model in Figure 1(a) are: there is a transition between s_0 and s_1 ($R(s_0, s_1)$); there is no transition between s_0 and s_3 ($\neg R(s_0, s_3)$); p is true in s_1 ($I(s_1, p)$), etc.

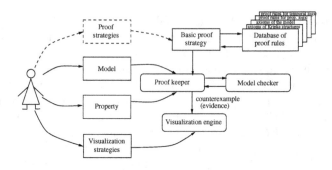

Fig. 4. Overview of the framework

$$\frac{a \quad b}{a \wedge b} \wedge\text{-rule} \qquad \frac{\exists t \in S \cdot R(s,t) \wedge [\![\varphi]\!](t)}{[\![EX\varphi]\!](s)} EX \qquad \frac{[\![\psi]\!](s)}{[\![E[\varphi \ U_0 \ \psi]]\!](s)} EU_0$$

$$\frac{a}{a \vee b} \vee\text{-rule} \qquad \frac{\exists n \cdot [\![E[\varphi \ U_n \ \psi]]\!](s)}{[\![E[\varphi \ U \ \psi]]\!](s)} EU \qquad \frac{f(d)}{\exists x \in D \cdot f(x)} \text{one-point rule}$$

$$\frac{b}{a \vee b} \vee\text{-rule} \qquad \frac{[\![\psi \vee (\varphi \wedge EX E[\varphi \ U_{n-1} \ \psi])]\!](s)}{[\![E[\varphi \ U_n \ \psi]]\!](s)} EU_i$$

Fig. 5. Some CTL proof rules

The proof system is then extended with proof rules for each temporal operator. In this paper, we only show proof rules for EX and EU, and refer the reader to [12] for a complete description of the proof system for CTL and for results on its soundness and completeness. The proof rule for the EX operator follows directly from its definition, i.e., to prove $EX\varphi$ at a state s, we need to find a state t which is a successor of s and in which φ holds. Note that this proof rule introduces an existential quantifier, which is later eliminated by the application of the one-point rule. The completeness of the proof rule for the EU operator follows from the fact that our models are finite. Thus, any path witnessing an EU formula has a bounded length. Finally, the proof rules for the bounded EU operator simply unroll it according to the bound, using the definitions of EU_0 and EU_i given in Section 2.

4.2   Generating Proofs

For a given property φ, a proof of its validity is constructed by applying the basic proof strategy: (1) the database of the proof rules is consulted to find all applicable proof rules based on the syntax of the property; (2) a model-checker chooses those for which the valid proof can be constructed; (3) the rule to be applied is randomly chosen from the resulting set. In [12], we give more detail on the use of the model-checker to guide an automatic proof construction and show that the above strategy is terminating for CTL.

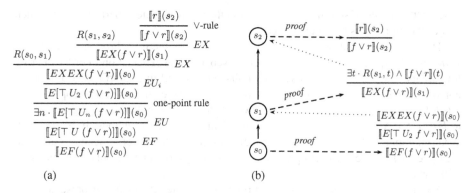

Fig. 6. (a) Proof of $[\![EF(f \vee r)]\!](s_0)$; (b) Proof-like witness of $[\![EF(f \vee r)]\!](s_0)$

For example, the construction of the proof of the validity of $[\![EF(f \vee r)]\!](s_0)$ of the Button module, shown in Figure 6(a) (where some proof steps are skipped for clarity), proceeds as follows. First, the EF operator is expanded according to its definition into the EU operator, and the proof rule for EU is applied. This results in the subgoal $\exists n \cdot [\![E[\top\ U_n\ (f \vee r)]]\!](s_0)$. The model-checker is then used to find the smallest bound on n, which is just the number of iterations required for a model-checking algorithm to converge, and in our example it is 2. Applying the EU_i rule twice, we reduce the proof to $[\![EXEX(f \vee r)]\!](s_0)$.

After one application of the EX rule, we want to prove that $EX(f \vee r)$ holds in state s_1, which reduces to $\exists t \in S \cdot R(s,t) \wedge [\![EX(f \vee r)]\!](s_1)$. The model-checker is then used to find a successor s_2 of s_1 in which $f \vee r$ holds, allowing us to eliminate the existential quantifier (this step is skipped in Figure 6(a)). Finally, to prove $[\![f \vee r]\!](s_2)$, the model-checker is called once again to determine which of the two $\vee$-rules to apply.

4.3 Visualization Engine

The visualization engine converts the proof into a witness or a counterexample, and presents it to the user in a proof-like style of [12]. The proof-like presentation combines the advantages of both proofs and traditional counterexamples by highlighting the behavior of the model that is used to justify the result of the model-checker. This is achieved by extracting the set of model execution traces from the proof, and labeling each state of the trace with the part of the proof that depends on it. For example, a proof-like witness for the property $[\![EF(f \vee r)]\!](s_0)$ is shown in Figure 6(b). This property is witnessed by a 3-state path s_0, s_1 and s_2. The proof in state s_0 tells us that a state in which $f \vee r$ holds is reachable in exactly two steps, since the EF operator is explained by an EU with the bound 2. In the last step of the proof in state s_0, the dotted arrow connecting the formula $EXEX(f \vee r)$ and the state s_1, tells us that s_1 is the witness for the outermost EX operator. The proof attached to state s_2 tells us that the formula $f \vee r$ holds in it because r is true.

The parts of the proof attached to each state can be seen as summaries that explain what is going to follow. For example, the proof attached to the state s_0 in Figure 6(b) can be summarized as "the next state is an intermediate one, and then we reach the desired state". Other types of summaries indicate whether a given state is part of a loop, which part of the property is being explained, etc.

The visual presentation of the result is controlled by the user through *visualization strategies*. A typical strategy is to restrict the scope of the explanation in order to bring forward its most useful parts. This is accomplished by specifying a starting and a stopping condition for the visualization. For example, to restrict the witness of the property $\varphi = EGEF(x \wedge EXx)$ to the EF operator, we set the starting and the stopping conditions to $EF(x \wedge EXx)$ and $x \wedge EXx$, respectively. In the proof-like witness in Figure 6(b), specifying that $f \vee r$ is the stopping condition removes the proof attached to the state s_2. If we let $f \vee r$ be the starting condition instead, s_2 would be the only displayed part of the witness.

A visualization strategy can also control how the state information is presented. For example, we can request to show all variables in each state, refer to each state by a unique name (as in Figure 6(b)), show only those variables that change between states, or always display some specific variables. Furthermore, the strategy can control the verbosity of the proof annotations, or completely replace the actual proof with a more suitable explanation. For example, we can replace the proof attached to the state s_0 with its (English) summary.

The result can be examined in a traditional forward fashion – starting from the initial state and proceeding in the direction of the trace execution to an error condition. Alternatively, the user can start the exploration at the error condition and use the proof annotations to move backwards along the trace. This corresponds to constructing the proof of the property from the basic axioms of the system.

The visualization engine that we presented in this section enables users familiar with model-checking to define strategies for counterexample generation and exploration. It also allows users who are comfortable with simple proofs to search through the counterexample effectively using the proof view. Yet, it is very simplistic – it is virtually a back-end visualizer. To be useful, our visualization engine must be extended with additional visual cues, e.g., as suggested in [9, 8] (see Section 7).

5   Adding User-Specified Strategies

The ability of a user to understand why desired properties hold or fail in the model can be greatly enhanced if the user can control the kind of evidence that gets generated as part of the explanation. This approach also makes proof generation much more scalable: only the fragment of the proof that the user wants to see gets generated and displayed.

Consider the example in Figure 6. The presented witness goes through the state s_2 of the Kripke structure in Figure 1(a), whereas the user may have preferred it to go through s_3 instead. This is a *model-based* decision that comes from the fact that several states may satisfy $[EX\varphi](s_1)$, for some property φ. The user can choose which of these (or whether all of these) are used in the proof.

The second decision type comes from explicit choices in *properties*, via a disjunction operator, e.g., $[EFp \vee EGr](s_3)$. If both disjuncts are true, as in the model in Figure 1(a), the proof of which disjunct should be shown? Controlling this is especially useful during the *specification debugging* phase of the verification.

```
1: void buildProof (Strategy st)
2:   st.init ()
3:   repeat until  leaves ≠ ∅
(a)4:   l = st.pickLeaf (leaves)
5:     r = st.pickRule (getRules (l), l)
6:     result = apply (r, l)
7:     st.ruleApplied (r, l, result)
8:   end repeat


1: class BasicStrategy extends Strategy
2:   Node pickLeaf (Set leaves)
(c)3:     return randomElmnt(leaves)
4:   Rule pickRule (Set rules, Node l)
5:     return randomElmnt(rules)

1: class PickExplored extends Strategy
2:   void init ()
3:     N = s₀
```

(e)
$$\text{4:   addRule}(\frac{[\![EX\varphi \wedge N]\!](s)}{[\![EX\varphi]\!](s)} \ Q)$$

```
5:   Rule pickRule (Set rules, Node l)
6:     if Q ∈ rules then
7:       return Q
8:     end if
9:   void ruleApplied(Rule r, Node n, Node r)
10:     s =getState(r)
11:     N = N∪{s}
12:     update rule Q
```

```
1: class  Strategy
2:   void init ()
3:   Node pickLeaf (Set leaves)
(b)4:   Rule pickRule (Set rules, Node l)
5:   void ruleApplied (Rule r,Node n, Node r)


1: class PickDisjunct extends Strategy
2:   Rule pickRule (Set rules, Node l)
(d)3:     pick Q in rules s.t.
4:       size(tryApply(Q,l)) is minimal


1: class Sequence extends Strategy
2:   void init ()
```

(f)
$$\text{3:   addRule}(\frac{[\![EX\varphi \wedge c_1]\!](s)}{[\![EX\varphi]\!](s)} \ Q_1)$$

$$\text{4:   addRule}(\frac{[\![EX\varphi \wedge c_2]\!](s)}{[\![EX\varphi]\!](s)} \ Q_2)$$

```
5:   c₁_state = true
6:   Rule pickRule (Set rules, Node l)
7:     if c₁_state = true then
8:       if Q₁ ∈ rules then
9:         c₁_state = false
10:         return Q₁
11:       end if
12:     else
13:       if Q₂ ∈ rules then
14:         c₁_state = true
15:         return Q₂
16:       end if
17:     end if
```

Fig. 7. Proof strategies

Typically, a proof proceeds by decomposing the top-level goal into simpler subgoals. For example, to prove $[\![p \wedge r]\!](s_2)$, we need to prove $[\![p]\!](s_2)$ and $[\![r]\!](s_2)$ separately. Yet, if the aim of generating the proof is *debugging*, we can often find the source of the error without expanding all of the subgoals. The choice of the order in which subgoals are to be expanded is the third type of decision that the user may want to make when generating proofs. We give the pseudocode of the proof generation in the method buildProof(), shown in Figure 7(a). The basic proof strategy, described in Section 4 and shown in Figure 7(c), makes all choices at random. Users can affect the proof generation by creating other strategies.

The simplest form of a strategy is to stop and ask the user to choose every time a decision needs to be made. Users can be aided in making decisions by proof summaries

$$\frac{[\![p]\!](s)}{[\![p \vee EFq]\!](s)} Q_1 \qquad \frac{[\![EFq]\!](s)}{[\![p \vee EFq]\!](s)} Q_2 \qquad \frac{[\![EX\varphi \wedge c]\!](s)}{[\![EX\varphi]\!](s)} EX_c$$

$$\frac{B \Rightarrow p}{[\![p]\!](B)} \text{atomic-rule} \quad \frac{\exists B_1, B_2 \cdot [\![\varphi]\!](B_1) \wedge [\![\psi]\!](B_2) \wedge (B \Rightarrow (B_1 \vee B_2))}{[\![\varphi \vee \psi]\!](B)} \vee\text{-rule} \quad \frac{\exists B_1 \cdot \mathcal{R}(B, B_1) \wedge [\![\varphi]\!](B_1)}{[\![EX\varphi]\!](B)} EX$$

Fig. 8. Additional proof rules

generated by the model-checker. For example, when choosing the part of the formula $[\![EFp \vee EGr]\!](s_3)$ to expand, the user may want to note that $[\![EFp]\!](s_3)$ converged in one iteration and $[\![EGr]\!](s_3)$ converged in two, and thus pick $[\![EFp]\!](s_3)$. Strategies can also be automated, with decisions based on summaries, observed history of the execution, or other user preferences. In this section, we discuss various types of strategies and their support in our framework.

5.1   Specifying Strategies

A user-specified strategy is created by implementing the `Strategy` interface shown in Figure 7(b). In particular, the strategy can modify the default proof system before the proof generation begins using `init()`, determine which subgoal is to be expanded using `pickLeaf()`, and determine which rule out of the applicable ones is to be applied using `pickRule()`. Finally, after the application of any proof rule, the strategy can execute its own `ruleApplied` method. In addition, strategies have full access to the proof system: they can examine the current proof, add or remove proof rules, and examine the result of any rule application. Thus, they can affect the behaviour of the prover based on the current subgoal, proof rules that have already been applied, other historical information, subgoals yet to be proven, etc.

We now demonstrate how a few useful strategies can be specified in our framework.

Choosing the Smallest Subgoal. The goal of this strategy is to always pick a rule that results in a subgoal with the least number of temporal operators. For example, suppose our current subgoal is $[\![p \vee EFq]\!](s)$, and there are two applicable proof rules for disjunction (see rules Q_1 Figure 8(a),(b)). Clearly, applying rule Q_1 results in a shorter proof, and therefore a shorter witness. An implementation of this strategy is shown in Figure 7(d), and is accomplished by overriding `pickRule()` to pick the rule that results in the new subgoal with the minimal number of temporal operators. The method `tryApply()` allows the strategy to determine the new subgoal without modifying the proof tree. Note that this is a *greedy* strategy – choosing the subgoal with the shortest length does not guarantee the shortest witness or counterexample.

Preferring Explored Part of the Model. This strategy attempts to guide the witness towards the part of the model that already appears in the proof. In general, a strategy can control which states of the model are used as part of a witness by introducing additional proof rules for the EX operator. For example, to ensure that all states of the witness satisfy a propositional constraint c, the strategy must add the proof rule EX_c (see Figure 8) during its initialization, and then ensure that this rule is always applied whenever possible.

The strategy `PickExplored`, shown in Figure 7(e), maintains a list of all states visited by the proof in the list N, adds a new EX proof rule Q that prefers elements of N, and modifies `pickRules()` so that Q is always picked when it is applicable. Finally, the strategy updates the list of visited states via the `ruleApplied()` method. This is an example of a strategy that uses the proof history in order to augment its behavior.

Sequential Constraint. The goal of this strategy is to ensure that states that satisfy some condition c_1 alternate with states that satisfy another condition c_2 on every path of the witness. As with the `PickExplored` strategy, it begins by adding new proof rules for the EX operator. Its `pickRule` method uses an additional boolean variable c_1_state to remember which of the two new rules was applied last, and augment its behavior based on that. In general, one can automatically generate such a strategy from a state machine that encodes a desired sequencing of constraints, e.g., one advocated in [2].

5.2   Discussion

The users of the framework do not have to interact with the proof engine explicitly. Instead, the interaction is based on the concepts that are already familiar to the engineers.

Some strategies are packaged for manual interaction. For example, the default implementation of the method `pickLeaf` allows the user to choose which part of the witness to extend by clicking on it. Some strategies are completely generic and serve as heuristics that are applicable to any model. For example, to ensure the shortest witness, we can combine strategies to pick the simplest subformula to explain, trying the current state first when choosing the next state, guiding the witness through already visited states, etc. Some other strategies, e.g., the one that ensures that every path of the witness satisfies a given constraint, are parameterized. In this case, the user specifies the constraint, and the interaction with the proof engine is automated. For example, the user can provide the desired constraints in the form of a finite-state automaton, which is sufficient to generate code for the appropriate `Sequence` strategy that deduces which proof rules to add and when to apply them.

Typically, model-checkers implement some greedy strategy to generate a witness or a counterexample. However, users can specify efficient strategies that use backtracking. The complexity of these is controlled by restricting the number of applications of backtracking. For example, a strategy for generating a shortest witness for $[\![EXEFp]\!](s)$ can be specified to pick the successor of s from which EF has the shortest bound.

Strategies are also essential for producing *partial* witnesses when full witnesses are too large to be practical. For example, consider a witness to a property AFp which in the worst case can be of the size of the entire model. The strategy might be to expand only those paths for which the path to the state where p holds is at most x steps long. Since the size of the underlying proof is proportional to the number of steps in the witness, strategies ensure that usable proofs can be generated even for very large models.

6   Abstract Counterexamples

It is often convenient to see all counterexamples or witnesses to a given property at once [7]. For example, consider the property $[\![EFr]\!](s_0)$ evaluated on the Button module from Figure 1(a). There are two witnesses of length 3 that justify this property: leading to states s_2 and s_3, respectively, as shown in Figure 1(b). The information provided by these witnesses can be summarized using an *abstract witness* resulting from merging

$$\frac{\mathcal{R}(s_0, s_1) \qquad \dfrac{\mathcal{R}(s_1, \{s_2, s_3\}) \qquad \dfrac{r \wedge \neg f \Rightarrow r}{[\![r]\!](\{s_2, s_3\})}}{[\![EXr]\!](s_1)}}{[\![EXEXr]\!](s_0)}$$

$$\frac{}{[\![EFr]\!](s_0)}$$

Fig. 9. Proof of $[\![EFr]\!](s_0)$ for the model in Figure 1(a)

the states at the same depth. In Figure 1(b), these states are identified via dashed boxes. Each state in this abstract witness corresponds to one or more states of the model, and can be expressed by a propositional formula. In our example, we obtain that the first state of the witness must satisfy $\neg p \wedge \neg r \wedge \neg f$, whereas the second and the third state should satisfy $p \wedge \neg r \wedge \neg f$ and $r \wedge \neg f$, respectively. There is a disagreement on the value of p between states s_2 and s_3, and thus p is not part of the formula describing the third state.

Propositional formulas provide a very compact presentation of all of the witnesses at once, which in turn helps focus the attention of the user to the more relevant parts of the explanation. For example, by examining the constraint of the third state, we see that the value of p is irrelevant. In [7], it was shown that such a presentation can dramatically reduce the time required by the engineers to locate the real cause of an error.

In the rest of this section, we show that our framework can be used to generate abstract witnesses for reachability properties, or equivalently, abstract counterexamples for safety properties. Any reachability property can be expressed using a combination of EX, and EU operators and propositional connectives [4]. To construct a proof that captures all witnesses at once, we need to extend the corresponding proof-rules from single states to sets of states.

For notational convenience, we write $[\![\varphi]\!](B)$ to stand for $\forall s \in B \cdot [\![\varphi]\!](s)$, where φ is a temporal logic formula, and B is a set of states. Furthermore, we extend the transition relation R to sets of states and write $\mathcal{R}(B, C)$ to stand for $\forall b \in B \cdot \exists c \in C \cdot R(b, c)$. To prove that a propositional formula p holds in all states of a set B (written as $[\![p]\!](B)$), we need to show that B is a subset of the set of states defined by the formula p. That is, p is compatible with the propositional constraints imposed by B. Formally, we obtain the atomic-rule, shown in Figure 8. For example, the fact that r holds in the set of states $\{s_2, s_3\}$ of the Button module follows from the relation $(r \wedge \neg f) \Rightarrow r$. To prove that $\varphi \vee \psi$ holds in a set of states B, we need to show that there exists a partitioning of B into sets B_1 and B_2, such that φ holds in all elements of B_1, and ψ holds in all elements of B_2. The above is captured by the $\vee$-rule, shown in Figure 8. Note that user-specified strategies can influence the choice of this partitioning. For example, if a property φ is more complicated than ψ, the user may prefer B_1 to be empty, if possible.

To prove that $EX\varphi$ holds in a set of states B, we need to identify the successor states of each state in B and prove that φ holds in them (see the EX rule in Figure 8). In practice, the set B_1 can be easily computed from the intermediate results of a symbolic model-checker. For example, it can be instantiated to the set of all states that satisfy φ, and that are successors of states in B. Once again, the user can control the exact choice of B_1 using a proof-strategy, where picking the *largest* such set leads to an abstract witness capturing all possible witnesses.

Recall from Section 4.1 that proof-rules for the EU operator are derived by reducing it to a formula containing a disjunction, a conjunction, and an EX operator. Thus, it can be trivially extended to sets of states using the rules defined in this section.

A sample proof produced via the above proof rules for the property $[\![EFr]\!](s_0)$ evaluated in the Button module, is shown in Figure 9. This proof captures all 3-step witnesses for this property.

7 Conclusion

In this paper, we presented a general framework for generating and exploring witnesses and counterexamples of temporal logic properties. The framework is based on building evidence in the form of a proof and controlling which portions of the proof are expanded and shown to the user either interactively or via user-specified strategies. Proofs also facilitate easy generation of conventional witnesses, which in our case are augmented with summaries describing which part of the property is being explained, whether a given state is part of a loop, how many steps separate a given state from the one in which a subproperty becomes true, etc. We have also created KEGVis – a prototype implementation of the framework.

We are currently looking at ways to connect exploration strategies with temporal logic property patterns [10]. Further, our preliminary experience with KEGVis indicates that users often make similar choices during their interactive exploration of witnesses. An automated strategy assistant that attempts to learn user preferences from previous interactions with the system and suggest an appropriate strategy would greatly enhance the potential usability of our framework. Finally, we are interested in how strategies can be used for understanding the impact of changing a model.

We view our current implementation as a back-end for a successful evidence exploration tool and, in its current form, it is by no means ready to be applied in an industrial setting. To enable such an application, the tool must become much more user-friendly. Most engineers find proofs too difficult, and, although proof-like witnesses bridge the gap between proofs and models, the concept of a proof is currently central to node summaries and some parts of the manual exploration.

For the sake of generality, our work has been on the level of the lowest common denominator of the interaction between the user and the model-checker. Namely, we assumed that the model of the system is given by a Kripke structure, and properties of interest are specified directly in temporal logic. This makes it possible to easily combine our approach with many of the existing model-checking tools. However, this also makes the actual technique appear more complex than it really is.

For example, in software model-checking, the user interacts with a model-checker by providing a source code of the program, and the model-checker automatically extracts a Kripke structure from it. Clearly, in this case, it is not helpful to explain the result of the model-checking run using states of this Kripke structure. Instead, such states should be converted back to what they are meant to represent, namely, line numbers of the program and values of relevant variables. Furthermore, sequences of states can be conveniently presented via interactive debug sessions. The proof part of the explanation is still useful in such cases: it can be used to annotate the debug trace, e.g., to explain why a particular branch of the program is taken next, or that the model-checker discovered a non-terminating loop in the program. Presentation of many of such proof aspects can also be tailored to a particular domain. For example, "an error in 3 steps" can become a graphical icon in the annotation of the trace.

Overall, we feel that the presented framework is flexible enough to enable creation of truly user-friendly tools that can facilitate effective model exploration and debugging using model-checking technology.

References

1. T. Ball, A. Podelski, and S. Rajamani. "Boolean and Cartesian Abstraction for Model Checking C Programs". *STTT*, 5(1):49–58, November 2003.
2. S. Barner, S. Ben-David, A. Gringauze, B. Sterin, and Y. Wolfsthal. "An Algorithmic Approach to Design Exploration". In *Proceedings of FME'02*, volume 2391 of *LNCS*, pages 146–162. Springer-Verlag, July 2002.
3. M. Chechik, B. Devereux, and A. Gurfinkel. "XChek: A Multi-Valued Model-Checker". In *Proceedings of CAV'02*, volume 2404 of *LNCS*, pages 505–509, July 2002.
4. E. Clarke, O. Grumberg, and D. Peled. *Model Checking*. MIT Press, 1999.
5. E.M. Clarke, O. Grumberg, K.L. McMillan, and X. Zhao. "Efficient Generation of Counterexamples and Witnesses in Symbolic Model Checking". In *Proceedings of DAC 95*, pages 427–432, 1995.
6. E.M. Clarke, Y. Lu, S. Jha, and H. Veith. Tree-Like Counterexamples in Model Checking. In *Proceedings of LICS'02*, pages 19–29, July 2002.
7. F. Copty, A. Irron, O. Weissberg, N. Kropp, and G. Kamhi. "Efficient Debugging in a Formal Verification Environment". In *Proceedings of CHARME'01*, volume 2144 of *LNCS*, pages 275–292. Springer-Verlag, September 2001.
8. Y. Dong, C.R. Ramakrishnan, and S. A. Smolka. "Evidence Explorer: A Tool for Exploring Model-Checking Proofs". In *Proceedings of CAV'03*, volume 2725 of *LNCS*, pages 215–218, 2003.
9. Y. Dong, C.R. Ramakrishnan, and S. A. Smolka. "Model Checking and Evidence Exploration". In *Proceedings of ECBS'03*, pages 214–223, April 2003.
10. M. Dwyer, G. Avrunin, and J. Corbett. "Patterns in Property Specifications for Finite-State Verification". In *Proceedings of ICSE'99*, May 1999.
11. A. Groce and W. Visser. "What Went Wrong: Explaining Counterexamples". In *Proceedings of SPIN Workshop on Model Checking of Software*, pages 121–135, 2003.
12. A. Gurfinkel and M. Chechik. "Proof-like Counterexamples". In *Proceedings of TACAS'03*, LNCS, April 2003.
13. K. Namjoshi. Certifying Model Checkers. In *Proceedings of CAV'01*, volume 2102 of *LNCS*. Springer-Verlag, 2001.
14. D. Peled, A. Pnueli, and L. Zuck. From falsification to verification. In *FST&TCS*, volume 2245 of *LNCS*. Springer-Verlag, 2001.
15. M.C. Plath and M.D. Ryan. "SFI: A Feature Integration Tool". In R. Berghammer and Y. Lakhnech, editors, *Tool Support for System Specification, Development and Verification*, Advances in Computer Science, pages 201–216. Springer, 1999.
16. L. Tan and R. Cleaveland. Evidence-Based Model Checking. In *Proceedings of CAV'02*, volume 2404 of *LNCS*, pages 455–470. Springer-Verlag, July 2002.

Using Annotations to Check Structural Properties of Classes

Michael Eichberg, Thorsten Schäfer, and Mira Mezini

Software Technology Group,
Department of Computer Science,
Darmstadt University of Technology, Germany
{eichberg, schaefer, mezini}@informatik.tu-darmstadt.de

Abstract. The specification of meta-information, by using attributes in .NET or annotations in Java, along with the source code is gaining widespread use. Meta-information is used for different purposes such as code generation or configuration of the environment in which a class is deployed. However, in most cases using an annotation also implies that constraints, beyond those defined by the language's semantics, have to be followed. E.g., a class must define a no-arguments constructor or the parameters of a method must have specific types. Currently, these constraints are not checked at all or only to a very limited extend. Hence, a violation can remain undetected and result in deployment-time or even subtle run-time errors. In this paper, we present a user-extensible framework that enables the definition of constraints to check the properties of annotated elements. Further, we demonstrate the application of the framework to check the constraints defined in the EJB 3.0 specification, and an evaluation of the approach based on checking the xPetstore-EJB3.0 project from within Eclipse to test the performance.

1   Introduction

The term *meta-information* refers to information about other information. In the context of programming languages it denotes information about program elements, which in turn represent information about an application domain. Meta-information on program elements is generally used by runtime environments and tools.

In Java, numerous examples of proprietary mechanisms to add meta-information to programs exist. Examples are tags like @author or @version used by the Javadoc tool to generate the class documentation. A similar approach is used by other tools such as XDoclet[1], Commons Attributes[2], JBoss AOP[3], or SGen[4]. Another example of extensive use of meta-information in Java are the various XML files in technologies such as Enterprise JavaBeans (EJBs)[5], Java Data Objects (JDO)[6], or Java Management Extensions (JMX)[7]. This information is used to configure the environment in which a class is to be deployed.

Currently, standard mechanisms are emerging to add meta-information to source code. In C#, [8] meta-information for source code artifacts like classes,

M. Cerioli (Ed.): FASE 2005, LNCS 3442, pp. 237–252, 2005.

methods, fields, etc. can be specified by means of *attributes* and in J2SE 5.0 by means of *annotations* [9]. The Java specification specifies six built-in annotations, how to declare annotation types, how to annotate declarations, and how to read those annotations later on. In addition to built-in annotations, there is also support to create and use user-defined annotations. Each annotation is considered a Java modifier and can be applied to annotate package, type, constructor, method, field, parameter, and local variable declarations. An annotation has a type and defines zero or more member-value pairs, each of which associates a value with a different member of the annotation type. E.g., in the following example the declaration of the class `CategoryX` is annotated with the annotation `@Entity`, whose member `access` is set to `AccessType.FIELD`, i.e., the container should access the entity's state using field access:

@Entity(access = AccessType.FIELD) public class CategoryX {...}

J2SE 5.0 annotations will have a fundamental effect on the way we program in Java. This is indicated by current development efforts on future versions of standard libraries. Major upcoming Java standards such as EJB 3.0[10], JDO 2.0[11], Java Web Services[12], or JDBC 4.0[13] will heavily rely on annotations. Further, a specification request exists to develop a set of annotations that apply across a variety of individual J2SE and J2EE technologies [14]. In the context of these specifications, annotations will be used for different purposes such as driving code generation, or supporting configuration. The rationale for the fast and widespread adoption of annotations is the expectation that their use will make the development process of components more lightweight and will flatten the learning curve of the supporting technologies.

However, a fact that is overseen by these efforts is that the use of annotations often imposes certain implementation restrictions on the decorated program constructs. Consider, e.g., the `java.lang.Override` annotation of Java 5, which can be used to annotate non-abstract methods to state that they that must be overridden in any subclass. Since `java.lang.Override` is a built-in annotation the implied implementation restriction is enforced by the Java compiler.

This is, however, not true for user-defined domain-specific annotations. An example for such annotations are those that will be part of the EJB 3.0 specification. In EJB 3.0, beans can be written as Java classes annotated with the specified EJB annotations. Based on these annotations, the container will generate the corresponding home and remote interfaces and extract the configuration information it needs. However, the effect of annotating a bean with, e.g., entity should go beyond driving the generation of its interfaces and providing configuration information to the container. It should also mean that implementation restrictions implied by the annotation, as explicitly stated in the specification, should be checked for, just like restrictions implied by built-in annotations are enforced by the compiler. An example of such a restriction on an entity bean is: *"An enterprise bean must not use thread synchronization primitives..."*.

From the discussion so far, it follows that automated annotation-based checking of implementation restrictions is needed. The *contribution of the work presented in this paper* is to provide support for this need. We present a user-extensible tool to bind checks of implementation restrictions to specific annotations. The tool is the first application which builds upon Magellan [15] - a generic platform for cross-artifact information retrieval during the software development process. Magellan enables to define queries over a uniform representation of all artifacts of a software project by mapping the artifacts of a project to XML representations and storing them in a database. Then XQuery, a functional query language for XML documents, can be used to query the database.

We extend this generic platform to check implementation restrictions based on Java annotations. The extension employs a time-efficient evaluation of checks by enabling a two-step querying process. In the first step, queries are run that select those program elements that are of common interest for queries evaluated in the second step. Certain implementation restrictions apply, e.g., only to entity beans. A query of the first step will select all entity beans. The result of this query determines the context for queries of the second step which encode the logic for checking different implementation restrictions. Hence, information that is needed by multiple queries is evaluated only once for all queries that need this information. Since the queries evaluated in the first step define a context for the evaluation of the subsequent queries they are called *context-defining queries*.

We also demonstrate the applicability of the proposed approach. As a proof of concept, we implemented queries to check the implementation restrictions defined by the EJB 3.0 draft[1]. These checks serve two purposes: (1) they demonstrate that the query capabilities used in our approach are sufficient for practical purposes, (2) they were used to evaluate the performance of our tool by running them against the xPetstore-EJB3.0 project. The results of this evaluation indicate that the tool can be used to check restrictions for annotated declarations on-the-fly for small to mid-sized projects ($< 100\text{-}200$ project classes), that is while the checks are performed in the background it is possible to continue editing in the foreground. Propositions about bigger projects cannot be done currently since there are no such projects publicly available that already use Java annotations. We will, however, provide some insights with this regard later in the paper.

This paper is structured as follows. The following section discusses the data model and the query language XQuery. Then queries to check implementation restrictions are discussed in Sec. 3. In Sec. 4 the architecture of the tool is presented and how queries are evaluated. In Sec. 5 we evaluate the performance and memory characteristics of our tool to show the feasibility of our approach. Related work is discussed in Sec. 6. Sec. 7 summarizes the paper and shortly discusses areas of future work.

---

[1] A prototype of the tool, including the checkers, is available as an Eclipse plug-in and can be downloaded from http://www.st.informatik.tu-darmstadt.de/pages/projects/Magellan.

2   Data Model and Query Language

2.1   Data Model

In this section, we discuss the data model that is the basis for the development of checkers. Since one goal of our approach is to provide a user-extensible tool, the selection of a comparable easy to comprehend data model is crucial. Due to the widespread knowledge of XML technologies we decided to build it upon an XML representation. A second reason for choosing XML is the free availability of industry-strength query languages. However, choosing XML as the underlying data format is not sufficient on its own. Additionally, we had to decide what kind of data should be represented. For the representation of Java code basically two choices exist. Either an XML representation of the abstract syntax tree (AST) of the source code can be used or a byte code based representation. At a first glance a representation based on the AST might look advantages because it is closer to what a standard Java programmer is used to. However, a bytecode representation has two advantageous. First, bytecode is less variform. E.g., in Java a field can be initialized directly, in an initializer, or in a constructor, but in bytecode all fields are initialized in a constructor. Hence, in bytecode the number of different cases how certain functionality can be expressed is smaller. This makes the development of checkers easier because it is not necessary to take multiple different possibilities into account. A second important point against choosing an AST-based representation is that checking an implementation restriction might require access to pre-built libraries that are not always available in source code (e.g., to determine inter-class relationships); so, some integration with a byte code representation would be needed anyway.

Our decision was to use an XML representation of the bytecode which is generated by BAT$_2$XML [16]. As a result the development of a checker might require some knowledge about Java bytecode and its XML representation in particular. Let's make an example to show how the XML database containing a representation of a Java class looks like. Assume we have the following class which declares a variable and a method, and uses annotations:

```
1  package xpetstore.domain.catalog.ejb;
2
3  @javax.ejb.Entity public class Category implements Serializable {
4      private Long categoryId;
5
6      @javax.ejb.Id public Long getCategoryId() {
7          return categoryId;
8      }
9  }
```

Listing 1.1. Category.java

The XML representation of this class, generated by BAT$_2$XML, is shown in listing 1.2 from line 6 to line 28.[2] The class itself is represented by the class element in line 6, while the method (line 16) is represented by a method element, and a field by a corresponding element (line 14). The attributes of these elements are self-explaining and define the properties of the declarations. The implementation of the method is shown in line 22 - 25; the field read access (`categoryId`) is represented by the get element (line 23).

```
 1  <db:all>
 2  <db:document type="source"
 3    documentID="file://[PATH]/xpetstore/domain/catalog/ejb/Category.class"
 4    tag="de.tud.xirc.processor.input.ClassFileInputProcessor" >
 5
 6    <class
 7        name="xpetstore.domain.catalog.ejb.Category"  visibility="public" ...>
 8      <annotations> <runtime_visible>
 9        <annotation type="javax.ejb.Entity"/>
10                    </runtime_visible> </annotations>
11      <inherits> <class name="java.lang.Object"/>
12                  <interface name="java.io.Serializable"/> </inherits>
13
14      <field type="java.lang.Long" name="categoryId" visibility="private" .../>
15
16      <method name="getCategoryId" visibility="public" ...>
17        <annotations> <runtime_visible>
18          <annotation type="javax.ejb.Id"/>
19                      </runtime_visible> </annotations>
20        <signature> <returns type="java.lang.Long"/> </signature>
21        <code>
22          <load index="0" />
23          <get declaringClassName="xpetstore.domain.catalog.ejb.Category"
24              fieldName="categoryId" type="java.lang.Long" />
25          <return />
26        </code>
27      </method>
28    </class>
29  </db:document>
30  </db:all>
```

Listing 1.2. XML representation of the byte code of the `Category` class in the database

The `db:all` element (line 1) is the root element of the database and the `db:document` element (line 2 - 4) is used to structure all documents in the

---

[2] The compiler generated default constructor is omitted for brevity.

database. Its attributes define necessary information that are required for maintaining the database (line 3) and to enable further processing of query results (line 4).

2.2   Query Language

After choosing the data format we decided to use XQuery to implement the checkers. XQuery [17] is a query language especially well suited for XML data sources. While XQuery is a functional language comprised of several kinds of expressions that can be nested and composed with full generality, we will only elaborate on the features relevant to this paper. The most important among them is the notion of *path expressions*[3]. In a nutshell, a path expression selects nodes in a (XML-)tree.

For illustration, consider the previous XML document (Listing 1.2). We can parse this document by accessing the top-level document node (`db:all`) of the corresponding tree. Then the path expression `db:all/db:document/class/method/code/get` selects the `get` nodes, resulting in the node spanning line 23 to line 24 in Listing 1.2.

In general, a path expression consists of a series of *steps* separated by the slash character. The previous path expression has the steps, namely the *child* steps, `db:all`, `db:document`, `class`, `method`, `code` and `get`. The result of each path expression is a sequence of nodes. XQuery supports different directions in navigating through a tree, called *axes*. In the path expression above, we have seen the *child* axis. Other axes that are relevant for this paper are the *descendant axis* (denoted by "`//`"), the *parent axis* (denoted by "`..`"), the *ancestor axis* (denoted by "`ancestor::`") and the *attribute axis* (denoted by "`@`"). Using the descendants/ancestor axis rather than the child/parent axis means that one step may traverse multiple levels of the hierarchy. For example, the above query could be rewritten as: `//get`.

The attribute axis selects an attribute of the given node, whereas the parent axis selects the parent of a given node. For example, the path expression `//method/../@name` selects the `name` attribute of the declaring class of a method. Another important feature of XQuery is its notion of *predicates* – (boolean) expressions enclosed in square brackets to filter a sequence of values. For instance, the query `//method[@name="getCategoryId"]` selects all methods with the name `getCategoryId`. One can bind query results to variables, which in XQuery are marked with the `$` character, by means of a `let` expression, as illustrated below.

```
let $entityAnnotations := //annotation[@type="javax.ejb.Entity"]
return $entityAnnotations/ancestor::class[@final = "true"]
```

XQuery also offers a number of operators to combine sequences of nodes, namely `union`, `intersect` and `except`, with the usual set-theoretic denotation,

---

[3] This subset of XQuery is a separate standard called XPath [18].

except that the result is again a sequence in document order, if required. The last relevant feature of XQuery is its notion of a function definition. For illustration, the function `directSupertypes` is shown below, which, being passed a set of class definitions, returns the classes that are directly inherited.

```
declare function xirc : directSupertypes ( $classes as element()*) as element()* {
    db: all /db:document/(class| interface )
                [@name =$classes/inherits/( class | interface )/@name]
};
```

3   Checking Implementation Restrictions

In the following, we exemplary discuss the implementation of some checks on top of the discussed data model and query language to illustrate the possibilities offered by our approach, and to give an idea how to define new checks. Basically, a checker is just a query that selects elements which violate a restriction. Let us consider a simple check first. The EJB 3.0 draft specification[10] states in section 6.1 [Requirements on the Entity Bean Class] that:

> The entity bean class must not be final. No methods of the entity bean class may be final.

A possible checker is shown in the next listing. The first line selects all classes that have the `javax.ejb.Entity` annotation and stores the result in the variable `$ebs`. The variable `$xirc:project-files` is the set of all classes that are not defined in a library (`.jar` file). After that, line two determines for all entity beans (`$ebs`) the set of classes and methods that are declared final.

```
1  let $ebs := $xirc : project − files / class [./ annotations//@type ="javax.ejb.Entity"]
2  return $ebs[ @final = "true"] union $ebs/method[@final ="true"]
```

Certain annotations can only be used in combination [19]. E.g., annotating a method with `javax.jws.WebMethod` requires that the class is annotated with `javax.jws.WebService`[12]. To check this dependency the following query first selects all classes that declare a method with the `WebMethod` annotation (line 1) and then subtracts (line 2) all classes that are annotated with the `WebService` annotation (line 3). The set of classes that have `WebMethods` but do not declare to be a `WebService` is returned.

```
1  $xirc : project − files / class [.// annotations//@type ="javax.jws.WebMethod"]
2  except
3  $xirc : project − files / class [./ annotations//@type ="javax.jws.WebService"]
```

The queries discussed so far could also be implemented using Java reflection, though the corresponding Java implementation would be harder to read and would require more effort: Explicit iteration over all classes and methods and checking each class' and method's modifiers. Fully checking the following restriction is no longer possible using Java Reflection because it requires information about a method's implementation, which is not exposed by Java Reflection. The EJB 2.1 specification (which is referenced by EJB 3.0) states in section 25.1.2 [Programming Restrictions]:

> *An enterprise bean must not use thread synchronization primitives to synchronize execution of multiple instances.*

The following query checks that (a) no method is synchronized (line 2), that (b) synchronize is not used (line 3) - using Java's synchronize statement manifests in monitorenter and monitorexist instructions at Java bytecode level -, and that (c) none of the wait or notify methods is called (line 4 - 7).

```
1  let $c := $xirc : enterprise −beans()
2  return  $c/method[@synchronized="true"]
3          union $c/method/code//monitorenter
4          union $c/method/code//invoke[@declaringClassName="java.lang.Object"
5              and (@methodName="wait" or
6              @methodName="notify" or @methodName="notifyAll")]
```

The queries discussed so far are self-containing, i.e. the queries can be executed as is against the database. However, during the development of the EJB 3.0 checkers we realized that many queries have identical parts. E.g., the queries to check an entity bean's implementation restriction nearly always started with a path expression to determine all classes that are entity beans:

```
let $ebs := $xirc : project − files / class [./ annotations//@type ="javax.ejb.Entity"]
```

Even more important, these parts required a significant amount of a query's evaluation time: In the case of a simple query up to 80-90%. To improve the performance of the query evaluation as well as to support a better modularization of the common part of queries we introduce context-defining queries. A context-defining query is a standard XQuery query where each node in its result set defines a context node for the subsequent evaluation of other queries. This node is passed to the query and can be accessed by using the "." operator. Multiple queries for checking implementation restrictions together with one context defining query are defined in a so-called Query Container.

For example, in Listing 1.3 lines 3-9 define a context defining query, which selects all classes that are enterprise beans. For each enterprise bean returned by the context-defining query the query defined in lines 14 - 16, which represents an implementation restriction, is evaluated. At the beginning of line 15 the context node, i.e. a class that is an enterprise bean, is accessed and used to select a finalize() method, if present. The listing also shows how to associate additional information (line 11 - 13) with a query.

```
1   < implementation_restriction_container >
2     < context_definition_type >query</context_definition_type>
3     < context_definition >
4       /db: all /db:document[@type = "source"]/class[
5                         ./ annotations//@type = "javax.ejb. Stateless "
6                   or ./ annotations//@type = "javax.ejb. Stateful "
7                   or ./ annotations//@type = "javax.ejb. Entity"
8                   or ./ annotations//@type = "javax.ejb.MessageDriven"
9     </ context_definition >
10    < implementation_restriction   id="FinalizeMethod" >
11      <title>An enterprise bean must not define the  finalize () method.</title>
12      <description>(see EJB 3.0  specification )</description>
13      <severity>error</severity>
14      <query>
15        ./ method[@name="finalize"' and empty(./signature/parameter)]
16      </query>
17    </ implementation_restriction > ...
18  </ implementation_restriction_container >
```

Listing 1.3. CommonEJB.XML; Query Container Definition

4   Architecture

As mentioned before, our tool is based upon Magellan [15], an open, cross-artifact information engineering platform integrated into the Eclipse IDE. Magellan provides the following services. Documents (in particular Java class files) are converted into corresponding XML-based representations and stored into a database. Changes to documents are tracked to keep the internal database up to date. In addition, a basic query facility is provided. When a client executes an XQuery query the corresponding XML nodes are returned as the result.

To check implementation restrictions our tool (XIRC) builds upon the Magellan platform and uses the provided services. For increased usability, XIRC is also developed as an Eclipse plug-in; however, the concept is also applicable to any other front-end, e.g., an integration with ANT. A user can enable the checking functionality on a project basis. If checking is enabled, the tool then creates special folders for managing the queries. Besides creating new query definitions in those folders and dropping existing query definitions in them it is also possible to include predefined checkers from a third party plug-in. This enables cost-effective reuse of checkers for common tasks, e.g., the checkers for EJB 3.0 are available as such a plug-in. Checking is triggered any time a resource, i.e. a Java class file or a checker, changes. Immediately after a change the Magellan plug-in synchronizes the database as discussed. Next, all queries found in the folder structure or provided by a plug-in are evaluated. The results of each query are passed to a special handler that is responsible for processing the resulting XML nodes. In this case, the handler maps the nodes back to the corresponding locations in the source code (e.g., to a class / method / field declaration or to a

Fig. 1. Violations of constraints implied by annotations in Eclipse

line number in the source code). Additional information defined along with the query, such as the severity of the restriction or a problem description, are used to inform the developer about the broken restriction (see Figure 1).

Figure 1 shows an example of the results from multiple queries. In the lower half of it the standard problem view of Eclipse is shown with multiple violated restrictions for class CategoryX. The developer can see the severity, a description and the location where the violation occurs. ¿From the second last entry in the problems view it can be seen that it is possible to navigate to the corresponding location in the source code by selecting an entry.

5   Evaluation

Before we will discuss the performance, we first discuss the effort necessary when developing new checkers. We made the experience that the biggest effort when writing queries is to learn to use XQuery. The effort was not to understand the XML representation generated by BAT$_2$XML. This is probably due to the fact that most checkers do not require sophisticated control-flow or data-flow analysis and that it is sufficient to simply take a look at the XML representation of a class to write the query. A detailed knowledge of the execution semantics of bytecode instructions is not necessary. Hence, we expect that developers familiar with XQuery and Java can immediately start writing queries to check structural

Table 1. Evaluation times of queries

SHORT DESCRIPTION	SECONDS
CommonEJB.xml	$\sum$ 0.643225
context defining query	*0.023961*
an EJB must not start threads	0.017519
signature of call back method is invalid	0.069257
the chosen transaction attribute cannot be used	0.011743
an EJB must have a no-arg constructor	0.010397
a business method must not start with "ejb"	0.012741
an instance that starts a transaction must complete the transaction before it starts a new transaction	0.385770
`(get│set)RollbackOnly` should be called only in bean methods that execute in the context of a transaction	0.044467
`UserTransaction` is unavailable to EJBs with CMT demarcation	0.011552
a `TransactionAttribute` can only be specified with CMT demarcation	0.012814
EJBs should not handle concurrent access on their own	0.013553
SessionEJB.xml	$\sum$ 0.831755
context defining query	*0.204696*
for update / delete operations a transaction context is required	0.047968
argument and return types must be legal types for RMI/IIOP	0.476183
argument and return types must be legal types for JAX-RPC	0.027315
multiple business interfaces should be annotated as `Local` or `Remote`	0.046658
this `SessionContext`'s method cannot be called	0.024672
EntityEJB.xml	$\sum$ 1.928637
context defining query	*0.147486*
persistent field has invalid type	0.463888
persistent properties with `@Basic` may not be an entity association	0.016634
invalid dependent class	0.159400
a protected field is to accessed by the defining class only	0.032637
an entity bean that is a subclass of another entity bean must have the same primary key	0.155760
entity beans must have getter/setter-methods for persistent fieds	0.099020
collection-valued persistent properties must have type `java.util.Collection` or `java.util.Set`.	0.737543
invalid type for primary key	0.080830
MessageDrivenEJB.xml	$\sum$ 0.015559
context defining query	*0.011637*

properties and that those checks can be written in a reasonable amount of time, that is implementing and testing a query requires less than an hour.

To assess the potential, performance, and memory consumption of our approach we have developed a full set of queries to check the constraints defined in the EJB 3.0 draft specification[10]. The queries were evaluated against a demo release of the xPetstore project[20][4] project that was updated by Bill Burke and Gavin King for EJB 3.0.

The following measurements were taken on an Intel Celeron 2.40 GHz system with 504 MB RAM running Windows XP and using J2SE 5.0, Saxon 8.1 and Eclipse 3.1M2 as the underlying platform. The XML database had 2833 class entries, which represented all public classes and interfaces of all Java APIs[5] delivered with Java 5, except for classes in the `javax.swing.*` and `java.awt.*` packages. Additionally, all necessary JARs to compile the xPetstore project were included. The evaluation for the original xPetstore project which run without any error being signaled required 1.97 seconds. To make the evaluation more realistic, we injected some more or less severe problems into the project code. The evaluation of all 48 queries against the messed project code generated correctly 53 messages and was executed in 3.56 seconds. In both cases, the time required by Eclipse to recompile the source file and to update the Magellan database should be added, which amounts to another 1-2 seconds. To keep the Magellan database in memory approximately 40 MB are required.

Detailed execution times are shown in Table 1; the table lists the times required to evaluate the query containers (printed bold) as a whole, as well as the times required for the evaluation of each context defining query, and the times for the queries to check the constraints along with a short description of the checked constraint. Queries that took less than 10 milliseconds to evaluate are omitted for brevity. The descriptions were shortened; the messages shown to developers are more detailed.

The result of this preliminary analysis shows that the overhead (less than five seconds and running in a non-blocking background process), generated by checking all implementation restrictions, is acceptable for a day-to-day usage. Further, the evaluation shows that the implementation restrictions defined by EJB 3.0 can be checked by using a declarative, though functionally complete, query language; it is not necessary to write the checks as imperative meta-programs in a "standard programming language" such as Java.

6   Related Work

The purpose of FindBugs[21] is to find bugs or potential bugs in existing projects based on control and data flow analysis. In contrast to our tool, FindBugs does not enable to write declarative queries. Instead, to detect a bug a visitor[22] has to be written that visits the in-memory representation of a class' bytecode and reports errors and warnings. JLint[23] and JiveLint[24] are further tools to detect bugs, which are similar in scope and functionality to FindBugs. However, while these tools are concerned with identifying general bugs that are independent of the usage of specific frameworks our approach is targeted at identifying specific implementation restrictions that need to be checked if and only if a specific framework is used.

---

[4] xPetstore-EJB3.0: http://cvs.sourceforge.net/viewcvs.py/jboss/xpetstore-ejb3.0/

[5] Classes starting with `com.*` are irrelevant for the checks and were not included.

IRC [25] is similar to FindBugs in the respect that a *checker* also analyses the in memory representation of a class' bytecode. But in contrast to FindBugs a sophisticated framework exists to programmatically construct queries to check the code. So, while evaluation speed is explicitly targeted by IRC writing a query still involves writing Java code and requires detailed knowledge of the internal representation of the byte code. Based on a comparison of the development of checkers using IRC and our new tool XIRC our experience is that writing, maintaining and evolving declarative queries on top of an XML representation is easier and can be done in less time. The development of checkers (for EJB 2.1) for IRC needed approximately double the time than the development for XIRC; though, the preconditions were comparable: The students who developed the checkers had no knowledge about the framework or the byte code representation in case of IRC and no knowledge about XQuery or the XML representation of byte code in case of this work.

AspectJ[26] can also be used for constraint checking[27]. However, AspectJ was not primarily designed to do it and, as we have argued in [25], the possibilities offered by static pointcuts to detect violations of constraints are too limited to be useful in general.

PMD[28] is similar to our tool in the respect that it also supports to write declarative queries by using XPath, which is an important part of the XQuery language. However, PMD operates on the abstract syntax tree of a program and its primary goal is to check the style of a program and not the semantics. In particular, the used abstract syntax tree does not contain resolved type information, e.g., the types of the formal parameters of a method are not available from looking at a method call node in the AST. This makes writing queries that take type information into relation or that need to span multiple classes tedious and error-prone. Checkstyle[29] is similar to PMD and suffers from the same problem.

The idea of Splint[30] is to annotate the source code (ANSI C) to make design decisions or implementation restrictions explicit. E.g., to annotate a parameter with @notnull to indicate that the parameter should never be null. Splint will then perform a static analysis of the code using the annotations and report violations. Splint is designed as a compiler; extensibility by users was not a goal. However, it would be an interesting exercise to develop a set of similar Java annotations and checks that can be used by developers to make implementation restrictions explicit in their code and which are checked.

ESC/Java2[31] also uses annotations of the Java source code to enable an extended static analysis. Since ESC/Java is based on theorem proving the evaluation times are very high [32]; on-the-fly evaluation is out of scope.

7   Summary and Future Work

With the standardization of annotations in J2SE 5.0, a common metadata facility is now available for the programming language Java. Forthcoming standards in the Java landscape such as EJB 3.0, JDBC 4.0 and Web Services Metadata show the widespread adoption of annotations. As argued previously, the usage of meta information in program code often implies that specific implementation restrictions have to be obeyed by the annotated declarations to guarantee that the program will work properly. Though, implementation restrictions are not new we argue that annotations represent perfect join points in the source code where to start checking restrictions.

We have shown that our tool can check structural properties of classes by using annotations, and that the checks themselves can be defined using declarative queries. For evaluation we applied our framework to the EJB 3.0 specification and, as our evaluation suggests, the performance is already good enough to use it for small to mid size projects. The tool is user-extensible and fully integrated into the Eclipse IDE enabling checks during the development process.

To the best of the authors knowledge, we presented a first fully-integrated tool which is capable of on-the-fly checking of properties based on Java's new annotation facility.

Currently, all queries are always evaluated against the entire database, which is reasonable fast for small to mid sized projects. But for large projects with hundreds of classes the achieved performance may be too slow; even though the evaluation is executed in the background, evaluation times beyond 10 to 15 seconds are not acceptable. The problem is that a long-running build process may prevent other (background-)processes from execution and may finally require the developer to stop the work until the processes have completed. To achieve faster evaluation times we are going to investigate queries that are evaluated per changed document, i.e., a changed document is set as the context node for the query evaluation. However, in this case it is necessary to keep track of all documents visited by a query in order to know when to reevaluate it. The question is, if the necessary effort for tracking and managing these information finally pays off.

Acknowledgments

The authors would like to thank Cuma Ali Gencdal, who implemented parts of the support for annotations in BAT$_2$XML and most of the queries for EJB 3.0.

References

1. Team, X.: XDoclet: Attribute-Oriented Programming. (http://xdoclet.sourceforge.net/)
2. Foundation, A.S.: Commons attributes. jakarta.apache.org/commons/attributes/ (2004)
3. Inc., J.: JBoss AOP 1.0 beta3. http://www.jboss.org (2004)
4. Beust, C.: SGen. http://www.beust.com/sgen/ (2004)
5. DeMichiel, L.G.: Enterprise JavaBeans Specification, Version 2.1. SUN Microsystems (2003)
6. Russell, C.: Java Data Objects, Version 1.0. SUN Microsystems (2002)

7. Sun Microsystems: Java management extensions. White paper, Palo Alto, California, USA (1999)
8. Archer, T.: Inside C#. Microsoft Press (2001)
9. Bloch, J.: A metadata facility for the java programming language. Java Specification Request 175, SUN Microsystems (2002)
10. DeMichiel, L.G.: Enterprise javabeans specification, version 3.0. Java Specification Request 220 (2003)
11. Russell, C.: Java data objects 2.0 - an extension to the jdo specification. Java Specification Request 243 (2004)
12. Zotter, B.: Web services metadata for the java platform. Java Specification Request 181 (2004)
13. Bruce, J.: Jdbc 4.0 api specification. Java Specification Request 221 (2004)
14. Mordani, R.: Common annotations for the java platform. Java Specification Request 250 (2004)
15. Eichberg, M., Mezini, M., Ostermann, K., Schäfer, T.: A kernel for cross-artifact information engineering in software development environments. In: Proceedings of 11th IEEE Working Conference on Reverse Engineering (WCRE), IEEE Computer Society (2004) to appear.
16. Eichberg, M.: Battoxml. http://www.st.informatik.tu-darmstadt.de/BAT (2004)
17. Boag, S., Chamberlin, D., Fernández, M.F., Florescu, D., Robie, J., Siméon, J.: Xquery 1.0: an xml query language. Working Draft 23 Juli 2004, (W3C)
18. Clark, J., DeRose, S.: XML Path Language (XPath) Version 1.0. (http://www.w3.org/TR/1999/REC-xpath-19991116)
19. Cepa, V., Mezini, M.: Declaring and enforcing dependencies between .net custom attributes. In: Proceedings of the Third International Conference on Generative Programming and Component Engineering. (2004)
20. Tchepannou, H., McSweeney, B., Cooley, J.: xPetstore. http://xpetstore.sourceforge.net (2003)
21. Hovemeyer, D., Pugh, W.: Finding bugs is easy. SIGPLAN Notices **December** (2004)
22. Gamma, E., Helm, R., Johnson, R., Vlissides, J.: Design Patterns. Professional Computing Series. Addison-Wesley (1995)
23. Artho, C.: Finding faults in multi-threaded programs. http://artho.com/jlint/ (2001)
24. Sureshot: JiveLint v1.22. (http://www.sureshotsoftware.com/javalint/)
25. Eichberg, M., Mezini, M., Schäfer, T., Beringer, C., Hamel, K.M.: Enforcing system-wide properties. In: Proceedings of the 15th australian software engineering conference (ASWEC), IEEE Computer Society (2004)
26. Kiczales, G., Hilsdale, E., Hugunin, J., Kersten, M., Palm, J., Griswold, W.G.: An overview of aspectj. In: Proceedings of the 15th european conference on object-oriented programming (ECOOP). Volume 2072 of Lecture Notes in Computer Science., Budapest,Hungary, Springer (2001) 327–355
27. Shomrat, M., Yehudai, A.: Obvious or not? regulating architectural decisions using aspect-oriented programming. In Kiczales, G., ed.: Proceedings of 1st international conference on aspect-oriented software development (AOSD), Enschede, The Netherlands", ACM Press (2002) 3–9
28. PMD. (http://pmd.sourceforge.net)
29. Kühne, L., Studman, M., Burn, O., Sukhodolsky, O., Giles, R.: Checkstyle. http://checkstyle.sourceforge.net/ (2004)

30. Evans, D., Larochelle, D.: Improving security using extensible lightweight static analysis. IEEE Software **January / February** (2002)
31. Cok, D., Kiniry, J.: Esc/java2. http://www.cs.kun.nl/sos/research/escjava/ (2004)
32. Rutar, N., Almazan, C.B., Foster, J.S.: A comparison of bug finding tools for java. In: 15th IEEE International Symposium on Software Reliability Engineering (ISSRE'04). (2004) to appear.

Improving System Understanding via Interactive, Tailorable, Source Code Analysis

Vladimir Jakobac[1], Alexander Egyed[2], and Nenad Medvidovic[1]

[1] Computer Science Department, University of Southern California,
941 W 37th St, Los Angeles, CA 90089, USA
{jakobac, neno}@usc.edu
[2] Teknowledge Corporation, 4640 Admiralty Way, Suite 1010,
Marina Del Rey, CA 90292, USA
aegyed@teknowledge.com

Abstract. In situations in which developers are not familiar with a system or its documentation is inadequate, the system's source code becomes the only reliable source of information. Unfortunately, source code has much more detail than is needed to understand the system, and it disperses or obscures high-level constructs that would ease the system's understanding. Automated tools can aid system understanding by identifying recurring program features, classifying the system modules based on their purpose and usage patterns, and analyzing dependencies across the modules. This paper presents an iterative, user-guided approach to program understanding based on a framework for analyzing and visualizing software systems. The framework is built around a pluggable and extensible set of clues about a given problem domain, execution environment, and/or programming language. We evaluate our approach by providing the analysis of our tool's results obtained from several case studies.

1   Introduction

Adding new functionality to an existing software system starts with a process of understanding the system's architecture, i.e., its structure, behavior, and key non-functional properties [12,13]. This becomes difficult in the case of large systems for which the documentation does not exist or is outdated. Many low-level details in the source code obstruct the process of creating a system's high-level, architectural abstraction, which aids in reasoning about the system.

A number of software "clustering" techniques have been developed to cope with this problem [9,10,11,14] but these techniques fail to provide much rationale behind the architecture. This becomes particularly important if we consider that the source code may actually contain accidental or emergent functionality and relationships which are not intended by the system's developers. Furthermore, clustering approaches are not always effective tools for performing architectural recovery. For example, our experience [9] has shown that in layered systems these approaches do not actually recover the layers, but tend to "slice"

M. Cerioli (Ed.): FASE 2005, LNCS 3442, pp. 253–268, 2005.

across them since the clustering is usually based on the existence of strong coupling (inter-layer) relationships.

For this reason, we posit that architectural recovery, and software clustering in particular, need to be accompanied by a system understanding activity, which includes the use of semantic information before any syntactic dependencies are considered, and whose goal is to help engineers control the architectural recovery process, and identify and correct any inconsistencies therein. Various representations can be used to describe successive levels of system's abstractions. Incited by Perry and Wolf's observation [12] that the key architectural elements of a software system are (1) processing, (2) data, and (3) connecting, we have developed ARTISAn, a tool-supported, pluggable framework intended to aid program understanding and, ultimately, architectural recovery.[1] Our approach is based on both structural and semantic analysis, where various design- and implementation-level constructs, termed *clues*, are used to classify, label, and collapse the system's elements (e.g., classes) into the three major categories.

The ARTISAn framework is tailorable. It comprises replaceable components to accommodate the exact programming environment. For example, the framework is instantiated with different components for various programming languages or off-the-shelf "utility" technologies such as middleware. ARTISAn provides a rich, interactive web of information to an engineer, allowing her to add, remove, or change both the clues and other analysis rules (and then reapply them), manually relabel any analysis results (and then observe how that new information is affecting the rest of the system), enact "what if" scenarios to identify key relationships and dependencies in the system, all the while being able to "undo" any changes. ARTISAn can also be further tailored for situations in which the division of system elements into processing, data, and connection may be overly general.

We have developed a prototype of ARTISAn targeted at Java systems. The tool is integrated with IBM Rational Rose®. We have applied ARTISAn on a number of third-party software applications to date, and report on those results.

This paper is organized as follows. Section 2 introduces an example application used to explain the approach, which is described in Section 3. In Section 4 we provide an evaluation of our approach. Section 5 presents related work and Section 6 summarizes our contributions and opportunities for future work.

2   Case Study

In this paper we are using a case study to illustrate our approach. The ANTS case study (Autonomous Negotiating agent TeamS) is an embedded agent negotiation system in which multiple, intelligent (software) agents negotiate over the best use of available resources (radars) to track a series of targets [2, 3]. The system was implemented in Java, and comprises over 200 classes developed by

---

[1] ARTISAn stands for Architectural Recovery via Tailorable, Interactive Source-code Analysis.

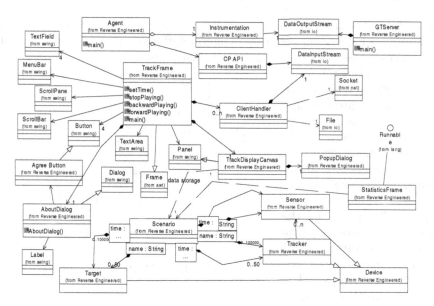

Fig. 1. UML class diagram for the ANTS Visualizer system

several organizations. The main components of the system are *Agent, GTServer, CPAPI* and a real-time *Visualizer*. While we used the entire ANTS system to evaluate our approach, the illustrations used in this paper are limited to its non-trivial visualization subsystem. Figure 1 depicts the class diagram of the ANTS Visualizer subsystem, where Agent, GTServer, and CPAPI components are depicted as single classes due to their complexity. These components communicate over the network via TCP/IP. There are three different types of input devices: *Sensor, Target,* and *Tracker*. While sensors track targets, trackers use sensor data to estimate targets' locations. Each data item is stored in a new *Device* instance and it is the responsibility of the *Scenario* class to keep track of both the current state and the change history of all devices. Finally, *TrackFrame* is used with other GUI-based classes to process and visualize the data.

3 Approach

Our approach (Figure 2) comprises three steps that are initially performed sequentially but may then be revisited in any order by the user. The first step, termed *initial labeling*, results in a classification of individual elements into *processing* (P), *data* (D), and *communication* (C) [12] based on ARTISAn's *clues*. The result obtained during the initial labeling phase and a pluggable set of propagation *rules* provide input to the *propagation labeling* step. During this phase, some non-labeled elements become labeled (i.e,. classified as P, D, or C), based on the recognition of structural patterns and relationships with other, already labeled elements. Furthermore, this step also identifies possible structural inconsistencies among labeled elements and alerts the user about them. Initial labeling and propagation labeling result in an interpretation of the system that suggests the *purpose* of each of the system's individual elements.

Finally, during the *def-use analysis* phase, regions of related elements are identified based on invocation and inheritance relationships. The obtained regions distinguish between elements that are shared across regions and those that are exclusive to a region. The result of this phase is a system's *usage* view representation, which provides information on parts of the system that could be grouped together based on their usage scenarios.

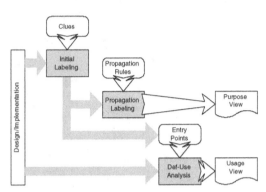

Fig. 2. The ARTISAn framework

Individually, the purpose and usage views provide the user with a classification of elements and their grouping based on usage analysis, respectively. These two views also complement each other. For example, if some unlabeled elements from the purpose view end up belonging to the same region with labeled elements of a single type, then one can surmise the purpose of the unlabeled elements. In total, our approach gives the user a better understanding of the system, and an opportunity to faster locate its parts that are of particular interest (e.g., for maintenance purposes).

The remainder of this section provides the rationale of our approach and describes each of the steps depicted in Figure 2 in more detail.

3.1 ARTISAn Clues and Initial Labeling

At the most general level, software systems integrate *processing* elements that exchange *data* via *communication (connecting)* elements [12]. By determining the type of a system element, one can distinguish elements with application-specific functionality from those with application-independent functionality. Typically, processing elements provide application-specific functionality as they implement the system's requirements. On the other hand, communication elements typically provide application-independent interaction facilities. In Java, for example, classes interact by invoking each other's methods and/or sharing data through public variables, regardless of the classes' functionality. In addition, a number of off-the-shelf communication elements (e.g., middleware) are available. A useful starting point in understanding the source code of a system is thus in the reusable, application-independent nature of its communication elements. Similarly, data elements only contain the information that is used or transformed by processing elements. Therefore, by identifying and then abstracting away data

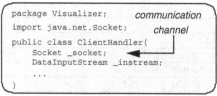
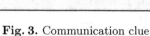

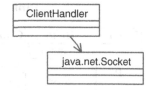

Fig. 3. Communication clue

Fig. 4. An excerpt from the ANTS Visualizer class diagram

elements, the reasoning about the system is improved (e.g., applications built using the pipe-and-filter architectural style).

Software systems are generally described by their design or implementation models (e.g., class diagrams). Often, the models are too detailed, so that their understanding becomes obscured. In ARTISAn, constituent elements of these models (e.g., classes) are at first classified into the three aforementioned categories (<u>P</u>rocessing, <u>C</u>ommunication, and <u>D</u>ata), providing an engineer the opportunity to quickly gain an overview on the purpose of individual elements and the structure of their composition. The process of classifying system elements into one of the three categories is termed *labeling*. The labeling is based on various design and implementation snippets, termed *clues*. Clues carry syntactic, semantic, and possibly domain-specific information, which is searched for in a system's model.

Figure 3 depicts a segment of Java source code from the ANTS system that illustrates how clues are identified. In the example, there is an attribute _socket that declares a use of the standard network socket library *java.net.**. This information is a clue to the existence of a communication channel, which is directly used by this class. We should note that clues could also be identified from a system's graphical model representation (e.g., its class diagrams), which enables the potential easy integration of our approach with already available visualization tools. For example, the same communication clue exists in Figure 4, which represents an excerpt from the ANTS Visualizer class diagram.

Each clue is represented as a 4-tuple: (1) *Impact*: if found, what is the meaning of a clue, i.e., is the element of type P, or C, or D? (2) *Base*: describes the software artifact in which we expect to find a clue (e.g., method, class, procedure); (3) *Condition*: a condition that must be satisfied for a clue to be found (e.g., a class whose name starts with *"java.net"*); (4) *Language*: the programming language to which clue applies. For example, the Java "Socket" clue, described above, is defined as *(C, class, class.name = "java.net.Socket", Java)*.

Although it is difficult to automatically understand the exact purpose of a processing element, it is possible to recognize such an element's existence through source code declarations. There are several clues that could be used in the detection of processing elements. For example, all classes that implement the static method *main*, or inherit from the library class *java.lang.Thread*, or implement the *java.lang.Runnable* interface are likely to be processing elements. Applied

Table 1. Domain-independent clues

Impact	Base	Condition
P	class.method	name= "main"
	class	implements= "java.lang.Runnable"
		extends= "java.lang.Thread"
		extends.startsWith("java.awt")
C	class	name.startsWith("java.io")
		name.startsWith("java.net")
D	class	parent.type= "D"
		no methods other than constructor(s)
		extends= "java.lang.Exception"
		name= "java.util.Vector", "java.util.Hashtable", ...
		implements= "java.net.Serializable"

to our case study example, this means that all classes in a model that have the "main" method are classified as processing classes, such as *TrackFrame*, *Agent*, and *GTServer* in Figure 1. In a similar way, *ClientHandler* is labeled as a processing element since it implements the *Runnable* interface. Additionally, system elements that provide the GUI functionality are considered as a subcategory of processing elements. They are easily recognized based on the use of dedicated GUI libraries (e.g., *java.awt.**). Similarly, ARTISAn defines data-element clues. For example, all classes with only a constructor method and non-empty attribute list are likely to serve as data stores.

The clues described above all belong to ARTISAn's extensible and pluggable set of clues. We expect each programming paradigm and language, domain, and/or application to have their own set of clues. Those clues would be identified by language and domain experts and integrated into the framework. ARTISAn distinguishes between the following clue categories: (1) *Domain-independent* clues, such as the *Socket* class being classified as C, or a class with no methods being recognized as D; (2) *Domain-specific* clues, e.g., in case a system is built on top of a known middleware platform (e.g., an element of the *Siena* middleware is classified as C and the classes having access to the *Siena* are appropriately marked); and (3) *Application-specific* clues, such as a class of name "*jigsaw.Resource*" in the Jigsaw Web server being recognized as D.

Table 1 lists the Java-based clues that we have used to evaluate our approach. All the clues listed in Table 1 fall into the category of domain-independent clues. They can be applied to a wide range of (Java) software systems and can be naturally complemented by the more narrowly applicable domain- or application-specific clues.

We should note that, in general, ARTISAn does not require application-specific source code to follow any pre-defined naming conventions. However, ARTISAn provides support for using naming conventions in situations where such a collection of rules is available, such as with standardized libraries.

ARTISAn uses different colors to represent different classes' labels on the class diagram, or combinations of these colors if a class has more than one label.

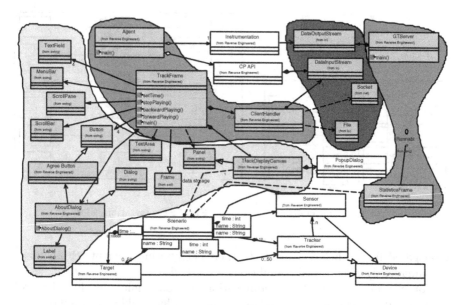

Fig. 5. The resulting diagram after the initial labeling step

Unlabeled classes remain transparent. However, in order to increase the readability of the illustrations in this paper, we additionally edited the diagrams by gray-scaling the labeled classes and drawing filled boundaries around classes of the same color. Figure 5 depicts the ANTS Visualizer diagram obtained after the initial labeling step is performed. Classes such as *Agent, TrackFrame,* or *GTServer*, which are inside the medium-gray boundary, indicate processing components. Classes such as *DataOutputStream* or *Socket,* inside the dark-grey boundary, indicate communication-based connectors. Finally, classes bounded by the light-grey shape indicate GUI elements, i.e., a subcategory of processing elements.

It should be noted that the clues are designed in such a way that applying them may identify one or more categories that an element belongs to, but also one or more categories to which the element does not belong. We refer to the former as an inclusion set, and to the latter as an exclusion set. For example, the *Socket* class will have C in its inclusion set, and P and D in its exclusion set. In other words, while this element is labeled as communication element, we also know that it cannot be processing or data. This information is of particular importance during the propagation labeling phase.

3.2   ARTISAn Rules and Propagation Labeling

It is very likely that not all elements in a system can be labeled based on ARTISAn clues. However, the existing knowledge about a system could be used to reason additionally about the system. Information obtained from clues can be

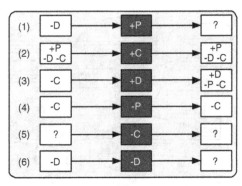

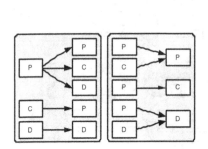

Fig. 6. Propagation scenarios   **Fig. 7.** Propagation rules

propagated from labeled elements to their neighboring elements (both labeled and unlabeled) when certain conditions are satisfied.

For example, as a result of an application of a communication clue, the ANTS *DataOutputStream* class is labeled as C, while no clue could be applied to the *Instrumentation* class (5). However, vital to the understanding of *Instrumentation* is its relationship to *DataOutputStream*. This relationship is a UML association and it indicates that *Instrumentation* uses *DataOutputStream*. Based on this observation we can deduce that *Instrumentation* cannot be a data element because a data element, by its definition, is not capable of such processing (i.e., a data element is perhaps allowed to do minor processing such as data checking, conversion, and storage, but not application-wide communication). Furthermore, *Instrumentation* is not an off-the-shelf communication element because we do not expect two such elements in a domain-independent system, such as ANTS, to be able to integrate and call each other directly. Thus, it follows that *Instrumentation* must be a processing element.[2]

We refer to this kind of reasoning as *clue propagation*. Clue propagation serves as a basis for the ARTISAn *propagation rules*. The pluggable set of propagation rules and the result obtained during the initial labeling phase provide input to the *propagation labeling* step (Figure 2). During this phase, some non-labeled elements become labeled, based on the application of the propagation rules. Propagation rules are derived from structural and interaction patterns involving different types of elements. Figure 6 illustrates these patterns.

The left-hand side of Figure 6 shows that a processing (P) element could call other processing, communication (C), and data (D) elements. In other words, there are no restrictions on what type of elements might be called by a processing element. On the other hand, our experience has shown that in case of domain-independent applications off-the-shelf communication elements usually

---

[2] This discussion is based on the understanding that there are no application-specific communication elements in the ANTS system. If there are, then they would be recognized as processing elements using ARTISAn's existing clues.

do not invoke any other element (e.g., socket-based communication) but if they do, the invoked elements could only be processing elements (e.g., COM-based communication element). We should note here that some technologies that are used to bridge across different computing platforms (e.g., the Java to COM bridge) may involve communication elements calling other communication elements. However, in those cases we would be dealing with specialized solutions that would allow us to recognize such situations on a case-by-case basis. Furthermore, these cases would be amenable to capture by specialized domain- or application-specific propagation clues and rules, which would result in an appropriate identification and labeling of all such elements. Finally, data elements are expected to be passive entities that may perform some rudimentary internal processing, but are otherwise not interacting with processing or communication elements. To describe the propagation rules in a more formal way, we will use the right-hand side of Figure 6, which is a transpose of its left-hand side (e.g., only P or C can call P).

Based on the caller-callee relationships in Figure 6, we can deduce six propagation rules, which are depicted in Figure 7. For example, rule 1 in Figure 7 states that if an element is known to be a processing element (denoted by +P in the middle box), then all elements that call it (its callers) cannot be data elements (denoted by D). The rationale for this is as follows: from the right-hand side of Figure 6 we know that either a P or a C can call another P. This implies that the caller cannot be D. Since we do not know whether the actual caller is P or C, we only write that it is not D. In this way we avoid having to make an early (but possibly incorrect) decision. The question mark in the right-hand column of rule 1 indicates that we cannot say anything about the elements being called by that element (its callees). Similarly, if an element is known not to be a processing element (-P), as in rule 4, then neither the caller nor the elements being called can be communication elements. This rule is again derivable from Figure 6. If an element is not P then it is either C or D. We know that C can be called only by P, and that D can be called by P or D. It follows that C or D can be called by at most the union of their callers, which is P or D. Since we do not know whether it is P or D, we simply write that it is not C. All other rules can be derived in a similar way.

As a result of the propagation labeling step, two additional classes in the ANTS Visualizer were recognized as processing elements: *Instrumentation* and *CPAPI*.

The algorithm for applying propagation rules is based on the changes in the inclusion and the exclusion sets for each of the system's elements. All elements are being processed, and as long as there are changes in any of the two sets (e.g., an unlabeled element becomes labeled, or a processing element becomes classified as non-connecting element), an appropriate propagation rule is run. Since the inclusion and exclusion sets for each element are finite, it is obvious that this algorithm terminates. Its running time is linear, because no decisions are ever undone (no backtracking).

This step also provides support for identifying any potential rule conflicts. For example, if a class is identified as a processing element through one propagation rule, but also as not a processing element using another rule, then either the clue or one of propagation rules was erroneous. Conflicts are easily identifiable due to their simple implementation representation (+P and -P) and ARTISAn reports all inconsistencies to the user. At that point, the user has the choice to manually label the elements if they are of a known type, ignore the discovered conflict (e.g., in case when a helper class of known functionality has conflicting labels), or use that information to modify the set of clues, and rerun the propagation labeling step. In the last case, both the user and the tool are "learning" about new clues that could be used for other systems.

3.3   Def-Use Analysis

The next step in our approach is the identification of regions, i.e., groups of system elements that are closely related, or independent of other parts of the system. To this end, we adapt *def-use analysis*. Def-use analysis is an approach that has already been used in literature and illustrates the use of dominance analysis for identification of regions of related modules [8, 10]. These regions indicate parts of a system that are exclusively used by its other part(s) and those that are shared. Each of the identified regions has an *entry point*, which is a module where processing starts (e.g., a class with the main() method). Entry points in ARTISAn are obtained from the initial labeling step (Figure 2). Those are all elements that satisfy the "main" clue, but also include elements that are able to create a new processing thread. The rationale for this lies in the fact that systems often spawn their own subsystems by creating separate processing threads. We can identify spawning using clues which were discussed previously.

In addition, ARTISAn supports a richer set of relationships among elements by analyzing class inheritance together with class association and dependency relationships. For example, the *Tracker* class inherits from the *Device* class, which makes the *Tracker* able to invoke the methods of the *Device*. Furthermore, if there is a class that declares a variable of type *Device*, that variable is then able to hold either an instance of *Device* or any of its subclasses (e.g., *Tracker*). This means that the variable holder class can invoke any of subclasses' methods, which is interpreted in ARTISAn as another type of calling relationship.

The information about regions enables an engineer to more easily recognize system elements that belong together. The *usage view* thus complements the *purpose view* by combining information about high-level functionality of individual elements with information about regions of related elements.[3]

3.4   Intervention of a Knowledgeable User

Since program understanding is an activity that inherently involves humans, it is vital for a tool such as ARTISAn to provide support for user intervention. AR-

---

[3] The example is omitted due to space limitation and can be found in [5].

TISAn is built with the premise that the information about the system provided by the user can be used by the tool to provide a richer set of results.

For example, in the case of the ANTS Visualizer system, the labeling phases were unable to classify the classes *Tracker, Target, Sensor, Scenario,* and *Device.* The result of a def-use analysis shows that these classes form a region, but the purpose of this entire region is still unknown (Figure 5). Yet, if a user knows that *Device* is a data class then she may provide this information to the AR-TISAn tool. This information is then instantly propagated to other elements of the system that have a relationship with the *Device* class, which results in all subclasses of the *Device* class (*Tracker, Target, Sensor*) being labeled as data classes. Furthermore, since the *Scenario* invokes data elements, we know that it cannot be a communication element (because its exclusion set contains C).

Moreover, the users have an opportunity to add/remove clues, and update the elements' labels (both inclusion and exclusion sets) as well as information about entry points. All the changes are performed immediately, i.e., the tool does not expect the user to restart and repeat the whole analysis. In addition, changes can be undone to further support "what if" scenarios.

4   Evaluation

This section evaluates our approach by discussing our tool's ability to label all the classes in a system (recall rate) and do so correctly (precision rate).

Table 2 lists a representative subset of several case studies (applications) that we have used to evaluate the approach to date. The meaning of each column header and value is described throughout the section. Since our tool currently supports the object-oriented paradigm, we chose to analyze various Java applications that span different domains, including middleware, such as MobiKit, which is built on top of Siena [15]. The first two case studies listed in the table have already been described in the paper. The Jigsaw web server was built by a third party and is available as open source. In all cases we either used the existing design model, if it was available, or reverse engineered its class diagram from the implemented system.

Table 2. Evaluation results

Case study	Classes	Initial labeling		Propagation labeling		
		Initial recall rate	FP	Total recall rate	Total FP	Inconsistencies
Visualizer	37	75%	0	81%	0	0
ANTS	211	67%	0	69%	0	0
DeSi	64	68%	0	93%	0	0
TimeWeaver	120	55%	4	60%	4	0
MobiKit	34	32%	3	58%	3	0
Jigsaw	1009	25%	?	47%	?	4

There are two columns in the table that show the measure of completeness of our approach, one for each of the two labeling steps (*initial* and *total recall rate*). The values in these columns range from 25% (initial labeling in the Jigsaw case study) to more than 90% (after the propagation labeling in DeSi case study).

To validate the correctness of labeled classes we looked at the number of false positives produced (denoted by *FP* in the table), for each of the two steps. All system classes being labeled incorrectly are considered to be false positives. As a reference set to which we compared the ARTISAn-generated labels, we used the labels obtained from the programming environment's chief developer (in case such a person was available), or the results obtained by conducting a survey. We created a collection of over 50 randomly chosen Java source code classes from 4 of the case studies, and asked 20 graduate-level computer science students who are proficient in Java to manually inspect and label the classes into the four categories: P, D, C, and "don't know". Each of the classes had 12 votes on average and we found that our tool produced a low number of false positives (0 to 4), and that their number did not increase from one labeling step to another. ARTISAn correctly labeled 72% of classes that were given to students. We also asked the students to provide a rationale for their decisions. We noticed that the classes for which the students' answers were unanimous and which our tool was unable to label were predominately application-specific processing classes. For example, the classes identified by the students as processing elements had implemented complex algorithms internally, or had mnemonic names (including method names), which all served as a rationale for classifying them. This type of information is currently outside ARTISAn's scope, but can be embedded in additional (domain- or application-specific) clues and rules.

The propagation labeling phase added a significant advantage to labeling as the total recall rate rose to an average of 68% compared to 53% of initial labeling. To validate the set of propagation rules, we compared the ARTISAn's results to the students' responses and also observed the number of inconsistencies discovered by the tool after the propagation-labeling step (the last column in the table). Our results showed that, except in one case, there were no inconsistencies in any of the conducted case studies.

While we believe that these results are already encouraging, we found that several of the identified problems could be avoided to a large degree through better reverse engineering. We relied on the off-the-shelf IBM Rational Rose tool for analyzing the source code, but found early on that it did not discover all class relationships well. Therefore, in some cases we had to manually investigate the code to add missing relationships, which is a labor-intensive and error-prone activity. We also found that Rose did not distinguish between class invocations and class references. This caused inconsistencies in Jigsaw where variable references and calling references did not always coincide. Finally, we found that Rose did not capture calling relationships among methods that belong to different classes. This was a problem whenever a class was identified as, say, both a processing and a data element, i.e., in cases when some of its methods indicated it to be a processing and other methods a data element. This problem then led to inconsistencies within the "data is not allowed to call processing" rule since our tool could not distinguish whether the processing methods of the class invoked the other class or the invocations originated from the data methods.

It should also be noted that we only used a set of domain-independent clues (Table 1) in our case studies. This is because we wanted to use only the clues that are applicable to all case studies and keep their number as small as practical. We found that we could have improved the total recall measure if we had extended our set of clues with other domain- or application-specific clues, such as those based on the use of middleware solutions and naming convention. For example, this way the *jigsaw.Resource* or *Siena.Notification* classes (and all their subclasses) could be recognized as data elements. However, since we were not involved in the development of, nor are we intimately familiar with, any of the mentioned domain-specific case studies, we decided to present results obtained only from using the domain-independent clues.

5   Related Work

Among the numerous program understanding techniques that have been proposed in the literature (i.e., inspection, visualization [6, 7], reading), our work is mostly related to those that achieve the goal of better program understanding and visualization through various architecture recovery methods. This section focuses on this area.

X-ray [10] is an exploratory reverse engineering approach which aids programmers in recovering architectural runtime information from existing software artifacts of a distributed system. Similarly to ARTISAn's notion of clues, X-ray allows the definition of syntactic program patterns, and an associated pattern-matching mechanism. Although the search of program patterns in X-ray would result in the recognition of a more abstract program feature, there is an obvious trade-off in terms of the generality of the approach, the richness of its set of rules, precision, and hit rate. For example, unlike ARTISAn, an interaction mechanism in the form of shared data might not be able to be recognized by X-ray. Furthermore, the lower abstraction level of clues in ARTISAn resulted in its inherent support for "what if" scenarios. The main similarity between ARTISAn and X-ray is in the recognition of program entry points, followed by the application of the study of the dominance relation (usage or reachability analysis), which is well-known and has been used elsewhere in the literature [8].

Similarly to ARTISAn, Lanza and Ducasse [7] propose a categorization of classes, based on class blueprints, as a way to visualize the internal structure of classes. All methods and attributes are distributed among five layers (initialization, interface, implementation, accessor, and attribute) and categorized based on their blueprints. However, this categorization does not try to understand the functionality of a class, but just its static structure.

ManSART [4, 17] is a Software Architecture Recovery Tool that uses special query language routines, called recognizers, to extract and analyze style information from an abstract syntax tree representation of the source code. Similarly to ARTISAn, the result is given as a collection of different architectural views. Architectural representation in ManSART is obtained by manipulating and combining (e.g., merging) different views or, like in ARTISAn, by finding connected subsets of a view.

ACT [1] is an architecture recovery method that combines clustering with pattern-based techniques. Similarly to ARTISAn, it proposes the use of architectural clues that serve as footprints of the high-level design of a system. However, the clues in ACT are small structural patterns (e.g., Façade) that refer to architectural patterns (e.g., Client-Server), which makes them less frequently present and more difficult to recognize, mainly because of their higher complexity and granularity.

Rigi [14] is a program-understanding tool that provides support for the discovery and hierarchical representation of subsystems. Subsystem composition, based on artifacts that are extracted and then stored in an underlying repository, depends on the purpose, audience, and domain [11]. For program understanding purposes, the approach uses low coupling and strong cohesion; alternatively, components can be identified by maintenance personnel based on their experience or qualifications. Unlike ARTISAn, the composition criterion depends on the application that is being re-documented. The use of domain knowledge is unavoidable and the recovery is usually done by persons who are familiar with the application (e.g., its developers).

DiscoTect [16] is a technique for solving the problem of dynamic architectural recovery by mapping low-level implementation style constructs to more abstract architectural operations when predefined run time patterns are recognized. However, the patterns used for search, unlike in ARTISAn, are often very specific, and depend on the application or the environment under inspection.

6   Conclusion and Future Work

This paper discussed ARTISAn, an exploratory and tailorable framework that helps in program understanding tasks. The framework comprises replaceable components to accommodate the exact programming environment and supports developers in understanding large-scale, multi-language source code. The approach is twofold: it provides both a high-level functionality view (i.e., purpose) and a usage view of system elements. In tandem, these views provide the user with a better understanding of the system, and an opportunity to faster locate the parts that are of particular interest (e.g., for maintenance purposes). The first two steps of our approach are evaluated by providing the analysis of the tool's results obtained from several case studies. To evaluate the def-use analysis step, or the correctness of the resulting set of rules, more formal methods are needed. For example, the former can be achieved by comparing the usage view with results of other similar approaches). Finally, determining the overall correctness of the approach requires a deep understanding of the functionality and behavior implemented by each element of a system, which is beyond the capabilities of a light-weight approach, such as ARTISAn.

There are numerous ways to improve our technique. Some of them include the use of reliability metrics that would depend on the reliability of each of the clues and rules applied, and then be used to (automatically) resolve any of possible inconsistencies that result from the labeling process. The other direction of improvement is in providing a richer set of domain- and application-independent clues. For example, the fact that delegating classes act as facades or wrappers to other classes, might turn up to be useful in recognizing communication-processing relationships. Furthermore, the presented rule set can be extended by additional rules that support subcategories of the three major element groups (P, C, and D), such as GUI (P) and interruptible communication (C) type elements. Such a richer propagation rule set would lead to a better understanding of the purpose of a system's elements.

References

1. M. Bauer and M. Trifu, "Architecture-Aware Adaptive Clustering of OO Systems," in *Proc. of the Eighth European Conference on Software Maintenance and Reengineering* (CSMR 2004), Tampere, Finland, March 24-26, 2004
2. A. Egyed, "Compositional and Relational Reasoning During Class Abstraction," In *Proceedings of the 6th International Conf. on the UML*, Oct. 2003, San Francisco.
3. A. Egyed, B. Horling, R. Becker, and R. Balzer, *"Visualization and Debugging Tools,"* *Distributed Sensor Networks: A multiagent perspective*, pp. 33 - 41, editors: Victor Lesser, Charles Ortiz, and Milind Tambe, Kluwer Academic Publishers, 2003
4. D. R. Harris, A. S. Yeh, and H. B. Reubenstein, "Extracting Architectural Features from Source Code," In *Automated Software Engineering* 3, 1996, pp. 109-138.
5. V. Jakobac, A. Egyed, and N. Medvidovic, "ARTISAn: An Approach and Tool for Improving Software System Understanding via Interactive, Tailorable Source Code Analysis", TR USC-CSE-2004-513, December 2004, USC, USA
6. D.F. Jerding and S. Rugaber, "Using Visualization for Architectural Localization and Extraction," In *Proc. of the Fourth WCRE,* pp. 56-65, Oct. 1997
7. M. Lanza and S. Ducasse, "A Categorization of Classes based on the Visualization of their Internal Structure: the Class Blueprint," In *Proceedings of the 2001 ACM OOPSLA*, October 14-18, 2001, Tampa, Florida, USA
8. T. Lengauer and R. E. Tarjan, "A Fast Algorithm for Finding Dominators in a Flowgraph," *ACM Trans. on Programming Languages and Systems,* Vol. 1, No. 1, pp. 121-141, July 1979
9. N. Medvidovic and V. Jakobac, "Using Software Evolution to Focus Architectural Recovery," In *J. of Automated Software Engineering,* To appear. 2005
10. N. Mendonca and J. Kramer, "An Approach for Recovering Distributed System Architectures," In *J. of Automated Software Engineering,* vol. 8, pp. 311-354, 2001
11. H. A. Müller, K. Wong, and S. R. Tilley "Understanding Software Systems Using Reverse Engineering Technology," In *The 62nd Congress of L'Association Canadienne Francaise pour l'Avancement des Sciences Proceedings (ACFAS)*, 1994
12. E. Perry and A. L. Wolf, "Foundations for the Study of Software Architecture," *ACM SIGSOFT SOFTWARE ENGINEERING NOTES,* vol 17 no 4 Oct 1992
13. M. Shaw and D. Garlan, *"Software Architecture: Perspectives on an Emerging Discipline"* Prentice-Hall, 1996

Kaveri: Delivering the Indus Java Program Slicer to Eclipse[*]

Ganeshan Jayaraman, Venkatesh Prasad Ranganath, and John Hatcliff

Department of Computing and Information Sciences,
Kansas State University,
234 Nichols Hall, Manhattan KS, 66506, USA
{ganeshan, rvprasad, hatcliff}@cis.ksu.edu

Abstract. This tool paper describes a modular program slicer for Java built using the Indus program analysis framework along with it's Eclipse-based user interface called Kaveri. Indus provides a library of classes that enables users to quickly assemble a highly customized non-system dependence graph based inter-procedural program slicer capable of slicing concurrent Java programs. Kaveri is an Eclipse plugin that relies on the above library to deliver program slicing to the eclipse platform. Apart from the basic feature for generating program slices from within eclipse along with an intuitive UI to view the slice, the plugin also provides the capability for chasing various dependences in the application to understand the slice.

1 Introduction

Program slicing is a well known analysis that can be used to identify parts of the program that influence or are influenced by a given set of program points (slice criteria). There have been a large number of publications along with a small number of implementations for languages such as FORTRAN, ANSI C, and Oberon. [1] Most of the implementations have been targeted to particular applications of program slicing such as program comprehension, testing, program verification, etc. Moreover, only few robust slicing tools exist for languages like Java and C++.

From our experience we have found that the properties required of a slice depend on the application. For example, the program slice needs to be executable for program verification applications such as Bandera[2] but not for program comprehension purposes. Similarly, the slice needs to be "residualizable" for some applications and such transformations can again be constrained by the application. Hence, program slicers need to be modular and flexible (customizable) as opposed to being monolithic and rigid.

---

[*] This work was supported in part by the U.S. Army Research Office (DAAD190110564), by DARPA/IXO's PCES program (AFRL Contract F33615-00-C-3044), by NSF (CCR-0306607) by Lockheed Martin, and by Intel Corporation.
[1] Please refer to Jens Krinke's Dissertation[1] for a brief informative overview of available implementations.

M. Cerioli (Ed.): FASE 2005, LNCS 3442, pp. 269–272, 2005.

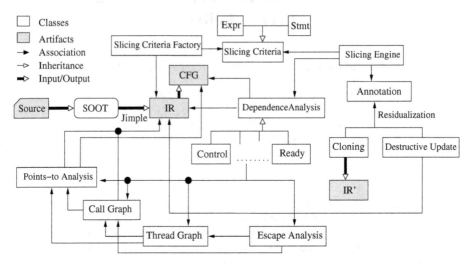

Fig. 1. Bird's eye view of classes and artifacts in Indus Java Program Slicing Library

2   Indus Java Program Slicer

Drawing from the our experience with Bandera slicer, we have implemented a program slicing library that can handle almost full Java[2]. To the best of our knowledge, this is the first publicly available Java implementation of a program slicer for Java.

Indus modules work on Jimple (SOOT [3]) representation of Java programs and bytecode.

The key features of Indus Java Program Slicing library apart from generating backward and forward slices are as follows.

Batteries Included. The program slicing library, directly or indirectly, requires various high level analyses such as escape analysis [4], monitor analysis, safe-lock analysis [5], and analyses to calculate and prune various dependences – intra- and inter-procedural data dependence, control [6] dependence, interference [7] dependence, ready dependence and synchronization dependence [5]. These high level analyses rely on low-level information such as object-flow information [8], call graph, and thread graph [4]. All of the above analyses and other related analyses are available in Indus.

Modularity. Most of the above mentioned analyses are available as independent modules. Hence, the user can use only the required analyses. Each analysis implementation is decoupled from it's interface to enable easy experimentation with various implementations. This is a recurring theme in Indus which is leveraged in the slicer.

Non-SDG Based. Most slicing related work is based on program/system dependence graphs (PDG/SDG) that contain dependence edges to account for various aspects of the language such as unconditional jumps, procedure calls, aliasing, etc. This can be an obstacle for reusability. Instead, in Indus, the logic to handle such aspects is encoded

---

[2] With the exception of dynamic class loading, reflection, and native methods.

in the slicing algorithm to decrease coupling and increase cohesion. As a result, dependence information is readily reusable, fine-tuning of slicing algorithm is simplified, and maintenance becomes easy.

Program Slicing = Analysis. In Indus, program slicing is considered to be pure program analysis – program slicing only calculates the program points that belong to a slice. This simplifies the slicing algorithm and enables the same slicing algorithm to be used with different transformations as required by the applications.

Inter-Procedural and Context-Sensitive. The slicer considers calling contexts (where possible) to generate precise inter-procedural slices. The user can generate context-sensitive slice criteria to further improve precision. *Scoping*, a feature that can be used to control the parts of the system that need to be analyzed, can be used to to restrict the scope of slicing to a single method, a collection of methods, a collection of methods belonging to a collection of classes, etc.

Concurrent Programs. This implementation can slice concurrent programs by considering data interference and other synchronization related aspects that are inherent to concurrent programs. Information from escape analysis and monitor analysis is used to improve the precision of concurrent program slices.

Highly Customizable. Using Indus libraries, the user can assemble a slicer that is customized for the end-application. For example, the user may choose cloning based residualization for differencing purposes or destructive-update based residualization for program verification purposes.

To verify that our library is indeed customizable to multiple application domains and also to realize a long term goal of having an UI to visualize program slices, we developed Kaveri.

3   Kaveri: A Program Slicing Plugin for Eclipse

Kaveri is a plugin that contributes program slicing as a feature to Eclipse [9]. Kaveri utilizes the Indus program slicing library to perform slicing, thereby, hiding the details of assembling a slicer customized for the purpose of program comprehension. As a program comprehension aid, Kaveri contributes the following features to Eclipse.

Slice Java Programs by Choosing Slice Criteria. The user can pick the criteria, generate the program slice, and view the slice all using the Java source editor. The plugin handles the intricacies such as mapping from Java to Jimple and driving the slicer.

View the Slice in the Java Editor. The part of the source code included in the slice is highlighted in the editor. This aids slice-based program comprehension.

Perform Additive Slicing. "What program points are common to slices based on criteria b and c?" is a common question during program comprehension. It can be answered by intersecting the slices based on criteria b and c. In Kaveri, the user can achieve this by associating different highlighting schemes to slices based on b and c, and viewing both the slices in the editor at the same time. Similarly, *Chop*s can be realised by intersecting backward and forward slices.

Support for Program Comprehension. Understanding dependence relations between various program points helps understand the generated program slice. In Kaveri, this is achieved by "chasing" dependences.

- The user can view which program points in a Java statement/expression are included in the slice via *slice comprehension view*, an eclipse view displays the Java-to-Jimple mapping for a Java statement/expression along with Jimple level slice annotations.
- As Kaveri annotates the parts of the source file in the editor, the user can use the built-in annotation navigation facility in Eclipse to keep track of dependence navigation. However, to compensate for the genericity of this facility, Kaveri maintains the dependence-based path taken by the user. The user can navigate this path and backtrack on it via a *dependence history view*.
- Kaveri also supports *path queries* that can be used to find sequences of program points that are related via a pattern of dependences and other relations specified by a language such as regular expressions.

The user can also generate a scoped slice based on scope specifications to understand the relation between certain program points independent of external influences.

Perform Context-Sensitive Slicing. In Kaveri, the user can identify calling contexts (from a inverted call tree of a finite depth) to be used in the generation of context-sensitive program slices.

We have successfully used Kaveri with code bases of $\leq$ 10K lines of Java application code ($<$ 80K bytecodes) (excluding library code). All software and related artifacts pertaining to Indus and Kaveri are available at [10].

References

1. Krinke, J.: Advanced Slicing of Sequntial and Concurrent Programs. PhD thesis, Fakultät für Mathematik und Informatik, Universität Passau (2003)
2. Corbett, J.C., Dwyer, M.B., Hatcliff, J., Laubach, S., Păsăreanu, C.S., Robby, Zheng, H.: Bandera: Extracting finite-state models from Java source code. In: Proceedings of the 22nd International Conference on Software Engineering (ICSE'00). (2000) 439–448
3. Sable Group: Soot, a Java Optimization Framework. (http://www.sable.mcgill.ca/soot/)
4. Ranganath, V.P., Hatcliff, J.: Pruning interference and ready dependences for slicing concurrent java programs. In: Proceedings of Compiler Construction (CC'04). Volume 2985., Springer-Verlag (2004) 39–56
5. Hatcliff, J., Corbett, J.C., Dwyer, M.B., Sokolowski, S., Zheng, H.: A formal study of slicing for multi-threaded programs with JVM concurrency primitives. In: Proceedings on the International Symposium on Static Analysis (SAS'99). (1999)
6. Ranganath, V.P., Amtoft, T., Banerjee, A., B.Dwyer, M., Hatcliff, J.: A new foundation for control-dependence and slicing for modern program structures, Springer-Verlag (2005) *To appear in the* Proceedings of European Symposium On Programming (ESOP'05).
7. Krinke, J.: Static slicing of threaded programs. In: Proceedings ACM SIGPLAN/SIGFSOFT Workshop on Program Analysis for Software Tools and Engineering (PASTE'98). (1998) 35–42 ACM SIGPLAN Notices 33(7).
8. Ranganath, V.P.: Object-Flow Analysis for Optimizing Finite-State Models of Java Software. Master's thesis, Kansas State University (2002)
9. OTI: Eclipse, an open extensible IDE written in Java. (http://www.eclipse.org)
10. SAnToS Laboratory: Indus. (http://indus.projects.cis.ksu.edu)

Non-local Choice and Beyond: Intricacies of MSC Choice Nodes*

Arjan J. Mooij, Nicolae Goga, and Judi M.T. Romijn

Technische Universiteit Eindhoven,
Department of Mathematics and Computer Science,
P.O. Box 513, 5600 MB Eindhoven, The Netherlands
{a.j.mooij, n.goga, j.m.t.romijn}@tue.nl

Abstract. MSC is a visual formalism for specifying the behavior of systems. To obtain implementations for individual processes, the MSC choice construction poses fundamental problems. The best-studied cause is non-local choice, which e.g. is unavoidable in systems with autonomous processes. In this paper we characterize two additional problematic classes of choice nodes. Based on these three classes we point out some errors in related work. Extending our work on pragmatic implementations of non-local choice, we motivate a different choice semantics which allows a little more behavior. Finally, inspired by practical case studies, we present the first implementation approach for non-local choice nodes that can handle arbitrary numbers of processes.

1 Introduction

Message sequence chart (MSC, see [11, 17]) is a visual formalism that is used to specify the behavior of a collection of processes. An important property of MSCs is that behaviors are described from a full-system's perspective. Then an immediate question is whether an implementation can be extracted that has the same behavior but expressed in terms of the processes in the system.

To obtain such an implementation, the behavior specified for the full system must be established by the independent processes in a distributed way. The usual way to obtain an implementation for each process is to project the MSC on each single process. However, in general, implementations with exactly the same behavior do not exist (see e.g. [13]). Typical problems that arise in naive implementation attempts are additional behaviors [19] and deadlocks [20].

Then one can conclude that the MSC formalism is inappropriate for protocol specification, but there are also some approaches to really address the problem. First, the obtained implementations can be compared with their specifications to find inconsistencies [20]. A second option is to identify and detect properties of MSCs that may cause problematic implementations, and then label such MSCs

---

* This research is supported by the NWO under project 016.023.015: "Improving the Quality of Protocol Standards".

M. Cerioli (Ed.): FASE 2005, LNCS 3442, pp. 273–288, 2005.

as being pathological [7]. Finally, alternative semantics of the MSC constructions are studied such that these constructions become implementable [5, 15].

In this paper we address the latter two approaches for the very topical issue of choice nodes. The best-studied property leading to implementation problems is non-local choice. In addition to this property about locality of a choice, we define two classes of problems related to propagation of the choice. These three classes together arise naturally from a single process' perspective, and we use them to point out some errors in related work.

To handle non-local choice we motivate a different kind of choice semantics, viz. one that allows a little more behavior than the standardized semantics, but in a controlled way. Based on this modified semantics we address approaches to implement choice nodes. Such approaches are highly needed, since non-local choice is inevitable in MSC specifications of systems with autonomous processes. In our cooperation with protocol standardization committees (see e.g. [15]) we have noticed that currently there are insufficient applicable solutions.

We present a generalization of our approach [15] to implement non-local choice in systems with two processes. We also introduce a new implementation approach for non-local choice that, as far as we know, is the first one that can deal with arbitrary numbers of processes. The MSC patterns required for both approaches are inspired by our experience with practical case studies.

Preliminaries. Instead of hMSCs (high-level MSCs or hierarchical MSCs), in this paper we use the mathematically more convenient notion of a message sequence graph (MSG). Since these concepts are equally expressive (see [8]) this is a valid and common strategy. An MSG is a finite directed graph in which each node is labeled with a bMSC (basic MSC), and there is one initial and one terminal node. We use the term MSC to refer to an MSG together with its bMSCs.

For simplicity reasons and without loss of generality, we assume the MSG to be normalized such that if a node has more than one outgoing edge, then the bMSC associated with the node is an empty bMSC. In this way the choices in the MSG are made explicit in (choice) nodes without an associated bMSC.

We use the following nomenclature for MSCs. There are four kinds of actions (or events): an internal action, asynchronously sending a message m (denoted by $!m$), receiving a message m (denoted by $?m$) and termination. A process is said to have initiative, if a possible next action for the process is an initiating action like an internal action, sending a message or termination. Note that finding the collection of possible next actions of a process might require considering the entire MSG.

Overview. In Section 2 we give our characterization of three properties that may cause problems when implementing MSCs with choice nodes, and we discuss some related literature. In Section 3 we discuss ways to handle the best-known class, viz. non-local choice. Section 4 contains a summary of our earlier work [15] on dealing with non-local choice in systems with only two processes, and it contains a small generalization. This summary also serves as an introduction to Section 5, in which we present an approach to implement non-local choice for an arbitrary number of processes. Finally Section 6 gives some conclusions and directions for further work.

2   Problematic Choice Node Properties

In this section we present our characterization of three problematic choice node properties. On this basis we discuss and comment on some related literature, and in Section 5 we exploit it to isolate one of the classes.

2.1   Characterization of Choice Synchronization Problems

As mentioned before, the core implementation problem is that one collective choice is specified, while it must be implemented in a distributed way. If in a choice node all possible initiating actions can be performed by only one of the processes, this single process can simply perform the system's decision about the choice. However, in general it is not sufficient to ensure that one process makes the decision. It is also important that the processes agree on the decision, so the decision must be properly *propagated* to the other processes. So far this has not really been recognized, and the propagation issue is frequently ignored.

In the remainder of this section, we study the implementation problem for a single choice node from the perspective of a single process. An important concept will be the set of successor nodes for the process, i.e. the nodes that contain the process' possible first action after the choice node. Note that the definition of successor node for a process is not restricted to the direct successors of the choice node. Namely, if the process is not involved in some direct successors in the graph, also nodes that can be reached further on must be considered.

Non-local Choice. A first question is whether the process should initiate some behavior or it should just wait to receive a message. When several processes independently decide to initiate behavior, they might start executing different successor bMSCs. This possibility easily leads to non-specified behaviors, and it is usually called *non-local choice* (NLC). An example of non-local choice can be generated with the bMSCs in Figure 1 by constructing a choice node from which only the bMSCs msc_base and msc_NLC can be chosen.

More formally, a node is a non-local choice node for the two distinct processes p and q if the following holds: there are two different successor nodes k and l for process p and q respectively, such that p has initiative in k and q has initiative in

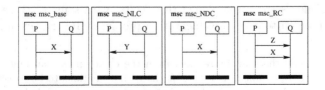

Fig. 1. bMSCs to illustrate the classification

l, and such that each (acyclic) path to node k without any action of p is disjoint with each (acyclic) path to node l without any action of q.

Non-deterministic Choice. Then assume that there is only one process that has initiative in the node, and this process performs the system's decision on the choice. Suppose in each successor node the first action of the process under consideration is a receipt, and suppose a matching message arrives. A question is whether this first receipt is sufficient to derive the decision made about the choice. In case some of the successor nodes have a common first receipt, then this is clearly not the case; we call it *non-deterministic choice* (NDC). An example of non-deterministic choice can be generated by constructing a choice node from which only the bMSCs msc_base and msc_NDC in Figure 1 can be chosen.

More formally, a node is a non-deterministic choice node for a process p if there are at least two different[1] successor nodes for p with the same receipt action as first action of p.

Race Choice. Absence of non-deterministic choice is not enough for a process to derive the choice decision on the basis of the first arriving message. Namely, in case messages *arrive* in a different order than in which their *receipt* is specified in the bMSC (which in itself is not an error, just a property of the underlying communication system), the process may incorrectly derive which decision has been made. So the first message receipt in one node, may actually have been sent according to *another* node in which the receipt is not the first action of the recipient; we call it *race choice* (RC). An example of race choice can be generated by constructing a choice node from which only the bMSCs msc_base and msc_RC in Figure 1 can be chosen.

More formally, a node is a race choice node for a process p if the following holds: there are two different[2] successor nodes k and l for process p such that p's first action in k is a receipt of message m and in l it is a receipt of a different message n, and such that starting with node l a message m may be sent to p before process p performs any action.

Examples with a combination of these properties NLC, NDC and RC can be generated with the bMSCs in Figure 1 by constructing a choice node from which only msc_base and the bMSCs for the selected properties can be chosen.

Distinguishing between the two propagation-related properties, viz. non-deterministic choice and race choice, may look somewhat arbitrary, but it is based on an essential difference. Intuitively, non-deterministic choice is a static property of the MSC, while race choice takes into account the dynamics of the communication network.

Finally it needs to be mentioned that MSCs with some of these properties are not guaranteed to give implementation problems [16]. For example, in case

---

[1] A successor node that can be reached from the choice node via multiple paths, is considered only once since we assume paths without actions to be irrelevant.

[2] Note that we exclude order problems that are not caused by a choice (e.g. within a bMSC), which falls under implementability of a single bMSC.

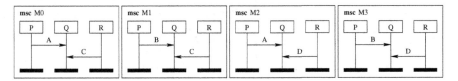

Fig. 2. Non-local choice without implied behaviors

all potential "additional" behavior has already been included in the MSC, or in case agreeing on the decision is not really important for the further execution.

2.2   Related Problems and Solutions

In this section we discuss various related issues from the literature and we point out some errors in related work.

Communication Infrastructure. Especially in small systems, the problems caused by non-local choice and race choice can be solved by extra assumptions about the underlying communication system [12, 4]. Typical properties that may help are communication synchrony, message order preservation, bounded buffer capacities and confirmed communications. In specific cases, such assumptions on the underlying system are both valid and useful.

Definitions of Non-local Choice. A frequently referenced paper for the definition of non-local choice is [2]. Although much literature suggests the equivalence of the various definitions in [2], we show that they are inconsistent. The informal introduction contains the following description:

> "When the wait-and-see strategy can be used to resolve a non-determinism within each process, we call the branching a *local branching choice*. Otherwise, when explicit synchronization between the processes is necessary to resolve a non-determinism, we call the branching a *non-local branching choice*."

After introducing a formal semantic definition and a formal syntactic characterization (equal to ours), the following informal explanation of the syntactic version is given:

> "An MSC specification has no non-local branching choice iff at each of its branching points, the first events in all bMSCs are sent by the same process."

Usually, this last version is used for definition purposes, but the first one is assumed when it comes to implementation. It is easy to see that these two definitions are different by studying a choice node with the two successor bMSCs msc_base and msc_RC from Figure 1. Since process P is the only process that can

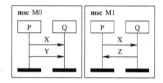

Fig. 3. Hidden non-local choice

initiate an action, it is local according to the second definition. Then according to the first definition all non-determinism should be resolved, but process Q shows the contrary.

Implied Scenarios. Implied scenarios are scenarios that are not contained in the MSC specification, but that are contained in implementations of the MSC. Although implied scenarios can result from propagation problems, only the relation with non-local choices (according to the syntactic definition of [2]) has been studied. In [18] the following two observations are made:

1. "Non-local choices are implied scenarios;"
2. "nevertheless the converse is not the case."

In contrast, [16] makes the following two observations:

3. "Notice that a non-local choice is not enough to have an implied scenario."
4. "To have an implied scenarios these conditions[3] hold: i) there is a non-local branching choice in the MSC specification so that ii) ..."

There are two contradictions here. Observation 3 falsifies observation 1, which can be shown using a choice node with as successors the bMSCs from Figure 2, where more than one process has initiative but no implied behaviors result. In turn, observation 2 falsifies observation 4, which can be shown with a choice node node with the two successor bMSCs msc_base and msc_RC from Figure 1. Implementations of this example, without non-local choice, contain implied scenarios with the prefix $!Z \cdot !X \cdot ?X$. Another example can be found in [18].

Delayed Choice. The widely accepted solution to non-deterministic choice is to use delayed choice semantics instead of ordinary choice semantics. Since this solution is effective quite often (though not always), it has become part of the MSC standard. Sometimes, it can even eliminate non-local choice by factoring out a common non-local prefix of the bMSCs after which a local choice remains.

However, we could not find any warning for its possible side-effects. Namely, delayed choice can also expose non-local choice, e.g. in a choice node with the two successor bMSCs from Figure 3. So although the MSG itself contains no non-local choice, after applying delayed choice the non-local choice pops up.

---

[3] This is the basis of [16]'s procedure for detecting implied behavior.

3 Dealing with Non-local Choice Nodes

In this section we address some ways to deal with the best-known choice problem from Section 2, viz. non-local choice. We motivate a class of solutions, of which only some instances have been described so far.

3.1 Traditional Approaches

Non-local choice is usually addressed by syntactically detecting (e.g. [2]) the non-local choice nodes, or by detecting the resulting implied behaviors by generating them (e.g. [16]). However, these approaches do not really address how to *solve* the problems with non-local choice. An obvious approach might be to change the MSC into a similar MSC with only local choice nodes. Since in that case at each node only one process has initiative, systems with autonomous processes cannot be specified. Another way to overcome the problems resulting from non-local choice is to explicitly include all implied behaviors in the MSC. Although this eliminates the implicit additional behaviors caused by implementing non-local choice nodes, the MSC becomes more complicated, which is definitely not desired from a practical point of view.

The problems with non-local choice nodes can also be seen as implementation issues, and hence they should not even be addressed in a specification. Then to obtain an implementation, some additional coordination protocol needs to be introduced (e.g. [2]). Although this leads to a nice layered design, it is problematic if some processes represent human beings, on which no additional protocol should be imposed. Also for protocol standardization this approach is undesired, since the additional protocol is not part of the MSC description.

3.2 Adjusted Semantics for Choice Nodes

The source of the problems with non-local choice nodes is that the underlying system is distributed. Since the processes are independent computational units, a coordination problem arises when the processes *together* need to make a transition in the MSG. Nowadays this problem is mainly noted in choice nodes, but in fact, it also arises for pure (or synchronous) sequential composition of bMSCs in an MSG. The latter issue has been solved by defining its semantics to be *weak* (or asynchronous) sequential composition, which usually corresponds to the intentions of the developer of the MSC. For choice nodes, the changes in their semantics (like delayed choice) are not (yet) sufficient.

Suppose all processes have reached a given non-local choice node. Since the processes are independent, we need to conclude that in general it cannot be avoided that the execution of several different bMSCs is initiated. This means that an *implementable* semantics of choice must allow, to some degree, parallel execution of the bMSCs. Of course, the amount of additional parallel behavior should be minimal, and as soon as possible the behavior should converge to the behavior of a conventional (or synchronous) choice.

As far as we know, this theoretical motivation for starting with parallelism and converging to synchronous choice has not been revealed before, but two of its instances have been discovered in [5, 15]. These instances mainly differ in the way in which the additional parallel behaviors are interpreted. In [5] this behavior is ignored, while in [15] it is stored to be used at the next choice node. The main limitation of both approaches is that only systems of two processes can be addressed. In Section 5 we describe the first implementation of such a semantics for an arbitrary number of processes.

4   Approach from [15] and a Generalization

In this section we summarize the approach for implementing non-local choice nodes from [15] for two reasons. First, this approach for two processes is a nice prelude to our approach for multiple processes in Section 5. Second, we show how the MSG pattern required for [15] can be generalized.

4.1   Pattern and Its Generalization

For application of the approach of [15], the MSC must match a certain pattern both with respect to its bMSCs and to its MSG. Two special kinds of bMSCs are distinguished, viz. RC-like bMSCs (Request-Confirm scenario) and A-like bMSCs (Announce scenario). These bMSCs contain as a prefix the structure as depicted in Figure 4, in which P and Q denote the names of the two processes.

These two kinds of bMSCs can be seen as negotiation scenarios: process P can send a Request message to process Q, but Q is the arbiter process that decides whether to send a Confirm message and continue the execution of the RC-like bMSC or to send an Announce message and execute an A-like bMSC. More details are discussed together with the implementation in Section 4.2.

With respect to the MSG, the successor bMSCs of each non-local choice node M must be partitioned into RC-like bMSCs and A-like bMSCs, but such that the Request and Confirmation messages in the RC-like bMSCs do not occur in the A-like bMSCs. The main restriction of [15] is that after an A-like bMSC, a similar choice node as node M is reached again. This is depicted in Figure 5 (including the dashed arrows): after each A-like bMSC, an S node is reached that is in fact identical to node M. This MSC pattern turns out to occur frequently.

However, the MSG pattern is too strong, since it only needs to ensure that when process P has sent a Request message, it still makes sense for process Q

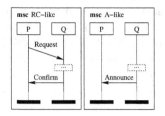

Fig. 4. Prefixes of the bMSCs for [15]

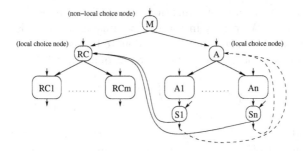

Fig. 5. MSG pattern for [15] and a generalization

to receive the message after execution of an A-like bMSC. Hence, after an A-like bMSC, only node RC is required to be reachable and we propose to *generalize* the pattern by eliminating the dashed arrows in Figure 5. After each A-like bMSC an S node is reached from which at least the previous series of RC-like bMSCs is reachable (via node RC). In addition, via the open outgoing edge also extra RC-like bMSCs and an arbitrary series of A-like bMSCs may be reachable.

4.2   Implementation

We summarize the proposed implementation for both the original pattern (see [15] for more details) and its generalization at the same time. Process Q becomes a kind of arbiter, with the usual implementation. However, the implementation for process P is slightly different: If process P receives an Announce message from process Q, it executes the corresponding A-like bMSC. Even if process P sends a Request message of an RC-like bMSC, it may still receive Announce messages from process Q that indicate that some A-like bMSC must be executed. Eventually, the Confirmation message corresponding to the Announce message will arrive, and then execution of the RC-like bMSC can be completed.

Note that in this implementation, between sending and receiving a Request message several executions of A-like bMSCs are possible. Observe also that after process P has sent a Request message, the remaining choice is in fact a local choice, viz. for arbiter process Q.

5   A New Approach to Deal with Non-local Choice Nodes

This section describes a way to implement the semantics proposed in Section 3.2 for systems with an *arbitrary* number of processes. Like in [15], the additional parallel behavior is interpreted as behavior that must be stored to be used at the next choice node. As far as we know, this is the first pragmatic implementation of non-local choice for an arbitrary number of processes. Furthermore this approach can deal with bMSCs in which several processes have initiative, and it is inspired from both examples in the literature and industrial protocol standards.

The description of our formalization is based on process algebra extended with two operators. We briefly introduce them using characteristic examples, in which a and b denote actions and s and t denote terms. The first operator is the delayed choice operator $\mp$ (see [1, 17]) with as quantifier $\overline{\Sigma}$:

$$a \cdot x \mp b \cdot y \quad = \quad \begin{cases} a \neq b: & a \cdot x + b \cdot y \\ a = b: & a \cdot (x \mp y) \end{cases}$$

The second operator is the partial synchronization operator $\cap$ (see [10, 3]) with a (hidden) set of actions S on which this operator synchronizes:

$$a \cdot s \cap b \cdot t \quad = \quad \begin{cases} a \in S \land b \in S \land a = b: & a \cdot (s \cap t) \\ a \in S \land b \in S \land a \neq b: & \delta \\ a \in S \land b \notin S & : & b \cdot (a \cdot s \cap t) \\ a \notin S \land b \in S & : & a \cdot (s \cap b \cdot t) \\ a \notin S \land b \notin S & : & a \cdot (s \cap b \cdot t) + b \cdot (a \cdot s \cap t) \end{cases}$$

In the remainder of this section, we first introduce a running example. Then we address the MSC pattern we assume, followed by a description of our proposed implementation. Finally we relate it to a proposed MSC extension.

5.1   Running Example

As an example to illustrate our approach, we use a simplified version of the well-known ATM example [20]. We have restricted it to its core non-local choice problem, as depicted in Figure 6. For later use, the MSCs contain some extra annotations; in particular the bMSCs have been split by a horizontal line.

We briefly explain the functionality of this simplified ATM. In node A some repetitive behavior is started with bMSC *Request*. It consists of inserting a card and entering a password, followed by verifying the bank account. Then choice node B is reached, in which the user can choose to:

- interrupt and cancel the account verification, which corresponds to: bMSC *Interrupt1* → node C → bMSC *Interrupt2* → node A;
- wait for a balance report and press the cancel button to end the session: bMSC *Response1* → node D → bMSC *Response2* → node A.

5.2   Pattern

To keep non-local choice manageable, we isolate it from other problematic choice properties. This motivates the classification in Section 2, and from now on we ignore propagation issues. In the remainder of this section, we exploit that the MSG is normalized as discussed in Section 1 by interpreting the MSG as a graph in which the edges are labeled with (concatenated) bMSCs, and in which the nodes indicate choices.

To apply our approach, each bMSC must be split into a (preferably small) *front* part that may be executed in parallel, and the remaining *tail* part that

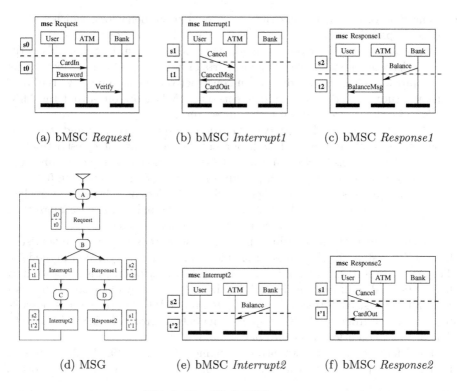

(a) bMSC *Request*   (b) bMSC *Interrupt1*   (c) bMSC *Response1*

(d) MSG   (e) bMSC *Interrupt2*   (f) bMSC *Response2*

Fig. 6. Simplified ATM example

will be part of a real choice. To solve non-local choice, in each node the choice between the successor bMSCs without their fronts must be a local choice. This can be achieved as follows:

1. *choose a process to become the "arbiter"*, which is typically a non-human process that occurs in each bMSC in an early stage;
2. *split the bMSCs* into a front and a tail, such that apart from the front, only the arbiter process has initiative, unless the bMSC can only be reached from a node with only one outgoing edge. (If the tail is empty for a process, also successor nodes are involved in deciding which processes have initiative.)

The splitting of the bMSCs must be such that the following conditions hold:

1. for each node and for each two of its outgoing edges e and f with different fronts, the node reached via edge e is no terminal node and the node has an outgoing edge with the same front as edge f;
2. for each two edges e and f with different fronts, the events in the front of edge e do not occur in the front of edge f;
3. for each two edges e and f, the events in the front of edge e do not occur in the tail of edge e nor in the tail of edge f.

The first condition reflects that additional front behaviors, which are the additional parallel behaviors, can indeed be used in next choice nodes. If it does not hold, a wrong arbiter process might have been chosen. But more likely the MSC lacks some unavoidable behavior, parts of which must be made explicit for our approach. Thus this condition can constructively help to improve the MSC without studying the process implementations. A last option is that the MSC needs to be slightly rearranged to fit our pattern.

The motivation for the last two conditions is quite technical and it will be discussed upon their use. Although our pattern contains some restrictions, it includes the patterns of Section 4 and it fits well-known examples as an ATM (see the running example), and a producer-consumer pair (see Section 5.4).

Let us apply this to our running example. All choices have been made explicit in the empty choice nodes A, B, C and D, and the only node with more than one outgoing edge, viz. node B, suffers from non-local choice.

To check the pattern, an arbiter process must be chosen. Using the heuristics from the first step, the ATM process should be an appropriate arbiter for node A. The next step is to split the bMSCs according to this arbiter. This is depicted by horizontal dashed lines in the bMSCs in Figure 6. This way of splitting turns out to fulfill the first condition, e.g. in node B after bMSC $Interrupt1$ it is possible to execute the front of bMSC $Response1$ namely as front of bMSC $Interrupt2$. The last two conditions also turn out to hold.

For reference purposes, we introduce names $s0$, $s1$, $s2$, $t0$, $t1$, $t2$, $t'1$ and $t'2$ for the bMSC parts as indicated in Figure 6. For example, for the $User$ process:

$s0 = \epsilon$	$s1 = \ !Cancel$	$s2 = \ \epsilon$
$t0 = \ !CardIn \cdot !Password$	$t1 = \ ?CancelMsg \cdot ?CardOut$	$t2 = \ ?BalanceMsg$
	$t'1 = \ ?CardOut$	$t'2 = \ \epsilon$

5.3   Implementation

In general it is complicated to directly define our proposed implementation in terms of a finite state machine. It turns out to be easier to use techniques from constraint-oriented programming (see e.g. [3]), from which for concrete examples a finite state machine can be obtained using operational semantics (see e.g. [3]).

In the remainder of this section, we concentrate on only one of the processes since their implementations are independent. Furthermore we use V for the set of nodes, and E for the set of labeled edges. More specific, we represent each edge as a four-tuple $(v, m, n, w) \in E$ as follows: the edge is directed from node v to node w, and m and n are the front and the tail respectively of the corresponding bMSC projected on the process to be implemented.

Our implementation is described in Figure 7, where the smallest solution of $I.v$ denotes the implementation of node v for the process. It is defined as the synchronized execution of the terms $I_i.v.m$ for each individual front m, where $I_i.v.m$ expresses where front m may be executed in relation with all tails. The partial synchronization operator $\cap$ only synchronizes on the events in the tails, for which we exploit the last two conditions mentioned above.

$$
\begin{array}{ll}
I.v & = (\bigcap_{m:(\exists v,n,w:(v,m,n,w)\in E)} \ I_i.v.m) \\[2ex]
I_i.v.m & = \begin{cases} (\exists_{n,w} \ \ (v,m,n,w) \in E) : & I_a.v.m.\epsilon \\ (\forall_{n,w} \ \ (v,m,n,w) \notin E) : & (\overline{\Sigma}_{m',n',w': \ (v,m',n',w')\in E} \ \ n' \cdot I_i.w'.m) \end{cases} \\[3ex]
I_a.v.m.p & = \left(\overline{\Sigma}_{m',n',w': \ (v,m',n',w')\in E} \ \begin{cases} m \neq m' : & I_a.w'.m.(p \cdot n') \\ m = m' : & (p\|m') \cdot n' \cdot I_i.w'.m \end{cases} \right)
\end{array}
$$

Fig. 7. Formalization of a single process implementation

The term $I_i.v.m$ describes the implementation in node v with respect to the *inactive* front m. If m is the front of a successor bMSC of node v, its execution can be started and hence it becomes active. Otherwise it remains inactive, and a usual choice is performed on the tails of the successor bMSCs of node v.

The term $I_a.v.m.p$ describes the implementation in node v with respect to the *active* front m. The additional parameter p is used to accumulate the series of executions of tails since front m's execution was allowed to start. In case the tail of a bMSC with front m is executed, then it is required that front m was executed along the path p to node v, which is expressed by the term $(p\|m')$.

To illustrate this approach on our ATM example, we first apply it to the high-level description in terms of s and t. Afterwards, the specific details can be substituted to obtain the final process implementations. First we give the instantiations of some of the formulas:

$$
\begin{array}{ll}
I.A & = I_i.A.s0 \cap I_i.A.s1 \cap I_i.A.s2 \\
I_i.A.s1 & = t0 \cdot I_i.B.s1 \\
I_i.B.s1 & = I_a.B.s1.\epsilon \\
I_a.B.s1.\epsilon & = (\epsilon\|s1) \cdot t1 \cdot I_i.C.s1 \ \mp \ I_a.D.s1.(\epsilon \cdot t2) \\
I_i.C.s1 & = t'2 \cdot I_i.A.s1 \\
I_a.D.s1.(\epsilon \cdot t2) & = ((\epsilon \cdot t2) \| s1) \cdot t'1 \cdot I_i.A.s1
\end{array}
$$

After simplification we obtain the following implementation per process:

$$
\begin{array}{ll}
I.A & = I_i.A.s0 \cap I_i.A.s1 \cap I_i.A.s2 \\
I_i.A.s0 & = s0 \cdot t0 \cdot (t1 \cdot t'2 \ \mp \ t2 \cdot t'1) \cdot I_i.A.s0 \\
I_i.A.s1 & = t0 \cdot (s1 \cdot t1 \cdot t'2 \ \mp \ (t2\|s1) \cdot t'1) \cdot I_i.A.s1 \\
I_i.A.s2 & = t0 \cdot ((t1\|s2) \cdot t'2 \ \mp \ s2 \cdot t2 \cdot t'1) \cdot I_i.A.s2
\end{array}
$$

By substituting the actions of the three processes and eliminating the $\cap$ operator, the following final implementations are obtained:

$$
\begin{array}{ll}
I^{User} & = !CardIn \cdot !Password \cdot (!Cancel \cdot (?CancelMsg + ?BalanceMsg) + \\
& \qquad ?BalanceMsg \cdot !Cancel) \cdot ?CardOut \cdot I^{User} \\
I^{ATM} & = ?CardIn \cdot ?Password \cdot !Verify \cdot \\
& \qquad (?Cancel \cdot !CancelMsg \cdot !CardOut \cdot ?Balance + \\
& \qquad ?Balance \cdot !BalanceMsg \cdot ?Cancel \cdot !CardOut) \cdot I^{ATM} \\
I^{Bank} & = ?Verify \cdot !Balance \cdot I^{Bank}
\end{array}
$$

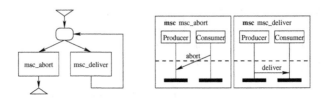

Fig. 8. Producer-consumer example

The implementation for the *ATM* (which is the arbiter process) and for the *Bank* are the usual ones. The possible behavior of the *User* has been extended, but it is intuitive in relation to Figure 6. In particular after pressing *Cancel*, the user can get a *BalanceMsg* instead of a *CancelMsg*. Using the model checker SPIN [9], we have verified that the normal implementation contains deadlocks, and that the above implementation is indeed free of deadlocks.

5.4   Relation with Compositional Message Sequence Charts

Our proposed implementation of non-local choice nodes typically contains behavior that is difficult to describe efficiently using current MSC. In [6] a syntactic extension of MSC is proposed called "compositional message sequence chart". The example in [14] to illustrate the usefulness of this extension, can also be generated using our approach and the MSC in Figure 8. Although the version of [14] gives a more precise specification (i.e. closer to an implementation), our version is simpler and more intuitive for system *specification* and still allows a (unique) implementation using the technique presented in this section.

6   Conclusions and Further Work

We have structured a number of choice node properties that may lead to implementation problems, viz. non-local choice, non-deterministic choice and race choice. This has resulted in a natural classification of these properties which covers initiative and propagation problems for choice nodes.

Further work is to address completeness of the classification. It needs to be studied whether choice nodes without any of these properties can indeed be implemented without introducing extra deadlocks or implied behaviors.

We have also focused on the best-known problematic property, viz. non-local choice, which we propose to handle by slightly changing the choice semantics. We have given the first implementation approach for non-local choice in systems with an arbitrary number of processes. This is a pure generalization of the current choice node semantics in the sense that for MSCs without choice problems it produces the normal implementation.

Further work is to study alternative formalizations of this approach. In particular the general properties of this approach need to be investigated. It would be interesting to investigate whether ignoring the additional parallel behavior (as in [5]) can be integrated and also whether other initiative and propagation issues can be addressed.

Acknowledgements. We thank the anonymous referees for the helpful comments.

References

1. J.C.M. Baeten and S. Mauw. Delayed choice: an operator for joining Message Sequence Charts. In *Formal Description Techniques*, pages 340–354, 1995.
2. H. Ben-Abdallah and S. Leue. Syntactic detection of process divergence and non-local choice in Message Sequence Charts. In *Tools and Algorithms for the Construction and Analysis of Systems*, number 1217 in LNCS, pages 259–274, 1997.
3. H. Brinksma. Constraint-oriented specification in a constructive specification technique. In *REX Workshop on Stepwise Refinement of Distributed Systems*, volume 430 of *LNCS*, pages 130–152, 1990.
4. A.G. Engels, S. Mauw, and M.A. Reniers. A hierarchy of communication models for message sequence charts. *Science of Computer Programming*, 44:253–292, 2002.
5. M.G. Gouda and Y.T. Yu. Synthesis of communicating finite-state machines with guaranteed progress. *IEEE Transactions on Communications*, COM-32(7):779–788, July 1984.
6. E.L. Gunter, A. Muscholl, and D.A. Peled. Compositional message sequence charts. In *7th Conference on Tools and Algorithms for the Construction and Analysis of Systems*, volume 2031 of *LNCS*, pages 496–511. Springer, 2001.
7. L. Hélouët. Some pathological message sequence charts and how to detect them. In *10th SDL Forum*, number 2078 in LNCS, pages 348–364, June 2001.
8. J.G. Henriksen, M. Mukund, K. Narayan Kumar, and P. S. Thiagarajan. Towards a theory of regular MSC languages. BRICS Report RS-99-52, Department of Computer Science, Aarhus University, Denmark, 1999.
9. G.J. Holzmann. The model checker Spin. *IEEE Transactions on Software Engineering*, 23(5):279–295, May 1997.
10. International Standards Organization. *Information Processing Systems – Open Systems Interconnection – LOTOS - A Formal Description Technique Based on the Temporal Ordering of Observational Behaviour*, 1989. ISO 8807:1989.
11. ITU-T. Message sequence chart. Recommendation Z.120, ITU-T, 2000.
12. F. Khendek, G. Robert, G. Butler, and P. Grogono. Implementability of message sequence charts. In *Workshop on SDL and MSC*. SDL Forum Society, 1998.
13. M. Lohrey. Realizability of high-level message sequence charts: closing the gaps. *Theoretical Computer Science*, 309(1–3):529–554, 2003.
14. P. Madhusudan and B. Meenakshi. Beyond message sequence graphs. In *21st Conference on Foundations of Software Technology and Theoretical Computer Science*, volume 2245 of *LNCS*, pages 256–267, 2001.
15. A.J. Mooij and N. Goga. Dealing with non-local choice in IEEE 1073.2's standard for remote control. In *SAM 2004: SDL And MSC*, LNCS 3319. To appear.
16. H. Muccini. Detecting implied scenarios analyzing non-local branching choices. In *Fundamental Approaches to Software Engineering*, number 2621 in LNCS, pages 372–386. Springer Verlag, 2003.
17. M.A. Reniers. *Message Sequence Chart: Syntax and Semantics*. PhD thesis, Technische Universiteit Eindhoven, June 1999.

18. S. Uchitel. *Incremental Elaboration of Scenario-Based Specifications and Behaviour Models Using Implied Scenarios.* PhD thesis, Faculty of Engineering of the University of London, February 2003.
19. S. Uchitel, J. Kramer, and J. Magee. Detecting implied scenarios in message sequence chart specifications. In *Proceedings of the 8th European software engineering conference*, pages 74–82. ACM Press, 2001.
20. S. Uchitel, J. Kramer, and J. Magee. Synthesis of behavioral models from scenarios. *IEEE Transactions on Software Engineering*, 29(2):99–115, February 2003.

Coverage Criteria for Testing of Object Interactions in Sequence Diagrams

Atanas Rountev, Scott Kagan, and Jason Sawin

Ohio State University
{rountev, kagan, sawin}@cse.ohio-state.edu

Abstract. This work defines several control-flow coverage criteria for testing the interactions among a set of collaborating objects. The criteria are based on UML sequence diagrams that are reverse-engineered from the code under test. The sequences of messages in the diagrams are used to define the coverage goals for the family of criteria, in a manner that generalizes traditional testing techniques such as branch coverage and path coverage. We also describe a run-time analysis that gathers coverage measurements for each criterion. To compare the criteria, we propose an approach that estimates the testing effort required to satisfy each criterion, using analysis of the complexity of the underlying sequence diagrams. The criteria were investigated experimentally on a set of realistic Java components. The results of this study compare different approaches for testing of object interactions and provide insights for testers and for builders of test coverage tools.

1 Introduction

Object-oriented software presents a variety of new challenges for testing, compared to testing for procedural software [1]. For example, programs contain complex interactions among sets of collaborating objects from different classes. It is not sufficient to test a class in isolation—testing the interactions between instances of different classes is of critical importance [2, 1, 3]. A variety of techniques can be employed to test different aspects of object interactions. Several existing approaches for such testing [3, 4, 5, 6, 7] are based on *UML interaction diagrams*. UML defines two kinds of semantically-equivalent interaction diagrams: sequence diagrams and collaboration diagrams [8, 9]. In this paper we discuss only sequence diagrams; Figure 1a contains an example of such a diagram.

A sequence diagram shows the messages that are exchanged among several objects, as well as other control-flow information (e.g., if-then conditions that guard messages). Such diagrams capture important aspects of object interactions, and can be naturally used to define testing goals that must be achieved during testing. The testing requirements are related to certain elements of the diagrams. For example, it may be required to exercise all relationships of the form "object X send message m to object Y". More aggressive approaches consider not only individual messages, but also *sequences of messages*—for example,

M. Cerioli (Ed.): FASE 2005, LNCS 3442, pp. 289–304, 2005.

all possible start-to-end message sequences in a diagram. Section 2 discusses in detail the previous work that proposes such approaches.

With the help of reverse-engineering tools, sequence diagrams can be extracted from existing code. Design recovery through reverse engineering is necessary during iterative development [10] and for evolving systems in which the design documents have not been updated to reflect code changes. Commercial tools already provide some functionality for such reverse engineering, both for class diagrams and for sequence diagrams. In addition, several static analyses proposed in the literature have considered various aspects of reverse engineering of sequence diagrams [11, 12, 13, 14]. Reverse-engineered sequence diagrams are a natural source of program-based coverage criteria for testing of object interactions. If a reverse-engineering tool is used to construct a sequence diagram, a coverage tool can use this diagram as a basis for defining and measuring of coverage metrics during subsequent testing. Such a diagram reflects precisely the up-to-date state of the code, and therefore can be used for early and frequent testing.

The first goal of our work is to define *a family of coverage criteria for object interactions* based on reverse-engineered sequence diagrams. The criteria are generalizations of traditional control-flow criteria such as branch coverage and path coverage, and are defined in terms of the sequences of messages exchanged among a set of collaborating objects. Some of these criteria have appeared in previous work. However, there have been no attempts to define a unifying framework for such criteria and to use it for systematic investigation and comparison of different techniques for testing of object interactions. The work presented in this paper defines such a framework. At the center of the proposed approach is a data structure which we refer to as *interprocedural restricted control-flow graph* (IRCFG). This data structure represents in a compact manner the set of message sequences in a sequence diagram, and can be easily constructed as part of the reverse engineering of such a diagram. The IRCFG allows us to define systematically the family of test coverage criteria.

Our second goal is to design *a run-time analysis* based on the IRCFG. The run-time analysis observes the behavior of the code while tests are being executed, and gathers coverage measurements with respect to each criterion. Automated coverage measurements are essential for any program-based coverage criterion, and the run-time analysis is an important complement to the criteria.

The third goal of this work is to perform a comparison of the different criteria. We aim to obtain an estimate of the effort required to achieve high coverage for each criterion, and to compare these estimates. For each criterion c, we propose an approach which determines a lower bound p_c on the number of start-to-end IRCFG paths that guarantee the highest possible coverage for c. If for a given sequence diagram the value of p_c is very high, this indicates that the effort required to achieve high coverage for c may be prohibitive, and therefore weaker criteria should be used. Having such estimates provides valuable insights about the differences between the criteria, which in turn could allow better planning and management of the testing process.

The fourth goal of the work is to perform an experimental study that determines the values of p_c for different criteria on a set of realistic software components. Our experiments use 18 components from various Java libraries. The comparison of p_c across a diverse set of components provides insights into the inherent relationships between the different coverage criteria, and into the effort required to achieve high coverage for these criteria.

2   Testing and Sequence Diagrams

Several testing approaches proposed in the literature consider testing of object interactions based on sequence diagrams (or the semantically-equivalent collaboration diagrams). Binder [3] considers the set of all start-to-end paths in a sequence diagram, and defines a criterion for choosing a subset of paths to be covered during testing. The criterion requires coverage that is similar to traditional branch coverage: each decision outcome within the diagram must be covered by at least one start-to-end path. For example, if a message is sent under some condition c, the set of test cases should ensure that at least one path covers the case when c is true, and at least one path covers the case when c is false. We will refer to this criterion as the all-branches criterion; a precise definition of this approach is presented later in the paper.

Consider the sequence diagram in Figure 1a. This diagram represents the set of possible behaviors when message m1 is sent to object a. Conditions c1, c2, and c3 guard certain messages: for example, m6 is sent to b only if c3 is true. A start-to-end path in the diagram can be represented by the temporal sequence of messages that are exchanged between objects. For example, one such path is (m1,m2,m4,m6,m2,m3,m4). To satisfy the all-branches criterion, testing must execute enough start-to-end paths to cover all conditional behavior. One possible set of paths that satisfies this requirement is $p_1 = (\text{m1}, \text{m2}, \text{m3}, \text{m4}, \text{m5})$, $p_2 = (\text{m1}, \text{m2}, \text{m4}, \text{m6}, \text{m2}, \text{m3}, \text{m4})$, and $p_3 = (\text{m1}, \text{m2}, \text{m4}, \text{m6}, \text{m2}, \text{m4}, \text{m5})$.

Other testing approaches consider not only individual messages and their guarding conditions, but also entire sequences of messages. Jorgensen and Erickson [15] consider testing that exercises method-message paths and atomic system functions. A method-message path is a sequence of events of the form "method m_1 invokes method m_2; during this invocation, m_2 invokes m_3; during this invocation, m_3 invokes $m_4 \ldots$". For example, in Figure 1a, the left-to-right sequence of messages (m1,m6,m2,m3) corresponds to a message-method path. In the subsequent discussion, we will use the more common term *call chain* to refer to such a sequence. An atomic system function, as defined in [15], is equivalent to the set of all start-to-end message sequences in a sequence diagram.

Abdurazik and Offutt [4] consider collaboration diagrams created during design, and define an approach for static checking and testing of the interactions among the diagram objects. Their technique requires coverage of start-to-end sequences of messages in the diagrams. Basanieri and Bertolino [16] define a testing approach that considers all message sequences in a sequence diagram and applies the category-partition method to choose the appropriate test data for exercising these sequences. Fraikin and Leonhardt [6] describe the SeDiTeC tool for testing based on sequence diagrams. Their approach requires coverage of all possible sequences of messages in a set of related sequence diagrams. The diagrams are augmented with information about expected input and output values for method invocations, and these values are checked during test execution.

Briand and Labiche [5] consider functional system testing based on use cases and sequence diagrams (or collaboration diagrams) constructed during object-oriented analysis. Each scenario within a use case corresponds to a start-to-end path in the sequence diagram for that use case. They construct a regular expression that represents all start-to-end message sequences (i.e., all scenarios), and require coverage of all such sequences during testing. Wu et al. [7] propose an approach for testing of component-based software which uses UML collaboration/sequence diagrams and statecharts. One of the suggested techniques requires testing of all possible sequences of messages in a collaboration diagram.

3   Criteria for Reverse-Engineered Sequence Diagrams

The testing approaches discussed in the previous section are based on interaction diagrams that are constructed during analysis or design, before the corresponding implementation code is written. In general, there is no guarantee that design activities will produce a complete set of diagrams for all interactions in the system. An incomplete set of diagrams is a weak basis for comprehensive testing of object interactions. Another potential problem is that during code construction, the implementation often diverges from the original design. For example, in iterative development, tools for reverse engineering of design artifacts from the code are often necessary to make the design documents consistent with the actual implementation.

This paper considers sequence diagrams that are constructed automatically from existing code, using static analyses for reverse engineering [11, 12, 13, 14]. Problems due to incomplete or outdated diagrams can be avoided with the use of reverse-engineered diagrams. Such diagrams can be constructed automatically from the latest version of the code, and for all relevant parts of the system. Furthermore, since the diagrams are created from the code, a coverage tool can easily determine what kinds of code instrumentation will be necessary in order to obtain run-time coverage metrics during test execution.

The approaches from Section 2 (with the exception of Binder's work [3]) have a common element: the requirement that all message sequences in an interaction diagram should be covered. This requirement is either used as a stand-alone coverage criterion, or as part of more general testing goals. When considered in the context of reverse-engineered sequence diagrams (rather than diagrams created during analysis or design), the requirement for all-paths coverage raises concerns similar to the ones from traditional CFG path coverage. Typically, CFG path coverage is considered to be infeasible in practice due to the potentially large number of paths. A similar question can be asked for testing of object interactions: is it practical to require coverage of all start-to-end paths in a reverse-engineered sequence diagram? In fact, the reason Binder considers the weaker all-branches criterion is because, as he states, "the number of paths can easily reach astronomical numbers" [3].

This section presents a formal definition of three coverage criteria that are weaker versions of the all-paths criterion; one of them is the all-branches criterion. The criteria provide several options with different tradeoffs between testing effort and test comprehensiveness. Having such options is important in the presence of resource constraints for the testing process. Depending on these constraints, different criteria for systematic testing of object interactions can be employed. The criteria are generalizations of traditional control-flow-based criteria such as CFG branch coverage and CFG path coverage. We first define the notion of an *interprocedural restricted control-flow graph* (IRCFG), which can be thought of as the equivalent of a CFG for a sequence diagram. Figure 1b shows the IRCFG for the diagram from Figure 1a. Paths through the IRCFG correspond to sequences of messages in a sequence diagram. The proposed coverage criteria for object interactions are then defined formally based on the IRCFG.

3.1   Interprocedural Restricted Control-Flow Graph

An IRCFG contains a set of *restricted CFGs* (RCFGs), together with edges which connect these RCFGs. Each RCFG corresponds to a particular method and is similar to the CFG for that method, except that it is restricted to the flow of control that is relevant to message sending. In Figure 1b, each RCFG is shown within a rectangular box. For example, the top RCFG in the figure corresponds to method m1, which is invoked as a result of sending message m1 to object a. A node in the RCFG for some method m represents a method invocation in the body of m. For example, the node labeled m2 in the top RCFG in Figure 1b corresponds to some call to m2 in the body of method m1. In the reverse-engineered diagram from Figure 1a, this call is represented by the message m2 sent from a to c. The RCFGs also contain artificial nodes start and end. The start node represents the moment when the run-time execution enters the method, and the end node represents the moment when the flow of control returns back to the caller.

RCFG edges, shown with solid arrows in Figure 1b, represent the sequencing relationships between nodes. In Figure 1a, after the execution enters method m1, method m2 is invoked. This is represented by the edge (start,m2) in the RCFG for m1. After this invocation of m2 completes, either m6 is invoked by m1, or m1 completes without invoking m6. These two possibilities are represented by RCFG edges (m2,m6) and (m2,end) respectively. Sometimes we will refer to RCFG edges as *intraprocedural edges*. RCFGs are connected with *interprocedural edges*, shown in Figure 1b with dashed arrows. An interprocedural edge connects an RCFG node n with a start node that corresponds to some method that could be invoked by n. Note that due to polymorphism, there could be multiple interprocedural edges coming out of n. The interprocedural edges define a tree in which the nodes are RCFGs; we will refer to that tree as the *RCFG tree*.

Clearly, all information in the IRCFG is entirely based on the structure of the corresponding sequence diagram. Since we consider sequence diagrams that are

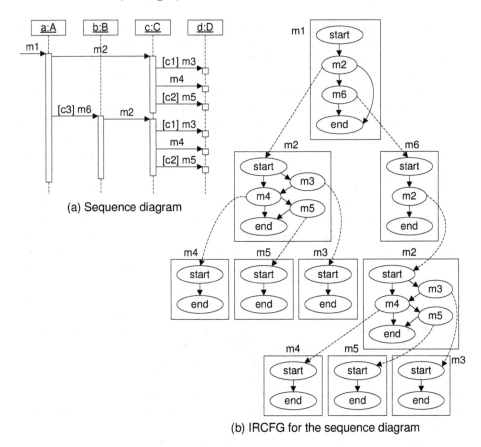

(a) Sequence diagram

(b) IRCFG for the sequence diagram

Fig. 1. Sample sequence diagram and the corresponding IRCFG

constructed from existing code using some reverse-engineering static analysis, it should be straightforward to construct the IRCFG by augmenting the static analysis. Our implementation (described later) uses this approach: it extends an existing reverse-engineering analysis to construct the IRCFG.

3.2   Coverage Criteria

The IRCFG introduced in the previous section serves two purposes. First, it allows precise formal definition of coverage criteria for the corresponding sequence diagram. Second, it is the basis for a run-time analysis that measures the coverage achieved during testing. In this section we focus on the definition of the criteria; the run-time analysis is outlined in Section 4.

The all-paths criterion, which we will refer to as *All-IRCFG-Paths*, requires coverage of the entire set of complete IRCFG paths. Each complete path is a start-to-end traversal of the IRCFG. An example of such a path is

$$(\text{start}_{m1}, m2, \text{start}_{m2}, m4, \text{start}_{m4}, \text{end}_{m4}, m5, \text{start}_{m5}, \text{end}_{m5}, \text{end}_{m2}, \text{end}_{m1})$$

Let p be a sequence of RCFG nodes in which the first and the last node are **start** and **end** in the root RCFG, respectively. We will refer to p as a *complete IRCFG path* if it has the following property. Consider some node n_i in p, and let R be the enclosing RCFG for n_i. If the next node after n_i in the sequence p is node n_j, then one of the following must hold:

Case 1. If n_i is the start node of R, there must exist an intraprocedural RCFG edge (n_i, n_j) in R

Case 2. If n_i is not the start or the end node of R, then
- there exists an interprocedural edge (n_i, n_j), where n_j is the start node of some child of R in the RCFG tree, or
- there are no interprocedural edges starting at n_i, and (n_i, n_j) is an intraprocedural edge in R

Case 3. If n_i is the end node of R, then the parent of R in the RCFG tree contains an intraprocedural edge (n_k, n_j), and there is an interprocedural edge from n_k to the start node of R

The second alternative in Case 2 represents a situation when the body of the method invoked by n_i is not included in the diagram. For example, it is common to "stop" the reverse-engineered diagrams at library methods; in this case there is no interprocedural edge coming out of n_i.

It is important to note that not all complete IRCFG paths necessarily correspond to feasible run-time executions. Of course, this is a standard issue for any program-based criterion that uses some abstracted model of the tested code. For example, in traditional CFG path coverage, some CFG paths may be infeasible and complete coverage may not be possible. Even though it is impossible to completely eliminate infeasibility, there is a wide range of effective static analysis techniques that can reduce significantly the degree of infeasibility in program models such as CFGs and IRCFGs. For example, points-to analyses (e.g., [17]) can produce very precise calling-context-sensitive information about the calling relationships between methods, and branch correlation analysis (e.g., [18]) can identify certain classes of infeasible CFG paths. Static analyses for reverse engineering of sequence diagrams can employ such techniques to identify infeasible subpaths in the diagrams and in their corresponding IRCFGs. The investigation of this issue is beyond the scope of this paper, and the subsequent discussion assumes that all IRCFG paths are feasible.

An interesting question is how many complete IRCFG paths exist in a given IRCFG. Consider the example in Figure 1b. The invocation of m2 from m1 could lead to four distinct IRCFG subpaths. Similarly, the invocation of m6 from m1 may proceed along four distinct subpaths. Therefore, there are 16 complete IRCFG paths in which m1 calls m2 and m6. When we also consider the case in which m6 is skipped, the total number of paths becomes 20. This example illustrates one fundamental concern with the *All-IRCFG-Paths* criterion: the number of paths could easily grow exponentially.

Next, consider all RCFG paths in an IRCFG. An *RCFG path* is a sequence of RCFG nodes within some RCFG R, beginning with the start node of R and finishing with the end node of R. Each pair of adjacent nodes in the path must correspond to an intraprocedural edge in R. For example, for the root RCFG in Figure 1b, there are two such paths: (start,m2,end) and (start,m2,m6,end). A complete IRCFG path could cover several RCFG paths. For example, consider again path

$$(\text{start}_{m1}, \text{m2}, \text{start}_{m2}, \text{m4}, \text{start}_{m4}, \text{end}_{m4}, \text{m5}, \text{start}_{m5}, \text{end}_{m5}, \text{end}_{m2}, \text{end}_{m1})$$

This complete path covers the following RCFG paths: $(\text{start}_{m1}, \text{m2}, \text{end}_{m1})$ in the root RCFG, $(\text{start}_{m2}, \text{m4}, \text{m5}, \text{end}_{m2})$ in the left child of the root, and the trivial start-end paths in the two leftmost leaves.

The *All-RCFG-Paths* criterion requires testing to exercise enough complete IRCFG paths to cover all RCFG paths. In Figure 1b, coverage for this criterion can be achieved with five (but not fewer) complete IRCFG paths. Coverage of all RCFG paths is similar to traditional CFG path coverage. Of course, unlike a CFG, an RCFG represents only a subset of the flow of control within a method (e.g., conditions that are irrelevant for calls are ignored). Furthermore, the criterion takes into account the calling context of a method. For example, for m2 there are two RCFGs in Figure 1b—corresponding to call chains (m1,m2) and (m1,m6,m2)—and each start-to-end path in each of the two RCFGs should be covered.

Another potential source of exponential growth is the fact that the number of RCFG paths could be exponential in the size of the RCFG. We can eliminate this source by defining a criterion that requires coverage of all RCFG edges rather than all RCFG paths. This *All-RCFG-Branches* criterion is equivalent to Binder's approach discussed in Section 2. For our running example, the criterion can be satisfied with three complete IRCFG paths.

It is possible to define an additional simplification that leads to an even weaker (and easier to achieve) criterion. Consider the case when the tree contains several RCFGs for the same method, and each graph is associated with different calling contexts for the corresponding method. If we require coverage of each RCFG edge regardless of the calling context, this defines a coverage criterion that is a simplified version of *All-RCFG-Branches*. In essence, we consider each unique RCFG edge regardless of how many times it occurs in the IRCFG, and require at least one occurrence to be covered by a complete IRCFG path. The new criterion will be denoted by *All-Unique-Branches*. For Figure 1b, this criterion can be satisfied by two complete IRCFG paths—for example,

$$(\text{start}_{m1}, \text{m2}, \text{start}_{m2}, \text{m3}, \text{start}_{m3}, \text{end}_{m3}, \text{m4}, \text{start}_{m4}, \text{end}_{m4}, \text{m5}, \text{start}_{m5},$$
$$\text{end}_{m5}, \text{end}_{m2}, \text{end}_{m1}) \text{ and } (\text{start}_{m1}, \text{m2}, \text{start}_{m2}, \text{m4}, \text{start}_{m4}, \text{end}_{m4}, \text{end}_{m2},$$
$$\text{m6}, \text{start}_{m6}, \text{m2}, \text{start}_{m2}, \text{m4}, \text{start}_{m4}, \text{end}_{m4}, \text{end}_{m2}, \text{end}_{m6}, \text{end}_{m1})$$

The preceding discussion defines four different coverage criteria based on the IRCFG. Clearly, these criteria form a subsumption hierarchy. (Criterion c_i *subsumes* criterion c_j if complete coverage for c_i also achieves complete coverage for c_j.) The criteria were defined under the assumption that each RCFG is acyclic. If an RCFG contains a cycle, the number of RCFG paths is of course infinite. Due to space limitations, the handling of this case is discussed in detail elsewhere [19].

4   Run-Time Coverage Analysis

This section defines a coverage analysis for *All-RCFG-Paths*, *All-RCFG-Branches*, and *All-Unique-Branches*. We are in the process of building a coverage tool for these criteria, and this paper describes the design of the run-time analysis algorithm used in the tool. For brevity, the description outlines the ideas behind the algorithm without providing an in-depth discussion of all relevant details. At present we have no plans to implement coverage tracking for *All-IRCFG-Paths*, because the experimental results presented later in the paper raise questions about the practicality of this criterion.

The code instrumentation required to perform the run-time tracking is fairly straightforward. Immediately before each call site, we insert instrumentation to identify the method that is about to be invoked. We also insert instrumentation immediately after each call site, in order to know at run time that the invocation has just completed. The run-time events triggered by the instrumentation are used to traverse the IRCFG while the tests are being executed. The analysis maintains a "current" RCFG node which reflects the current state of the run-time execution. Immediately before a call site is about to make a call, the corresponding interprocedural edge in the IRCFG is traversed downwards and the current node is changed to the start node of the RCFG for the called method. The execution within the callee method proceeds until the flow of control reaches the exit of that method. At this point of time, the current node in the coverage analysis is **end** in the RCFG for the callee. The return to the caller triggers an instrumentation event which shows that the call has just completed. As a result, the current node becomes the corresponding RCFG node in the caller method.

Based on the current RCFG node in the analysis, it is easy to compute coverage metrics for *All-RCFG-Branches* and *All-Unique-Branches*. To compute path coverage for *All-RCFG-Paths*, we use a variation of an approach for intraprocedural path profiling proposed by Ball and Larus [20]. Their technique assigns a unique integer path id to each distinct start-to-end path in a CFG. Instrumentation at CFG edges is used to update the value of a run-time integer accumulator. At CFG exit the accumulator contains the id of the executed path. We can use a similar technique for RCFG path tracking: each RCFG has an associated accumulator, which is initialized every time the flow of control enters the start node of the graph.

5   Minimum Number of Paths

In this section we define techniques for estimating the testing effort inherent in each of the four criteria discussed earlier. Given some IRCFG, for each criterion c we want to compute *a lower bound on the number of complete IRCFG paths* whose run-time coverage would guarantee the best possible coverage for c. This bound is an indication of how many complete IRCFG paths a tester may need to consider for coverage in order to satisfy c.

IRCFG Paths. First, what is the total number of complete IRCFG paths in a given IRCFG? The computation of the number of paths can be done in bottom-up fashion on the RCFG tree. Starting from the leaves, we can compute the number of IRCFG subpaths in each subtree. Consider some RCFG R in the tree, and suppose that we have already computed the number of IRCFG subpaths for each of the subtrees rooted at R's children. To compute the number of subpaths for the subtree rooted at R, we can traverse R in topological sort order. During the traversal, when we visit an RCFG node n in R, we compute the number $p(n)$ of all IRCFG subpaths from the start node of R to n. In the beginning of the traversal, $p(start_R) = 1$ for the start node of R. For each visited node n, we have

$$p(n) = \sum_{(n',n) \in R} p(n') \times q(n')$$

Here n' is an intraprocedural predecessor of n and $q(n') = \sum_{R'} p(end_{R'})$ where the sum is over all RCFG R' that are called by n' (i.e., there is an interprocedural edge from n' to the start node of R'). In the case when there are no such R', let $q(n') = 1$.

In this computation, for each intraprocedural edge (n', n) in R, we consider the number of IRCFG subpaths $p(n')$ from the start of R to n'. For each RCFG R' that is called by n', we examine the value $p(end_{R'})$ computed earlier for the end node of R'. There are a total of $p(n') \times p(end_{R'})$ IRCFG subpaths that start at the beginning of R, lead to n', continue downwards into R', and eventually return back to n in R. The total number of complete IRCFG paths is the value $p(n)$ computed for the end node of the root RCFG.

RCFG Branches. To find the minimum number of complete IRCFG paths that contain all RCFG edges, we define an integer linear programming problem. Consider some hypothetical set S of complete IRCFG paths. For each RCFG edge e, let the integer value $v(e) \geq 0$ represent the number of times e is covered by all paths in S (i.e., the edge frequency of e in S). For each call node n in the IRCFG, we define equation **E1**: $\sum_{e \in In(n)} v(e) = \sum_{e \in Out(n)} v(e)$. Here $In(n)$ denotes the set of all intraprocedural edges (n', n), and $Out(n)$ is the set of all intraprocedural edges (n, n''). Equation **E1** shows that the number of times n is entered by paths in S is equal to the number of times n is exited.

For each call node n that has outgoing interprocedural edges, we also need to model the execution of the corresponding children RCFGs. This is done by equation **E2**: $\sum_{e \in In(n)} v(e) = \sum_{e \in Call(n)} v(e)$. Here $Call(n)$ denotes the set of all interprocedural edges $(n, start)$ entering the children RCFGs. Equation **E2** encodes the fact that the number of times n is covered by S is equal to the number of times the children graphs are covered by S. We also model the execution frequencies of the edges coming out of each start node, using equation **E3**: $v(e') = \sum_{e \in Out(start)} v(e)$, where e' is the single interprocedural edge entering $start$.

For the *All-RCFG-Branches* criterion, we define a system that combines **E1**, **E2**, and **E3** with the following equation: $v(e) \geq 1$ for each edge e in each RCFG. Given this system, we solve a linear programming problem that minimizes the objective function $\sum_{e \in Out(start_{root})} v(e)$, where $start_{root}$ is the start node of the root RCFG. This value represents the total number of times the start node is traversed by S, which is equal to the size of S. Let p^* be the minimum value for the objective function, as computed by a linear programming solver. It can be proven that p^* is the minimum number of complete IRCFG paths that contain all RCFG edges.

Unique Branches. When considering unique RCFG edges, **E1**, **E2**, and **E3** are combined with equation $v(e_1) + v(e_2) + \ldots + v(e_k) \geq 1$. Here e_i are RCFG edges that are equivalent: they belong to different RCFGs for the same method, and all of them represent transitions between equivalent pairs of RCFG nodes. It can be proven that a linear programming problem with the same objective function as before produces the minimum number of complete IRCFG paths that contain each unique RCFG edge.

RCFG Paths. Recall that an RCFG path is a start-to-end sequence of intraprocedural edges inside an RCFG. Let S_R denote the set of all such paths in some RCFG R. For each edge $e \in R$, let $w(e)$ be the number of times e occurs in S_R. Suppose we combine **E1**, **E2**, and **E3** with the following equation: $v(e) \geq w(e)$ for each edge e in each RCFG. Using the same objective function as before, it can be proven that a linear programming solver will produce the minimum number of complete IRCFG paths that cover all RCFG paths.

To construct the system, we need to compute $w(e)$. Given an RCFG R, the values of $w(e)$ for all $e \in R$ can be computed in time linear in the size of R. First, a topological sort order traversal is used to compute the number $p'(n)$ of paths from the start node of R to any node $n \in R$. Clearly, $p'(n)$ is equal to the sum of $p'(m)$ for all predecessor edges $(m, n) \in R$. Similarly, using a traversal in reverse topological sort order, we can compute the number $p''(n)$ of paths from n to the end node of R. For an edge $e = (n_i, n_j)$, the value $w(e) = p'(n_i) \times p''(n_j)$.

6   Experimental Study

The approach described in this paper was implemented as part of the ongoing work on the RED tool for reverse engineering of sequence diagrams. The goal of this tool is to provide high-quality support for reverse engineering of UML sequence diagrams from Java code and for testing based on such diagrams. The tool uses several static analyses, including call graph construction [21, 17], call chain analysis [22], control flow analysis [13], and object naming analysis [14]. IRCFG construction was implemented as a straightforward extension of these existing analyses. The lower bounds described in Section 5 were computed with the lp_solve linear programming solver (groups.yahoo.com/group/lp_solve).

The 18 subject components used in the study are listed in Table 1. The components come from a variety of domains and typically represent parts of reusable libraries. Columns labeled "Methods" show the number of non-abstract methods in each component. For each component, we considered the set of methods that would normally be used to access the functionality provided by that component.

Table 1. Subject components

Component	Methods	IRCFGs	Component	Methods	IRCFGs
checked	15	3	pushback	20	11
bigdecimal	33	26	vector	38	22
gzip	41	11	boundaries	74	13
io	86	12	zip	118	38
decimal	136	30	date	136	37
calendar	152	60	collator	157	17
message	176	59	math	241	156
jflex	313	93	sql	350	22
mindbright	488	161	bytecode	625	333

For each such method we constructed an IRCFG starting at the method (i.e., the root RCFG was for this method). RED uses a parameter k to control the length of call chains in the reverse-engineered diagrams. Given some k, the number of messages in call chains is restricted to be at most k—that is, the depth of the corresponding RCFG tree is at most k, where the depth for the root is 0. We ran all experiments with the value $k = 3$. RCFGs were created only for component methods: if a component method called code external to the component, the corresponding RCFG node did not have a child RCFG. This restriction is part of the design of RED, and it allows a tool user to define a "scope of interest" and to ignore code that is outside of this scope. Columns "IRCFGs" show the number of IRCFGs that had non-trivial flow of control: at least one RCFG node had two or more outgoing edges. The total number of such IRCFGs for all components was 1104.

For each IRCFG counted in columns "IRCFGs" in Table 1, we determined the minimum number of complete IRCFG paths for the different criteria, as described in Section 5. Table 2 shows the distribution of these numbers for the entire set of 1104 IRCFGs. Each column shows the percentage of IRCFGs for which the minimum number of complete IRCFG paths was in the corresponding range. For example, the last column shows the percentage of IRCFGs that had a minimum number of complete paths greater than 1000.

The results from Table 2 lead to some interesting observations. In a substantial number of cases, the number of complete IRCFG paths is rather large. In fact, for several IRCFGs this number is very large (e.g., more than a million). Thus, even for the limited diagram depth of $k = 3$, and with the limited scope of the diagrams to component-only code, in many cases the *All-IRCFG-Paths* criterion is clearly impossible to achieve in practice. These results confirm experimentally Binder's intuition [3] that the number of all start-to-end paths may be too large. The use of less demanding coverage criteria is one way to address this problem. Our results indicate that the three other criteria require less testing effort, and therefore are useful alternatives to *All-IRCFG-Paths*. For example, for *All-Unique-Branches*, almost all IRCFGs have a minimum number of paths that is ≤ 100, and for half of the IRCFGs this number is ≤ 5. The results suggest that each criterion provides a different tradeoff between testing effort and test

Table 2. Minimum number of IRCFG paths

Criterion	1–5	6–10	11–100	101–1000	>1000
IRCFG-Paths	29.1%	10.3%	16.8%	10.2%	33.6%
RCFG-Paths	40.8%	14.9%	27.4%	2.6%	14.2%
RCFG-Branches	45.5%	19.6%	31.9%	2.9%	0.2%
Unique-Branches	49.9%	22.1%	27.4%	0.5%	0.0%

Table 3. Reduction in the number of paths

Ratio	1	(1, 2]	(2, 10]	(10, 10^3]	$> 10^3$
$\frac{IRCFG-Paths}{RCFG-Paths}$	35.1%	13.0%	12.7%	20.2%	19.0%
$\frac{RCFG-Paths}{RCFG-Branches}$	51.3%	26.2%	7.6%	13.2%	1.7%
$\frac{RCFG-Branches}{Unique-Branches}$	65.6%	23.5%	10.8%	0.2%	0.0%

comprehensiveness, and therefore a tester may benefit from having tool support for each criterion.

For each IRCFG counted in columns "IRCFGs" in Table 1, we computed the ratios between the minimum number of paths for different pairs of criteria, as shown in the first column of Table 3. Each of the remaining columns in that table shows the percentage of IRCFGs for which the ratio was in the corresponding range. For example, the last number of the first row in the table shows that for 19% out of the 1104 IRCFGs, the minimum number of complete IRCFG paths for *All-RCFG-Paths* is more than 1000 times smaller than the total number of complete IRCFG paths. The results in Table 3 are an indication of the reduction of testing effort when replacing a stronger criterion with a weaker one. All pairs of criteria exhibit substantial degrees of reduction, and the most significant change is from *All-IRCFG-Paths* to *All-RCFG-Paths*.

The results of the study can be summarized as follows. First, there is strong indication that the number of start-to-end paths in reverse-engineered sequence diagrams is often quite large, and therefore simpler (and easier to achieve) criteria should be available as options to testers. Second, the remaining three criteria appear to be good candidates for such options because they provide different tradeoffs for testing effort and comprehensiveness.

7 Related Work

As discussed in Section 2, several testing approaches are based on interaction diagrams that are constructed during analysis or design [3, 15, 4, 16, 6, 5, 7]. Our work applies similar techniques to diagrams that are constructed automatically from existing code. We define a spectrum of coverage criteria that could provide a tester with several options for the targeted test coverage.

The IRCFG used in our approach is based on two popular data structures: interprocedural CFG [23] and calling context tree [24]. An interprocedural CFG contains the CFGs for individual procedures, as well as edges connecting these CFGs. Unlike an IRCFG, an interprocedural CFG contains nodes for all statements in the procedures, and the edges between the individual CFGs do not form a tree. In a calling context tree, a node represents a procedure and the chain from the node to the tree root represents a call chain for that procedure. Similarly, the RCFGs in our approach form a tree that represents call chains.

Binder's all-branches approach [3] is based on a flow-graph representation of a sequence diagram which is similar to an RCFG. The discussion of the approach is limited to a single method, while our IRCFG combines information about several methods and their calling relationships. Briand and Labiche [5] represent an UML activity diagram with a directed graph in which paths correspond to sequences of use case that are considered for testing. The sequence diagram for a use case is represented by a regular expressions that captures the possible sequences of messages in the diagram. In order to automate the construction of the regular expression, the authors suggest modeling the sequence diagram with a labeled graph in which labels correspond to messages, similarly to our use of the RCFGs.

The traversal of the RCFG tree during the run-time analysis is similar to the dynamic profiling analyses from [24, 22]: in both cases, the sequence of methods on the run-time call stack is "simulated" by the analysis. The coverage of intra-RCFG paths uses the efficient techniques for path profiling from [20], with the appropriate modifications to ignore statements irrelevant to calls. Melski and Reps [25] present a general approach for interprocedural paths profiling which may be possible to adapt in order to obtain run-time coverage information for complete IRCFG paths.

8   Conclusions and Future Work

This work presents a family of control-flow-based coverage criteria for testing of object interactions in reverse-engineered sequence diagrams, together with a corresponding run-time coverage analysis. The experimental study highlights the inherent difficulty of criteria based on sequences of messages (i.e., path coverage). The study also indicates that less demanding criteria (e.g., based on branch coverage) may be a more practical choice for testing of object interactions. In our future work we plan to measure the coverage for these criteria that is achieved by real-world test suites, and to investigate the test weaknesses exposed by the different coverage statistics.

References

1. Binder, R.: Testing object-oriented software: a survey. Journal of Software Testing, Verification and Reliability **6** (1996) 125–252
2. Perry, D., Kaiser, G.: Adequate testing and object-oriented programming. Journal of Object-Oriented Programming **2** (1990) 13–19

3. Binder, R.: Testing Object-Oriented Systems: Models, Patterns, and Tools. Addison-Wesley (1999)
4. Abdurazik, A., Offutt, J.: Using UML collaboration diagrams for static checking and test generation. In: International Conference on the Unified Modeling Language. (2000) 383–395
5. Briand, L., Labiche, Y.: A UML-based approach to system testing. Journal of Software and Systems Modeling 1 (2002)
6. Fraikin, F., Leonhardt, T.: SeDiTeC—testing based on sequence diagrams. In: International Conference on Automated Software Engineering. (2002) 261–266
7. Wu, Y., Chen, M.H., Offutt, J.: UML-based integration testing for component-based software. In: International Conference on COTS-Based Software Systems. (2003)
8. Booch, G., Rumbaugh, J., Jacobson, I.: The Unified Modeling Language User Guide. Addison-Wesley (1999)
9. Fowler, M.: UML Distilled. 3rd edn. Addison-Wesley (2003)
10. Larman, C.: Applying UML and Patterns. 2nd edn. Prentice Hall (2002)
11. Kollman, R., Gogolla, M.: Capturing dynamic program behavior with UML collaboration diagrams. In: European Conference on Software Maintenance and Reengineering. (2001) 58–67
12. Tonella, P., Potrich, A.: Reverse engineering of the interaction diagrams from C++ code. In: IEEE International Conference on Software Maintenance. (2003) 159–168
13. Rountev, A., Volgin, O., Reddoch, M.: Control flow analysis for reverse engineering of sequence diagrams. Technical Report OSU-CISRC-3/04-TR12, Ohio State University (2004)
14. Rountev, A., Connell, B.H.: Object naming analysis for reverse-engineered sequence diagrams. In: International Conference on Software Engineering. (2005) to appear.
15. Jorgenson, P., Erickson, C.: Object-oriented integration testing. Communications of the ACM 37 (1994) 30–38
16. Basanieri, F., Bertolino, A.: A practical approach to UML-based derivation of integration tests. In: 4th International Quality Week Europe. (2000)
17. Milanova, A., Rountev, A., Ryder, B.G.: Parameterized object sensitivity for points-to analysis for Java. ACM Transactions on Software Engineering and Methodology (2004) to appear.
18. Bodik, R., Gupta, R., Soffa, M.L.: Refining data flow information using infeasible paths. In: ACM SIGSOFT International Symposium on Foundations of Software Engineering. (1997) 361–377
19. Rountev, A., Kagan, S., Sawin, J.: Coverage criteria for testing of object interactions in sequence diagrams. Technical Report OSU-CISRC-12/04-TR68, Ohio State University (2004)
20. Ball, T., Larus, J.: Efficient path profiling. In: IEEE/ACM International Symposium on Microarchitecture. (1996) 46–57
21. Rountev, A., Milanova, A., Ryder, B.G.: Points-to analysis for Java based on annotated constraints. In: Conference on Object-Oriented Programming Systems, Languages, and Applications. (2001) 43–55
22. Rountev, A., Kagan, S., Gibas, M.: Static and dynamic analysis of call chains in Java. In: ACM SIGSOFT International Symposium on Software Testing and Analysis. (2004) 1–11

23. Sharir, M., Pnueli, A.: Two approaches to interprocedural data flow analysis. In Muchnick, S., Jones, N., eds.: Program Flow Analysis: Theory and Applications. Prentice Hall (1981) 189–234
24. Ammons, G., Ball, T., Larus, J.: Exploiting hardware performance counters with flow and context sensitive profiling. In: ACM SIGSOFT Conference on Programming Language Design and Implementation. (1997) 85–96
25. Melski, D., Reps, T.: Interprocedural path profiling. In: International Conference on Compiler Construction. LNCS 1575 (1999) 47–62

Tools for Secure Systems Development with UML: Security Analysis with ATPs

Jan Jürjens* and Pasha Shabalin

Software & Systems Engineering, Dep. of Informatics,
TU Munich, Germany

Abstract. We present tool-support for checking the security requirements associated with UMLsec stereotypes. A framework supports implementing verification routines, based on XMI output of the diagrams from UML CASE tools. Advanced users of the UMLsec approach can use this open-source framework to implement verification routines for the constraints of self-defined stereotypes. We focus on a verification routine that automatically verifies sequence diagrams with cryptographic algorithms for security requirements by using automated theorem provers.

The analysis suite for UMLsec [Jür04] models available at [UML04] is illustrated in Fig. 1. The developer creates a UML 1.5 model and stores it in the XMI 1.2 file format (an upgrade to UML 2.0 is in development). Note that some UML CASE tools do not implement XMI correctly, in which case one might have to correct the format for example with a script. The file is imported into the tool's repository, using the data-binding framework MDR. By using MDR, the framework can handle all UML constructs for which a translation to XMI exists in the relevant DTDs released by the OMG. The tool accesses the model through the JMI interfaces generated by the MDR library. Static checkers parse the model and verify it directly for static requirements. Dynamic checkers translate the relevant fragments of the UML model into the input language of several analysis engines (such as model-checkers and automated theorem provers). That way, the UML models can be analyzed for dynamic requirements, which may be formulated in temporal logic, or potentially using OCL. The analysis engines are spawned by the UML suite as external processes. Their results, and possibly a counter-example in case a problem was found, are delivered back to the error analyzer. For the dynamic checkers, a reference semantics for a simplified fragment of UML exists in [Jür04], which is however not enforced by the framework but at the responsibility of the tool developer, as well as achieving semantic consistency between different tools. The error analyzer uses the information received from both the static checkers and dynamic checkers to produce a text report for the

---

* http://www4.in.tum.de/~juerjens. This work was partially funded by the German Federal Ministry of Education, Science, Research and Technology (BMBF) in the framework of the Verisoft project under grant 01 IS C38. The responsibility for this article lies with the author(s).

M. Cerioli (Ed.): FASE 2005, LNCS 3442, pp. 305–309, 2005.

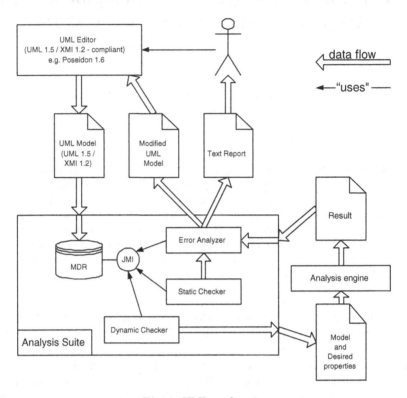

Fig. 1. UML tools suite

developer describing the problems found, and a modified UML model, where the found errors are visualized and, as far as possible, corrected. There currently exist various analysis plugins for the UMLsec tool framework, including:

- a tool-binding to the model-checker Spin to verify cryptographic protocols,
- a tool-binding to first-order logic (FOL) automated theorem provers,
- a test-sequence generation for subsystems, sequence diagrams, activity diagrams, and statechart diagrams, and
- a checker for the static security constraints in UMLsec.

Advanced users of the UMLsec approach can use this framework to implement tools for constraints of self-defined stereotypes. The developer can concentrate on the verification and need not become involved with the input/output interface. A tool only needs to obey the following assumptions made to keep framework and tools simple but retain as much functionality as possible:

- It is given a UML model as input and may load further models if necessary.
- The tool exposes a set of commands which it can execute.
- A command is non-interactive. It receives parameters, executes, and returns its output.

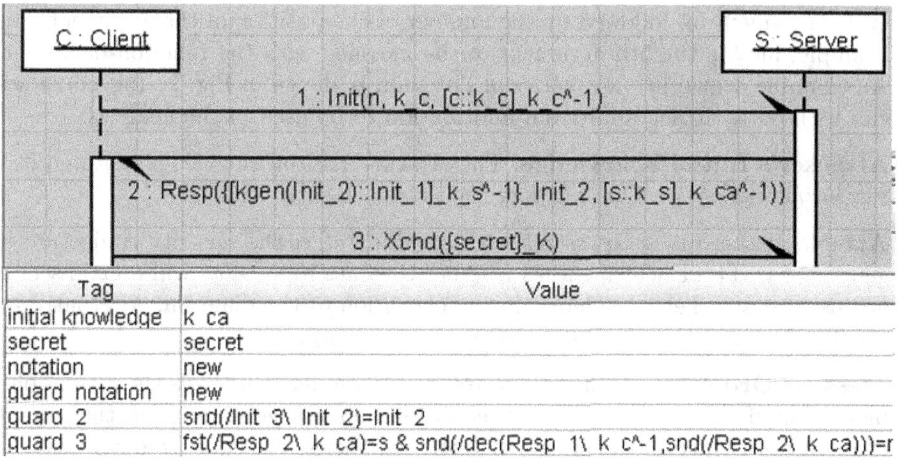
C: Client
S: Server
1 : Init(n, k_c, [c::k_c]_k_c^-1)
2 : Resp({[kgen(Init_2)::Init_1]_k_s^-1}_Init_2, [s::k_s]_k_ca^-1))
3 : Xchd({secret}_K)
Tag
Value
initial knowledge
k ca
secret
secret
notation
new
guard notation
new
guard 2
snd(/Init 3\ Init 2)=Init 2
guard 3
fst(/Resp 2\ k ca)=s & snd(/dec(Resp 1\ k c^-1,snd(/Resp 2\ k ca)))=r

Fig. 2. Example

- Each time the tool is called with a UML model, it may give back a text report and also a UML model.
- The tool can execute several commands consequently; the internal state of the MDR repository and all tools is preserved between command calls.
- The set of commands available for each tool may vary depending on the execution history and current state.

On any Java-enabled platform, the tool can run as a console application (interactive or batch mode), a Java Servlet on a webserver, and a GUI application executed locally. For this, each tool integrated in the UML framework must only implement one common interface. We now focus on a tool which automatically verifies sequence diagrams including cryptographic algorithms for security requirements by using automated theorem provers.

Sequence Diagram Analyzer Using ATPs. The sequence diagram to be analyzed is drawn using a UML CASE tool. The analyzer produces an abstract interpretation of the execution semantics of the diagram, and the security requirement to be verified, as a FOL formula in the TPTP format. TPTP is an input notation used by many automated FOL theorem provers such as e-Setheo and SPASS. More information about the security analysis method can be found in [Jür05]. Here we concentrate on the tool issues. A more comprehensive tutorial can be found at [UML04]. The following notation is supported for cryptographic algorithms: The encryption of the expression E under the key K is written as $\{E\}_K$, the decryption of E using K as $<E>_K$, the signature of E using K as $[E]_K$, the extraction of the signature E using the verification key K as $/E\backslash_K$, and the private key belonging to the public key K is written as K^{-1}. To use an argument in another message or guard, one can make use of the variables in which incoming values are stored. Each variable is named by the name of the operation which it is the argument of, followed by the number of the position of the argument. For example, Init$_5$ is the 5th argument of the message with the function-name Init. An example drawn in the UML tool Poseidon is shown in Fig. 2. Tagged values can be used to attach additional information to be used in the analysis:

Attacker's Initial Knowledge. The attacker's initial knowledge is stored in a tag *initial knowledge*. One tag is defined for each such value.

Attack. If there is a tag *secret* with a value *value*, the security conjecture is generated in TPTP which checks whether the data item *value* will remain secret against the attacker considered during execution of the diagram. Alternatively, the TPTP conjecture can be stored in the tag *conjecture*.

Message Ordering. With the tag *order*, one can determine whether the implementation of the sequence diagram enforces the message ordering at the receipt of messages (which is the standard UML semantics for sequence diagrams), or not (which is what is implemented for example at many smart-cards, see [Jür05]. By default, the order is respected.

Variable Notation. With the tag *notation*, one may switch between different ways of definining the variable names that store the incoming arguments.

Guard Notation. For UML CASE tools which do not directly support the use of guards in sequence diagrams (such as Poseidon 1.6), one can include them in front of the stimulus labels, or as tagged values with the tag-name *guard_NR*, where *NR* is the number of the stimulus in the diagram to which the guard belongs. The tag may be defined at any model element in the diagram. Using the tag *guard_notation* one can switch between these two alternatives.

Facts. First-order formulas in the TPTP notation can be added as axioms to the TPTP file by storing them in tagged values with the tag-name *fact*.

Related Work. There seems to be no work yet on connecting ATPs to UML CASE tools. Work on providing security analysis tool support for UML is performed by the DEGAS project [DEG01]. More generally, there have been a number of approaches for tool-support verifying general properties of UML diagrams, mostly by connecting UML CASE tools to model-checkers, including [LP99, SKM01].

Conclusion. The framework has been used in several industrial applications: for example, the binding to the automated theorem prover e-Setheo has been used to verify the Common Electronic Purse Specifications and a biometric authentication system. Experiences have been favorable (see [Jür05]).

Acknowledgements. Fruitful collaboration with the UMLsec group members, especially Andreas Gilg, on implementation issues is gratefully acknowledged.

References

[DEG01]   Degas, 2001. http://www.omnys.it/degas.

[Jür04]   J. Jürjens. *Secure Systems Development with UML*. Springer, 2004.

[Jür05]   J. Jürjens. Sound methods and effective tools for model-based security engineering with UML. In *ICSE 2005*. IEEE Computer Society, 2005.

[LP99]   J. Lilius and I. Porres. Formalising UML state machines for model checking. In *UML 1999*, volume 1723 of *LNCS*, pages 430–445. Springer, 1999.

[SKM01]   T. Schäfer, A. Knapp, and S. Merz. Model checking UML state machines and collaborations. In S.D. Stoller and W. Visser, editors, *Software Model Checking*, volume 55 of *ENTCS*. Elsevier, 2001.

[UML04]   UMLsec tool, 2002-04. Open-source. Accessible at http://www.umlsec.org.

Maintaining Life Perspectives During the Refinement of UML Class Structures

Alexander Egyed[1], Wuwei Shen[2], and Kun Wang[2]

[1] Teknowledge Corporation, 4640 Admiralty Way,
Suite 1010, Marina Del Rey, CA 90292, USA
aegyed@teknowledge.com
[2] Dept of Computer Science, Western Michigan University, USA
{wwshen, kwang}@cs.wmich.edu

Abstract. Models provide an alternative perspective for the understanding of a software system. However, models reflect the state of the system at the time of their creation (or last updating) but they do not reflect intermediate changes during the system's evolution. Depicting perspectives without showing changes is like watching a movie through a small set of still pictures (i.e., no motion). This paper demonstrates this problem on an existing technique for the automated simplification (abstraction) of class diagrams. We will show that it is computationally feasible to maintain a set of abstract perspectives of a class structure such that evolutionary changes to the class structure are instantly perceived through its perspectives. For developers, this provides the ability to understand changes to systems from the modeling perspectives they care about. It also gives the developers the confidence that their modeling perspectives remain up-to-date with the system even while the system evolves.

1   Introduction

Software is more than source code and software development is more than programming. Software development generates and maintains a wide range of artifacts, such as documentation, requirements, or design models; all of which are valuable to the understanding of a software system. These artifacts help developers in understanding the software system through different perspectives (i.e., representing different goals or problems). In doing so, these perspectives emphasize certain development concerns and ignore others that are momentarily not of interest. For example, the design is an abstraction of the implementation and it often omits language-specific programming details that are not necessary to the understanding of the system. Our notion of perspectives is similar to the notion of views, however, a view typically hides parts of a model whereas our perspectives interpret the hidden information.

Perspectives separate concerns and thus cope with the complexity of software development. Perspectives reduce the complexity of software development

M. Cerioli (Ed.): FASE 2005, LNCS 3442, pp. 310–325, 2005.

as they limit the amount of information the developers have to be aware of at any given time (i.e., instead of having to understand the entire system, developers only need to understand the perspectives). In this paper, we discuss perspectives of UML (v1.3) class structures [14]. With modern software systems becoming increasingly complicated, developers can easily lose their vision of the structure of the system while diving into the implementation details. It is thus common practice to retain abstractions of the class structure (sometimes referred to as higher-level designs or architectures [15]). These higher-level perspectives typically represent snapshots of the lower-level design, omitting lower-level details. It is not uncommon to retain different perspectives of the same lower-level design, to, say, represent different requirements, development concerns, or aspects (aspect oriented software development [11]).

While developers derive tremendous value from perspectives, they are not free. There is a cost in creating perspectives and a cost in maintaining them (i.e, new or changing goals or needs [4]). If a perspective cannot be updated promptly based on the changes made in a software system then the perspective no longer correctly reflects the system. This lack of correctness may then mislead developers.

Like many others [5, 12], we have investigated techniques for creating and maintaining perspectives. This paper builds on one such technique for the automated class abstraction [7]. This technique simplifies (=abstracts) UML class structures where developers can decide which classes to keep and which ones to temporarily "hide." This technique solves a range of concerns that will be discussed in Section 2. For example, the hidden classes have to be reinterpreted in terms of their effect on the remaining, non-hidden classes. Our technique has the benefit that developers may derive perspectives when they are needed. However, our technique does not maintain the correctness of the perspectives thereafter (i.e., during evolutionary changes). Of course, perspectives could be recreated instantly after design changes but this is computationally infeasible because class abstraction is not cheap computationally, there are potentially many perspectives, and iterative software development [4] encourages changes to be frequent. Relatively minor but frequent changes thus lead to costly re-transformations.

As an alternative, this paper discusses on how to efficiently update perspectives by only propagating changes (additions, removals) [3]. This paper thus contributes a technique for the instant and incremental abstraction of class structures to keep perspectives up to date continuously at a low cost. It works on the same rules as the original abstraction technique (batch abstraction) but it only updates changes. That is, any change to the system is evaluated in terms of its impact onto all perspectives. The change is then propagated to every perspective separately such that only those parts of the perspectives are updated that have changed.

This paper also contributes a new philosophy to working with perspectives. Since the perspectives are updated instantly, they provide developers with an instant understanding on the high-level effect(s) of their changes. Developers now instantly become aware about the impact of their low-level changes in context of the perspectives they care about. Previously, this could only be done after a costly batch re-abstraction and comparison. Even then, it was often not possible to tell exactly what had changed (e.g., if the name of two classes are swapped then an after-the-fact comparison might confuse this with the movement of its relationships).

This paper is organized as follows: Section 2 defines perspectives for class abstraction and provides background for generating them automatically. Section 3 discusses our approach to the incremental and instant class abstraction. Section 4 shows results of several case studies. Finally we draw our conclusions in Section 5.

2   Background

2.1   A Need for Perspectives

Fig. 1 shows a class diagram of a simplified hotel management system (HMS) taken from [7]. The role of the HMS is to provide support for hotel reservations, check-in/check-out procedures, and associated financial transactions. The class diagram depicts details on how a guest is a person (inheritance), how every person has an account or how payment and expense transactions are associated with accounts.

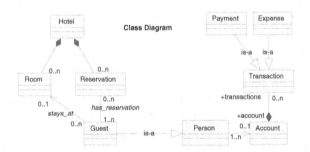

Fig. 1. Refinement of a Class Structure

While this class diagram is simple enough for human comprehension, we have worked with class diagrams that include thousands of classes and many more relationships [13]. It is impossible for humans to comprehend such class structures and developers resort to abstraction as a means of coping with this complexity. Abstraction depicts a class structure from a particular point of view, concern, requirements, or other form of interest. We refer to such an abstraction as a perspective of the class structure. Fig. 2 depicts four such perspectives of the class structure in Fig. 1.

Naturally, the perspectives in Fig. 2 are class structures themselves albeit simplified ones. A trivial form of a perspective is to represent a subset of the class structure only. For example, Fig. 2 (a) simply depicts the classes Guest,

Reservation, and Hotel (and their relationships) from Fig. 1 by omitting all other classes and their relationships. These forms of trivial "perspectives" (i.e., sometimes referred to as views) are supported in many modeling tools, i.e., in form of diagrams. Yet, it must be understood that deriving perspectives is not just about eliminating details but also about re-interpreting the hidden details. For example, Fig. 2 (b) depicts the classes Guest, Payment, and Expense (as taken from Fig. 1) but it also depicts relationships among these three classes that are not to be found in Fig. 1. These relationships are the abstract interpretation of the hidden information. Fig. 2 (c) and (d) depict yet other perspectives that "slice" across the classes in Fig. 1. Clearly, there are a range of benefits associated with working with perspectives. Each perspective is easier to understand than the original class diagram.

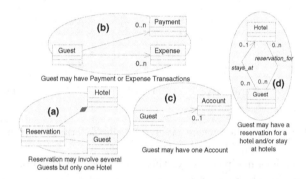

Fig. 2. Perspectives of the HMS system

Yet, without instant and incremental abstraction, it would be computationally infeasible to maintain these perspectives consistent with the system while the system evolves. That is, a change in Fig. 1 instantly renders all perspectives obsolete unless this change is propagated to all affected perspectives. Such propagation has the benefit that the perspectives continue to reflect the system accurately (i.e., important for decision making); and it has the benefit that the developers understand their system change(s) in terms of its impact onto the various perspectives. For example, if the cardinality from Person to Account changes from 0..1 to 0..n in Fig. 1 (i.e., a person may have many accounts and not just one) then which perspectives need updating? Does this change affect the Guest-Payment relationship in Fig. 2 (b)? Or does it change the Guest-Account relationship in Fig. 2 (c)?

2.2 Automated Abstraction

We previously developed a transitive reasoning technique in collaboration with Rational Software [10]. The technique takes arbitrary complex class structures and infers transitive relationships among its classes. A transitive relationship is the semantic equivalent of a collection of normal relationships. For example, if

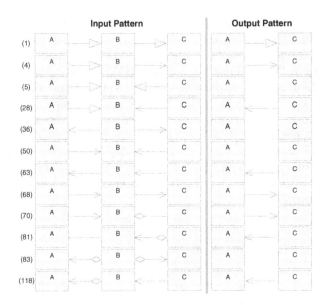

Fig. 3. Subset of Transitive Abstraction Rules for UML relationships [6]

A calls B and B calls C then, transitively, A calls C. Transitive relationships are thus indirect relationships between classes.

A transitive relationship is always the result of a collection of direct relationships. By composing the properties of a collection of direct relationships one can infer properties of the transitive relationship. Properties of relationships include the direction of the call, the type of relationship, or the cardinality of association ends. If, say, two relationships have the same type and the same calling direction then transitively the two relationships can be composed into a single one of the same type and direction (see Rule 70 in Fig. 3). Transitive relationships are thus a form of abstraction where the transitive relationship is semantically equivalent or weaker (less constrained) than the direct relationships it composes. Fig. 3 gives an excerpt of about 121 transitive relationships defined in [6]. For instance, rule 1 states that if A inherits from B and B inherits from C (input pattern) then, transitively, A inherits from C (output pattern). Or Rule 118 states that if C depends on B, A is a part of B (diamond head), and A is called by B (arrowhead) then, transitively, C depends on A.

The given transitive abstraction rules are simple in nature. Most rules describe a collection of two input relationships that are composable into a single output relationship (or not composable if the output pattern does not have a relationship). What makes this abstraction technique powerful is the large number of simple rules (121 rules for three types of class relationships and various properties). Given the simplicity of the rules, the abstraction algorithm is fast (see empirical studies in [6]); however, at the expense of precision. UML relationship semantics are not well-treated in the current UML specification which may lead to uncertainties during transitive reasoning (e.g., A calling B and B calling C may not imply A calling C always; see validation in [6]). While we cannot guarantee the correctness of all abstraction results, we found that we can guarantee completeness. That is, the lack of an abstraction result true means that there is no transitive relationship. Furthermore, validation showed that it was a two-orders of magnitudes (100 fold) saving in checking the correctness of abstraction results manually versus having to abstract by hand.

As input, the algorithm takes an arbitrary complex class structure and a list of "important classes". The list of important classes emphasizes the classes that should not be hidden. In Fig. 3, the classes A and C are important and the class B is not important as it gets replaced (together with its relationships) by a higher-level relationship. A human has to make the decision what classes are important as it depends on the circumstances and usage of the perspectives.

Important classes are not used for transitive reasoning during abstraction. They remain untouched during abstraction but their relationships to other, important classes are derived through transitive reasoning by hiding and re-interpreting unimportant classes (=helper classes). Fig. 4 shows the use of transitive reasoning in understanding the relationship between the important classes Guest and Payment (from Fig. 1). Although the two important classes are not directly related to one another, a transitive relationship can be derived by eliminating the helper classes Person, Account, and Transaction. Fig. 4 shows that the application of Rule 4 eliminates the class Person, the subsequent application of Rule 70 eliminates the class Account, and, finally, rule 28 eliminates Transaction. This results in an incremental abstraction where the previous result is then abstracted further if needed. The resulting abstraction is depicted in the bottom of Fig. 4. It depicts the two untouched, important classes and a single relationship between them that is semantically equivalent to the now-hidden helper classes.

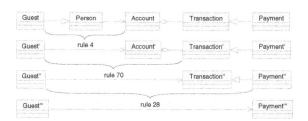

Fig. 4. Transitive Relationship between Classes

In summary, transitive reasoning merges low-level classes and relationships into higher-level relationships. This form of abstraction is necessary in cases where lower-level classes are the result of refining a relationship. For instance, the low-level class Account is important for implementing the HMS system but it is not needed on a higher-level abstraction to convey the point that a guest may have payment transactions. The class was thus hidden together with other classes and the hidden information was then re-interpreted through higher-level relationships. It is also possible to merge classes into higher-level classes (instead of relationships) and our approach is capable of doing so but its discussion is not of importance in this paper [8].

In the remainder of the paper we refer to the class structure in Fig. 1 as the design and to the abstractions in Fig. 2 as the perspectives. Abstraction assumes the existence of the design and a list of important classes in order to compute perspectives. The design and list of important classes must be provided by the developer.

3   Approach

Automated abstraction gives the developer the ability to create one perspective at a time. This perspective is then consistent with the design (assuming the rules for abstraction are accurate) but any change to that design may render any and all perspectives obsolete. Naturally, developers may re-compute perspectives to make them consistent again; however, many automated techniques, such as ours are computationally not cheap. It is thus infeasible to update perspectives continuously while the design changes.

This paper extends our previous work through incremental abstraction. Instead of updating perspectives in their entirety (batch abstraction), we only update changes. The basic goal of our approach is depicted in Fig. 5. Incremental abstraction understands both the design and its perspectives such that it can reason about a change in the design in terms of its impact onto the perspectives. It then updates the perspectives by deleting obsolete information or adding new ones. Compared to the abstraction of entire perspectives, we find this incremental approach to be much more efficient.

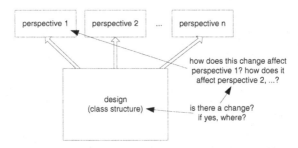

Fig. 5. Instant and Incremental Abstraction to maintain the Consistency between a Design and its Perspectives

Incremental abstraction is a two-step process in that one has to understand 1) when and where changes happen in the design (class structure) and 2) how such changes affect the given perspective(s). While a change to the design is a constant, its impact is dependent on the particular perspectives at hand. This section explores these two issues and discusses our solution.

3.1   When and Where Changes Happen

To understand when and where changes happen in a design, we need to instrument its drawing tool (e.g., the design capture tool). Of interest is information about the creation, modification, and deletion of classes, their relationships, and associated properties (e.g., methods, attributes). This task is only moderately complex if the source code of the drawing tool is available. However, we previously demonstrated a capability for "spying" into commercial-off-the shelf tools to elicit these kinds of information [9]. In particular, we demonstrated on IBM Rational Rose [1] and Matlab/Stateflow [2] how to convert low-level keyboard and mouse events into the kinds of events discussed above (e.g., class creation, renaming, and relationship moving).

This technology has been published in [9] and is not described in more detail here aside to say that we have built a tool support, called the UMLInterface, that enables us to use the commercial tool IBM Rational Rose as a drawing tool for class structures and is able to observe developer changes. Fig. 6 depicts the architecture of our tool schematically where design changes from inside Rose are forwarded to our abstraction tool, which then responds by updating the perspectives in Rose. It is important to note that Rose maintains both the design and its perspective(s) and our tool simply propagates the changes. Therefore, all the visible activities happen inside Rose and the developer is never aware of our tool.

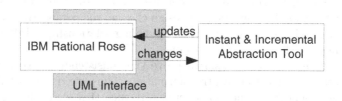

Fig. 6. IBM Rational Rose and the Instant & Incremental Abstraction of Changes

Since Rose is used as both a design drawing tool and a perspective visualization tool, we had to define logical structures for separating them. We also had to define a way for developers to designate "important classes." Recall from Section 2 that perspectives must define lists of important classes. We found a way of capturing this information inside Rose. However, these details are not discussed here as they do not contribute to the main topic of this paper.

3.2   How Changes Affect Perspectives

Incremental abstraction assumes the existence of a design and its perspectives. Changes to the design then cause updates to the perspectives. This approach assumes that perspectives are initially consistent with the design. The change to the design then causes an inconsistency and the simple propagation of the change is sufficient to re-establish consistency. However, there are situations

Table 1. Perspective Changes in Response to Design Changes

Impact of design onto perspectives			Perspective			
			Class		Relation	
			Add	Remove	Add	Remove
Design	Class	Add	no	no	no	no
		Remove	no	yes	no	yes
		Upgrade	yes	no	yes	yes
		Downgrade	no	yes	yes	yes
	Relation	Add	no	no	yes	no
		Remove	no	no	no	yes

where it is incorrect to assume initial consistency. For example, if a developer loads an existing class diagrams then we need to ensure initial consistency by abstracting all perspectives in their entirety. We refer to this process as the initial batch abstraction which is, in our case, the same as the normal class abstraction discussed in Section 2.

After the initial consistency between design and perspective is ensured, a change to the design requires no more than the abstraction of the change to again guarantee consistency. The kinds of changes in a design made by developers during software include: adding a class, removing a class, upgrading a class in a design from a helper class to an important class and downgrading a class (there are also other changes but are not discussed here). Table 1 depicts design changes in the rows. In response to a design change, the perspective may change by adding/removing classes and adding/removing relationships. Table 1 depicts these perspective changes in the columns.

We do not have a mechanism to prove the consistency between the batch transformation and incremental transformation. Thus, we tested batch abstraction and incremental abstraction concurrently such that we could compare differences. Fortunately, changes in the design have limited ways on how they affect a perspective. The fields in Table 1 indicate what kinds of perspective changes are caused by what kinds of design changes. For example, removing a class from the design may remove classes and/or relationships from the perspective (e.g., if the class was important then the perspective may loose a class; if the class was unimportant then the perspective may loose relationships). It is interesting to observe that class and relationship changes in the design have few effects onto the perspectives but class upgrades/downgrades are more complex. Table 2 summarizes and discusses these impacts in more detail.

Changing a Class in the Design
Adding a new class to a design does not add any new relation to that design. Therefore the perspective remains unchanged. However, deleting a class from a design may result in a change in the perspective. For example, if a developer decides that the class Person (Fig. 1) is no longer required in the design then this also changes some of the perspectives. For example, the perspective "Guest may have Payment or Expense Transactions" becomes out of date because Person is

Table 2. Design Changes and Impact onto Perspectives in More Detail

User Action	Changes based on perspective
Add a class	No change
Remove an important class	Delete class from the perspective. Also remove the relations between the class and all other important classes.
Remove a helper class	Delete relations from the perspective whose abstractions used the helper class.
Add a relationship between two classes	Find paths between important classes that pass through the relationship. Abstract these new paths into relations.
Remove a relation between two classes	Delete relations from the perspective that were abstracted from the removed relation.
Upgrade a class from a helper class to an important class	Add class to the perspective. Delete relations from the perspective that were abstracted from the upgraded class (the previous helper class). Also find paths between the new important class and other important classes. Abstract these new paths into relations.
Downgrade a class from an important class to a helper class	Remove class from perspective. Find paths between important classes that pass through the downgraded class. Abstract these new paths into relations. Also delete relations from the downgraded class to other important classes.

a helper class in that perspective and its removal affects the paths from Guest to Expense and Payment (recall Fig. 4). Consequently, there are no longer abstract relations among these classes and the perspective needs to be updated.

Since the removed class is a helper class, incremental abstraction only removes those relations in the perspective that were abstracted from it. Fig. 7 shows a design (left) and its perspective (right) with X and Y being important classes. If developers remove the helper class A in the design then our approach deletes the relation (2+A+3)' because this helper class was used to derive that relation.

Removing an important class in a design obviously results in its removal from the perspective. As a side-effect of the removal of an important class, all relations connecting to the important class must be removed also. For example, in Fig. 7 the removal of the design class X instead of A would delete the perspective class X' and all its relationships.

Changing a Relationship in the Design

There are two situations related to changing a relation in a design: adding a relation and deleting a relation. The addition of a design relation implies that there are potentially new paths among the important classes. This in turn may result in new relationships in the perspective. For example, if a developer adds a

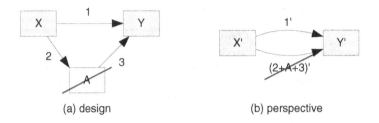

(a) design   (b) perspective

Fig. 7. Remove a helper class from a design

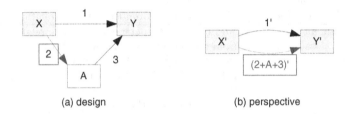

(a) design   (b) perspective

Fig. 8. Add/delete a relation in a design

relation between the Transaction and Account classes then this again affects the perspective "Guest may have Payment or Expense Transactions". The addition of the relation creates new paths among Guest, Expense, and Payment. Thus, we need to find all new paths between the important classes that pass through the new relation and abstract them.

Fig. 8 shows a general case for adding a new relation. If the new relation "2" is added between classes X and Y (Fig. 8 left) then we need to search for new paths among the reachable important classes (X and Y in this case) that pass through the relation. There is one such path (2+A+3)' which is then abstracted and added to the perspective.

The deletion of a relation is similar to the deletion of a helper class. If a developer deletes a relation from the design then incremental abstraction only removes those relations in the perspective that were abstracted from it. For example, if relation 2 in Fig. 8 is now removed from the design then the relation (2+A+3)' in the perspective must be removed also. While the removal of a design class may affect both perspective classes and relations, the removal of a design relation only affects perspective relations.

Upgrading and Downgrading a Class in the Design

Upgrading a class changes it from a helper class to an important class. Upgrading affects perspectives more than class and relation changes (recall Table 1). However, upgrading is not complex but simply the concatenation of class and relation changes. If a developer changes a helper class to an important class then three things have to be done. First, the newly-important class has to be added

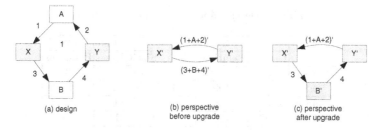

Fig. 9. Upgrade a class A

to the perspective (i.e., because important classes are not hidden). Second, all relations in the perspective that were abstracted from it need to be removed. And, third, all paths between it and other important classes must be found, abstracted, and added to the perspective.

For example, if developers are not only interested in "Guest may have Payment or Expense Transactions" but also in "Guest may have Transaction" then the helper class Transaction should be upgraded. The paths among the classes Guest, Expense, and Payment have to be removed from the perspective because they all pass through Transaction which is no longer a helper class. Transaction also needs to be added to the perspective and all paths between Transaction and Guest, Expense, and Payment need to be found and abstracted.

Fig. 9 (a) shows a general case for upgrading the class B in a design where classes X and Y are important. Before the upgrade, the perspective had two classes (X' and Y') to reflect the important classes of the design, and it had two relations between them to reflect the two paths through A and B (see Fig. 9 (b)). After class B is upgraded to an important class, incremental abstraction adds B' to the perspective, eliminates all relations in the perspective that were abstracted from B (e.g., (3+B+4)'), and adds relations from B' to all other important classes if it can find abstractable paths (see Fig. 9 (c)).

Downgrading an important class to a helper class is the exact opposite of upgrading a class (simply reverse the before/after picture in Fig. 9). The downgrading of a class removes that class from the perspective and with it all its relations to other important classes. Furthermore, it searches for paths among the important classes that pass through the downgraded class.

4   Validation

Software development changes have side effects. Yet these side effects are localized in that single changes in the design typically only cause small changes to their perspective(s). It is thus computationally wasteful to dispose of abstractions in their entirety simply because of small changes in the design. We evaluated the design models of four software systems (see Table 3) ranging between 9 classes and 127 classes to investigate this trade-off.

Table 3. Design Models used for Cases Study

	Design			Perspective	
	Classes	Relations	Model Size	Classes	Relations
Hms	9	9	104	3	3
Vod	65	199	1683	7	15
Visualizer	50	92	823	6	17
iTalks	107	127	1270	11	25

Fig. 10 (left) depicts the impact of design changes onto perspectives. As was discussed previously, there are essentially three types of changes of interest: up/downgrading, class changes (add/remove a class) and relationship changes (add/remove a dependency, association, or generalization). We subjected these models to over 800 random changes and observed their impact. For example, a change to a trace dependency in the iTalks design impacted in average 2.5 perspective elements (at least one and at most 8); or a change to a relationship impacted in average 0.9 perspective elements (0-5). The other three systems exhibited similarly small impact numbers which confirms our initial claim that design changes typically only have small impacts onto the perspectives for class abstraction. This observation is important for scalability.

While Fig. 10 (left) depicts up/downgrading, class, and relationship changes independently, there are situations where they occur together. For example, in IBM Rational Rose, the deletion of a class also causes the deletion of all its relationships and knowledge of its important/unimportant markers. Or the copy-and-paste action supported in many modeling tools allows a set of classes, relationships, and, perhaps, important/unimportant markers to be pasted at once. We thus conducted over 280 random changes that involved the deletion and creation of classes with relationships and important/unimportant markers. Fig. 10 (right) depicts the averaged results of these tests. For example, a typical deletion of a class in the vod system also deleted three design relations and 0.2 "important" markers (i.e., every 5th class deleted an important class). We refer to this deletion as a group deletion. In response, a group deletion changed elements in the perspectives. In the vod system, in average 0.2 classes and 2.3 relationships were changed per group deletion. These numbers demonstrate that the grouping of elements has only mild negative effects onto the impact of changes.

It must be noted however that a single copy-and-paste could involve an entire class structure which would then result in a change to the entire perspective. However, these kinds of changes are rare and so is their associated computational penalty.

Fig. 10 (left) also depicted another interesting observation. In all four systems, the up/downgrading had more severe effects onto the perspectives than relationship changes, which in turn had more severe effects than class changes. The differences are quite strong in that a relationship change impacts in average 3.5 times more perspective elements than a class change; and a up/downgrade impacts in average 2.9 times more elements than a relationship change (one order

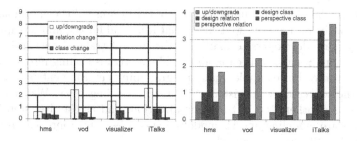

Fig. 10. Average, Min, Max Number of Perspective Changes per Design Change (left) and Grouping of Design Changes and Perspective Changes (right)

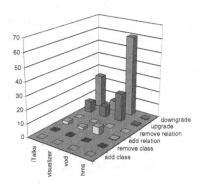

Fig. 11. Average number of Path Re-Evaluations for Design Changes

of magnitude difference). The differences are caused by the path re-evaluations that are part of class abstraction.

Fig. 11 depicts the average numbers of path re-evaluations for all four systems and it is obvious that up- and downgrading are particularly expensive. However, it must be noted that the path re-evaluations during incremental abstraction are cheap in comparison to the existing approach to abstraction (the batch abstraction of entire class structures). Also, we believe that trace changes are much less likely than relationship or class changes. After all, the four systems contain only 27 traces but almost 700 classes and relationships.

5 Conclusion

Abstraction, as in the simplification of complexity, plays an important role during software development. This paper demonstrated on UML class structures that it is possible and computationally feasible to maintain "life" perspectives that change instantly with system changes. The foremost advantage of instant transformation is that perspectives never become obsolete. Another advantage is that developers can observe system changes through their perspectives. The latter, in particular, is not common practice today because of the enormous cost of instant transformation. Yet, we believe that it is vital for the uninterrupted work flow of software developers to maximize the instant transformation of all kinds of information. Some of this capability is already transitioning into software development today. For example, many programming environments are capable of keeping the source code consistent with GUI modeling tools. We therefore see this work as another step in the same direction; and as the first step in doing so for software modeling and its model perspectives. The approach discussed in this paper is fully tool supported.

It is our future work to investigate the coupling of the instant and incremental abstraction discussed in this paper with the instant and incremental comparison for scalable consistency checking. That is, instead of checking the validity of entire models, we believe it is computationally much cheaper to check the consistency of models incrementally. Using instant and incremental abstraction to guide this instant and incremental consistency checking has not been attempted yet. It is our future work to investigate how to formally prove the consistency between batch and incremental transformation.

References

1. IBM Rational Rose. http://www.rational.com.
2. Matlab and Stateflow by Mathworks. http://www.mathworks.com.
3. R. Arnold and S. Bohner. Software Change Impact Analysis. In *IEEE Computer Society Press*. 1991.
4. B. Boehm, A. Egyed, J. Kwan, and R. Madachy. Using the WinWin Spiral Model: A Case Study. In *IEEE Computer*, pages 33–44. 1998.
5. B. Cheng, E. Y. Wang, R. H. Bourdeau, and H. A. Richter. Bridging the Gap Between Informal and Formal Approaches to Software Development. In *Proceedings of Software Engineering Research Forum, November 1995*. 1995.
6. A. Egyed. Semantic Abstraction Rules for Class Diagrams. In *Proceedings of the 15th IEEE International Conference of Automated Software Engineering (ASE)*, Grenoble, France, 2000.
7. A. Egyed. Automated Abstraction of Class Diagrams. In *ACM Transactions on Software Engineering and Methodology*, volume 11, pages 449–491, 2002.
8. A. Egyed. Compositional and Relational Reasoning During Class Abstraction. In *Proceedings of the 6th International Conference on the Unified Modeling Language (UML)*, pages 121–137, San Francisco, USA, 2003.
9. A. Egyed and B. Balzer. Integrating COTS Software into Systems through Instrumentation and Reasoning. In *Journal on Automated Software Engineering (JASE)*, accepted for publication.
10. A. Egyed and P. Kruchten. Rose/Architect: A Tool to Visualize Architecture. In *Proceedings of the 32nd Hawaii International Conference on System Sciences (HICSS)*, 1999.
11. G. Kiczales, J. Lamping, A. Mendhekar, C. Maeda, C. Lopes, J. Loingtier, and J. Irwin. Aspect-Oriented Programming. In *European Conference on Object-Oriented Programming (ECOOP)*, pages 220–242, 1997.

12. F. D. Racz and K. Koskimies. Tool-Supported Compression of UML Class Diagrams. In *Proceedings of the 2nd International Conference on the Unified Modeling Language (UML)*.

13. W. Roll. Towards Model-Based and CCM-Based Applications for Real-Time Systems. In *Proceedings of the 6th IEEE International Symposium on Object-Oriented Real-Time Distributed Computing*, pages 75–82, Hakodate, Hokkaido, Japan, 2003.

14. J. Rumbaugh, I. Jacobson, and G. Booch. *The Unified Modeling Language Reference Manual*. Addison Wesley.

15. M. Shaw and D. Garlan. *Software Architecture: Perspectives on an Emerging Discipline*. Prentice Hall, 1996.

Automated Compositional Proofs
for Real-Time Systems*

Carlo A. Furia, Matteo Rossi, Dino Mandrioli, and Angelo Morzenti

Dipartimento di Elettronica e Informazione,
Politecnico di Milano,
32, Piazza Leonardo da Vinci, 20133, Milano, Italy
{furia, rossi, mandrioli, morzenti}@elet.polimi.it

Abstract. We present a framework for formally proving that the composition of the behaviors of the different parts of a complex, real-time system ensures a desired global specification of the overall system. The framework is based on a simple compositional rely/guarantee circular inference rule, plus a small set of conditions concerning the integration of the different parts into a whole system. The reference specification language is the TRIO metric linear temporal logic.

The novelty of our approach with respect to existing compositional frameworks — most of which do not deal explicitly with real-time requirements — consists mainly in its generality and abstraction from any assumptions about the underlying computational model and from any semantic characterizations of the temporal logic language used in the specification. Moreover, the framework deals equally well with continuous and discrete time. It is supported by a tool, implemented on top of the proof-checker PVS, to perform deduction-based verification through theorem-proving of modular real-time axiom systems.

As an example of application, we show the verification of a real-time version of the old-fashioned but still relevant "benchmark" of the dining philosophers problem.

Keywords: Formal verification, modular systems, real-time, compositionality, rely/guarantee, axiom systems.

1 Introduction

Formal methods are more and more recognized to be a useful tool for the development of applications, as they allow their users to precisely verify the correctness of systems in their early development phases, before uncaught mistakes become overly costly to fix. One drawback often attributed to formal methods, however, is that they do not "scale up", i.e. when the system grows in complexity, they are too cumbersome and unwieldy to be used effectively. A natural solution

---

* Work supported by the MIUR project: "Quack: Piattaforma per la qualità di sistemi embedded integrati di nuova generazione."

M. Cerioli (Ed.): FASE 2005, LNCS 3442, pp. 326–340, 2005.

to this problem is to apply well-known software engineering principles such as modularity and separation of concerns to the verification of formal models. A compositional framework can help in this regard, in that it allows one to focus on the single parts of the system at first, and then analyze their mutual interactions at a later moment with a smaller effort than it would be required if all aspects (local and global) of the application were taken into account at once.

This paper presents a compositional inference rule for the TRIO language [5] that is suitable to formally prove the correctness of the behavior of a modular system from the behavior of its components. TRIO is a metric temporal logic for modeling and analysis of time-critical systems, and has been used in a number of industrial projects. Its advanced modular features are useful in writing specifications of complex systems. Our framework combines these features with the compositional inference rule through some application methodology that facilitates its practical use in structured specifications.

The approach followed in this paper belongs to the general framework of axiom systems, where a specification consists of a set of logic formulas and the verification consists in formally demonstrating that certain desired properties follow deductively from the specification formulas. This framework is indeed very general and abstract, as it does not rely on specific semantic assumptions and is independent of any notion of underlying computational model (to be considered when moving from specification towards implementation). In fact, proofs in our framework are to be intended as in classic logic deduction [15], and are supported and semi-automated by the theorem proving tool PVS [18]. Also, even if the reference language is TRIO, the results can be easily extended to any logic formalisms for the description of real-time axiom systems.

The paper is structured as follows: Section 2 shortly introduces the TRIO language; Section 3 presents a proof-oriented compositional framework for TRIO; Section 4 applies the framework to a timed version of Dijkstra's dining philosophers problem [8]; Section 5 reviews the most important compositional rules and frameworks in the literature, and points out where our approach differs from previous works on this subject; Section 6 draws conclusions and outlines future research.

For reasons of space, some of the formulas and proofs discussed in the paper have been omitted. The interested reader can find these details in an extended version of the paper, available online [11].

2   TRIO

TRIO [5] is a general-purpose specification language suitable to describe real-time systems. It is a first-order linear temporal logic that supports a metric on time. In addition to the usual propositional operators and quantifiers, it has a basic modal operator, called *Dist*, that relates the *current time*, which is left implicit in the formula, to another time instant: given a time-dependent formula F (i.e. a term representing a mapping from the time domain to truth values) and a term t indicating a time distance, the formula $Dist(F, t)$ specifies that F holds

Table 1. TRIO derived temporal operators

OPERATOR	DEFINITION
$Past(F,t)$	$t \geq 0 \wedge Dist(F,-t)$
$Futr(F,t)$	$t \geq 0 \wedge Dist(F,t)$
$Som(F)$	$\exists d : Dist(F,d)$
$Alw(F)$	$\forall d : Dist(F,d)$
$AlwP(F)$	$\forall d > 0 : Past(F,d)$
$AlwF(F)$	$\forall d > 0 : Futr(F,d)$
$Lasted(F,t)$	$\forall d \in (0,t) : Past(F,d)$
$Lasts(F,t)$	$\forall d \in (0,t) : Futr(F,d))$
$Within(F,t)$	$\exists d \in (0,t) : Past(F,d) \vee Futr(F,d)$
$WithinP(F,t)$	$\exists d \in (0,t) : Past(F,d)$
$WithinF(F,t)$	$\exists d \in (0,t) : Futr(F,d)$
$Since(F,G)$	$\exists d > 0 : Lasted(F,d) \wedge Past(G,d)$
$Until(F,G)$	$\exists d > 0 : Lasts(F,d) \wedge Futr(G,d)$
$UpToNow(F)$	$\begin{cases} \exists d > 0 : Lasted(F,d)) & \text{if dense} \\ Past(F,1) & \text{if discrete} \end{cases}$
$NowOn(F)$	$\begin{cases} \exists d > 0 : Lasts(F,d)) & \text{if dense} \\ Futr(F,1) & \text{if discrete} \end{cases}$
$Becomes(F)$	$UpToNow(\neg F) \wedge (F \vee NowOn(F))$

at a time instant whose distance is exactly t time units from the current instant. Notice that, in this paper, we deliberately do not formally specify a semantics for the interpretation of TRIO formulas: in fact all the discussion is independent of how the modal operator $Dist$ is interpreted, and of which computational model is chosen, since it involves only syntactic manipulation of formulas.

A number of *derived* temporal operators can be defined from the basic $Dist$ operator through propositional composition and first-order logic quantification. Table 1 shows those used in this paper. Notice that TRIO operators predicating on intervals by default do not include the interval boundaries. We define variations that may or may not include such boundaries by using the subscripts i (included) or e (excluded). E.g. $AlwP_i(F) \equiv \forall d \geq 0 : Past(F,d)$, $AlwP_e(F) \equiv AlwP(F)$, $WithinF_{ei} \equiv \exists d \in (0,t] : Futr(F,d)$, $WithinF_{ii} \equiv \exists d \in [0,t] : Futr(F,d)$, etc.

TRIO is well-suited to deal with both dense and discrete time. For specifying large and complex systems, and to support encapsulation, reuse and information hiding at the specification level, TRIO has the usual object-oriented constructs such as classes, inheritance and genericity. The basic encapsulation unit is the class, which is a collection of parameters, basic items, formulas and an interface.

Items are the primitive elements of the specification, such as predicates, time-dependent variables, functions, etc. *States* and *events* are time-dependent items with a particular temporal behavior: events are predicates that are true only at isolated time instants; states are predicates which are true on non-empty time intervals (see [12] for a more precise definition).

We illustrate TRIO's features by introducing the specification of the *dining philosophers problem* [8]. Our solution is based on a philosopher class and assumes a continuous time model. Continuous time introduces some peculiar difficulties in the specification and verification phases, which we will handle exploiting an axiomatic-deductive approach. The basic items of the class are the event item start for the system initialization, and the items take(s) and release(s), with $s \in \{l, r\}$, indicating, for each philosopher, the action of taking or releasing the left or right fork. Other items are the state eating, which is true when the philosopher is eating, and the states holding(s) and available(s), meaning that the philosopher is holding a given fork or that the fork is available (i.e. not held by the adjacent philosopher). The philosopher class is parametric with respect to three constants t_e, T_e, T_t. They denote, respectively, the minimum eating time, the maximum eating time and the thinking time after an eating session, before becoming hungry again. Obviously, we assume $T_e > t_e > 0$.

For each TRIO class, formulas are divided into three categories: axioms, assumptions and theorems. Axioms postulate the basic behavior of the system, assumptions express constraints we must discharge by means of other parts of the system (external to the current class) and theorems describe properties that are derived from other formulas. Any TRIO formula is implicitly universally quantified with the *Alw* operator.

We formalize the basic behavior of a philosopher through axiom formulas. For the sake of space limit, we do not present explicitly all the formulas of the example, but just give an informal presentation of some of them. The interested reader can find the complete example in the extended version of this paper available online [11]. We postulate that each philosopher always takes and releases both forks simultaneously (axiom holding_synch); consequently, if only one fork is available, the philosopher waits till the other fork becomes available as well.[1] A philosopher becomes "hungry" when he/she has not eaten for a period longer than T_t. If he/she is hungry and if the forks are available, two situations are possible: either he/she takes both forks, or nondeterministically one of his/her neighbors takes a fork at that very time, so that the fork is not available anymore and the philosopher "loses his/her turn". This is formalized by axiom hungry.

Axiom 1 (hungry) $Lasted(\neg eating, T_t) \wedge UpToNow(available(l) \wedge available(r))$
$\Rightarrow (take(l) \wedge take(r)) \vee NowOn(\neg available(l) \vee \neg available(r))$.

Axioms eating_def and eating_duration state that, when a philosopher succeeds in acquiring both forks, he/she eats for a time duration of more than t_e and less than T_e time units, after which he/she releases both forks. Whenever a philosopher holds both forks we consider him/her eating. When he/she is not eating we say he/she is thinking (axiom thinking). Finally, a thinking session which has just begun lasts T_t time units (axiom thinking_duration).

Each TRIO class has an interface, defined as the set of items and formulas that are externally *visible*. The user can declare each item to be visible or

---

[1] We introduce this simplification with respect to the traditional formulation because our example aims at proving a *real-time, non starvation property*, rather than the absence of deadlocks.

non-visible; henceforth all the formulas predicating on visible items *only* are considered as visible, while all the other formulas are considered as non-visible outside the class. The interface is synthetically represented with a graphical notation: Figure 1 illustrates the interface of the philosopher class.

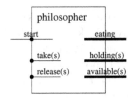

Fig. 1. Interface of the philosopher class

A structured TRIO specification is a collection of *modules*, i.e. instances of TRIO classes. The behavior of the overall composite system is given by the combination of the behaviors of its modules (i.e. it is defined by the logical conjunction of the axioms). We compose $N \geq 2$ instances of the philosopher class into the new composite class dining_N. The N modules of the philosopher class are instantiated in an array Philosophers indexed by the range $[0..N-1]$. The modules are connected so that the available item of each philosopher corresponds to the negation of the holding item of the philosopher on his/her left/right.

3   A Compositional Framework in TRIO

In this section, we introduce a compositional framework for axiom systems, and the TRIO language in particular. The rationale of our approach is the following. The specification of a complex system is structured into classes. The fundamental behavior of each class is captured by axiom formulas. The derived behavior of each class can be expressed by theorem formulas. In general, according to the rely/guarantee paradigm, we want to relate the derived behavior of a class with certain properties of the (external) environment we assume to hold. When we compose the class with other classes constituting its actual environment, we have to discharge (i.e. prove) the assumption formulas by means of formulas of other classes. If the assumptions on the environment are temporally closed formulas (i.e. they express time-invariant properties), we may use TRIO assumption formulas to represent them; then, when discharging them, it is important to avoid circularities, in order to guarantee the soundness of the composite specification. If, on the other hand, we have to express assumptions on the environment that are directly temporally related with the derived behavior they guarantee,[2] we need a new operator: the $\rightarrow\!\!\!\!\rightarrow$ operator (called *time progression*) for the TRIO language, introduced in Section 3.2. When we compose the class with other classes,

---

[2] Notice that this is likely to happen when specifying real-time systems.

rely/guarantee formulas expressed using the $\twoheadrightarrow$ operator are composed using an *ad hoc* inference rule which handles temporal circularities correctly, according to the semantics of the operator. Finally, once the local assumptions have been discharged, we can infer the global specification from the logical composition of the (valid) local specifications.

Notice that the $\twoheadrightarrow$ operator, while similar to the operators presented in [1, 16], differs from them in that it does not impose any constraints nor conditions on the properties involved and the underlying computational model of the formalism. Section 5 discusses this issue in more detail.

3.1 Rely/Guarantee Specifications

Let us consider the rely/guarantee specification of a TRIO class C written according to the following guideline. The basic behavior of C is defined in terms of axioms over both visible and non visible items, which rely on no assumptions, since they just state the very basic behavior of the class. Then, we wish to derive a number of remarkable properties of the class as theorems. These theorems often depend on assumptions about the behavior of the environment. In TRIO, these assumptions can be stated using the language construct of the *assumption* formula. Let us name $\mathcal{AX}_C$, $\mathcal{AS}_C$ and $\mathcal{TH}_C$ the set of all axioms, assumptions and theorems of class C, respectively, and let $\mathcal{F} = \mathcal{AX}_C \cup \mathcal{AS}_C \cup \mathcal{TH}_C$ be the set of all formulas of C. Furthermore, for each set of formulas $\mathcal{F}$, we define $\mathcal{F}^\vee \subseteq \mathcal{F}$ to be the set of *visible* formulas in $\mathcal{F}$, i.e. the formulas predicating over visible items only (see Section 2). Therefore, the complete specification of C is represented by the formula $\mathcal{AX}_C \wedge \mathcal{AS}_C \Rightarrow \mathcal{TH}_C$.

Let us map these ideas on the philosophers example. Section 2 showed some axioms of the philosopher class. A derived property of the class we want to state is that there is always a time interval in which both forks are available to the philosopher. In our axiomatization, it suffices to show that this time interval ends at a time distant at most $T_t + 2T_e$ time units. The above property is expressed by the following TRIO formula.

Theorem 2 (fork_availability)
$WithinF_{ei}(UpToNow(\text{available}(l) \wedge \text{available}(r)), T_t + 2T_e)$

The validity of this theorem cannot be guaranteed regardless of the behavior of the environment of this class. Therefore, we introduce three assumption formulas that suffice to deduce Theorem 2. First of all, each fork has to become available within $T_t + T_e$ time units or be already available and remain so for a sufficiently long (i.e. $\geq T_t$) amount of time. Second, we want each fork to be available, for a non-empty time interval, within T_e time units. This is basically like assuming that the adjacent philosophers eat no longer than T_e time units. Finally, when a fork becomes available, we assume it to stay so for (at least) T_t time units, i.e. the thinking time of the neighbor philosophers is no shorter than T_t. These three assumptions are formalized by three formulas named availability, availability_2 and lasting_availability (not shown here for brevity).

Let us now formalize what happens when composing TRIO classes. Let us consider n modules $C_1, \ldots, C_n$. For all $i = 1, \ldots, n$, module C_i has a rely/guarantee specification expressed synthetically by the formula $\mathcal{AX}_i \wedge \mathcal{AS}_i \Rightarrow \mathcal{TH}_i$. Let C_{glob} be the class obtained by composing the n instances C_i as modules of C_{glob}. The composition of the n modules is described by the logical conjunction of all the local specification formulas. Therefore TRIO classes are compositional, in that the semantics of the composition of classes is given by the logical conjunction of the semantics of the classes which are put together. In general, class C_{glob} has its own axioms, assumptions and theorems, besides those of its modules, to allow the recursive application of the method. Hence, C_{glob} is described by the formula $\mathcal{AX}_{glob} \wedge \mathcal{AS}_{glob} \Rightarrow \mathcal{TH}_{glob}$.

We seek a way to prove:

$$\mathcal{AX}_{glob} \wedge \mathcal{AS}_{glob} \wedge \bigwedge_{j=1,\ldots,n} (\mathcal{AX}_j \wedge \mathcal{AS}_j \Rightarrow \mathcal{TH}_j) \Rightarrow \mathcal{TH}_{glob}$$

Hence, we want to find a way to *discharge* the local assumptions of each class by means of visible formulas of other classes, so that we can in turn use the validity of the local visible theorems to deduce global results. As it is simple to realize, this kind of reasoning involves a circularity between assumptions and guarantees of the modules, so that a naïve rule does not guarantee soundness, in general. We want to rule out these invalid reasonings in order to obtain a valid rule for composition. To this end we introduce a new temporal operator suitable to express rely/guarantee compositional specifications, and different conditions on the initial validity of the environment assumptions and on how to discharge them. Through these elements, we finally provide a valid compositional rule for rely/guarantee reasoning in TRIO.

3.2   A Rely/Guarantee Inference Rule

Let us introduce the $\twoheadrightarrow$ "time progression" operator for the TRIO language, suitable for expressing temporal relationships between assumptions and guarantees. Let P and Q be two time-dependent formulas. We define the $\twoheadrightarrow$ operator as a shorthand for the formula:

$$P \twoheadrightarrow Q \quad \triangleq \quad \begin{cases} \text{if dense} : AlwP_e(P) \Rightarrow AlwP_i(Q) \wedge NowOn(Q) \\ \text{if discrete} : AlwP_e(P) \Rightarrow AlwP_i(Q) \end{cases}$$

Informally speaking, $P \twoheadrightarrow Q$ means that Q lasts at least as long as P does and even "a bit longer".

Now, we consider rely/guarantee specifications whose semantics is given in terms of the $\twoheadrightarrow$ operator. Therefore, if E is the environment assumption and M is the guarantee, the rely/guarantee specification is written as $E \twoheadrightarrow M$. Notice that we now admit temporally open formulas to be assumptions and guarantees.

Let us state, without proof, the following property of the $\twoheadrightarrow$ operator; the interested reader can find a proof in [11–Appendix A]. Note that the lemma holds both in dense and in discrete time models.

Lemma 1. *For any formulas P, Q and R, if:*

1. $Som(AlwP_e(P))$
2. $Alw(Q \wedge R \Rightarrow P)$

then:

$$Alw(P \twoheadrightarrow Q) \Rightarrow Alw(R \twoheadrightarrow Q)$$

The following proposition states a sound inference rule[3] for the $\twoheadrightarrow$ operator.

Proposition 1 (Rely/Guarantee Compositional Inference Rule). *If, for $i = 1, \ldots, m$ ($m \in \mathbb{N}^+$):*

1. $Som(AlwP_e(E_i))$ *(that is E_i is initialized)*
2. $E \wedge \bigwedge_{j=1,\ldots,m} M_j \Rightarrow E_i$
3. $\bigwedge_{j=1,\ldots,m} M_j \Rightarrow M$

then: $Alw\left(\bigwedge_{j=1,\ldots,m}(E_j \twoheadrightarrow M_j)\right) \Rightarrow Alw(E \twoheadrightarrow M)$.

Proof. Assume $Alw(\bigwedge_{j=1,\ldots,m}(E_j \twoheadrightarrow M_j))$. It is simple to realize, by considering the definition of the time progression operator, that this implies $Alw\left(\left(\bigwedge_{j=1,\ldots,m} E_j\right) \twoheadrightarrow \left(\bigwedge_{j=1,\ldots,m} M_j\right)\right)$. Moreover, hypothesis 2 implies that $Alw(E \wedge \bigwedge_{j=1,\ldots,m} M_j \Rightarrow \bigwedge_{j=1,\ldots,m} E_j)$, since it holds for every $i = 1, \ldots, m$. Finally, hypothesis 1 implies that $Som(AlwP_e(\bigwedge_{=1,\ldots,m} E_i))$, since there exists a base interval such that the conjunction of the E_i's is true on it[4].

Therefore, we can apply Lemma 1 by substituting $\bigwedge_{j=1,\ldots,m} E_j$ for P, $\bigwedge_{j=1,\ldots,m} M_j$ for Q and E for R. We get:

$$Alw\left(\left(\bigwedge_{j=1,\ldots,m} E_j\right) \twoheadrightarrow \left(\bigwedge_{j=1,\ldots,m} M_j\right)\right) \Rightarrow Alw\left(E \twoheadrightarrow \left(\bigwedge_{j=1,\ldots,m} M_j\right)\right).$$

Finally, by combining it with hypothesis 3 and with the definition of the time progression operator, we get the desired result.   □

Furthermore, we introduce a variation of the $\twoheadrightarrow$ operator for dense time domains: the $\twoheadrightarrow_i$ operator. $P \twoheadrightarrow_i Q$ is defined as $AlwP_i(P) \Rightarrow AlwP_i(Q) \wedge NowOn(Q)$, and Proposition 1 is valid for $\twoheadrightarrow_i$ as well. This variation will be used in Section 4.

---

[3] As it is often the case with compositional rules (and formal languages in general), there is a trade off between (relative) completeness and simplicity and ease of use [16, 14]. In this work, we have chosen to privilege the latter over the former, so that the inference rule in Proposition 1 is *incomplete*, as several other compositional rules in the literature [16, 4]. For the sake of space limit, we do not discuss this issue in depth, leaving it for future extensions of this work.

[4] Consider the intersection of the intervals on which each of the E_i's is individually true; this intersection is non-empty, since all intersected intervals are unbounded on the left, because of the $AlwP$ operator.

3.3   Integrating TRIO Modules

Let us consider the composition of n modules $C_1, \ldots, C_n$. We want to show briefly how the inference rule of Proposition 1 can be used in a large TRIO specification, integrating it with generic TRIO formulas. In general, each of the n modules we compose may have one or more rely/guarantee formulas of the form $E \twoheadrightarrow M$ among its theorems. For each module $j = 1, \ldots, n$, let $\mathcal{TH}_j^{rg} \subseteq \mathcal{TH}_j$ be the set of theorems in the form $E \twoheadrightarrow M$ of class j. More formally, for each theorem formula $F \in \mathcal{TH}_j$, $F \in \mathcal{TH}_j^{rg}$ if and only if F can be written as $F \equiv E \twoheadrightarrow M$ for some formulas E and M. Let us also define m to be the number of such formulas over all classes: $m = \sum_{j=1,\ldots,n} |\mathcal{TH}_j^{rg}|$. Moreover, $\mathcal{TH}_j^{nrg}$ is defined as the complement set $\mathcal{TH}_j \setminus \mathcal{TH}_j^{rg}$ for all $j = 1, \ldots, n$. The composite class C_{glob} also has its own rely/guarantee formula $E_{glob} \twoheadrightarrow M_{glob}$ among its theorems $\mathcal{TH}_{glob}$.

Now, we have to define what is a dependency between two formulas. Let us consider a formal proof π: it consists of a finite sequence of formulas, together with their *justifications* (see, for example, [15]). We say that a formula χ *directly depends upon* another formula ϕ in the proof π, and write $\phi \leadsto_\pi \chi$, if and only if ϕ appears before χ in the proof and χ is the result of the application of an inference rule which uses ϕ. The transitive closure $\overset{\star}{\leadsto}$ ("depends upon") of the $\leadsto$ relation $\phi \overset{\star}{\leadsto}_\pi \chi$ is defined as usual. The notion of dependency can be extended to a set of proofs Π: for any two formulas ϕ, χ we say that $\phi \overset{\star}{\leadsto}_\Pi \chi$ if and only if there exists a proof $\pi \in \Pi$ such that $\phi \overset{\star}{\leadsto}_\pi \chi$.

Finally, we can formulate a "checklist" to follow when verifying our composite specification. The rationale is that we avoid circularities in discharging temporally closed assumptions, and we resolve possible circularities between $\twoheadrightarrow$ specifications by using the inference rule of Proposition 1. More precisely, one should proceed as follows.

1. Verify each local specification, that is prove that for all $k = 1, \ldots, n$: $\mathcal{AX}_k \wedge \mathcal{AS}_k \Rightarrow \mathcal{TH}_k$. From our perspective, this step is considered to be atomic, but obviously the compositional approach can be applied recursively to each module.

2. Show that the local assumptions can be discharged by means of global formulas, local axioms and theorems, and visible formulas of other classes. In formulas, this corresponds to proving that for all $k = 1, \ldots, n$: $\mathcal{F}_{glob} \wedge \mathcal{AX}_k \wedge \mathcal{TH}_k \wedge \bigwedge_{j=1,\ldots,n \wedge j \neq k} \mathcal{F}_j^\vee \Rightarrow \mathcal{AS}_k$.

3. Prove that the global non-rely/guarantee theorems (i.e. not involving the $\twoheadrightarrow$ operator) follow from the local visible formulas and from the global axioms, assumptions and other (i.e. rely/guarantee) theorems. In formulas, this means proving $\mathcal{AX}_{glob} \wedge \mathcal{AS}_{glob} \wedge \mathcal{TH}_{glob}^{rg} \wedge \bigwedge_{j=1,\ldots,n} \mathcal{F}_j^\vee \Rightarrow \mathcal{TH}_{glob}^{nrg}$.

4. Show that each local rely/guarantee formula has an assumption which satisfies the initialization condition (as in hypothesis 1 of Proposition 1). In order to prove the initialization condition, we can use global and local formulas, plus any visible formula of any other class of the system. In formulas, this corresponds to proving that for all $k = 1, \ldots, m$: for all $j = 1, \ldots, n$: if $(E_k \twoheadrightarrow M_k) \in \mathcal{TH}_j^{rg}$ then $\mathcal{F}_{glob} \wedge \mathcal{F}_j \wedge \bigwedge_{i=1,\ldots,n} \mathcal{F}_i^\vee \Rightarrow Som(AlwP_e(E_k))$.

5. Show that each local rely/guarantee formula has an assumption that can be discharged by means of global and local formulas, or by the global assumption, or by means of guarantees of other classes. This corresponds to hypothesis 2 in Proposition 1. In formulas, this is proving that for all $k = 1, \ldots, m$: for all $j = 1, \ldots, n$: if $(E_k \twoheadrightarrow M_k) \in \mathcal{TH}_j^{rg}$ then: $\mathcal{F}_{glob} \wedge \mathcal{F}_j \wedge \bigwedge_{i=1,\ldots,n} \mathcal{F}_i^{\vee} \Rightarrow Alw(E_{glob} \wedge \bigwedge_{i=1,\ldots,m} M_i \Rightarrow E_k)$.

6. Show that the global guarantee follows from the local guarantees of all modules and from global formulas and local visible formulas of any class. This corresponds to hypothesis 3 of Proposition 1. In formulas, this is proving $\mathcal{F}_{glob} \wedge \bigwedge_{j=1,\ldots,n} \mathcal{F}_j^{\vee} \Rightarrow Alw(\bigwedge_{j=1,\ldots,m} M_j \Rightarrow M_{glob})$.

7. Be sure that in all the above proofs there are no circular dependencies among any two closed formulas. Formally, this corresponds to checking that in the set Π of all the above proofs, for all formulas $\phi \in \bigcup_{k=1,\ldots,n}(\mathcal{AS}_k \cup \mathcal{TH}_k) \cup \mathcal{TH}_{glob}$: $\neg(\phi \overset{*}{\rightsquigarrow}_{\Pi} \phi)$.

From the application of the above steps, thanks to the inference rule of Proposition 1 and the absence of circularities, we conclude the validity of the global specification $\mathcal{AX}_{glob} \wedge \mathcal{AS}_{glob} \Rightarrow \mathcal{TH}_{glob}$

4   Compositional Dining Philosophers

This section illustrates an analysis of the *dining philosophers problem*, with the compositional proofs of some relevant properties, as an example of compositional specification and verification in TRIO using the rely/guarantee paradigm. Even if the example does not constitute an "industrial-strength in-the-large" case study, we believe that, after several decades of successful application, it is still an insightful and thought-provoking example to assess the validity of — not only — our compositional rule in the short space of a conference paper. All details of the proofs have been checked with the encoding of the TRIO language in the PVS proof checker [18] (see [12, 10] for some details of this encoding), even if we present them succinctly (due to space limit) and in human-readable form.

4.1   One Rely/Guarantee Philosopher

Assumptions availability, availability_2 and lasting_availability of Section 3.1 express the suppositions that each philosopher makes about the behavior of his/her neighbors. In turn, the philosopher must guarantee to them that he/she will not be unfair and will periodically release the forks. This requirement is expressed by two theorems, taking_turns and taking_turns_2 (not explicitly shown), that are analogous to the assumptions availability and availability_2, while assumption lasting_availability corresponds to axiom thinking_duration (see Section 2). For the sake of brevity, the proofs of these two theorems, which are directly derivable from the axioms of the philosopher class only, are not discussed here.

The *local* non-starvation property requires that, assuming a regular availability of the forks, we can guarantee that, after the system starts, the philosopher eats regularly. This requirement can be formalized using the $\twoheadrightarrow_i$ operator, relating the availability of the forks in the past to the occurrence of the eating sessions in the immediate future. In our case, $E_k = WithinF_{ei}(UpToNow(\text{available}(l) \wedge$ $\text{available}(r)), T_t + 2T_e)$ and $M_k = SomP_i(\text{start}) \Rightarrow (\exists t > t_e : Within_{ii}(Lasts$ $(\text{eating}, t), T_t + 2T_e))$. The following theorem expresses the local non-starvation property, whose proof we omit for brevity. Notice that the proof assumes that the thinking time of each philosopher is larger than twice the eating time: $T_t > 2T_e$. After all, they are philosophers, not gourmands! (Unless they are Epicureans, one may argue...). This condition allows to avoid the race conditions.

Theorem 3 (regular_eatings_rg).
$WithinF_{ei}(UpToNow(\text{available}(l) \wedge \text{available}(r)), T_t + 2T_e)$
$\rightarrow_i \quad (SomP_i(\text{start}) \Rightarrow (\exists t > t_e : Within_{ii}(Lasts(\text{eating}, t), T_t + 2T_e)))$

Up to this point, we have proved that $\mathcal{AX}_{phil} \wedge \mathcal{AS}_{phil} \Rightarrow \mathcal{TH}_{phil}$, which corresponds to step 1 of Section 3.3.

4.2   A Table of Philosophers

The *global* non-starvation property is expressed by theorem liveness_rg below. It simply states that each philosopher in the array eats regularly, unless he/she has not started yet. Notice that in our example $E_{glob} = \text{true}$ since the composite system is closed, and M_{glob} coincides with the following liveness_rg theorem.

Theorem 4 (liveness_rg) $SomP_i(\text{Philosophers[i].start}) \Rightarrow$
$(\exists t > t_e : Within_{ii}(Lasts(\text{Philosophers[i].eating}, t), T_t + 2T_e))$

In Section 4.1 above, we completed step 1 of Section 3.3. Now, let us consider step 2. Each local assumption is discharged by either a global assumption or by a visible theorem or axiom of the modules adjacent to the current philosopher. Therefore, step 2 is completed without circularities involved, since thinking_duration is an axiom and taking_turns[_2] are both proved directly from axioms local to each class.

Step 3 is empty in our example, since the only global theorem we want to prove is theorem liveness_rg in $\mathcal{TH}_{dining\_N}^{rg}$. Let us consider step 4, where we have to prove that each environment assumption E_k is initialized, that is we have to show that hypothesis 1 of Proposition 1 holds. Since the local theorems have already been proved without circularities, we can use fork_availability to complete this step. The theorem simply states that the desired property $E_k = WithinF_{ei}(UpToNow(\text{available}(l) \wedge \text{available}(r)), T_t + 2T_e)$ always holds, which subsumes the initialization condition. Step 5 requires to discharge the E_k's by means of other formulas, in order to fulfill hypothesis 2 of Proposition 1. Once again, the theorem fork_availability for class k works correctly since it predicates the validity of the E_k's over the whole temporal axis. Step 6 is also very simple, since $M = \forall k \in \{1, \ldots, n\} : M_k$, so that the implication of this step holds trivially. As a consequence, hypothesis 3 of Proposition 1 is shown to hold.

As discussed above, no circularities arise in proving the local formulas, so we conclude that theorem liveness_rg holds as a consequence of the inference rule of Proposition 1 and following the steps in Section 3.3.

4.3   Complexity of the Proofs

Let us briefly evaluate the complexity of the global proof outlined above, using the proof checker PVS. The PVS proofs of the dining_N system required a total of 926 prover commands; approximately half of them where devoted to the proof of the theorem regular_eatings_rg. Let us compare the cost of this verification with the cost of a non-compositional one.

The basic problem with a non-compositional proof is that we cannot exploit encapsulation and reuse. Therefore, there is no distinction between local and global items and everything is "flattened" at the same level of visibility. In the case of the dining philosopher problem, we can overcome this problem by "simulating" modularization at the global level. In other words, we have to carefully parametrize each item with respect to an index which separates different "instances" of the philosopher. Moreover, and most importantly, we must devise a way to replace the use of the $\rightarrow$ operator by temporally closed formulas only. This unstructured solution has been implemented; the result has been a proof of length comparable to the compositional one, but fragmented into more intermediate lemmas, with more assumptions and more intricate proof dependencies. Another feature that distinguishes the compositional proof from the non-compositional one is the fact that the former is repetitive while the latter is intricate. In other words, the compositional proof has a structure made of several similar parts, indicating that it is indeed simpler to manage for the human user who can easily understand when previous proof patterns can be applied again with minor modifications. All in all, even if the number of proof commands where not dramatically different in the two proofs, the complexity of the non-compositional one, considering also the mental effort and difficulty in managing the proof, was much greater. Furthermore, our experience with the compositional proof of the same property has guided and helped the building of the non-compositional one: we believe that doing the non-compositional proof first would have been really hard and time-consuming.

5   Related Works

A compositional analysis technique applies some, possibly formal, method to infer global properties of a large, complex system through a hierarchical and iterative process that exploits the system's modular structure. A general (and historical) introduction to compositional methods can be found in [6, 7]. Without aiming at exhaustiveness, this section briefly reviews some of the most important contributions about compositional reasoning and shows how the approach of this paper differs from them.

An issue still largely unexplored in the present literature on compositionality is the consideration of hard real-time aspects, which require a metric modeling of time. A first noticeable exception is Ostroff in [17], where the metric temporal logic RTTL is embedded in a compositional framework. Nonetheless, the approach is rather different from ours, being focused on refinement aspects rather than on *a posteriori* composition that exploits reuse. Furthermore, time is treated as a separate variable and is discrete, while in our approach time is an implicit item of the language and can be either continuous or discrete.

The need for compositionality has become indisputable in the formal methods community, so that almost every newly introduced formalism encompasses some sort of compositional technique or permits compositional specifications. However, to the best of our knowledge, all proposed compositional frameworks are deeply rooted on some particular, often restrictive semantic assumptions, and depend explicitly on the underlying computational model. In this regard, formalisms typically assume either an interleaving semantics (e.g. [1, 9, 16]) or a synchronous semantics (e.g. [3]) for the concurrent components of the system.

A rather different compositional framework to support the top-down development of real-time systems based on logical formulas at the semantic level is studied by Hooman [13]. In a sense, Hooman's framework is independent of semantic assumptions, even if its set-theoretic model of semantic primitives naturally relates to interleaving semantics models. However, the framework is focused on the refinement (i.e. decomposition) aspect and basically consists of an inference rule that permits to deduce that the decomposition of a module into its refined parts correctly implements the original (unrefined) module. Another important difference between Hooman's framework and ours is that the former does not adopt the rely/guarantee paradigm, and is therefore suitable only to write specifications of modules who do not rely on a constrained behavior of the environment to function correctly.

More typical solutions to the problem of formulating a sound rely/guarantee compositional rule involve the use of an *ad hoc* operator to write rely/guarantee specifications so that they satisfy certain specific characterizations.

For example, the above approach is followed by Abadi and Lamport [1], who analyze the rely/guarantee compositional paradigm using TLA as the reference specification language. The authors introduce the TLA operator $\xrightarrow{+}\!\!\!\triangleright$ to write rely/guarantee specifications that can be soundly composed. Notice that our paper also introduced a suitable operator (the *time progression* operator $\rightarrow\!\!\!*$) to write rely/guarantee specifications. The crucial difference is that our time progression operator is applied in inference rules independently of any assumption on the semantics of processes and also of any semantic characterization of formulas (its application does not need notions such as safety, closure, etc., which are instead integral part of (among others) Abadi and Lamport's framework). This renders our framework purely *syntactic* and very general. In particular, even if the inference rule of [1] is usable for general properties, the conditions of the rule are hard to prove if they are not safety properties; such a distinction does not apply to a syntactic rule such as ours.

Abadi and Merz [2] propose an abstract generalization of rely/guarantee inference rules, in an attempt to treat compositionality syntactically. To this extent, a modal operator to write rely/guarantee inference rules is introduced with minimal semantic assumptions. However, the use of the operator in inference rules and the consequent soundness proofs are possible only *after* the abstract framework is specialized by choosing a semantic model and a computational model. On the contrary, in our framework the soundness of the inference rule is completely proved without assumptions of this kind.

Amla et al. [4] present an abstract compositional framework which can be considered as a generalization of several concrete compositional frameworks in the literature. In particular, they succeed in formulating an inference rule which does not rely on an *ad hoc* operator to be sound, and is therefore simpler than others. However, their framework still relies heavily on semantic assumptions, such as downward closure, on the set of behaviors describing a process. Therefore, our framework does not fit the models in [4], since it pursues the alternative (and new) approach of using a rely/guarantee operator, but independently of any semantic assumptions on the behavior of the components of the system, according to the axiomatic approach.

6   Conclusions

We presented a compositional framework for the TRIO specification language that supports verification through automated theorem proving. The framework is based on a formal notion of composition of TRIO modules, which is used to prove that the mutual interactions between components of a complex system guarantee some property for the global application, after the components are integrated into the system. The compositional rule has been proved sound and has been applied to the classic example of Dijkstra's dining philosophers as a simple, but not simplistic, example. The compositional framework has been encoded into the logic of the PVS theorem prover.

With respect to other approaches to compositionality in formal methods, our own emerges as more suitable for real-time modeling, it encompasses both continuous and discrete time to better model physical processes, and it is conceived for axiom systems and deductive verification. Therefore, the approach is very general and abstracts away from specific assumptions about process semantics and the underlying computational model.

Future work in this line of research will follow three main directions. First, the framework presented here is being applied to several real-life industrial case studies to experimentally evaluate its effectiveness. Second, alternative weaker — or stronger — inference rules will be investigated. In particular, we are exploring variations and generalizations of the $\rightarrow$ operator, better suited to be applied on certain classes of systems, different inference rules which do not use a time progression operator at all, and complete inference rules (which sacrifice some simplicity of application). Third, automated support for the framework will be improved and extended.

Acknowledgements

The authors thank the anonymous reviewers for their remarks.

References

1. M. Abadi and L. Lamport. Conjoining specifications. *ACM TOPLAS*, 17(3):507–535, 1995.
2. M. Abadi and S. Merz. An abstract account of composition. In *MFCS'95*, volume 969 of *LNCS*, pages 499–508, 1995.
3. R. Alur and T. A. Henzinger. Reactive modules. *Formal Methods in System Design*, 15(1):7–48, 1999.
4. N. Amla, E. A. Emerson, K. S. Namjoshi, and R. J. Trefler. Abstract patterns of compositional reasoning. In *CONCUR'03*, volume 2761 of *LNCS*, pages 431–445, 2003.
5. E. Ciapessoni, A. Coen-Porisini, E. Crivelli, D. Mandrioli, P. Mirandola, and A. Morzenti. From formal models to formally-based methods: an industrial experience. *ACM TOSEM*, 8(1):79–113, 1999.
6. W.-P. de Roever. The need for compositional proof systems: a survey. In *COMPOS'97*, volume 1536 of *LNCS*, pages 1–22, 1998.
7. W.-P. de Roever, F. de Boer, U. Hannemann, J. Hooman, Y. Lakhnech, M. Poel, and J. Zwiers. *Concurrency Verification: Introduction to Compositional and Noncompositional Methods*. Cambridge University Press, 2001.
8. E. W. Dijkstra. Hierarchical ordering of sequential processes. In *Operating Sys. Tech.*, pages 72–93. 1972.
9. B. Finkbeiner, Z. Manna, and H. B. Sipma. Deductive verification of modular systems. In *COMPOS'97*, volume 1536 of *LNCS*, pages 239–275, 1998.
10. C. A. Furia. Compositional proofs for real-time modular systems. Laurea degree thesis, Politecnico di Milano, 2003.
11. C. A. Furia, M. Rossi, D. Mandrioli, and A. Morzenti. Automated compositional proofs for real-time systems. Full version with appendices available online from `http://www.elet.polimi.it/upload/furia`, 2005.
12. A. Gargantini and A. Morzenti. Automated deductive requirement analysis of critical systems. *ACM TOSEM*, 10(3):255–307, July 2001.
13. J. Hooman. Compositional verification of real-time applications. In *COMPOS'97*, volume 1536 of *LNCS*, pages 276–300, 1998.
14. P. Maier. Compositional circular assume-guarantee rules cannot be sound and complete. In *FOSSACS'03*, volume 2620 of *LNCS*, pages 343–357, 2003.
15. E. Mendelson. *Introduction to Mathematical Logic*. Chapman & Hall, 1997.
16. K. S. Namjoshi and R. J. Trefler. On the completeness of compositional reasoning. In *CAV'00*, volume 1855 of *LNCS*, pages 139–153, 2000.
17. J. S. Ostroff. Composition and refinement of discrete real-time systems. *ACM TOSEM*, 8(1):1–48, 1999.
18. S. Owre, J. M. Rushby, and N. Shankar. PVS: A Prototype Verification System. In *CADE-11*, volume 607 of *LNCS*, pages 748–752, 1992.

Iterative Circular Coinduction for CoCasl in Isabelle/HOL

Daniel Hausmann, Till Mossakowski, and Lutz Schröder

BISS, Dept. of Computer Science, University of Bremen

Abstract. Coalgebra has in recent years been recognized as the framework of choice for the treatment of reactive systems at an appropriate level of generality. Proofs about the reactive behavior of a coalgebraic system typically rely on the method of coinduction. In comparison to 'traditional' coinduction, which has the disadvantage of requiring the invention of a bisimulation relation, the method of *circular coinduction* allows a higher degree of automation. As part of an effort to provide proof support for the algebraic-coalgebraic specification language CoCasl, we develop a new coinductive proof strategy which iteratively constructs a bisimulation relation, thus arriving at a new variant of circular coinduction. Based on this result, we design and implement tactics for the theorem prover Isabelle which allow for both automatic and semiautomatic coinductive proofs. The flexibility of this approach is demonstrated by means of examples of (semi-)automatic proofs of consequences of CoCasl specifications, automatically translated into Isabelle theories by means of the Bremen heterogeneous Casl tool set Hets.

Introduction

Coalgebra is emerging as a standard unifying framework for the specification of reactive systems [11], complementing the use of universal algebra for the specification of the functional correctness of programs. Following this paradigm, several coalgebraic specification languages have recently been designed, e.g. the *Coalgebraic Class Specification Language* CCSL, which is geared towards object oriented programs, and the algebraic-coalgebraic specification language CoCasl [7], which extends the standard algebraic specification language Casl [1, 8] and thus allows not only the specification of both functional and reactive requirements, but also the intercombination of inductive datatypes and coinductive process types.

This work forms part of an effort to provide proof support for CoCasl. To this end, an existing embedding of Casl into the semiautomatic theorem prover Isabelle/HOL [9] has been extended to CoCasl, so that proofs about CoCasl specifications can now be conducted in a well-developed higher order logical environment. This embedding is the basis for the development of automatic tactics that serve to simplify the actual proof work.

In the same way as proofs about algebraic datatypes typically involve induction, the standard proof method for coalgebraic process types is coinduction. The

M. Cerioli (Ed.): FASE 2005, LNCS 3442, pp. 341–356, 2005.
© Springer-Verlag Berlin Heidelberg 2005

coinduction principle states that bisimilar, i.e. observationally indistinguishable states are actually equal. While inductive proofs of simple assertions are usually easy to mechanize, the automatization of coinduction is faced with the problem that standard coinduction requires the invention of a bisimulation relation. A variant of coinduction that lends itself more easily to mechanization is the method of circular coinduction [10], which works by 'reducing the claim to itself' adhering to certain restrictions in the permissible proof steps. Here, we introduce an implementation of a related proof method where the bisimulation is built up inductively from the proof goal. This process may be performed either automatically or, in cases where this fails, semiautomatically, with the inductive construction guided by the user by means of specialized tactics. The inductive completion process has the advantage that specifications are not limited to (conditional) equational logic, as with circular coinduction (as realized in BOBJ).

The use of this method is illustrated by means of example specifications in CoCasl. It turns out that many simple goals can indeed be solved automatically, and that more complicated goals require only a moderate amount of user interaction.

The material is organized as follows. Basic facts and notions concerning coalgebra and coinduction are reviewed in Sect. 1. Section 2 gives a brief introduction to CoCasl. The method of the iterative construction of a bisimulation, called iterative coinduction, is introduced in Sect. 3. Section 4 discusses the implementation of this method in Isabelle/HOL and the example proofs.

1   Coalgebra and Coinduction

We now briefly recall some basic notions from coalgebra.

Definition 1 (coalgebra). Let $\mathbf{C}$ be a category, and let $T : \mathbf{C} \to \mathbf{C}$ be a functor. A T-*coalgebra* (A, α) (or, somewhat imprecisely, just A) consists of an object A of $\mathbf{C}$ and a morphism $\alpha : A \to TA$. A *homomorphism* between two T-coalgebras (A, α) and (B, β) is a morphism $h : A \to B$ such that $\beta \circ h = (Th) \circ \alpha$. A T-coalgebra Z is called *final* if for each T-coalgebra A, there exists a unique homomorphism $A \to Z$.

Final coalgebras admit *corecursive definitions*: given an object A of $\mathbf{C}$, a function $f : A \to Z$ into the final T-coalgebra Z can be defined by exhibiting a T-coalgebra structure α on A. The function $f : A \to Z$ thus defined is then the unique homomorphism $(A, \alpha) \to Z$. Examples of corecursive definitions are given below.

There is also a principle of *coinductive proof* which relies on a coalgebraic notion of bisimulation and is particularly suitable for proving properties of corecursively defined functions.

Definition 2 (bisimulation and full abstraction). Let $\mathbf{C}$ be a category. A *relation* between two objects A and B of $\mathbf{C}$ is a subobject R of $A \times B$; equivalently, R is given by the two projection morphisms $\pi_1 : R \to A$ and $\pi_2 : R \to B$. If

A and B are coalgebras for a functor $T : \mathbf{C} \to \mathbf{C}$, then such a relation R is called a *bisimulation* if there exists a T-coalgebra structure on R that makes π_1 and π_2 into coalgebra homomorphisms. A coalgebra A is called *fully abstract* if every bisimulation on A is contained in the identity relation, i.e. the diagonal $\Delta : A \to A \times A$.

In the special case $\mathbf{C} = \mathbf{Set}$, the notion of relation as defined above coincides with the usual notion. In this case, elements of coalgebras are called *bisimilar* if there exists some bisimulation that relates them. Full abstractness of A means that we have the following *coinduction proof principle* on A:

If x and y are bisimilar elements of A, then $x = y$.

As indicated in the introduction, this proof principle, while indeed essentially dual to induction, carries the disadvantage that a bisimulation R relating x and y must actually be invented. Coinduction is always available on final coalgebras, and hence on their subcoalgebras:

Lemma 3. *Final coalgebras are fully abstract.*

Example 4. Let T be the set functor given by $TX = A \times X$ for a fixed set A. The final T-coalgebra $Z = (A^{\mathbb{N}}, \langle hd, tl \rangle : A^{\mathbb{N}} \to A \times A^{\mathbb{N}})$ has the set $A^{\mathbb{N}}$ of all infinite streams of elements from A as its carrier and the combined head and tail function as its coalgebra structure. We can define corecursive functions $odd, even : A^{\mathbb{N}} \to A^{\mathbb{N}}$ and $zip : A^{\mathbb{N}} \times A^{\mathbb{N}} \to A^{\mathbb{N}}$ by the equations shown in Fig. 1 below (where $A^{\mathbb{N}}$ corresponds to $Stream[Elem]$). In the case of odd, these equations correspond to requiring that odd is a homomorphism $(A^{\mathbb{N}}, \langle hd, tl \circ tl \rangle) \to Z$, i.e. to commutation of the diagrams

$$
\begin{array}{ccc}
A^{\mathbb{N}} \xrightarrow{\ odd\ } A^{\mathbb{N}} & \qquad & A^{\mathbb{N}} \xrightarrow{\ odd\ } A^{\mathbb{N}} \\
hd \downarrow \qquad \downarrow hd & & tl \circ tl \downarrow \qquad \downarrow tl \\
A \xrightarrow[\ id\ ] A & & A^{\mathbb{N}} \xrightarrow[\ odd\ ] A^{\mathbb{N}}
\end{array}
$$

similarly for *even* and *zip*. By Lemma 3, the claim that $zip(odd(s), even(s)) = s$ for all $s \in A^{\mathbb{N}}$ can be proved by coinduction as follows. We have to define a bisimulation R which relates $zip(odd(s), even(s))$ and s for all $s \in A^{\mathbb{N}}$. To this end, we put $R = \{(zip(odd(s), even(s)), s) \mid s \in A^{\mathbb{N}}\}$. Showing that R is a bisimulation amounts to proving that $s \, R \, t$ implies $hd(s) = hd(t)$ and $tl(s) \, R \, tl(t)$. The former goal is solved trivially by just applying the definitions. The latter is shown as follows:

$$
\begin{aligned}
tl(zip(odd(s), even(s))) &= zip(even(s), tl(odd(s))) \\
&= zip(even(s), odd(tl(tl(s)))) \\
&= zip(odd(tl(s)), even(tl(s)))) \\
&R \; tl(s),
\end{aligned}
$$

where we have used the lemma

$$even = odd \circ tl.$$

This proof illustrates two difficulties w.r.t. mechanizability: not only did we have to invent the said lemma, we also had to apply this equation in two different directions during the calculation of $tl(zip(odd(s), even(s)))$. This point will be discussed in more detail below.

A further difficulty appears in the following example. Let $bzip : A^{\mathbb{N}} \times A^{\mathbb{N}} \times Bool \rightarrow A^{\mathbb{N}}$, where $Bool$ is the set $\{\top, \bot\}$ of truth values, be corecursively defined by

$$hd(bzip(s,t,b)) = \begin{cases} hd(s) & \text{if } b \\ hd(t) & \text{otherwise} \end{cases}$$

$$tl(bzip(s,t,b)) = \begin{cases} bzip(tl(s),t,\neg b) & \text{if } b \\ bzip(s,tl(t),\neg b) & \text{otherwise.} \end{cases}$$

Then the equation $zip(s,t) = bzip(s,t,\top)$ can be proved by coinduction. However, the initial guess at a bisimulation, $R = \{(zip(s,t), bzip(s,t,\top)) \mid s,t \in A^{\mathbb{N}}\}$, in fact fails to be a bisimulation. A bisimulation is obtained only by the improved guess $R' = R \cup \{(zip(t,s), bzip(s,t,\bot)) \mid s,t \in A^{\mathbb{N}}\}$.

Circular Coinduction

A coinduction proof principle similar to the one described above has also been introduced for behavioral specifications in the framework of hidden algebra. Roşu [10] has noted that coinduction based on behavioral rewriting loops for proof goals like $zip(odd(s), even(s)) = s$. He has therefore introduced *circular coinduction*, a proof rule that avoids looping by stopping whenever a subgoal is reached that is an instance of a proof goal that has already been decomposed using the observers. Circular coinduction has been implemented in the BOBJ system [10]. Our iterative coinduction method introduced below is very similar to circular coinduction, the essential difference being that it is tailored towards integration in a semiautomatic theorem prover like Isabelle (while a direct integration of the circular coinduction rule into Isabelle would actually lead to less automation because true narrowing instead of just rewriting would be needed).

2   CoCASL

The algebraic-coalgebraic specification language CoCASL has been introduced in [7] as an extension of the standard algebraic specification language CASL. For the basic CASL syntax, the reader is referred to [1, 8]. We briefly explain the CoCASL features relevant for the understanding of the present work using the example specification shown in Fig. 1.

Dually to CASL's datatype construct **type**, CoCASL offers a **cotype** construct which defines coalgebraic process types; it is formally proved in [7] that one can indeed define for each cotype signature a functor T such that models of

---

spec STREAM1 [**sort** *Elem*] =
  cofree cotype
       Stream ::= *cons*(*hd* : *Elem*; *tl* : *Stream*)
  ops *odd*, *even* : *Stream*[*Elem*] → *Stream*[*Elem*];
      zip : *Stream*[*Elem*] × *Stream*[*Elem*] → *Stream*[*Elem*];
  vars s, s_1, s_2 : *Stream*[*Elem*];
      • $hd(odd(s)) = hd(s)$
      • $tl(odd(s)) = odd(tl(tl(s)))$
      • $hd(even(s)) = hd(tl(s))$
      • $tl(even(s)) = even(tl(tl(s)))$
      • $hd(zip(s_1, s_2)) = hd(s_1)$
      • $tl(zip(s_1, s_2)) = zip(s_2, tl(s_1))$
  then %**implies**
    var s : *Stream*[*Elem*]
    • $zip(odd(s), even(s)) = s$
  end

Fig. 1. CoCasl specification of streams

the cotype correspond to T-coalgebras. A simple example is the cotype *Stream* defined in Fig. 1. Like a type declaration, a cotype declaration is just a short way of declaring operations; specifically, the declaration of *Stream* produces two operations $hd : Stream \rightarrow Elem$ and $tl : Stream \rightarrow Stream$. Models of the cotype *Stream* are essentially coalgebras for the functor $\lambda X. Elem \times X$.

Cotypes can be qualified by keywords expressing further constraints. In particular, the keyword **cofree** qualifying the cotype of streams in Fig. 1 has the effect of restricting the models of *Stream* to the final coalgebra (uniquely up to isomorphism), i.e. the set of streams. In particular, one thus has a coinduction principle for *Stream*, which we could also express by using the weaker constraint **cogenerated** instead of **cofree**. Moreover, the corecursive definitions of the functions *odd*, *even*, and *zip* indeed constitute a definitional extension, i.e. do not actually affect the model class.

We now recall some notions from the formal semantics of Casl and CoCasl: A *many-sorted* Casl *signature* $\Sigma = (S, TF, PF, P)$ consists of a set S of sorts, two $S^* \times S$-indexed sets $TF = (TF_{w,s})$ and $PF = (PF_{w,s})$ of total and partial operation symbols, and an S^*-indexed set $P = (P_w)$ of predicate symbols. Function symbols in $TF_{w,s}$ are written $f : w \rightarrow s$.

Models are many-sorted partial first order structures, interpreting total (partial) function symbols as total (partial) functions and predicate symbols as relations. Homomorphisms between such models are so-called *weak homomorphisms*. That is, they are total as functions, and they preserve (but do not necessarily reflect) the definedness of partial functions and the satisfaction of predicates.

Definition 5 (Σ-cogeneration constraint). Given a signature $\Sigma = (S, TF, PF, P)$, a *cogeneration constraint* $\Theta = (\bar{S}, \bar{F})$ over Σ consists of a set of *observable* sorts $\bar{S} \subset S$ and a set of *observer* operation symbols $\bar{F} \subset TF \cup PF$.

Definition 6 (Observation functional). Let $\Theta = (\bar{S}, \bar{F})$ be a Σ-cogeneration constraint. The *observation functional* Obs_Θ computes the image of a relation under all observers with observable result. Formally, if M is a Σ-model and $R \subset |M| \times |M|$ is an S-sorted binary relation, $Obs_\Theta(R) = \{(f_M(x), f_M(y)) \mid (x, y) \in R, f \in \bar{F}_{w,s}, s \in \bar{S}\}$.

Definition 7 (Transition functional). Let $\Theta = (\bar{S}, \bar{F})$ be a Σ-cogeneration constraint. The *transition functional* $Trans_\Theta$ computes the image of a relation under all observers with non-observable result. Formally, for $R \subset |M| \times |M|$, $Trans_\Theta(R) = \{(f_M(x), f_M(y)) \mid (x, y) \in R, f \in \bar{F}_{w,s}, s \notin \bar{S}\}$.

Definition 8 (Θ-bisimulation). Let M be a Σ-model. A binary relation R on M is called a Θ-*bisimulation* if

$$Obs_\Theta(R) \subset \Delta \text{ and } Trans_\Theta(R) \subset R$$

for the Σ-cogeneration constraint Θ (Δ denotes the identity relation). Two elements of M are called Θ-*bisimilar* if they are in relation for some Θ-bisimulation. The constraint Θ is *satisfied* in a Σ-model M (written $M \vDash \Theta$) if each Θ-bisimulation on M is contained in the equality relation (this model M is then also called *cogenerated* by Θ).

If the cogeneration constraint Θ corresponds to the functor T (cf. [7]), then the notion of a bisimulation for T-coalgebras and the notion of a Θ-bisimulation coincide. The coinduction proof principle from Definition 2 thus takes the following form:

> Let Θ be a Σ-cogeneration constraint and let R be a Θ-bisimulation. Then $(x, y) \in R \Rightarrow x = y$ (i.e. $R \subset \Delta$).

Thus it suffices to exhibit a Θ-bisimulation R which relates two elements x and y of a cogenerated model of Σ in order to show that $x = y$. The difficulty is, again, in finding a suitable R.

Remark 9. The satisfaction of cogeneration constraints is defined in [7] in terms of co-congruences rather than in terms of bisimulation relations. For arbitrary functors, the arising coinduction principle is stronger than coinduction principles based on bisimulation, so that the method of coinductive proof described in Sect. 1 remains sound. For the more restricted functors considered here, the two notions are equivalent.

3   Iterative Construction of the Bisimulation

A first approach to the construction of a bisimulation R in coinductive proofs is as follows. Given a proof goal $\forall X. t_1 = t_2$,

1. Let $R = \{(x, y) \mid \exists X.\, x = t_1 \wedge y = t_2\}$ (following [2], we call R the current *trial bisimulation*).
2. Try to prove $Obs_\Theta(R) \subset \Delta$ and $Trans_\Theta(R) \subset R$ (i.e. try to show that R is a Θ-bisimulation).
3. If this succeeds, the proof is finished.

However, this approach will often fail:

Example 10. Consider again the example of infinite streams $A^\mathbb{N}$ of elements from A defined using the functor $TX = A \times X$. The corresponding signature is $\Sigma = (\{Elem, Stream\}, \{hd, tl\}, \emptyset, \emptyset)$. The observation functional for the Σ-cogeneration constraint $\Theta = (\{Elem\}, \{hd, tl\})$ is defined as $Obs_\Theta(R) = \{(hd(x), hd(y)) \mid (x, y) \in R\}$, the transition functional is defined as $Trans_\Theta(R) = \{(tl(x), tl(y)) \mid (x, y) \in R\}$. The attempt to prove $\forall s.\, zip(odd(s), even(s)) = s$ from Θ fails if the above algorithm is used:

1. Let $R = \{(x, y) \mid \exists s.\, x = zip(odd(s), even(s)) \wedge y = s\}$
2. Try to prove $Obs_\Theta(R) \subset \Delta$ and $Trans_\Theta(R) \subset R$. In order to prove the first inclusion, we have to prove $\forall s.\, hd(zip(odd(s), even(s))) = hd(s)$, which can be done by just rewriting the left term. For a proof of the second inclusion, one would have to prove $\forall s.\, tl(zip(odd(s), even(s)))\, R\, tl(s)$, which is indeed true. However, $tl(zip(odd(s), even(s))) = zip(even(s), odd(tl(tl(s))))$ and the latter term cannot be simplified any further, so that a proof attempt by mere rewriting fails.

It is hence necessary to use a 'larger' relation which *explicitly* contains $(zip(even(s), odd(tl(tl(s)))), tl(s))$ for all s (there is no harm in the fact that these pairs are indeed already contained in the original relation). A similar situation arises in the proof of the identity $zip(s, t) = bzip(s, t, \top)$ (cf. Example 4), where the original trial bisimulation actually fails to be a bisimulation and hence needs to be properly extended.

A more effective proof method is the iterative extension of the trial bisimulation: First one tries to prove that the current trial bisimulation is a bisimulation, and if this fails, one adds a new pair to the relation and again tries to show that the new relation is a bisimulation. This is done repeatedly until the proof of the fact that the current trial bisimulation is a bisimulation succeeds.

We now present an algorithm called *iterative coinduction* that uses this approach. Assuming the cogeneration constraint Θ, the proof goal $\forall X.\, t_1 = t_2$ is dealt with as follows.

1. Let $R = \{(x, y) \mid \exists X.\, x = t_1 \wedge y = t_2\}$, and let $n = 0$.
2. Let $R_n = R \cup Trans_\Theta(R_{n+1})$, with R_{n+1} a metavariable which can later be instantiated.
3. Try to prove $Obs_\Theta(R_0) \subset \Delta$ and $Trans_\Theta(R_0) \subset R_0$ by instantiating R_{n+1} with $\emptyset$ (i.e. try to prove that R_0 is bisimulation).
4. If this does not succeed, then set n to $n + 1$ and continue with 2.

5. Otherwise conclude by the coinduction proof principle that $\forall X. t_1 = t_2$, since $\forall X. t_1 R_0 t_2$.

Example 11. The proof attempt for $\forall s . zip(odd(s), even(s)) = s$ succeeds if the above algorithm is used:

1. Let $R = \{(x, y) \mid \exists s . x = zip(odd(s), even(s)) \wedge y = s\}$, let $n = 0$.
2. Let $R_0 = R \cup Trans_\Theta(R_1)$, with R_1 a metavariable.
3. Try to prove $Obs_\Theta(R_0) \subset \Delta$ and $Trans_\Theta(R_0) \subset R_0$ by instantiating R_1 with $\emptyset$. As discussed above, the first inclusion can be discharged by rewriting, while a rewriting proof of the second inclusion fails, although the inclusion does hold.
4. Thus set n to 1 and let $R_1 = R \cup Trans_\Theta(R_2)$ with R_2 a metavariable (now $R_0 = R \cup Trans_\Theta(R \cup Trans_\Theta(R_2)))$.
5. Try to prove $Obs_\Theta(R_0) \subset \Delta$ and $Trans_\Theta(R_0) \subset R_0$ by instantiating R_2 with $\emptyset$. Since Obs_Θ and $Trans_\Theta$ distribute over unions, the following proof goals arise:

$$Obs_\Theta(R) \subset \Delta \qquad\qquad Trans_\Theta(R) \subset R \cup Trans_\Theta(R)$$
$$Obs_\Theta(Trans_\Theta(R)) \subset \Delta \quad Trans_\Theta(Trans_\Theta(R)) \subset R \cup Trans_\Theta(R)$$

The goal for $Obs_\Theta(R)$ was already discharged in step 3, and the goal for $Trans_\Theta(R)$ is trivial. The goal for $Obs_\Theta(Trans_\Theta(R))$ can be discharged by rewriting the left side. In order to establish the last inclusion, we have to prove that for all s, $tl(tl(zip(odd(s), even(s)))) R_0 tl(tl(s))$. Now

$$tl(tl(zip(odd(s), even(s)))) = tl(zip(even(s), odd(tl(tl(s)))))$$
$$= zip(odd(tl(tl(s))), even(tl(tl(s))))$$
$$R \ tl(tl(s)),$$

which establishes the last goal.
6. We conclude by coinduction that $\forall s. zip(odd(s), even(s)) = s$.

The method of iterative coinduction is thus able to complete the proof. Furthermore, the method succeeds in proving the theorem $\forall s_1, s_2. zip(s_1, s_2) = bzip(s_1, s_2, \top)$ from Example 4. During the proof, the algorithm adds the pairs $(zip(s_2, tl(s_1)), bzip(tl(s_1), s_2, \bot))$ for all s_1, s_2 to the trial bisimulation $R = \{(zip(s_1, s_2), bzip(s_1, s_2, \top)\}$. These pairs constitute an actual extension of the trial bisimulation, i.e. they were (in contrast to the situation in the proof of $\forall s. zip(even(s), odd(s)) = s$) not previously contained in the relation.

Notice that the above coinduction method is not guaranteed to terminate, i.e. it is possible that the method just keeps adding new pairs to the trial bisimulation. Such looping may have different causes: firstly, of course, if the proof goal is not a consequence of the considered specification, the method will not be able to prove it and hence fail to terminate (however, if the inclusion $Obs_\Theta(R_0) \subset \Delta$ becomes false at some stage, then the method can actually be used to disprove the incorrect goal). The algorithm may fail to terminate also on correct goals in cases where the iterative construction of a bisimulation requires infinitely many steps (see [2] for examples). Such goals can typically be solved by generalization: A more general proof goal is stated, which one may then, in turn, attempt to solve with the algorithm.

4   Iterative Coinduction in Isabelle/HOL

As part of the Bremen heterogeneous tool set Hets [6,5], a translation of Co-CASL specifications into Isabelle/HOL theories has been implemented in order to allow for the interactive proving of properties of reactive systems (see e.g. Figure 2). This includes a translation of cogeneration constraints, so that coinductive proofs about CoCASL specifications in Isabelle/HOL are made possible in principle. Making coinductive proofs practically feasible requires a set of custom-tailored proof procedures, called *tactics* in Isabelle. Specifically, tactics have been implemented to support the method of iterative coinduction as introduced in the previous section. The *iterative-coinduction* tactic assembles the smaller tactics into one complex tactic which succeeds in proving a relatively large variety of different theorems over different cotypes automatically. In cases where this fails, it is usually possible to construct simple semi-manual proofs by means of the semiautomatic tactics provided by the implementation. The following automatic and semiautomatic tactics have been implemented:

- **The coinduction tactic:** Let the proof goal be $\forall X. t_1 = t_2$. This tactic then automatically chooses the basic relation R such that $(x, y) \in R \Leftrightarrow \exists X. x = t_1 \wedge y = t_2$. The appropriate cogeneration axiom is applied afterwards while instantiating R_0 with $R \cup Trans(R_1)$ where R_1 is an uninstantiated metavariable. The *coinduction* tactic generates two subgoals: the first subgoal states that R_0 is a bisimulation, and the second states that $(t_1, t_2) \in R_0$.
- **The init tactic:** The *init* tactic automatically proves $(t_1, t_2) \in R_0$ and thus solves the second of the two subgoals generated by the *coinduction* tactic.
- **The breakup tactic:** The *breakup* tactic splits a subgoal of the schematic form $(x, y) \in (R \cup Trans(R_n)) \Rightarrow C$ for some natural number n and formula C up into two subgoals $(x, y) \in R \Rightarrow C$ and $(x, y) \in Trans(R_n) \Rightarrow C$.
- **The close-or-step tactic:** This tactic tries to solve the current subgoal by simplification while speculating that R_n may be chosen as $\emptyset$ (this attempt is also called the *close*-part of the tactic). If this fails, the tactic instantiates R_n with $R \cup Trans(R_{n+1})$ (this is also called the *step*-part of the tactic).
- **The force-finish tactic:** The *force-finish* tactic instantiates R_n with the empty predicate and afterwards applies simplification steps in order to solve the last remaining subgoal.
- **The iterative-coinduction tactic:** This tactic combines the previous five tactics in order to allow for automatic proofs.

4.1   Examples

We will now demonstrate the use of the tactics described above by several example proofs.

Recall the CoCASL specification of streams of type *Elem* as shown in Fig. 1. This specification contains corecursive definitions of functions *odd* and *even*, which given a stream s return the stream of elements of s at odd or even positions, respectively. Furthermore, a function *zip* is defined which merges two streams s_1 and s_2 into a stream which alternatingly contains elements from s_1 and s_2. Finally, the specification contains a theorem (marked as such by the CASL semantic annotation %**implies**) stating that for all streams s, $zip(odd(s), even(s)) = s$.

```
typedecl "Elem"
typedecl "Stream"

consts
"hd"   :: "Stream => Elem"
"tl"   :: "Stream => Stream"
"even" :: "Stream => Stream"
"zip"  :: "Stream => Stream => Stream"
"odd"  :: "Stream => Stream"

axioms
odd_hd: "!!s::Stream.(hd(odd s)) = (hd s)"
odd_tl: "!!s::Stream.(tl(odd s)) = odd(tl(tl s))"
even_hd: "!!s::Stream.(hd(even s)) = (hd(tl s))"
even_tl: "!!s::Stream.(tl(even s)) = even(tl(tl s))"
zip_hd: "!!s1::Stream.!!s2::Stream.(hd(zip s1 s2)) = (hd s1)"
zip_tl: "!!s1::Stream.!!s2::Stream.(tl(zip s1 s2)) = zip s2 (tl s1)"

ga_cogenerated_Stream: "!! R :: Stream => Stream => bool.
!! u :: Stream. !! v :: Stream. ! x :: Stream. ! y :: Stream.
R x y --> (hd x = hd y & R (tl x) (tl y)) ==> R u v ==> u = v"

theorem Stream_Zip: "!! s :: Stream . zip (odd s) (even s) = s"
```

Fig. 2. Isabelle translation of the CoCASL specification of streams

Figure 2 shows the automatic translation of this CoCASL specification into an Isabelle theory, generated by Hets. This theory first declares the types Elem| and Stream| together with the observers and additional functions odd|, even| and zip|. This is followed by axioms arising from the coinductive function definitions. Let $\Theta_{Str} = (\{Elem\}, \{hd, tl\})$. The axiom ga_cogenerated_Stream states that every Θ_{Str}-bisimulation R is contained in the equality relation. This axiom constitutes the coinduction proof principle on which the subsequent proofs

```
theorem Stream_Zip: "!! s :: Stream . zip (odd s) (even s) = s"
apply(coinduction)
apply(init)
apply(breakup)
apply(close_or_step)
apply(force_finish)
done


theorem Stream_Zip2: "!! s :: Stream . zip (odd s) (even s) = s"
apply(iterative_coinduction)
done
```

Fig. 3. Two proofs of $zip(odd(s), even(s)) = s$

are based. (The existence part of the finality constraint expressed by the keyword **cofree** is irrelevant for coinductive proofs and presently ignored by the translation.) The theorem $zip(odd(s), even(s)) = s$ is translated as an open goal. Figure 3 shows two proofs of this theorem using the tactics for iterative coinduction. The first proof uses the semiautomatic tactics in order to con-

```
spec BINTREE1 [sort Elem] =
  cofree cotype BinTree ::= (left : BinTree; node : Elem; right : BinTree)
  op  mirror :  BinTree[Elem] → BinTree[Elem];
  vars  t : BinTree[Elem];
       • left(mirror(t))  =  mirror(right(t))
       • node(mirror(t))  =  node(t)
       • right(mirror(t)) =  mirror(left(t))
then %implies
  var  t : BinTree[Elem]
   •   mirror(mirror(t)) = t
end
```

Fig. 4. CoCASL specification of infinite binary trees

duct the proof step by step. The *coinduction* tactic automatically applies the ga_cogenerated_Stream axiom to the current goal, yielding two new subgoals by instantiating the relation variable in the axiom with $R \cup Trans_{\Theta_{Str}}(R_1)$. The first subgoal states that $R_0 = \{(x, y) \mid \exists s :: Stream. \, x = zip(odd(s), even(s)) \wedge y = s\} \cup Trans_{\Theta_{Str}}(R_1)$ is a Θ_{Str}-bisimulation; the second subgoal states that R_0 relates $zip(odd(s), even(s))$ and s. The *init* tactic solves this second (trivial) subgoal and transforms the first subgoal into a form to which the *breakup* tactic can be applied.

After the execution of the *breakup* tactic, there are two new subgoals. The first subgoal states that R is mapped into R_0 under hd and tl, i.e. that $hd(x) = hd(y)$ for any $(x, y) \in R$ and that $(tl(x), tl(y)) \in R_0$ for $(x, y) \in R$; the second subgoal makes the corresponding statement for $Trans_{\Theta_{Str}}(R)$ in place of R. The *close-or-step* tactic fails to prove the first subgoal by simplification, and thus applies the *step*-part, instantiating R_1 with $R \cup Trans_{\Theta_{Str}}(R_2)$ and automatically succeeds by assuming $R_2 = \emptyset$ to show that $R_0 = R \cup Trans_{\Theta_{Str}}(R)$ is closed under hd and tl and is hence a bisimulation. The remaining subgoal is trivialized by applying the *force-finish* tactic. The proof is thus finished and can be completed by executing *done*.

The second proof uses the automatic *iterative-coinduction* tactic which combines the smaller tactics and finishes the proof without requiring user interaction.

```
typedecl "BinTree"
typedecl "Elem"

consts
"cons" :: "BinTree => Elem => BinTree => BinTree"
"left" :: "BinTree => BinTree"
"mirror" :: "BinTree => BinTree"
"node" :: "BinTree => Elem"
"right" :: "BinTree => BinTree"

axioms
mirror_left: "!!t::BinTree.(left(mirror t)) = (mirror(right t))"
mirror_node: "!!t::BinTree.(node(mirror t)) = (node t)"
mirror_right: "!!t::BinTree.(right(mirror t)) = (mirror(left t))"

ga_cogenerated_BinTree: "!! R :: BinTree => BinTree => bool.
!! u :: BinTree. !! v :: BinTree. ! x :: BinTree. ! y :: BinTree.
((R x) y) --> (((R (left x)) (left y)) & (node x) = (node y) &
((R (right x)) (right y))) ==> ((R u) v) ==> u = v"

theorem BinTree_Mirror: "!! t :: BinTree. (mirror (mirror t)) = t"
```

Fig. 5. Isabelle translation of the CoCASL specification of infinite binary trees

A CoCASL specification for the cotype of infinite binary trees with nodes labelled in a set *Elem*, together with a corecursively defined function *mirror* which keeps the value of the current node and replaces the left subtree with the mirrored right subtree and the right subtree with the mirrored left subtree, is shown in Fig. 4. Figure 5 contains the corresponding Isabelle theory obtained by automatic translation in Hets. The axiom `ga_cogenerated_BinTree` states that any Θ_{Tree}-bisimulation is contained in the equality relation. The proof goal arising by translation of the %**implies** part of the CoCasl specification states that *mirror* is self-inverse, i.e. that for all infinite binary trees t, $mirror(mirror(t)) = t$.

Two proofs of this theorem are shown in Fig. 6. The proofs use the tactics in an equivalent way as the proofs in Fig. 3.

```
theorem BinTree_Mirror: "!! t :: BinTree. (mirror (mirror t)) = t"
apply(coinduction)
apply(init)
apply(breakup)
apply(close_or_step)
apply(finish)
done

theorem BinTree_Mirror2: "!! t :: BinTree. (mirror (mirror t)) = t"
apply(iterative_coinduction)
done
```

Fig. 6. Two proofs of $mirror(mirror(t)) = t$

Table 1 shows a selection of theorems which have been proved using the iterative-coinductive proof tactics in a similar manner as in the examples above[1]. The depth of a coinductive proof is the number of iterations required in order to arrive at a bisimulation (including the initial guess). The example goals concerning streams, largely taken from [2], make use of further corecursively defined functions: $swap(a, b)$ is the stream $(a, b, a, b, \ldots)$; $const(a)$ is the stream $(a, a, a, \ldots)$; $iterate(f, a)$ is the stream $(a, f(a), f^2(a), \ldots)$; and $inflist(a, g, f)$ is the stream $(g(a), g(f(a)), g(f^2(a)), \ldots)$. The *bswitch* function interchanges even and odd positions in the stream it receives as its first argument, starting at the first or the second position depending on its boolean second argument. The function *bzip* is defined as in Example 4. Other function names should be self-explanatory.

The proofs of the theorems $zip(s, t) = bzip(s, t, \top)$ and $zip(s, t) = bswitch(zip(t, s), \top)$ are typical examples where the trial bisimulation has to be extended by pairs not previously contained in it; the additional pairs are correctly 'guessed' by the iteration mechanism. As can be seen from Table 1, the proofs presently have to be conducted at the semiautomatic level; however, the proofs do not actually require substantial user interaction, so that further fine-tuning of the *iterative-coinduction* tactic is expected to produce a fully automatic proof of these goals.

The theorems on bitstreams shown in Table 1 mention a function $flop : Bit \to Bit$ which toggles bits, and a function $flip : BitStream \to BitStream$

---

[1] Proof scripts and tactic implementations available under http://www.informatik.uni-bremen.de/~hausmann/cocasl

Table 1. Theorems proved by iterative coinduction in Isabelle

Cotype	Theorem	Depth	Automatic
Streams	$zip(even(s), odd(s)) = s$	2	Yes
	$zip3(first(s), second(s), third(s)) = s$	3	Yes
	$zip4(one(s), two(s), three(s), four(s)) = s$	4	Yes
	$zip(const(a), const(b)) = swap(a, b)$	2	Yes
	$zip(s, t) = bzip(s, t, \top)$	2	No
	$zip(even(s), odd(s)) = bswitch(s, \top)$	2	No
	$zip(s, t) = bswitch(zip(t, s), \top)$	2	No
	$odd(zip(s, t)) = s$	1	Yes
	$even(zip(s, t)) = t$	1	Yes
	$iterate(f, f(a)) = map(f, iterate(f, a))$	1	Yes
	$const(a) = odd(swap(a, f))$	1	Yes
	$const(a) = map(identity, const(a))$	1	Yes
	$inflist(a, identity, identity) = const(a)$	1	Yes
	$map(g, iterate(f, a)) = inflist(a, g, f)$	1	Yes
	$map(compose(f, g), l) = map(f, map(g, l))$	1	Yes
	$const(f(a)) = map(f, const(a))$	1	Yes
	$const(a) = even(const(a))$	1	Yes
	$const(a) = iterate(identity, a)$	1	Yes
	$const(a) = swap(a, a)$	1	Yes
BitStreams	$flip(b) = map(flop, b)$	1	No
	$tick = flip(tock)$	1	Yes
	$flip(flip(b)) = b$	1	Yes
NatStreams	$streamadd(s, s) = map(double, s)$	1	Yes
	$streamadd(s, t) = streamadd(s, t)$	1	Yes
Binary Trees	$mirror(mirror(t)) = t$	1	Yes
TreeStreams	$swap(mirror(mirror(t)), t) = const(t)$	2	No

which toggles all bits in a stream; the corecursive definition of $flip$ uses a case distinction over $hd(b)$ in the clause for $hd(flip(b))$, i.e. does not use $flop$. The theorem $flip(b) = map(flop, b)$ for all bit-streams b has to be proved semiautomatically because explicit case distinction needs to be performed in the course of the proof (an approach for further automation of proofs which involve case distinction is described in [4]). Using this theorem in simplification, the goals $tick = flip(tock)$ (where $tick$ and $tock$ are the two alternating bitstreams) and $flip(flip(b)) = b$ can be proved automatically.

Another point where the fully automatic tactic fails is nested coinduction. An example is the theorem $swap(mirror(mirror(t)), t) = const(t)$ for all infinite trees t, where during a coinductive proof over streams, a second coinductive proof – this time over trees – becomes necessary. This requires a semiautomatic proof in which the user explicitly tells the system when to start the second coinductive proof. The iterative coinduction tactics automatically choose the right coinduction principle needed in the current situation.

5   Conclusion

We have proposed a method of coinduction by iterative construction of bisimulations. This method, which postulates only the standard coinduction principle, produces proofs that are similar in spirit to circular induction. As part of the proof support for the algebraic-coalgebraic specification language CoCASL, corresponding proof tactics have been implemented in Isabelle/HOL; iterative coinductive proofs are supported by both an all-out automatic tactic and a set of semiautomatic tactics that allow user-guided initiation, continuation, and completion of the iterative construction.

Compared with circular coinduction as realized in BOBJ [10], our approach is suitable for specifications written in full first-order (and even higher-order) logic, not just conditional equations. Moreover, while the degree of automation that we achieve is comparable to that of BOBJ [10] and CoClam [3], the availability of semiautomatic tactics means that user interaction may help to complete proofs that fail with a completely automatic proof procedure (in particular, missing lemmas appear as open subgoals and can be proved on-the-fly, possibly with another coinduction; cf. the *TreeStreams* example). Last but not least, the realisation of circular coinduction as a proof tactic in Isabelle/HOL means that correctness of the implementation only relies on the rather small and long-tested kernel of Isabelle.

Example proofs have been conducted on CoCASL specifications, automatically translated into Isabelle theories by the Bremen heterogeneuous tool set Hets [5, 6]. Simple proof goals can typically be discharged automatically; typical features that require user interaction are case distinction and nested coinduction. The further automation of case distinction, as in BOBJ, is not expected to cause fundamental difficulties.

Continued work on the CoCASL proof environment includes fine-tuning the automatic proof tactics and extending the implementation (which currently only works for the single-sorted case) to many-sorted coinduction and datatype-valued observers, as well as developing proof support for advanced CoCASL features, in particular CoCASL's modal logic and structured cofree specifications.

Acknowledgements

We thank Grigore Roşu for discussions on circular coinduction, Horst Reichel for organizing a very fruitful workshop on coinductive proof techniques, and Markus Roggenbach and Horst Reichel for collaboration on CoCASL. Furthermore we would like to thank Erwin R. Catesbeiana for conceptual help with circular proofs.

References

1. M. Bidoit and P. D. Mosses, CASL *user manual*, LNCS, vol. 2900, Springer, 2004.
2. L. Dennis, *Proof planning coinduction*, Ph.D. thesis, Edinburgh University, 1998.

3. L. Dennis, A. Bundy, and I. Green, *Using a generalisation critic to find bisimulations for coinductive proofs*, Automated Deduction, LNAI, vol. 1249, Springer, 1997, pp. 276–290.

4. J. Goguen, K. Lin, and G. Rosu, *Conditional circular coinductive rewriting with case analysis*, WADT 02, LNCS, vol. 2755, Springer, 2003, pp. 216–232.

5. T. Mossakowski, HETCASL – *heterogeneous specification. Language summary*, 2004.

6. _____, *Heterogeneous specification and the heterogeneous tool set*, Habilitation thesis (draft), University of Bremen, 2004.

7. T. Mossakowski, L. Schröder, M. Roggenbach, and H. Reichel, *Algebraic-co-algebraic specification in* COCASL, J. Logic Algebraic Programming, to appear.

8. P. D. Mosses (ed.), CASL *reference manual*, LNCS, vol. 2960, Springer, 2004.

9. T. Nipkow, L. C. Paulson, and M. Wenzel, *Isabelle/HOL — a proof assistant for higher-order logic*, LNCS, vol. 2283, Springer, 2002.

10. G. Rosu, *Hidden logic*, Ph.D. thesis, University of California at San Diego, 2000.

11. J. Rutten, *Universal coalgebra: A theory of systems*, Theoret. Comput. Sci. **249** (2000), 3–80.

Formalisation and Verification of Java Card Security Properties in Dynamic Logic

Wojciech Mostowski

Department of Computing Science,
Chalmers University of Technology,
SE-412 96 Göteborg, Sweden
woj@cs.chalmers.se

Abstract. We present how common Java Card security properties can be formalised in Dynamic Logic and verified, mostly automatically, with the KeY system. The properties we consider, are a large subset of properties that are of importance to the smart card industry. We discuss the properties one by one, illustrate them with examples of real-life, industrial size, Java Card applications, and show how the properties are verified with the KeY Prover – an interactive theorem prover for Java Card source code based on a version of Dynamic Logic that models the full Java Card standard. We report on the experience related to formal verification of Java Card programs we gained during the course of this work. Thereafter, we present the current state of the art of formal verification techniques offered by the KeY system and give an assessment of interactive theorem proving as an alternative to static analysis.

1   Introduction

Java Card [8] is a technology designed to incorporate Java in smart card programming. The main ingredient of this technology is the Java Card language specification, which is a stripped down version of Java. In recent years Java Card technology gained interest in the formal verification community. The two main reasons for this are: (1) Java Card applications are safety and security critical, and thus a perfect target for formal verification, (2) due to the relative language simplicity Java Card is also a feasible target for formal verification.

In this paper we show how common Java Card security properties can be formalised in the Dynamic Logic used in the KeY system and proved with the KeY interactive theorem prover (the background of the KeY project is given in Sect. 2). The properties in question are a rather large subset of properties that are of interest to the smart card industry [18]. We demonstrate the formalisation and verification of the properties on two real-life Java Card applets (the case studies are described in Sect. 3). After giving the detailed description of the properties we formalised and proved (Sect. 4), we report on the experience we gained during the course of this work and analyse the main difficulties we encountered. In an earlier paper [12] we reported on the verification of transactions related safety properties based on a somewhat simplified example of a

M. Cerioli (Ed.): FASE 2005, LNCS 3442, pp. 357–371, 2005.
© Springer-Verlag Berlin Heidelberg 2005

JAVA CARD purse applet. We proposed the approach of *design for verification*, where we argue that certain precautions have to be taken into account during the design and coding phase to make verification feasible. In this work however, we concentrate on source code verification of already existing JAVA CARD applications without any simplifications whatsoever, and we discuss wider range of security properties than before. In particular, one of the assumptions we made, is that we should be able to specify properties and perform verification without modifying the source code of the verified program. Thus, this work presents the current state of the art of automated formal verification techniques offered by the KeY system for industrial size JAVA CARD applications with respect to meaningful, industry related security properties. This is discussed in Sect. 5. The main conclusion is that full source code verification of JAVA CARD applications is absolutely possible and in most part can indeed be achieved automatically, however, such verification requires deep understanding of the specification issues, including full understanding of the application being verified and the specificities of the JAVA CARD environment. Therefore, we consider the KeY system, assuming the approach we present in this work, mostly suitable for experienced users. The properties that we consider here, originate from the area of static analysis [18], however, to the best of our knowledge, no static analysis technique for thorough treatment of those properties has been developed. We managed to formalise and verify almost all of the properties using the KeY interactive theorem prover. For the remaining properties we give concrete suggestions on how to treat them with the KeY system. We give arguments why we think that interactive theorem proving is a reasonable, and in fact in some ways better, alternative to static analysis. This discussion is included in the second part of Sect. 5.

2   Background

The KeY Project. The work presented here is part of the KeY project[1] [1]. The main goals of KeY are to (1) provide deductive verification for a real world programming language and to (2) integrate formal methods into industrial software development processes.

For the first goal a deductive verification tool for JAVA source programs, the KeY Prover, has been developed. The main target of the KeY system is the JAVA CARD language – a stripped down version of JAVA used to program smart cards (e.g., JAVA CARD does not support concurrency or large primitive data types, and has a very small API). The verification is based on a specifically tailored version of Dynamic Logic – JAVA CARD Dynamic Logic (JAVA CARD DL), which supports most of sequential JAVA, in particular the full JAVA CARD language specification including the JAVA CARD transaction mechanism. JAVA CARD DL and the KeY Prover are designed to make the verification process as automated as possible.

For the second goal, the KeY Prover was integrated into a commercial CASE tool, which uses UML (Unified Modelling Language) as the design language

---

[1] http://www.key-project.org

and OCL (Object Constraint Language) as the specification language. For the present work however, due to specificities of the security properties in question, and the necessity to operate on relatively low level of the specification, we took the approach of using JAVA CARD DL directly as a specification language.

JAVA CARD Dynamic Logic with Strong Invariants. We give a very brief introduction to JAVA CARD DL. We are not going to present or explain any of its sequent calculus rules. Dynamic Logic [13] can be seen as an extension of Hoare logic. It is a first-order modal logic with parametric modalities $[p]$ and $\langle p \rangle$ for every program p (we allow p to be any sequence of legal JAVA CARD statements). In the Kripke semantics of Dynamic Logic the worlds are identified with execution states of programs. A state s' is *accessible* from state s *via* p, if p terminates with final state s' when started in state s.

The formula $[p]\phi$ expresses that ϕ holds in *all* final states of p, and $\langle p \rangle \phi$ expresses that ϕ holds in *some* final state of p. Since JAVA CARD programs are deterministic, there is exactly one final state (p terminates) or no final state (p does not terminate). In JAVA CARD DL termination forbids exceptions to be thrown, i.e., a program that throws an uncaught exception is considered to be non terminating (or, terminating abruptly) [5]. The formula $\phi \rightarrow \langle p \rangle \psi$ is valid if, for every state s satisfying precondition ϕ, a run of the program p starting in s terminates, and in the terminating state the postcondition ψ holds. The formula $\phi \rightarrow [p]\psi$ expresses the same, except that termination of p is not required, i.e., ψ needs only to hold *if* p terminates. On top of that, a "throughout" modality ($[\![\cdot]\!]$) has been introduced to JAVA CARD DL. As opposed to the box and diamond modalities, the throughout modality requires that a certain property is maintained at *all intermediate* program states, so for the throughout modality the semantics of a program is a sequence of all states the execution passes through when started in the current state (its *trace*). This allows us to ensure that a certain property should hold even in case of an unexpected/abrupt termination (e.g., when the smart card is ripped out from the terminal). We call such properties *strong invariants*. Strong invariants are the central part of one of the discussed security properties.

JAVA CARD DL is axiomatised in a sequent calculus to be used in deductive verification of JAVA CARD programs. The detailed description of the calculus can be found in [2]. The calculus covers all features of JAVA CARD, such as exceptions, complex method calls, or JAVA arithmetic. The full JAVA CARD DL sequent calculus is implemented in the KeY Prover. The prover itself is implemented in JAVA. The calculus is implemented by means of so-called taclets [3], that avoid rules being hard coded into the prover. Instead, rules can be dynamically added to the prover. As a consequence, one can, for example, use different versions of arithmetic during a proof: idealised arithmetic, where all integer types are infinite and do not overflow, or JAVA arithmetic, where integer types are bounded and exhibit overflow behaviour [6]. Full treatment of strong invariants also required formalisation of JAVA CARD transactions in the logic. The transaction mechanism [8] ensures that a piece of JAVA CARD program is executed to completion or not at all. The theoretical aspects of integration of the throughout modality and transactions into JAVA CARD DL are discussed in [4].

Related Work. For us, the most interesting formal approaches to JAVA CARD application development are those considered with source code level verification, based on static checking and various program calculi. The work of Jacobs et al. [14] is most closely related to our work and can partly serve as a brief overview of verification techniques targeted at source code. It reports on successful verification attempts of a commercial JAVA CARD applet with different verification tools: ESC/JAVA2 [10], KRAKATOA [16], JIVE [19], and LOOP [15]. The security property under consideration, one of the properties we discuss in this paper, is that only ISOExceptions are thrown at the top level of the applet. The analysed applet is a commercial one, sold to customers. There are no technical details revealed about the applet, so it is difficult to compare its complexity to our case studies. Jacobs et al. detected subtle bugs in the applet with respect to a possible uncaught ArrayIndexOutOfBoundsException (with LOOP and JIVE tools), as well as full verification (no exceptions other than ISOException, satisfied postcondition, and preserved class invariant) of single methods with the KRAKATOA tool. The paper admits that expertise and considerable user interaction with the back-end theorem provers (PVS and COQ) were required. It is also noted that the provers are the performance and scalability bottlenecks in the verification process. We will relate to those issues while we present our results.

3 Case Studies

In the remainder of this paper we will use two JAVA CARD case studies. The first one is a JAVA CARD electronic purse application *Demoney*[2] [17]. While *Demoney* does not have all of the features of a purse application actually used in production, it is provided by *Trusted Logic S.A.* as a realistic demonstration application that includes all major complexities of a commercial program, in particular it is optimised for memory consumption, which, as noted in [12], is one of the major obstacles in verification. The *Demoney* source code is at present not publicly available, so we are not able to disclose some of the technical details necessary to fully discuss the verification problems associated with *Demoney*, but we hope that what we present is convincing enough.

The second case study is an RSA based authentication applet for logging into a Linux system (SafeApplet). It was initially developed by Dierk Bolten for JAVA Powered iButtons[3] and was one of the motivating case studies to introduce strong invariants into JAVA CARD DL. Here, we use a fully refactored version of SafeApplet, which is described in [20].

4 Security Properties

The security properties that we discuss here are directly based on the ones described in [18], which we will refer to as the *SecSafe* document in the rest

---

[2] We thank Renaud Marlet of Trusted Logic S.A. for providing the *Demoney* code.

[3] http://www.ibutton.com

of the paper. We considered all of the properties listed there, but few of them we did not yet analyse in full detail. However, we still discuss those remaining properties and the possibilities of handling them in the KeY system at the end of this section. Let us start with a brief overview of the five properties that we do discuss in detail.

Only ISOExceptions *at Top Level (Sect. 3.4 of the SecSafe document).* The exceptions of type ISOException are used in JAVA CARD to signal error conditions to the outside environment (the smart card terminal). Such an exception results with a specific APDU (Application Protocol Data Unit) carrying an error code being sent back to the card terminal. To avoid leaking out the information about error conditions inside the applet, a well written JAVA CARD applet should only throw exceptions of type ISOException at top level.

No X Exceptions at Top Level. Due to its complexity, the first property is proposed to be decomposed into simpler subproperties. Such properties say that certain exceptions are not thrown, including most common ones (e.g., NullPointerException). A special case of this property is the next one.

Well Formed Transactions. This property consists of three parts, which say, respectively: do not start a transaction before committing or aborting the previous one, do not commit or abort a transaction without having started any, and do not let the JAVA CARD Runtime Environment close an open transaction. The JAVA CARD specification allows only one level of transactions, i.e., there is no nesting of transactions in JAVA CARD. As we show later, this property can be expressed in terms of disallowing JAVA CARD's TransactionException.

Atomic Updates (Sect. 3.5 of the SecSafe document). In general, this property requires related persistent data in the applet to be updated atomically. In the context of our work this property is directly connected to the "rip-out" properties and strong invariants, which we will use to deal with this property.

No Unwanted Overflow (Sect. 3.6 of the SecSafe document). This property simply says that common integer operations should not overflow.

In the following we will go through these security properties one by one. For each of the properties we will give a general guideline on how to formalise it in JAVA CARD DL, give an example based on one or both of the case studies, give comments about the verification of a given property and possibly discuss some more issues related to the property. Due to space restrictions and the lengthy code snippets in our examples, we are going to show abbreviated versions of the examples. A technical report discussing all the examples in full detail is available [21].

4.1   Only ISOExceptions at Top Level

The KeY system provides a uniform framework for allowing and disallowing exceptions of any kind in JAVA CARD programs. We explain this with a general example. Given some applet MyApplet one can forbid aMethod to throw any exception other than ISOException in the following way (this is the actual syntax used by the KeY Prover, we will explain it shortly):

```
java {"source/"}

program variables { MyApplet self; }

problem {
 preconditions ->
  <{ method-frame(MyApplet()): {
      try { self.aMethod(); } catch(ISOException ie) {}
    } }> true }
```

This is a proof obligation that is an input to the KeY Prover. The first section in the file tagged with java tells the prover where the source code of the program to be verified is. The program variables section defines all the program/JAVA variables that are going to be used in the proof obligation. The problem section defines the actual proof obligation. The string preconditions is a place holder for the preconditions necessary to establish the correct execution of aMethod. One of the obvious conditions to put there, is that the self reference is not null: !self = null. With this proof obligation we want to prove that a call to aMethod either terminates normally or with an exception of type ISOException. The actual call to the method, self.aMethod(), appears inside the diamond modality (<{}>) and is wrapped with some additional statements. The diamond requires the program to terminate normally – the trivial postcondition true is only satisfied if no exceptions are thrown. So, to specify that a program throws a certain kind of exception only, one wraps the actual program with a try-catch statement catching the particular kind of exception. This way, if our method terminates normally or throws an ISOException (only), the program inside the diamond still terminates normally, making the proof obligation valid. In case any other kind of exception is thrown the proof obligation becomes invalid. The method-frame statement tells the prover that our program is executed in the context of the MyApplet class (e.g., such information is necessary if aMethod is private). The method-frame statements is one of the extensions to JAVA syntax used in JAVA CARD DL to deal with scopes of methods, method return values, etc. We want to stress here, that this extension is a *superset* of JAVA, not a subset – any valid JAVA/JAVA CARD program can be used inside the modality.

Let us now demonstrate this property with real examples. First we give a specification of *Demoney*'s method verifyPIN. This method is common to almost every JAVA CARD applet, it is responsible for verifying the correctness of the PIN passed in the APDU. If the PIN is correct the method sets a global flag indicating successful PIN verification and returns, otherwise an ISOException with a proper status code (including the number of tries left to enter the correct PIN) is thrown. The proof obligation below specifies that verifyPIN is only allowed to throw ISOException. The example is abbreviated; however, no important issues are omitted:

```
program variables {
  fr.trustedlogic.demo.demoney.Demoney self;
  javacard.framework.APDU apdu; ... }

problem {
  // General preconditions for verifyPIN, e.g., !self = null & ...
  // PIN well formed preconditions: !self.pin = null & ...
  // ISOException well formed preconditions: ...
  -> <{ method-frame(fr.trustedlogic.demo.demoney.Demoney()): {
         try{ self.verifyPIN(apdu,offset,length); }catch(ISOException ie){}
       } }> true }
```

There are numerous preconditions to guard the execution of `verifyPIN`. It took some trial and error steps to get all the preconditions right (we discuss this issue in detail in Sect. 5). Missing even the smallest one renders the program not terminating normally. This proof obligation is proven automatically by the KeY Prover in slightly more than 3 minutes[4] with less that 10 000 proof steps.

The *SecSafe* document requires that exceptions other than `ISOException` are not thrown as a result of invoking the entry point of the applet. For us, it means that we would have to prove our property for the applet entry method `process`. At the current stage of our experiments we found it technically difficult to perform a proof of this kind for the applet of the size of *Demoney*. We know however, that such a proof can be modularised (see next example).

The second example is based on `SafeApplet`. Among other things, `SafeApplet` keeps a table of registered users that can be authenticated with the applet. For each user a unique user ID and a set of RSA encryption keys are stored. Method `dispatchDeleteKeyPair` is responsible for unregistering a given user ID, it takes an APDU, which stores the user ID to be unregistered. In case no user with such an ID is registered an `ISOException` with a proper code (`SW_USER_UN-REGISTERED`) is thrown, otherwise the proper entry in the user table is removed:

```
// APDUException, ISOException well formed, ...
& !self = null & !self.temp = null & ...
-> <{ method-frame(SafeApplet()):{
        finishedWithISOEx = false; finishedOK=false;
        try { self.dispatchDeleteKeyPair(apdu); finishedOK = true;
        }catch(ISOException e1){ finishedWithISOEx = true; }
    } }> (finishedOK = TRUE | (finishedWithISOEx = TRUE &
        ISOException.instance.theSw[0] = SafeApplet.SW_USER_UNREGISTERED))
```

Among other things, the precondition says that the entries in the user table are not `null`. In the postcondition we also want to specify that the `ISOException` that might be thrown contains the right status code. Because of this, we need to distinguish between two cases in the postcondition: *either* the method terminates normally *or* an `ISOException` is thrown with a proper status code – two boolean variables (`finishedOK` and `finishedWithISOEx`) keep track of this. The way the program in the modality is constructed ensures that those two variables cannot be `true` at the same time (this can also be verified).

---

[4] All the benchmarks presented here were run on a Pentium IV 2.6 GHz Linux system with 1.5 GB of memory. The version of the KeY system used is available on request.

Proof Modularisation. This proof obligation is proved automatically with the KeY Prover in about 15 minutes with less than 40 000 proof steps. This may seem to be a lot. The reason for such performance is threefold. First of all, there is a loop involved, which goes through the table of users. This loop is symbolically unwound step by step and the proof size depends on the actual constant value of MAX_USERS (equal to 5). Secondly, the method performs a lot of preliminary work before the users table is modified. Finally, for this particular benchmark result, there was no proof modularisation used whatsoever – when a method call is made in a program the prover replaces the call with the actual method body and executes it symbolically. Instead, one can use the specification of the called method – it is enough to establish that the precondition of the called method is satisfied, and then the call can be replaced with the postcondition of the called method. Obviously, one also has to prove that the called method satisfies its specification. One limitation of this technique is that the method specification have to include so called modification conditions [22, 7] – a complete set of attributes that the method possibly modifies. Factoring out method calls this way shortens the total proof effort even in the simplest cases – although a method might be called only once in a program, due to proof branching, it may need to be analysed in the proof multiple times. For comparison, we applied such modularisation to our last example – we used specification for just one method that contains a loop. The resulting proof took less that one minute (5 000 proof steps), the side proof establishing that the factored out method satisfies its specification took less than 2 minutes (12 000 proof steps) – the time performance increased 5 times.

4.2   No X Exceptions at Top Level

As already mentioned, the KeY system provides a uniform framework for dealing with exceptions. The JAVA CARD DL calculus rules and the semantics of the diamond modality require that no exceptions are thrown whatsoever. In particular, the calculus is carefully designed to establish that each object that is dereferenced is not null, that the indices used to access array elements are within array bounds, etc. So, as long as the total correctness semantics is used, the KeY Prover establishes absence of all possible exceptions. Still, for the sake of consistency, one can disallow only one kind of exception this way:

```
preconditions & unwantedException = FALSE ->
  <{ method-frame(MyApplet()): {
     try { self.aMethod(); } catch(Exception e) {
       unwantedException = (e instanceof UnwantedException); } }
  }> (unwantedException = FALSE)
```

Here, the boolean variable unwantedException will become true only when the undesired exception is thrown in aMethod, thus the above proof obligation states that no UnwantedException is thrown by aMethod.

4.3   Well Formed Transactions

The first two parts of this property say that a transaction should not be started before committing or aborting the previous one, and that no transaction should be committed or aborted if none was started. This boils down to saying that no `TransactionException` related to well-formedness is thrown in the program. Since in our model of JAVA CARD environment we do not consider transaction capacity, we can simplify this part of the property to "No `TransactionException` is thrown in the program." – a special case of the previous property.

The last part of the property says that no transactions should be left open to be closed by JCRE. The information about open transactions is kept track of by JCRE and can be accessed through the JAVA CARD API (static attribute `JCSystem.transactionDepth`). It is quite straightforward to specify that a given method does not leave an open transaction:

```
preconditions & JCSystem.transactionDepth = 0
-> <{ method-frame(MyApplet()): { self.aMethod(); }
   }> (JCSystem.transactionDepth = 0) }
```

The precondition states that there is no open transaction before `aMethod` is called. This is necessary in case `aMethod` is top-level and does not check for an open transaction before it starts its own. After `aMethod` is finished we require the `transactionDepth` to be equal to 0 again, this ensures that there is no open transaction. Also, what is implicit, is that no `TransactionException` is thrown. We will briefly illustrate this property with a real example in the next section.

4.4   Atomic Updates

This property requires *related* persistent data in the applet to be updated atomically. Strong invariants seem to be the right technique to deal with this property – as we stated already, they are used to specify consistency of data at all times, so that in case an abrupt termination occurs, the data (in particular, related data) stay consistent. We will illustrate this property briefly with the same example that is discussed in full in [12], for this work however we were able to use the real *Demoney* applet instead of the simplified one used in [12]. One of the routines of the electronic purse is responsible for recording information about the purchase in the log file. Among other things, the current balance after the purchase is recorded in a new log entry. As the *SecSafe* document points out accurately, when atomic consistency properties are considered, one has to be able to say what it means for the data to be related. In our example we want to state that the current balance of the purse is always the same as the one recorded in the most recent log entry. By using JAVA CARD transaction mechanism, method `performTransaction` is responsible for debiting the purse balance and updating the log file in one atomic step. In JAVA CARD DL, to express that a strong invariant is preserved, the throughout modality is used:

```
JCSystem.transactionDepth = 0 & !self = null & ...
// Strong Invariant: The current balance of the purse is equal to the
// balance recorded in the most recent log entry: self.balance = ...
-> [[{method-frame(fr.trustedlogic.demo.demoney.Demoney()): {
     self.performTransaction(amount, apduBuffer, offsetTransCtx); }
   }]] // Strong Invariant: same as above
```

An important part of the precondition is the one saying that the strong invariant holds before the method is executed. This proof obligation is proved automatically in 12 minutes with less than 12 000 proof steps. This particular method uses two loops to copy array data, which were not factored out with modularisation, so we consider this a relatively good result. Modularisation has been used for some other, simple methods, however, we have to point out here, that in case of proof obligations involving the throughout modality and transactions using method specifications is not possible in general, and in cases where it is possible it has to be used with caution.

This proves that the related data stays consistent throughout the execution of performTransaction. Since a JAVA CARD transaction is involved in this method it is also desirable to prove well-formedness of transactions for performTransaction, as stipulated in the previous section:

```
// Mostly the same preconditions as for the previous proof obligation
-> <{method-frame(fr.trustedlogic.demo.demoney.Demoney()): {
        self.performTransaction(amount, apduBuffer, offsetTransCtx); }
    }> (JCSystem.transactionDepth = 0)
```

This is proved automatically in 11 minutes with less than 12 000 proof steps.

We proved a similar property for SafeApplet, saying that all the registered users have a properly defined set of private and public encryption keys at all times. Here we only make two comments about the proof. First, there are no transactions used in SafeApplet to ensure data consistency, instead additional fields in objects associated with consistency property are used and accessing of those objects is carefully coded. This results in a more complex proof. Second, during the proof, some small amount of manual interaction with the prover was necessary, namely 8 manual quantifier instantiations were required, otherwise the proof proceeded automatically and took 3 minutes to finish.

4.5   No Unwanted Overflow

Finally, we deal with a property related to integer arithmetic: additions, subtractions, multiplications and negations must not overflow. To deal with all possible issues related to integer arithmetic, in particular overflow, the KeY Prover uses three different semantics of arithmetic operations [6]. The first semantics treats the integer numbers in the idealised way, i.e., the integer types are assumed to be infinite and, thus, not overflowing. The second semantics bounds all the integer types and prohibits any kind of overflow. The third semantics is that of JAVA, i.e., all the arithmetic operations are performed as in the JVM, in particular they are allowed to overflow and the effects of overflow are accurately modelled. Thus, to deal with overflow properties, it is enough for the user to choose appropriate integer semantics in the KeY Prover. Based on the *SecSafe* document, below is an example of a badly formed program with respect to overflow:

```
inShort(balance) & inShort(maxBalance) & inShort(credit) &
balance > 0 & maxBalance > 0 & credit > 0 ->
  <{ try { if (balance + credit > maxBalance) throw ie;
          else balance += credit;
    }catch(ISOException e){} }> balance > 0
```

The problem is that the `balance + credit` operation can overflow making the condition inside the `if` statement false resulting in a `balance` being less than 0 after this program is executed. When processed by the KeY Prover with the idealised integer semantics switched on, this proof obligation gets proved quickly. When the arithmetic semantics with overflow control is used, this proof obligation is not provable. The fix to the program to avoid overflow is to change the `if` condition to `balance > maxBalance - credit`. The modified proof obligation is provable with both kinds of integer semantics.

4.6   Other Properties

We have just shown how to formalise and prove five kinds of security properties from the *SecSafe* document. Here we briefly discuss the remaining ones.

Memory Allocation. Due to restricted resources of a smart card, one of the requirements on a properly designed JAVA CARD applet is the constrained memory usage: bounded dynamic memory allocation and no memory allocation in certain life stages of the applet. This seems like a problem suitable for static analysis – in general there is no need for precise analysis of the control flow, although, for example, if memory allocation is performed inside a loop, a precise analysis is required to find out the loop bounds. Either way, we believe that this property in general can be formalised and proved with the KeY system as well. The main idea is the following. The KeY Prover maintains a set of implicit attributes for every object to model certain aspects of the JAVA virtual machine, in particular object creation. There is no obstacle to introduce a new static implicit attribute to our JAVA model that would keep track of the amount of allocated memory or the possibility to allocate memory. However, due to optimisation of inheritance and interface representation in JVM, the actual memory consumption may differ for each JVM implementation. Thus, keeping precise record of the allocated memory is not so simple and thorough treatment of this problem requires further research. At the moment, we could only give approximate figures for memory usage.

Conditional Execution Points. This property says that certain program points must only be executed if a given condition holds. Again, this is a subject to static analysis (e.g., ESC/JAVA2 provides means to annotate and check conditions at any program point), but it can also be done with theorem proving by introducing a generalised version of the throughout modality. The throughout modality requires that a property holds after every program statement. For the generalised case, such a property would have to hold only in certain parts of the program. So there are no theoretical obstacles here, but due to less priority this has not yet been implemented in KeY.

Information Privacy and Manipulation of Plain Text Secret. Those two properties fall into the category of data security properties. As it has been shown in [9], formalising and proving data security properties can in general be integrated into interactive theorem proving, however no experiments on real JAVA CARD examples were performed so far.

5   Discussion

Lessons Learned. Here we sum up the practical experience we gained during the course of this work. The main lesson is that the current state of software verification technology that at least the KeY system offers makes the verification tasks feasible. Schematic formalisation of the security properties from the *SecSafe* document was easy, however, applying it to concrete examples was much more tricky. We found getting right all the preconditions to guard the execution of a given method very difficult. This particularly holds when normal termination is required. Constructing the preconditions requires deep understanding of the program in question and the workings of the JCRE. However, calculation of the preconditions can be tool supported as well:

In [14] ESC/JAVA2 is used to construct preconditions. In short, the tool is run interactively on an unspecified applet, which results in warnings about possible exceptions. Such warnings are removed step by step by adding appropriate expressions to the precondition. Alternatively, as [14] suggests, the weakest precondition calculus of the JIVE system could be used by running the proof "backwards", i.e., by starting with a postcondition and calculating the necessary preconditions. This however, has not been presented in the paper and to our understanding the approach has certain limitations.

The KeY system itself provides a functionality to compute specifications for methods to ensure normal termination [23]. The basic idea behind computing the specification is to try to prove a total correctness proof obligation. In case it fails, all the open proof goals are collected and the necessary preconditions that would be needed to close those goals are calculated. There are two disadvantages to this technique: (1) for the proof to terminate the preconditions that guard the loop bounds cannot be omitted, so there is no way to calculate preconditions for loops, they have to be given beforehand, (2) proofs have to be performed the same way for computing the specification as it is done when one simply tries to prove the obligation, so computing the specification is in fact a front-end for analysing failed proof attempts in an organised fashion. Moreover, the specifications produced can be equally hard to read as is analysing the failed proof attempt manually. Despite all this, we still find the specification computation facility of the KeY system quite helpful for proof obligations that produce small failed proof attempts or at least ones containing only few open proof goals.

Proving partial correctness also requires caution. A wrong or unintended precondition can render the program to be always terminating abruptly. This makes any partial correctness proof obligation trivially true. Thus, in cases where a partial correctness proof is necessary (e.g., strong invariants), one should accompany such a proof with an additional termination property, as we did in Sect. 4.4.

To enable automation, the KeY Prover and the JAVA CARD DL are designed in a way not to bother the user with the workings of the calculus and the proof system. However, we have realised that proper formulation of the DL expressions can further support automation. We have also introduced a small number of additional simplification rules for arithmetic expressions. Such rules considerably simplify the proof, but introducing them, although being relatively easy, requires a little bit more than the basic understanding of Java Card DL. Moreover, each introduced rule has to be proven sound. The rules are very simple and we have means to do it automatically with the KeY system [3], but due to constantly changing set of those rules, we decided to leave the correctness proofs out for the time being.

Our experimental results show that proof modularisation greatly reduces the verification effort. The problem of modularising proofs using method specifications has been well researched [22, 7], but has been implemented in the KeY system only recently, thus, we gained relatively little experience here. So far we have learnt that using method specification in the context of the throughout modality is not always possible and has to be done with care.

Finally, one of the goals of formal verification is to find and eliminate bugs. So far, we have not found any in our case studies. We believe the reason for this is twofold. First, the properties we considered so far were relatively simple and the methods were expected not to contain bugs related to those properties. Second, neither of the applications we analysed as a whole, only parts of them. In particular, the bugs often occur at the points where the methods are invoked, due to an unsatisfied method precondition.

Static Analysis vs. Interactive Theorem Proving. The results of this paper show that we are able to formalise and prove all of the security properties defined in the *SecSafe* document. Many of the properties would require quite advanced static analysis and, as far as we know, no such static analysis technique has been developed so far. Moreover, we believe that some properties go beyond static analysis, e.g., certain aspects of memory allocation (Sect. 4.6) require accurate analysis of the control flow. Furthermore, each single property would probably require a different approach in static analysis, while the KeY Prover provides a uniform framework. For example, all properties related to exceptions are formalised in the same, general way, and in fact can be treated as one property. Also, dealing with integer overflow is done within the uniform framework of different integer semantics, that cover all possible overflow scenarios.

Therefore, we consider interactive theorem proving as a feasible alternative to static analysis. More generally, deep integration of static analysis with our prover is a subject of an ongoing research [11]. One argument that speaks for static analysis is full automation. However, our experiments show that the KeY system requires almost no manual interaction to prove the properties we discussed. Also, the time performance of the KeY prover seems to be reasonable, although the work on improving it continues. On the other hand, as we noticed earlier, constructing proof obligations require some user expertise. In our opinion however, this is something that is difficult to factor out when serious formal verification attempts are considered, no matter if theorem proving or static analysis is used as the basis.

6   Summary and Future Work

We have shown how most of the security properties of the industrial origin for JAVA CARD applications can be formalised in JAVA CARD DL and proved, for the most part automatically, with the KeY Prover. Most of the properties were illustrated by real-life JAVA CARD applets. Considerable experience related to formal verification has been gained during the course of this work. This experience indicates that JAVA CARD source code verification, at least using the KeY system, has recently become a manageable and relatively easy task, however, for scenarios like the one presented in this work, user expertise is required. Two main areas for improvement are clearly the modularisation of the proofs and tool support for calculating specifications (more precisely, preconditions). Our future work will concentrate on those two aspects, to reach full, truly meaningful verification of JAVA CARD applications with as much automation as possible. We feel that the performance results should already be acceptable by software engineers, however, the work on improving the speed of the prover will continue. Finally, our experience clearly shows that interactive theorem proving is a reasonable alternative to static analysis – we plan to further explore this area by concentrating on the few properties we only discussed briefly here.

References

1. W. Ahrendt, T. Baar, B. Beckert, R. Bubel, M. Giese, R. Hähnle, W. Menzel, W. Mostowski, A. Roth, S. Schlager, and P. H. Schmitt. The KeY tool. *Software and Systems Modeling*, April 2004. Online First issue, to appear in print.
2. B. Beckert. A dynamic logic for the formal verification of JAVA CARD programs. In I. Attali and T. Jensen, editors, *JAVA on Smart Cards: Programming and Security. Revised Papers, JAVA CARD 2000, International Workshop, Cannes, France*, volume 2041 of *LNCS*, pages 6–24. Springer, 2001.
3. B. Beckert, M. Giese, E. Habermalz, R. Hähnle, A. Roth, P. Rümmer, and S. Schlager. Taclets: a new paradigm for constructing interactive theorem provers. *Revista de la Real Academia de Ciencias Exactas, Físicas y Naturales, Serie A: Matemáticas*, 98(1), 2004. Special Issue on Symbolic Computation in Logic and Artificial Intelligence.
4. B. Beckert and W. Mostowski. A program logic for handling JAVA CARD's transaction mechanism. In M. Pezzè, editor, *Proceedings, Fundamental Approaches to Software Engineering (FASE) Conference*, volume 2621 of *LNCS*, pages 246–260, Warsaw, Poland, April 2003. Springer.
5. B. Beckert and B. Sasse. Handling JAVA's abrupt termination in a sequent calculus for Dynamic Logic. In B. Beckert, R. France, R. Hähnle, and B. Jacobs, editors, *Proceedings, IJCAR Workshop on Precise Modelling and Deduction for Object-oriented Software Development, Siena, Italy*, pages 5–14. Technical Report DII 07/01, Dipartimento di Ingegneria dell'Informazione, Università degli Studi di Siena, 2001.
6. B. Beckert and S. Schlager. Software verification with integrated data type refinement for integer arithmetic. In E. A. Boiten, J. Derrick, and G. Smith, editors, *Proceedings, International Conference on Integrated Formal Methods, Canterbury, UK*, volume 2999 of *LNCS*, pages 207–226. Springer, April 2004.

7. B. Beckert and P. H. Schmitt. Program verification using change information. In *Proceedings, Software Engineering and Formal Methods (SEFM), Brisbane, Australia*, pages 91–99. IEEE Press, 2003.

8. Z. Chen. *JAVA CARD Technology for Smart Cards: Architecture and Programmer's Guide*. JAVA Series. Addison-Wesley, June 2000.

9. Á. Darvas, R. Hähnle, and D. Sands. A theorem proving approach to analysis of secure information flow. Technical Report 2004–01, Department of Computing Science, Chalmers University of Technology and Göteborg University, 2004.

10. C. Flanagan, K. R. M. Leino, M. Lillibridge, G. Nelson, J. B. Saxe, and R. Stata. Extended static checking for JAVA. In *Proceedings, ACM SIGPLAN 2002 Conference on Programming Language Design and Implementation, Berlin*, pages 234–245. ACM Press, 2002.

11. T. Gedell. Integrating static analysis into theorem proving. Available from `http://www.cs.chalmers.se/~gedell/publications/satp.ps`.

12. R. Hähnle and W. Mostowski. Verification of safety properties in the presence of transactions. In G. Barthe and M. Huisman, editors, *CASSIS'04 Post Workshop Proceedings*, volume 3362 of *LNCS*, pages 151–171. Springer, 2005.

13. D. Harel, D. Kozen, and J. Tiuryn. *Dynamic Logic*. MIT Press, 2000.

14. B. Jacobs, C. Marché, and N. Rauch. Formal verification of a commercial smart card applet with multiple tools. In *Proceedings, Algebraic Methodology And Software Technology, Stirling, UK*, volume 3116 of *LNCS*, pages 241–256. Springer, July 2004.

15. B. Jacobs and E. Poll. JAVA program verification at Nijmegen: Developments and perspective. In *Software Security – Theories and Systems: Second Mext-NSF-JSPS International Symposium, ISSS 2003, Tokyo, Japan, November 4–6, 2003. Revised Papers*, volume 3233 of *LNCS*, pages 134–153. Springer, 2003.

16. C. Marché, C. Paulin-Mohring, and X. Urbain. The KRAKATOA tool for certification of JAVA/JAVA CARD programs annotated in JML. *Journal of Logic and Algebraic Programming*, 58(1–2):89–106, 2004. `http://krakatoa.lri.fr`.

17. R. Marlet and C. Mesnil. Demoney: A demonstrative electronic purse – Card specification. Technical Report SECSAFE-TL-007, Trusted Logic S.A., November 2002.

18. R. Marlet and D. L. Métayer. Security properties and JAVA CARD specificities to be studied in the SecSafe project. Technical Report SECSAFE-TL-006, Trusted Logic S.A., August 2001.

19. J. Meyer, P. Müller, and A. Poetzsch-Heffter. The JIVE system – Implementation description. Available from `http://softech.informatik.uni-kl.de/old/en/publications/jive.html`, 2000.

20. W. Mostowski. Rigorous development of JAVA CARD applications. In T. Clarke, A. Evans, and K. Lano, editors, *Proceedings, Fourth Workshop on Rigorous Object-Oriented Methods, London, U.K.*, March 2002. Available from `http://www.cs.chalmers.se/~woj/papers/room2002.ps.gz`.

21. W. Mostowski. Formalisation and verification of JAVA CARD security properties in Dynamic Logic. Technical Report 2004–08, Department of Computing Science, Chalmers University of Technology, Göteborg, Sweden, October 2004. Available from `http://www.cs.chalmers.se/~woj/papers/secprop.pdf`.

22. P. Müller. *Modular Specification and Verification of Object-Oriented Programs*. PhD thesis, FernUniversität Hagen, 2001.

23. A. Platzer. Using a program verification calculus for constructing specifications from implementations. Minor thesis, Karlsruhe University, Computer Science Department, February 2004.

Author Index

Lecture Notes in Computer Science

For information about Vols. 1–3339

please contact your bookseller or Springer